FOUR WORLDS OF WRITING
INQUIRY AND ACTION IN CONTEXT
Fourth Edition

Janice M. Lauer
Purdue University

Andrea Lunsford
Stanford University

Janet Atwill
University of Tennessee

Thomas Clemens
Heartland Community College

William Hart-Davidson
Rensselaer Polytechnic Institute

Debra Jacobs
University of South Florida

Lisa Langstraat
University of Southern Mississippi

Libby Miles
University of Rhode Island

Tim Peeples
Elon College

Nan Uber-Kellogg
Sonoma State University

Pearson
Custom
Publishing

Addison
Wesley
Longman

Copyright Acknowledgments

Brief Contents

1 Introduction   1

Part I: Writing as Inquiry and Action   11

The Everyday World
2 Area of Inquiry: Relationships   13
3 Area of Inquiry: Free Time   61

The Public World
4 Area of Inquiry: Issues in Groups   115
5 Area of Inquiry: Local Cultures   161

The Academic World
6 Area of Inquiry: Fields of Study   245
7 Area of Inquiry: Technology   295

The World of Work
8 Area of Inquiry: Workplace Problems   393

Part II: Alternative Strategies, Genres, Collaboration, and On-line Resources   435

9 Invention Strategies   437
10 Research Strategies   459
11 Reading and Interpretive Strategies   479
12 Situation, Drafting, and Revising Strategies   487
13 Using Genres   523
14 Collaborating Effectively   543
15 Inquiry, Writing, and Technology   549

Detailed Contents

Preface		xvii
Acknowledgments		xxi
1	Introduction by Janice Lauer	1
	What the Text Offers	1
	Part I	1
	Focus on Inquiry	1
	Focus on Action in Contexts	1
	Focus on Process, Strategies, and Collaboration	2
	Focus on Alternative Genres	2
	Part II	2
	Focus on Maximum Flexibility: Multiple Uses, Multiple Voices	2
	Questions the Text Helps You Answer	2
	Why Write?	3
	Writing to Inquire	3
	Inquiry Starts with Questions	3
	Inquiry Involves Probing Your Cultural Assumptions	4
	Inquiry Takes Time	4
	Writing in Four Worlds	4
	Writing to Act in Context	5
	Writing in Everyday Contexts	5
	Writing in Public Contexts	5
	Writing in Academic Contexts	6
	Writing in Workplace Contexts	6
	Learning to Inquire and Act in Contexts	6
	Using Strategies	6
	Studying Examples	7

Gaining Experience in Real Contexts 7

Collaborating in Writing 8

Collaborating on This Book: Our Story 8

Part I: Writing as Inquiry and Action 11

The Everyday World

2   Area of Inquiry: Relationships by Nan Uber-Kellogg 13
    Why Write about Relationships 13
    Examples of Writing for Inquiry and Action 13

    Reading for Inquiry and Action 14
    A Fabricated Mexican (excerpt) by Rick P. Rivera
    Questions for Analysis 16

    A Case: Jonathan's Inquiry 17
    Questions for Analysis 32

    Writing for Inquiry and Action 33
    The Writing Assignment 33
    Your Writing Process 33

    Starting: Selecting a Relationship; Getting in Touch with
    Dissonance; Locating Your Relationship in a Context;
    Questioning; Su's Questions; Workshop 33

    Exploring: Investigating from Three Perspectives;
    Miranda's, Shelby's, and Jim's Explorations; Workshop 36

    Positioning Writers and Readers: Setting Writer and
    Reader Positions; Amanda's Positions; Workshop 43

    Selecting Genres: Selecting a Genre and Examining
    Its Implications; Gregg's Genre; Workshop 46

    Focusing: Stating Your Subject and Point of Significance;
    Alfredo's Focus; Workshop 49

    Organizing: Trying Different Modal Plans: Whole/Parts;
    Time Segments; Grouping; Setting Criteria; Alfredo's Plan;
    Workshop 50

    Drafting: Writing Drafts; Jeff's Letter; Workshop 52

    Responding: Responding to Peers' Drafts; Jeff's Self-Assessment;
    Instructor's Response; Workshop 54

    Revising: Making a Plan and Revising; Jeff's Plan
    and Revision; Workshop 57

3   Area of Inquiry: Free Time by Libby Miles   61

    Why Inquire into Free Time?   61

    Examples of Writing for Inquiry and Action   63

    Readings for Inquiry and Action   64
    "The Globalization of Michael Jordan" by Walter Lafeber
    Questions for Analysis   73

    A Case: Jennie's Inquiry   75
    Questions for Analysis   91

    Writing for Inquiry and Action   91
    The Writing Assignment   91
    Your Writing Process   92

    Starting: Telling Stories; Noticing Packages; James' Package
    and Story; Workshop   92

    Exploring: Listing Key Terms and Contrasting Terms;
    Telling a Contrastive Story; Listing Puzzlement; Analyzing
    Target Groups; Jerry's Exploration; Workshop   95

    Questioning: Posing Questions; Diane's Questions   101

    Positioning Writers and Readers: Locating in a Context;
    Setting Positions; Diane's Context and Reader and
    Writer Positions   102

    Selecting Genres: Picking a Genre;
    Diane's Selection of a Poster   104

    Focusing and Organizing: Stating a Focus and Planning an
    Organization; Diane's Focus and Organization; Workshop   105

    Drafting: Writing Several Drafts; Scott's Critical Essay   107

    Responding: Using a Reader Response Guide; Shari's Response
    to Scott's Plan   110

    Revising: Formulating a Revising Plan and Revising;
    Scott's Plan and Revision; Workshop   111

The Public World

4   Area of Inquiry: Issues in Groups by Janet Atwill   115
    Why Write about Issues?   115
    Examples of Writing for Inquiry and Action   115

    Readings for Inquiry and Action   116
    Letter to *Birmingham News* by Ora Lee Gaines   116
    Questions for Analysis   118

A Case: David's Inquiry 119
Questions for Analysis 131

Writing for Inquiry and Action 132
The Writing Assignment 132
Your Writing Process 132

Starting: Questioning; Locating in a Context; Cassandra's Issue; Workshop 132

Exploring: Taking Different Perspectives; Cassandra's Exploration; Workshop 136

Positioning Writers and Readers: Setting Positions; Cassandra's Positions; Workshop 139

Selecting Genres: Analyzing a Genre; Cassandra's Letter to a Newspaper; Workshop 141

Focusing: Focuses for Action, Awareness, and Attitude; Cassandra's Focus; Workshop 142
Developing Rhetorical Appeals: Constructing Credibility, Affective, and Rational Appeals; Cassandra's Appeals; Workshop 144

Organizing: Making Persuasive Plans; Cassandra's Plan; Workshop 151

Drafting: Writing Drafts; Using Cohesive Devices; Using Concrete and Connotative Languages; Cassandra's Letter; Workshop 153

Responding to Texts: Using a Reader Response Guide; Group Responses; Workshop 155

Revising: Revising Strategies; Cassandra's Plan and Revision; Workshop 158

5   Area of Inquiry: Local Cultures by Lisa Langstraat 161
Why Write about Local Cultures? 161
Examples of Writing for Inquiry and Action 163

Readings for Inquiry and Action 164
"Social Class, Tipping, and Alcohol Consumption in an Ann Arbor Cocktail Lounge" by Suzanne Faber 164
Questions for Analysis 169

A Case: Terri's Inquiry 169
Questions for Analysis 204

Writing for Inquiry and Action 205
The Writing Assignment 205
A Process of Writing about Your Local Culture 205

Starting: Selecting a Local Culture and Context;
Marcus' Questions; Workshop   206

Exploring: Taking Different Perspectives on Your Local Culture;
Hanna's Biker Pack   212

    Using Ethnographic Research; Observations of
    Steven's Engineering Program; Workshop   215
    Compiling an Annotated Bibliography; Mark's Annotated
    Bibliography; Workshop   217
    Interviewing; Bernice's Interview with a University
    Counselor; Workshop   220

Positioning Writers and Readers: Alicia's Reader and
Writer Positions   222

Focusing and Selecting a Genre: Amy's Focus about
Tanning Salons; Workshop   223

Organizing: Ethnographic Organization; Heather's
Organization Plan; Workshop   224

Drafting: Steven's Ethnography on His First-Year
Engineering Program   227

Responding: Using a Reader Response Guide for an
Ethnography; Steven's Responses from His Group   233

Revising: Steve's Revision Plan and Revision   236

The Academic World

6   Area of Inquiry: Fields of Study by Debra Jacobs   245
    Why Write about Fields of Study?   245
    Examples of Writing for Inquiry and Action   246

Readings for Inquiry and Action   247
    "History as Imagination" by James Axtell   247
    Questions for Analysis   251

    A Case: Rhonda's Inquiry   251
    Questions for Analysis   270

Writing for Inquiry and Action   271
    The Writing Assignment   271
    Your Writing Process   271

Starting: Selecting a Subject; Locating in a Context; Questioning;
Mark's Choice of the Field of History; Workshop   271

Exploring: Taking Different Perspectives; Mark's Exploration;
Workshop   275

Positioning Writers and Readers: Setting Positions; Sue's Reader and Writer Positions; Workshop   280

Selecting Genres: Examining a Genre's Implications; Mark's Brochure; Workshop   283

Focusing: Stating Focuses; Sue's Focus on Nursing and Mark's on History; Workshop   287

Organizing: Setting Alternative Plans; Sue's and Mark's Plans; Workshop   289

Drafting: Writing Drafts; Mark's Brochure on History; Workshop   291

Responding: Using a Reader Response Guide; Group and Instructor Responses to Mark; Workshop   292

Revising   293

7   Area of Inquiry: Technology by Tom Clemens   295
    Why Write about Technology?   295
    Examples of Writing for Inquiry and Action   295

Readings for Inquiry and Action   296
    "To Start a Dialogue: The Next Generation of America's Schools" by James A. Mecklenburger   296
    Questions for Analysis   301

A Case: Mark's Inquiry   302
Questions for Analysis   330

Writing for Inquiry and Action   331
    The Writing Assignment   331
    Your Writing Process   331

Starting: Selecting a Subject; Locating in a Context; Questioning; Joselyn's Choice of Intranets; Workshop   331

Exploring: Taking Different Perspectives; Joselyn's Exploration; Workshop   336

    Exploring through Library Research: Working Bibliography and Annotations; Note Taking; Online Indexes; Online Data Bases; Carol's Working Bibliography and Notes; Workshop   343

    Exploring through Internet Research; Browsers; Hypertext Connections; Bookmarks; Joselyn's Working Bibliography and Notes   353

    Exploring through Field Research   358

Positioning Writers and Readers: Joselyn's Reader and Writer Positions; Workshop   359

Selecting Genres: Joselyn's Choice of Research Paper; Workshop   361

Focusing: Joselyn's Focus; Workshop   362

Organizing: Joselyn's Plan; Workshop   364

Drafting: Writing Drafts; Citations; Quotations; Style; Joselyn's Research Paper   366

Responding: Using a Reader Response Guide; Carol's Responses to Joselyn's Paper   381

Revising: Revising; Joselyn's Revising Plan and Revision   384

The World of Work

8   Area of Inquiry: Workplace Problems by Tim Peeples   393
     Why Write about Workplace Problems?   393
     Examples of Writing for Inquiry and Action   393

Readings for Inquiry and Action   394
     "It's Just a Matter of Time: Twentysomethings View Their Jobs Differently Than Boomers" by Helen Wilkinson   394
     Questions for Analysis   397

A Case: Myndee, Natasha, and Nicole's Inquiry   397
     Questions for Analysis   411

Writing for Inquiry and Action   412
     The Writing Assignment   412
     Your Writing Process   412

Starting: Selecting Workplace Problems and Needs; Locating in a Context; Formulating Questions; Audrey's Questions; Workshop   412

Co-Authoring: Project Planning Strategy; Audrey, Sara, and Shanna's Project Plan; Workshop   417

Exploring: Collaborative Investigations; Library and Field Research Methodologies   422

Positioning Writers and Readers: Setting Positions in the Workplace   423

Selecting Genres and Focusing: Workplace Genres; Solutions to Problems   423

Designing a Document: Planning the Page; Document Hierarchies and Persuasiveness for Readers; Audrey, Sara, and Shanna's Document Design   424

Organizing: Group's Organizing Memo; Workshop   430

Drafting: Writing Documents; Audrey, Sara, and Shanna's Flyer/Memo   431

Responding and Revising: Using a Reader Response
Guide for Workplace Documents; Revising; Audrey, Sara, and
Shanna's Revision;
Workshop 432

Part II: Alternative Strategies, Genres, Collaboration, and On-line Resources 435

9   Invention Strategies by Janice Lauer and Andrea Lunsford   437
    Starting Strategies 437
      Questioning Strategy 437
      Focused Freewriting 441
      Project Planning 441
    Exploring Strategies 444
      Three Perspectives Guide 445
      Strategies for Developing and Evaluating Persuasive Appeals 448
      Toulmin's System of Analysis 450
      A Deductive Chain 451
      The Journalistic Formula 454
      The Pentad 454
      The Classical Topics or "Places" 455
      Brainstorming 455
      Speed Writing 455
      Looping 456
      Meditating 456
      Keeping a Journal 456
      Clustering 456

10   Research Strategies by Janice Lauer   459
    Library Research 459
    Compiling a Working Bibliography 459
      Annotating Selected References 463
      Note Taking 466
      Documenting Sources Using the Conventions 469
    Field Research 472
      Observing and Note Taking 472
      Analyzing Your Observations 473
      Interviewing Strategy 474
      Using Surveys 478

11   Reading and Interpretive Strategies by Janice Lauer   479
    Interpreting Written Texts 479
    Reading Guide 481
    Interpretive Guide for a Poem 482
    Interpretive Guide for a Short Story 483
    Interpretive Guide for a Nonfiction Essay 484
    A Semantic Calculator for Bias in Rhetoric 485

12 Situating, Drafting, and Revising Strategies by Janice Lauer   487
    Strategies for Considering Readers and Writers   487
        Writer/Reader Positioning Strategy   487
        Forum Analysis   490
        Designing for a Reader   491
    Focusing Guides   492
        Focusing Strategy   492
        Focusing Strategy for Persuasion   494
        Nutshelling   495
    Organizing Plans   495
        Modal Plans   495
        Persuasive Plans   498
        Sentence Outline   501
        Topic Outline   502
        Ethnographic Organization   502
        Document Design   503
        Document Organization   506
        Building an Idea Tree   508
    Drafting   509
        Writing Several Drafts   509
        Using Cohesive Devices   509
        Using Concrete and Connotative Language   510
        Drafting Researched Papers   511
        Writing Essay Examinations   514
        Writing a Project Proposal   516
    Responding Guides   517
    Reader Response Strategy   517
    Revising Plans   519
        Revising Strategy   520

13 Using Genres by Andrea Lunsford   523
    Why Consider Genre?   523
        Genre Strategy   524
        Selecting a Genre   524
        Examining the Implications of Genres   525
        Features of Fifteen Genres   527

14 Collaborating Effectively by Andrea Lunsford   543
    Why Collaborate?   543
    Why Collaborate On and In Writing?   543
    Collaborative Strategies   544
        Establishing Your Group   544
        Focusing on Effective Group Interactions   544
        Managing Conflict   545
        Enacting Collaboration   546
            Planning Groups   546

Peer Response Groups 546
Co-Authoring Groups 547

15 Inquiry, Writing, and Technology by William Hart-Davidson 549
The Strategic Use of Writing Technologies 550
Simple . . . and Not So Simple Searches 551
Planning Your Online Research 553
Selecting Search Terms for Inquiry 554
Getting in Touch with Dissonance 554
Locating Sources 555
Locating Tools and Sources for More Advanced Searches 555
Formulating a Good Query 558
Organizing Your Search Strategy 562
Sorting and Reflecting On Your Inquiry Results 563
Evaluating Your Research Goals 563
Reviewing Your Search Results 563
Organizing Your Search Results 564
Evaluating and Positioning Your Sources 565
Evaluating Your Sources 565
Positioning Yourself, Your Readers, and Your Sources 566

Index 569

Preface

INTERACTING WITH STUDENT WRITERS
IN REAL CONTEXTS

In the fourth edition of *Four Worlds of Writing: Inquiry and Action in Context,* we again foreground students writing to inquire and to act in a real context. Although this book can be used in many ways, we demonstrate how teachers and students can INTERACT with the student writers in the text.

You can observe students making many choices throughout their writing processes.

You can study them as they:

1. engage in inquiry (reach new understanding) or critique
   - by raising questions in a writing context they choose
   - by exploring their question
   - by positioning themselves as writers
   - by setting positions for their readers
   - by trying different focuses (answers to their questions)
2. select their genre
3. plan an organization
4. draft
5. receive responses
6. plan revisions
7. revise

You will find students struggling, facing the results of their choices, and making changes. You can discuss their efforts.

The question foremost in these students' minds as they write is NOT "What does the teacher want?' But instead "What do my readers, my focus, context, and intended action call for?" Grading with this emphasis acknowledges whether or not you meet these expectations. You and your teachers are encouraged to work together to help you accomplish YOUR actions.

STUDENTS USING STRATEGIES

You can observe them using powerful strategies to guide different acts during their inquiry. Because each student works with strategies in his or her own way, you can notice how they adapt and modify guides to their own styles.

STUDENTS COLLABORATING IN GROUPS

We show students working in groups throughout their writing process, helping each other to make decisions, to change plans or drafts. You can decide whether the advice is helpful or not.

CLASSES STRESS INTERACTION WITH STUDENT EXAMPLES AND YOUR OWN WORK

Classes are shown centering around discussions of the students' work in the text and your work as you inquire, draft, respond and revise. One student's writing process is presented as a narrative reading at the beginning of each inquiry chapter.

COMPOSITION THEORY IN FOUR WORLDS OF WRITING, 4TH EDITION

The fourth edition of *Four Worlds of Writing: Inquiry and Action in Context,* is based on premises derived from rhetorical and composition theory:

- that writing is a way of learning or making knowledge
- that writing is action accomplishing something
- that every writing assignment is best done in actual contexts
- that meaningful writing grows from the writer's own pressing questions
- that learning to write in different worlds is important for every writer
- that students can use writing to examine the cultures which help form them
- that the composing process is a series of acts that can vary in sequence and are often recursive, even though they are ordered in certain ways in a text
- that choice of genre and organization are interdependent
- that stylistic choices vary with different contexts, genres, readers, and focuses
- that specific skills such as paragraph building and grammatical conventions are best developed within the framework of the whole writing process.

Throughout we have merged theory with all of our practical experience and that of college instructors who have developed, tested, and refined that theory in their classrooms.

NEW FEATURES IN THE FOURTH EDITION

More Co-Authors

Eight new authors join our team. Each has taught this pedagogy, as well as several others, over several years in different colleges, universities, and community colleges. Each one contributes one area-of-inquiry chapter based on his or her experience and selection of student work.

New Areas of Inquiry

Four of the seven areas of inquiry are new in this edition: Free Time, Local Cultures, Fields of Study, and Technology. Three continue: Relationships, Issues in Groups, and Workplace Problems.

New Student Work

All of the student work is new. Each chapter presents one student's "inquiry and action in context" as a narrative at the beginning of each chapter in part one. Many student writings pervade the second half of these chapters, which engage you in writing your own texts.

New and Revised Strategies

In Part I all the strategies have been revised. Many new strategies have been added, including the Genre Selection Strategy, Telling Stories, Noticing Packages, Listing Key Terms and Contrasting Terms, Ethnographic Research, Project Planning, and Document Design. In Part II, many new strategies have been added to those from the previous edition, to offer you a repertoire of guides as you write. Included there are guides for writing interpretations of poetry, fiction, and non-fiction, and for taking essay exams.

New Chapter on Collaboration

Based on recent work in the field, this chapter offers you many helps in working with others in groups. It also gives advice about how to deal with conflict.

New Chapter on Genre

In this chapter you will find a helpful explanation of the notion of genres and their importance for writing. Because this text encourages writers to select their genre, the chapter offers descriptions of frequently used genres in different worlds.

New Chapter on Inquiry, Writing, and Technology

This chapter illustrates specific ways in which you can use the internet when engaging in research.

Acknowledgments

We are grateful to the students whose work is featured in this text: Delia Akins; Nikki Arakelian; Audrey Arihood; Jerry Bracken; Shanna Brown; Greg Buczkowski; Kimberly Carter; Jonathan Felber; Scott Fisher; Amanda Foresman; Ryan Gilbert; Mark Herman; James Hatcher; Jonathan Hasse; Shelby Hileman; Cassandra Johnson; James Keeth; Jennie Lane; James Maggart; Rebecca Majeske; David May; Vita Malcolm; Jeffrey May; Kelly Newman; Myndee Paddock; Su Perera; Alfredo Pivoral; Michele Raibley; Benson Rho; Julie Sheer; Sue Simmons; Matthew Spotts; Sara Steffin; Leslie Stewart; Amy Tisdale; Diane Watkins; and Steven Welsh. We are also indebted to all of the teachers and students who worked with this edition as it was being developed and all the reviewers of the text. We wish to acknowledge the role Addison Wesley Longman played in supporting the planning of the text and the help of Pearson Custom Publishing, especially Jo-Anne Weaver and David Daniels in bringing the book to completion. Janice Lauer wishes to acknowledge the indispensable support of her late husband David Hutton through the many phases of the text's composition. Finally we are grateful to all of our families and friends for their support.

1

INTRODUCTION

JANICE LAUER

WHAT THE TEXT OFFERS

Part I focuses on inquiry, contexts, process, and collaboration

Focus on Inquiry

Part I provides sites in which you can investigate your own questions, issues, and cultural assumptions. In each chapter, you are encouraged to initiate and pursue your own inquiry, helped by the comments, suggestions, and advice of your teacher and peers. You can investigate your own subjects, can change actual readers' views, and initiate action in your own communities. To help you accomplish these goals, the text shows other writers engaging in a process of inquiry—beginning with their own compelling questions and investigations and reaching their own conclusions.

A Focus on Action in Contexts

This book encourages you to use every writing assignment to act—to accomplish something with actual readers in real situations. Actions take different forms such as increasing understanding or commitment; gaining new insight; changing a point of view or an attitude; changing behavior or policy; taking a new position or rejecting a position; and reaching a solution. In every writing process you can aim to bring about changes in the context you choose. Writing here has serious stakes.

This text shows other students in writing contexts that were important in their own lives. Each chapter in Part 1 includes two readings. The first is by a professional writer who is addressing a subject related to the chapter's area of inquiry. The second reading is a case, unique to this book—the story of one student engaging in inquiry and action important to her or him. The cases follow the progress of these students, showing their struggles, decisions, interactions with instructors and group members, and work with a number of writing strategies. The cases also interweave on-going narratives with the students' actual writing as they progress from questions to final revision, including students co-authoring a report. Unlike most textbooks which show only snippets of students' work, a draft or a piece of planning, the case allows you to follow the developing text so that you can see, for example, how a writer's early decisions about contexts, readers, or genre impact later efforts. After both the professional and student readings, questions help you analyze these readings *as processes of inquiry and action.*

Focus on Process, Strategies, and Collaboration

The chapters guide you through a writing process, suggesting strategies and illustrating them with student examples. Strategies highlight for you some ways effective writers inquire, draft, and revise. The chapters also illustrate collaboration in action, showing how other students help each other in workshops, offering advice, responses, ideas, and criticism. Throughout, periodic workshops list activities to guide group work.

Focus on Alternative Genres

While many textbooks pose assignments which require you to master a type of discourse like description or cause-and-effect, this text allows you to select the genre that will work best for your subject, readers, and context. To show you that genres are means not ends, the text : a) illustrates more than one genre in each chapter, b) shows students writing in different genres, c) presents a repertoire of generic options in Part II, and d) illustrates how genres can serve your objectives.

Part II emphasizes accessibility and alternatives

This part offers a collection of alternative strategies and genres that you can use in any area of inquiry. The chapter on genres details not only the features of many genres but also their impact on your inquiry, focus, and readers. Part II also includes a chapter on collaboration, providing ideas about how groups can work together successfully at various points during writing, including advice about conflicts and co-authoring.

Focus on Maximum Flexibility: Multiple Uses, Multiple Voices

In order to help you follow your own leads and select strategies you find useful, Part II catalogs numerous alternative guides and genres.

Chapter 15 discusses on-line resources

The chapter shows you how to use internet resources in conjunction with the strategies the text illustrates. It introduces you to the strategic use of writing technologies you'll be engaging in and provides you with the basic information you need to access and use on-line resources.

Questions the Text Helps You Answer

This text addresses some important questions about writing. If you agree with the answers, then the book will help you meet your writing needs.

Why write?

This book gives two answers to that question: 1) you write to go beyond what you already know, and 2) you write to accomplish something in the contexts in which you live. Both of these answers claim that writing is powerful. This book will back up these claims by showing you how you can use writing to reach these ends. The first power of writing is expressed by the word *inquiry* in the title. The second power is captured by the words *action* and *context*. The two sections below explain these powers.

Writing to Inquire

You may be skeptical about the power of writing to create new knowledge. You may think that scientific research, historical investigations, or repeated experience create new knowledge. Or you may view writing as a tool to communicate what you already know. While both of these ideas are true, they do not tell the whole story about the power of writing. Writing as inquiry has long range benefits. Some students at the end of their college days feel that they have missed something, that they have lived so fast that they don't remember or understand what happened to them. But writers as inquirers sense this loss less than most. Why? Because each piece of writing has given them the chance to catch those swiftly passing moments of loving, encountering, learning, wondering, and fearing and to hold them long enough to find personal meaning. Writers save the meaning of their lives by dealing with that meaning in writing. Writers as inquirers not only find what is unique in their experiences, they also find patterns and structures in their lives similar to those they have heard or read about. They learn what makes them unlike anyone else who has ever lived, as well as what makes them like all others who have ever lived. They become aware of their cultural assumptions and the ways in which their values have been shaped by larger cultural forces around them. So what does writing as inquiry mean? How does writing as inquiry differ from other writing?

Inquiry Starts with Questions

Starting your writing process with questions is different than beginning with a thesis or a focus. A question implies that you are curious, puzzled, or intrigued by something that you haven't figured out yet. In that frame of mind, you can write to gain insight and to share it with readers. Beginning with questions has a richer payoff for you and your readers because you both learn something new. For example, when Cassandra, one of the students presented in this book, raised questions about rap music's impact on attitudes toward black women, she didn't have an answer at first. After her inquiry, however, she had reached a new understanding and was able to share the conclusions she reached with readers of the *Black Student Newspaper*.

Because schools usually reward correct answers instead of good questions, you probably haven't developed the power to shape such questions. This ability is crucial, however, because unless you can articulate what you *want* to know and *don't know* yet about a subject, you can't begin the process of inquiry. But not just any old question will do. If you want to use your precious time well, it is also critical that you raise questions about a subject that is of vital interest to you and your readers—one whose answer will make an important difference to you. Why? In your busy life as a student, you have little time to reflect on the meaning of your experience, to examine in depth an issue that plagues you and others close to you, to critically examine your relation to your culture and the larger cultures around you, and to follow up on puzzlement that occurs in your classes. Most of the time, you whirl from class to your room, to jobs, or parties. A writing course is an oasis in which you can take time to reflect on and construct meanings about a few of these aspects of your busy life. Not only does it give you an opportunity to create new understanding, but it offers you a record of your insights that you can review later. Writing also helps you to effect some change in the world around you. So selecting a subject for inquiry has consequences. Only a real, burning question needs a full inquiry process guided by sophisticated strategies. You don't need high-powered guides to dash off writing on what you already know.

Inquiry Involves Probing Your Cultural Assumptions

Writing as inquiry also develops the power to analyze your culture: the values inculcated by your family, your assumptions about relationships, your expectations about work, and the goals of your social class. Without examining the social, political, economic, racial and gender factors that permeate a subject, you limit your chances of creating a meaningful understanding. This book will help you to raise questions about inconsistencies between cultural values such as freedom and civil rights on the one hand and subtle or obvious discriminatory practices of racism or sexism on the other. If the question you raise is important to you, don't ignore important avenues for insight. This book will help you to understand your cultural assumptions and to look at your culture(s) in new ways.

Inquiry Takes Time

Investigation of a serious question requires *time* for exploration—to take a fresh look at your subject from different angles, to draw on your imagination and memory, and to make notes. You will need time to record observations, to relate ideas, to take your readers' views into consideration. You will need time to mull over emerging answers and to articulate and ponder different insights. You will need time to position your readers, select your genre, and write drafts. This book gives you that time, suggesting two or more weeks for each writing experience. The process of inquiry requires, then, considerable time from initial questioning to revision.

Writing in Four Worlds

This book shows students inquiring in four different worlds. In their everyday worlds, they raise questions about relationships, family, home, neighborhoods, and free-time activities, probing to uncover the personal and cultural sources of what they value in these areas. In their public worlds, they interrogate complex and controversial issues that have touched their lives, seeking new or more qualified positions. They study local cultures in which they have participated. In their academic worlds of different disciplines, they question ideas, theories, or practices that are puzzling or apparently incompatible. They conduct research about technology, seeking to reach and share new understanding. In their worlds of work, they describe problems in their places of employment, noticing the gaps that sometimes exist between the objectives and practices in these organizations. This book illustrates that inquiry can be conducted in many worlds.

Writing to Act in a Context

Another reason for writing is to have an impact on contexts in which you live. And why shouldn't you take the opportunity to make a difference in several of your own contexts? That is one of writing's important powers—to effect change. In order to make that happen, however, your writing has to reach readers in these contexts—whether they are in your neighborhood or family, political or religious groups to which you belong, your classes, or your workplace.

But writing in real contexts is not always automatic in a composition course. You have to be free to choose the readers and the genre that you think most appropriate for your context. Instead of being required to write papers only to the instructor in a specified type of writing such as an academic essay, critical paper, research paper, and so forth, this text encourages you to decide on your readers and genre. To guide you in making those decisions and carrying them out, the book presents strategies to help you consider your readers, and to select and analyze your genre. Each chapter illustrates writers, readers, and genres in action in different areas of inquiry. The question you choose to investigate normally arises from the world of writing and context you inhabit. Below are some of the contexts in which students presented in the text conducted their inquiries.

Writing in Everyday Contexts

- Jonathan investigated a long-time concern of his—how competitive his relationship with his best friend Chad had become. Because he realized that any change in their relationship had to be mutual, he chose as his writing context his long distance friendship with Chad, selecting a personal letter as the most appropriate genre.
- Jennie examined the ways in which her favorite free-time activity, swimming, was "packaged." She shared her findings with her classmates.

Writing Public Contexts

- David, an older student and experienced karate instructor, was irritated by the rising violence in his community and the apparent contribution karate was making to it, despite karate's philosophy of non-aggression and self-discipline. He conducted an inquiry into this situation, selecting his karate school as his writing context.
- Cassandra had been debating the issue of rap music with her friends in the black community. Although she liked many types of rap, especially as black music, she and some of her friends disliked the way some rap music demeaned women. As her writing context for her inquiry, she selected the Black Student Association and ultimately as her genre an editorial in the association's *University Newspaper*.

- Terri started watching a soap opera daily with a group in the Student Union at her university. Although she enjoyed this activity, she was irritated by the attitudes of others toward soap operas and those who watch them. She conducted an ethnographic inquiry into this local culture of soap opera viewing. As her readers she chose a number of students who were skeptical about soaps.

Writing in Academic Contexts

- Rhonda chose to investigate the field of accounting, which she had planned to study until her cousin Keandra, a high school student, challenged her because this field didn't seem to fit Rhonda's vibrant personality. With the context of her former high school in mind, she decided to communicate the results of her inquiry in a brochure on accounting.

Writing in Workplace Contexts

- In Myndee's job at the Fifth Street Diner, she wanted to help the owners increase their patrons. Collaborating with two group members, Natasha and Nicole, she developed a report on the use of a Web Page to attract customers from beyond the immediate neighborhood. In this workplace context, the group planned and wrote a report to the owners, detailing the advantages and feasibility of a Web page.

Notice that in all of the contexts, the students used writing to investigate questions about important aspects of their lives that they wanted to understand and change. They chose the genres that were appropriate (letter, newspaper item, brochure, ethnographic account, etc.) and the readers they wanted to affect. In each case, they were able to act through writing.

LEARNING TO INQUIRE AND ACT IN CONTEXTS

Using Strategies

The power to inquire and act through writing effectively doesn't usually develop naturally. To develop these more sophisticated writing powers, this text offers you a range of strategies. Strategies are flexible directives that guide you through complex writing acts such as positioning your readers or revising. Instead of just expecting you to inquire and write well, we offer you guides. These directives make explicit (demystify) the tactics of effective writers. They are flexible for two reasons: you can adapt them to your own style, and you don't have follow them strictly. These strategies help you with starting, exploring, positioning writers and readers, selecting genres, focusing and organizing, drafting, and revising. But it is important to remember as you are learning strategies that they are means, not the end of writing. You will have to invest time in learning a strategy before you can use it effectively and make it your own, tailoring it to your own style. If you decide to include a strategy in your repertoire, try it out with different types of writing. Can you adapt it? Does it increase your ability to explore or organize or revise? This text offers you many guides so that you can find those that fit your writing process.

Using strategies, however, can be dangerous unless you know the difference between a strategy and a formula. Formulas have to be used exactly, step by step. Strategies are flexible and can be changed to suit the user and the task. If you use a strategy as a formula, not adapting it to your own style, it becomes rigid. For example, the text offers several exploratory guides. What is important is that you use these guides to examine your questions from more than one point of view. Choose whatever guide helps you to do this well. Perhaps a guide works better with one subject than another. When you first try out a guide, it's often helpful to use it as illustrated in the text, and then when you feel comfortable, alter it to suit your needs.

Studying Examples

Many writers also benefit from studying examples. We introduce two kinds of examples: 1) real student cases that illustrate writers' entire processes of inquiry and action and 2) separate samples of students' work with different strategies. These students raise questions about relationships, family, home, and neighborhoods that have influenced their development, probing to uncover the personal and cultural sources of what they value in these areas. They interrogate complex and controversial issues that have touched their lives, seeking new or more qualified positions that they persuade others to share. They raise questions about their fields of study and identify problems in their places of employment, noticing the gaps that sometimes exist between the objectives and practices in these organizations. The cases allow you to see the decisions made by writers throughout the process and the importance of these decisions on the outcome of the inquiry. Studying the student cases and examples will also show you what worked well and what was problematic. You can see how posing a question in one way impacts everything that follows. You can observe writers using some ideas and rejecting others in their explorations, decisions that change the course of their writing process. You can follow the way that a focus directs the shape and organization of the text. You can compare the results of two students' revisions. Student examples also illustrate different genres at work—letters, reports, essays, research papers. In each case, you can watch students struggling to make their writing accomplish something.

Gaining Experience in Real Contexts

Strategies and models are helpful when learning to write, but they need to be put into practice in actual contexts over and over again. You need to have the chance to write to readers who will give you responses so that you can see whether your intended action took place. Exercises on artificial subjects will not give you this experience. In this text, every writing assignment encourages you to effect some change in one of your actual contexts. You, however, have to seize that opportunity and choose subjects that are significant to readers in your contexts. You have to size up these readers and make crucial choices about the genre and language choices that will work. You have to experiment with reader positions to find out whether readers can assume those positions. While classroom writing (writing to your composition class and instructor) is a real context, we encourage you to write in a variety of contexts so that your instructor and workshop members can help you to become effective in diverse writing situations. While a full inquiry process takes time (at least two weeks or more depending on the genre), you still have the chance to write in several contexts in a given semester. Learning to write as inquiry is challenging and you will make some mistakes, but they are part of learning if you benefit by them.

Collaborating in Writing

Writers are often pictured alone at a table, but research shows us that writing involves several kinds of collaboration: during planning, while working in response groups, and in co-authoring texts. Circulating in every text you compose, either directly or indirectly, are the authors you have read, the programs you have watched, and the many voices you have encountered. As you plan your papers, we encourage you to discuss your investigations with your writing group, whose ideas and suggestions find their way into your text. If you interview or conduct research, these sources are also collaborators. And most important are your dialogues with your readers as you shape your writing. Once a draft is complete, you can profit by your group's feedback, not as proofreaders but as collaborators, helping you to make large changes in the light of your focus and intended readers. This book also provides you with experience in co-authoring a piece of writing as a group, producing a common text through collaborative planning, drafting, and revising. Because co-authoring is increasingly used in many fields of study and workplaces, this opportunity will help you to develop valuable co-authoring writing strategies.

Collaborating on This Book: Our Story

We do not just advocate collaborating, we illustrate it in this text, which is the result of extensive collaboration among ten co-authors. We have taught writing for a number of years in different kinds of schools and parts of the US. Each of us has special expertise, a unique teaching style and personality, and has developed diverse materials and syllabi for teaching. We decided to form a team that would generate a new edition of *Four Worlds of Writing*. The prospect was exciting yet challenging because as far as we knew, a composition textbook had not been written with this many co-authors. Little did we anticipate the adventures ahead. It took us two years and four lengthy meetings to frame the book's guiding principles, decide on the number and nature of the areas of inquiry, to plan how to divide our labors, and to agree on terminology. At our first meeting, we agreed on the principles that we thought important for this edition.

- The book should foreground writing as a process of inquiry beginning with students' own compelling questions, not assigned types of writing.

- It should help students select genres that are appropriate for their inquiry and context.
- The book should help students understand themselves as located in actual situations specific to each student.
- It should demonstrate students in action, students from our classrooms.
- The book should offer students opportunities to expand and interact with the text on-line via a World Wide Web site and Internet discussion groups.

We also had a lively discussion about which *writing powers* we would emphasize in the book. Here are the ones we agreed on. The power to:

- frame and pursue questions for investigation
- create new understandings
- effect change in actual contexts
- increase consciousness about cultural influences

Also at our first meeting, we decided that our book should continue to offer guidance at critical points in the writing process when writers face difficult tasks. The critical points we identified included:

- choosing subjects and raising questions
- exploring memory or conducting library, on-line, or field research
- positioning themselves and their readers
- focusing and organizing
- selecting an appropriate genre
- drafting, responding, and revising

Even harder was our effort to reach consensus on the *writing strategies* we would illustrate in the chapters because all of us had worked with many writing guides. Although we concurred that it was essential to continue to offer guides to students during these challenging writing tasks, we also feared that some students might use the strategies as formulas. We decided, however, that in our combined experience, the benefits of strategies to students outweighed the risks. We also knew that students need the opportunity to try different guides, to gain confidence with them and to adapt them to their own style. It would be challenging to demonstrate that process of individualizing in a book.

   At our second meeting, we agreed upon the kind of *teaching practices* that would be either explicitly represented in our book or implied. We were able to agree on the following:

- centering class periods on students' own writing
- fostering effective collaboration
- devoting writing assignments to students' ongoing papers, not exercises

- allowing students to choose their own subjects, genres, readers, and contexts
- introducing a repertoire of strategies and genres
- helping students with their individual problems in grammar, spelling, and punctuation

By the third meeting we had framed several *areas of inquiry*—each an important site of students' lives: relationships with others, issues in their groups, free time activities, academic life, local cultures, reading texts, workplaces, and on-line activities. By choosing this array of areas for inquiry, we hoped to communicate that writing can be used for inquiry and action in many spheres of students' experience. Each co-author assumed responsibility for part of the text, even though everyone agreed to read and criticize all of the chapters. Janice Lauer wrote the Preface, Introduction, and Chapters 9 to 12 in Part II, and coordinated our project; Andrea Lunsford wrote Chapters 9, 13 and 14 in Part II; Nan Uber-Kellogg, Chapter 2; Libby Miles, Chapter 3; Janet Atwill, Chapter 4; Lisa Langstraat, Chapter 5; Debra Jacobs, Chapter 6; Tom Clemens, Chapter 7; Tim Peeples, Chapter 8; and Bill Hart-Davidson, Chapter 15, the book's technological connections. All of us read and critiqued several drafts of the manuscript, based upon our experiences with it in our own classes and those we supervised. A number of ideas also came from other teachers who tested the book in classes. Thus, *Four Worlds of Writing: Inquiry and Action in Context* is the product of many writers, readers, teachers, and students.

Part I

Writing as Inquiry and Action

2

AREA OF INQUIRY: RELATIONSHIPS

NAN UBER-KELLOGG

WHY WRITE ABOUT RELATIONSHIPS?

To be human is to have relationships with other people. Understanding your most important relationships is central to living well. Reflecting on your relationships, deciding what you want to change, communicating feelings and suggestions, all go into keeping relationships thriving. Many times, though, relationships are confusing or puzzling. The reasons for confusion are often hard to uncover when you are caught up in the daily rush of activities. For instance, you may seldom have time to think about a particular friend because you are taking classes and working practically every day. Furthermore, your relationships occur within large, intricate social systems. These systems, and the values they foster, influence your relationships as well, perhaps in ways you don't usually notice.

Writing can give you an opportunity to think about your relationships. When you write, you can ask questions about your relationships; sort out experiences and characteristics; make connections between your relationship and larger cultural forces. Your relationships matter to others as well as to you, so writing to them can help strengthen your ties.

EXAMPLES OF WRITING FOR INQUIRY AND ACTION

- Jim examines his surprisingly close relationship with his roommate whose biker lifestyle is different from his own, which he thinks of as a "typical" middle class, Midwestern lifestyle. He will share his exploration with his family to let them in on what he has learned about the value of having a friend so different from himself.

- Recently, Su is having conflicts with her boyfriend, Nirosh, over his traditional views on the role of women. She will explore their conflicts within the context of women friends from Sri Lanka who, like herself, left traditional roles behind to seek a college education and career. Su thinks that by sharing her story, she can show her friends why it's important that they stick with their decisions to pursue nontraditional options.

- Now that Miranda has started college, living at home with her mom has become uncomfortable. She notices that her mom still treats her as though she were in high school. What's more, Miranda is realizing how little either one of them talks to the other. She decides to explore the causes of their poor communication within the context of her family, in hopes of starting a dialogue with her mother.

- Sharon Hamilton, in *My Name is not Susie*, reflects on her relationships with students of hers who come to school to pursue a better life. She recalls her own drive to overcome a childhood in foster homes by becoming literate and writes a book on literacy within the context of college educators, in order to increase their understanding of the struggles of some of their students.

- Greg Sarris, a member of the Kashaya Pomo tribe of Northern California, had listened to fellow tribe member Mabel McKay's stories since he was a child. On one visit home from college he began to wonder about what she was really teaching him with the stories. He wrote *Keeping Slug Woman Alive* to explore how Mabel and others use story telling to build relationships with those around them. He wrote the book within the context of people interested in Native American literature to share his new understanding of the role of storytelling in Kashaya Pomo culture.

READINGS FOR INQUIRY AND ACTION

A FABRICATED MEXICAN (excerpt) by Rick P. Rivera

In this autobiographical novel, Mr. Rivera explores important relationships he experienced while growing up in two contexts: his Hispanic farm-worker community and the Anglo world of school.

The first time I saw him, there was blood all over his face. The coach said, "I think your nose is broke, David. That ball took a wicked hop. I don't think you should play today."

"I think I can handle it, coach," he replied as he attempted to wipe flowing blood from his mouth and chin. "At least let me try the first couple of innings."

David played the entire game and hit a home run and a triple. He also flawlessly fielded everything hit to him. That day he replaced Bob Hayes, the world's fastest human, as my hero. I had a vested interest in this athlete as he was my sister's boyfriend and the talk of the local baseball enthusiasts. It concerned me that the relationship was a strong one, because to know David was to know a local star.

Newspapers frequently wrote about him and featured pictures of his outstretched body parallel to the ground as he speared searing ground balls, recovered, and threw out frustrated runners at first. Other newspaper pictures captured him at the plate in the middle of his sweet, fluid swing.

He was a modest star and that's what I really liked about him. His kind blue eyes always greeted me with an attention that caused deep sighs of adulation. He was not loud and did not ever admit that he was an attraction to other young boys like myself, or to budding high school girls who envied my sister's luck.

His mannerisms were complacent. He would wave by holding up a still hand at about shoulder height for a few seconds, then return to whatever it was he was doing.

I knew this ballplayer was a special person as he had the respect of my brothers who thought Al Capone was a sissy for getting caught. It was my brothers who collectively agreed that to "deny, deny, deny" was the best way out of anything accusatory. Then use force if necessary.

David once gave me his baseball mitt. It was a Rawlings with Clete Boyer's autograph. Even though I never played on a baseball team, I once made it to the final cuts with that glove. For a short, bittersweet time, I became a better baseball player because of that talismanic glove. David spent hours with me, teaching me how to hit and field, but mostly infusing my life with a confidence that I frequently tried to deny.

Of course, my sister had a headlock on the relationship. And at times I felt I was competing for something that rightfully belonged to her. Whenever David was around, my sister would attempt to shoo me away so they could be alone. But I was like a bothersome fly; I would disappear for a little while and then return to catch David's tentative hand holding my sister's hand.

One of my proudest moments was when my sister announced that she and David would be getting married. Through the residual effect of being my sister's little brother, I could flaunt that David, a future big leaguer, would be my brother-in-law. I, in turn, announced to Eddie Brown, Jesse Comenares, and Alberto Balderas that, yes, it was true, David the star would be related to me. For weeks I walked around with a hubris that was nauseating to my friends, especially since I was never talented enough to make it on a baseball team despite five humiliating attempts.

During those days of my infatuation with baseball and my future brother-in-law, little else attracted my attention. I would scan the sports section of the local paper after every game that David played to see how he had done. When I could attend his games, I was his personal statistician. I had a little piece of paper with columns denoting bats, hits, type of hit, runs, and runs batted in. Upon returning home, I would log the figures into the cumulative totals that I kept on a large piece of cardboard tacked to my bedroom wall. I never kept track of any errors that David made. I ignored errors—which were too few anyway—and always convinced myself and any others who would listen that the ball must have taken a wicked hop.

Questions for Analysis

The Narrator's Insights

1. What questions might the narrator be investigating about his relationship with David by writing about him?

2. What new understandings about his relationship with David does the narrator reach?

The Readers

3. The number and types of details that a writer includes about the subject are tailored to the readers' familiarity with the subject. Looking at the details the narrator provides about baseball and about several American cultural icons, how old do you think he imagines his readers to be, and what level of familiarity with baseball does he assume? Explain your assessment by pointing out details that support it.

4. Rivera writes about a personal world in a genre—the novel—that will be read by people whom he does not know. Some of the details in this excerpt are quite personal and reveal some of the narrator's weaknesses. If you were to take material from your life and fashion it into a work of fiction, are there details that you would be able to share more easily than if you were writing directly to your family and friends? Why or why not?

Cultural Values

5. Based on this passage, what do you think are the qualities of a hero for the narrator?

6. How does the narrator indicate where his values come from in this passage? Point to specific passages.

7. What are some qualities of heroes with which you are familiar, either from your own experience or from media representations of heroes? How are they similar to the narrator's? Different?

8. Who are your heroes/heroines? Why? What larger cultural networks such as your family, your school, and commercial television promote these same heroes/heroines?

Genre

9. Rivera chose to write a novel. What does the genre of the novel allow him to write about that he might not have been able to write in, say, a sociology report on the role of sports in the lives of young boys?

A Case   JONATHAN'S INQUIRY

Jonathan was a twenty-two-year-old Anglo American engineering student partici-
pating in the Air Force ROTC. He wanted to become an Air Force pilot. When
Jonathan learned that he was going to be investigating an important, puzzling
relationship in his writing class, he considered several relationships: his mother
and two others from his younger years. Jonathan's instructor set up the writing
project as an inquiry—a project that is driven by a question. Jonathan used the
Questioning Strategy to choose a relationship, identify confusions about it, and
generate a question to guide his inquiry.

Jonathan's Questions

Possible relationships:

- My high school football coach. He really influenced me, and I miss having his guidance. I want to figure out how I can go on from here without his guidance every day.

- My best friend from home, Chad. We keep competing with each other about everything, and it gets in the way of our friendship. I want to figure out why we do this.

- My mother. We've always been close, and I know when things are bothering her. Lately she seems unsatisfied with her work. I want to encourage her to try something new, but I don't know how she will take this suggestion from me.

- The relationship that puzzles me the most: my relationship with Chad.

- The relationship I would most like to understand better: my relationship with Chad.

- The relationship that holds the most consequences: my relationship with my mother.

I choose my relationship with Chad because I would really like to figure out what's going on before I see him again.

Chad and I have been best friends since the sixth grade, even though our families moved to opposite sides of town. We've done so many things together—snowmobiling, going on vacations with my family, competing in sports, being in honors classes in high school. He's been a good friend, but there was always something that bothered me about our friendship; I couldn't figure out what it was while I was still in high school. I was too close to the whole situation.

Once I got to college and developed new friendships, I realized that Chad and I competed about everything all the time, even things like parties; if one of us got invited to a party, we wouldn't tell the other one about it, so they would be left out. The more I thought about it, the more I realized what a drag it was, and how much I would like things to change. But I drew a blank at first over how to do anything about it because I couldn't figure out what the sources of our competition were. It all seemed so jumbled up—there were so many possible causes.

Relationship with my friend Chad

My Experience	My Values	Cultural Sources	Dissonance
• Chad and I spent a lot of time together	• Spend time with your friends	• Family, Friends are important to your development	• No dissonance
• He was in many activities I was in. He seemed to be following me around	• Follow your own interests	• Parents; their work as teachers. They thought kids went around in packs too much & didn't think for themselves	• It bothered me; he picked things because I did
• We have both always been very competitive academically & in sports	• Competition is good	• Family: we'd have family snowmobiling races • School: they'd encourage us to get the best GPA • Sports: the coaches pitted us against each other for spots on team	• Our friendship was at times hindered by the fact that we compete so much
• My parents took us on snowmobiling vacations & to Mexico; his parents didn't include me much	• Include your friends in your family activities	• Family: Our house was always the place where all us kids hung out with our friends	• Differences in incomes meant they couldn't include me on trips
	• Parents should take an active interest in their kid's life and friends		• Differences in values meant Chad's parents didn't take the time to do things with him

Locating my relationship within a writing context:

- My family. They know both of us well and care what happens to our friendship.
- My friends back home. They have known us too, but they are scattered all over at school
- My new friends at school. They're more mature than my friends back home, but they don't know Chad, so they might not be able to help me sort out what's going on.

My choice for a context
My family

Questions I want to answer

- What first started the competition between Chad and me, and what has caused it to continue?
- Do the differences in our families' incomes and child-rearing practices promote competition between us?
- What cultural influences might reinforce our competition?

- Could I say something to him which could help reduce the competition between us without upsetting anyone?
- How could Chad and I end the competition?

My choice
What first started the competition between Chad and me and what has caused it to continue?

Jonathan met with two other students in his composition class, Alfredo and Ben, to talk over their Questioning Strategies. Alfredo, from Guatemala, was in his first semester at the large American university. Not an immigrant, he planned to return to his country after graduation. Ben, an Asian-American from the Midwest, was also a first-year student. He had wrestled in high school.

Alfredo and Ben thought that Jonathan's choice of a writing context—his family—made sense if he really needed help sorting things out. Alfredo and Ben thought that cultural attitudes about competition played a factor in Jonathan and Chad's relationship. As an athlete himself, Ben thought, "the sports system encourages competition, and it might have intensified the competition between you two." Jonathan, though, thought the differences between Chad's and his families were more relevant. He told his group mates: "My parents are both educators and really promote learning. Chad's parents aren't so interested in education, and they were always busy with work. Chad wanted some adults in his life to take an interest in his school work, so he spent a lot of time at our house talking with my mom and dad." Jonathan's instructor, an Anglo-American woman, encouraged him to investigate the family differences, as well as to follow Alfredo and Ben's suggestion to pay attention to larger cultural sources of competition. She also asked him whether the difference in their families' incomes made Chad vulnerable to an economic dynamic that encourages Americans to tie their personal value to wealth.

When it came time for Jonathan to choose a question, Alfredo and Ben encouraged him to ask what factors started the competition. His instructor suggested he expand his question about differences in income and child-rearing practices since she thought that he might benefit from looking for cultural connections that would explain the pressures they felt to compete. Jonathan decided to use the question about what first started the competition since he was just beginning to notice sources of the tensions.

Having settled on a question, Jonathan next explored his relationship from three perspectives, to try out ways of looking at the relationship. He brainstormed in writing, jotting down many memories, images, ideas, and looking for cultural underpinnings to his relationships.

Jonathan's Exploration

Three Perspectives Guide

Describe and Distinguish

Physical & personality features that characterize people in my investigation

- Chad: Chad's about 5′10″, medium build, and brown hair. He's got a good build for playing soccer. He sort of hunches his shoulders up some of the time, like he's protecting himself. And sometimes he stands back and kind of squints at people, like he's sizing them up.

   Chad could be considered to be moderately self-centered. He's intelligent, especially in chemistry and physics, and he's good with machines. He's got a drive for success. Whenever he starts something, he keeps at it until he proves he's the best.

- Me: I'm 5′11″, medium build, with black hair. I played wide receiver. I'm pretty athletic and like other sports too. I don't hunch up like Chad; I tend to stand up pretty straight. My friends kid me that I'm at attention all the time.

   I could be considered self-centered at times too. I'd say I'm as intelligent as Chad, but my strong areas are math and history. I have a drive for success also, but I try to compete with myself more than with my friends, although, I guess I do compete with them. I'd say I'm pretty easy going, though.

Day–to–day interactions I associate with person involved in my investigation

Since we have been in college, our day-to-day interaction is nonexistent except during vacations. In high school, we had basically identical schedules. Chad would ask me what I was going to take each semester, and then he'd sign up for the same schedule. We were involved in the same extracurricular activities: we both were on student council, and in the snowmobiling club, and hung out with the same people, but participated in different sports. I played football, and Chad played soccer. A typical day back then was we'd meet in home room, go to classes, have lunch together with other friends, go to our sports practices, then meet up at my house and work on homework or relax until supper. We used to go to parties together or go on double dates. This daily, all day long interaction while we were younger could have been one of the sources of the competition since every thing we did we did together.

Trace Moves and Changes

How my experience with my relationship began

- Chad and I became close friends around the fourth grade. At that time, both Chad and I were close friends with a neighbor of mine. Chad and I would sometimes hang out together, and sometimes we would hang out with Matt but without the third person. This could have been a possible beginning to the competition between ourselves concerning friends we had in common.

- We got to be the leaders of our sixth grade class, and other kids looked up to us. It seemed like the only way for us to compete was with each other, so we did.
- When we got into snowmobiling, we competed over who had the better one, and who could race the best.
- Throughout high school, we played different sports and we were always arguing or teasing each other about how our sport was better than the sport which the other person played.

How my relationship has changed

- My family moved into a subdivision and built a house on a private lake. Chad's family also built a new house, but not in a subdivision and not on a lake. Chad used to hate staying at his house, so he'd hang out at our house as much as he could. Once he started doing that, it seemed like he wasn't so sure of himself and had to keep challenging me. That bothered me.
- For my part, I would sometimes get irritated with him for following me around so much, and I'd use our competition as a way to express my irritation.
- Since the passing of my grandfather, my family came into a lot of money which then passed on to me. Chad seems to get a little annoyed when I get something new.
- Chad and I have obviously matured a great deal which has toned down the competition, but nonetheless it still exists. When we get together on vacations, we talk up our exploits at school, and we always challenge each other to a race or a game of tennis. If one of us gets invited to a party, we sometimes don't tell the other so they're left out.

Changes in my attitude and feelings

I have realized that our competition is foolish and unnecessary. It is not necessary to compete when it gets us nowhere and only gets between our friendship. We're both smart and doing well, so why compete with each other?

Larger cultural changes that have influenced my relationship

- Chad's mom and dad both work in the automotive industry which keeps going through changes. They don't think their jobs are stable, so they worry a lot and don't spend lots of time with Chad. Consequently, Chad hung out with my family. So, in a way, the automotive industry has influenced our relationship.
- The rising cost of tuition meant that Chad's parents weren't able to send him out of state to the school he really wanted to go to. My parents had more money and were able to help send me to my top choice school out of state.

Map Networks and Relationships

Cultural narratives that apply to my subject

I think that in society people are brought up to compete with each other and for their place in the world. Another cultural narrative might be that parents instill competitiveness into their children so their children can be better than their friends.

Some of the assumptions and stereotypes

- Looking at our friendship from the outside, someone might assume that it would be normal for two guys to compete with each other, especially honors students who are varsity athletes like we were.

- Since we're guys, there might be an assumption that we would only be friends by doing things together, not by talking about personal things.

- I guess if someone were going to stereotype me, they could use upper middle class white male because my family lives in a really nice area and takes vacations to Mexico; money isn't really a problem, and I'm getting a good education.

- If someone were to stereotype Chad, they'd use more of a middle class/working class white male stereotype. His dad went to vocational/technical school, and his mom didn't do much college at all. They both work blue collar jobs. They have a nice house, too, but not in as fancy a place as we do. They aren't that involved with Chad's schooling unlike my parents who are educators.

An analogy

- We're like twins joined at the hip; wherever one goes, the other goes.
- We're like two lions competing to take over the pride.

When Jonathan met with Alfredo and Ben again, they looked over each other's explorations like detectives searching for clues. Alfredo, who was examining a relationship with a friend having family problems back home in Guatemala, was alert to the economic differences between Jonathan's and Chad's families. Therefore, Alfredo thought that Jonathan's observations about the two families might help him gain new insight. Ben was still on the trail of athletic competition. He suggested Jonathan expand his answers to Physical and Personality features by adding more about how the two of them act when they are competing in sports. Alfredo and Ben thought there were other cultural influences encouraging competition as well. To help Jonathan expand his thinking about cultural forces, Alfredo offered a stereotype of an honors student: "They are people who study a lot, are very responsible, admirable. They compete for the best grades, the best schools." Ben thought the stereotype of an athlete could be something that Jonathan and Chad were trying to live up to: "You have to be a hard worker and practice all the time and try to be the best even though you are working as a team member."

Jonathan's instructor asked him, "Why don't you describe specific interactions you had with Chad, ones that could have sparked competition?" And since Jonathan had mentioned the economic differences between his family and Chad's as a larger cultural factor, she suggested he consider still other cultural factors like perceived threats to white males' opportunities. Jonathan decided to explore both of these avenues.

Before Jonathan moved on to drafting, his teacher asked him to next look more closely at his writing context, or the community of people to whom he would write. His teacher asked him to choose positions to help him think about the kind of information he wanted to share and the relationship he wanted to establish in his text with his readers. He used the Writer/Reader Positioning Strategy to select positions for himself and his readers.

Jonathan's Writer/Reader Positioning

My choice for a context

My family

My question

What first started the competition between Chad and me and what has caused it to continue?

Setting my writer position

- *Positions I have written from within this context:* I have generally written as the college student, youngest son, youngest brother
- *Excluded positions:* I'm excluded from the position of full adult, from older brother or older son
- *Positions left behind:* the young bright teenager, and the little kid of six brothers
- *Writer Position I will adopt:* None of those positions really fits this inquiry. It doesn't matter that I'm the youngest; none of my brothers has gone through the kinds of things Chad and I have, so my being youngest doesn't matter. Instead I'll adopt the position of maturing son because that position will allow me to emphasize how I'm changing my views to more adult ones.

Setting my reader position

- *Reader positions in my writing context:* family member, brother, parent, adult, teenager
- *People who benefit:* My family would probably benefit from what I have to say because they would understand me better, however, I believe that I will benefit more than anyone from what I will say as it will give me a chance to more clearly understand the situation.
- *The position I choose for my reader:* Within the context of my family, I think my parents would be the most helpful to me in understanding this situation. My brothers and I have competed, too, and they might not be that sympathetic, whereas my parents would be. Since my parents have seen the situation between Chad and me and understand what has taken place between us, I will choose the position of "parent" and gear my writing towards them.

> - *The values and background I associate with my reader position:* Values: watch out for children; listen to children's problems; hold high hopes for their children's futures; hope their children will turn out to be decent people; want their kids to be happy. Background: parents bring children into the world and raise them; they watch their children grow up; they get to know their kids' friends; they develop opinions of their kids' behavior.

Jonathan's group met and offered feedback on the writer/reader positions each had chosen. Alfredo thought that Jonathan's writer position was good, but suggested he change his context and reader position: "Maybe it would be better to change your context to your friends back home and within that context write directly to Chad since he is the one that has to know how you really feel." Ben agreed. Jonathan decided he had learned enough about what caused their competition so that he could write directly to Chad. Jonathan switched his context to friends back home and changed his reader to Chad. This change meant he had to alter his writer and reader positions. He changed them both to "friend." Jonathan was eager to write to Chad, but he quickly realized that there were issues he would have to treat carefully, especially the way Chad followed him around and the differences in their families' incomes. "It would hurt his pride if I don't do it just right," he told Alfredo and Ben.

Just as his writer and reader positions shaped what he could write about, so too did the genre he chose.

Jonathan's Selection of a Genre

> *Possible genres*
>
> letter; essay; e-mail message
>
> *Implications of these genres*
>
> - *letter:* I am very familiar with this genre, and I have enough time to write one. I could write about our past experiences and share private thoughts about our situation; my writer & reader positions would work
>
> - *e-mail message:* I could be both personal and more formal, but there's always the possibility that an e-mail message will get sent places you don't want it to, so it could be risky.
>
> *Question I am trying to answer*
>
> What started the competition between Chad and me, and what has caused it to continue?
>
> *My genre choice*
>
> I'll write a letter.
>
> *Implications of the genre*
>
> The parts of my exploration that will be good to include are the ones that include stories of our competition; also, the parts that make links

between our competition and social practices. In a letter I can include lots of details about our past and remind him of how important our relationship is. A letter is compatible with lots of organizing plans, so that gives me flexibility. I can be casual in tone. It will be written and go via snail mail, so Chad will have it to look over and keep if he wants to (or burn!)

In their small group, all supported Jonathan's choice, as did his instructor.

Next Jonathan began to answer his questions using the Focusing Strategy. Jonathan's focuses reflected his deepening understanding of the role of competition in their friendship.

Jonathan's Focusing

My question

What first started the competition between Chad and me, and what has caused it to continue?

My focuses

Subject	Point of Significance
• Chad's and my competing in sports	may have caused our competition to spread to other parts of our lives
• The college majors chosen by Chad and me	shows evidence that Chad has followed me around through life
• The noticeable decline in our competition and the improvement in our relationship	proves that competition has been a hindrance to our friendship
• A number of Chad's recent behaviors	have been rude and unfriendly.

The group met to talk over the focuses they had generated and to offer each other advice about which focus to pursue. Jonathan wasn't sure what insight he wanted to emphasize. He told Alfredo and Ben, "I need to try developing the focuses before we make a decision." Alfredo and Ben protested. "It's up to you to choose, not us." His instructor asked, "What if you think again about what you hope to accomplish by writing to Chad, to help you decide?"

Later that afternoon, after ROTC drills, Jonathan was hanging out with some of the older ROTC guys. They were talking about how they were going to try to get good commissions. "You've go to do everything that comes your way," said one of them. "Otherwise you just get passed over. There aren't enough good commissions to go around." Something clicked for Jonathan. Wasn't this situation one where a larger cultural factor was influencing them all? Weren't they having to compete? Suddenly his investigation of his relationship with Chad looked different. He wanted to understand what cultural factors had helped keep their competition going. He developed a new focus that allowed for social forces: "The competition between Chad and me over the years—can be partly explained by several factors." Jonathan developed an organizing plan for this focus.

Jonathan's Organizing

Focus	*Point of Significance*
The competition between Chad and me over the years ———————	—— can be partly explained by several factors, including larger social forces.

Organization

- The competition ————————————— began when we were both friends of Matt's.
- The competition ————————————— was increased by the fact that we did practically all the same things together.
- The competition ————————————— was encouraged in sports. (larger social forces at work here)
- The competition ————————————— was encouraged in our honors classes. (here too)

In their small group, Jonathan told Alfredo and Ben about his new direction. They were surprised but enthusiastic. Jonathan wondered, though, "Why write to Chad? I'm going to benefit more than he will." Alfredo answered, "The letter could be helpful to Chad, too." Ben agreed. "Maybe Chad is wondering the same thing and would be relieved to have it out in the open." Jonathan saw their point and decided to go ahead and write to Chad.

Jonathan used his draft to do several things: to express his appreciation to Chad, to call attention to their problem, to speculate on the sources of the competition, and to ask that they stop competing so much. He included all of these elements.

Jonathan's Polished Draft

Dear Chad:

We have been friends for quite some time. I still remember the first times we started hanging out together. Those were the days! In the sixth grade, Shannon, Tina, you and I were considered kings of the school as we were captains and lieutenants of patrol. Also in sixth grade, I left our good friend Matt bleeding on the street after our little brawl and intervened and helped Matt back to his house. After I moved to River Oaks in the seventh grade, the distance separating our friendship was great considering we were only thirteen years old. Our years in junior high tested the strength of our friendship in many ways, however, our friendship prevailed, possibly stronger than ever. Junior high school brought on the snowmobiling craze. First I bought one, then you topped me by buying your Indy Sport. It wasn't even a year until I topped you with my more powerful Indy Sport. During this same time period, we went on many vacations together and constantly hung out together. High school brought many new times and memories. We both desired to excel in our classes and in sports. We had practically the same schedule for three years, participated in the same school clubs, and we both loved playing sports. Since high school we have both survived through two years of college, and we are now looking at our futures and places in this world.

All those years and memories were great, however, there is one thing which has been bothering me about our relationship. Our friendship has been constantly and consistently hindered by the competitive natures which reside in both of us. This competition has inadvertently been the source of many arguments between us and many uncomfortable moments.

After analyzing our situation, I have come to many possible reasons and solutions to our competition. For as long as I can remember, we have had similar interests in everything we do, similar motivations, and similar talents. We both are physically active, and we both wish to succeed in life. I believe that our uncanny similarities first caused the competition between us and those similarities have driven the competition until now. However, those similarities weren't the only cause. During high school we each played separate sports which were important to each of us. The coaches encouraged that competition, to fire us up. We wanted our sports to seem more important than the other person's. In high school, since we were in the same honors classes, the thought of outdoing the other person was never far off in our minds. That thought had help from our teachers, who made a big deal out of the importance of each of us excelling.

While we have been in college, the competition which coexisted in our lives from the time when we first met until our high school graduation has decreased significantly, however, even as sophomores in college, we still continue to foolishly compete with each other. Though I understand that our competition will never completely end between us, I hope that by my bringing up this issue, the stupid incidents which result from our competition no longer take place. Friendship is a delicate thing; it is sometimes hard to establish, but can be easily broken. You have been a great friend to me, and I thank you for it. Next time I am in Wisconsin, let's head over to the ice arena, and I bet you that you can't beat me in some one-on-one.

Your friend,
Jonathan

The instructor asked each writer to analyze his own text before receiving responses because they were the experts on their own goals and texts.

Jonathan's Self Assessment

Overall response

I think this paper shows I am concerned about the relationship and want to end the competition. It also shows understanding of the causes.

Focus

"The competition between you and me—has been caused by several factors." All parts of the letter fit this focus because they have to do with our relationship and reasons for competing.

Development for reader

The reader position is friend. Detail is sufficient for this position as far as our history goes. Add more about the cultural factors that foster competition between us.

Organization and coherence

Organizing starts with brief history of our relationship and then attempts to explain why there has been competition between us.

Main emphasis for revision

Add more about the cultural factors that foster competition between us.

Compiled Reader Responses to Jonathan's Draft

Overall response

Ben: I think you describe your friendship with Chad really well. You describe different events that you both enjoy. It's hard to tell, though, what the point of the letter is in the first paragraph.

Alfredo: This letter shows definite concern for your friendship. You could include examples of how the competition was hard on your relationship.

Instructor: A good start towards explaining to yourself and to Chad the causes and costs of competing. You could explore the sources of the competition further.

Focus

Ben: "Our friendship is constantly hindered by our competitive natures." First paragraph doesn't fit because it doesn't talk about the problem. Rest does.

Alfredo: "Throughout out friendship, competition—has hurt our relationship." Hard to see how first paragraph fits.

Instructor: You have 2 going: "Our friendship—has continued through many events." The first paragraph fits this focus. Your second focus is "The hurtful competition in our friendship— can be attributed to several causes." The rest of the letter fits this focus.

Development for readers

Ben: Writer and Reader position: friend. You provide enough detail about your early friendship, but you don't tell what happened that bugged you. You could add that in.

Alfredo: The Writer and Reader positions are close friends. You could add an example of an argument that was caused by competition. You could write more about the cultural sources of the need to compete because I don't think Chad would get it with what you've included here alone. He hasn't been thinking about it the way you have.

Instructor: Writer position—friend. Reader position—friend. In your first paragraph you remind Chad of some key events in your friendship. The events you highlight all connect to competition in some way and lead up to the second half of your letter. Could you make a more direct bridge between the remembered events and what you are writing about? A good place to bridge would be after your last sentence of P 1. Why has the issue of competition become important to you now? You could write about that. Could you give an example of an argument you have had in P. 2? And in P. 4? Also, in your Three Perspectives Strategy, you considered some larger cultural sources of the competition. Could you elaborate on those here? It may be that Chad hasn't considered them either and would like to hear from you about them.

Organization and coherence

Ben: First paragraph is organized chronologically; rest is organized by grouping of causes. You went back to sixth grade & moved to the present, so the order seems right for the first part. In the second part you went from smaller to bigger parts which makes sense.

Instructor: No clear organizational structure, although you are working with a chronological order in the first paragraph. Paragraphs 3 & 4 suggest a grouping organization would work well, one that supports your second focus. Opening to first paragraph does not introduce the focus of the letter, so it could be rewritten to signal what's to come.

Language choices

Ben: Some parts are casual, like the last sentence of the letter. Since the person you are writing to is the same age, language choices are good here. But in other places, you sound like you are writing for school rather than for a friend. Ex: "the distance separating our friendship was great considering we were only thirteen years old." You could drop some of the big words and use words that people our age use when talking with each other.

Instructor: Mix of informal and formal; probably too formal in places where you are explaining competition. See last sentence of Paragraph 2.

Conventions

Instructor: No real problems

Main emphasis for revision

Ben: Redoing organization. Adding examples of over-competition. Rework language choices.

Alfredo: Focus: Rework so you have just one. Development: Add examples of arguments and say more about the cultural sources.

Instructor: Settle on one focus; develop an organizing plan that supports the focus; develop the discussion of the cultural sources of the competition; add details about the arguments you've had.

Jonathan compared his own response with Alfredo's, Ben's, and his instructor's. Jonathan agreed that he could rework the text so that all the material reflected the focus. He also planned to add examples and to elaborate on the cultural sources. He hadn't noticed how the organization didn't really work, so he decided he would redo that part as well. Their instructor asked them to devise a revising plan.

Jonathan's Revising Plan

1. The best advice I received was to continue developing the cultural sources of competition and to build the letter around that part more.

2. I need to work on using just one focus. I also want to expand the cultural sources part and to redo the organization.

3. Then I will include the parts that Alfredo and my instructor suggested. Next I will fix the organization.

4. I have learned that many things influence a relationship. You have to look at the cultural influences and investigate a situation in depth in order to understand it.

5. By writing about my relationship, I am seeing more clearly how much competition interfered, and it is making me wonder about other relationships that have been affected by competition.

Jonathan thought about the responses he received, and the plans for revision he had made. He changed the letter in the several ways he planned. However, as he worked on revising, he noticed more things he wanted to change that no one had suggested. He saw how the earlier draft didn't focus on the cultural sources as much as he wanted it to. He made changes in this area, too.

Jonathan's Revision

Dear Chad,

We have been friends for quite some time. Friendship is a delicate thing; it is sometimes hard to establish but can be easily broken. You have been a great friend to me, and I thank you for it. I still remember the first times we started hanging out together. All the years and memories were great, however, there is one thing which has been bothering me about our relationship. We compete with each other all the time, and it hinders our friendship. It's been the source of many arguments between us and many uncomfortable moments. Remember when I gloated over buying a snow-mobile before you? Really rubbed it in? You then worked extra hard to earn enough money for your Indy Sport. You didn't tell me until you had it, and you showed up on the trails with it. Then you constantly rubbed it in. These incidents hurt our friendship.

When we were living at home, I never really noticed how much competition got in our way. Since I've been at college, I've seen it more clearly, and I started wondering what caused it. At first I thought it was just because we were so alike in our interests and abilities and drive. But lately, after analyzing our situation, I have come to many possible reasons for our competition.

These reasons are larger than we are. One reason is that middle school promotes unofficial popularity contests by giving out special privileges. Those were the days! In the sixth grade, Shannon, Tina, you and I were considered kings of the school as we were captains and lieutenants of patrol. We were rewarded for outdoing others, and it egged us on to compete for more glory. Our sports activities promoted individual competition big time even though we were supposedly making a team effort. Remember how they kept track of everyone's records and gave awards to the best individual effort even though we were supposed to be team members? Remember how each of our coaches encouraged us to think that our sport was the best? We didn't invent that stupid football/soccer rivalry all by ourselves, but it sure made its way into our friendship, and we let it get the best of us.

Then there were academics in high school. Being in honors classes, we were expected to excel by outdoing everyone else in class. Our teachers really drooled all over anyone who aced out everyone else. That essay contest that happened when we were juniors is a good case in point. We kept boasting to each other that we could write a better essay; we slipped into slamming each other's work and ended up not talking for a week. It's a good thing neither of us won. Who knows what we would have done to each other! When you think about it, our teachers and the principal didn't really support us working together; they wanted us to do things on our own. So, even if we wanted to cooperate, we were told to compete. I ask myself why they did that, and I come up with the same reason—they think we are going to have to compete with everyone once we get out into the job market, and they want us to be prepared.

And there's another thing. You know how my grandfather had a lot of money even though he didn't have a fancy job? Well, your parents and my parents all have to work to make ends meet. The economy has changed, and our teachers and coaches know that we may have a harder time finding and keeping a job. OK, so maybe we do have to compete more for work. Does that mean you and I have to compete all the time about everything? I don't think so. I've been hanging out with my ROTC buddies, and we do something different. We work hard together as a team but help each other out afterwards with homework and fixing cars and stuff. I'm thinking you and I could lighten up, too. What do you think? Our competition may have gotten started because we spent so much time from a young age doing things together, and because we're so much alike. But it really got fueled by the people leading the activities we participated in and school policies. We took it too far and made it a 24-hour a day mission. We don't have to let competition ruin our friendship; we can cooperate on things too.

By the way, next time I am in Wisconsin, let's head over to the ice arena and have some fun. I bet you that you can't beat me in some one-on-one.

Your friend,
Jonathan

Jonathan met with his instructor after the project was finished. He told her how amazed he was by the way his understanding of competition in their relationship had grown. "I thought I could attribute our competition to a few quirks of our history and our personalities. But the more I looked at it, the more I saw these other factors. I never would have guessed I would have ended up here." His instructor congratulated him for his persistence, and joked with him: "If Chad had been in the class, do you think he would have worked as hard as you did to uncover the sources of competition?" Jonathan laughed and shook his head. "I don't know," he said. "But I won't be surprised if I get a letter back trying to explain it in a different way!"

Questions for Analysis

1. Did Jonathan's writing process engage him in a genuine inquiry—pursuing an important question for which he did not have an answer at the beginning? Why or why not?

2. Did Jonathan locate himself in a real writing context, one in which he could actually send his letter to his friend? Why or why not? Was it the best context for the question he was trying to answer?

3. Which aspects of his writing process contributed most to Jonathan's inquiry?

4. At several points Jonathan made critical decisions. What were they? What impact did they have on the rest of his process?

5. During his process, Jonathan analyzed some cultural practices and assumptions that surrounded his question. What observations would you add to his analysis? What other cultural factors would you include?

6. Imagine a conversation between Ricky, the narrator in "A Fabricated Mexican," and Jonathan about sports heroes and competition. What could Ricky contribute to Jonathan's analysis?

7. Jonathan's group and instructor gave him feedback and advice along the way during his planning. What advice was especially helpful in your view? What feedback was misleading or unhelpful? Why?

8. He also received reader responses to his draft. What responses do you think were most useful? Which were misguided or ineffective?

9. Based on what you know about Chad, would he be receptive to the letter? Why or why not?

WRITING FOR INQUIRY AND ACTION

THE WRITING ASSIGNMENT

Choose an important relationship, explore it through writing, and address your text to a person or persons who are interested in your relationship. Select a relationship that is genuinely puzzling to you, so that you can create a new understanding. Examine ways your relationship brings you face to face with values promoted by the culture at large.

YOUR WRITING PROCESS

Inquiring into a puzzling relationship is more challenging than writing what you already know, but it's also more rewarding. In this chapter you will be introduced to several writing activities to help you with your inquiry. These activities are guided by powerful strategies that can be used in many other writing contexts as well.

STARTING

Why pose questions about relationships?

When you work in this context, you are using writing to investigate puzzling aspects of a relationship that matters to you. You are also communicating with others who care about you in an effort to bring about new understandings or positive changes. A good beginning can involve the following: choosing a puzzling relationship, noting confusions, choosing a context in which to write, and posing a question to guide your inquiry. The Questioning Strategy below has four directives that can help you begin well.

QUESTIONING STRATEGY

Select a Relationship / Get in Touch with Dissonance / Locate Your Relationship in a Writing Context / Raise Questions / Workshop

---

SELECTING A RELATIONSHIP FOR INQUIRY

For some of you, one relationship may leap out as an obvious choice. For others, you may be thinking of many options. In either case, here is a way to help you choose well. Start by listing several relationships so that you have a chance to consider more than just the most obvious one. Once you've got a list, look at what's at stake in each case. Jot down your reactions to each relationship since your responses are clues to what matters to you. Having brainstormed about each relationship, go back and compare them before you pick one. You might ask yourself which relationship puzzles you the most; which one you would like to understand better; and which one holds the most consequences for you if you investigate it. Remember, there's not much point in writing about a relationship you already understand well. Then make your decision. See also Part II.

GETTING IN TOUCH WITH DISSONANCE

Having chosen a relationship, you can now develop an inquiry. Often a good inquiry emerges from a dissonance, or tension, in a relationship. Dissonance occurs when your experience is different from your expectations and your values. In order to locate dissonances in your relationships, you can begin by reviewing experiences you've had that have puzzled you. Once you have noted those experiences, you might write down your expectations for that type of relationship and the values that underlie those expectations. Next, in order to make connections between your values and larger cultural forces, name some institutions or social structures such as family, church, and school where values for this type of relationship are discussed. Describe how the value is promoted in each institution. Finally, identify whether your puzzling experience reflects your value, fails to do so, or exceeds it. If it fails to do so, or exceeds your values, you have a dissonance occurring between your values and the other person's. That dissonance may be worth investigating. You can chart your answers to make it easier to find connections. See the example. For more on Dissonance see Part II.

LOCATING YOUR RELATIONSHIP IN A CONTEXT

Writing is never done in a social vacuum. You might think of writing as a form of conversation. When you write, you are responding in some way to people and events that have come before, and you are directing your ideas back towards those people. In this book we describe this dynamic interaction as taking place in a context. The word derives from the Middle English *con tere* meaning "to braid together." You participate in any number of contexts, and each one shapes the way you write and the content you include. Your family forms a context, for instance. Your family's unique attributes and history will most likely lead you to choose material tailored especially to it. If you wrote to a group of friends instead, the context you and they share would guide you to create a quite different message.

Context is especially important when you are using writing for inquiry and action. The context you choose—the people to whom you write—will shape your questions. List the possible contexts you could choose, reflect on what each one allows you to investigate, and select one. For more on Context see Part II.

RAISING QUESTIONS FOR INQUIRY

A good question makes all the difference in your inquiry because it sets the direction of your entire effort. To develop strong questions, you can return to the dissonances you've identified, and select one that puzzles you the most, or which you would most like to understand, or which holds the most consequences for you if you investigate it.

Now that you have chosen a dissonance, you can move on to developing a question about it. The way you raise your questions will lead to different kinds of answers. There are several types of questions. A *new understanding* question is one that leads to an explanation for a confusing relationship. A *cultural sources* question guides you to an understanding of cultural values and practices that affect your relationship. A *solution to a problem* question helps you to solve a problem in your relationship. A *course of action* question maps positive steps to take. Try posing at least one of each of these types for your dissonance. When you have several questions, select the one that holds the most chances for new knowledge, matters most to you and your context, and can be addressed in the time you have.

Example: Su's Questions about Her Boyfriend

Selecting a Relationship

Relationships that matter to me:

My best friend, Nirosh, who is also my present boyfriend
- I transferred to [this school] from England to be with him. He doesn't seem to realize the trouble I endured.
- I am quite westernized whereas he is not that liberal; he expects me to be a typical Asian girl in certain issues.

My mother
- I see her once a year when I go home to Sri Lanka. We can't call because it's expensive. I miss her.
- I feel out of touch with the family, and when she writes she never tells me what's really going on. I wonder how we can stay close.

My advisor back at the university in England
- she advised me against moving to the US to follow Nirosh because she thought I had more opportunities at that school.
- I refused to stay, and once I made my mind up, she supported me and helped me transfer by writing a letter.
- I still feel that there's some tension between us, and I would like to explain to her once again why I moved and how things are here. I'd like to be able to write to her about how confusing things are here, but I feel like she'll tell me that she warned me.

- Relationship that puzzles me the most: Nirosh
- Relationship that I would like to understand better: Nirosh
- One that holds the most consequences for me: Nirosh

My choice:

My relationship with Nirosh

Getting in touch with my dissonance

My Experience	*My Values*	*Cultural Sources*	*Dissonance*
• We both want to be at the top of our chosen fields of study	• self-actualization	• Family: both parents are respected professionals • School: Western prep school and university promote excellence	• we share this value; no dissonance here
• Nirosh wants me to do most of the housework.	• People should compromise	• Family: we talk about problems & compromise • Religion: teaches tolerance & respect	• my value is not being met, but will probably continue to be a problem

35

| • Lately he has taken over the chores some of the time | • Men & women should share housework | • Western education that stresses equality between the sexes | • Same as above |

My questions

- Why do I get so angry with Nirosh over housekeeping?
- What are the cultural sources of the differences between Nirosh and me?
- How can we resolve our differences?

The question I choose:
- How can we resolve our differences?

WORKSHOP

In a small group, take turns explaining to one another the relationship you have chosen, the contexts you are considering, and the question you have selected for your inquiry. For each group member, answer the following questions:

1. Is the context a realistic one? Can the writer actually reach the readers? Why or why not?

2. Does the question represent a genuine inquiry? Does the writer currently not have an answer and want to find one? Why or why not?

EXPLORING

Why explore relationships from different perspectives?

Oftentimes a dissonance in a relationship persists because you approach the relationship in the same way over and over. Exploring a relationship with a variety of approaches may provide you with new ways of thinking about the relationship, and these fresh angles may lead you to new insights. This book offers you many exploratory guides to use in different writing experiences. The Three Perspectives Strategy is introduced below.

THREE PERSPECTIVES STRATEGY
Investigate Your Question from Three Perspectives / Review Your Ideas and Highlight Those that Answer Your Question / Allow Your Ideas to Incubate / Workshop

To avoid getting stuck in habitual ways of solving problems, try out the Three Perspectives listed below. Keep your question and context in mind by writing it at the beginning of this strategy. It will help your group members and your instructor recall what you are investigating.

DESCRIBE AND DISTINGUISH

This perspective helps you create a description of important and relatively unchanging details in your relationship. Distinguishing features of the particular relationship are emphasized. These features may help you describe the most significant elements of your relationship. To help you think about what these distinguishing features might be, here are some attributes to consider: The physical or personality characteristics of the people involved may alert you to factors that play a big part in the relationship. They may reveal central, enduring features of your relationship and help to explain its power. Day-to-day interactions among the people involved may also provide clues for understanding the dissonance you are experiencing. These interactions could consist of small, repeated activities, like a brother leaving his things on the kitchen table each night, that create a predictable irritation.

Having identified relatively unchanging features of your relationship, you can go on to describe what features *distinguish* your relationship. A relationship may be distinctive because it's unlike other relationships you are familiar with, or the distinctive characteristics may be those that make the relationship important to those involved.

A dissonance occurs when an expectation or value is not met, or is exceeded. Your attitude towards such a value may prove important when you investigate your relationship. Explain your attitude so that you are in a position to explain why it is important to you. Describing the feelings that the relationship arouses can also help.

A very different way to characterize your relationship is to ask yourself what recurring images come to mind when you think of it. Images are non-linear, complex ways of understanding relationships. You can use images to describe your relationship more succinctly and emotionally than you might with the other approaches described above. For example, when you think of your boss, you might think of a mountain top because she seems inaccessible and concerned with things that don't have much to do with what you and your co-workers deal with every day.

TRACE MOVES AND CHANGES

This perspective emphasizes the ways your relationship and your culture have changed over time, perhaps as they have been affected by significant events. To engage this perspective, you might describe the beginning of your relationship so you can trace its entire history and explain how your relationship became important to you. Next, noting how your relationship and your question about it have evolved over time can provide you with a way to recall events that contributed to the dissonance. In addition, explaining how your attitude has changed may help you describe what has shifted for you, especially if many features of the relationship have not altered.

Reviewing changes in your relationship gives you much valuable material, but it doesn't necessarily help you make connections between your experience and larger cultural changes that may have influenced it. You may be thinking that no larger changes have influenced your relationship. It may be hard to connect your personal experience with events and issues you read about. However, keep in mind that the values we hold are continuously promoted or discouraged by society's institutions, like universities, governments, even shopping malls. In addition, all media presentations promote values, attitudes, and practices. We not only make decisions about our own relationships, but we may follow soap operas or listen to songs that deal with loyalty and deception, selfishness and watching out for the family, juggling children and careers. Regardless of whether you can see a direct connection between larger cultural issues and your own relationship, take some time to list issues that you have noticed receiving media attention lately. You may find a connection later. (Remember, the point of this strategy is to look at your relationship in ways you might not yet have tried.)

Just as with values that are being addressed by the media, there are also shifting trends in the economy, in politics, in life styles that may have some bearing on your relationship. Some may seem to be directly related to your situation: a change in student loan policy may affect whether you or the person about whom you are writing can go to college. Others may not seem to relate, but might: shifting job patterns may mean that the career you are pursuing seems less certain, adding stress to your life which surfaces in other ways in your relationship. Here, too, it's not important to make connections between your relationship and the events right away, but to identify and describe some events that have caught your interest lately. That way you have materials available later when you begin to answer your question.

MAP NETWORKS AND RELATIONSHIPS

This perspective makes more specific connections between your relationship and cultural values and practices.

List cultural narratives or basic stories being told over and over in the culture that apply to your relationship. One common cultural narrative about romantic relationships is "boy meets girl, boy gets girl, boy loses girl, boy gets girl back, and they live happily ever after." While you may not believe your relationships follow this pattern, you still encounter these stories in movies and novels. Therefore, you deal with them in some way if only to ignore them. Identifying cultural narratives, then, can help you notice cultural values you have to negotiate.

Note some assumptions and stereotypes being played out in the cultural narratives. In the boy meets girl narrative, a number of assumptions, or unquestioned ideas, are operating: relationships only involve one test, and after it has been past, the resulting marriage lasts forever; family and friends have no influence over relationships; relationships are heterosexual. In this example, a stereotype about boys is they are assertive; girls react to boys' advances.

Identify some of the social practices and institutions that frame your relationship, values, and question. Some institutions that may shape the way you go about dating are businesses that provide entertainment like restaurants and bars. These institutions facilitate couples going off away from their families and require a couple to make enough extra money to be able to go there. Describing the practices and institutions your relationship is affected by can give you a chance to question how much of your behavior is set by larger cultural practices and institutions.

Describe another relationship that is similar to yours and one that is opposite. This suggestion is designed to help you notice the features your relationship shares with other relationships. Once you have noticed similarities and differences, go on to classify your relationship. Classifying involves noting the general characteristics of your relationship, grouping it with other relationships that share the same general features, and giving the whole group an identifying name. Your relationship with your boy or girl friend could be classified a romantic relationship or a friendship. Classifying a relationship allows you to think about it more abstractly, moving away from the specific details, and looking for shared commonalties with other types of relationships. Sometimes these shared characteristics can help you make connections between cultural forces, especially economic ones, that shape relationships.

Create an analogy or metaphor for your relationship. Use your imagination to connect your relationship to whatever pops into your mind. It could be an object, animal, place, or event. Then list ways your relationship is like that other thing. This activity is similar to thinking of an image and makes it possible to create non-linear ways of thinking about your relationship and to get in touch with powerful feelings.

REVIEW YOUR IDEAS AND HIGHLIGHT THOSE THAT ANSWER YOUR QUESTION

Take time now to look over your Three Perspective notes with the idea of searching for pieces of answers to your question. Do you detect patterns in your notes or see potential answers? Highlighting them now can give you a starting point for developing an answer later.

ALLOW YOUR IDEAS TO INCUBATE

Allow yourself time to set aside your inquiry and let your unconscious mind explore for answers. Your unconscious can continue the search for connections, answers, insights if you give yourself sufficient time.

Example: Miranda's Exploration of Her Relationship with Her Mother

My question

Why is it that my mom and I don't talk or do things together?

Describe and distinguish

Physical and personality features that characterize the people involved in my investigation

- *Mom:* She is 45 years old, about 5'3", thin, and energetic. She is friendly, even to strangers. She is a very neat person. Her house has to be clean and she even tells me to clean my room.

- *Me:* I am 19 years old, 5'3", and fairly skinny. Like my mom, I am energetic and neat. I am a little shy when it comes to talking to strangers until I get to know them better. I am not a very open person, which deals with my relationship in that this lack of openness might be a reason my mom and I don't have many personal conversations.

Day-to-day interactions I associate with my mom

- My mom asks me how my day went, and I kind of shrug her off and simply say, "fine." I don't go into detail to try making conversation.
- When mom asks me to do something, I sometimes get mad and say I don't want to do it, instead of just doing it.

Features of my relationship that are distinctive to me and my context

- I want to be closer to my mom, like you see on television shows with mothers and daughters.
- I need someone to talk to, like my friends talk to their moms.

My attitude toward the value this relationship calls into question

- I value this relationship highly. I feel it is important that a mother and daughter be close and am willing to try to change it for the better.

Recurring images that have come to mind

- Busybody without much time to listen and talk with me.
- A tough outer skin because she doesn't say what she is feeling. I don't say what I'm feeling either.

Example: Shelby's Exploration of Her Relationship with Her Brother

My question

How can I explain to Brock that our relationship needs to change?

Trace moves and changes

How my relationship has changed

- After my mother died of breast cancer, I had to take care of Brock.
- Father became involved and took his part in our lives again.
- Older brother Bud became more and more buried in his feelings of guilt.
- Financial: We went from not being able to buy new things to being able to get whatever we want.
- Parental: We went from having a loving and caring mother and a mostly absent father to having a father who learned how to be there for us, and a step mother who didn't want us.
- Educational: Brock has excelled more than we could have ever dreamed. He is considered a genius. I have continued to work hard at the good grades I get.

Changes in my attitude and feelings

- I had to become more responsible for my family because no one else cared.
- Brock became really distant; he was afraid that we would all leave him. He didn't understand that his mother wasn't coming back.

Cultural changes that have influenced my relationship

- In this day and age divorce is common and people don't think much about faithfulness to families.
- Also, people are starting to realize that disease and cancer affect us all.
- We are more aware of our health.
- Breast cancer is one of the top five killers of American women.
- In the last few years implants that were given to women who had their breasts removed proved to be dangerous.

Example: Jim's Exploration of His Relationship with His Roommate

My question

What causes my roommate and me to be such good friends even though we are so different?

My networks and relationships

Cultural narratives that apply to my relationship

- Roommates respect each others' belongings.
- Roommates need to talk about their problems instead of keeping things inside. Compromise is very important; if they have different tastes in music, then they learn to share the stereo and try to play an equal amount of music that they both like. If one roommate wants to have a friend stay over, then they should inform the other person about their plans.
- The only way to get a good roommate is to know the person beforehand.
- Friendship between roommates is important.

Some of the assumptions and stereotypes operating in this cultural narrative

assumptions:

- Roommates are alike and have the same interests.
- Good roommates are friends forever.
- Bad roommates are your worst nightmare come true.

Stereotypes:

- *Me:* I could be stereotyped as the middle class, Republican Midwesterner who's straight laced and church going and interested in stability and a good safe career

- *My roommate:* he could be stereotyped as a long-haired punk/biker dude who's mostly interested in loud music and bikes and doesn't care about the future so much

Some of the social institutions and social practices framing my relationship
Institutions:

- If you don't have a friend from back home to room with, you just put in your name and hope for a good match. The housing office puts you together with someone; you don't have much say.
- If you're a freshman at this school, you pretty much have to live in the dorms.
- All of the dorm rooms are two-person rooms, so there's no getting around living with a roommate.
- Having two-person rooms makes living expenses a lot lower, and with college expenses the way they are, most people have to double up anyway

social practices that grow out of the institutional structure:

- Roommates eating meals together and discussing their days.
- Talking about problems with your roommate.
- Somebody to go home to and yell at.
- Talking about major events going on in their lives. Staying up late at night because one or both cannot fall asleep. Ending up talking for two hours until 2 A.M.

Other relationships that are similar/different from this one
Similar:

- army buddies. You are assigned to a platoon in the army. You don't get a say in who you work with; you have to make the best of it.

Different:

- choosing a spouse. In this country you get to choose who you marry. These days, if things don't work out, you can choose to separate.

An analogy/metaphor for my relationship

- night and day
- the Odd Couple

WORKSHOP

1. Bring copies of your Three Perspectives Strategy for each of your group members, and ask them to highlight sections that help answer your question. Discuss the sections they highlight. You might look for:

   - What sections provide background information for the inquiry? (information that you may need to include to explain the situation to your readers)
   - What material is surprising, unexpected? (this material may yield answers to your question)
   - Where do links exist between personal experience and larger cultural practices?

2. Help each other by pointing to areas where the writers have not elaborated as fully as they might. Make suggestions regarding details they might add.

POSITIONING WRITERS AND READERS

Why position writers and readers when writing about relationships?

A position is a role, like student or daughter. While you have many positions, one or more of them may be dominant in a given situation. For example, when you enter a classroom, your position of student comes to the fore. When you spend time with your mother, the position of daughter may be emphasized. Each position carries with it certain expectations about how one will and won't behave. These expectations come from a mixture of sources: the culture at large, groups within the culture, and individuals. Some positions have more room for variation than others, but all can be characterized by conduct that people agree is fitting. When you write, you also adopt a position. Furthermore, you assign a corresponding position to your readers. This assigning is known as positioning. Your choices of writer and reader positions shape the material you include and the writing style you choose.

When you write to a person with whom you have a relationship, you may very well select one of the positions you occupy when you are with that person. When you write to your sister, for instance, you might take on the position of brother. Your choice of writer position will most likely determine your reader's position. If you write as a brother to your sister, her reader position will be sister. Why work with positions? They help you construct a text that not only answers your question but also engages your readers in ways that are relevant and meaningful to them. Furthermore, choosing a position for yourself and for your readers helps you reinforce the relationship you wish to develop with them throughout the text. The Writer/Reader strategy calls for a review of positions you and your readers occupy in relationships as well as in your writing to one another. It helps you consider which positions are best suited to your writing project.

WRITER/READER POSITIONING STRATEGY
Position Yourself / Position Your Readers / Workshop

POSITIONING YOURSELF

Beginning by considering possible writer positions that you could adopt will make it easier to select a corresponding reader position. Even if you have not written to the members of your writing context before, you can draw upon the positions you have taken or been placed in. Any such positions can be used when writing. It's useful, though, to consider positions you no longer take, and ones you have been excluded from in order to identify the limitations that your usual positions may be placing on you. For more on Positioning, see Part II.

Consider the status, or standing, of the people in your context in relationship to one another and to yourself. Who has key status? Who has no status? Once you've identified the various levels of status, think about which writer positions are connected with each level of status and determine which ones you can adopt. For instance, if you are writing to your parents, the positions might be child, daughter, and adult, with adult carrying the most status. Can you convincingly use the adult position, and, more to the point, would it help you achieve your goal for your writing?

Using the analysis you have just developed, decide which positions you could adopt for use in this context and why. Think, too, about which ones you will avoid and why. Having examined each one, choose a writer position to adopt for this inquiry.

POSITIONING YOUR READER

You can now consider the positions available to your readers and consider which reader position works best with your writer position and your question. The readers, who are members of your writing context, probably occupy a number of positions. Begin by listing those positions since you will most likely select a position from them. Think over the advantages and disadvantages of each position for your readers. Consider who is excluded (not written to or spoken of) with each position; who benefits from each position; and who might be harmed or angered. Reflect on which position will most likely enhance your relationship.

Based on the analysis you have just done, select a position for your readers. The position should be one that you can address easily from your writer position. It should also be one that will help your readers come to a desirable understanding of your relationship. Having set your reader position, list characteristic values and backgrounds you associate with that position. The general values and backgrounds that typically go with the position can help you make decisions about what kinds of arguments to use, what examples to include, and what kinds of language choices to make.

Example: Amanda's Writer and Reader Positions, Writing about Her Relationship with Her Mother

Positioning myself

My question
- Why did I move in with my father?

Positions I have written from within my context of family
- daughter   • middle child   • the "boss"

Positions I have been excluded from
- Since I am writing to my mother, I must avoid friend and sister.

Positions I have left behind
- I no longer write as though I'm a little girl.

Position I will take as a writer
- I will take the positions of daughter and grownup because as a grownup I can talk about new issues that I now understand as daughter. This can be a woman-to-woman issue.
- I will not take the position of middle child because I have more responsibility and more maturity than either of my brothers.

Positioning my readers

Reader positions available in my writing context
- mother   • adult   • friend

My reader position
mother

The values and background I associate with my reader position of mother
Values:

- understanding. A mother values making efforts to understand her children
- trusting. A mother values setting up a trusting environment so that her children can come to her and discuss problems

Background:
- has learned from the mistakes she made
- grew up in one family and now has her own
- has gone through some of the same situations her children have
- has watched her children grow up

WORKSHOP

Share your Writer/Reader Strategy with your group members. For each group member, address the following questions:

1. Do the writer and reader positions match? If not, suggest an adjustment to one or both positions.

2. What additional values and experiences can you name for each reader position? Keep in mind that these values and experiences are for the position, not for the particular people the writer is writing to. Share your suggestions with each writer and have each writer add them to his or her work.

SELECTING GENRES

Why select a genre when writing about a relationship?

Genres are commonly used forms of writing. Examples are a letter, essay, and report. The genre you choose will influence your text's content and style. The genre will have an impact on your readers, and on how they regard your message. In the context of relationships, letters and personal essays support the sharing of personal, even intimate, thoughts and experiences. A report, which generally restricts the sharing of personal information, might be a difficult genre to use in this context. Choosing a suitable genre, therefore, contributes to the effectiveness of your writing effort. Your choice might seem obvious, but the Genre Strategy helps you consider the implications of the genres for this context.

GENRE STRATEGY

Select a Genre / Probe the Implications of the Genre / Workshop

---

SELECTING A GENRE

Often you have a choice of more than one genre to use for a writing project. Since the genre has significant impact on your project, take time to consider your options. Begin by listing three or four genres you might use. Before you think about the implications of using each one, review the work you have done so far. What question are you trying to answer? Who are your readers, and what position have you set for them? You can use the suggestions that follow to guide your selection. For more information on genres, see Part II.

Writer and Reader Positions in Your Context

Genres allow for the use of some writer and some reader positions but exclude others. For instance, the writer position of student researcher might not fit the genre of personal letter. Does each genre accommodate your chosen positions?

Genres in Your Context

Just as writers have different status, so do genres. Are there some genres that are considered out of reach for people with low status in your context? Your answers to these questions will help you recognize which genres are accessible to you given your status. You can also determine if you need to choose a genre based on whether it will help to elevate your status. If, for example, the writers with key status in your context generally use the personal essay genre, you might choose it as well. List the major genres used in your context. Which ones are valued most? Are any devalued or discredited?

Briefly Analyze These Alternative Genres

Think, too, about how each genre can be used: to change another's point of view, share a new insight, initiate a change in relationship. Note when the genres are used: weekly, to share news; rarely, to communicate major happenings. Based on your analysis of each genre, identify which genres might fit your question, readers, and writer position in this context. Revise your list of genres if necessary.

Practical Issues in Genre Selection

Next, think about the logistics of your particular project. Is the genre practical and realistic for you to use? Do you know enough about the genre to use it well? Do you have enough time to use it? How will you distribute this genre (via mail, on-line)? Does the genre work for your writer position? Are there aspects of your writer position that would be excluded in the genre?

Development Issues in Genre Selection

Development refers to the kind of content and the level of detail found in a text. For each genre, what types of evidence are regarded as legitimate? What details will you need to include? Leave out?

Format and Organization

Most genres have characteristic formats. What format characterizes each genre? What are typical ways the genre is organized? What is the normal length of this genre? How will these features help you? limit you?

Level of Formality

Some genres call for a formal use of language and a formal presentation style; others are more casual. What kinds of language choices are appropriate for each genre? Is the genre typically written in first, second, or third person? Does the writing require typing? Handwriting?

Range of Variation

Some genres allow for a wide range of variation in format, level of formality, development; others are quite limited. How wide is the range of variation in the genre? How well will it allow you to achieve your goals? How far can you go in "stretching" this genre or in blurring it with others?

EXAMINING THE IMPLICATIONS OF YOUR GENRE

All of the factors you have just analyzed have a bearing on the genre you choose. Using your analysis, consider how receptive your readers might be to each genre and make a selection.

USING THE FEATURES OF YOUR GENRE TO
MAKE DECISIONS ABOUT YOUR TEXT

Now that you have chosen a genre, you can consider how you can use it to make decisions about your text. Review your Multiple Perspectives Strategy in light of your genre and your readers. What kinds of development are best suited to this genre? Most compelling for your readers? Examples from your own experience? Family stories? Shared knowledge? Reflect, too, on language choices that will work best for your genre. Will you use first, second, or third person? Will you use formal, standard English, or casual language choices?

Example: Greg's Genre for Writing to His Family about His Relationship with His Brother

Possible genres

letter, essay

Implications of each genre

- *letter:* My readers are used to reading and writing letters, so they will be able to concentrate on the message instead of on the genre. Letters can be personal; I can write about family matters easily; I can use my writer and reader positions; they are used to writing and receiving letters, so I can easily write about family matters. Language can be informal; I can count on their familiarity with letters, so they will be able to concentrate on the message

- *essay:* I know how to write essays and have enough time to write one. Essays can have personal material in them, but they also often refer to the writings of others and involve taking a step back from personal experience and connecting it to others' experiences. I may not want to refer to others' experiences in this context. The typical format involves 3–5 pages of word processed text. The language can be somewhat casual, but not so casual as in a letter.

My choice

I'm going to choose a letter because a letter is a much more personal form of writing.

Making decisions about my text based on my chosen genre

- *kinds of development:* They like to hear about experiences I'm having and to know my thoughts. Also, we have several important family stories that we refer to in situations like this, so I'll use one of those.

- *what level of formality is accepted:* it can be pretty casual, but it depends on how serious the subject matter is.

WORKSHOP

Share your choice of genre with your group. For each group member, answer the following questions:

1. Will the writer be able to use the writer and reader positions she has selected in this genre? Why or why not?

2. Are the writer's readers likely to expect him or her to use this particular genre to write about a relationship? Why or why not? How might the writer use the readers' expectations/surprise to communicate effectively?

FOCUSING
Why focus when writing about relationships?

A focus is a succinct statement of your current, overall new understanding. A focus is an answer to your question. Sometimes the answer is tentative, sometimes more definite. Focusing marks a shift from asking questions and gathering material to constructing a text. A focus sets the direction for the entire text. Generating responses to your question and testing out those responses before drafting lets you try to develop your new understanding with your readers in mind because a focus sets the stage for the text you will write.

Why focus? It can save you effort and time because focusing allows you to map out an entire text before you write it. When you begin writing without a focus, you may uncover problems that require you to rethink your direction. You may find your reasoning doesn't hold together; your approach won't reach your readers; or your examples don't fit. Encountering such problems when you are in the middle of a draft can be frustrating; and starting over can be time consuming and discouraging. Focusing can help you anticipate and avoid these problems.

FOCUSING STRATEGY
State Your Focus / Workshop

STATING YOUR FOCUS

A focus is a two-part statement that sets the stage for your text. Like a regular sentence, it must have a subject and a verb. The first part, *a subject,* names the situation you are investigating. The second part, *the point of significance,* presents your understanding of the situation and contains the verb. For more on focusing, see Part II.

Keep your question on hand because you will be generating focuses that state your tentative answer to your question. Next, review your exploration. At this point, do any parts of your exploration supply an answer? Now formulate focus statements for your question. Try for several focuses reflecting different answers you may have reached in your exploration.

Example: Alfredo's Focus about His Relationship with a Friend

My question

Why does Rodrigo end our relationship because of something that neither of us control—his parents' divorce?

My context

My friends including Rodrigo

My tentative focuses

Subject	*Point of Significance*
• Several aspects of Rodrigo's behavior ——	are creating problems for us.
• Rodrigo's attitude———————————	reflects pressures put on families going through a divorce in Guatemala.
• Over time, Rodrigo's parents' divorce ——	resulted in Rodrigo breaking up our best friendship.
• Rodrigo's behavior since the divorce———	isn't acceptable for a best friend.

WORKSHOPS

Share your focuses and compare them with your question for inquiry.

1. Does each focus have a subject and a point of significance? If not, help one another restate them.

2. Which focuses address the most important aspects of your inquiry?

3. Which focus do you recommend?

ORGANIZING

Why construct an organizing plan when writing about relationships?

An organizing plan is a skeleton for the text you will write. When you develop an organizing plan, you have a chance to test out the focus before committing yourself to writing an entire draft. Like a focus, these plans can save you lots of time and effort and allow you to test out several ways to organize your text without having to write full drafts. Organizing plans also give you an opportunity to select examples and details that suit your focus and your readers. This book suggests several ways of organizing (See Part II). This chapter shows students using modal plans.

MODAL PLANS

Organize by Whole and Parts / Organize by Time Segments / Organize by Setting Criteria / Organize by Grouping / Workshop

ORGANIZING BY WHOLE AND PARTS

Whole and parts organization involves explaining aspects of a relationship, one at a time. This plan can be used to explain important details that will help your readers to understand your focus. It involves giving readers a sense of the whole and delineating the parts and their connection both to the whole and to each other. Notice that each statement in the modal organizing plans has the same structure as a focus, namely a subject and a point of significance.

ORGANIZING BY TIME SEGMENTS

This strategy presents a series of time segments. You can use this plan to present a series of events, emphasizing changes over time. It can be effective when you want to demonstrate how a relationship has changed.

ORGANIZING BY SETTING CRITERIA

This plan involves listing criteria and relating them to the subject. It helps you evaluate a relationship.

ORGANIZING BY GROUPING

Grouping places the subject within larger categories. Grouping consists of a series of connections between the particular subject and other subjects or groups. It can be used in this context to establish links between your particular relationship and cultural values and practices. Variations include ordering by comparison, contrast, or analogy.

Example: Alfredo's Organization Plan

Parts of a whole

Focus

Several aspects of Rodrigo's behavior ———— are creating problems for us.

Organization

- Rodrigo's telling me that it is his problem — cuts me out of the most important thing happening to him.
- Rodrigo getting angry with me ———— hurts and confuses me and keeps us distant.
- Rodrigo refusing to see me ———— leaves me sad; I don't have him to talk with about my problems.
- Rodrigo cutting off our friendship ———— means he loses a best friend & has to sort things out on his own.

Grouping

Focus

Rodrigo's attitude ———————— reflects pressures put on families going through a divorce in Guatemala.

Organization

- Rodrigo's attitude———————— buys into the idea that in Guatemala divorce is so shameful that families have to keep to themselves.
- Rodrigo's attitude———————— accepts the idea that family is more important than friends.
- Rodrigo's attitude———————— is a reaction against the fact that in Guatemala, everyone knows everyone else's business because we all live where we grew up.

Time segments

Focus

Over time, Rodrigo's parents' divorce ——— resulted in Rodrigo breaking up our best friendship.

Organization

• Before the divorce, ——————— we did everything together: school work, sports, & talking to girls.

• When problems between his parents started, ——————— Rodrigo's attitude changed a little, but still we did things together, always at my house.

• After Rodrigo's parents divorced, ——— he would hardly ever talk to me. When he did talk to me he got so mad after some time we both had to go home. I offered advice but he just ignored me. He just does not want me near him.

Criteria

Focus

Rodrigo's behavior since the divorce ——— isn't acceptable for a best friend.

Organization

• His mostly refusing to see me——————— contradicts the idea that friends stick together in good & bad times.

• His getting mad at my advice & help——— doesn't go along with friends needing each other.

• His not letting us just be friends ——— violates the idea that best friends adjust their relationship as needed.

WORKSHOP

Share your organizing plans. Help each other determine:

1. if each organization fits with the focus and remains consistently in the chosen mode. If not, help each other adjust them.

2. if each statement in your organizing plan has a subject and point of significance.

3. which focus and organization best suits your inquiry and your context.

DRAFTING

Why draft when writing about relationships?

Coming to a new understanding for yourself is one thing; sharing that insight with your readers is quite different. In order to reach your readers effectively, you may have to try several versions even when you have tested several Focuses and Organizing Plans.

DRAFTING STRATEGIES

Review Your Exploration / Follow Your Organizing Plan / Write Several Drafts / Workshop

FOLLOWING YOUR ORGANIZING PLAN

Your Organizing Plan will predict the content and order of your text. You can use it as a template for the draft.

REVIEWING YOUR EXPLORATION

Since the process of generating a new understanding of your relationship is ongoing, you may want to review your exploration once more to look for additional materials that help you answer your question.

WRITING SEVERAL DRAFTS

Use your planning work to guide your writing of your drafts. Develop the draft as far as you can on your own. Give your small group members and your instructor the most polished draft you can so they can help you with things you can't find on your own. For more information on drafting, see Part II.

Example: Jeff's Letter to His Sister about Their Relationship

Dear Jenny,

From the beginning, we have always had our disagreements. When we were young, it was looked at as a normal sibling relationship. Brothers and sisters are supposed to argue. Now, later in our lives, we still have a hard time communicating. Lately, with the death of Grandma, I've felt like we need to resolve this problem between us. You never know how much time we have left between us.

I understand we've both led completely different lives. You've always been the one to take life cautiously; I've always jumped in head first. We've never connected on many issues due to this. I thought, at first, that the problem was a difference in values. The more I considered this, the more I think it's false. Mom and Dad instilled good values in us both. Through our differences, we still have had the same quality upbringing. One of the values we were taught is to stand our ground. This stubbornness is a prime reason for our disagreements. Compromise is a word that is not in either of our vocabularies. Maybe it should be.

All through high school you resented me for constantly doing what I wanted and still getting by. While I was out with my friends, you were home studying or in bed. I know that you had to struggle for all the accomplishments you've earned. I respected you for that. You thought I looked down on you for all of the effort you had to put forth. The truth is I admired you for it. Later in life you'll benefit from your constant struggles. I'll have to come to you for advice later, and I hope we're close enough that you'll give it to me without resentment.

Although we've had our differences, I believe our relationship is salvageable. I don't want to go through life just being friendly when we happen to see each other at Christmas or other holidays. We truly are alike. If we would put our petty differences behind us we could have a lasting quality relationship. All I'm asking is that we both try a little harder at getting things to work. With the death of Grandma, it just scares me to think that you could be gone without us ever working this out.

Yours Truly,
Jeff

WORKSHOP

Often drafting is done alone, but if you do meet during the drafting process, you can share your drafts and your thoughts and questions as you draft. You might consider the following sorts of questions:

1. Am I staying with the original focus, or am I developing a new insight?

2. Am I staying with the focus and organizing plan I chose, or is my writing veering away from the plan?

3. Am I using the writer and reader positions I chose to decide the type and level of detail to include?

4. How can I make connections between my experiences and larger cultural values and practices?

RESPONDING

Why respond to texts when writing about relationships?

Writing to readers about a relationship is a complex task. A writer, engrossed in the process of composing, may not notice all the ways the text works. Sympathetic readers, like writing group members familiar with the project, can help a writer see the text better. Responders tend to benefit their own writing as well, gathering ideas about writing styles and identifying writing problems they encounter, too. Even when you have others to respond to your text, you can respond also and strengthen your ability to revise.

READER RESPONSE STRATEGY
Use the Reader Response Strategy / Tailor the Reader Response Strategy / Workshop

---

USING THE READER RESPONSE STRATEGY

The Reader Response Strategy gives you a way to guide your readers' feedback to you. It separates the types of feedback from each other so that they aren't jumbled together. The types of feedback are arranged according to the degree of influence they have over the entire text: more fundamental aspects of the text are addressed first; less crucial aspects come later. Here are the categories for the Reader Response Strategy:

- *Overall response:* Give your reaction to the content and the presentation of the text.

- *Focus:* State the focus and indicate whether all parts of the text fit the focus.
- *Development for readers:* Name the writer and reader positions and discuss the degree to which the writer supplies sufficient and appropriate information for the reader position.
- *Organization and coherence:* Identify the kind of organization, note whether the order of the text follows the organization type, and discuss the transitions and how they support the organization.
- *Language choices (words and sentences):* Keeping in mind the writer and reader positions, discuss the appropriateness of the language choices. Also, comment on the variety of sentence structures.
- *Conventions:* Identify any problems with grammar, spelling, and punctuation.
- *Main emphasis for revision:* Of all the levels you have discussed, suggest which one you think the writer ought to emphasize.

TAILORING THE READER RESPONSE STRATEGY

The Reader Response Strategy can be adjusted to suit your project. You can add categories for response or emphasize features of the text for which you want feedback. For instance, in this context, you might want to know whether your responders think you have answered your guiding question. You could add a place for them to address this issue.

You can also use the strategy to respond to your text yourself. By responding to your own text, you can identify those aspects you think work well and those that need more work. This self-assessment can make it easier to use reader responses from other readers since you know the areas for which you want help.

Example: Jeff's Self-Assessment

Overall response

Overall, I think it's a very heartfelt letter. It cuts right to the point and doesn't drag on. But it doesn't yet explain connections between what we do and larger cultural influences

Focus

"From the beginning, disagreements have been part of our relationship." I think I stick with that focus, but I also talk about how I want to change our relationship. I may have to decide if I want to emphasize my call for a change more, and if so, how I will change the focus.

Development for readers

The reader position is obviously a sibling. I think I've developed my text for my reader well. I think reminding her of the way she used to stay home and resent me, and the way I used to go out but admire her will help her know exactly what I'm talking about.

Organization and coherence

The organization tries to take on groups of reasons for us not getting along, one by one. The order is also chronological. It starts from when we were young and goes to the present time.

Language choices (words and sentences)

I feel my language sounds natural and conveys my usual directness.

Conventions

I wonder if I've used commas correctly. Instructor will comment.

Main emphasis for revision

Overall, I'm pleased with the letter. I want to rethink the focus. I also think I would change the fact that I didn't ask if she even sees the same problem I do in our relationship.

What I want feedback on

I want to know whether the responders think I have made enough suggestions about how we can change.

Example: Responses to Jeff's Draft from His Teacher

Overall response

Your framing of the letter around your grandmother's death gives it a compelling urgency. You remind her of disagreements but don't explain the sources of agreements.

Focus

"Our relationship is hurt by our disagreements." You maintain this focus in most places, but in other places, you move into something like: Changing our relationship is something we ought to do.

Development for readers

The reader position is sibling. In the third paragraph you provide specific examples of your difference. Try to provide comparable examples throughout the letter.

Organization and coherence

Time segments—works well for documenting the continuing puzzlement of the situation. Yet a time segments plan doesn't help you explain the sources well. How about shifting to a grouping plan?

Language choices (words and sentences)

Your word choices seem largely suitable. They are not too academic. You don't use many words with warm, friendly, or conciliatory connotations. Would you like to? You use a combination of simple and compound sentences which works well. You also use parallel construction to show the contrast in your two ways of doing things. This technique is especially effective here.

Conventions

OK.

Main emphasis for revision

- Focus: rework it to fit whole letter and to emphasize causes
- Organization: Switch to grouping plan
- Development: Include what you and your sister argue about and why you think these arguments occur.

What you wanted feedback on

What you wanted feedback on: "Have I made enough suggestions for changes in the letter?" You give general suggestions for change, which may be the appropriate thing for a letter introducing the idea of change. In the long run the suggestions you give may not be detailed enough. What would happen if you made a more specific suggestion about how you two could take a next step, with the understanding that you will come up with more concrete suggestions together?

WORKSHOP

After you have done your self assessment and Reader Responses for the members of your group, take turns discussing your responses. If responders disagree, try to determine why.

REVISING

Why revise when writing about a relationship?

The relationship you are investigating and the reader(s) you have chosen matter to you. There may be significant consequences for you as a result of writing this text. Therefore, making the revised draft as clear and as compelling as possible is important. The emergence of insights into a significant question can occur incrementally rather than in one sudden flash. Revising your text gives you another opportunity to deepen your developing understanding.

REVISING PLAN
Construct a Revising Plan / Carry out Your Revisions /
Write a Revision / Workshop

CONSTRUCTING A REVISING PLAN

A revising plan is just what its name says: a plan for revising. In it you describe not only what you are going to revise but in what order. Ordering your revisions reinforces the idea that some changes are more central to the text than others and ought to be done first. For instance, it makes more sense to revise your focus first than to correct grammar errors since the focus change may lead you to delete some of the text with grammar errors.

Begin by reviewing the feedback you received and decide which feedback you want to use. Identify the changes you plan to make to the text in as specific detail as you can manage. Once you have named all the revisions, establish an order for making them. If you are uncertain which changes to make first, refer to the Reader Response Strategy. This order is a good one to follow.

Example: Jeff's Revising Plan

- rethink focus
- switch to grouping organizing plan
- explain causes of conflicts
- offer plan of action for us

CARRYING OUT YOUR REVISIONS

Your revising plan serves as a guide for what to do. Follow your plan for an orderly revising process; for advice on revising your focus; for dealing with problems with unity, development, organization, and coherence; for advice on problems with cohesion, sentence variety, grammar, spelling, and punctuation. For more information, see Part II.

Example: Jeff's Revision

Dear Jenny,

From the beginning, we have always had our disagreements. When we were young it was considered a normal sibling relationship. Brothers and sisters are supposed to argue. Now, later in our lives, we still have a hard time communicating. Lately, with the death of Grandma, I've felt like we need to resolve this problem between us. You never know how much time we have left between us. I want us to get along. If we understand the causes of our disagreements and try to change our behavior, I think we can make things better.

I thought, at first, that our disagreements were caused by a difference in values. The more I considered this possibility, the more I thought it was false. Mom and Dad instilled good values in us both. Despite our differences, we still have had the same good upbringing. One of the values we were taught was to stand our ground. Mom and Dad really reinforced this value, and we heard and saw plenty about this value each time the whole Jensen clan got together. It's a way of life in our family. You and I took standing our ground into stubbornness, and this stubbornness is a prime reason for our disagreements. Compromise is a word that is not in either of our vocabularies. Maybe it should be. If we even considered the other one's opinion, I think things would be a lot less rocky between us.

Many times our arguments were just over stupid things when we were young. We would argue about everything. I can remember our elementary school teachers having to separate us in the lunch room. Day after day we were all over each other for anything. I know that our disagreements couldn't have been that important in themselves because I can't even remember half the things we argued about. I think those arguments were tied to our being so close in age and having to jostle for attention at home.

I never saw any real reasons behind our arguments until we came to high school. That is when I noticed a distinct change in you from just arguing for argument's sake, to resenting my actions for some reason. Now I think I understand what you resented. I understand we've both approached life differently. You've always been the one to take life cautiously; I've always jumped in head first. All through high school you resented me for constantly doing what I wanted and still getting by. While I was out with my friends, you were home studying or in bed. I can see now how irritating it must have been to have me, your big brother, going out whenever he wanted while you worked so hard. The differences in our personalities have been a big source of our disagreements. I don't think either one of us will change, but if we acknowledge our different approaches, we could get along better.

We've never connected on many issues due to this difference in our personalities. For example, you thought I looked down on you for all of the effort you had to put forth. The truth is I admired you for it. I know that you had to struggle for all the accomplishments you've reached. I respected you for that. Later in life you'll benefit from your constant struggles. I'll have to come to you for advice later, and I hope we're close enough that you'll give it to me without resentment.

Although we've had our differences, I believe our relationship is salvageable. I don't want to go through life just being friendly when we happen to see each other at Christmas or other holidays. We truly are a lot alike. Our differences are minor compared to the big picture. If we learn to work with differences, we could have a lasting quality relationship. I think we both deserve it. All I'm asking is that we both try a little harder at getting things to work. With the death of Grandma, it just scares me to think that you could be gone without us ever working this out.

Yours Truly,
Jeff

WORKSHOP

Share your revising plan with your group members and ask for feedback on the order in which you plan to revise, as well as for additional suggestions for revision.

If you also have time to share your revisions, ask your group members to comment on where you have or have not followed your revising plan.

Discuss the revised version of your text, offering general reactions and comments on how you think the intended readers will respond. If you share your text with the intended readers, you might share their reactions with your group.

CONCLUSION

Inquiring into important, puzzling relationships through writing is challenging, but can yield unexpected insights and pave the way for taking action, changing your relationship for the better. The writers you have encountered here each took some uncomfortable risks to examine their relationships, yet they each gained a deeper understanding. Among the most rewarding new understandings for them were their increased insights into the cultural sources of some of the conflicts they experienced. They carried with them a new alertness to the cultural dimension of all of their experiences; in short, they became more astute participants in their various contexts, more able to choose whether they wanted to buy into these values.

Jonathan sent his letter to Chad and got a phone call from him a few days later. Chad agreed that they let competition take over their relationship sometimes, and that it wasn't good for their friendship. He thanked Jonathan for writing, and invited Jonathan to come over to his house and talk things over more the next time Jonathan came home for a visit.

As you finish your project, take some time to reflect on and review your own writing project. You have just used writing to inquire and to take action. What specifically have you learned about your relationship? What action have you taken as a result of your writing? What changes have taken place in your context, in your relationship?

The strategies you used here are powerful when used to conduct a meaningful inquiry and to generate new ways of thinking about your relationships. These strategies can be used in many other writing contexts as well. In the following chapters, you will have opportunities to use them again.

3

AREA OF INQUIRY: FREE TIME

LIBBY MILES

WHY INQUIRE INTO FREE TIME?

"I'd Rather Be Flying." "I'd Rather Be Golfing." "I'd Rather Be Sailing." "I'd Rather Be Sleeping." Sometimes I feel I'd rather *not* be reading what other people would rather be doing on their car bumpers every time I drive. But those bumper stickers often tell us a lot about the person who owns the car. *"My Other Car is a Mercedes Benz." "My Other Car is in the Shop." "My Other Car is a Broom."* Maybe the driver has pretensions of grandeur; maybe she just has a sense of humor. *"My kid is a CHS Honor Student." "My kid beat up your Honor Student."* Regardless, bumper stickers most often reflect something about what drivers value in their free time: their hobbies, their kids, their associations, their political affiliations. In other words, what do people do when their time is their own? What do people value so much they feel the urge to proclaim it on the backs of their cars?

Free time is one of those parts of our lives that many of us feel we have some control over. "Free," after all, seems to indicate that the time is ours to do with as we please. It also seems to indicate that there is no *cost* associated with the way we choose to occupy that time. As it turns out, neither of these assumptions is necessarily true.

As an example, no matter where I am, I would almost always *rather* be playing Frisbee with my dog. I have a big backyard, and even though my dog is small, he is really good at catching sizeable disks in his mouth. When I drive home from a long day at work, the first thing I do when I get home is grab his Frisbee and spend some time with him in the backyard. It's a very nice way to come home. We both enjoy it.

That's the happy version, a telling of this story that makes my time with my dog sound quite "free" and relaxing. But you know it isn't the whole story. If I have been teaching and going to meetings on campus all day, my dog has been cooped up in the house all those hours. I really *have* to take him outside as soon as I get home unless I want him to make a mess in the living room. I don't actually have a choice about taking him outside when I get home, then; it is a responsibility that comes with owning a dog. After all, dogs need outdoor time, and dogs need exercise. So our daily Frisbee game is not really my choice; we don't just play whenever *I* feel like it, in *my* free time. Often, there are hidden responsibilities and constraints conditioning the way we spend our free time—even if it is just playing Frisbee with a little dog.

But what about the money? My afternoon playtime with my dog doesn't seem like it would cost me a cent. Actually, however, the Frisbee wasn't cheap; it's a special chew-proof dog Frisbee with some kind of scent on it that dogs like. Furthermore, the dog was technically "free" from the Humane Society, but it still cost me $65 to have him neutered right away. Then we spend at least $30 a year for his annual vet visit and at least $20 a month for food, heartworm medicine, and flea prevention. On top of such basic costs, we also have to pay for assorted emergency vet visits when he eats something that makes him sick, or to have his cataracts removed (that last operation was in the neighborhood of $1400). I may not have to pay every time I throw the disk to him, but there has been a substantial start-up and maintenance cost.

So my "free" time isn't really free after all. It is often occupied by a responsibility, and one that costs money at that. Nonetheless, I still value it highly, and I feel strongly about keeping it in my daily routine. Why is that?

Every time I throw that Frisbee, I am participating in a network of values. I am living up to my responsibility as a pet owner, and I am supporting the Humane Society by doing so. I am also making sure that *I* get time outside, since I value the property where I live. I take notice when the lawn needs to be mowed, or the trees need to be pruned, or the paint is chipping off the garage. In other words, playing Frisbee with my dog allows me to live up to some of the values that I hold dear: honoring my responsibilities, spending time outside, maintaining a healthy and productive home, and appreciating the environment around me.

This exploration of a seemingly simple and inconsequential act—throwing a Frisbee to a small dog—demonstrates several reasons why "Free Time" is a context worthy of your inquiry. First of all, the demands on your time have most likely increased dramatically now that you are taking college classes. As a result, you probably have even less free time to do with as you like; this means that every decision you make about how to spend your free time should be a thoughtful one. Secondly, you will most likely have even less money to spend on those activities you choose; so, again, each choice should really count for something. Third, it seems that even the area of our lives that we often feel we have the most control over, and the most freedom, is actually quite constrained by responsibilities, economic conditions, and physical limitations. As I said above, the word "free" is misleading. Fourth, each choice we make about spending our free time has rippling effects from the values it embraces; such choices are too socially important to make lightly. As long as you are participating in a network of values, it is important that you can identify and support that network.

Writing, then, can be an action through which you begin to understand the implications of how you might spend your free time, and writing can help you turn that understanding into better choices and more conscious social action. You will have the chance to inquire into the ways your free time actions support—or don't support—those values that are important to you and to your readers. Once you have explored the implications of your free time, and the values associated with it, you can make conscious choices about which ones you want to support, and which ones you plan to reshape or reject. Since writing is to be shared, others will benefit from your inquiry as well.

EXAMPLES OF WRITING FOR INQUIRY AND ACTION

- James, a 28-year old first-year student who has spent several years in the army, will be getting married at the end of the school year. It is his responsibility to choose their honeymoon location, so he uses this area of inquiry as a way to think more seriously about his options. He locates honeymoon advertisements on the Internet and in magazines; he analyzes the values those possibilities seem to promote; he makes his decision based on his critique; and he writes an analytical "report" for his fiancée.

- Nikki, a 18-year old first-year student, really likes the alternative band 311. At the same time, she is getting increasingly interested in World Wide Web sites, especially fan pages for music groups. Since she is thinking about making a page herself, she analyzes an existing home page for 311, critiques it, and lists the features she would like to use in her own page. In the proposal she writes to her classmates as potential visitors to her home page, she models what such a Web site might look like, and she recreates an interactive design in which the fans can talk directly with the band members.

- Steve, a 17-year old first year student whose parents immigrated from China, has recently been questioning his commitment to playing the violin. He inquires into the values his parents promoted by having both their children spend so much of their childhood practicing music, and he finds that his parents' good intentions outweighed the annoyance he feels with them. Having gained some insight into his parents' values, Steve writes a letter to his brother encouraging him to keep up his violin playing and not to follow his example by quitting once he gets to college.

- Terry, an African-American novelist, writes an analysis of *The Wizard of Oz* directed at her daughter. Terry's strong feelings about the values promoted by Dorothy's adventures are both good and bad, and through her essay she inquires into the reasons her reactions are so mixed.

- Bob, a freelance copyeditor, has been a movie buff for years. He watches them with a appreciative but critical eye, and he likes to teach others to watch movies critically as well. When he started working for the local newspaper, he asked if he might write some movie reviews for their "Arts" section. His reviews, a mixture of plot summary, critical evaluation, and educational movie-watching tips, are now a standard feature every week.

READINGS FOR INQUIRY AND ACTION

"THE GLOBALIZATION OF MICHAEL JORDAN," *Michael Jordan and the New Global Capitalism* by Walter LaFeber

When Michael Jordan joined them in the autumn of 1984, the Chicago Bulls were on the ropes. They had won twenty-seven and lost fifty-five games the previous year. A typical crowd filled only one-third of the Chicago Coliseum's seats. The franchise's estimated worth was $18.7 million—only a fraction of some other franchises—and dropping. Television audiences were disappearing.

Within the next ten years, Jordan became the most widely recognized and probably wealthiest athlete on earth. The Bulls sold out the old Coliseum, then their new United Center, and had thousands of names on a wait-list for season tickets. The franchise's worth exceeded $190 million and was climbing. The NBA meanwhile became a television goldmine not only in the United States, but globally. It was quite a decade—an era made possible by Jordan's athletic skills, his marketing instincts, a new type of corporation exemplified by Nike, and the technology of communication satellites and cable that made the globe into one mammoth television audience.

The outlook was not rosy in 1984–1985. Jordan had led the 1984 U.S. Olympic team to a gold medal in men's basketball. He charmed hundreds of millions of television viewers when he placed his gold medal around Deloris Jordan's neck. The publicity that trumpeted him into Chicago, however, did not endear him to his veteran teammates. Nor, more importantly perhaps, did his all-out intensity during practices, or his refusal to drink or take drugs afterwards. If some of the Bulls were losers on the court, they were self-styled champions off the court in Chicago's Rush Street and other late-night hangouts. Jordan seldom joined them.

"The first NBA game I ever saw was the one I played in," he later told reporter Bob Greene. In that contest Jordan scored 16 points as the Bulls defeated Washington 109–63. During his first season, one writer later observed, "Jordan mesmerized crowds with his Nijinskyesque physical artistry and, especially, his balletic slam-dunks." Experts were awed by his all-around game, including rebounding and, especially, defense. He shut down the other team's best guard or forward, while displaying uncanny talent for intercepting passes.

Critics who searched for weakness soon thought they had discovered it: Jordan seemed not only unable to bring his teammates up to a championship level, but he often alienated them with his intensity, the parading of his skills, and his commercial successes off the court. These successes appeared at the start when, for $200,000, he endorsed a basketball for Wilson Sporting Goods. Wilson then terminated agreements with other stars including Detroit's Isiah Thomas. At the 1985 All-Star game in Indianapolis, Jordan stood out as the only rookie elected to the Eastern Conference's starting team. When he appeared for a shooting contest, however, the rookie wore clanking gold chains and a sweatsuit loudly bearing the Nike logo. It proclaimed another highly profitable endorsement. Thomas, Magic Johnson, Larry Bird, and others froze Jordan out of their company. In the game itself, the West All-Stars targeted and humiliated Jordan. His teammates looked the other way.

The Bulls' young star proved to be a quick study. The gold chains disappeared. Humility and deference to his elders on the basketball floor replaced the swaggering. He went on that season to become only the third person in NBA history to lead a team in scoring, rebounding, and assists. Home attendance doubled.

Jordan, Bird, Johnson, Thomas, and other stars were meanwhile propelling the once down-and-nearly-out NBA to new heights of popularity. Basketball was challenging baseball and football as the national sports pastime. In 1986, much of the game's hope, charm, and popularity was captured in the film *Hoosiers,* starring Gene Hackman, Barbara Hershey, and Dennis Hopper. The film told the real-life David-and-Goliath story of tiny Milan defeating taller and deeper large-city teams to win the 1954 Indiana State High School Championship. Basketball was acquiring a kind of mythic quality. With grit and discipline honing talent, anything was possible.

Anything, that is, except a Chicago championship. Krause manipulated the draft so he could obtain Scottie Pippen, a forward from the University of Central Arkansas. The youngest of eleven children, Pippen, like Jordan, spent much of his childhood in the non-urban South. And like Jordan, he could shoot from any distance, pass, rebound, and play exquisite defense. Phil Jackson, then a Bulls assistant coach, believed that "Scottie had a near-genius basketball IQ." Jackson also noticed that while other players seemed reluctant to get too close to Jordan, Pippen tried to learn all he could from the star. As the two became friends, over the next decade Pippen developed into arguably the second-most valuable player in the NBA.

During the 1987–1988 season, the Bulls won fifty of eighty-two games. Jordan became the first NBA player to win both the Most Valuable Player and Defensive Player of the Year awards. In April 1988, as the Bulls had nearly tripled their attendance since 1984, Reinsdorf and Krause quadrupled Jordan's annual salary to $3.25 million over a new eight-year contract. But again, despite the presence of Pippen, the Bulls quickly fell in the playoffs to Detroit in the second round. The first round, against Cleveland, however, became legendary. Jordan won the pivotal game with what became known as simply "The Shot." Behind one point with three seconds to play, he took a pass, and, as *Sports Illustrated* later described it, "spins to the top of the key [the foul circle] and hits a hanging, double-clutch, 18-foot jumper . . . at the buzzer" to stun 20,000 Cleveland fans.

On July 7, 1989, Krause fired Doug Collins and promoted Phil Jackson to head coach. Thus began both an extraordinary friendship between Jackson and Jordan and one of sports' best coaching records. A substitute on the New York Knicks' championship team of 1973, Jackson was an unusual person and coach who read widely and meditated daily. He learned from both his meditating and the Knicks' successes that teams, not individuals, won championships. "The day I took over the Bulls," he wrote in his autobiography, "I would create an environment based on the principles of selflessness and compassion I'd learned as a Christian in my parents' home; sitting on a cushion practicing Zen; and studying the teachings of the Lakota Sioux" in his home state of North Dakota. Lakota warriors, Jackson emphasized, did not try to be stars, but helped others, regardless of the cost, so the group could succeed. Owner Jerry Reinsdorf once told Jackson that most people were motivated by either fear or greed. Jackson replied that he thought they were also "motivated by love."

Translated, the new coach planned to install a new system in which all the Bulls, not just Jordan, would be fully involved in both offense and defense. Jackson's intricate system was beautiful to watch, but difficult and frustrating to learn. It did turn the 47–35 record of the year before into 55–27 in 1989–1990. Nevertheless, Chicago again suffered an embarrassing defeat in the spring 1990 playoffs at the hands of the championship Detroit team. Almost as bad, Jordan had grown to dislike Detroit's intimidating stars—Isiah Thomas, Bill Laimbeer, and Dennis Rodman—personally. He publicly attacked his teammates for not standing up to Detroit's brutal style of play.

Jordan was becoming obsessed with winning the championship in 1990–1991. The obsession did not stem from his need for money but his need to be the best. Between his $3.25 million Bulls salary and his endorsements, the $17 million total probably made him the world's richest athlete. A U.S. advertising-industry analysis further revealed that he was tied with another African-American, television superstar Bill Cosby, as the best-known and best-liked celebrity in the country. Increasing amounts of Jordan's celebrity and money came from selling Nike sneakers in the United States and, indeed, around the globe.

Enter the Transnational Corporation

By the 1990s, teenagers shot and sometimes murdered each other to steal Nike's Air Jordan sneakers and other athletic clothing. The shoes, which cost well under fifty dollars to make in Southeast Asian factories paying some of the lowest manufacturing wages in the world, cost up to three times that in stores. Customers of all ages willingly paid the huge profit to Nike because of Jordan's name, the highly advertised technology that went into the shoe, and the almost supernatural aura that seemed to surround Nike's world-famous Swoosh symbol and motto, "Just Do It"—which, critics claimed, was exactly the advice gun-toting teenagers followed to obtain their Nikes.

After Jordan had become the world's most glamorous athlete in the mid-1990s, Nike was a $9 billion company with about half its sales overseas. It spent nearly $50 million in research and development and more than a half-billion dollars on advertising and marketing worldwide, a figure that dwarfed the spending of such competitors as Reebok, Fila, and Adidas. Nike churned out profits not only by dominating its markets. The Beaverton, Oregon, company exemplified something new and most significant in American history: a corporation that made nearly all its products abroad and sold half or more of those goods in foreign markets. In other words, although known as an American corporation, most of its laborers and its sales were abroad.

Multinational corporations are not new. In the late nineteenth century, such U.S. firms were rising from the ashes of the Civil War to dominate markets. These included Standard Oil in petroleum products, Eastman Kodak in film, Singer in sewing machines, and McCormick in farm harvesters. But these companies differed from their late-twentieth-century descendants in at least five respects.

First, the 1890s firms largely employed Americans to produce their product; in the 1990s, the firms extensively employed foreign labor and made the overwhelming bulk of their goods abroad. By 1980, a stunning 80 percent of these U.S. corporations' revenues came from overseas production, and less than 20 percent arose from exporting American-made goods to foreign markets.

Second, while the late-nineteenth-century firms largely traded in natural resources (oil, iron) or industrial goods (steel, paint), the late-twentieth-century firms traded in designs, technical knowledge, management techniques, and organizational innovations. The key to success was not so much the goods, as it was knowledge: the quickly formulated and transferred engineering and marketing information, the control of advanced, rapidly changing technology (such as how to make computer software—or Air Jordans).

A third revolutionary characteristic of transnationals, such as Nike or Coca-Cola, was their increasing dependence on world markets—not solely U.S.—for profits. For the corporations that drove the U.S. economy, and on which nearly all Americans depended directly or indirectly for their economic survival, relied in turn on global markets. In 1996 for example, the Atlanta, Georgia-based Coca-Cola Company, that most American of all firms, stopped dividing its markets between "domestic" and "international." Instead, it organized sales along the lines of specific regions and, in this regard, "North America" was not substantially different from, say, "Southeast Asia." This new policy was logical: in 1996 four of every five bottles of Coke were sold outside the United States.

A fourth difference followed: as the Nike budget demonstrated, transnationals of the late twentieth century depended on massive advertising campaigns to make people want their products. The advertising, too, was revolutionary in that by the late 1980s it could be instantaneously seen on as many as thirty to five hundred television channels in many countries through the new technology of communication satellites and fiber-optic cable. Such advertising often sold not merely a product (as sneakers) but a lifestyle ("Just Do It") that in most instances was based on American culture. Standard Oil petroleum or McCormick harvesters were not uniquely American products; they challenged other cultures far less in the 1880s than did Nike athletic equipment and its accompanying advertising lifestyle advice, which vividly illustrated the freedom (even the ability to fly through the air with a basketball) that seemed to come with the equipment.

Finally, because the old multinationals were not only headquartered, but produced and/or sold much of their product, in the United States, they could usually be made accountable to the government in Washington. Even the richest of all Americans, John D. Rockefeller, learned this hard lesson when the government broke up his Standard Oil monopoly into a number of smaller companies in 1911. The new transnational, however, became so global by the 1980s that a single government had power over only a part of the firm's total operation. The size of many transnationals, moreover, dwarfed the size of many governments. Of the hundred largest economic units in the world of the 1980s, only half were nations. The other half were individual corporations. Thus, for example, when the makers of athletic equipment were found in the 1990s to be exploiting low-paid Southeast Asians who worked in horrible conditions, the U.S. government's power to remedy the problem was limited. The transnational was, as its name declared, transcending the boundaries of individual nations.

Enter the Swoosh

Phil Knight certainly had no idea that his company might be involved in such a transformation when he founded Nike in the 1960s. Knight, a red-haired and quite mediocre distance runner at the University of Oregon in the late 1950s, was also highly observant of the efforts of the legendary Oregon coach, Bill Bowerman, to produce a lighter, better track shoe. Knight recalled how the gruff, outspoken coach once painstakingly measured exactly how many strides a runner took in running a mile, then calculated that if just one ounce could be shaved from the shoes' weight the runner would be freed of 550 pounds during the race.

Knight carried this memory with him when at Stanford Business School a professor instructed his students to write a paper about how they would create a new company. Knight wrote a detailed analysis arguing that profits could be generated by importing cheap but well-made running shoes from Japan. Athletic footwear had been around since the 1860s when the British began wearing lightweight canvas leisure shoes. By the 1920s, Converse had turned these into the most popular and profitable sneaker in the United States. From then until the 1960s, nearly all basketball players wore Converse shoes. In the 1950s, however, German-made Adidas and Puma sneakers began to challenge Converse by giving free shoes to top runners who, in turn, would promise to wear them in competition. Thus German companies gave birth to the athletic endorsement several decades before Michael Jordan made it globally famous.

Phil Knight believed he could change American styles by using the Japanese to defeat the Germans. In 1963, while working in a Portland, Oregon, accounting firm, he went on an around-the-world trip. Knight carefully set time aside to visit Kobe, Japan, where the Tiger running shoe was produced. When the skeptical Japanese asked which sports company he was with, Knight made up a name on the spot—Blue Ribbon Sports. He asked for some Tigers to take back to Oregon. The tough Bill Bowerman admitted, "These shoes aren't half bad." Knight believed he had found his opportunity. He and Bowerman each invested five hundred dollars to purchase Tigers then Knight traveled around to regional track meets and sold the shoes from his car. The first year Blue Ribbon Sports sold one thousand pairs and cleared about $364.

By 1969, Knight's sales had leaped to a million dollars. He now worried that the Japanese, whose own transnationals were rapidly spreading around the world, might drop him so they could sell Tiger shoes directly to American customers. The two men, however, were determined to find better shoes. One Sunday morning, with his wife at church, Bowerman poured melted rubber into the family's waffle iron. Waffle-soled, square-cleated athletic shoes, made of lightweight fabric, were the ultimate result. Knight decided to concentrate on the shoes he and Bowerman were developing. But he needed a name, a trademark, an easily recognized symbol. One of his young designers, Jeff Johnson, had a bad night's sleep during 1971 in which he dreamed of Nike, the Greek winged goddess who symbolized victory. Without any better idea, Knight decided to try Johnson's suggestion.

The next year, a Portland State University design student, Carolyn Davidson, sketched a fat, floating check-mark as a symbol for the running shoes. "I don't love it," Knight told her, "but maybe it'll grow on me." He bought the design from her for thirty-five dollars. Nike employees called it the "Swoosh." By the 1990s, when it was worn by Nike endorsers Michael Jordan, golfer Tiger Woods, and tennis champion Pete Sampras, among many others, the Swoosh had become the most recognizable commercial logo in global sports. Davidson later received Nike stock from Knight, and rightly so. Her design made it possible for people in faraway lands whose languages did not easily translate the word "Nike," to identify Nike products simply by the Swoosh. Only an image, not words, was needed to reap profits in other cultures.

In the late 1970s, the American addiction for physical fitness, especially by jogging, helped drive Nike sales from $10 million to $270 million. Half of all running shoes sold were Nikes. But Knight wanted more. He was determined to smash Adidas and Reebok, his main competitors.

To overwhelm Adidas and Reebok, Knight also thought he needed more imaginative advertising. He did not reach this conclusion easily. Indeed, he had considered advertising large a waste of money, even a fraud. Any product's success, Knight preached, should depend on its quality, not on slick advertising gimmicks. But Adidas and Reebok employed advertising, so in 1980 he visited a local ad agency. "I'm Phil Knight," he greeted Dan Wieden and David Kennedy, "and I hate advertising." Wieden and Kennedy overlooked this unusual introduction to design superb advertisements.

For a number of reasons, Nike promptly went into a nosedive. Reebok quadrupled sales revenues to become the number one shoe. In 1985–1986, Nike profits plummeted 80 percent. Part of the problem turned out to be the need for more focused advertising. The much larger problem was that Nike employed nearly all men, who designed shoes for men. Women, however, were now buying as many athletic shoes as were men. Reebok shrewdly designed apparel for this booming female market. In 1986, Knight returned to Wieden & Kennedy. He brought with him Nike's new breakthrough, a basketball shoe with an air pocket in the inner sole. Knight agreed to advertise the new footwear on television. Dan Wieden came up with a slogan: "Just Do It." Two young women on Wieden & Kennedy's staff devised an ad with no words, only the Swoosh logo and the blasting music of the Beatles' "Revolution." They had found how the transnational corporations could sell goods in vast overseas markets, even in the many lands where English was not spoken. Nike sales soared. They doubled between 1987 and 1989 to $1.7 billion.

Michael Jordan wore the new shoe, but, as Knight recalled, "it was so colorful that the NBA banned it—which was great! We . . . welcome the kind of publicity that pits us against the establishment." And Jordan, of course, "played like no one has ever played before. . . . Sales just took off." The Bulls' star was used to sell the new shoes, Knight emphasized, because "It saves us a lot of time. . . . You can't explain much in 60 seconds, but when you show Michael Jordan, you don't have to. People already know a lot about him. It's that simple." Jordan, in other words, was an image much like the Swoosh.

David Falk had brought Knight and Jordan together in 1984. A 1975 law-school graduate, Falk and his ProServ agency were among the first professional agents who not only represented athletes in contract negotiations (in which ProServe took about 4 percent of the player's salary for negotiating the deal), but in obtaining endorsements (where ProServe could receive as much as 25 percent). Falk knew what Oscar Robertson had learned the hard way: many companies did not want African-American athletes to represent them. In 1982, however, basketball great Kareem Abdul-Jabbar received an unprecedented fee, $100,000, for endorsing Adidas sneakers. Then Jordan's North Carolina teammate, James Worthy, received $1.2 million over eight years to wear a New Balance shoe.

Falk speculated that the right athlete could do more than merely wear a particular sneaker: that athlete could actively enter the marketplace, drive sales upward, then profit handsomely from those sales. He believed Jordan could be such a pioneer. The North Carolinian was not only a special player but a respected person with good values instilled by strong parents. "The thing about Jordan," a competitor of Nike later observed, "is that he doesn't alienate anybody." The All-American, moreover, was willing to work cheaply. At his first meeting with Knight, Jordan announced that in return for his endorsement he wanted, most of all, an automobile. Falk had considerably more expensive terms in mind.

The timing was perfect. Not only was Knight searching, and Jordan newly available, but the NBA had just appointed an ambitious, imaginative new commissioner. David Stern fervently believed that professional basketball could be promoted globally and be highly profitable. He later compared the NBA with Disney: "They have theme parks, and we have theme parks. Only we call them arenas. They have characters: Mickey and Goofy. Our characters are named Magic and Michael. Disney sells apparel; we sell apparel. They make home videos; we make home videos." As one observer later noted, Stern "grasped the root law of capitalism: grow or die." The new commissioner, as Jeff Coplon wrote, had nothing less than a "manifest destiny regime."

A key to making that destiny manifest, critics claimed, lay in the NBA achieving what historian John Hoberman called "virtual integration": white executive business control combining with African-American athletic domination to create a "crossover appeal" among millions of white and black viewers. Once the idea that the NBA was (in the words of one of its African-American executives) "too black," and "too drug infested," was "turned around," then the "new personalities" of Johnson, Bird, and Jordan could become moneymaking machines.

Nike and Wieden & Kennedy found another African-American who had crossover appeal. The movie director Spike Lee scored a major success with all audiences in 1986 with his film *She's Gotta Have It*. The lead male character, Mars Blackmon (played by Lee himself), was such an obsessed fan of Michael Jordan that he even wore shoes endorsed by the Bulls' star to bed. Lee filmed advertisements (turned out by a young sports-addict-turned-writer, Jim Riswold) that brought "Mars" and Jordan together in some of the funniest and most popular commercials of the late 1980s. These combined with ads showing Jordan flying through the air for what seemed to be forever. "His Airness," as he became known, and the Air Jordan shoe became one. In 1987, Falk negotiated a seven-year contract with Nike. Phil Knight not only guaranteed Jordan $18 million, but a royalty on every Air Jordan shoe sold—a royalty that would amount to far more than $18 million.

Knight then took another step to flummox his competitors. He signed not just individual stars, but entire colleges. These schools, famous for their sports teams, promised to use Nike equipment nearly exclusively in return for large sums of money. Football powerhouse University of Miami was first in 1989. As Nike's historian, Donald Katz, described it, Knight wanted "to vertically integrate all sports"—much as John D. Rockefeller's Standard Oil Company had vertically integrated the oil industry from exploration and drilling to selling gas at the pump. Knight was becoming the Rockefeller of the sports world.

Nike's next step to crush competitors was especially significant. Knight launched massive global advertising campaigns. As he explained, "To paraphrase Willy Sutton [a criminal who said he robbed banks because that's where the money was], we're going out into the world because that's where the feet are." Nike had begun major advertising in Europe during 1985, then increased the pace until its shoes dominated that market. Jordan, now famous for both his Olympic basketball feats and his Nike ads, could no longer walk down many European streets by 1988 without drawing a crowd. In Japan, an all-out advertising campaign in 1989 made the Air Jordan shoe number one and, along with Coca-Cola, one of the two items teenagers said they most wanted.

Nike also joined the many who had for decades, indeed centuries, lusted after the great China market. In 1978, the Communist government slowly began delicate reforms aimed at opening China to capital investments, while maintaining tough Communist Party political control. Nike became one of more than fifty thousand joint ventures between transnational corporations and the Chinese. By 1995, China was second only to the United States in receiving direct foreign investment. With annual growth rates of 8 percent and more (the average annual U.S. rate has historically been about 3 percent), the world's most populous market was booming.

Many Chinese could now watch foreign television, notably shows from British-governed Hong Kong. When Nike opened its new store in the giant boomtown of Shanghai, hundreds lined up during the night to buy clothing. Knight put on a spectacular opening: "six scantily clad women—the few clothes they were wearing came from Nike's line—did aerobics," according to the staid *Far Eastern Economic Review,* "to the tune 'New York, New York,' and Madonna's 'Material Girl,' fitting songs for the dawning of the age of the Chinese consumer."

Enter the Communication Satellite

"Now the experience of sports is everywhere," Knight observed. "It's all-encompassing and instantaneous. It's right there beside you from cradle to grave" and is "the culture of the world." It was a remarkable claim: sports was the culture that linked the peoples around the globe. He could exhibit some persuasive evidence. Exhibit A was Michael Jordan. "I never knew it could be like this," the star remarked. He had been popular as a high school senior and especially in college, "but I never knew it could be nation-based—or, if you want, world-based."

In the late 1970s and early 1980s, just as Jordan appeared on the scene, commercial television began to jump over national boundaries. A decade later, NBA games, especially those of the Chicago Bulls, could be seen in ninety-three countries. This exposure was made possible by the direct broadcast satellite (DBS). The first DBS was launched in May 1974 by the U.S. National Aeronautic and Space Administration (NASA), which in 1969 had put the first men on the moon. DBS was to have a much greater impact on the day-to-day lives of people around the world than did the moon landing. Launched into orbit so it would float in space over the west coast of South America, the first broadcast satellite relayed information from specialists on health and education into previously isolated areas, such as parts of Alaska and the Rocky Mountains. The experiment was so successful that private companies stepped in to launch their own satellites. The companies, as usual, made their profits by selling advertising.

Thus new technology led the world's people into a new era of globalization, paid for by a new advertising. By the 1980s, the technology became even more dazzling—and profitable. DBS went into the home of the television viewer through one of two routes. One route sent the signal from, say, the stadium where the game was being played, to the satellite, then back to earth to individual receivers (or "dishes") owned by a viewer. In the 1980s and 1990s, however, the more common route was from the stadium to the satellite and then to a receiving station on earth where the signal went into cables. The cables carried the game into individual homes. Thus whoever controlled the cable service could go far in controlling the television markets.

The potential profits of those markets skyrocketed in the 1980s when fiber-optic cables were developed.

Now the possibilities were breathtaking. A single direct-broadcast satellite could transmit to earth all of the *Encyclopedia Britannica* in less than a minute. The contents could even be picked up and placed before the viewer by a cable relay station whose cost in 1975 had been $125,000, but in 1980 was less than $4,000 because of the quick technological advances. Profits promised to have no limit. As cable and satellites created international television in the 1980s, so did advertising, whose profits for cable companies shot up more than ten times.

These new systems seemed to resemble magic cash registers as they churned out the money.

Whenever innovative technology appears, swashbuckling entrepreneurs quickly materialize to exploit it. In the 1880s and 1890s, it had been the robber barons (Rockefeller, steelmaker Andrew Carnegie, banker J. P. Morgan), whose understanding of industrial technology's potential made them very rich. In the 1980s and 1990s, those made very rich by satellite and cable included Michael Jordan and Phil Knight, but also such media barons as American Ted Turner and Australian Rupert Murdoch. For it was the few, led by Turner and Murdoch, who created the satellite-cable networks on which Jordan and Knight sold the NBA and Nike shoes to the many around the world. . . .

Questions for Analysis

1. This essay begins by describing a low point in the history of the Chicago Bulls—few victories, low attendance, diminishing television

market. Why do you think the author begins this way? What does the historical perspective help LaFeber accomplish in his argument?

2. Later, LaFeber recounts Michael Jordan's early days in the NBA. What characterizes Jordan's first few years? In what way did Michael become a "quick study"?

3. LaFeber credits some of the growing interest in basketball through the 1980s to "real-life" movies like *Hoosiers,* which helped generate a desire for basketball. What other social factors might have helped the sport's popularity grow? What free time activities might certain movies or television shows be advocating now?

4. In the next section of the essay, LaFeber describes five features of transnational corporations. Why does he do this? What argument is he able to make because of this section? What connections do you see between his discussion of transnational corporations and your favorite pastime?

5. LaFeber discusses the Nike/Jordan alliance as a combination of a good product, provocative marketing, and a number of other social factors. What are those factors, and what is their significance? Which additional social movements might you add to LaFeber's list?

6. Michael Jordan was able to build on the advances in race relations forged by African American athletes before him, as LaFeber describes. Are black/white divisions still an issue in professional sports? What seem to be the major divisions in your free time activities: are there problems with gender, socioeconomic class, or ethnicities? Explain your answer.

7. According to LaFeber, what were the most significant impacts of the communications industry on the "globalization of Michael Jordan"? Do you see similar changes in other sports or other free time activities?

8. LaFeber uses the phrase "magic cash registers" when he discusses the response to cable-driven communications technologies. What other provocative phrases does he invent in this essay? Which ones have the greatest impact on you as a reader? Why? Can you think of similar phrases that might work in your own writing?

9. In the final paragraphs, LaFeber ends by looking back historically at "robber barons" in American history. What does this look backward achieve for the writer?

10. By the end of the essay, LaFeber has explained a convergence of factors leading to Michael Jordan's phenomenal economic success: talent, drive, a willingness to learn from mistakes, marketing and advertising, improved race relations, expansion to worldwide markets, links with a product, advances in telecommunications, and so on. What other factors can you add to this list? What other side effects have resulted from the globalization of Michael Jordan?

A Case   JENNIE'S INQUIRY

In high school, Jennie was a competitive swimmer who spent about 20 hours a week practicing to prepare for meets. Because of the intensity of her commitment, Jennie rarely had time to spend with friends who were not a part of the swim team. These friends often asked Jennie if all the work was worth it since her free time was so filled with such a big responsibility to the team. Now that she is in college, Jennie has started to ask herself the same question. When Jennie's writing instructor assigned an inquiry into free time, Jennie decided to take a look at her swimming.

Jennie's instructor had asked the class to investigate the marketing and packaging that accompanied their free time. After the class generated a list of their activities, the class began to write out some of the ways their free time is sold to the public. As a class, the students discussed what packaging meant, and each writer made his or her own list for two of their activities. Next, the instructor taught them a new story-telling guide which would help them to step back and take a fresh look at their selected free time activity.

Jennie's Starting Strategy

Free Time Activities List

- swimming
- skiing
- listening to music
- watching TV, especially on Thursday nights
- talking on the phone with friends from high school
- water polo
- running
- dancing at parties
- hanging out with friends by the fountain

I'll choose swimming.

Swimming Packages

- magazine *Swimming World*
- boxes that competition swimsuits come in: small with lots of waves, water, American flags, and company logos on them
- SPEEDO stores, with athletic-looking mannequins in the windows
- brightly colored suits
- goggles: advertised as aerodynamic—look great, and feel right
- swim caps: always attention-getters with the name of the team, words of wisdom or psych-out slogans, uplifting, gets you psyched to swim your best
- canvas bags: sporty, will hold everything you need and more
- POWERBARS for energy, lots of advertisements
- T-shirts for each team. Same goal as the swim caps.

A Story from My T-Shirt

As I pull off my team T-shirt, the tension mounts. There are some big girls here, and we are all here for one reason only. As I stretch out, I am pulled out of my concentration when the starter says, "Next heat, varsity girls 500 Free up to the block." I slowly step forward as I place my goggles down over my eyes. As I think about the message on our team T-shirt, "Reaching for Excellence One Stroke at a Time," I feel confident that I can do my best. I stretch my neck as a shake my arms and legs. I can feel the adrenaline flowing throughout my body from the snug fit of the goggles down to my toes on the scratchy starting block. I remember the feel of that 100% cotton shirt, and I visualize the stance of the swimmer in the picture. Arm up, perfect arc, precise form. I can do it.

"Swimmers, take your mark . . . beep!" We're off.

As I hit the water a feeling of complete control overcomes me. As I reach my pace speed after the first 150, I breathe more often to keep an eye on my competitors. Feeling the power—the excellence—through every single stroke. The counter on deck sends me messages with the counter at the end of the pool: 11, 13, 15 . . . the race is almost over . . . speed it up and drive it home hard with everything you have left! Don't leave anything behind; don't hold anything back. Legs speed up as I feel more power with every perfect stroke. The last 100 yards is an all-out sprint. As I speed up, I feel my muscles tightening up, and there is an aching-burning sensation now. As I turn to my last 25 yards, I hold my breath and drive hard. The wall is approaching and every stroke reaches to touch it. I stretch once more and tag the wall. Exhausted and breathing hard, I pull the goggles off my head and I glance up at the time board. 5:25:63. Best time ever! One stroke at a time—I did it!

After working through the story-telling guide, Jennie and her writing partner, Brandi, met to discuss the work they had done so far. Brandi said that she liked Jennie's work, but she had a couple of questions and suggestions. First of all, she wasn't sure what was going on in the story. Was it a true story about Jennie's swimming, or was it about one of her packages? Brandi thought it was interesting, but she didn't see how the story highlighted a way swimming was packaged. Jennie replied that her story was a combination of both—she picked up on the phrases and images in the team T-shirt (like "Reaching for Excellence One Stroke at a Time," and the graphic of the precise swimmer), and she played out what might happen if the T-shirt really did possess the power to make her swim differently. Her dream-like story, though, really did happen, and was one of the proudest moments in her swimming life.

To help them further investigate how their free time was packaged, the instructor next asked the class to write out a list of words that described their packages and then create a list of the "opposites" or "contrasts" for each term. These contrasts would help them see what was *not* in the package, and they would suggest a number of different stories which are left out in the packaging.

After that, each writer was to compose another story—this one using the contrasting terms instead of the key terms. Exploring through key terms, contrasts, and a contrasting story might open up some puzzlements or dissonances.

Jennie's Terms and Contrasts

Key Terms on the T-shirt	*Contrasts*

Red, White, and Blue (team colors)	other country's flag colors
	    Purple, Black, and Orange (opposites on
	    the color wheel)

lone swimmer	entire team no swimmer shown
goggles, cap, and suit in the picture	old-fashioned swimming dresses skinny-dipping
Lake Valley (name of our team)	forest mountain shopping center
"Reaching for Excellence One Stroke at a Time"—team logo	"Losing badly all together" "Slacking miserably all at once"
water in the picture	sand land air
perfect technique	clutzy sloppy, no precision
discipline	out of control not with the rest of the team
summer	fall winter
warm	cold over 115 degrees in the shade
star (red) sky in the picture	black hole in the ground yellow moon in the sky
waves with the swimmer	calm smooth
female	male
freestyle	butterfly stroke dog paddle relay
racing	warm up cool down
100% cotton	mostly polyester 50/50

Contrasting Story from the Contrasting Terms of the T-shirt

The world seemed to be all black, purple, and orange—like a polyester disco in the 1970s. It wasn't a disco, though, it was a community pool in a shopping center, and it seemed like it was filled with all the clutzy people of the world. All of them were out of shape, and they were sweating in their polyester outfits. It was 115 degrees in the shade, and all those people wanted to get cool, but they couldn't figure out how to get into the pool. And if they had all tried to get into the pool, it would have overflowed. The pool itself was like a black hole in the ground, waiting to swallow all these masses of people. In the still air, there wasn't a ripple in the surface of the pool. Instead, the only water that flowed was the sweat running off those hundreds of backs as they rolled around in their neon jumpsuits.

After several hours of this lolling around, one of the clutzy guys figured out that things would be cooler in the pool. He stripped down to nothing and jumped in the shallow end. Everyone watched, horrified. The guy shouted and flailed around and eventually started doggy paddling around in circles. Another guy thought it looked like fun, and he cannonballed into the pool with the largest splash you have ever seen. One after another, all the people took off their polyester jumpsuits and got in the pool. It was chaos. Eventually, the fire department had to come and rescue people who were being trampled in the pool.

The following day, Jennie's class discussed their contrasting terms and stories. The instructor asked the class if anyone had found puzzlements or dissonance. Jennie, in fact, had noticed something that bothered her. The team T-shirt she was examining portrayed only a single swimmer, which meant that the word "team" was on the contrasting side. Jennie knew that wasn't right since everything the team teaches and supports is the team concept—all for one and one for all. Jennie's explorations showed her an ideological conflict between the valued "individual" in the package (the team T-shirt) and the value of "team unity" espoused by all the coaches. Her contrasting story, on the other hand, was the one that included lots of people; the initial story was only about a lone swimmer.

Jennie and Brandi discussed their key terms and contrasts a bit more. Brandi agreed with Jennie's observations, especially after Jennie showed her the actual T-shirt. Brandi felt that the dominant values in the T-shirt were *discipline, hardwork,* and *commitment*—but *teamwork* was nowhere to be found. On the contrary, *individual perfection* was more prominent than any kind of team effort. With Brandi's feedback, Jennie was able to articulate quite a few puzzlements.

Puzzlements—

- Team unity is very important, but so are individual performances. Unity isn't represented in the picture on the T-shirt, though.
- The shirt is supposed to represent the team not the individual. There's no "I" in "team."
- I often swim year-round not just in warm weather. Why does the shirt just show the warm weather when it's easier? We are supposed to uphold a solid year-round work ethic.

Jennie's instructor next introduced another way to inquire into free time packaging: a target group analysis. The instructor showed the class how to use a grid that broke society into segments that the students could identify. The grid is arranged to foreground various cultural categories, like race, class, and gender; it is also divided into columns that illustrate who is being included, and who has been left out of the target group. In other words, what kinds of people were the manufacturers targeting with their packaging efforts? The class practiced this analysis as a whole with an advertisement the instructor brought in, then they worked on their own packages in their workshop groups. Jennie and Brandi worked together on one another's packages, and by the time they were finished, they both felt ready to write questions that would guide the rest of her inquiry.

Jennie's Target Group Analysis

Target Group Analysis

Cultural Category	*Range of Possibility*	*Who's Included*	*Who's Excluded*
age	6–under; 7–8; 9–10; 11–12; 13–14; 15–18; older	7–12 (younger swimmer on shirt)	the older range of swimmers, adults
race	white, black, Hispanic, Asian, Indian	white	all the rest
gender	male, female	female	male
economic class	poor, middle class, rich	middle class	anybody in poverty
sexual orientation	straight, gay, bi	straight (kids)	can't tell
education level	preschool, elementary, jr. high, high school, college, grad school	pre-school through high school	college and beyond (too old)
religious affiliation	Christian, Jewish, Mormon, etc.	can't tell	can't tell

Discussion of Target Group Analysis

- White, female, middle to upper class family. She is straight, between the ages of 6–12, religion unknown.
- The values associated with this target audience are friendship, sports, activities, and their own religion. They also seem to value the work of the individual—everyone for himself. Or herself.
- The value of teamwork and unity is excluded. This sport of swimming takes the effort and support of the whole team not just one individual.
- What is good, ideal, and acceptable is exercise, hard work, training, discipline, and sticking with the team. We highly value working hard to perfect your stroke, and staying dedicated to precision.
- What is bad, deviant, or unacceptable is not having a good work ethic and just being out for yourself.

My Position within the Package

- I do fit the image on the shirt: I am female, white, middle-to-upper class, straight, and Catholic.

- I'm 18 now and in college. I will soon be too old to compete in this group. I am also someone who believes strongly in teamwork and working as a group.

- The manufacturer/designer assumes that you are a hardworking individual striving for the perfect technique and work discipline. I want to be that kind of person, work hard while you work and play hard while you play. Determination, dedication, discipline, and commitment to the team is the kind of person I want to be.

- I do not agree with the fact that the shirt glorifies the "individual"

When Jennie and Brandi discussed their target group analyses, Jennie said she was starting to feel that she was a part of an elite target group of young, white, upper middle class women. Was swimming really limited to a certain group? Brandi admitted that her image of swimmers fit the target group that Jennie had described. Jennie was starting to realize there were several possible questions she could pursue.

Jennie's Questions

Questions

- I've noticed a diverse range of people participating in swimming, so the shirt shouldn't portray only a white female. Why can't the shirt include others?

- How can we change the shirt in the future to stress the importance of teamwork in a team sport?

- Why does the T-shirt glorify the individual instead of supporting the team concept?

When it came time to compose a guiding question, Jennie decided she could not go with the one that only asked about showing more types of swimmers; the larger issue, in her mind, was the matter of the *individual* versus the *community*. The more she and Brandi talked about it, the more they both realized their questions about the T-shirt really reflected a tension in American society. Their analysis was leading them both toward an understanding of some contradictory societal values. After this discussion, Jennie was able to pose a useful guiding question.

My Question:

Why does the team T-shirt glorify the individual instead of supporting a team concept?

Now that Jennie had completed her exploration and formulated a good question, she considered possible writing contexts, reader and writer positions and appropriate genres.

Jennie's Writing Contexts

Locating Writing Contexts for Writing about the T-shirt

swimmers

- college team here
- my old high school team
- people who buy T-shirts and caps
- US Olympic team

others

- my writing class
- those who sell swimming goods
- students on my dorm floor
- my non-swimming friends from high school

My context choice:

I would like to write for this class, because I think I can say things to them that I wouldn't be able to say to other swimmers. I want to write about some of the social implications Brandi and I have been talking about, and I think the class is my best context for that.

Brandi questioned why the swim team wouldn't make a good reader for Jennie's writing. They shared many of the same values and experiences, so they might really be interested in Jennie's perspective. After their discussion, Jennie decided that Brandi had a good point, but she still preferred to write to the class. Jennie felt that the class would be more open to the kind of analysis that she was starting to do, especially since each member of the class was conducting a parallel inquiry. Jennie's inquiry into a swimming package, the team T-shirt, was leading her to some insights about American culture; she hoped that the class would be able to share and learn from one another's insights.

Jennie's Writer and Reader Positioning and Genre Selection

Positioning Myself in the Class

Positions I have written from in this class: I haven't yet written *to* the class, since all of my other projects have been in other contexts.

Positions I have been excluded from: Technically, I'm not the teacher, but sometimes I do play the role of informing and teaching others (especially Brandi).

Positions I have left behind: I can't be a quiet and nervous student since there is always work to be done in this class, and everybody has to participate in the groups. We are supposed to participate as equals in a conversation, so I shouldn't take on a role where I am talking up or down to my classmates.

Position I will take: I will take the position of a conversational equal in a critical environment. This means that I need to explain certain things about my subject that the others may not know, but I can assume that they will understand certain terms that I might use that are common to the class. I can also assume that they will be interested in cultural insights.

Reader Positions

Reader positions available in the context of this class: Fellow students who know a little about swimming, fellow cultural critics who have been exploring the implications of their free time, fellow students who might be influenced by the tension between individual and society that I am writing about.

My choice of reader position: I choose fellow cultural critics.

The values and background I associate with my reader position of cultural critics: I know that they won't say that I'm reading too much into things since they have gone through the same learning process that I have. They will want to know what I learned, just as I hope to learn from them. We are like a team.

Genre Selection

Possible genres in the context of my class:

- a new, redesigned T-shirt
- a critical essay explaining the contradictions and their cultural sources

My Genre choice:

- I could just go ahead and redesign next year's shirt, to make sure that "TEAM" is really an obvious value, but then I wouldn't be explaining why I made the changes I did. And it wouldn't give me a chance to write about the social value stuff Brandi and I talked about.
- My genre is a critical essay. I want to discuss the shirt, and I know that I need to talk about how the shirt mirrors other things in society. The critical essay lets me do both.

Features of the critical essay:

- Critical essays look like academic papers: double-spaced, neatly type-written, with 1" margins on all sides. They are usually at least 3 pages long, and they can be really long.
- Sometimes they have catchy beginnings, which make you want to read more.
- They usually have paragraphs that are about the same size, and each paragraph talks about one main idea.
- They usually have a focus statement somewhere near the front, although some don't mention the focus until the very end (building up to it like a surprise).
- They usually have a strong conclusion that leaves the reader thinking about the main point.

Having decided to go with the genre of a critical essay, Jennie found it helpful to think through some of her earlier work in light of larger societal issues dealing with individualism and teamwork. She wrote more on key terms and contrasts, and she was able to come up with a number of supporting examples by thinking about some new stories. In particular, she identified a list of contradictions within the sports world that she thought would reinforce her position on the T-shirt. Going back through her earlier work with new insight and a careful eye enabled Jennie to easily craft a focus statement and two possible organizational plans.

Jennie's Focus and Organization

Focus Statement

My swim team T-shirt reflects a contradiction in American society: we say that we value teamwork, but we are most usually rewarded for individual efforts.

Possible Organizational Plans

Grouping plan (with comparison and contrast)

1. Introduce the T-shirt and the team (using story?)
2. Describe the contradiction between the T-shirt and the team handbook
3. Give examples of sports that show contradictions:
   a. Olympic women's basketball, baseball, and soccer teams
   b. NBA basketball teams and free agency
   c. Famous swimmers (bring back my subject of swimming)
4. Conclude

Narrative plan

1. Begin with images of individualism from early age, conflict with learning to share
2. Talk about first experience with swim team, conflict with badges and honors
3. Talk about progress through the team, conflict with promotions to assistant and coach
4. Talk about how T-shirt is a symbol of the tension—pictures louder than words
5. Conclude

Jennie felt that either plan would work, but she thought that more of the work she had done with her writing process so far could go into the first plan. Since she liked it the best and it made sense to her, she went with it. She and Brandi weren't able to meet before the polished draft was due, so Jennie had to make this decision on her own.

Jennie's Polished Draft

Polished Draft

As I pull off my team T-shirt, the tension mounts. There are some big girls here, and we are all here for one reason only. As I stretch out, I am pulled out of my concentration when the starter says, "Next heat, varsity girls 500 Free up to the block." I slowly step forward as I place my goggles down over my eyes. As I think about the message on our team T-shirt, "Reaching for Excellence One Stroke at a Time," I feel confident that I can do my best. I stretch my neck as a shake my arms and legs. I can feel the adrenaline flowing throughout my body from the snug fit of the goggles down to my toes on the scratchy starting block. I remember the feel of that 100% cotton shirt, and I visualize the stance of the swimmer in the picture. Arm up, perfect arc, precise form. I can do it.

"Swimmers, take your mark . . . beep!" We're off.

As I hit the water a feeling of complete control overcomes me. As I reach my pace speed after the first 150 I breathe more often to keep an eye on my competitors. Feeling the power—the excellence—through every single stroke. The counter on deck sends me messages with the counter at the end of the pool: 11, 13, 15 . . . the race is almost over . . . speed it up and drive it home hard with everything you have left! Don't leave anything behind, don't hold anything back. Legs speed up as I feel more power with every perfect stroke. The last 100 yards is an all-out sprint. As I speed up I feel my muscles tightening up and there is an aching-burning sensation now. As I turn to my last 25 yards, I hold my breath and drive hard. The wall is approaching, and every stroke reaches to touch it. I stretch once more and tag the wall. Exhausted and breathing hard, I pull the goggles off my head, and I glance up at the time board. 5:25:63. Best time ever! One stroke at a time—I did it!

The story that I just told was real. I am a member of the Lake Valley Swim team, and the day I've described was one of the best of my swimming career. Swimming is something that I really like to do, and I have worked my way though the different levels of the team. I started when I was a kid, and now I am actually a coach. I used to think that I liked everything about the swim team until I started to look seriously at the team T-shirt. Now, I'm not so sure anymore. In all the years I've been swimming with Lake Valley, I have learned from the coaches and from our team handbook that one thing is important above everything else, teamwork. As a swimmer, the sense of teamwork made me more disciplined, more precise, more competitive against other teams. As a coach, I also stressed the values of hard work and team unity. One of the most exciting parts of the early season for us is when we get our T-shirts for the season. The T-shirts are supposed to bring us all together, to make us look the same, and give us a unified look. They are also supposed to psych out the other team. I guess you could say that the T-shirt sends a message to the other team, and it also sends a message to us. Every time we put on that shirt, we think about what it means to be part of the Lake Valley family. I have always thought that Lake Valley represented team unity, support, dedication, commitment, and hard work. I assumed our T-shirt represented the same things.

I have been thinking about our team shirt for a while now, and I have found that it puzzles me because it doesn't represent what Lake Valley is all about. Sure, I agree with the meaning of "Reaching for Excellence One Stroke at a Time," but my disagreement is with the image on the front of the shirt. By using a single individual swimmer we fail to represent the importance of the team. It would appear to others the Lake Valley Swim Team glorifies "individuals" rather than the "family" of 250 swimmers that we know we have here. Think about it a minute. When has one person been responsible for Lake Valley's success? Never. Our success is the combination of the effort and performance of every person on the team. Whether 4 or 18 years old. Everybody contributes to the overall outcome of our success. We work hard together during practices and we participate 100% in all our activities. We are not swimming for personal glory; we swim for the team.

Since I respect my coaches and teammates so much, I really had to think hard about why they would have created such a contradicting image for our T-shirt. The more I thought about it, the more I realized that our whole society is filled with contradictions just like the one on the Lake Valley Swim Team T-shirt. American Society has lots of slogans that indicate we are supposed to act like a team: "We must all hang together or surely we will all hang separately," "All for One and One for All," "The whole is greater than the sum of its parts." At the same time, however, we tend to praise, remember, and reward individuals rather than team efforts. This summer's Olympics proved that to me.

Since swimming is what got me thinking about all of this, I am going to stick with sports for my examples. Supposedly this year's Olympics was the year of the American Women's Teams. Well, it was. They all did really well and won lots of gold medals, from softball to soccer to gymnastics to basketball. And that made me really proud to watch. Since I am such a believer in teamwork, I was so happy to see all these women's teams doing so well.

After the medals were won, however, I couldn't help but notice that even though the Sportscasters kept saying nice things about the team, there were clearly individuals that they *really* liked better than the team effort. Those individuals got the microphone, the media spotlight, the special interest stories, and the Wheaties boxes. What do you remember from the gymnastics team? Kerri Strug and her ankle injury. The softball team? Dr. Dot Richardson who took a year off from her hospital work to play softball. The basketball team? Lisa Leslie and Rebecca Lobo. All individuals who contributed to the team but were somehow held above it for special attention.

Contradicting the team effort slogans, then, are the competing stories about rugged individuals, pulling yourself up by your bootstraps, and making a name for yourself. Even in sports, we all know more about Michael Jordan (and his salary) than we do about the Bulls. We know a lot more about Mark Spitz (and how many gold medals he won) than the rest of his Olympic teammates or even his college teammates. Same story with Janet Evans and Summer Sanders. And Ireland's Michelle Smith pretty much won everything all by herself with no team to back her up. It seems like the American slogan might be "Reaching for Gold Medals One Individual at a Time." In other words, the focus is on the "one" rather than the "reaching."

In conclusion, I can understand why our Lake Valley T-shirt was a contradiction between the team and the individual. Our society seems to be filled with the same contradiction. Even though the team handbook stresses team unity, unfortunately the T-shirt undermines that message. The same holds true in American society. Even though we are encouraged in some ways to "hang together," the bigger rewards go to those who set themselves apart. Unfortunately, pictures speak louder than words, whether the picture is on a television set or on a T-shirt.

Brandi was really impressed with Jennie's paper, and she told her about the things she liked in the Reader Response Guide. She also suggested some areas for improvement. Likewise, Jennie's instructor recognized Jennie's good work, and she offered her own advice for revision.

Reader Responses from Brandi and the Instructor

Overall:

Brandi—Jennie, I really like this paper. I especially like the way you work slogans in with your cultural analysis.

Instructor—Jennie, this is terrific work. You have done a marvelous job of finding an important insight into your culture; that's not easy to do. Excellent draft.

Focus:

Brandi—Your focus is clear in all parts of the paper: that our society says it values teams, but really it's the individual that gets all the glory.

Instructor—I agree with Brandi that your focus is clear and consistent: that Americans give lip service to valuing teamwork while rewarding individual efforts. Great focus!

Development for Readers:

Brandi—For the most part, I thought you were writing to the class, but other times I thought you might be talking to your team-mates. (I've marked those places on your paper.) You supported your focus with a lot of good examples and not just from the T-shirt but from sports figures that everyone in the class knows.

Instructor—Your supporting information is terrific. You use plenty of specific examples, mixing examples known to the class as well as objects that aren't as familiar. I also agree with Brandi about your reader position; it does seem to shift once in a while. Two points of development could use some revision. First, don't forget that the Wheaties box did show the entire women's gymnastics team. Second, you might want to do more to tie the opening story in with the rest of the paper. Maybe refer to it once in a while at appropriate points in the paper?

Organization and Coherence:

Brandi—I followed your paper fine. Everything except the story fits your focus.

Instructor—You might want to try re-arranging some paragraphs as I've noted on your paper. The organization is good, but you have some other possibilities that might help everything link together better. You might also consider adding transitions from one section to another that are more obvious.

Language Choices:

Brandi—Fine.

Instructor—Great for the most part; see a few places on your paper.

Conventions:

Brandi—I've circled some places that I thought you might have some mistakes.

Instructor—Good work here.

Main Emphasis for Revision:

Brandi—Make sure you stay with your reader position throughout the entire essay.

Instructor—Work on tying the whole piece together. You are so close!

Having gotten feedback from her writing partner and her instructor, Jennie wrote the following self-assessment and revision plan.

Jennie's Self-Assessment

OVERALL RESPONSE: Overall, I'm pretty happy with what I've done. I think I got the main point across pretty well, and I like how I learned something new while writing.

FOCUS: "The Lake Valley Swim Team T-shirt does not represent what the team really is, and this is because we get mixed messages from the American Culture." The story is just an intro, but all of the other paragraphs support that focus. I want to change the story so it leads to the focus a bit better, and I'll refer to it again later in the paper.

DEVELOPMENT FOR READERS: I'm afraid my reader position does flip around, especially in the paragraph where I describe the team. I'll work on that by taking out references that seem to be directed to my teammates. I think I've provided a sufficient amount of material and examples. I don't think I ever took a strong position on the package, though.

ORGANIZATION AND COHERENCE: I'll test my organization by making sure every paragraph has something to do with the focus, and I'll make sure I put in transitions between major ideas.

LANGUAGE CHOICES: Sometimes I'm not really academic enough—but I don't want to be stuffy.

CONVENTIONS: My instructor said she liked the way I used fragments, so I want to keep some of them there. Some of the other sentences, though, are a little too complicated. I'll rewrite the ones that she marked.

MAIN EMPHASIS FOR REVISION: I want to re-read my paper out loud so that I notice the places I don't have good transitions. I will correct the part about the Wheaties box, and I'll do more to involve my opening story at the end.

Having formulated a self-analysis and revision plan, Jennie revised her paper below.

Jennie's Revision

Wheaties Does It Right:
The Image of Champions

My father saved an old Wheaties box from a long time ago. It is mostly orange, and it has a picture of Mark Spitz on it after he won all his gold medals in the Olympics. Underneath, the caption reads "The Breakfast of Champions." Growing up, I kept that picture of Mark Spitz in the back of my head I as went to swimming practice every day. Stories like this would run through my mind:

> As I pull off my team T-shirt, the tension mounts. There are some big girls here, and we are all here for one reason only. As I stretch out, I am pulled out of my concentration when the starter says, "Next heat, varsity girls 500 Free up to the block." I slowly step forward as I place my goggles down over my eyes. As I think about the message on our team T-shirt, "Reaching for Excellence One Stroke at a Time," I feel confident that I can do my best. I stretch my neck as a shake my arms and legs. I can feel the adrenaline flowing throughout my body from the snug fit of the goggles down to my toes on the scratchy starting block. I remember the feel of that 100% cotton shirt, and I visualize the stance of the swimmer in the picture. Arm up, perfect arc, precise form. I can do it.
>
> "Swimmers, take your mark . . . beep!" We're off.

As I hit the water a feeling of complete control overcomes me. As I reach my pace speed after the first 150, I breathe more often to keep an eye on my competitors. Feeling the power—the excellence—through every single stroke. The counter on deck sends me messages with the counter at the end of the pool: 11, 13, 15 . . . the race is almost over . . . speed it up and drive it home hard with everything you have left! Don't leave anything behind, don't hold anything back. Legs speed up as I feel more power with every perfect stroke. The last 100 yards is an all-out sprint. As I speed up, I feel my muscles tightening up, and there is an aching-burning sensation now. As I turn to my last 25 yards, I hold my breath and drive hard. The wall is approaching and every stroke reaches to touch it. I stretch once more and tag the wall. Exhausted and breathing hard, I pull the goggles off my head and I glance up at the time board. 5:25:63. Best time ever! One stroke at a time—I did it!

As it turns out, the story that I just told became a reality. I am a member of the Lake Valley Swim team, and the day I've described was one of the best of my swimming career. In all the years I've been swimming with Lake Valley, I have learned from the coaches and from our team handbook that one thing is important above everything else—*teamwork*. As a swimmer, the sense of teamwork made me more disciplined, more precise, and more competitive against other teams. As a coach, I also stress the values of hard work and team unity. Early every the season, we get a team T-shirt for the year. The T-shirts are supposed to give us all a unified look as well as psych out the other teams. You could say that the T-shirt sends a message to the other team, and it also sends a message to us. Like the Wheaties box, it gives us an image of ourselves that we should keep in mind as we compete. I had always thought that since Lake Valley represented team unity, support, dedication, commitment, and hard work, our team T-shirt represented the same things.

I have been thinking about our team shirt for a while now, and it puzzles me because it doesn't represent what Lake Valley is all about. Sure, I agree with the meaning of "Reaching for Excellence One Stroke at a Time," but my disagreement is with the picture of a single swimmer on the front of the shirt. By using a single individual swimmer we fail to represent the importance of the team. It would appear to others the Lake Valley Swim Team glorifies "individuals" rather than a "family" of 250 swimmers all working together. Think about it a minute. When has one person been responsible for an entire team's success? Never. Lake Valley's success is the combination of the effort and performance of every person on the team. Whether 4 or 18 years old. We are not swimming for personal glory; we swim for the team. That's not the message of our shirt, though.

Since I respect my coaches and teammates so much, I wanted to understand why they would have created such a contradicting image for our T-shirt. The more I thought about it, the more I realized that our whole society is filled with contradictions just like the one on the Lake Valley Swim Team T-shirt. Americans have lots of slogans that indicate we are supposed to act like a team: "We must all hang together or surely we will all hang separately," "All for One and One for All," "The whole is greater than the sum of its parts." At the same time, however, we tend to praise, remember, and reward individuals rather than team efforts.

For example, images of rugged individuals (like Dennis Rodman), pulling yourself up out of a slump (like Darryl Strawberry), and making a name for yourself (like Charles Barkley) compete with all the advice we get about being a team player. What's more famous: Michael Jordan (and his salary) or the Bulls? Mark Spitz (and his gold medals) or the rest of his Olympic team? He's the one on the Wheaties box, after all. Same story with Janet Evans and Summer Sanders in more recent Olympics. And Ireland's Michelle Smith pretty much won everything all by herself with no team to back her up. It seems like the American slogan might be "Reaching for Gold Medals One Individual at a Time." In other words, the focus is on the "one" rather than the "reaching."

This summer's Olympics proved that to me that American society says it values teamwork while it really rewards individuals. For example, newspapers proclaimed that this year's Olympics was the year of the American Women's Teams. And in many ways it was. They all did really well and won lots of gold medals, from softball to soccer to gymnastics to basketball. And that made me really proud to watch. Since I am such a believer in teamwork, I was so happy to see all these women's teams doing so well.

After the medals were awarded, however, I couldn't help but notice that even though the Sportscasters kept saying nice things about the teams, they obviously liked to tell stories about certain individuals more than stories about the team effort. Those individuals got the microphone, the media spotlight, the special interest stories, and the Wheaties boxes. What do you remember from the gymnastics team? Kerri Strug and her ankle injury. The softball team? Dr. Dot Richardson who took a year off from her hospital work to play softball. The basketball team? Lisa Leslie and Rebecca Lobo. All of them are individuals who contributed to the team but were somehow held above it for special attention.

Unfortunately, pictures speak louder than words, whether the picture is on a television set, on a T-shirt, or on a cereal box. Until this year, all of those pictures have glorified the individual at the expense of the team. This year, however, Wheaties decided to put the entire US Women's Gymnastics team on their box instead of just focusing on Kerri Strug. We need more of these kinds of images.

In conclusion, I can understand why our Lake Valley Swim Team T-shirt illustrated a contradiction between the team and the individual. After all, our society seems to be filled with the same contradiction. Even though the team handbook stresses team unity, unfortunately, our T-shirt undermined that message. The same holds true in American society. Even though we are encouraged in some ways to "hang together," the bigger rewards go too often go to those who set themselves apart. Pictures have the power to make us dream, like that antique Wheaties box did for me. I only wish that my dream had been one for the whole team rather than one of personal glory.

Questions for Analysis

1. Did Jennie's writing process engage her in a genuine inquiry? Did she learn something through the process of analyzing and questioning through writing that she did not already know? Why or why not?

2. What aspects of her writing process contributed most to her inquiry? Which parts seem to have taught her the most?

3. At several points, Jennie had to make crucial decisions about her inquiry. What were those points? How did those decisions impact the rest of her process? Did she reverse any of those decisions? If so, why?

4. Was Jennie thorough enough in her exploration using the contrasting strategy? Were there places where you would have said something different? What would you have added to her work?

5. Likewise, did Jennie consider the implications of the target group carefully enough? Are there issues of race, economic class, gender, sexual orientation, education level, age, and religion that might have resulted in more insight?

6. Jennie worked through the strategies in a particular order, following a particular timeline. What was that pacing? Do you find it was helpful? If so, explain how you might try a similar pace; if not, explain what you would do differently.

7. Did Jennie locate herself in a real writing context? Explain your response.

8. How helpful was the feedback Jennie received from her writing partner and her instructor throughout her writing process? Which responses were particularly useful? Which were misleading or unhelpful? Why?

9. How successful was Jennie's paper in helping her reach new understanding about her own values, as well as the values within her social contexts? Explain your response.

10. What do you think of Jennie's final version, having worked with her through every step of her inquiry. Do you find her writing interesting, or persuasive, or thought-provoking? What adjectives would you like others to use in describing *your* writing?

WRITING FOR INQUIRY AND ACTION

THE WRITING ASSIGNMENT

Select an aspect of your free time and inquire into it through writing using the guidelines and strategies below. Pick a free time activity that raises some questions in your own mind; this assignment might allow you to better understand the basis of your discomfort. Through your inquiry, you will examine the values promoted by your free time activity, and you will articulate your values in relation to the communities around you.

YOUR WRITING PROCESS

The goal here is to help you make active and conscious choices about how you "spend" your free time and at what cost. This chapter will show you some strategies for inquiring into your free time and for writing within the context of your free time activities. You will learn some new strategies, like the Story-Telling Strategy and the Contrasting Strategy, in addition to the strategies you have used already. Instead of following one student through a writing process, this chapter will illustrate the strategies using several writers.

Starting

In the first chapter in this book, you started your writing by creating a good question to guide your inquiry. In this chapter, you will select your subject through a process of **story-telling**, considering several possibilities at once, and you won't actually pose a question until later in the process.

As you work through the strategies that follow, notice which ones you find most enjoyable or useful—you may want to use them again in other contexts. Notice, too, which strategies you've already learned that you would like to use here and supplement your work with anything that you know works. Keep track of which strategies really work for you and in what situations; after all, knowing *when* to use *which* strategies and *in what way* is an important part of becoming an actively inquiring writer.

Why Tell Stories?

Since you have probably already tried starting with the questioning strategy several times, it is now time to try something different. Just as probing for dissonance by following prompts can lead you to good questions, so can telling stories about what you perceive. Stories that we make up often unearth insights, feelings, or odd connections that we might not notice otherwise. For instance, I might be bothered by the shape of the dog bone imprinted on the top of the Frisbee I use every afternoon, but I wouldn't be able to answer questions about *why*. If I were to compose a little story about that Frisbee in which the bone imprint played a prominent role, I might get at my discomfort indirectly. In addition to fostering insight, story-telling also allows your creativity free reign; play with your style, your tone, and your attitude. Perhaps best of all, you can make it as weird as you like, and it won't detract from your final grade. Most importantly, have some fun with your stories—it will only make your writing better.

STORY-TELLING STRATEGY
List Activities / Notice Packages / Compose Stories / Workshop

---

LISTING ACTIVITIES

To begin thinking and writing about your free time, make a list of those activities and responsibilities that occupy you when you aren't at school or work. If you can't come up with more than five, feel free to be as silly or as un-academic as you like; after all, since this paper might be *about* fun, there's no harm in trying to make it fun. What would you *really* like to do if you only had more time? What do you most look forward to doing either every week, every month, or even just once a year? What are your wildest dreams for spending time?

It might help to think systematically through different periods of your life. What did you love to do when you were 5 years old? 10 years old? 15 years old? Now? Likewise, consider each season of the year: what do you look forward to doing in winter, spring, summer, and fall? How about different days of the week? You might have a biking club every Wednesday, band rehearsals on Mondays and Thursdays, and Big Brother/Big Sister outings on Saturdays. What do you like to do at different times of the day? Are mornings for exercising, evenings for eating pizza and watching rented movies? Think through your life systematically until you have a full list of hobbies, interests, and activities.

NOTICING PACKAGES

Once you have at least five alternative free time activities (more is better, though), try to list at least five different ways each of those activities is packaged. In other words, how are your activities made into something that can be marketed, sold, and bought? What can you buy related to this activity? And what do you *have* to purchase in order to participate? Likewise, how is the activity represented in other forms of popular culture? Does it show up in TV commercials or magazine ads for other products? If so, which ones?

This strategy works best if you cast a wide net when listing the types of packages that you might consider for your analysis. The broader you think, the more fruitful your inquiry will be. For example, if one of your activities is listening to Mary-Chapin Carpenter's music, your list of packages might include:

- her CDs
- T-shirts sold at her concerts
- music videos showing on MTV and VH-1
- a TV special she produced about women in country music
- fan magazine and band newsletters
- official or unofficial Websites on the Internet
- the commercial she did promoting baseball, in which she sings "Take Me Out to the Ballgame"
- ads for her next concert tour in *Rolling Stone* magazine

Try to think of anything you can; you can always eliminate options later.

For the five (or more) activities you listed above, take the two that you find have the most promising and interesting packages. If you can only list a couple of packages for a particular activity, that one will probably not be a good choice for this assignment.

COMPOSING STORIES

After noticing the kinds of packages related to several of your activities, you can look at the packages themselves. What do the physical packages look like? What strikes you about the boxes, or the CD covers, or the colors on the T-shirts? The packages you should select for your inquiry should be portable in some way since you will need to examine it closely—repeatedly. In other words, make sure you have something you can actually carry into class. If you are choosing a song, make sure you have it on tape or CD; if you have a television commercial, make sure you have a copy of it on video.

Select the two packages you find most intriguing or interesting. Write the stories you think the packages are telling. For example, if we were to turn the Mary-Chapin Carpenter CD cover into a movie, what would happen? What would the set look like? What would people do there? What might they say? Let's say the cover shows her sitting in a dark corner playing her guitar, with a single ray of sunlight at her feet. Why is she there? What happened right before this picture was taken? What will happen next? What song is she singing (or writing) right now? Does anyone hear it?

Feel free to make your story as weird or imaginative as you like. Definitely don't worry about "reading too much into nothing," since sometimes the most extreme interpretations open wonderful lines of inquiry. Have some fun with this part.

Example: James' Story about Travel

Activities I Enjoy

- Spending time with Rachel, my fiancée
- Spending time outdoors (especially after all those months in a submarine!)
- Traveling around the country and the world
- Playing pick-up basketball
- Watching re-runs of old sitcoms on Nick at Nite

I will choose traveling and how it's packaged

- Travel magazines like *Honeymoon*
- Airline commercials on television
- Cruise line brochures from travel agencies
- Luggage advertisements
- The World Wide Web site for *Traveler*
- Ad for the North Carolina State Tourism Board in *Outside*
- Promotional videos for specific places (like Disney World)

A Story (about a Cruise Liner brochure)

Do you long for the nostalgia of the past? You have just entered into the twilight zone and have been flashed back from the colorful nineties to the classic days of black and white.

You can now roam the beaches and frolic in the waves of those in "From Here to Eternity." You lose track of time as your ship slips through the gentle waves toward the setting sun. You are closer to your lover than ever before. You notice that every time you take a dip in the ocean you feel different. It is as if you are more alive. All of your senses are intensified. Love has never been as good as it is now. You wonder if this saltwater is an aphrodisiac.

And finally, as you drift off to sleep in each other's arms, you think that it really is different out here. You hope this feeling will last forever.

WORKSHOP

Since you have been working with several possibilities for your inquiry up to this point, your group can help you select which one will probably work most fruitfully.

1. Circulate the work you've done so far, asking your group to help you fill in more packages, more details in your stories, and more contexts for writing.

2. Decide as a group which package, and which story, seem like the best bet to help fulfill the assignment described earlier in this chapter.

Exploring

CONTRASTING STRATEGY
List Key Terms / Generate Contrasting Terms / Compose Contrasting Story / List Puzzlements / Analyze Target Group / Workshop

Why Consider Contrasts?

In this chapter you will use a **contrasting strategy** to try to figure out what it *not* there in your package. In other words, it is up to you to figure out what might **contrast** with your package. What are the possible *opposites* of what is pictured on your package? As it turns out, sometimes when writers try to figure out what is *not* represented somewhere, they learn more about what *is* included. Think of this, then, as another inquiry strategy to add to your growing collection.

Some activities for considering contrasts are described here: list key terms, generate contrasting terms, compose a contrasting story, list puzzlements, and analyze the target group.

LISTING KEY TERMS

You might want to start by writing down a quick description of the package you have chosen to work with (or, if you are still choosing between two equally promising alternatives, do this for both). If you like, refer back to the story you wrote earlier. The point of this process is to generate as many **key terms** as you can for your package. In other words, what words or phrases are really important in your description? Which details are so integral to the design of your package that you can't describe it without mentioning them? If the skis you are looking at come in a really large box, then *really large box* is a key term. And if the colors on it are day-glow green and orange, then *day-glow green* and *day-glow orange* are key terms.

In order for this part of the strategy to work, you will need to list between 15–20 key terms for your package. Make sure you look really closely at the design elements on that package; after all, somebody chose them for a certain effect, and your job is to figure out each element. Pay close attention to the name of the product, any pictures on the package, and any descriptions of the product found on the package. Key terms can be words, images, colors, sizes, shapes, textures, or even scents.

If you get stuck, or if you aren't able to list very many key terms, try answering the questions listed below. If that still doesn't work, you might consider getting a different package—one where you can clearly identify more terms to list right away.

- What activity or product is being sold?
- What else does the package seem to be promoting in addition to that activity or product? What elements in the package make you think something else is being sold?
- What are the important words in the text? And what are the important pictures and images in the text?
- How would you describe the main characters, if any are shown. Young? Old? Cartoonish? Super-models? Students? Executives? Animals?
- What actions are suggested by this package (look at your story again to see what you thought when you first looked at it)? And what reactions might follow from those actions?
- What kind of world does this package seem like it belongs in? High-tech? Organic? Urban? Suburban? Rural? Fantasy? Over-populated? Idyllic? What elements lead you to envision that kind of world?
- What kind of economic bracket does this created world assume? Do the people (or creatures) in it have a lot of money? A lot of free time? Or is it a frugal world, in which people are just getting by?
- What details are included in the background?

GENERATING CONTRASTING TERMS

Now that you have scrutinized what your package contains, it is time to consider what is *not* included—perhaps because alternative images tell too different a story and are purposefully excluded.

To find out what is *not* there, you can write **contrasting terms** next to each **key term**. In other words, what is the opposite of each key term? What would provide the greatest contrast? For example, if you have written *really large box* as a key term, then a contrast might be *tiny little bag*. Next to *day-glow orange* you might write *beige* or *brown* or *faded yellow*. Obviously, there's no right answer here, and most key terms will have a wide range of contrasting terms. Write down any you think of; don't limit yourself to just one.

As you generate your contrasting terms, you may find that you begin to see additional key terms. That's great—just add them to the list and find some of their contrasts. It is very possible that thinking about what is *not* pictured can help you see more of what *is* represented.

COMPOSING CONTRASTING STORY

Just as you wrote a story based on your first examination of your package, you can now write a **contrasting story** based on the terms in your **contrasting terms** list. What kinds of stories do those terms evoke? Write at least one such story, using as many of the contrasting terms as you can.

After you've written your contrasting story, compare it with the first story you wrote. Does the contrasting story offer any insight into the world the package is creating? What can you learn about the values the package is promoting by comparing the two versions? Is there anything grossly inadequate, unfair, or too utopian in the original version? If it is too good to be true, jot down some of the reasons you think so.

LISTING PUZZLEMENTS

Sometimes the process of exploring through telling stories or generating contrasts can point out places in the original package that might cause some discomfort, puzzlement, or dissonance for you. Any puzzlements or dissonances that you list now might make good questions to shape the paper you will write. Any of the conclusions you reached after comparing your two versions of the story are good candidates.

For example, notice if there are any images presented in the package that don't match your experience with the activity at all. Remember that in the case reading, this is the point at which Jennie articulated her dissonance with the swim team T-shirt, since it pictured an individual even though the swimmers had been told to value the team. You might also find puzzlements by looking through your list of key or contrasting terms to find terms that cancel each other out or contradict one another. Of course, as you read through the contrasting story, you might see that your package is making some value judgments with which you disagree. If so, include those disagreements in your list of puzzlements. You will come back to this list when it is time to craft a guiding question for your polished draft.

ANALYZING TARGET GROUP

Since your project is to consider the packaging of your free time, you will also need to explore the consumer profile that your product's manufacturers and advertisers seem to be appealing to. **Target Group** (or "target audience") is a term used in marketing to define the type of person that might be a good customer. Many companies run elaborate analyses to figure out what kind of person would be most interested in their product or service—and then they create packaging to appeal to that kind of person. It follows, then, that if you can figure out a product's target group, you can gain insight into the values promoted by that package. Then, too, you can begin to see *why* certain values are present and why others are not. Finally, you can decide whether or not you want to belong in that target group. Do you already? Do you support all of the values your membership in the target group indicates you would hold? As a potential member of the target group, you can make choices about your relationship to the values being promoted by the packaging you have been analyzing.

Analyzing Cues on the Package. Your first step might be to look at the package as a whole (rather than taking it apart one **key term** at a time). When you look at the package, you are looking at a world that the text and images have created. What are the values supported in that world? What would members of that world consider "good" or "ideal" or "acceptable"? Likewise, what would they consider "bad" or "deviant" or "unacceptable"? Do you disagree with any of these stances? If you can't answer these questions yet, feel free to move on to the next set of questions.

Narrowing the Range of Possibility. Another way to inquire into the target group is to break the package down into the **cultural categories** it seems to represent, as well as those it excludes. Since there are an infinite amount of target group profiles, the grid below might help you narrow the field from the immense array of possibilities. Fill it in to the best of your ability, keeping in mind that not all the categories will fit your package (most will however, so look closely!). If the grid seems difficult to figure out, take a look at Jennie's example at the beginning of the chapter.

Cultural Category	Range of Possibility	Target Group	Who's Excluded
Age:			
Race:			
Gender:			
Social Class:			
Sexual Orientation:			
Education Level:			
Religious Affiliation:			

Putting Yourself in the Package. What, then, is the precise profile of the target group using the categories listed above? Do you fit that description? If so, how? If not, where are you excluded? In other words, in what ways do you *not* conform to the expectations of that group? What kind of person does the package expect you to be? Is that the kind of person you *want* to be?

What do you think are the primary values of the target group? Do you share them? Are there issues on which you might disagree with members of the target group?

Example: Jerry's Analysis of a Garth Brooks CD Cover

List Key Terms and Generate Contrasting Terms

Key Terms in the Package	Contrasting Terms
Garth Brooks	Snoop Doggy Dogg Alison Krauss Michael Jackson Lawrence Welk
Red, White, and Blue	black and gray green and yellow
American	Japanese German Russian
Male	female "Pat" (can't tell, unisex)
White	ethnic
Country Music	Heavy metal Classical Grunge
"The" hits	there's more than one option "some" hits
the "Hits"	garbage flops the "B-sides"
CD	8-track tape vinyl
cowboy	businessmen waitress Indian
hard working	lazy
black background	white background multi-colored
his face	other parts of his body impersonal
stars and stripes	rising sun hammer and sickle swastika
cowboy hat	hard hat fedora baby bonnet
famous	no-name notorious, infamous
sincere	lying
"limited time only"	anyone can get it, anytime easy access

Compose Contrasting Story

The colors are so bright in here—it makes my head hurt. I see this mass of people: all shapes, sizes, races, religions, colors, ages, and so on. I'm not sure what I'm doing here. There is loud music playing, and it's not very pleasant. Discordant sounds fill the air. It's some weird cross between Lawrence Welk and Snoop Doggy Dogg (how did they get together anyway?). It just sounds like garbage to me, but all these people around me seem to like it.

I move to get a closer look at the stage, and it is just as strange. The lead singer is dressed like a 1950s waitress, kind of like in the B-52s. Her backup band is all dressed in business suits from Wall Street; it's kind of a reversal of Robert Palmer's Babe Band. They sure sound terrible. How often do they practice?

All of a sudden, the music stops and the waitress welcomes everyone to the political rally. A flag is lowered from the ceiling. It is bright red and has a swastika on it. How on earth did I get here? And how do I get out? As I run for the door, I hear the waitress/singer saying: "Hey, come one, come all. We are open to everybody! Tell your friends!"

List Puzzlements

- My contrasting story is very confusing to me for several reasons. First, it seems like Garth Brooks is representing what is American and good, but the final line of the story is that the contrasting terms are the ones inviting everyone to participate. Is that a contradiction? I thought America was the great participatory nation.

- Second, the contrasting story includes all races and ages and religions. Again, this seems like a contradiction since the USA is the great melting pot. Is Garth Brooks excluding people who aren't like him?

- I feel like country music should appeal to everyone. I think it is the best kind of music we can listen to today. This contrasting story seems to indicate that it might not be so universal after all.

Analyze Target Group

Cultural Category	*Range of Possibility*	*Target Group*	*Who's Excluded in the Package*
Age:	kids, teens, adults, middle-aged, elderly	late teens–mid 30s	kids, elderly
Race:	black, white, brown, yellow, etc.	white	all others
Gender:	male, female, can't tell ("Pat")	men	women, Pats
Social Class:	poor, working class, middle class, upper middle class, lower upper class, really rich	working class to middle class, maybe upper middle	really rich (even though he's rich now), and really poor

Cultural Category	Range of Possibility	Target Group	Who's Excluded in the Package
Sexual Orientation:	heterosexual, gay, bi	heterosexual	all others
Education Level:	junior high, high school diploma, college, grad school, seminary, med school, law school	all levels	nobody (except maybe second grade drop-outs)
Religious Affiliation:	Jewish, Christian, Buddhist, Muslim, ??	Christian	all others

WORKSHOP

Sometimes others can see things a person working alone might miss. Share your analysis so far with your group members and ask to help you where you think you could benefit the most from their perspective. As a group, select two of the following options:

1. Ask your group members to add more key terms and contrasting terms, so you have a fuller analysis of the package.

2. Focus on the target group analysis, adding more refinement to the work you have done on your own. Help each other create the most precise target group profile you can.

3. Discuss and clarify the values that emerge from your analysis so far (including the key terms, contrasts, stories, and target group analysis). As a group, craft a "value statement" that articulates the primary values of each package. In other words, write out a description of the network of values captured in your package.

Questioning
Why ask questions *now?*

In the other inquiries you have written so far, your questions have come earlier in your writing process. You may have noticed that you haven't formulated a question about this paper just yet. Those of you who have revised your questions substantially after exploring or focusing know that sometimes it isn't possible to ask questions without knowing more about your subjects. Other times, you need more information before you even know what kinds of questions can be answerable. Since you have explored the implications of your packages in several different ways, you are now ready to formulate informed questions. Chances are, you've been jotting down questions as you have been working through the various strategies. Now is a good time to go back and look at that work again.

POSING QUESTIONS

Depending on the analysis you have done, there are a number of different kinds of questions you can ask that will shape your responses in writing. Your analysis now works on several different levels, all leading to different kinds of questions:

- What *images* and *values* are being sold along with the product?
- What do you choose to buy, and what do you choose to reject?
- In what ways can you reject or modify the images and values you are buying?

The questions you choose to guide your paper can reflect any—or all—of these directions. You should now be able to pose questions that capture the kinds of responses you seek, just as you have with the other contexts in this book. As you know, the way you pose your question will lead to different kinds of responses.

Compose at least three different questions that combine the elements above: the product, the images and values it promotes, and your response to them. As in other areas of inquiry, your question might lead you to a **new understanding**, the **cultural sources of a gap between your analysis and your experience**, a **course of action**, or a **solution to a problem**. See Questioning Strategy, Part II.

Example: Diane's Questions about the "Buns of Steel" Exercise Video

Pose questions

- Why do I and so many other women so badly wish to obtain the image of the "body of perfection" that is presented in the packaging of aerobic exercise?
- What can I do to help other females realize that doing aerobics only for the purpose of looking like Barbie shouldn't be the only motivation for leading an active lifestyle?
- How might I help the Co-Rec sell the value of "health" and not a body image that is "perfect"?

My choice:

How might I help the Co-Rec sell the value of "health" and not a body image that is "perfect"?

Positioning Writers and Readers

LOCATING IN A CONTEXT

Now that you have a good guiding question, you should be able to think about good writing contexts. You may have thought of some as you have worked through the strategies so far. In addition to those ideas you may have already had, complete the Locating in a Context Strategy in Part II.

SETTING WRITER & READER POSITIONS

A range of writer and reader positions are available to you within the context you choose. What are the possibilities for your writer and reader positions? After identifying a variety of options, select the most appropriate positions for your inquiry.

Review the **Writer/Reader Positioning Strategy** in Part II, and work through that strategy as you find it helpful.

Example: Diane's Writer and Reader Positions

Locate in a context

- I could write to the people at the Co-Rec suggesting a better plan of action
- I could make a poster for the Co-Rec and hang it between the women's locker room and the aerobics room
- I could write in to the student newspaper about the right reasons for exercising
- I could make a brochure for the Co-Rec that would be distributed at the main desk

My context choice: The context I choose is the Co-Rec because that is where the most people go who are concerned about their body images. Most of the people I want to reach go there, and the highest concentration of them are involved in the aerobics classes.

Positioning myself at the Co-Rec

Positions I have written from at the Co-Rec: I haven't really done much writing at the Co-Rec, since I just go there to exercise. I had to fill out some forms to get a locker, and I had to read through the brochures to figure out which classes I wanted to attend. Really, I do more reading there than writing. I look through the "nutrition notes" and the posters before class, and I sometimes take the newsletters home and read them afterwards.

Positions I have been excluded from: I'm not the aerobics instructor, and I am not an employee of the Co-Rec. I am much more of a casual exerciser who cares than a professional or expert. I think I am a typical person there—I'm not one of the crazies who feels like she has to go every day.

Positions I have left behind: In high school, I was more of the expert fitness type. I was usually the leader; here I am a follower. I am no longer the person that others have to listen to—now I have to work harder to get somebody to pay attention.

Position I will take as a writer: I will put myself in the shoes of the other students attending aerobics classes. I will write to them as an equal, although, I have a strong point of view that I want to get across. My position, then, is fellow exerciser who cares about overall health.

Reader positions

Reader positions available in the context of the Co-Rec: fellow exercisers who feel the same way I do about health; fellow exercisers who do it for the wrong reasons (just to look good); sheep who follow the herd without question; exercise experts who are missing the big picture.

My choice of reader position: I choose fellow exercisers who do it just to look good.

The values and background I associate with my reader position of exercisers who do it for the wrong reasons: This may sound mean, but I assume they are kind of shallow. I don't think they pay very much attention to things if they still think that the only benefit of exercise is that you can look better to the opposite sex! They are motivated (especially the ones who go every day!), and they probably diet all the time. It is safe to assume that they see "images of perfection" everywhere (just like I do), but that they don't see many other positive images. I hope to make them aware that there are other more important reasons to do aerobic exercise besides trying to look like Barbie. I hope that they come to realize that being active and healthy should be motivated by the other positive aspects they are gaining from exercise—better health, longer life, better attitude, more energy, better discipline, more confidence.

Selecting Genres

Given the writer and reader positions you have set, certain genres may be the most probable means to communicate effectively with the readers you have chosen. The selection of the appropriate genre, then, is crucial. Remember that some genres allow for longer texts and fuller analyses, while others require that you present your work in short takes with plenty of graphics. Given the analysis you have already done, what is the best way to reach your readers? At this point, you might find it helpful to refer back to the **Genre Strategy** in Part II.

Example: Diane's Genre Selection

List several possible genres

- pamphlets, posters, flyers, newsletters, and aerobics schedules.
- less frequently, there are once-a-week articles in the student paper.

Briefly analyze alternative genres

- Most of the texts are in the form of flyers and posters. They are short and to the point. The message is expressed through key phrases or sentences with drawn or photographed images.
- The flyers and brochures have to be picked up at the front desk, and not a lot of people bother to get them. The posters, however, hang right outside the aerobics area, so people look at them while they are waiting for the earlier class to get out.
- Newspaper editorials would reach more people, but they aren't as focused in on my specific readers. I don't need for everybody to read it, just those who exercise for the wrong reasons.

My genre choice:

- I want to design a poster that will catch the attention of the people in my exercise community. I also feel this would be the best way to reach my readers. I'm reluctant to write a lengthy letter because I seriously doubt my readers would pay any attention. The poster could be displayed on the bulletin board in the central stairway of the Co-Rec.

> *Features of a poster:* The best posters in a gym are colorful, large, and have some kind of attention-getting graphic. The words are short and to the point, usually lists rather than full sentences. And there is a catchy phrase somewhere to reinforce or explain the main picture.

Focusing

COMPOSING A FOCUS

Having explored your package through several methods, set your writer and reader positions, and selected the best genre, now is a good time to compose your focus statement. In addition to the **Focusing Strategy** in Part II, you might also want to try responding to the following prompts.

Considering Your Power as a Writer and Citizen. One possible way to arrive at your focus is to figure out what kinds of responses to your analysis you can actually control: as a writer, as a consumer, as a citizen. For starters, respond to the following questions:

- In what ways can you continue to support the promotion of certain images?
- In what ways can you react against those images you think are wrong or unfair?
  What strategies do you have at your disposal? Purchasing power? Informing friends? Writing to the company? Altering your own behavior? Influencing others' behavior? Volunteering for a certain cause? Giving donations to certain organizations?
- Which actions might interest your readers the most? Which might they not think of on their own, without your insights?

Selecting Values to Accept, to Reject, and to Change. If there are parts of the package you like, but others that are too contradictory for you to accept, isolate those aspects you support from those you reject. Craft your focus statement around your simultaneous acceptance and rejection of the values in the package. Is there anything you can do to alter those images or values?

Example: Diane's Focus

> *Compose a focus*
>
> *My main question:* What can I do to help other females realize that doing aerobics only for the purpose of obtaining the image of the "body of perfection" shouldn't be the only motivation to lead an active lifestyle?
> In what ways can I continue to promote certain images and values? I feel that leading an active and healthy lifestyle is very important. I can emphasize that image of health in my poster.
>
> *In what ways can I react against those images I think are wrong or unfair?* I can concentrate on the positive areas and express how the wrong ideal can lead women to exercise for the wrong reasons.

> *What strategies do I have at my disposal?* After looking at my free time activity of aerobic exercise in a different way, I have begun to alter my own attitude and behavior. In effect, I hope to create a new awareness among my peers.
>
> *Which values do I choose to accept, and which to reject?* Accept: hard work, determination, dedication, commitment, the health benefits to leading an active lifestyle. Reject: doing aerobic exercise only for the purpose of trying to get a "perfect body"
>
> *Focus statement:* Doing aerobic exercise (subject) shouldn't be just to get a "body of perfection" but to lead an active and healthy lifestyle (point of significance).

Organizing

TESTING YOUR FOCUS WITH ORGANIZATION PLANS

Now that you have a focus statement and a clear course of action, you can begin to test your focus with several different organizational plans. Your choice might require you to employ certain arrangements; if you find the genre too constrictive, you might reconsider your genre choice. Refer to Part II for more advice on different organizational plans and remember that these strategies work best if you try several alternative plans before committing to one in your polished draft.

Example: Diane's Organization Plan

> *Test focus with organization plan*
>
> *Introduction:* The Wrong Reasons—I reject the values of doing aerobic exercise only to get a particular body shape that is probably impossible anyway. I reject that body image that is packaged with exercise.
>
> *The Consequences*—Since the "body of perfection" is only a packaging myth anyway, it can be discouraging for women who exercise a lot. Therefore, they need other reasons to keep them motivated.
>
> *Shifting to Another Perspective*—With a healthier motivation, the exercise means more, lasts longer, and feels better.
>
> *The Right Reasons*—Confidence, energy, health, future health, fun, good feeling.
>
> *Conclusion*—Do it for Yourself!!

WORKSHOP

At this stage in the writing process, it is often helpful to check with your group before proceeding. As a group, decide which of the following questions you will answer with one another:

1. Is your focus statement a strong one, which helps respond to your inquiry question and suggests your stance on the product and the values promoted by the packaging?

2. Which organizational plan works best for your writing context, your focus, and your genre? If any of those earlier decisions need to change, which should change? And how?

3. If your writing group is also your reader, ask them which parts of your plan might need more detail, more examples, or more explanation.

4. Ask your group to suggest other sources or related products that might support your inquiry so far. Are there television shows, or videos, or magazine articles that you might be able to use as further evidence? Are there other types of products that use similar images to those you are studying that might support your focus statement?

Drafting

WRITE SEVERAL DRAFTS

Look back through your starting and exploring strategies, your workshops, your focuses, and your organizational plans. You may see some features in the work you have already done that you would like to add; this sometimes happens as writers gain more insight into their subjects. If you see some contradictions or issues that you did not notice before, take the time to write a paragraph about it. Later, you can "cut and paste" it into your paper.

Since you have written several stories, consider using pieces of them, or descriptions of the images in your packaging, to provide a framework for your text. For example, you might want to begin your text with a snapshot of the "positive" story and end on a sour note with the "contrasting" story. Or you can take images from the package itself and suggest revisions to those images as part of your conclusion.

Drafting

If you have been working on a computer, now is a good time to learn any "cut-and-paste" features in your word processor. Since you have generated so much writing already—before you've even sat down to compose a formal paper—feel free to use that writing you have already done, revising appropriately for your reader, your genre, and your writer position.

Likewise, you might want to experiment with graphics in this paper. Are there parts of your package that you should illustrate (or copy) in order to strengthen your points? Are there images from the package that you want to visually represent in your paper? What pictures might your reader need? Where should they be placed for the best results?

Example: Scott's Critical Essay on Fitness Magazines for His Classmates

Polished Draft

Fitness Magazine Headlines: Contradicting?

Are you overweight or feeling out of shape? Has spring break fever hit you, but the thought of wearing a swim suit knocked you out? Then get fit fast! Lose your gut for good! Train 30 days for a peak physique! Even hair loss solutions! These contradicting headlines are what fitness magazines claim.

To a stranger of the fitness world, this will have your blood flowing with envy. Not only do you see the eye-catching headlines in bold letters, but a prima donna figure lies in awe beside them. His muscular features and washboard abs are oiled down underlying his dark tanned skin. This sight makes the headlines even more attractive.

Living in a fast paced society, everyone seeks quick results. You would think from these headlines that this is possible. Expectations rise only to fall lower than before after results aren't attained from following these headlines. You ask yourself, why? The headlines said it could be done. The man on the cover looked great. Were these headlines not applying to him? No, he did not follow any easy "get fit fast" program or "30 days to a peak physique" program! Although he gloatly exposes his shirtless, perfect, and desirable physique, this is what sells fitness to society.

To attain the physique that you desire takes time, patience, dedication, and what I call the total fitness package. The latter I will describe further in this issue. Time, get fit fast! This is one of the biggest oxymorons of the fitness world. I've spent years in fitness, which has proven to me that only time and dedication produces results. One cannot go into the gym and expect it to pay off immediately. You can't start out lifting maximum pounds at maximum repetitions and sets. For the beginner or expert who has taken time off from training, must ease their body into it. The body is not conditioned enough to handle all the stress at once. Working out consistently will give the muscle the endurance to accept the heavier weight and increased repetitions and sets. I'm not claiming that it takes years to get into shape, but it will take all of that time, if not more, to look like the prima donnas that are exposed to us. Although, I will claim from experience that results will be noticed right away in the aspect of feeling healthier and more energized.

Has fat overtaken your abdominal area? Then lose your gut for good! The magazine headline boasts this. The abdominal area is the first place men put on fat. There is no way to lose your gut for good without maintaining a regular workout schedule that consists of regular abdominal exercises. If you quit training, your gut will probably return in more abundance than before.

The total fitness package, which is overlooked if not unheard of, is required for maximum results. I classify the total fitness package as weightlifting, aerobic exercise, rest and recuperation, and dieting. You cannot only lift weights, only participate in aerobic exercise, or lose your gut without one main ingredient: proper dieting. Dieting plays as much of a role in fitness as does weightlifting and aerobics. Aerobic exercise is just as important as weightlifting and vice-versa. They all feed off each other with no one being more important than the other. Weightlifting alone will build muscle, but you will not look any better if a layer of fat exists on top of it. Aerobic exercise alone will shed off excess fat, but will not build great looking muscle tone. This is why being fit involves a combination of the two. You will not feel like doing either weightlifting or aerobic exercise without proper rest and recuperation. Rest will allow the muscle to recuperate and grow between workouts. Dieting now comes into play. From my experience, dieting is 60% of the package with the other mentioned items combining for the other 40%. I don't mean dieting in the aspect of limiting the intake of food, but rather the kind of food. Foods low in fat and high in protein and carbohydrates are needed. Protein is needed for muscle growth while carbohydrates fuel the body for energy. The expectations set in your mind will never be reached without proper dieting! This is why I say dieting is worth 60% of the package. I can not emphasize enough how important all of this is for maximum results. After all, if you're going to spend time in the gym, you may as well get the most from it.

Fitness resulting in hair loss solutions. Does this mean certain exercises will grow hair? Is a man of baldness any less healthy than a man with a full head of hair? No, fitness and exercise will not grow hair, and it is not known that health depends on how much hair one has on his head. Back to the man on the cover. He has a full head of hair and he works out. What this headline is actually doing is advertising special creams and surgical operations, at a price of thousands of dollars, that result in hair growth. I say to these magazines, "Stick to fitness and health issues as their name implies!"

You will achieve the physique desired by keeping the total fitness package in mind. If you are in the search of hair growth, I suggest you see a doctor. When you run across these headlines boasting of fitness in no time, hair loss solutions, and super looking models selling fitness, keep a sound mind and stay in the world of reality. Remember the old saying, "If it sounds or looks too good to be true, it probably is." Do not set your expectations too high that you can't reach them. The health and fitness magazines that claim these contradicting headlines are out for one thing: to sell magazines.

Responding

READER RESPONSE

Solicit specific kinds of responses from your instructor and your writing group. Let them know which parts of your text were the most difficult to write and which parts make you the most uncomfortable or uncertain. The more you can guide them, the more they can help you.

Refer to the **Reader Response Guide** in Part II for more guidance.

Example: Shari's Response to Scott's Critical Essay

OVERALL: Scott, your paper has a lot going on in it—I learned so much by reading it! You give plenty of examples, and you back up everything you say.

FOCUS: Your focus is that people need a good balance of exercise, diet, and weights in order to be really healthy. You also talk about the fitness magazine headlines, but that part doesn't seem to be as important as your suggestions to your readers. Actually, it seems like there are two focuses here, and I'm not sure which one is more important to you. Maybe you should pick one and emphasize it more.

DEVELOPMENT FOR READERS: I'm not sure who your readers are. I had thought that you were writing to the class, but there are several places you go right over my head. (I've marked them on your paper.) Sometimes, then, you go into too much detail about the health stuff, especially since you seem to talk less about the magazines as the essay goes on. I guess I'm not sure about your development since I'm not completely sure about your focus.

ORGANIZATION AND COHERENCE: This seems pretty well organized, especially when you get into the parts about what people should do. Your transitions between sections seem clear to me.

LANGUAGE CHOICES: Sometimes it seemed like you were making fun of the magazines. I like that part—do more of it.

CONVENTIONS: I was confused at the beginning because you have all these questions and sayings. I couldn't tell where they came from. Are they from the magazines, or did you make them up? If they came from the magazines, maybe you should make them look like headlines, or at least put them in quotation marks.

MAIN EMPHASIS FOR REVISION: The main thing is your focus. Pick one and go with it and make it clear all throughout the essay what your focus is.

Revising

Now that you have gotten feedback from your group and your instructor, you can formulate a **Revising Plan**. What will you change for the next version? How will you go about making those changes? For more help with Revising plans and with the revising process, see Part II.

Example: Scott's Revising Plan

OVERALL: I'm pretty happy with the contradictions and false claims I found, but I'm afraid that my main point isn't strong enough. Reading through it again, I seem to have some strange sentences that don't make sense to me anymore.

FOCUS: Shari is right—I do switch between two kinds of focuses. I thought that I had integrated the one about what people *should* do into my main focus about the false claims, but that seems to be more confusing than effective. I will do a better job of stating my focus up front and sticking with it throughout the essay.

DEVELOPMENT FOR READERS: Since my focus isn't quite clear, I have to go through and pick the sections of the essay that really support it and which ones just tell the class what else they should be doing. I can make this more clear through better transitions and by stating what I am doing more strongly. Then, if I haven't explained any of the contradictions, I need to do that.

ORGANIZATION AND COHERENCE: Because of the section on exercise, the essay seems disorganized. Once I take care of that part, the rest should be okay.

LANGUAGE CHOICES: Shari marked the places my wording sounds funny, and I'll rewrite those sentences.

CONVENTIONS: I have to fix the bit about the quotation marks around the magazine titles. Somehow, I have to indicate that the phrases are from titles of magazines, and that they are stupid.

MAIN EMPHASIS FOR REVISION: I will work on sharpening my focus, and I will make sure that every section of the essay supports it.

Example: Scott's Revised Critical Essay

Fitness Magazine Headlines:
Contradicting Common Sense?

"Get fit fast!" "Lose your gut for good!" "30 days for a peak physique!" "Hair Loss Solutions!" "How to Live to 100!!"

Don't these claims sound crazy? Too good to be true? Well, they are too good to be true. I am writing this to make sure that you aren't taken in by these false claims, no matter how enticing they might be. If you think about it, common sense tells you that these promises are impossible to keep. Not everybody thinks with common sense, however, sometimes our desires make us believe things we shouldn't. Imagine the following scene with me.

You are skimming through a magazine rack, and these headlines have your blood flowing with hope and excitement. Not only are the eye-catching headlines in large bold letters, but a perfectly formed man stands beside them waiting for your admiration. His muscular features and washboard abs are oiled down, emphasizing his dark tanned skin. His hair, styled with mousse, drapes lazily past one eye. Next to the promises of the headlines, his look seems attainable, even easy. You could do these things, and look just like him—quickly.

We live in a fast-paced society, which promotes quick results. If you believe the headlines on these fitness magazines, you might begin to think that quick results are possible. Unfortunately, many people have expectations that rise only to fall lower than before when the promise results don't come through. They may ask themselves, why isn't this working? The magazine said it could be done. The man on the cover looked great, and so did all the other guys inside the magazine. Don't the same rules apply to them?

Well, yes and no. The same rules apply to them that apply to each of us. The difference is that the rules are not what the headlines promise. These guys did *not* follow any easy "get fit fast!" program, or a "30 days for a peak physique!" plan. However, as the cover model exposes his perfect and desirable physique and gazes at the headlines, it certainly looks like he owes it all to these bogus programs. This is what society buys as "fitness."

What society should be buying instead, I argue, is what I call a "total fitness package." Rather than easy solutions for quick results, the total fitness package takes time, patience, dedication, and attention to a well-rounded program. These are more difficult, and they won't guarantee the exact body of the man on the cover, but the results are still worth it. Let me explain the total fitness package in more detail, contrasting it with the ridiculous promises the magazines make.

"Get fit fast!" This is one of the biggest oxymorons in the fitness world. Working out simply does not pay off immediately. I've spent years in fitness programs, which has proven to me that only consistency and dedication over time will produce results. It is not wise to start out with maximum weight at maximum repetitions and sets. The body is not conditioned enough to handle all that stress at once. Both beginners and experts who have taken time off from training must ease into it slowly, giving it time. Working out consistently will give the muscle the endurance it takes to accept the heavier weights and increased repetitions and sets. I'm not saying that it takes *years* to get into shape, but it won't happen as quickly as the headline indicates. And if you want to look as glorious as the cover model, it will certainly take more than "30 days." On the other hand, I can claim from my own experience that you will notice some results right away, like feeling healthier and more energized.

"Lose your gut for good!" Has fat taken over your abdominal area? The headline might lead you to think this is easily remedied. The abdominal area is the first place men put on fat. Put bluntly, there is *no* way to lose fat from the gut at all without maintaining a regular workout schedule that consists of regular abdominal exercise. And in order to lose it for good, you have to keep up these exercises your entire life; once training has stopped, fat often returns with even more abundance than before.

So far I have talked about the importance of time and consistency in the total fitness package. There is more to it than that. I also describe the total fitness package as a combination of weightlifting, aerobic exercise, rest and recuperation, and a proper diet. It is not recommended to only lift weights, only do aerobic exercise, only rest, or only cut down on your fat intake. For maximum results you must have all four components, consistently implemented over time. Many men don't realize that a proper diet plays just as important a role in fitness as weightlifting and aerobic exercise. In addition, many don't realize that aerobic exercise is just as important as weightlifting and vice versa. All the elements of the package feed off each other, with no one being more important than the others. After all, weightlifting alone will build muscle, but won't look better if there is a layer of fat covering it. And aerobic exercise may help you lose fat, but it won't build and tone your muscles. Finally, none of the elements work without proper rest between workouts, since muscles need time to recuperate and grow.

I need to reinforce the idea of a proper diet. From my experience, diet is 60% of the package, with the other elements combining for the other 40%. Fit bodies need foods low in fat, but high in protein and carbohydrates. Muscles need protein to grow, while the rest of the body needs the carbohydrates for energy. Even with a combination of weightlifting, aerobic exercise, rest and recuperation, practiced consistently and over time, you will not achieve your desired outcome without a proper diet; this is why I say diet is 60% of the package. After all, if you're going to spend time in the gym, you may as well get the most from it.

So let's look again at the man on the cover and the promising headlines. "Hair Loss Solutions!" And get this one—"How to Live to 100!!" Does this mean certain exercises will help you grow hair? Will working out make a person immortal? Of course not. Both claims are absurd. A bald man is no less healthy than one with hair. Since the man on the cover has a full head of hair, and he works out, it might seem like the two are related. In fact, the article behind the headline actually just advertises special creams and surgical operations—at the price of thousands of dollars—that supposedly result in hair growth. As for living to 100, it has been said that being fit will raise your *chances* of living longer, but it won't *promise* it. There are plenty of people out there who have lived to 100 without fitness being a part of their lives at all. (Some were even smokers.) I say to these magazines, stick to *Exercise & Health* and *Men's Health* issues as your names imply!

If you are in search of hair growth or longer life expectancy, I suggest you see a doctor. But if you want a healthier body and a nicer physique, go for the "total fitness package" I have described and stay away from the false promises of men's fitness magazines. When you see headlines boasting: "get fit fast!" "Lose your gut for good!" "30 days for a peak physique!" "Hair Loss Solutions!" "How to Live to 100!!," think of the old saying: "if it looks too good to be true, it probably is." Don't set your expectations so high they can't be reached. And remember that the health and fitness magazines making these contradictory claims are out for one thing—to sell more magazines!

CONCLUSION

By this point, you have read about writers who inquire into free time, and you have tried doing it yourself. You should now be in a better position to make clear and conscious choices about those values you support with your own free time and what changes you might want to bring about.

Jennie, as it turns out, did talk with the other members of her swim team family about the contradictory design of the T-shirt. The following year's shirt depicted a wave of arms synchronized with precise strokes, all swimming together. The team seems happy with the new shirt, and Jennie knows she was able to change a part of her life for the better. Her inquiry through writing did lead to social action within the context of her swim team.

4

AREA OF INQUIRY: ISSUES IN GROUPS

JANET ATWILL

WHY WRITE ABOUT ISSUES?

The title of this text promises to help you use writing not only to inquire into important aspects of your life, but also to act upon and change your world. Effectively acting upon your world usually involves group identities. Let's take an example. Suppose your student financial aid is affected by legislation in Congress, and you find it necessary to increase your hours in a part-time job to make up for the reduction in aid. The extra work begins to affect your grades, and you almost forget what it was like to participate in campus activities and spend time with friends. You can take action for change. You can write as a member of a campus political organization, seeking to organize a group of students to address your senators. In this case, you are writing from the position of a college student depending on financial aid, a person who is part of a very large group.

We are all parts of many different kinds of groups. We are born into some groups—familial, racial, and ethnic, for example. Some groups we join in a formal way, like clubs, sororities, fraternities, religious groups, and political organizations. Sometimes we are members of groups simply because of certain choices or activities. You may not have thought about enrolling in Midwestern University as joining a certain group, but by going to school, you became a member of that college community. You may also be a part of a smaller group within a large group, like returning students, part-time students, and international students. You may be surprised at the number of groups of which you are a member. Almost every role you play in your life can be related to a group affiliation.

EXAMPLES OF WRITING FOR INQUIRY AND ACTION

- As a former staff member and football announcer at his hometown radio station, Scott investigates the lack of broadcasting of football games.
- As a member of an ROTC Unit, Michael inquires about the apparent inequity in the policy of issuing ribbons.

- Vita studies an issue in two groups: Americans of East Indian descent, and Christians from India (AIC). Her Indian heritage was important to her; and she was an officer in the student branch of AIC. After marrying a white American, she heard members discuss the issue of marrying non-Indians and noticed that they didn't treat her quite the same.

- Laura, a graduate of a rural high school, found she had to work twice as hard in college as her new friends just to catch up with what they had been doing as juniors and seniors in high school. She made inquiries into her hometown's plans to consolidate high schools to make more resources, courses, and teachers available to students in this rural area.

READINGS FOR INQUIRY AND ACTION

"LETTER," *Birmingham News* by Ora Lee Gaines

Letter to Birmingham News *reprinted in C.A.R.E. newsletter (Coalition of Alabamians Reforming Education)*

Dear Editor,

God has blessed me to live over seven decades. During the years, I have witnessed children devalued and programmed to fail. We moved from no schools for black children to separate and unequal schools. Now the State Board of Education has adopted "new" graduation requirements that will cause separate and unequal classes for black, poor, and working class children of all races for another one hundred years. The new requirements mandate academic requirements but no similar advance requirements. Therefore, the children at the bottom level will be ill prepared professionally. Furthermore, the new recommendations have mandated a third Disability Act against disabled children which is humanely separate and unequal.

Last Thursday I sat in the Gordon Persons Building at the State Capitol and prayed that the black and white Board members would seize the opportunity to mandate a quality education for "all" children. I was filled with hope when Stephanie Bell, a white woman (who is said to be conservative) gave an incredible statement against the proposed system that would create three completely separate tracks. I was moved almost to tears when she spoke of the harm that tracking causes to children. She surprisingly understood the anguish and defeat of being placed in low levels and being told or treated like you're not as smart as the children at the top. She spoke eloquently but emphatically against the creation of dual classes in the base core curriculum. She amended Senator Hank Sanders' dynamic argument against having two ninth grade English, Math, and Social Studies classes. "These are not advanced subjects, but advanced classes of the same subjects," she argued. We support advanced courses, especially AP classes, but separating kids in grades 7, 8, 9 and beyond to take English, Math and Social Studies from the same book is suspect and terribly unfair. Even the Superintendent publicly admitted that blacks and poor whites would dominate the lower classes because of past race and class discrimination. He also acknowledged that these children are not likely to choose the high levels because of low expectations, low self-esteem, lack of self-fulfillment, and failure. Yet, the Superintendent nor the majority of the Board members were willing to take measures to get these children off the bottom who were there, not because they were inferior but because they and their parents have been subjected to an inferior public education generation after generation. At first I didn't understand. The Superintendent said the new requirements were raising the standards. Yet, these children would still be behind their more fortunate peers. In our legal system, people are compensated when they are injured through the fault of others. However, five adults voted to increase graduation standards without compensating victimized children with "catch up" resources and assistance. With the proper compensatory measures, most of these children could compete with their more fortunate peers in basic and core curriculum courses. Without additional help, many will not be able to meet the new requirements that are higher than the past, but far below what will be taught and expected of students who seek the advanced degree. When some fail, the failure will be used to justify and keep them at the bottom. The result is that the cycle of poverty and crime will continue.

I did not go to the State School Board meeting alone. I took forty children from McRae Learning Center, a school I direct in Selma, Alabama. A four year old read a first grade reader for the Board. Six year old students recited their twelve time tables. One student, Andrew Hill, told the Board how he was treated like he was dumb and, therefore, stopped trying to learn in public school. "I'm an A-B student at McRae," he proudly told the Board. At McRae, all children are expected to learn at high levels, and they do: the black ones, the brown ones, the white ones, and the poor ones. McRae has no dual system of education. If we can do it on a shoe string budget, why can't the public schools do it with million dollar budgets.

I was moved to tears by the children, and so were some of the Board members. David Byers, a white board member from Birmingham, Alabama, insightfully echoed the sentiments of Stephanie Bell, Senator Hank Sanders, Ronald Jackson, Dr. Carol Zippert, Rose Sanders and others who spoke against the dual system. I was also proud to see Rev. Abraham Woods, Rev. John Nettles of SCLC, a NAACP representative, and Malika Sanders of 21st Century Youth Leadership Movement in the audience. These people and organizations are members of C.A.R.E. (Coalition of Alabamians Reforming Education), which has lead the fight for true education reform in Alabama. To my surprise, Dr. Ethel Hall, Vice-Chair of the Board, voted for this dual system of education that would perpetuate separate and unequal education for the majority children in the State for the next one hundred years. How ironic!

On the eve of the 100th Anniversary of the Plessy decision, a black woman voted to keep black and poor children separate and unequal. I thought of Clarence Thomas and a few other blacks who have used their power and position to maintain the white status quo. Again, I was moved to tears.

I decided not to concentrate on the negative. I thought of Dr. Willie Paul, David Byers, and Stephanie Bell. No white official in the state spoke out against segregation thirty years ago when everyone knew that schools were terribly separate and unequal. Yet, a white conservative republican had spoken out loud and clear. I feel hopeful because I now believe that there are white officials in this state that will put aside race, politics, and class to serve the best interest of all children. The white board members who stood up for all children were not flaming white liberals who often act condescending and maternal when it comes to black people. Two white and one black bold visionary board members realized that you can't move Alabama forward and leave a majority of children of color and poverty behind. It was an exciting moment in history that the printed media failed to reveal. Thus this letter. The Greene County Democrat was the only newspaper present to capture and document it.

Hopefully, this letter will help alert the media and the public to the most historic moment for education in my seventh plus decade of living.

—Ms. Ora Lee Gaines' letter to the Birmingham News . . .
reprinted with permission.

Questions for Analysis

1. How clear is the persuasive response the writer is seeking? Do you think she is trying to create awareness, change an attitude, or provoke action? Is she seeking some combination of these responses?

2. One way to think of a writer's credibility is to see it as the picture the writer creates of herself in the text. What kind of person is depicted in this text? Do you think the writer created an honest or accurate picture of herself?

3. What emotions, if any, did the letter provoke in you? What examples do you find of emotional appeals?

4. Late in the second paragraph, the writer offers a very clear example of the appeal of contrast when she observes that our legal system has ways of compensating people for injuries, while our educational system has no similar responsibility or liability. What other logical appeals do you find in the text?

5. What group or groups do you think this writer was addressing? How would you describe her "writer position" in relation to these readers?

6. A political theorist named Iris Marion Young has made the case that people should look at social and racial difference in a far more flexible way. For example, you may find yourself in social situations where, for a time, you have great deal in common with people who

may be very different form you in other ways. How does the situation described by this writer illustrate looking at difference in a more flexible way? In other words, have the problems with tracking created alliances between groups that the writer seems to suggest are frequently alienated from each other?

7. What personal knowledge of or experience with tracking do you have?

8. What do you see as the advantage of tracking?

9. At what points do you agree with the writer's assessment of the problems with tracking? At what points do you disagree? What do you think about the principle of separate but equal?

10. What further actions for change do you think people in this situation, including the writer, will need to take?

A Case   DAVID'S INQUIRY

On the radio this morning as I was driving to class, I heard about what was being called an alleged robbery attempt. A car owner had seen a teenager near the passenger-side door, and the car alarm had been set off. The owner of the car happened to be a karate student; he attacked the young man, leaving him with an injury that could paralyze him for life. The young man was arrested, but the prosecutor was investigating the possibility of issuing charges against the owner of the car as well.

The story bothered me for several reasons. As a 40 year-old returning student, with a teen-aged son, I was concerned about the rise of violence in my community. I am also an Isshinryu karate instructor, and later in the day, I learned that the owner of the car is a student of one of my friends. I was troubled by the karate student's response. Karate is supposed to be an art of self-defense, and I wondered just how much danger the teenager had posed to the young man. Learning self-discipline is supposed to be just as important to karate students as learning the karate forms. The car had not been entered or tampered with. Was there any justification for the car owner's use of the potentially deadly force of karate? I decided to investigate this issue for my second assignment.

David started by identifying the group to whom this issue would matter. He knew that the community was concerned about rising violence, but he was specifically troubled about the role karate had played in this violent incident. As a way of investigating the relationship between karate and violence, David recorded another incident in which karate had played a role in violent confrontation. He decided to focus his inquiry on the values within the community of Isshinryu karate experts and teachers. Using a Questioning Strategy, David settled on three questions as he explored how these incidents had challenged his karate community's values.

David's Questions

My Possible Groups	My Possible Issues	
Isshinryu karate experts/teachers	Karate should be for self-defense only	
Parent	Community is getting more violent. My son does karate. Could this make him a danger to himself and others?	

My Experiences	My Values	Source of My Values
Hearing about karate student crippling high school student over the possibility of breaking into his car	Karate for self-defense	Karate philosophy Isshinryu philosophy Family
	Avoid violence	
Hearing about another blackbelt who witnessed an armed robbery in a record store. Blackbelt who ran after thief was shot and killed. Article in Isshinryu newsletter praised the blackbelt's bravery.	Getting killed over material possessions is stupid.	My common-sense

Writing context possibilities

Class: People in class were interested in subject when I discussed it. Most people are concerned about violence.

Class wouldn't have any way to act on the karate dimension of the problem. And that is most important to me

Isshinryu teachers and students: Would know subject, should care about violence problem. I have written short articles for the newsletter published by the International Isshinryu Karate Association (IIKA).

Letter to my son Jarrod: He would probably be turned off.

Context I will write in: Isshinryu teachers and students. If I want to see some change, this community makes the most sense. My kid reads the newsletter and is more likely to pay attention to something I say in print than in person.

Issues to investigate:

- increased violence in culture
- Isshinryu philosophy on violence, self-defense, protection of property
- the way Isshinryu philosophy is taught in local dojos

Questions:

What is making young people so violent?

To what extent in local karate schools is the Isshinryu philosophy of self-discipline and non-aggression being taught together with the karate forms?

To what extent is the Isshinryu perspective on violence, self-defense, and the protection of property a useful guide for behavior?

In his writing group, Vita and Laura reviewed David's questions and pointed out that the first one would be difficult to deal with in the two weeks they had to work on the project. David decided to focus on the last two questions. The question regarding how much Isshinryu philosophy was being taught in local schools would require some research—phone calls and discussions with students and teachers whom he knew. The last question, however, was one he could investigate using the resources he already had: experiences, knowledge, and understanding. The Three Perspectives Guide helped him recall what he already knew and believed; it also let him make new connections and re-evaluate his experiences and values.

David's Exploration

Three Perspectives Guide

<u>*Question and writing context*</u>

To what extent is the Isshinryu perspective on violence and self-defense a useful guide for behavior?
Writing genre: IIKA newsletter

<u>*Describing and distinguishing*</u>

- *Important elements:* martial artists, martial artist wanna-be's, teenagers and adult karate teachers, local karate schools, local martial arts schools—some do not stress philosophy, they encourage violence. Various weapons normally associated with self defense. "Karate" means "empty hands"—my weapons are my empty hands. Crime and violence in the neighborhood and the schools. The way karate is depicted in movies and on TV—Bruce Lee. Jarrod's karate teacher Samuel is a very gentle person who stresses self-discipline and concentration.

- *Images and Experiences:* I saw a young boy die from falling face first onto a sharp stub of a wild bush after being hit in a "boyish" after-school fight. I know what damage fists, feet, and weapons can inflict upon a human body; many people don't. Television and movies show a couple of big guys who slug it out for five minutes but shed no blood, lose no teeth, suffer no broken noses or jaws, etc. That ain't how it works

- *Perspectives within group:* Many karate instructors think that you should not show cowardice (they see discretion as cowardice) and promote violence as the solution to most problems. Others think you should be able to take a small amount of non-physical abuse, but not much

- *Perspectives outside the group:* There are many opinions about self-defense, ranging from total pacifism to outright violence. Texas just passed a law allowing anyone to carry a concealed weapon. Self-defense was the rationale behind the law. The law's opponents predicted that a minor traffic accident could result in murder if one or both of the persons involved had a gun. Their prediction came to pass shortly after the law was passed. One motorist shot the other following an argument and a brief fight. The proponents of the law still argue that the killing was justified. I say that if the man hadn't been carrying a gun both parties would be alive.

- *My Perspective:* Avoid conflict whenever possible. There may come a time when force is necessary, but the circumstances must be extreme.

Map networks and relationships

Categories/classifications:
Mine: personal well-being; self-defense
Others: Some see self-defense strictly as a physical act.
Comparisons/Contrasts:
avoidance/confrontation
safety/danger
health/injury
peace of mind/paranoia

Cultural stereotypes:
    A blackbelt is always a tough guy
    Self defense must be physical and violent
I have given many self defense seminars and demonstrations. Most people expect to see physical action. When I talk about avoidance, about running away from an assailant, leaving a situation, and facing possible embarrassment, I seem to lose their interest.

Trace moves and changes

- *My experience:* I used to think that self-defense always involved physical contact in a confrontational situation. Then, in the mid-1970s, I started studying Isshinryu karate. There was a lot of physical training and fighting techniques, but there was also the philosophy of Master Tatsuo Shimabuku. Some of his sayings were strange at first, but I put a lot of thought into them and came to realize that he promoted a peaceful existence through knowledge of power.

- *My attitudes:* I used to have a quick temper and be very willing to fight. Now, I believe I have a much more peaceful demeanor. I will fight only for a very good reason.

- *Changes in issue:* People are scared; many are just plain paranoid. Newspapers and TV reports are filled with violent images. Many have the perception, real or imagined, that violence is everywhere.

- *Effects:* More people are carrying weapons because of this fear. I believe that people with weapons have some "instant bravery" and are less likely to avoid confrontation. That leads to a greater chance of someone being killed or injured. It is redundant to say that your chances of being hurt are less if you avoid trouble.

David, Vita, and Laura read each other's explorations in class, highlighting material relevant to their questions and noting new values and attitudes that were emerging. Both Vita and Laura pointed out to David that his question [To what extent is the Isshinryu perspective on violence and self-defense a useful guide for behavior?] put the emphasis on Isshinryu philosophy, while his exploration dealt more with peoples' attitudes and commonsense issues concerning self-defense.

As all three writers moved closer toward drafting a text, they asked themselves "Who would listen to me about this issue?" "What response to the issue could those readers make?" The Writer/Reader Positioning Strategy helped them begin to answer these questions.

David's Writer/Reader Positioning

Positioning myself

- *My positions in context*—I've written a couple of articles for the IIKA newsletter. My position is that of a karate instructor for almost 15 years. I'm just a member of the association; I don't set policy. The newsletter contains a lot of things I don't agree with at times. Positions I've left behind—I'm not a student. If I want to see something changed, I need to do something about it. At 40, I am also older than many of the newsletter readers. My experiences as an older adult and even a father might be relevant.

- *Position I will take*—that of an experienced teacher and participant in the sport. This is an accurate description of my relationship to this group of people. I will avoid the position of either whiner (somebody else fix it) or know it all. This probably means I should let some of my personal experience "speak" for itself.

Positioning my reader

- *Possible positions:* karate students and teachers
  If I try to write only to students, I cannot focus on the attitudes of those who have the most influence—the instructors. Also, other instructors might feel that I am undermining their authority. Students would not necessarily feel ignored if I address my article primarily to teachers since my concern for students is at the heart of this issue.

- *Reader position:* Isshinryu karate instructors.
  What I would share with all instructors is a passion for the art. All teachers would also share concern for their students; teachers would also want to be respected by their students. I am probably more interested than a lot of instructors in the philosophy and mental attitudes of the founder of Shimabuku, Isshinryu's founder. I also truly believe in avoiding any form of violence. I used to have something to prove; I don't anymore. There are still a lot of instructors out there with macho attitudes. If I stress philosophy too much, some instructors will question my skill and proficiency.

In their group, David, Vita, and Laura asked the following questions about their writer and reader positions:

- Will readers feel comfortable in the positions defined for them by the writer?
- Will the position defined for the writer be most likely to elicit respect from readers?

David's Selection of Genre and Focus

Genre Selection

Medium: IIKA Newsletter
Genre Possibilities: Article or letter to the editor. I'll consult the genre chart/I'm choosing the article because letters aren't supposed to be very long.

Focusing

After reviewing my exploration and writer/reader positions, I've decided to change my question:

Why should Isshinryu instructors help students avoid violent confrontations?

Considerations:
I know that the karate instructors and teachers alike are aware of the problem of violent confrontation, so a "creating awareness" focus doesn't fit. I hope that my article will provoke an action on the part of Isshinryu instructors—that of teaching students how to avoid violent confrontations. But I'm aware that I will get resistance to teaching avoidance because of their macho attitude toward karate—one that's not very consistent with the teachings of Isshinryu's founder. I think I'll create a focus to "change an attitude"—the attitude that to avoid confrontation is to be a coward.

My focus

Teaching students to avoid violent confrontations is consistent with the philosophy of Isshinryu's founder, Shimabuku, and with being a good citizen.

David's group thought he had a workable focus and genre. The instructor then introduced three persuasive appeals that they could use to establish their credibility, to engage their readers' attitudes, and create arguments that would prompt readers to respond to a persuasive focus. They were encouraged to list an example that would enact each appeal.

David's Rhetorical Appeals

My Focus: Teaching students to avoid violent confrontations is not only responsible but also consistent with the philosophy of Isshinryu's founder, Shimabuku.

Rhetorical appeals

Credibility
1. Shared values
Values: love of karate; pride in mastery of techniques

2. Shared background/experience

Instructors have to go through training and examination to register officially as Isshinryu instructors. Anyone who has been involved in karate for very long would probably have witnessed or experienced a karate injury. They will only identify with me if they are confident my position is not based on fear or cowardice.

3. Reference to writer's position

I have some authority to speak on this subject because I am a blackbelt, with close to 20 years of karate experience. I have taught karate for almost 15 years.

Affective

1. Readers would have to believe that it takes as much courage to avoid violent confrontation as it does to engage it. Feelings of pride and self-confidence would probably help readers come to that belief.

2. Readers would be turned off if they feel I am talking down to them.

3. If I describe examples of violent confrontation, my language could make the examples more convincing.

Rational

1. Example, story, narrative

I have several stories about avoiding confrontation and unnecessarily engaging it.
Avoidance: my traffic accident where the other driver tried to pick a fight.
Engagement: kid crippled by blackbelt who thought he was breaking into his car; record store robbery; watching a young kid die from an accident during a fight

2. Definitions

Courage—is not just physical. It takes courage to use discretion even when you have the physical skills
Self-defense—is more than disarming or disabling an assailant; distance is the best self defense
Coward—someone who avoids trouble is not a coward

3. Model or Plan

I could propose some ways of integrating Isshinryu philosophical teaching with karate instruction.

4. Ideal, Premise, or Principle

Sometimes avoiding a fight takes more courage than fighting.
Discretion is a basic concept of self defense.

5. Causes/Effects

Violence begets violence.
The way karate is depicted in action movies supports the identification of a violent response with success, heroism, bravery.

When karate is taught without the lessons of self-control and inner harmony it simply becomes another form of fighting.

6. Consequences

Avoiding confrontation enhances the possibility of safety. The outcome of a situation is rarely predictable.

Bloodshed that usually occurs with physical engagement leaves the combatant at least open to possible HIV infection.

Accepting violent responses to situations has negative consequences: people do not solve problems through negotiation; people assume conflict rather than cooperation.

7. Connection between persons and actions

Shimabuku would not engage in physical contact unless there was no other alternative.

People who have self-respect do not have to prove themselves through physical engagement.

8. Means to ends.

Learning karate for self-defense is supposed to be the means to the end of personal safety.

Karate is supposed to lead to self-discipline and self-respect.

In movies, unfortunately, karate is often depicted as a violent means to an end.

9. Direction in a stage or process

Isshinryu karate is moving away from its roots. Less Isshinryu philosophy is being taught together with the karate. Bravado is no longer condemned. Successful physical engagement is now the primary objective of many Isshinryu students.

The self-discipline of karate leads to personal harmony; personal harmony brings about harmony in the world.

Physical engagement quickly raises the stakes in a situation. If the other party has a gun, you are out of luck.

10. Classifications

People sometimes assume that those who use their heads before their hands are not karate experts.

11. Comparisons and contrasts

The Isshinryu perspective on violence is comparable to commonsense principles for living in a community: lives are more important than property; peace should always be the first choice.

People use karate for self defense; they use guns for self defense; criminals also use guns. Karate cannot compete with a handgun.

12. Shared authority

The Karate Creed: I come to you with only "karate"—empty hands. I have no weapons: but should I be forced to defend myself, my principles or my honor . . . should it be a matter of life or death, or right or wrong, then here are my weapons—KARATE—my empty hands.

Shakespeare said that discretion is the better part of valor.

13. Analogy

No one would give a young person a gun for self-defense without careful instruction concerning when and how to use it.

In their workshop, Vita and Laura helped David to decide on which would be the most effective appeals for their texts. They used the following criteria: Which appeals were most directly related to the focus? Which appeals were most appropriate for the writer and reader positions? Vita and Laura had several questions about two of David's rational appeals. Was David's second consequences appeal about bloodshed and HIV really related to the focus, and did David have his facts straight about AIDS? They also questioned whether David's readers would accept Shakespeare as a "shared authority." David considered their responses, made some choices, and organized his appeals in a plan.

David's Organization Plan

Introduction:
- refer to the master of Isshinryu Karate to establish my credibility
- state the issue and my focus

First Point:
- establish contrast between current practice of physical contact and my philosophy of avoidance

Second Point:
- define discretion

Third Point:
- problems with guns—possible effects

Conclusion:
- give them a feeling of responsibility, especially for their students

David's instructor and his group thought he had a good start, but they noted that he had left out some very good appeals he had included in his planning, especially credibility and affective ones. David reexamined his list of appeals, wrote several drafts of his article, and shared it with his group and instructor.

David's Polished Draft

Isshinryu Karate:
An Art of Violence or Inner Peace?

The late Master of Isshinryu Karate, Tatsuo Shimabuku, taught a philosophy of inner power masked by outward peace. He promoted peace when possible, power when necessary. Lately, I have been wondering how closely instructors have been following Isshinryu teachings. Teaching students to avoid violent confrontations is not only responsible but also consistent with Isshinryu's philosophy.

Many karate and self-defense instructors focus exclusively on physical contact and the techniques needed in a confrontational situation. I believe more emphasis should be placed on the very basic self-defense technique of avoidance. Distance from danger is the best defense. This doesn't mean that you should always run from trouble, just that you should pick your fights wisely.

Discretion is a basic concept of self-defense. Karate teachers and self-defense instructors should teach discretion first and physical violence as a last resort, especially in situations where an attack is not instant or imminent. Please don't take me wrong; I believe in defending myself, my family, my friends, and, in some cases, strangers, by whatever means necessary. But, I am not going to use force unnecessarily; nor am I going to risk life or limb defending material goods or pride.

What about guns? More people than ever carry guns. Some states have even passed laws giving all citizens the right to carry concealed weapons. Guns give some people instant bravery, making them less likely to avoid trouble. If you are in a confrontation, you must consider the possibility of your opponent having a gun.

Those of us who have taken it upon ourselves to teach self-defense must recognize the responsibilities that go along with our position. In addition to teaching people how to fight, we must also teach them when to fight. Not every confrontation is life threatening, so not every self defense technique should involve injurious or deadly force. In fact, many situations, which at first may appear to be threatening, can be handled using discipline and discretion. Encourage your students to follow the teachings of Master Shimabuku. They may find that peace is possible in more situations than they had imagined.

David's group members and the instructor read his draft and give him responses. Below are Vita's responses.

Vita's Response to David's Polished Draft

Overall response

You made a lot of good points, but there were two main problems. Some material was unrelated to the focus. This distracted your readers from the persuasive response, and you didn't establish your credibility.

Focus

Your focus in the first paragraph was obvious. (Teaching students to avoid violent confrontations is not only responsible but also consistent with Isshinryu's philosophy.) But you had several problems. Your focus had two parts: one part relating to responsibility and the other to Isshinryu philosophy. But can you count on all Isshinryu instructors being equally committed to Isshinyru philosophy? Your writer/reader positioning strategy suggested that you couldn't. Did you explain enough Isshinryu philosophy to motivate the instructors unfamiliar with it to change an attitude? Probably not. Some appeals were good ideas, but since they were not related to the focus they did more harm than good. This was especially the case with the discussion of guns in the fourth paragraph.

Development for readers

Your reader position was karate instructor. Your article did address this position, but your important problem was the absence of many appeals, especially to your credibility. One advantage you had as someone older was experience. You are particularly experienced in karate, yet you barely mentioned that experience. Also you didn't use many good appeals that you had thought of.

Organization

Your organization was OK because you stuck to a different appeal in each paragraph, but your transitions didn't help at all to take your reader from one idea to the next.

Language choices

Your word choices were comfortably informal but not very personal considering all of your firsthand experience. Your readers need more connotative language to motivate them to share your concern.

Conventions

Good work.

In response to these comments, David decided on a different focus:

"Teaching students to avoid violent confrontations is consistent with the philosophy of Isshinryu's founder, Shimabuku, and with being a good citizen." He also selected more appeals.

David's Revision

Isshinryu Karate:
An Art of Violence or Inner Peace?

Last week, on my way to night school, I heard on the radio the story of a teenager who had possibly been crippled for life when a karate student attacked him, believing the teenager was trying to break into his car. A few days later, I learned that the owner of the car was an Isshinryu karate student. Almost nothing about the situation was easy to judge. The teenager had set off the car's alarm system. There was good reason for the karate student to think the teenager was going to harm his property. Still, the car hadn't been entered; no crime had really taken place. The only thing that was really clear about the situation was that the karate student had chosen violent confrontation as the first response. As a blackbelt and a teacher of self-defense and Isshinryu karate, I have thought about this incident for a long time. It is difficult to avoid concluding that violence as the first resort violates both Isshinryu philosophy and principles of responsible citizenship.

The late Master of Isshinryu Karate, Tatsuo Shimabuku, taught a philosophy of inner power and outward peace. He promoted peace when possible, power when necessary. Shimabuku maintained that one resorted to karate only when the life of one's family or oneself was in danger. For Shimabuku, mastering the art of karate was the same thing as mastering one's self. Shimabuku believed that self-discipline created a kind of harmony that was the first step to harmony with others. So, in many ways, the ultimate goal of karate is to promote situations where using the art is unnecessary.

We don't have to study Isshinryu philosophy for these principles to make sense. All we have to do is go to the typical action movie to see how violence is used as the first alternative to solve problems and meet challenges, and, unfortunately, karate is often depicted as a violent means to accomplish one of these ends. Accepting violence as a first choice has several dangerous consequences. People forget how to use thinking and talking to solve problems. Human life is no longer viewed as sacred. We no longer assume that trust and respect are what holds a community together. Instead we assume that the way to survive is to win.

I know that all of this is easier said than done. Not long ago, on my way to teach a karate class at a neighborhood recreation center, I was involved in a minor traffic accident in which a young man changed lanes suddenly and hit my car. He got out of his car and began a long series of curses directed at me. I just kept my distance—somewhat amused, at first, at his behavior. Finally, he stuck his chin toward me and said, "All right, let's just fight." I could have put a simple hold on him that would have shut him up without my risking assault charges. But I was not in danger. There was no legitimate need for self defense. Reacting to his taunt would be accepting his way of measuring self worth: that to be a real "man" you have to win, even if it entails violence.

Those of us who have taken it upon ourselves to teach self-defense must recognize the responsibilities that go along with our position. In addition to teaching people how to fight, we must also teach them when to fight. If we encourage our students to remember the teachings of Master Shimabuku and the principles that making living together possible, they may find that peace is possible in more situations than they had imagined.

Questions for Analysis

1. Was David's writing process a genuine inquiry—investigating an important issue for which he did not have a solution at the beginning? Why or why not?

2. What aspects of his writing process contributed most to his inquiry?

3. Did David write in a real writing context: one in which he could actually communicate with the karate instructors? Why or why not? Was it the best context for the question he was trying to answer?

4. Were the writer and reader positions he chose effective for his subject? Why or why not? What other more appropriate positions might he have set? Was an article in the newsletter an effective genre?

5. At several points David made critical decisions. What were they? What impact did they have on the rest of his process?

6. During his process, David analyzed a couple of cultural stereotypes that surrounded his question. How extensive was his analysis? What other aspects of culture (e.g., race, class and gender) could he have investigated? Why would they have been important for him to analyze?

7. How effective were David's credibility, affective, and rational appeals? Did he achieve a balance? What other appeals could he have used?

8. David paced himself throughout the writing process so that he had enough time to plan, draft, and revise. How did he divide his assignments? Was his pacing helpful?

9. David's group and instructor gave him feedback and advice along the way during his planning and in reader responses. What advice was especially helpful? What feedback was misleading or unhelpful? Why?

10. How successful was David in convincing his readers that teaching students to avoid violent confrontations was consistent with the founder's philosophy and with being a good citizen? Why or why not?

WRITING FOR INQUIRY AND ACTION

THE WRITING ASSIGNMENT

This assignment gives you the opportunity to explore and confront an issue faced by a group that is important to you. As you begin to explore, think about the situations that have challenged you and your group. Could writing help change those situations by motivating people either to act or view an issue in a new way? Exploring situations like these will lead you to examine the values held by you personally, by your group, and the culture at large.

YOUR WRITING PROCESS

Examining issues that concern a group can empower you to take action for change. However, influencing others' beliefs and motivating them to actions is a challenging task. In addition to strategies for inquiring into your issue, you will find strategies called persuasive appeals that will help you engage your readers' values.

Starting

QUESTIONING STRATEGY
Select a Subject for Inquiry / Probe for Dissonance and Action / Locate Your Issue in a Writing Context / Formulate Questions for Inquiry / Workshop

---

Why Pose Questions?

Writing to act upon your world does not mean that you don't have to change in the process. Inquiry is very important in persuasive writing. You will be more effective in writing for action if you have an informed, critical understanding of the issue you and your group find important. You may even find that after exploring the issue, you want to take a different stand. Combining inquiry with writing for action may allow you not only to change something in your world but also to create new possibilities.

SELECTING A SUBJECT FOR INQUIRY

One way to select a subject for this kind of inquiry is to make a list of important groups in your life. Think of groups into which you were born, groups you have joined because of decisions you've made or activities you have engaged in, and groups in which you have a formal membership. For example, what membership cards would someone find in your wallet? After you have made your list, ask yourself the following questions: Are any of those groups presently dealing with a challenge or conflict originating outside the group? What about challenges or conflicts originating in the groups? Have you been involved in any of these challenges or conflicts? Have you observed an important group in your life doing something very "right"—and you want them to continue doing so? For example a local museum, of which you are a student member, may have recently opened its doors for a number of public meetings and activities. You may think this is a wonderful way to make a museum a part of the everyday life of your city, and you may want to make sure the museum continues this service to the community.

Some of you may think that you don't belong to any significant groups. In this case, can you think of a recent conflict that has troubled you or an issue that has engaged you? Think about that conflict or issue. Who else is involved? Who else cares? Do you share some kind of group identification with any of these people? Pick one of your potential groups and brainstorm for a few minutes. If you find yourself having a hard time brainstorming about one group, choose another. Next let the following questions help you decide on a group issue you may want to explore and act on:

- Which of these issues most concerns you now?
- With which issues do you have personal experience?
- For which issues can you examine your own attitudes critically?
- Which issues are already being debated with written texts in a group you belong to? (personal letters, letters to the editor, newspapers, newsletters, magazines, comment/ response)
- Which issues could you realistically as a member of that group address in writing?

PROBING FOR DISSONANCE AND ACTION

Once you have settled on an issue in an important group, you are ready to begin exploring in order to understand it more fully and see it from different perspectives. To help you explore, write down experiences that are associated with the issue. Imagine trying to explain the issue to a classmate: what specific examples or experiences would you use to help someone understand this issue? Next, what are the values that are tied to something you care about? The things we care about are usually related to our values. What values are at stake for you? What values are at stake for your group? Where did these values come from? Were they instilled in you by your family when you were a child? Did you come to hold new values as you matured, as you encountered new experiences, or as you met new friends? The strategy illustrated below will help you explore yourself and your group as you try to relate specific experiences to the values that made these experiences important to you.

The issue you have chosen probably challenges the values of a group with which you identify. Sometimes these challenges come from within a group; sometimes the values of one group are challenged by the values of another.

LOCATING YOURSELF IN A WRITING CONTEXT

One reason you are invited to think of issues in groups is that you generally can only influence those who see you as having authority or experience with an issue. What contexts are possibilities for you? In other words, whom does it make sense to address about this issue? Would it make sense to address them in writing? How would you now define your issue and your group?

FORMULATING QUESTIONS FOR INQUIRY

If the issue you have chosen were easy to resolve, it probably wouldn't be an issue. This book invites you to make inquiry a part of the process of persuasion to help create new possibilities in complicated situations. Using questions to guide your inquiry is one way to enhance creative thinking. Think about questions that would lead you and your group to understand what is at stake in the issue. The best questions for persuasive inquiry meet the following criteria:

- help you reevaluate the issue, rather than only reinforce an opinion you already hold
- are important to you and your group
- can be investigated in the time available

Example: Cassandra's Group and Questions

Possible Groups

Cheerleaders at Southeastern U.

Black Student Association.

Issues

- When people find out I am a cheerleader, they assume I am not a serious student.
- Effect of controversies over rap music on the black community

My Issue for Inquiry

Issue: Rap music and the black community

Experience	*Values*	*Sources of Values*
Have grown up with hip-hop, like most of it, and love a lot of it	love music	family & culture
Have argued with my brother and others about the way some groups treat women in their lyrics	fairness, respect, equality	family, my education
Have seen the way this gets handled in the media: some disgusting lyrics are shown, some bad rap gets identified with all rap, and some people outside the black community just identify rap with "black music"	pride in my African-American community fair representation of African-Americans	family, community
Issue is back in the media again with political candidates saying rap is "killing the soul" of America. I don't like a lot of rap lyrics either, but I think this is becoming another "race card" issue.	Fair representation of black community; racial quality	my community
I know how my parents and grandparents have struggled for racial equality; some rap music just seems to be about how women can be used, bought, sold.	Equality—for all groups	family and education
Some friends say I just worry too much about what white people think.	I don't know; I guess I would like to see more unity in the black community	family and community

---

Possible Contexts

- university—letter to the editor in student newspaper
- city—letter to editor in city newspaper
- African-American students—comment/response in Black Student Associ-ation Newspaper; letter to editor
- composition class—essay

My Context

- Black Student Association—I'm choosing their newspaper because right now I look at this issue as a problem inside the black community. I have attended receptions, lectures, and parties at the Black Student Association. I always read their newspaper. Many different issues are dealt with there. Students write letters to the editor, and longer texts are always encouraged.

- Their values
  - equality for all groups—gender and racial
  - unity in the African-American community
  - pride in African-American achievements
  - gender equality

Possible Questions

To what extent does female rap and rap that treats women with respect outweigh the "bad" rap?

What impact does "hardcore hip-hop" have on the images people outside the community have of blacks?

To what extent can disagreements about rap music be reconciled with the desire for unity in the black community?

What impact does some rap music have on relations between men and women inside the black community?

How can the gender inequalities in some rap music be reconciled with the struggle for racial equality?

The questions I will consider:

How can the gender inequalities in some rap music be reconciled with the struggle for racial equality?

To what extent can disagreements about rap music be reconciled with the desire for unity in the black community?

WORKSHOP

In your group, use the following three criteria to help your members select a good question and context for inquiry.

A good question:

1. holds the most chances for new knowledge. (A subject with no questions or dissonances is not appropriate for writing as inquiry because you already have it figured out.)

2. matters to you and your community. (A subject to which you are indifferent does not merit the effort that the process of inquiry takes.)

3. can be investigated in the time available. (Some subjects require more time or resources that you have in the composition course. These subjects can be saved for later.)

Exploring

Why explore?

When you write to influence readers to either change an attitude or take an action, you need to have an informed understanding of the issue. You need to understand the issue from many different kinds of perspectives, from the perspective of analyzing the elements of the problem or issue, understanding its causes, effects, and consequences, and comparing and contrasting it to similar issues. These perspectives will give you a more complex understanding of the issue, point to various directions for responding to the issue, and help you experience how others might feel about the issue. You may use the Three Perspectives Strategy below or other exploratory guides.

THREE PERSPECTIVES GUIDE
Describe and Distinguish / Map Networks and Relationships / Trace Moves and Changes

---

INVESTIGATING YOUR QUESTION FROM THREE PERSPECTIVES

DESCRIBE AND DISTINGUISH

What are the important elements of your issue? What types of people, "concrete" objects, institutions, businesses, places, attitudes, etc., are involved? Give specific examples, "proper names." What images or experiences does the issue evoke for you? What different perspectives are held on the issue inside your group? Outside your group? How would you describe your own perspective?

MAP NETWORKS AND RELATIONSHIPS

In what categories or classifications can you place your issue? In what categories or classifications do others place the issue? Do different cultures classify the issue differently? How has the media classified the issue? What important comparisons and contrasts can you make concerning the issue? What cultural narratives, stereotypes, and assumptions appear in your issue? How have they shaped how different groups view the issue? Create an analogy or metaphor for your subject.

TRACE MOVES AND CHANGES

How did your experience with the issue begin and develop? How have your own attitudes concerning the issue changed? How has the issue itself changed? What causes, circumstances, and/or effects are at work in shaping the issue? What important effects can you determine?

Example: Cassandra's Exploration

My Questions

How can the gender inequalities in some rap music be reconciled with the struggle for racial equality?

To what extent can disagreements about rap music be reconciled with the desire for unity in the black community?

Writing Context: Black Student Association

Describe and Distinguish

Elements of issue:

People: Rap Groups: Sister Souljah, Dr. Dre', Snoop Doggy Dog, CJ Mac, Grand Puba Maxwell etc. Members and officers of Black Student Association—men and women in the organization. Feminists/ white women/ black women

Objects, institutions, businesses: CDs, radio stations, black radio stations: 92.3 The Beat, recording studios—Young "D" Boyz-River Records; Rap-A-Lot Records; Lil Fly-Rag Top Records; Black Student Association sound system for parties; tape and CD collection. Budget for music and parties. Black Student Association meetings

Places: Rap centers—New York, L.A., Flint, MI; Houston-Crazy C; Black Student Association; my church; the South/the Bible Belt—get more bothered about bad language in songs than bad treatment of blacks or women; SE University—small black student population

Attitudes: White students think that what a few black students on campus do or think represents all black people; white women judging black men; black men dissing black women; politicians using rap to stereotype black people; black women facing barriers—sexism in black community; racism in culture; sexism in culture; white people looking for reasons to condemn blacks; me—feel like I'm forced to look at almost every issue in terms of race, wonder if I do care too much about what white people think

Images/Experiences: Listening to men use the B- word in rap lyrics. Rap videos depicting women as prostitutes; Women depicted as sex objects; sexual violence against women suggested in some videos.

Perspectives inside/outside group:

Inside: Many blacks don't criticize rap because they think it reflects some of the black experience. Some blacks think that caving into criticism of rap is caving into white attitudes. Some black men don't see anything wrong with the way rap lyrics treat women. Some black women think that criticizing rap is undermining black men. Some members of the association will think I'm trying to cause division in the group.

Outside: Some white feminists think that black women can't be feminists unless they actively speak out on sexism in rap. Outside the Black Student Association, older black folks and older people in my church think that rap is a bad influence on young blacks; they are more concerned about this than sexism in rap.

My own perspective: I agree that a lot of rap reflects the black experience. I think rap is uniquely African-American. I guess I feel that unity within the black community is more important than my identification as a feminist. Because of this, I want to see the black community address sexism in order to fight off racial division.

Map Networks and Relationships

Categories/classifications:

Types of music/black music: rap, soul, gospel

Popular music that appeals to different types of people: white people buy as much rap as black people.

Social issues: racism, sexism, crime; some white people classify rap music as a crime problem; it's a small step to identifying black men with crime.

Media: sometimes tries to classify rap as a kind of social awareness music; at the same time it exploits sex and crime in rap; media doesn't discuss the economic issues very much.

Comparisons/contrasts:

Issues that have divided black community: Contrast Farrakhan with Jesse Jackson

Compare sexism with racism—they both deny people their humanity just because they are members of a group. Sexism is an issue people can rationally discuss.

Cultural narratives/stereotypes/assumptions:

Some black men won't deal with racism in rap because they think rap depicts the world a lot of black men have to live in.
A lot of black women are used to putting their needs second to black men's.

Metaphors/analogies:

Sexism in some rap music is like slavery: one group has complete power over another; one group is denied humanity; one group receives violence from another.

Denying that sexism is a form of discrimination is like denying your own house is on fire.

Trace Moves and Changes

My experience with the issue:
I listened to my brother's rap music when I was in junior high. I didn't pay as much attention to the lyrics then, but there wasn't as much sexism and violence in the rap music I used to listen to. I've watched a lot of rap videos and have seen the sexism. Black Student Association has some rap CDs that demean women. I got into a discussion with some of the association officers last month. There wasn't much agreement about the issue.

Changes in my attitude:
I liked rap music at first. I thought it was distinctly black music, like soul. I don't want the kind of sexism in some rap to be thought of as distinctly black.

Changes, causes, effects in the issue:
In the past few years, more rappers have landed in jail or prison—some for violent crimes against women. Social and economic injustice are the causes of many of the themes and attitudes in rap. Selfishness in some black men make them think that how women feel about some of this rap isn't important. Effects—encouraging a demeaning attitude toward women isn't going to strengthen black families.

WORKSHOP

1. When you finish exploring, take a break. Then review what you have written and highlight parts of your exploring that help you answer your question. Let your new insights simmer for awhile.

2. Sometimes others can find insights in your work that you have missed. Share your Exploration with your group members. Ask them to:

   - highlight material they think helps to answer your question

   - write down other attitudes toward the issue that occur to them.

Positioning Writers and Readers

POSITIONING YOURSELF

First decide on your own position by asking yourself how you are already viewed in your writing context. From what positions have you already written within this context? From what positions have you been excluded? What positions have you left behind? Are there new positions you can now take? Once you have answered these questions, write down the position you have chosen for yourself. Now, think about the consequences of writing from that position. What made you decide on that particular position? What positions will you now avoid? Why? On what parts of the issue will you concentrate because you have chosen the position? See the Writer/Reader Positioning Strategy, Part II.

POSITIONING YOUR READER

What positions are possibilities for your readers? Usually one position excludes other options. Think about the positions that are excluded by each of your options. How would the choice of each position influence what you would or would not discuss in your text? Once you have decided on a position that you are sure your reader can assume, think about the values and the background associated with that position. Understanding the values and background of your readers' position is one of the most important tasks in persuasive writing. Your readers will only be moved to care, change an attitude, or take an action if they know you understand and care about their values and experiences. Try to determine values and experiences that you share. What you determine about the readers at this point will serve as your guide in formulating a focus and choosing persuasive appeals.

Example: Cassandra's Writer and Reader Positions

> ## *Writer Positions*
>
> ### *Positioning myself*
>
> I've only written something for the Black Student Association Newspaper once, and that was just a notice about a Spike Lee movie series sponsored by the English department.
>
> ### *Positions I have been excluded from*
>
> I am not a staff member for either the newspaper or the Association. I don't have a lot of authority because of my non-official position in the group. I can have authority as a black women who is a member of the association and has studied the issue carefully. Since young African-Americans generally have a different perspective on rap than older members of the community, I want to write in the position of a young member of the black community.
>
> ### *Positions I have left behind*
>
> Sometimes when I confront this issue I feel I am a woman or a feminist first and a black person second.
>
> ### *Position I will take as a writer*
>
> I will take the position of a black person who is concerned about the health and unity of the African-American community. Obviously I also must take the position of a black women. I need to do that in a way that doesn't exclude black men.

Reader Positions

Possibilities: member of black community, member of Black Student Association, black men, black women.

Who is excluded: I don't want to write to only the reader position of a black woman because that would exclude black men. I don't want to address only the position of Black Student Association member since the issue goes far beyond the Black Student Association.

Who benefits, who is harmed? Addressing only the positions of black men OR black women could only highlight the way this issue can divide the sexes.

Position I choose for my readers: position of young member of the black community

Values

equality, inclusiveness, pride in black identity, respect

Background

Every black person has had some experience with discrimination and knows what it feels like to be excluded, treated as an unequal, shown disrespect.

As black students on this campus, we have experienced together what it's like to see our organization and activities treated as inferior to the others. We've heard white students argue that they should not be required to support the Black Student Association with their activities fee. We've heard some fraternities argue that if they have to support the Association, they should be able to fly the Confederate flag on campus. Every black student knows about the Confederate flag debate. We know what it is like when our feelings about an issue important to us are dismissed or ridiculed.

WORKSHOP

1. Share your Writer/Reader Positions with your group members.

2. Can group members think of any alternative positions you have missed?

3. What advantages and/or problems do they see with the positions you have determined?

Selecting Genres

When you write persuasively, you need to make decisions about both the type of writing you will choose and the medium in which that writing is found. For example, you may be confronting an issue in your context like the need for a stoplight at a certain intersection or a problem with city waste disposal. You may decide that members in the context need to be informed about the issue before it can be acted upon. Choosing the genre of essay, however, probably wouldn't make much sense because most newspapers don't publish persuasive essays. You might consider writing a news article, but unless you are on the paper's staff or payroll, you do not have the writer's position that is appropriate for a news article. Your local newspaper probably does have a section for letters to the editor and/or an opinion column that is an open forum for all readers of the paper. Make sure your readers can be addressed through the genre and medium on which you decide. The following questions should help you decide on the best genre. What genres are available to your writer position? Which of these is the most appropriate for the writer and reader positions you have selected? As you think about genres, you may realize you need to rethink the writer/reader positions. When you feel comfortable about your decisions concerning those positions and genres, think about the implications of those decisions for drafting your text. See Genre Strategy, Part II.

Example: Cassandra's Genre

Media Possibilities: University Newspaper, Black Student Association Newspaper, local city newspaper. The local newspaper is read by members of the black community, but since the black community in this city is small, they are not the primary readers. Because young and old tend to have very different attitudes toward rap, I want both writer and reader positions to be young African Americans. The local newspaper would not be a good choice. Also, since I really only want to address the African-American community on this issue, the University Newspaper is not a very good choice.

Genre Possibilities: University Newspaper and Black Student Association Newspaper have both opinion columns and sections for letters to the editor. I'll check the genre chart.

Most appropriate medium: Black Student Association Newspaper

Most appropriate genre: Letters to the editor in the Black Student Association can be only 400 words long. Since I think my text will be longer than that, I will choose the genre of opinion column.

WORKSHOP

1. Review your group members' genre selections using the following questions.

2. How appropriate are their selections to the writer/reader positions?

3. What is it appropriate to write about in these genres and media? What is inappropriate?

Focusing

Why focus?

As you learned in previous chapters, a focus is an answer to a question you find important; it expresses the result of your exploration and summarizes a new insight. When you write to bring about a change in your world, your focus also expresses the response or action you hope to elicit in your readers.

Writing to change your world doesn't mean that your only objective is to prompt your audience to take an action. Sometimes the first step toward action is becoming aware of an issue or a problem; and sometimes a change in attitude is necessary before a more concrete change can take place. Consequently, your focus may be somewhere on a continuum with creating an awareness at one end and eliciting an action on the other end.

create an awareness ◄———————change an attitude———————► take an action

As you prepare to state your focus, consider which type of persuasive response is most appropriate for your subject, the positions of your readers, and your own position as a writer.

FOCUSING STRATEGY
State Your Subject and Point of Significance

STATING YOUR FOCUS

Now you will begin to reap the benefits of your creative thinking. Return to the questions you wrote before exploring. As you review these questions, you may find that one is now clearly far more important than another. You may find that you would phrase the most relevant question in a different way. It may be helpful to rewrite the question you now think is the most important. Take some time to review your exploration and your writer/reader positions. How does your creative thinking there help you answer the question? Like the focuses in the preceding chapters, a persuasive focus has two parts. The first part of the focus defines your subject in a particular way, and the second part defines your new insight, or the point of significance. In this case, however, your point of significance should also define the persuasive response you hope to elicit from your readers.

The following focus aims at **eliciting an action** (i.e., refusing to play a certain kind of rap music). It is appropriate only for a reader who is in a position to take that action—in this case, leaders of the Black Student Association.

Rap music that is
demeaning to women   should not be played at Association
(Subject)   functions.
                                          (Point of significance/ persuasive response)

The focus below aims at **changing an attitude**. It is appropriate for readers who may not have looked at the issue this way.

"Gangsta rap" that
demeans women   hurts the black community
(Subject)   as a whole.
                                       (Point of significance/ persuasive response)

As you decide on your focus, think about what type of focus is most appropriate.

Example: Cassandra's Focus

Question: How can the gender inequalities in some rap music be reconciled with the struggle for racial equality?

Focus:

Images of gender inequality in hardcore rap *(Subject)*	hurt the efforts of African-Americans for racial equality. *(Point of significance/persuasive response)*

WORKSHOP

Share your focus with your group, asking them to help you determine if:

1. Your subject is a manageable and important aspect of your issue, and

2. Your point of significance goes beyond a statement of fact to a position that approaches changes in attitude or action.

Developing Rhetorical Appeals

Why develop appeals?

As a writer, you came to your focus by critically examining your issue and your own experiences and values. Your insight may be very reasonable, but it probably wasn't the result of only "reason." The insights that are most meaningful to us generally involve values about which we care deeply and our own unique experiences and attitudes. When you write to elicit a response or action, you are inviting your readers to take a similar journey in challenging and exploring their assumptions, ideas, and values.

The following strategies are designed to help you lead readers through that journey. They are divided into three categories: credibility, affective, and rational. These classifications will help you keep in mind the many assumptions, attitudes, ideas, and feelings people use when they make decisions about issues that are important to them. These appeals will be at the heart of the text you write. Be sure to keep your focus clearly in mind. You might want to write it down and keep it in front of you as you create the following appeals.

CONSTRUCTING CREDIBILITY APPEALS

Credibility appeals help you establish a relationship with your readers through the medium of your text. You took your first steps toward establishing that relationship when you determined writer/reader positions. These appeals should help you develop that relationship by prompting you to elaborate on shared values and background.

1. *Refer to shared values:* What principles and ideals do you share with your readers? What values do you share that are directly related to the issue?

2. *Refer to shared background and/or experience, usually pertaining directly to the issue:* "Background " usually includes things like the region in

which you grew up (urban, suburban, rural; the Northeast, the South); social experiences; level of family income; diversity (or lack of it) in regard to race and perhaps "class"; religion. . . . Would referring to any of those parts of your background build a bridge to your readers that would help them make the focus response? Be careful, you may have shared background that would alienate your readers if you raised it. What about shared experience, particularly with regard to the issue? Reminding your readers of these experiences might help your readers understand why it is important for them to make the focus response.

3. *Refer to the part of your position as a writer that will prompt readers to listen to you:* What authority, experience, or knowledge will confirm for your readers that you are worth listening to. Again, you want to be careful. If you seem to be bragging, you will probably alienate your readers. Your relevant experience and authority should be part of the writer position you set for yourself.

Example: Cassandra's Credibility Appeals

Focus: Images of gender inequality
in hardcore rap   hurt the efforts of African-Americans
for racial equality.

1. *Shared values:*
Values: pride in black accomplishment; concern for community
"As a pretty typical college student, I like a lot of popular music. As an African-American, I am especially proud of the role blacks have played in developing much of the American music we hear today. Black music has not only given us something to be proud of, it has also brought us together in times of oppression and adversity."

2. *Shared background/experience:* We share experience with discrimination; and students my age probably have experience listening to rap—and listening to the conflicts over it. We share the experience of having our feelings dismissed on campus on the issue of the Confederate flag.

3. *Reference to writer's position:* The part of my position as a writer that will make readers listen to me is the role we share as students and as members of the African-American community. If I act like a big authority, I take myself out of the role. I need to avoid claiming I have special knowledge or experience.

WORKSHOP

Share your credibility appeals with your group.

1. Do they help you advance you focus?

2. Do they strengthen your writer position?

CONSTRUCTING AFFECTIVE APPEALS

We don't really have emotions apart from our ideas and experiences. Consequently, crafting appeals to readers' emotions is more a matter of how we present credibility and rational appeals. It also involves avoiding arousing feelings that would alienate or anger readers.

1. *Prompting an emotional state that would move your readers* toward *the focus:* Dealing with your readers' emotions is a very complex task. No one likes to be told what to feel; no one likes to be manipulated. Suppose that your focus is concerned with implementing a drinking policy in your fraternity house—probably not a real popular effort. However, suppose you also spent a year working as an Emergency Medical Technician before you started college, and you were working the night a child died in the emergency room from injuries sustained in a car accident caused by a drunk college student who had been driving. A careful description of the child, his family, and the college student could impress on your fraternity brothers the seriousness of the issue. Most people who would read the description would feel sympathy for the child and his family. College students might also feel a lot of anxiety, knowing how easily they could have been that drunk driver.

2. *Avoiding emotional states that would be most likely to move readers* away *from your focus:* What feelings would "turn off" your readers? In persuasive writing, you also must be very careful not to raise emotions that would alienate your readers. Take the example above. A careful description of a long night in the emergency room with the dying child and a grieving family (as well as a grieving college student) could be very effective in impressing on readers the seriousness of irresponsible drinking. It is effective, however, because the vividness of the story does the "preaching." The writer is not judging the readers or trying to provoke feelings of guilt. Instead young people reading the story would probably feel both sympathy and anxiety—if they had reason to identify with the drinking college student.

3. *Use connotation, vivid language, and striking examples as you craft your text:* This appeal is a matter of how you present your credibility appeals and your arguments, or rational appeals. Again, the story about the drunk-driving student is effective to the extent that the writer brings the story to life with carefully chosen language and details. See Connotation, Part II

Example: Cassandra's Affective Appeals

1. *State of emotion you want readers to have:* I want my readers to feel almost disgusted with some of the images hardcore rap gives of men and women. At the same time my readers would have to feel some pride, ownership, even protectiveness of the black community.

2. *State of emotion you want to avoid:* Feeling of resentment that I am being condescending.

WORKSHOP

Share your affective appeals with your group.

1. Do they support your focus?
2. Do they invoke your reader's senses and feelings? How?

CONSTRUCTING RATIONAL APPEALS

Your rational appeals will provide the substance of your text. They are the arguments designed to move your readers to accept the persuasive focus. Consequently, as you craft these appeals you must keep in mind writer/reader positions and your specific focus.

1. *Use an example, story, or narrative:* When you provide concrete pictures of the ideas you put forth or tell stories that illustrate your point, you are providing examples. Examples are an especially important rational appeal because they can perform so many functions. An example can illustrate shared experiences and values. The way you describe something or tell a story can also raise or quell your readers' emotions. Examples can be as short as a sentence, or your whole text can be one extended story—or narrative—that brings your readers to the focus response.

2. *Provide a definition:* Often a debate turns on how the parties involved define an important term. For example, you point out that a disagreement is based simply on different definitions, while there may be significant agreement on other matters. Or you could argue that all sides accept a new or specific definition of an important term. Some people believe that democracy is defined by the freedom to make decisions based on individual interests; others believe that democracy is defined by the responsibility to ensure equal treatment to all.

3. *Propose a model or a plan:* A model or plan is often a kind of solution. For example, an issue like yours may or may not have been resolved in a different context. The way that issue was dealt with may serve as a model for your own issue. If your persuasive focus aims to provoke an action—that of accepting a solution—the major part of your text may be a description of that plan. As you will see, one of Cassandra's appeals is to explain how another student group solved the same problem she is confronting.

4. *State an ideal, premise, or principle:* These are usually "sayings" that embody ideals, principles, or values that you and your readers share. An example would be, "Nothing is ever accomplished without hard work."

5. *Describe causes/effects:* This is a very common rational appeal that can work in a number of ways. For example, making the case that an action has brought about an effect that is causing problems for your group may successfully influence your readers to look at that action in a particular way. Obviously, cause/effect relationships can be a matter

of opinion, and you must consider whether or not your readers would accept your basis for a cause/effect relationship. Tobacco giant R. J. Reynolds, for example, denied that there was sufficient evidence to establish a cause/effect relationship between smoking and lung cancer.

6. *Describe consequences:* Like cause/effect, consequences establish a relationship between two things. Consequences differ in that the relationship may not be as direct or immediate. Take the example of the Chernobyl radiation disaster. Most people would accept a cause/effect relationship between radiation and the exorbitantly high incidence of cancer in the Chernobyl area. One might also suggest that one consequence of the Chernobyl disaster has been the disintegration of the local economy. In this case, there is not a scientific link between radiation exposure and economic decline. Still, it is not hard to accept that the toll of radiation exposure on human health has had the further consequence of disrupting both agriculture and business in Chernobyl.

7. *Establish a connection between persons and actions or the lack of connection:* This appeal may take several forms. You might suggest that a certain type of person or a character trait is associated with a particular action. For example, in cases where one spouse is accused of murdering the other, a defense lawyer might argue that the heinous crime of murder is simply inconsistent with the defendant's ten-year history of being a loving spouse.

8. *Relate means to ends:* This appeal can be used in a number of ways. It can be simply descriptive, or it can express some form of the judgment that an end does or does not justify certain means. Those who believe in supply-side economics, for example, maintain that tax cuts are a means to the end of stimulating the economy.

9. *Show a direction in a stage or process:* This appeal can be used to analyze a present condition, evaluate what has come before, and suggest what may happen in the future. Those who do not believe in supply-side economics might argue that a tax cut is only another step toward economic inequality—putting more money in the hands of fewer people.

10. *Use classifications:* This appeal may involve putting your subject or an element of your issue in a certain group or classification; it may also involve arguing that it has been placed in the wrong group or classification. Some people believe, for example, that the issue of where their children attend school should be classified as a matter of private choice; from their perspective, it is legitimate to use tax money to support the choice of private schools. Others believe that anything involving tax money should be classified as public concern, and from their perspective, public funds should not be used to support a private education.

11. *Use comparisons and contrasts:* This appeal involves stressing similarities and differences. For example, those who believe that it is fair

to use tax dollars to support private schools could compare their issue to other cases where tax money pays for services provided by private businesses—road construction and military weapons are two of many examples.

12. *Appeal to shared authority:* This authority can be a person or reference source respected by you and your readers. For example, people on both sides of the supply-side economics debate refer to famous economists who support their perspective. In discussions about race, both Abraham Lincoln and Martin Luther King are frequently invoked by very different types of people often for very different reasons.

13. *Create an analogy:* An analogy is like a very creative comparison. Supply-side economics is sometimes called by both advocates and critics a "trickle down" theory of economics. According to this image, capital is compared to drops of water that may accumulate at the top of a mountain, but invariably runs "downstream." Supply-siders would say that when those who have lots of money spend it, those who have less money eventually benefit when they are compensated for goods and services they supply.

Example: Cassandra's Rational Appeals

1. *Example, story, or narrative:* For characterizations of women in hard-core "hip-hop" I could use Luniz's "Playa Hata" and "Pimps, Playas and Hustlas." I could summarize some songs and videos to point out how seldom women are the "playas."

   For an example to reinforce to my readers that gender equality in hip-hop is an issue worth thinking about, I could describe a recent community forum in Boston on the subject: "Rap Music—Is It The Music of Our Time?" It was sponsored by a chapter of the National Coalition of 100 Black Women, and it focused on rap's references to women and depictions of violence against women.

2. *Definition:* Discrimination means that one group believes another group does not deserve respect. Most of us know what it's like not to be treated with respect by people of other races. The same definition of discrimination applies, however, to the way we treat each other inside the black community.

3. *Model or a plan:* I know of a black student association in another state that dealt with this issue by sponsoring a series of "rap sessions on rap," where black men and women together could listen to and watch some of the more controversial rap artists. Then students in the group would just talk about what they heard and saw in the music. These sessions started an important conversation between black men and women.

4. *Ideal, premise, or principle:* Equality is the central value in a democracy. That principle has to be applied to gender as well as to race.

5. *Cause/effects:* Some of the conditions described in rap music are the effect of a tragic disregard for human life. The effects of this tragedy are only compounded when rap music itself devalues human beings.

6. *Consequences:* A lot of hip-hop celebrates life, music, friends, and relationships between men and women. That's the kind of hip-hop I'd like my own kids to grow up with. What kind of men or women could our kids become if they see violence and exploitation as the "normal" scene.

7. *Connection between persons and actions:* Listening to rap that demeans a particular group would be inconsistent with the kind of persons who are members of the Black Student Association.

8. *Means to ends:* Hip-hop music has been a means of sharing positive black experiences.

9. *Direction in a stage or process:* The commercial success of hip-hop is proof of the increasing influence of black culture and the rising affluence of black performers. We have to be sure that this is a step in the direction of making life better for all African-Americans.

   Accepting gender inequality in rap music is a step in the direction of accepting more notions of inequality.

10. *Classifications:* This issue isn't about what white people think about black people; it's about what black people think about themselves.

    This issue isn't just about men treating women badly. Women can also reinforce images of inequality. I think some of Smooth's songs are great, but sometimes she also exploits negative images of women.

11. *Comparisons and contrasts:* Everyone who has grown up with hip hop knows that most of it is about life on the streets, so often it is about violence, anger, oppression, and exploitation. But "telling it like it is" isn't the same thing as telling it like it's OK. It's no secret that women on the streets turn to prostitution, but that's different from making a pimp the hero of a video.

    Dismissing black women's feelings about these images isn't all that different from the white community dismissing the feelings of African-Americans concerning flying the Confederate flag.

12. *Shared authority:* Even rap magazines like *The Source* are saying it's time for the Hip-Hop nation to take responsibility for some of the messages it sends.

13. *Analogy:* Denying the images of gender inequality is like denying your own house is on fire.

WORKSHOP

Share your rational appeals with your group.

1. Do they supply arguments that advance your focus?
2. Are they appropriate for your focus, readers, and genre?

Organizing

Why create a plan?

Creating a persuasive plan allows you to forecast which appeals you will use and how you will arrange them. You can try different versions before drafting to see which will work best with your readers.

PERSUASIVE PLANS
Develop an Introduction / Order Your Appeals / Insert a Refutation / Add a Conclusion / Workshop

---

DEVELOPING AN INTRODUCTION

The introduction of a persuasive paper has at least three functions:

1. it establishes the credibility of the writer,
2. it begins the appeal to the reader's attitudes, values, and feelings, and
3. it announces the writer's focus.

Most of the introduction should be devoted to establishing your credibility. Here you can introduce the appeals that you selected for establishing your credibility within your chosen context and your issue. Normally the introduction concludes with your focus. Remember that your task in the introduction is to begin raising concern about your issue. You must build bridges, indicating why your readers should listen to you and why they should care about your subject.

Think of the reader as needing answers to four questions.

1. Why should I be interested in this *issue?*
2. What are you going to *argue* about this issue?
3. Why should I listen to *you?*
4. Why should I read this *now?*

ORDERING YOUR APPEALS

Your proof is the longest section of your document, usually several paragraphs in length in a typical academic paper. In this section you concentrate on interweaving your three kinds of appeals. At the core are your rational appeals. But these should be advanced with details, information, examples, and language that work to sustain your credibility and stimulate feelings and attitudes in your reader.

When creating a persuasive plan, you might (1) list all of the appeals you intend to use and then (2) indicate in what order or section of your document they will be employed. A plan helps you to determine how these appeals fit together, what transitions you will need, and what gaps may exist. A plan also enables you to check that all parts of your argument support your focus.

INSERTING A REFUTATION

Refutation anticipates and answers your reader's objections to the argument you are making about your issue. It can be made in a separate section or interwoven with the proof. If you have analyzed your reader's views of the subject, you will have some ideas about what can be refuted.

Refutation can add to the persuasive force of your document in several ways. First, you show that you are not ignoring opposing views on the issue, thus enhancing the plausibility of your argument. Second, if you state objections fairly and accurately, you add to your own credibility. Third, by acknowledging the reader's emotional involvement in the issue, you can defuse some of the potential hostility.

Kinds of Refutation

You can refute by directly attacking a reader's statement of facts or proof. You can *deny* the reader's position and maintain that the opposite is true. You can make a *distinction*, accepting a reader's position in one sense but denying it in another, more important sense. You can *retort*, using your reader's reasoning to draw a different conclusion.

You can also use indirect refutation, attacking the character, credibility, or reasoning of an author with an opposing position, *but only if this person is not your own reader;* otherwise he or she will stop listening to you.

ADDING A CONCLUSION

The ending of a persuasive document, especially an academic paper, requires the writer to summarize the proof and restate the major conclusion you have reached on the issue. In a short paper, these may be included in a single sentence. In a longer paper, the two may require a paragraph. The ending should be as brief as possible because a long summary irritates readers who have paid close attention to your proof.

Example: Cassandra's Persuasive Plan

My Persuasive Plan

Focus: Images of gender inequality in hard-core rap music hurt the efforts of African-Americans for racial equality.

Introduction
- Credibility appeals
  #1–pride in black accomplishment
- State focus

Paragraph #2

- Rational appeals
  #4–ideal of equality in democracy
  #2–definition of discrimination
  #1–examples of rap performers

Paragraph #3

- Rational appeals
  #11–contrast—telling it like it is/ like it is OK
  #5–cause/effect—disregard for human life
  #9–direction in stage—gender inequality / other types of inequality

Paragraph #4

- Rational appeals
  #1–example of National Coalition of 100 Black Women
  #12–shared authority—*The Source*

WORKSHOP

Share your persuasive plans with your group.

1. Have you selected strong appeals?
2. Have you argued them effectively?
3. Is the order of your appeals effective?

Drafting
Why draft?

Once you have developed a persuasive plan, you have a pretty clear idea of how your document will look and how you will incorporate your appeals into a persuasive argument. Nevertheless, once you begin drafting your document, you may discover that certain appeals need to be added, removed, or reorganized within your document. It is critical that you develop several drafts in order to produce your most effective persuasive document.

DRAFTING STRATEGIES
Use Cohesive Devises / Use Concrete and Connotative
Language / Workshop

USING COHESIVE DEVISES

In all kinds of writing, it is important for your readers to be able to find relationships among the ideas and in issues you discuss. Readers need to see how one idea is related to another. When those relationships are clear, your paper has the quality of coherence. It holds together. Crafting and reworking your organizational plan is one way to achieve coherence of ideas. Here are some very concrete ways to create coherence between your sentences and paragraphs.

Repetition

Repeat something in the preceding sentence or paragraph in the immediate sentence or paragraph. The thing repeated can be a word, a phrase, a clause, or the total statement of an idea. With obvious limits, it can be repeated exactly or approximately. For example, if the repeated element is a single word, you can repeat it exactly, substitute a pronoun for it, or use a synonym for it.

Add Transition Words

Transition words help alert the reader to any of several relationships:

> *Contrast:* but, although, yet, however, *etc.;*
> *Coordination:* similarly, likewise, just as, *etc.;*
> *Consequence:* consequently, therefore, thus, so, as a result, *etc.;*
> *Accumulation:* moreover, furthermore, in addition, for example, *etc.;*
> *Alternation:* or, either, *etc.;*
> *Sequence:* first, second, next, finally, *etc.*

Maintain Consistency by Avoiding Abrupt Shifts in Number, Person, or Tense

There are only two grammatical numbers in English—singular and plural. Coherence breaks down when, for example, pronouns and their antecedents don't agree in person and number. "Person" distinguishes the person speaking (first person— *I, we*), the person spoken to (second person—*you*), and the person or thing spoken of (third person—all other pronouns and nouns).

There are six tenses in English: present, present perfect, past, past perfect, future, and future perfect. Fortunately, they are usually easy to keep consistent. Discourse that begins in the past tense, for example, should continue in that tense except when a reference to another time requires a shift.

USING CONCRETE AND CONNOTATIVE LANGUAGE

As you draft, using concrete language will help you to be credible, while general and abstract language will convey vague, unsubstantiated opinion. A persuasive text may also contain humor, wit, and satire, probably because humor pleases readers and therefore makes them more receptive to the writer. Effective discourse may also contain figures of speech which are highly connotative. See Part II for helpful examples.

Example: Cassandra's Polished Draft

> Dear Members of the Black Community:
>
> I'd like to address an important problem in the black community: the way hard-core rap music disrespects black women. African-Americans have always had reason to be very proud of black music, but the very thing that once helped bring us together now threatens to divide us. Images of gender inequality in rap music hurt the effort of black Americans for racial equality.
>
> Equality is a central value in a democracy, and this principle has to be applied to gender as well as to race. Discrimination means that one group believes another group does not deserve respect. We know what it's like

not to be treated with respect by people of other races. The same definition of discrimination applies, however, to the way we treat each other within the black community. Rappers like Dr. Dre and Snoop Doggy Dog depict women as prostitutes or refer to women using the "b-word." How can we argue against racial discrimination when this kind of gender discrimination is so prevalent?

Rap music may represent the experiences of some black Americans. It's no secret that when women end up in the streets, some of them turn to prostitution. But telling it like it is isn't the same as telling it like it's OK. Just because some women end up as prostitutes, pimps don't have to be made the heroes of rap videos. Some of the conditions described in rap music are the effect of a tragic disregard for human life. The effects of this tragedy are only compounded when rap music itself devalues human beings.

Men who disrespect black women's feelings about sex discrimination in rap music can't expect others to respect their feelings about other kinds of discrimination. Accepting sex discrimination is a step in the direction of accepting more kinds of inequality. Do we want our children to grow up with these images of women?

Many women believe that it is time to do something about rap music that demeans women. A chapter of the National Coalition of 100 Black Women held a forum on rap's depiction of women. Even the rap magazine *The Source* has had articles on the negative images of women in rap. The Black Student Association can't expect for others to listen to our calls for racial equality when we allow gender inequality. Rap music that demeans women has no place in the Association's activities.

WORKSHOP

In your group,

1. analyze Cassandra's letter for its coherence and cohesion,

2. examine the letter for concrete and connotative language, and

3. discuss what could be done to improve cohesion and language.

Responding to Texts

Why seek response?

Responders can be very helpful if you are trying to persuade readers. They can let you know whether you have managed to establish your credibility and if you have moved them to take the action you want, to assume an attitude, or to change their position. They can also give you feedback on how strongly your rational appeals worked. The Reader Response Guide below shows you how to adapt the general guide to this kind of writing.

READER RESPONSE GUIDE
Use the Reader Response Guide / Workshop

USING THE READER RESPONSE GUIDE

Give an Overall Response

What is your total reaction to the piece of writing?
Would the readers find it powerful? Dull? Confusing? Other?

Comment on the Focus

What is the focus?
Does the point of significance include suggested reader action or change?
What sections support the focus?
What sections are unrelated to the point of significance?
How can they relate better to the focus?

Assess the Development for Readers

What is the reader position being invoked? What sections engage the reader well?
What is the writer position? Does the development seem appropriate from this writer position?
Has the writer made credibility appeal(s)?
What rational appeals has the writer used? What reader background and values do these appeals refer to? Which are the most effective? The least effective?
Has the writer used affective appeals? Which appeals could be developed in more detail?
Would any of the appeals create negative reactions in the readers?
Has the writer overlooked a value, issue, or objection that readers in this position are likely to have?
What is the genre? Does the writing suit this genre?

Examine the Organization and Coherence

What is the genre? Does the organization suit the genre?
Does the introduction set up credibility and establish a focus?
Are appeals arranged in the most effective order?
Does the conclusion reinforce focus, particularly persuasive response?
What parts fit well? What sections break the order?
Do the paragraphs help maintain the order?
What can be done to improve the order?
Is the paper consistent in person, number, and tense?
Where are transitions or other cohesive devices needed?

React to the Language Choices (words and sentences)

Is connotative language used for the affective appeal?

What choices of words work well for the genre, focus and reader position? Which need reworking?

Are the sentence patterns effective? Where could improvement be made?

Check the Conventions

What conventions are required by the genre? Does the writing observe these conventions?

Are there places lacking the conventions of standard written English—grammar, spelling, and punctuation?

Indicate a Main Emphasis for Revision

What is the most important thing for the writer to change for the revision?

Example: The Instructor's Responses to Cassandra's Polished Draft

Focus:

You seem to have two focuses: one as the last sentence of the first paragraph and one as the last sentence of the text.

Development for Readers:

Your most serious problem is the writer position you assume in the text. For example, in your Writer/Reader positioning strategy, you indicated that you wanted to avoid being condescending to your readers; you also noted that dividing your readers by gender—addressing *either* men or women—might only make the division between the sexes stronger. However, some appeals in the text are aimed specifically at men. You also don't have any credibility appeals that reinforced your identification with your readers. Moreover, the way you present your rational appeals seems to place you in a superior position to your readers. In other words, though you wanted to avoid being condescending to your readers, places in the text did suggest a condescending attitude. Your reader would also find it difficult to feel anything strongly. Perhaps you are concentrating on your own feelings and attitudes rather than your readers'. More examples would be helpful.

Organization and Coherence:

Overall, you have followed a good plan, but there are few transitions between and within paragraphs.

WORKSHOP

1. Using the Reader Response Guide, provide written response for your group members.

2. Share these responses in an oral discussion.

Revising

Revising allows you to make changes in your focus, development, organization, or style so that your writing better communicates with your readers, helping them to take the action you hope for. It also is a time to clean up mistakes in grammar, spelling, and punctuation. Some revisions are more important to make before moving on to others. For example, if you have a major problem with a section that is out of focus, there is little point in changing the word choices in that section because the whole part may be eliminated. See Revising Plan and Revision Strategies, Part II.

Example: Cassandra's Revising Plan

I will use a new focus aimed at creating awareness of the problems raised by the way women are depicted in some rap music. My new focus is : "The Black Student Association should confront the issue of gender discrimination in some rap music." I plan to put my focus close to the end of the text to avoid sounding like I am telling others what they should do.

I plan to develop new appeals designed to reinforce my identification with my readers and to lead them to examine the problem themselves rather than simply to accept my opinions. I will begin with an extended example that illustrates how the issue had already been raised in my group. I also want to avoid taking a condescending attitude, so I will be careful to avoid sounding preachy.

Example: Cassandra's Revision

As a pretty typical college student, I like a lot of popular music. As an African American, I am especially proud of the role blacks have played in developing much of the American music we hear today. Black music has not only given us something to be proud of, it has performed many important functions in the daily lives of black Americans. For example, spirituals not only provided comfort to blacks in slavery, they also served as a form of communication, providing information about secret meetings, revolts, and escapes. Music has played an important role in the black community. The very thing that once helped bring us together, however, now threatens to divide us. One example of that division occurred during the last association dance.

After everyone had danced for about an hour, the D. J. put on Snoop Doggy Dog. Several of the women stopped dancing, and a few of us went over to ask him to change it. We told the D. J. that we found the music offensive because it depicted women as prostitutes and was filled with the "b-word". He said that since only two people were complaining, most of the people there must like the music. Since we were outnumbered, he said that the majority should rule. A small group stepped outside to talk about the issue. One woman said that because rap music depicts the experience of some blacks, it was censorship to say that it couldn't be played at the dance. One of the guys pointed out that even women rappers used the "b-word." Someone else told me I needed to chill on the whole issue. What I remember most about the incident was the D. J. telling me that the majority should rule.

Last year the Association requested that a fraternity on campus stop flying a Confederate flag. The Pan-Hellenic Council said that we were the only ones complaining, and it was unfair for the opinions of a few to set rules for so many. I remember the first meeting the Association held after the Pan-Hellenic Council decided that the fraternity didn't have to take down their flag. We kept questioning the idea that the most important thing about democracy was that the majority should always have its way. Shouldn't democracy also mean that people have a responsibility to listen to other perspectives? Shouldn't it mean that the values of all members of the democracy should be respected in some way?

It is hard for me to see how the issue of sexism in rap music is all that different from the issue of the Confederate flag. I felt just as disrespected by the D. J. as the Association was by the Pan-Hellenic Council. I'm not writing to say that hardcore rap music should be banned at Association functions. I do believe, however, that it is time for the Black Student Association to confront the issue of gender discrimination in rap music. If we can't learn to listen to each other inside the Association, we can't expect others to listen to us outside.

A friend at a midwestern university told me that their black student organization held a series of discussions about sexism—and violence—in rap. A similar kind of discussion in the Black Student Association would be a first step in confronting an issue that many black men and women are saying can no longer be ignored. It would also be a first step in practicing the kind of democracy we would like to see in our country as a whole.

WORKSHOP

1. Share your Revision Plan with your group.
2. Exchange and discuss your revisions.

CONCLUSION

If you think back to the beginning of this chapter, you will remember that David's willingness to respond to the problem of violence and karate led him to reflect on his own understandings of Isshinryu philosophy. Similarly, Cassandra's willingness to confront what she saw as a problem for women and her student association led her to explore the complex layers of stereotypes involved in gender and racial discrimination. In attempting to change their world, these students changed in the process. By approaching persuasive writing as inquiry, they not only learned about their world, they helped make it better.

5

AREA OF INQUIRY: LOCAL CULTURES

LISA LANGSTRAAT

WHY WRITE ABOUT LOCAL CULTURES?

For many, the word "culture" denotes the customs of a group of people who share regional, ethnic, racial, and linguistic traits. For others, culture is what you acquire through education and training: the cultured person has acquired the good taste to enjoy the finer things in life, such as Shakespeare plays or classical music. But culture is much more complex than either of these definitions suggests. While your regional and ethnic background and traditions greatly affect the way you understand yourself and the world, you may be equally influenced by other cultures. And certainly you can be a cultured person if you've never listened to Vivaldi's *Four Seasons*. Indeed, some would argue that Vivaldi is no more "cultured" than Elvis!

If you think of culture as a way of life—the daily habits and experiences that give us a sense of belonging in our communities—you'll probably realize that you belong to many local cultures at this very moment. For example, based solely on your birth date, you might be considered part of the "generation Y" or "baby boomer" cultures. At the same time, you are a college student, and that means you belong to yet another culture. Perhaps you participate in a student organization for basketball players, single parents, or engineering majors. Perhaps you have a full- or part-time job, and that working community has a great impact on you. Perhaps you and your friends enjoy country, rap, or grunge music, and the culture of each musical community motivates your dress, speech, and actions. Every local culture you belong to helps shape who you are at different times and places in your life.

In this context, you will investigate a local culture, attempting to describe and analyze the values and behavior of a specific group of people in a specific time and place. Such research is no easy task because local cultures don't exist in isolation. Instead, they are part of a complex network of political, economic, and social values that shape our attitudes and, in turn, our identities. Researching a local culture, then, calls on you to inquire in new ways about activities and communities that may seem natural to you. To really understand your local culture, you must draw connections between its daily habits and the larger social values that inform those daily habits.

One of the best ways to enhance your understanding of a local culture is to engage in ethnographic research strategies. "Ethnography" literally means a "picture of a culture." Through vivid description, an ethnography reveals a culture's day-to-day behaviors, beliefs, and shared interests. Researchers in a variety of disciplines employ these ethnographic techniques to study both distant and local cultures. While there are many different approaches to and goals for ethnographic research, it requires many of the same skills as traditional research: deciding which aspects of the topic are most worthy of inquiry; gathering others' opinions and research on the subject; synthesizing and analyzing a large amount of information; and organizing your ideas for specific readers. However, ethnographies differ from traditional academic research in two important ways:

> *Your role as a participant/observer.* While traditional academic research might ask you to privilege the validity of published scholarship, ethnographic research begins with your experiences and perceptions. Ethnographers immerse themselves in the culture they are studying, and they become both participants and observers of that culture. The participant/observer role requires that researchers seriously consider their roles as researchers, for they cannot assume a position of pure objectivity. They use their senses—sight, sound, and feeling—to gain new understanding of a culture's practices and values.

> *Integrating a variety of research strategies.* Ethnographers employ several research techniques. In addition to gathering published, expert opinions, ethnographers also do field research. They closely observe cultures on a number of occasions, recording people's behaviors and concerns. They interview members of the culture as well as non-members (such as administrators or government officials) who interact with the culture. This field research allows the ethnographer to present vivid descriptions of people's daily lives and to include individual's voices and perspectives in their research.

Most ethnographers spend months, even years, working with the cultures they research, but you, of course, have different time constraints. Hence, you will employ ethnographic research strategies for a shorter study of a local culture to which you belong. Ethnographic techniques can help you understand more about your local culture's values, methods of self-expression, and relationships to dominant cultural institutions. Many business people, for example, employ ethnographic strategies to understand how employees communicate, how to improve working conditions, and how to meet consumer needs. Through ethnographic research, you can help others understand your local culture's values and purposes, and you can propose improvements to help your local culture meet its most important goals.

EXAMPLES OF WRITING FOR INQUIRY AND ACTION

- Literary critic Janice Radway conducted her research in the small, Midwestern community of "Smithton." Observing and interviewing a group of women who regularly read romance novels, Radway investigated how the publishing industry and cultural stereotypes about romance novels influenced the women's reading practices. She published her findings in *Reading the Romance: Women, Patriarchy, and Popular Literature*, a book critically acclaimed for its insights on the role of popular culture in people's daily lives.

- In 1981, the National Assessment of Educational Progress reported that as elementary school children improved their writing skills, their enjoyment and sense of competence in their writing tended to decline. Upon reading this report, writing teachers Susan Florio and Christopher Clark wanted to understand the causes for students' attitudes and feelings about writing, so they conducted an ethnographic study of students in a second- and third-grade open classroom. Florio and Clark worked with the students and teachers over a long period of time, gathered many different kinds of data (from student writing to classroom observation), and reached a variety of conclusions about the importance of collaboration and community in students' writing experiences. They published their findings in *Research in the Teaching of English*, a widely-read journal that influences English teachers from the elementary to the college-level.

- Susan Faber, a student in an anthropology course, analyzed the relationship between social class and the tipping behavior of customers at a cocktail bar where she worked as a waitress. Observing her customers' behavior and analyzing their responses to surveys, Faber discovered that lower-income people tend to tip more than high-income people, possibly because of social insecurity. In addition to sharing her findings with her fellow students, Faber's ethnographic research was included in *Researching American Culture*, a university-press book which features a variety of ethnographic studies and methods.

- Stephen, a new student at a large Midwestern university, studied the first-year engineering program in which he was enrolled. Steven examined the implicit and explicit values the program fostered, such as competition among students. Stephen shared his ethnography with several teachers in the first-year engineering program, encouraging them to rethink some of their competition-inducing practices.

- A political science student, Bernice, studied a group of African-American friends to determine if and how they had experienced racism on their campus, which had only a three percent African-American population. In the process of conducting her interviews and researching other universities' approaches for dealing with racial and ethnic difference, Bernice discovered avenues for becoming an activist and educating others about the problem of racism on her campus.

READINGS FOR INQUIRY AND ACTION

"SOCIAL CLASS, TIPPING, AND ALCOHOL CONSUMPTION."
Researching American Culture by Suzanne Faber

Suzanne Faber took advantage of her job as a cocktail waitress in a local bar to explore relationships between income level, alcohol consumption, and tipping. Her data are based on participant observation, observation of behavior in a public place, and formal questioning of informants. Her most significant finding is a tendency for lower-income people to tip more than middle- and high-income people, a pattern that may reflect social insecurity or their identification with the bar employee. As in the selections by Larson and Van de Graaf and Chinni, Faber uses quantitative data to substantiate her conclusions.

Social Class, Tipping, and Alcohol Consumption in an Ann Arbor Cocktail Lounge

Suzanne Faber

American culture is marked by diversity based on differential access to strategic resources. Various attempts have been made to prove that behavioral differences between representatives of the many social strata are observable. Speech patterns, style of dress, mannerisms, and so forth, have been analyzed as indicative of a particular background, a particular class. While class differences are indeed evident in many areas of behavior, questions nevertheless remain as to the specific circumstances in which differences may be discerned. Are class-based differences manifest in even the most commonplace, routine activities? The focus of my research is an attempt to answer precisely this question.

Through observation of individual behavior in a bar situation, based on examination of drinking and tipping habits, I have attempted to determine whether or not class-based behavioral differences in such routinized circumstances are apparent. Being employed as a waitress at a local bar has afforded me the opportunity to compile the necessary data.

Both the location and the atmosphere of this tavern proved conducive to comparative analysis of class. The fact that it is situated in a hotel implies that its patronage is not limited to local customers. It is located near an expressway off-ramp but still close to many large and small businesses. It is large, clean, and tastefully decorated. There is a dance floor and live entertainment, usually including the kind of pop and soft rock music that appeals to a variety of age groups. Compared to other bars in the area, it attracts customers from a fairly broad range of income groups, as will be demonstrated further on.

The data were compiled over four weeks, during which I worked ten shifts. I approached more than 150 people in order to recruit 100 participants. Due to the nature of my research, I did not wish to alter their normal behavior patterns. I explained that I was a student doing anthropological research involving income distribution of people who patronize local bars. They were unaware that I would be taking note of particular aspects of their behavior.

I needed to obtain three different types of information. Obviously I had to determine the individual informant's social class. Realizing that most people would respond to a direct inquiry about their social position by affirming their membership in the middle class, and recognizing the social unacceptability of asking such a question, I decided to use a less conspicuous approach. After showing them a card I had previously prepared, which listed five gross income groups, I asked them to write down on the back of their check the letter which corresponded to their own approximate gross income. The choices were as follows:

A. $0.00–$10,999
B. $11,999–$19,999
C. $20,000–$35,999
D. $36,000–$59,999
E. $60,000 and above

I chose to use such wide income margins primarily because I felt that if the list had been more specific or if I had asked the participants to write down their exact income, many would have felt the invasion of privacy too great and might have withdrawn their offer to participate. It is true that income level alone does not necessarily determine social class. However, since class is the sum total of a number of interrelated variables, including income, certain generalizations may be drawn. Usually someone who draws a relatively large income has better access to strategic resources and thus is in a higher class than someone who earns substantially less. Upper, middle, and lower classes, then, are not absolute concepts, but merely ways in which the sum of personal variables may be understood relatively. Accepting this as a premise, I divided the participants, on the basis of income, into the following categories:

A. Lower class
B. Lower middle class
C. Middle class
D. Upper middle class
E. Upper class

The second category of information needed for the study was alcohol consumption patterns. On the back of each participant's check I noted the number of drinks ordered and the frequency with which they were ordered. I discarded the information taken from participants who stayed for less than two hours. Classification of the participants with regard to consumption habits was as follows:

Four or more drinks per two hours = excessive
Three drinks per two hours = heavy

Two drinks per two hours = average
One drink or less per two hours = low

The third area of concern was tipping behavior. After the participants had left I made note on their check of the amount left as gratuity. The basis for classification here was as follows:

20 percent or more = excessive
15–20 percent = high
10–15 percent = average
10 percent or less = low

Upon completion of the data-gathering process I was able to correlate the results in an effort to determine whether or not class-based differences were indeed manifest in drinking or tipping behavior. The findings are documented in tables 1 and 2.

Examination of the data reveals some definite trends. Most striking are the class-based differences with regard to tipping. The pattern is that persons of the lower to lower middle class tipped more generously than individuals of the middle to upper classes. Excessive tipping is apparent among only 3 percent of the higher income groups, while among those with lesser means, about 30 percent left tips upward of 20 percent. (I should point out that one man who claimed to be in the bottom income category left a tip of $20.00 for a bill that totaled only $8.50.)

There are a few possible explanations for this. It may be that lower-class people, who are less confident about their social status than wealthier individuals, feel a need to overcompensate by tipping excessively. They may also feel a certain loyalty to their class and identify with their waitress, whom they see as another member of their own working class. Generous or excessive tipping may thus express a certain class "camaraderie." Conversely, high-income people, secure in their social and economic positions, are less likely to overcompensate. Most of them were cautious to leave a tip close to the traditional 15 percent.

Table 1   Alcohol Consumption by Social Class

Social Class	Drinks Consumed per Two Hours				Total People
	4	**3**	**2**	**1**	
Upper class	2	3	2	3	10
Upper middle class	4	8	9	7	28
Middle class	4	10	11	8	33
Lower middle class	4	6	8	5	23
Lower class	0	2	3	1	6
Total	14	29	33	24	100

Though it is difficult to pinpoint a specific cause for class-based differences with regard to tipping behavior, the trend is significant. The variation in the percentage of the bill left for the waitress implies that a number of other factors also dictate tipping behavior. These will be discussed further on.

The data fail to reveal any marked trend that might support the hypothesis that variations in alcohol consumption are class-based. Among all classes, between one-third and one-half drank at least three drinks per two hours, but most people consumed one drink per hour or less. It becomes clear that drinking is a cross-class phenomenon and that level of income has little to do with amount or frequency of consumption. (More significant, though not related to the current hypothesis, however, are the obvious implications of such enormous liquor consumption to American culture in general. The data support the notion that alcohol is the most widely abused drug in this country.)

Table 2   Tipping Behavior by Social Class

	Percent Tip			
Social Class	**20**	**15–20**	**10–15**	**10**
Upper class	0	30	70	0
Upper middle class	4	18	71	7
Middle class	3	18	61	18
Lower middle class	26	39	22	13
Lower class	33	33	33	0
All social classes	10	25	54	11

The data seem to indicate that class-based differences are indeed manifest in such routinized behavior as tipping. Yet, after completion of the data-gathering process, I must express my own skepticism about the validity of its results. The conditions under which information was taken were not conducive to either my own nor my informants' objectivity. My appearance, sadly enough, was a factor. The uniform I must wear for work is a lowcut black leotard and a slinky slit skirt. It certainly did not enhance my credibility as an anthropologist. Moreover, my dual role as waitress and researcher often conflicted, as customers who felt they had to wait too long for service subsequently did not cooperate. In addition, although I tried to be inconspicuous in determining participants' class, the fact that at least some of them were interested in making a positive impression (with others at the table and myself, too) makes me hesitant to accept their claims. For example, one of the men who claimed to earn over $60,000 per year left his room key on the table with a note that said he would be interested in discussing the results of my research.

More generally, too many variables could have affected both tipping and consumption data for me to be certain of their validity. Frame of mind, and desire to impress a member of the opposite sex, or a superior, are some of the many variables that operate in bar situations. My own frame of mind must also be considered. Those people who seemed anxious to cooperate in my research were naturally treated better than those who were reluctant. Tipping behavior therefore was not accurately or objectively expressed. In addition, although I tried to carefully monitor the consumption patterns of the participants, my personal dislike of overt drunkenness, along with my responsibility as a waitress, might have caused me to avoid tables where I felt the customer had drunk too much. It is for these reasons that I feel that a repetition of the experiment using a different researcher might not result in similar findings.

Although I am skeptical about the validity of the data, I am certain of other (nonquantitative) trends that became evident during data gathering. I noticed significant behavioral differences along class lines in both my approach to the customers and their reaction to me. Many of the better dressed, more sophisticated individuals I approached took great offense to my efforts to recruit them. I received many threats that the manager would be told of my behavior, and one gentleman went so far as to remind me of my "place." The vast majority of the overtly less sophisticated customers I approached greeted me with a great deal of warmth and enthusiasm. Recognition of the social boundaries reinforced by class differences was thus at least tacitly expressed.

Another phenomenon also became clear in my research. Many of the participants expressed difficulty in accepting the fact that I am both a student and a waitress. A waitress is seen as a lower-middle-class worker, socially stagnant, while students are perceived as being upwardly mobile, the inheritors of high social positions. My dual role was thus somewhat incongruous in the minds of many, and in almost every case, the customers expressed their great surprise.

It becomes difficult to draw any conclusions, based on either my statistical or qualitative findings. In the first case, I doubt the accuracy of the data (for the reasons stated previously), and the degree of subjectivity involved in the second case would make conclusions suspect. Nevertheless, after having done the field research, I must affirm my belief that class differences do indeed exist, even in the most routinized, commonplace activities. Perhaps, given more objective and scientific circumstances, this hypothesis may yet be proven.

Self-Evaluation

I began the project with the best of intentions. I later realized that my approach and methodology were naive. I was not fully aware of the complexities involved in any field research project and I am sure that is evident in the paper. I did, however, learn a great deal. I have begun to be much more aware of subtle class-based behavioral differences among people in all situations, not just in the bar. Yet I am disappointed by the fact that I spent a great deal of time and suffered a lot of aggravation for what turned out to be inconclusive. Some of the things that happened were, in hindsight, somewhat humorous. Some of the "regulars" who found out that I was doing research now refer to me as "Professor," and leave larger tips in an effort to help me with my tuition. One gentleman offered to fly me to the Caribbean with him so that I could research the natives there; his wife tipped me twenty dollars after I told him off.

Questions for Analysis

1. What are the hypotheses or questions guiding Faber's ethnographic research?

2. Characterize the reader-writer relationship in Faber's ethnography. Why might Faber have chosen this relationship for her work in a course called "The Anthropology of Contemporary American Culture"?

3. Describe Faber's participant/observer role. How does it inform her data analysis?

4. Faber chooses to collect the majority of her data through surveys, but she also includes observations of customers' behavior in analyzing her data. How might interviews and scholarly research change or enrich Faber's ethnographic study?

5. Evaluate Faber's survey. Does it seem comprehensive? Would you add or subtract questions? (See Part II for a discussion of surveys.)

6. Does Faber offer enough description to make her local culture vivid and realistic? Which details and observations seemed most striking? Why?

7. Faber suggests that her clothing and her social role as a waitress affect customers' responses to her. Do you think these issues undermine the validity of her research? Why or why not?

8. Faber states that while her research might be "inconclusive," it nonetheless suggests that customers of lower socio-economic class might be better tippers because they sympathize with their waitresses' class status. Would you interpret Faber's conclusions differently? Why or why not?

9. Go to a nearby restaurant and observe customer/employee relationships. What trends do you notice? What hypotheses might you develop based on those trends?

10. Informally interview several people about their tipping habits. Do their reasons for tipping well or tipping poorly correspond with Faber's conclusions?

A Case   TERRI'S INQUIRY

During the summer term I enrolled in this university. It seemed the logical thing to do: My hometown is less than an hour away, and I could save money by living with my parents. A few weeks after the semester started, however, I wondered if I'd made the right choice. Attending classes, studying at the library, driving home—everyday I suffered the same, monotonous schedule. This huge campus, like a foreign city with secret pathways, made me feel so alone. I enviously watched groups of friends who gathered in the quad, laughing with one another. They seemed perfectly formed, as if there were no room for another person. No room for me.

The summer semester drew to a close, and I still wandered around campus like an outsider. I talked to my parents about living in the dorms because it seemed like a good way to meet people, but I knew we couldn't really afford it. I realized I had to change my expectations for school. It would have to be a place to work, not a place to socialize. My fall schedule would be arranged for maximum efficiency: into classes, out of classes, then into my car for the long drive home. That schedule, however, was a pipe dream. I ended up with a dreaded two-hour break between classes every afternoon.

At first, I spent that time at the library studying and feeling miserable. But one day everything changed. There were hordes of people and no tables left in the cafeteria, so I went upstairs in search of a quiet place to eat and read. I passed by a lounge area, heard a familiar voice, and did a double-take. There, larger than life, was Bo! He had always been one of my favorite characters on *Days of Our Lives,* a soap opera I used to watch with my grandma. A dozen or more people were gathered around a big screen TV, laughing and talking. Pizza in hand, I settled in a chair at the back of the lounge and caught up with the lives of my favorite characters from the city of Salem.

Each day I went to the Union to watch *Days of Our Lives.* And each day, familiar faces appeared on the screen—and in front of it! This group of people tuned in Monday through Friday, and they were obviously having a good time. They joked about the characters, made bets about what would happen next, and seemed to be having a great time. I wanted to get to know them better, but I felt like I'd be butting my way in, so I stayed a safe distance in my comfy armchair.

A few weeks after I discovered the group, a woman, Kim, came up to me and said, "Can you clear up a bet we're having? I say that Carrie's been on the show for a long time, but Julie says she just started a few years ago. Do you know?" I thought for a moment and said, "Well, she was on the show when I first started watching. Let's see, I was around ten, so that was in '87 or so. Yeah, she's been on there a long time!" Kim smiled, thanked me, and asked me if I wanted to sit closer to the TV. As I picked up my soda and backpack, she introduced me to the group. "Guys, this is Terri, and she's one of us!"

Since then, I've been joining these fans for my daily dose of *Days.* I've made some life-long friends in the group, especially Kim who is also a computer science major. We have fun, share our *Days* trivia, and hang out together. I finally feel like I belong here!

When her teacher first discussed ethnographic strategies for inquiry, Terri felt confused about choosing a local culture for her research. New to the university and college life, Terri considered herself an independent person who didn't join clubs. As she began her inquiry, she was stumped. If she didn't belong to any student or work organizations, what did she know or care enough to write about? The answer came when she shared her initial questioning strategy with her writing group, Justin and Amy. By talking with them and seeing their list of possible subjects and issues, she realized she had a rather limited definition of what counted as a local culture. Her aerobics class, fellow computer majors who attended an introductory computer programming course, her group of friends who met everyday in the Student Union to watch their favorite soap opera—each could be considered a local culture because each group shared identifiable values, beliefs, and behaviors. As she discussed this insight with her group, Justin remarked, "Wow. You're a computer major, and you watch soaps? I thought only dippy people watch those shows!" This honest comment sealed Terri's decision: She would write about her group of friends who watched *Days of Our Lives* together, and she would address stereotypes about soap opera fans. Launching into her writing with enthusiasm, Terry used the questioning strategy to understand why people's belittling attitudes toward soaps bothered her so much.

Terri's Questions

My Local Culture:

My group of friends who meet everyday at the Union to watch *Days of Our Lives*. We are true soap fans who know everything about the show, but the way people stereotype us as sappy pushovers is really annoying.

My Experience	*My Values*	*Cultural Sources*	*Dissonance*
I meet with friends to watch Days every afternoon. It's a blast!	I value friendships, and I have made wonderful, close friends through *Days*.	Sharing interests helps you make friends, and we all love and know a lot about *Days*.	I only feel dissonance about people who don't understand our love of *Days* and think that my friends and I are "sappy" losers.
I sometimes feel self-conscious about watching *Days* in the Union. People walk by and say rude things like, "We could start a riot if we changed the channel on them!"	I value being open-minded about people who have different interests and life-styles. I think it is bigoted to judge people you do not know!	My family taught me to be open-minded, and they also taught me that soaps are not stupid. My grandma and I watched soaps together after school when I was young.	People stereotype us because they think all soaps are for people who have no lives of their own. This is not fair. I wouldn't put down someone who enjoyed opera music!

My Writing Contexts:

- My friends who watch *Days* with me.
- People in this class who think that watching *Days* is a waste of time and who stereotype soap fans.
- My grandma, since she got me hooked on *Days* and would probably like to know that I think of her when I watch it.

My writing context will be the people in this class.

My Questions for Inquiry:

New Understanding: What does my *Days* group think of the stereotype that soap fans are "dippy" time wasters?

Cultural Sources: Why do people stereotype soap fans? Do they think that just because people watch a show, they take it seriously and accept the values in it?

Solution to the Problem: How can my *Days* culture change people's minds and let them know that soap fans are intelligent people?

When Terri shared her planning with her group, Amy and Justin could see the sources of her dissonance and agreed that her guiding questions were driven by real concerns and consequences. Justin noticed that Terri used his term, "dippy," to describe stereotypical attitudes, and he was concerned that he had offended Terri. Terri assured Justin that he wasn't alone in his attitudes, and Amy agreed that she also felt some skepticism for fanatic soap fans—such as her sister, who recorded *All My Children* while she was at work and watched it each evening. Amy and Justin's input helped Terri recognize that people had different reasons for belittling soaps and their fans, and she decided to focus on her first question for new understanding. She kept this in mind as she explored her experiences using the Three Perspectives Strategy. As she wrote down memories and considered her local culture from several perspectives, she realized that since she was so dedicated to her fellow *Days* fans, she would have to be careful to give the "skeptics' view" serious attention.

Terri's Exploration

Three Perspectives Guide

Describe and Distinguish

Characteristics of my local culture

- There are anywhere from 10 to 35 people who gather in the Student Union to watch *Days* of Our Lives. We are 17–20 years old, and about 3/4 of the viewers are women. We are all college students, and many of us live off campus, so the Union is really the only place to go between classes.

- We all meet in a big, open area of the Union where there is a large-screen TV. The couches and easy chairs in the area fill up quickly, and lots of people sit on the floor. Some of us get there early and chat about school and our lives. We also talk a lot about the show—who Sami (the evil woman) will trap next, what Bo (the handsome good guy) will do about his love-life, and, of course, what everyone is wearing! To anyone who didn't know us, we would probably look like a group of friends hanging out and catching up.

- Our group is very emotional about the show! We laugh and talk as the actors pull their stunts on the big-screen, and we talk back to them as if they could hear us. Sometimes we are rowdy, and sometimes we are quiet and moved by the story lines on *Days*. Some people even schedule their classes so that they can watch *Days* with their friends every afternoon!

- On the surface, our *Days* culture has only one purpose: to watch the show. But there are other reasons why we get together. We talk about the show, but we also talk about ourselves. This is a large campus, and it isn't easy to find people who share your interests. In some ways, watching *Days* is just an excuse to make friends. But we also get a welcome escape from the reality of school- and life-problems for an hour every day because we see people with worse lives than our own, and it makes us feel better.

Membership in the Days *culture*

- Since we watch *Days* in a public place, anyone can become a member of our group—that's the best thing about it! People who were *Days* fans before they came to college have passed by, seen the screen, and joined us. Some shy people will start by sitting in the back of the room, but soon they get to know other viewers, and a friendship is born! Some of us bring friends who don't know anything about *Days*, and we love filling them in on the show's history.

- There seems to be no hierarchy of power here. Sometimes people who know the most about *Days* (by having watched it for years or reading *Soap Opera Digest*) are listened to more than others, but not always. A sense of humor and ability to make witty remarks makes you stand out in the group, too.

Trace Moves and Changes

The history of the Days *culture and my participation in it*

- I'm not sure when people started watching *Days* at the Union. Some of the current members have been meeting there for at least three years. The purpose has pretty much stayed the same: to watch the soap, make friends, and have good conversation.

- My participation in this culture started when my friend, Kim, asked me to join them. That was almost three months ago. At first I was shy because Kim was the only person I knew. But now I chat with everyone, and I'm one of the resident experts because I've been watching *Days* since I was ten—it was my grandma's favorite soap, and we always watched it together when I got home from school.

- My feelings about the culture haven't changed except now I realize how many people cut down soaps and fans. They feel free to make nasty comments to us while we're watching. But we always either ignore them or make comments back. There's safety in a group, and we band together against rude skeptics.

Cultural changes that affect the Days culture

- *Days* has been on the air for a long time (at least ten years), and it is one of the most popular soaps today. In that time, many cultural changes have affected and probably been affected by *Days*. Morals, for example. As morals become looser, the soaps show racier love scenes. Also, issues like interracial marriage, homosexuality, alcoholism, divorce, rape, AIDS, and wife abuse have become more public in our society, and the soaps have shown people dealing with them. This is one of the best things about *Days*, though sometimes they handle them in unbelievable ways.

- *Days* might include sensational stories to keep people hooked and to get younger generations interested. They try to keep up with the times and the situations that most affect people today.

- One of the traditions of soaps is to show people in constant torment and really outrageous situations. Like a character who is pregnant with her sister's boyfriend's child. Members of the *Days* culture don't really take these story lines seriously, but they are so much fun to make fun of!

The future of the Days culture

- As long as *Days* keeps entertaining us, we'll be watching! Every year new students join us at the Union, and *Days* is as popular as ever.

Map Networks and Relationships

Cultures similar to the Days culture

- Other groups of college students who get together to watch their favorite shows are like our culture. I have a friend who watches *X-Files* every week with people from her dorm floor. They have the same kinds of values: to spend time with friends and have fun watching shows they can relate to.

Cultural values and their impact on my local culture

- All the controversial topics of the day are included in soaps: characters who have abortions, die from AIDS, fight breast cancer, and all the rest. It is good that they show people in these situations because it lets you see the problems from a different perspective. Sometimes they only use the controversies to get their ratings up, and I do think that's not right, but it's what everyone in Hollywood does, really. Whatever sells.

- Fashion trends affect how the characters dress. This is one of the things that I like about the soaps, seeing all the gorgeous clothes and jewelry. It does get on my nerves when they show a girl who works as a waitress, but she wears all of these expensive clothes. But that's all part of the fantasy.

- Negative attitudes about soaps are probably caused by the fact that they were originally for women who didn't have outside jobs and were home during the day to listen to the radio. Soap operas are called that because soap companies sponsored them, and most of the commercials during the soaps are still aimed at women. It's like the soaps are emotional and "sappy" so guys wouldn't watch them. Or like they insult your intelligence because they are sensationalist, but so are most action movies today!

- I guess the only institutional practice that affects the *Days* culture at the Union is the business of soaps—how they want big ratings for the companies that advertise during the shows, etc. I don't know much about this yet.

After reading Terri's exploration, Amy and Justin began to understand why Terri enjoyed and defended the *Days* culture—it did sound like fun and a great way to make friends. As they helped one another identify significant issues in their explorations, Amy offered Terri an important insight: While Terri's original guiding questions concerned only the dissonance she felt about outsiders' views of soap fans, her exploration revealed that she also felt dissonance about the soaps themselves—such as their treatment of controversial issues, their "anything for ratings" attitude. Terri's instructor also commented on this dissonance; she found it odd that though one of the local culture's objectives was to "escape from reality," the soaps seemed to be addressing very real issues, like AIDS. Didn't this seeming contradiction affect members of the *Days* culture and their enjoyment of the soap? Terri found these insights valuable and decided to account for them as she continued her research.

Facing the difficulties of most participant/observer researchers, Terri knew that it would be a challenge to take close observation notes of the *Days* culture. She could easily lose herself in conversations with her friends and the characters' latest dilemmas. She developed two strategies to help her concentrate on the task of observing. First, she decided to sit at a small distance from the group. Second, she decided to articulate the issues she wanted to address through her observations: how the setting of the Union affected the *Days* culture, what personality characteristics the group shared, how members responded to *Days*' characters and story lines, what their responses say about their morals and values, and how outsiders responded to *Days* viewers. Terri observed the *Days* culture on three occasions to gather a variety of data.

Excerpts from Terri's Observations

Friday, Student Union: First observation visit

The group gathers around the big-screen TV upstairs in the Union. There are two couches and about ten chairs surrounding the TV, and they are full, so some people are sitting on the floor in front of the couch. There are 16 *Days* fans watching today. 12 are women, 4 are men, and all are students. Some live off campus and don't have time to get home to watch *Days,* but others just go to the Union because they can get lunch to eat while the show is on. Some people are sitting at tables and in chairs at the back of the room, but they are not here to watch the show.

As I take notes, some of my friends ask me what I'm writing down, and I tell them about my project. Kim begs me to interview her, and everyone thinks this is a great research project. They all want to help me with it.

Everyone is chatting about their classes, their lives, and their favorite *Days* stories and characters. Julie walks around taking a poll on who the cutest *Days* guy is. Everyone says Bo. Once the show starts, people settle down to watch and get very involved. At first they are quiet, but they soon start to whisper comments and jokes about the characters. When a bad character gets into a car wreck, a few people cheer and say she deserved it. They call her a -itch and say it would be good if she died. A few of the die-hard fans in front give them a dirty look. During the commercials, people run to get sodas or talk more about the characters. Most of the fans like Carrie (an actor about our age), and they talk about how great her clothes and hair are.

When the show comes back on, there is a love scene between two characters who are in their 50's. Kim and Jamie yell out that it is disgusting to see old people kissing, and that they should get off the screen. Some people laugh, and others hiss "Shhhhhh!" Joe asks them what happened to their sense of humor.

As we are talking this way, a few students walk by our group during the show and laugh at us. One guy who was reading at the table behind us starts a sarcastic running commentary on the show. He probably feels we are keeping him from studying, but his comments are very obnoxious, like "Oh, kiss me, kiss me, Sami!" We all quiet down to try to hear *Days,* and Julie walks up to him and politely asks him to be quiet, but he just laughs. He leaves during the next commercial.

When the show is almost over, people begin putting stuff in their backpacks, and some people have to leave early to make it to class on time. The rest of us sit and talk about the show a while longer, or we go downstairs to have lunch together.

Analysis: This is a typical day for the Days *culture. There were only 16 people present, but that is because it is a Friday, and some people have Mon /Weds/ Fri classes during* Days*.*

The setting

The Union is the most logical place for students to relax between classes. This setting is great because the TV is large, and the couches are comfy. I also think there is some fun watching the soap in public. The *Days* group has grown because of word of mouth, and many people migrated there because they just happened to pass by and see us watching. It's safety in numbers: you don't feel so foolish watching a soap that people put down if you watch it with a large group of people.

The fans and the mood of the group

- It was typical that people asked me what I was doing, encouraged me, and offered their help. I am not good friends with everyone in the *Days* culture, but we all smile at each other when we pass on campus. I think it again relates to the ways that soaps are put down—we band together.

- People were very emotional about the show. Yelling back at the screen and the characters—especially if they are bad guys—is typical. We get hooked by the never-ending story lines. The majority of the members have been watching the show since they were young, so they know a lot about it.

- I never noticed before how cultural attitudes affect the way people respond to the show. When Kim and Jamie got disgusted just because a love scene was between two older characters, I was disappointed in them. But really, I think they had that kind of response not just because they are young, but because the love scene was very intense and emotional. As I think about it, whenever there is a love scene (some are pretty explicit), someone has to break the tension with a joke. I think it's hard to watch something that intense in public without feeling uncomfortable and embarrassed. A joke makes the atmosphere lighter.

Outsiders' comments and interruptions

I guess to a certain extent, you can expect some interruptions from skeptics since we meet in a public place. As I was observing, I realized that members of the *Days* culture made more negative comments about the show than people passing by or the guy at the back of the room, but our comments are different. We say them to show how much we know and to entertain each other. We're not bashing the show when we cheer if a bad character gets what she deserves—we're just really into the show. The guy in the back who made all those comments was making fun of the love scenes and how emotional the characters were. The content of soaps can be unbelievable at times—especially if you don't get hooked on the stories. I can understand why people make fun of characters who constantly come back from the dead. (Stephano on *Days* has "died" too many times, and he keeps coming back with an amnesia or kidnapping excuse!) These things just don't happen in everyday life, but we still love the shows because they provide an escape from our everyday problems. It's no different from how unrealistic a James Bond movie is, but it's easier to make fun of soaps because they're on TV.

On the two other occasions when Terri observed the *Days* culture, she encountered similar behavior, and she started noticing resurfacing themes for analysis: the group seemed to form its identity and closeness in reaction to skeptics who ridiculed the soaps; watching *Days* in the Union provided a public forum for the group to perform for each other and those skeptics; and the group's ironic and humorous commentary was meant to entertain friends and show how much a viewer knew about the show, rather than to belittle the soap and its fans. When Terri, Justin, and Amy shared their observations and analyses, they helped each other look critically at their local cultures by asking pointed questions and offering alternative ways to analyze each culture's behavior and values. Justin noticed that most of the vocal skeptics Terri observed were male, and he wondered if the male soap fans reacted differently from the female fans; he explained that he'd always thought of soaps as women's shows and was surprised that as many as 10 guys were members of the *Days* group. Amy agreed, and asked if the story plots seemed to be more focused on women than men. She also wanted to know more about the group's values in terms of the story lines and controversial plots: did the soap's producers have to be careful not to go too far when dealing with controversial issues? In her library research, Terri decided to focus on these important issues as well as the resurfacing themes she identified while conducting her observations.

Terri was gratified to find over one hundred sources about soap operas in the library, but she also felt overwhelmed. She explained her dilemma to her instructor who suggested that Terri locate only those sources that would help her address her primary guiding questions that arose from her observation analyses. Terri decided to get information from both popular and academic sources to get background information on *Days,* to find out how soap producers make decisions about controversial story lines, if men and women have different attitudes about soap viewing, why so many people denigrate soaps, and why avid fans are dedicated to and defensive about their favorite shows. Including twelve sources in an annotated bibliography, Terri summarized and responded to each source, noting if it challenged her perceptions of the *Days* culture, if it included important quotes or facts, and if it would be useful in her ethnography. She chose to use MLA documentation format because she was familiar with it and found many sources from Humanities journals.

Excerpts from Terri's Annotated Bibliography

Davidson, Valerie. "Abortion, Homosexuality and Political Correctness." *Soap Opera Weekly* 22 Oct. 1996: 12+.

Davidson interviewed soap producers and writers who gave two reasons for presenting controversial topics like abortion, homosexuality, and AIDS: to educate their audience and to increase their ratings. The producers have to deal with pressures to be politically correct about depicting sexual scenes, alternative lifestyles, and characters of various nationalities, ethnicities, and disabilities. Davidson argues that the bottom line in depicting controversial issues is the soaps' revenue.

This article gave me a lot of information about behind-the-scenes decisions to use controversial topics in soaps. Soaps usually play it safe when showing controversy. Characters have only had abortions when they have been raped, and all of the AIDS victims on soaps have contracted the disease through heterosexual sex or IV's. I also found it interesting that there are some fanatic fans out there. When one *All My Children* character went into the Betty Ford clinic, hundreds of fans actually sent flowers to her! No one in my culture would go that far.

Lemish, Dafna. "Soap Opera Viewing in College: A Naturalistic Inquiry."
Journal of Broadcasting and Electronic Media 29.3 (1985): 275–93.

This is a study of soap opera viewers who met in a public college location. The author wanted to understand their interaction with the soap and whether the soap's values affected the audience. Lemish identified four types of viewers—the leader, the follower, the observer, and the challenger—and argued that public soap opera viewing is a form of social interaction with specific etiquette rules. The story lines adjust to the social needs and interests of younger audiences. Soap operas help viewers learn about controversial issues from a human perspective, but young audiences might get a skewed idea about problems like abortion and AIDS because the soaps tend to be conservative so they don't lose ratings.

I can't believe someone has done research like mine! It's great to know that others think soap cultures are important to understand. This article is very useful. I hadn't noticed that there are different types of soap viewers, but I will have to observe my group again to see who is the leader, etc. I also liked the way Lemish showed that the content of the soaps allows fans to gossip in harmless ways and establish social rules of behavior. I agree with Lemish about the way soaps talk about controversial issues, but at least they are getting the issues into the public eye.

Reviewing Terri's annotated bibliography, Amy and Justin shared her surprise that soaps had warranted so much study and discussion. Terry explained that she had learned a lot through her research, and she now realized how much soaps are influenced by larger cultural values and issues, such as traditional gender roles (for both viewers and soap characters) and the desire to make a profit. She felt more dissonance about the soaps than she had previously, and she could now understand why some people make fun of fanatic fans. The group suggested that Terri again observe the *Days* culture with these perspectives in mind, but Terri had beat them to the punch. Since she spent each afternoon with the *Days* culture, she had been re-observing them while she was compiling and reading her library sources. She noticed new patterns that both supported and challenged some of her sources' opinions. She noticed, for example, that Kim and Julie seemed to be "leaders" in the group—something she hadn't realized before.

Terri asked Amy and Justin's advice about choosing interviewees and creating interview questions. Since Terri's guiding questions had shifted to include the cultural values implied by controversial *Days* story lines, the way gender influenced viewing patterns and attitudes, and the social interaction of the group, Amy thought Terri should make decisions with these questions in mind. Justin suggested that Terri interview Kim or Julie, since they were leaders, and Joe, since he was one of the male regulars in the *Days* culture. Justin also offered to let Terri interview him, since he was an outsider to the culture, had been skeptical about it, but was trying to keep an open mind. Amy suggested that Terri interview a professor from Sociology or Communications who could offer expert opinions on how soaps influence viewers, but Terri decided against this; she had already gathered such perspectives through her library research. Terri's instructor agreed with her interviewee choices, and Terri set about developing interview questions that would capture each interviewee's knowledge and values about the *Days* culture.

Excerpts from Terri's Interviews

Kim H.: I interviewed Kim on Friday after *Days*. Kim is a leader in our group because she has been watching *Days* for years and knows a lot about it. She invites people to join the group, and she plans her class schedule so that she has a free hour during *Days*. Kim is a good friend, and I knew that she would give me honest and serious answers to my questions.

Q: **When and why did you begin watching *Days*?**

A: When I was about 8 and I visited my dad in the summer, my stepmom and I watched it together. We had a lot of fun talking about it, and I kept watching it. Now I know all about the characters' lives and histories. It's entertaining and a good way to forget everything for a few hours.

Q: **So you watch *Days* to escape from reality? Is that why you're hooked on it?**

A: Well, in the first place, I wouldn't say I'm addicted to it or anything. I don't go into withdrawal if I miss a day! It's more like it's a habit, and, yes, it does help me escape reality. But not because I take what happens on *Days* as real. Like Stephano—no one is going to accept that he has come back from the dead so many times as real! Part of the fun of soaps is the fantasy and the crazy story lines. You're not supposed to take it seriously. You're only watching it for entertainment.

Q: **Why do you watch *Days* in the Union rather than in a private place?**

A: Because we can do just about anything we want in the Union, and no one tells us to stop! Besides, it's a lot more fun watching it with a big group of people, and we can meet at the Union between classes and eat lunch while *Days* is on. I think we have made some good friends through *Days,* and it's not as much fun to watch it alone because you're expecting this person to make a snide comment or that person to laugh.

Q: **Many *Days* viewers get very emotional about the show. Why do you think that happens?**

A: Because most of the actors are really good looking! (Laughs.) I think we get emotionally involved because we really like the show. We can make fun of the characters who might remind us of people we know, and we can cry when someone dies or has problems similar to our own. It also has to do with the fact that we all watch it together. We laugh together and wonder what's going to happen next. We feel comfortable with each other.

Q: **When *Days* showed Kate and Victor in a love scene a few weeks ago, you said that seeing two older people kissing was "disgusting," and you yelled to get them off the screen. Why did you have that reaction?**

A: Was I that rude? (Laughs.) Well, I didn't mean it seriously. I was just trying to make people laugh because it was a pretty intense scene. It didn't really have anything to do with their ages.

Q: **According to Valerie Davidson, soap producers show controversial topics and story lines to increase their ratings. Do you watch the show for its controversies and tragic dramas?**

A: Sure. But *Days* isn't really as controversial as *All My Children* or some of the other soaps. It's pretty mild in comparison! I think it's more traditional—most of the time characters just fight over someone they love.

Q: **So you don't mind the fact that *Days* is out to get good ratings?**

A: Of course not. All shows want good ratings. *Days* educates people, too, about things like rape.

Q: **Soaps are often stereotyped as women's entertainment, and some scholars, like Diane Crispell, say that soaps show female characters as either victims or evil people. Do you agree?**

A: I suppose. I mean, part of the fun is that you have these people who are almost real, but not quite. You have to have your evil Sami's and your good Carrie's! In soaps, the good person almost always wins in the end. You just have to wait forever to see it because of all the twists in the plot. I do think that most of the stories are geared to women, but not all of them. You also get to see things from a guy's perspective. Like Austin. He married Sami, even though he didn't love her, just so he could take care of his son.

Q: **Why do you think so many people put down soaps and fans?**

A: Lots of reasons. They probably can't understand how people could have so much fun with the soaps, and they think we're fanatics or something. They think soaps are dumb, so anyone who watches them must be dumb, too. But they don't bother me unless they get so rowdy that we can't hear the show. My friends like *Days,* and I like *Days,* and no one takes it too seriously.

Analysis of Kim's interview

Reasons for belonging to the *Days* Culture: Kim is a typical member of the *Days* culture. She has been watching the soap for a number of years, and she prides herself on knowing a lot about it. For Kim, *Days* isn't just a show; it's a chance to get together with friends and have fun. She uses *Days* as a social event, and her comments confirmed my ideas that the *Days* culture bands together against skeptics, and that's one of the things that makes us all closer.

Attitudes toward cultural values in *Days*: Kim's responses were kind of contradictory. She said she doesn't take the story lines or the show's values about gender or controversial topics seriously. It's "just entertainment." But then she said that the soaps educate viewers on things like rape and guys' perspectives on fatherhood. She acts like she just ignores the stereotypes that are in the soaps themselves, but that conflicts with what a lot of my library research says: that we learn about relationships, roles, and values by watching the soaps. I think it's true that *Days* does have stereotyped characters. Kim says that's what you expect from a soap, and I guess if you analyze them too much it does take some of the fun out of it.

Opinions about outsiders and skeptics: Kim says they don't bother her too much, but I've seen her get really upset when people put *Days* down. She takes it personally. It's not so much that she defends the show as an important cultural event, but when people put down *Days,* they are also putting down its fans. I think she's right when she says people make fun of soaps because they don't know enough about them or the people who watch them. If they took time to understand why people watch, they might end up with more open minds.

In her writing group Terri discussed the transcripts and analyses of her interviews with Kim, Joe, and Justin. Amy wondered if Kim's interview proved that avid *Days* fans tend to deny the soap's cultural values and their effects on viewers. Justin, who had visited the *Days* group after his interview with Kim, disagreed; he explained that the group made fun of *Days'* cultural values, especially the really outrageous story lines. But Amy held her stand and said she noticed the same trend in Joe's interview, which argued that no one took the soaps seriously. Because of Amy's insights, Terri could see that Joe and Kim shared similar values, and she realized that she had overlooked this issue because, as a member of the *Days* culture, it was hard to keep other perspectives about the group in mind. She knew, however, that she would have to address perspectives such as Amy's in her ethnography if she were to help people understand her fellow soap fans' values.

As Terri began the process of drafting her ethnography, she felt overwhelmed. Having gathered so much research data from so many sources, Terri was experiencing the effects of "information overload." She knew she had to make some important decisions about the information most important to include in her ethnography, but she wasn't sure where to begin. However, as she selected a genre, a research essay, and wrote her reader/writer positioning and focusing strategies, she began to hone in on her readers' needs and the most important questions she wanted to address.

Terri's Context and Focus

People in this class who think that soaps and soap fans are silly and living in a fantasy world. Since I know many of my classmates feel that way, I'll write to the skeptics among us.

Setting my writer position

I am a member of my writing context because I am a student in this class. Since I have presented positive perspectives about soap operas, however, some people probably think I'm dippy, and I'll have to be careful to emphasize my credibility by taking my topic seriously and presenting many different perspectives about it. I want to avoid sounding angry with the skeptics in this class—I want to take the position of an intelligent woman who wants to help people understand why so many college students, like myself, become avid soap fans.

Setting my reader position

I am addressing my ethnography mainly to skeptics in this class because if I can challenge some stereotypes about soaps, I think they won't be so quick to judge us fans. Since everyone here is a college student, I think they will value openness to new ideas and perspectives. I also think that, since this is a college context, my readers will value good research and getting a variety of opinions about soaps. I am going to assume that they will be open-minded—but only if I present the *Days* culture in an intelligent and mature way.

My tentative focuses

Subject	Point of significance
The *Days* culture at the Union ————————	uses the soap to make friends and entertain one another.
Negative perceptions of soap fans————————	are caused by cultural stereotypes about gender and the value of popular television.
The *Days* culture at the Union ————————	challenges stereotypes about soap fans.
Soap operas ————————————————	have both positive and negative effects on their audiences.

When she met with Amy and Justin to discuss her Focusing Strategy, Terri expressed dissatisfaction. None of her tentative focuses seemed to capture the complex relationships and issues she wanted to explore in her ethnography. Justin asked Terri which focus she thought came closest to the mark, and she explained that her third focus seemed best because her subject wasn't soaps in general but the *Days* culture in particular. The point of significance, however, was just too general. Amy agreed but thought that a general point of significance might be necessary in Terri's ethnography; a focus should provide her readers with cues about the author's opinions and the major topics for discussion, but it couldn't capture every nuance of an author's topic. The group worked together to develop a new focus: A close look at the *Days* culture at the Union reveals that college students view soap operas in creative ways which both challenge and uphold cultural stereotypes about soaps and their fans. Terri felt more satisfied with this focus because it concentrated on the *Days* culture of college students, emphasized their viewing habits, and acknowledged the contradictory attitudes and issues which Terri uncovered in her research.

In the process of creating their Organization Plans, Terri, Amy, and Justin devised a strategy to help them wade through their collected research and identify the information which would best help them support their focuses. They reviewed their explorations, observations, annotated bibliographies, and interviews, using highlighters in several colors to code the information which seemed most significant. As she color-coded her research, Terri saw five important issues emerge: the background and shared characteristics of the *Days* culture, the complexities of her participant/observer role, the emotional responses of *Days* fans, the reasons why many "outsiders" are so skeptical of soaps in general and the *Days* culture in particular, and the interesting ways *Days* fans both support and dispel stereotypes about soap fans. These categories were still fuzzy in Terri's mind, but they gave her a place to start developing her organizational plan.

Terri's Organization Plan

An Ethnography of *Days of Our Lives* Viewers

Rationale:

- Introduce readers to *Days* group and its purposes.
- Explain questions for my research:

  Why did the people in the group begin watching soap operas, and why have they continued watching?

  What characteristics does the viewing audience share?

  Why has the atmosphere of the Union worked so well for the group?

  Why do so many outsiders of the group make fun of soap operas? How do soaps and their fans both support and challenge society's stereotypes about daytime drama?

- *Explain my focus:* A close look at the *Days* culture at the Union reveals that college students view soap operas in creative ways which both challenge and uphold cultural stereotypes about soaps and their fans.

Participant/observer role:

- Why I am an avid fan and how I made really good friends through the *Days* culture.
- How I have endured criticism for my devotion to soaps.
- Difficulties in observing and interviewing my friends.

Analysis:

- The characteristics group members and other viewing audiences share:

  students, friends; male-female ratio; length of viewing

  research on primary and secondary viewers (Lemish)

- Cultural influences that entice college students to start watching soaps:

  reasons for watching and soaps' appeal to young people (Lemish)

  soaps as a female entertainment form (Crispell and Waldrop and interview with Joe)

- Why viewers become emotionally attached:

  relating to lives of the characters (Kennedy)

  habit and addiction

  learning from soaps (Kennedy, Boeck & Vancura, Kim's interview)

- Why outsiders make fun of soap operas and fans:

  Stereotypes about fans and soaps (Justin's interview, Davidson)

  Stereotypes in soaps themselves (Davidson, Olsen, Joe and Kim's interviews)

  What fans do and don't believe about soaps

Days is a way to make friends and gossip.

Concluding remarks
- Overview of my findings and why I will continue watching
- Quote from Buckman on why soaps are positive

In their group, Terri, Amy and Justin talked over their Organization Plans, and Terri got some good ideas by reviewing her group members' strategies. She asked for advice about the Analysis section of her plan. It seemed skewed, not quite right to her, but she couldn't come up with an alternative. Justin and Amy thought she was including some very important issues, but they were concerned about how this information would meet her readers' needs. If her readers were skeptics about the *Days* culture, and if one of Terri's aims was to dispel stereotypes about soap fans, shouldn't she begin with a discussion of those stereotypes, then challenge them throughout the paper? Terri's instructor agreed with the group's suggestions, but Terri was unsure about such a strategy. She thought it would be better to first let her readers get to know the members of the *Days* culture as people, then to bring up negative attitudes about them. In that way, she reasoned, some of the readers' stereotypes would be implicitly challenged as she explained her friends' values about and interests in *Days of Our Lives*. Terri decided to follow her original plan and to see if she came up with an alternative in the process of writing her ethnography. As she wrote her first drafts, she knew the ethnography wasn't clicking, and she was very frustrated. But she pushed on and just got her central ideas about the *Days* culture down on paper. She shared her most polished draft with Amy, Justin, and her instructor.

Terri's Polished Draft

An Ethnography of *Days of Our Lives*' Viewers

I belong to a group of *Days of Our Lives* viewers who meet Mondays through Fridays in an upstairs area of the Student Union. This area contains a television with many chairs and couches around it. I wanted to study this group because I wanted to learn more about the reasons people become such loyal and avid fans of soap operas. Everyone in this group is hooked on *Days* and the lives of each character. I wanted to know why the people in the group began watching soap operas and why they have continued watching. I wanted to know what characteristics the viewing audience shares and why the atmosphere of the Union has worked so well for the group. Lastly, I wondered why so many outsiders of the group make fun of soap operas and accuse the people who watch them of being "sappy" time-wasters. Are we really poisoning our hearts and minds every time we tune in to *Days*?

The *Days* culture has been watching their favorite soap at the Union for several years now, and since it is open to any individual who would like to watch *Days* with them, it keeps growing in size. About five million college students watch soap operas at least once a week (Kissinger 100).

Days, which has been capturing the hearts of Americans for over thirty years, is especially popular among college students, and it is the number-one soap among 18 to 48 year-old women ("Nielsens" 9). The objectives of the group are to relax and enjoy their one hour of escaping from a hard day of classes. The group members also enjoy talking with one another about their problems, their day, and their show. As a member, and through observation, I have learned that we see the show as our own, as part of the *Days* of our lives. A close look at the *Days* culture at the Union reveals that college students view soap operas in creative ways which both challenge and uphold cultural stereotypes about soaps and their fans.

My Role as a Participant/Observer

I am a religious *Days* of Our Lives viewer, and I have been since I was ten years old and would watch the show everyday after school with my Grandmother. I now go to the Union so I can watch my favorite show in the company of good friends and fellow soap opera fans. I got involved with the *Days* culture by chance. I was new to campus, and one day when I was searching for a place to eat lunch in the Union, I happened to hear a familiar voice. I looked around, and on a big screen was one of my favorite *Days* characters, Bo. Each day I returned to the Union to catch up on the happenings in Salem, the city where *Days* takes place, and I eventually met and became good friends with members of the *Days* culture. They have become my closest friends, and we study, talk, and have fun together.

As a member of this culture, the questions guiding my research focused mainly on the curiosity that I hold about the reasons viewers become so emotionally attached to these widely popular and disputed dramas. Also, as a group member, I have endured much criticism for my devotion to soap operas. So, another important question that haunted me about this culture was why so many people think that soap operas are socially unacceptable in modern times.

My role in the group and the regularity of the meetings made it fairly simple for me to observe the members of the group. One conflict that occurred in my observations was that it was often difficult to concentrate on the group members' behaviors when the show was in progress. It was easy to forget about working and to just enjoy myself because I was friends with all the other viewers. But once I shared my research with people that make up the *Days* culture, I found that they were more than willing to participate in my research, especially my interviews. That says something about how the *Days* group is: we are friendly and open to helping each other with school and everyday problems.

Analysis

What characteristics do the group members and other viewing audiences share?

Members of the *Days* culture have many shared characteristics. We are all college students between the ages of 17 and 21, and we all enjoy the friendship we have found in our daily habit of watching our favorite soap together. There are anywhere from ten to thirty-five people who gather in the Union, and most are young women. Recently, there have been many new members who were complete strangers to us before we bonded through our common link, *Days of Our Lives*. Since we watch *Days* in a public place, many people just gravitate to our group by passing the screen and seeing their favorite characters on it. Just about anyone can become a member of our culture—they just have to be friendly and willing to join in the fun that revolves around *Days*.

Most avid soap opera fans get very emotionally attached to their favorite characters and story lines, and our *Days* culture is no different. We cry, yell, and laugh at the characters and plots. According to Dafna Lemish, who conducted a study of college-aged soap opera fans, the behavior of the *Days* culture at the Union is not that different from other groups who watch soaps in public university places. Lemish found that many loyal viewers talk about their favorite television shows with great eagerness and interest. Lemish's research shows that viewing audiences in college campuses around the nation share certain characteristics. There are, for example, primary and secondary viewers (281). Primary viewers watch the same show in the same place everyday, and they give their favorite soap all of their attentions. Secondary viewers are those who talk, eat, or do homework around the television. Among primary viewers, Lemish identified four types: leaders, followers, observers, and challengers (281–3). Leaders are enthusiastic to share knowledge about the history of the show, eager to predict plot development, and they often argue with the television. Followers are active conversationalists who usually ask questions towards the leader. Often, leaders and followers were complete strangers before they settled in to watch their soap together. Observers rarely initiate conversation, and they tend to focus more on how leaders and followers act during the show. Finally, the challenger is a type of viewer who makes stereotypical, often hostile remarks. Seemingly, this is done to put down the other viewers in order to protect their own image by disassociating themselves from the soap opera (283).

Lemish's categories of viewers fit our group to a T. Though many members of the culture drift in and out, depending on their schedules each semester, there remains a core of leaders, followers, and observers. For example, Kim H. is a leader who plans her schedule around *Days,* and since she has been watching it for years, she often instigates bets about upcoming story plots, actors' histories, and other important facts about the show. People ask Kim questions, and she'll know or find the answer. I am a follower, to a certain extent. Like many other members of our culture, I like asking questions and talking about anything *Days!* Each member of our culture seems to play a role that they enjoy, and that strengthens their friendship with their fellow die-hard fans. Joe L., a long-time member of the *Days* culture, is also a leader in the group. He explained, "The Union is the perfect place for our group, because we can do just about anything and nobody tells us to stop!" For Joe, this means cracking jokes throughout the show and making comments about what the women on the show look like. The other guys all laugh along with him.

What cultural influences entice college students to watch soap operas?

There are four primary motives for watching soap operas: exploring reality, escaping and releasing stress, entertaining and relaxation, and interacting socially (Lemish 276). The influences of mothers, grandmothers, aunts, friends, and even baby-sitters cause people to start watching. Kim, for example, started watching based upon her step-mother's influence and Joe L. started watching when he began dating his girlfriend, Julie. The content of soap operas stresses language and story lines that are alluring to young adults. This proves that soaps have adjusted to the interests of younger audiences, who have specific social needs. CBS recently launched a six-million dollar campaign to have people travel to colleges and deliver the message that it is "cool" to watch CBS soaps (Kissinger 100). When this much money is put into advertising to young people, you know that soaps are trying to cater to young viewers' interests.

As communications expert Austin Barbrow argues, young people enjoy soaps because of the social interaction of their peer groups; college-age viewers don't always watch their soaps in isolation the way that older soap audiences who were mainly stay-at-home housewives did (172). Soaps are not considered to have an audience including men in our society. However, the average daytime drama audience is comprised of a nearly 30 percent male audience (Crispell and Waldrop 30). Despite this fact, the majority of issues soap operas concentrate on are portrayed from a woman's point of view, and most of the advertisements on during afternoon soaps are directed toward a female audience. In an interview, Joe L. explained that it can be uncomfortable being a male viewer. First, the commercials during the soaps are sometimes embarrassing to him. But mostly, people look at him strangely or think there is something wrong with him when he sits with the *Days* group and yells at the screen. Joe, however, has come to enjoy the humorous story lines in the soap, and he tries not to let skeptics bother him. "I think a guy today can watch soaps and not be afraid about his masculinity. A lot of the guys on soaps are strong and good-looking, and it's also a lot of fun to check out the good-looking actresses and their love scenes." (I wonder how Julie would respond to that comment!)

Such a large percentage of male viewers would probably surprise many people who stereotype soap fans as sappy females. Though the content of daytime television is primarily for women, it by no means excludes a male audience!

Why have many viewers become so emotionally attached to *Days*?

The members of the *Days* culture become emotionally attached to the lives of the characters. We get so worked up over the show that we yell at the television. With her typical sense of humor, Kim suggested that the main reason for this attachment is that the actors are "really attractive." But when I pushed her to explain more, she said,

"I think we get emotionally involved because we really like the show. We can make fun of the characters who might remind us of people we know, and we can cry when someone dies or has problems similar to our own. It also has to do with the fact that we all watch it together. We laugh together and wonder what's going to happen next. We feel comfortable with each other."

Kim's comments echo what many soap opera experts say. As Lemish says, college students often watch soap operas because of the social interaction. Perse and Rubin, who studied why audiences get satisfaction from their favorite soaps, say that the way you feel about a certain show is related to your prior expectations and activity before you watch it (368). In other words, since Kim enjoyed watching *Days* with her step-mom, she has come to think of the soap as a never-ending story which she can share with other people. She doesn't really *believe* the truth of all of the plots and characters' actions. They are just a way of connecting with friends about her "friends" on the screen.

After the *Days* fans get to know a character, we feel like they are just like one of our own friends (or enemies). If a "good" character suddenly commits a crime, for instance, we are shocked and in disbelief. Most soap fans blame the show's writers for this kind of situation (Kennedy 48). That shows that we are not people who "have no life and want to experience something else." This was said by Justin P., a soap skeptic, when I asked him what he used to think about soap fans. Instead, we just like the experience of getting into a story and relating with some of the problems and joys that the soap characters experience. Lisa Kennedy, writer for the *Village Voice*, says, "Who needs existentialism or Freud's 'Mourning and Melancholia' to make ourselves familiar with loss? Who, when we could simply tune in tomorrow." This almost sarcastic remark supports my research that there is no harm in having some fun in a different world, the world of daytime drama. We do have lives of our own that we learn from, but we also learn through watching others deal with the conflicts of life.

Soap fans are also educated by the topics featured on their favorite daytime dramas. A *USA Today* chart called "Fans Say Soaps Educate, Too" was compiled by Scott Boeck and Cliff Vancura. They compiled statistics on the top issues that soap fans have learned about or changed their opinions on, including AIDS, rape, breast cancer, alcohol, spousal abuse, and interracial relationships. This has been true in our group. Joe, for example, said that when he watched a character go through a drug problem a few years ago, he could relate to it. He had a friend in junior high school who got hooked on drugs. Joe said that *Days* portrayed the situation so well he wished he had seen it while he was in junior high because he probably could have recognized his friend's problem and helped him sooner. It is true that some soaps present controversial topics like drug abuse, homosexuality, and abortion just to keep their ratings up. Valerie Davidson, a writer for *Soap Opera Digest*, argues that the bottom line in depicting controversial issues is ratings and revenue (14). She shows that soaps usually play it safe when featuring "hot topics." For instance, characters only have abortions when they have been raped, and all of the AIDS victims on soaps have contracted the disease through heterosexual sex or through IV's, not through homosexual sex (13). Still, as

Joe's example shows, soaps still educate their viewers, and that is one reason the *Days* group gets so emotionally involved in the soap.

Why do so many outsiders of the group disagree with and make fun of soap operas?

The content of daytime dramas can be unbelievable at times. They are stereotyped as having a circle of love, marriage, adultery, murder, and death. *Days* is no exception. One character, Stephano, has "died" several times, but he always returns to the show with stories of amnesia or kidnapping. It is understandable why this kind of unrealistic plot would make non-fans even more skeptical about avid fans' devotion to soaps. But there is more to the hatred that some people feel for soaps—and for our group. People feel free to walk by us as we're watching *Days* and to make rude comments or laugh at us. On one day when I observed the group, a student who I didn't recognize was making a sarcastic running commentary on the show, saying things like, "Kiss me, kiss me Sami" about a character who was telling her boyfriend how much she loved him. When Julie, a *Days* fan, politely asked him to be quiet, he just laughed and continued making rude comments until he finally left. What could cause this kind of rude behavior?

Justin, the soap skeptic I referred to before, told me that he thought too many soap fans were out of touch with reality: "I thought that they watched soaps to escape from reality, and I have to say that I thought most people who are addicted to soaps are not too bright."

It is true that some soap fans take it too far. For example, when a character on *All My Children* was portrayed with a drinking problem and eventually checked into the Betty Ford clinic, dozens of fans actually sent flowers to the show (Davidson 12)! Now, this is not normal behavior, but considering how many people watch soaps, those who sent flowers were a small percentage of the viewing audience. While those who did are out of touch with reality, most fans do not actually believe the story lines in soaps. As Kim said, *Days* does help her escape the reality of school pressures for one hour a day. But, she explained, "Part of the fun of soaps is the fantasy and the crazy story lines. You're not supposed to take [*Days*] seriously, you're only watching it for entertainment."

This is not to say that soaps do not have an effect on their audiences. Beth Olsen determined that many soaps portray sexual issues in a very romantic and, therefore, dangerous way. She determined that soap opera viewers may be more likely to ignore the need for contraception and protection against sexually transmitted diseases and are more likely to believe that active sexual behavior is appropriate for unmarried partners (107). People who watch television shows can't help being influenced by them. But the fact is, no matter what show you watch on TV, you will be somehow affected by it, whether it is a morning news show, an evening sit-com, or an afternoon drama. Soaps are in the business of making money, so they are going to give audiences what they want: sex, romance, and intrigue.

I think the problem is that skeptics have the reasons why soap audiences want these things all wrong. The *primary* thing that *Days* viewers get out of the soap is friendship. We build relationships with each other by sharing the *Days* experience, whether it is a sad story or a ridiculous and funny one. Peter Buckman, who wrote *All For Love: A Study in Soap Opera,* found that many soap fans use their favorite shows as relationship-builders. True, they immerse their own problems in someone else's for a short period of time, but they also use soaps as an opportunity to gossip about characters, make sense of their own experiences, and build friendships (210). This challenges the stereotype that soap fans are not living in reality or that they believe everything they see on TV.

For example, one day when I observed the *Days* culture, the show featured a woman who got into a car wreck. The character was an evil person who had caused a lot of pain to many other good people in Salem. When the car wrecked, cheers went up among the *Days* fans. Joe yelled, "I hope she dies! She deserves it!" Everyone laughed and agreed.

Now, to an outsider, this scene would probably make them think that we actually believed what was happening on the show. But that is not the case. We were making fun of the show and the character, and we were bonding together in our agreement that she deserved her car wreck. As Joe explained the situation, "When we yell at the TV, it's not because we actually believe the scene is real. Yeah, sometimes certain characters remind you of people you know, and you react. But the main reason is that we like to entertain each other. Sometimes it's like a contest who can make the most humorous remark."

In other words, we band together when we are watching the soap, and each comment or response from a fan reflects his or her personality. Joe compared it to being at a football game. When you yell about a play, you don't really expect the coach to hear you or take your advice. You are just letting off steam and showing off in front of your friends.

Both Kim and Joe said that it doesn't bother them when people make fun of them and other *Days* fans. But I disagree. It puts a damper on our group when people feel like they can put us and our soap down. We are loyal fans, but it's not just *Days* we are defending: It is our friends who watch soaps, and it is ourselves. We are not sappy people, out of touch with reality. We are friends who are having fun in front of the TV screen.

Conclusion

I have shown that soap opera fans have many reasons for tuning in to their daily doses of drama. The negative images of soap fans are everywhere, but with education, skeptics can learn to reevaluate their stereotypes. Justin experienced this. When I first told him that I was interested in *Days of Our Lives,* he was surprised because he didn't think computer science majors like me would be interested in soaps. But as we talked and he started to understand more of the reasons why *Days* fans are fans, he started changing his perspectives. I think more people should do the same and not be so quick to judge soap fans. As Buckman states,

"Soaps are a phenomenon, but that does not make their audiences freaks. The audience becomes not simply viewers and listeners, but story tellers too" (200). We can learn a lot from the theme to *Days*:

Like sands through the hourglass,
so are the *Days* of our lives.

In other words, life is too short to stereotype people!

Works Cited

Barbrow, Austin S. "An Expectancy-Value Analysis of the Student Soap Opera Audience." *Communication Research* 16 (1989): 155–78.

Boeck, Scott and Cliff Vancura. "Fans Say Soaps Educate, Too." *USA Today* 15 May 1995: 1.

Buckman, Peter. *All For Love: A Study in Soap Opera*. Salem, North Carolina: Salem House, 1994.

Crispell, Diane, and Judith Waldrop. "Daytime Dramas Demographic Dreams." *American Demographic* Oct. 1988: 29–31, 58.

Davidson, Valerie. "Abortion, Homosexuality, and Political Correctness." *Soap Opera Weekly* 22 Oct. 1996: 12+.

H., Kim. Personal Interview. 27 Oct. 1996.

Kennedy, Lisa. "Days and Confused." *Village Voice* 8 Feb. 1994: 48–49.

Kissinger, David. "CBS Hopes Soaps Wash at College." *Variety* 3 Sept. 1990: 1, 100.

Lemish, Dafna. "Soap Opera Viewing in College: A Naturalistic Inquiry." *Journal of Broadcasting and Electronic Media* 29.3 (1985): 275–93.

L., Joe. Personal Interview. 30 Oct. 1996.

"The Nielsens." *Soap Opera Weekly* 22 Oct. 1996: 9.

Olsen, Beth. "Soaps, Sex, and Cultivation." *Mass Communication Review* 21.1-2 (1994): 106–113.

P., Justin. Personal Interview. 26 Oct. 1996.

Perse, Elizabeth M. and Alan M. Rubin. "Audience Activity and Satisfaction with Favorite Television Soap Operas." *Journalism Quarterly* 65.2 (1988): 368–75.

When Terri met with Amy and Justin, she explained her concerns about her draft: it felt jumbled, and as she reviewed it, she wondered if her readers would be able to get a vivid picture of the culture and its members. She knew she had included some good information, but she wasn't sure if she had arranged it well enough to support her focus. She told Amy and Justin that writing the ethnography was like pulling teeth; she had to force herself to get each word down. Amy said that all writing was that way for her, but this process was even more difficult because she was so close to her local culture. Amy, Justin, and Terri traded their drafts and wrote reader responses for one another.

Compiled Reader Responses to Terri's Draft

Reader Response Guide

Overall Response

Amy: The beginning was kind of hard to follow, but you really get rolling near the end when you discuss skeptics and argue against them.

Justin: I learned a lot from your paper. Since I am one of your readers, I felt like you did convince me that I need to stop stereotyping soap fans.

Instructor: I can see that you've put a lot of hard work into this ethnography! You include some great information, but I didn't really get a vivid picture of the *Days* culture in action. Remember, such vivid descriptions are a central aim of ethnographic research.

Focus

Amy: Very good focus because it shows your need to let readers know they shouldn't stereotype fans.

Justin: "A close look at the *Days* culture reveals . . ." Good focus!

Instructor: Your focus attends to the local culture's values and structure. But you don't really follow the focus throughout the ethnography because it's not clear what stereotypes you are trying to challenge until the end of the paper. If you are trying to persuade readers that their stereotypes are wrong, you need to use your descriptions of the local culture to support your *claims* about the culture. Perhaps you might revise your focus to a more persuasive aim?

Development for Readers

Amy: You need to give more background information about the culture in your introduction. Your readers are skeptics of soap fans, but that doesn't show until the last two sections of your analysis. Good information from your research!

Justin: You use your interviews and library research well, but you don't really use your observations. You need to explain more what the culture is like on an everyday basis.

Instructor: Your introduction is underdeveloped. Your reader probably needs a glimpse of your local culture in action before you can begin dispelling stereotypes about *Days* viewers. Your participant/observer section seems to "float" in the ethnography. Can you connect it more to your focus? You have included some excellent research here (particularly from your interviews) and in certain sections (such as your "skeptics" section), I was impressed by the connections you made between that research and your focus. However, you need to make those connections explicit throughout the ethnography if you're going to convince readers that negative cultural assumptions about soaps lead to stereotypes about *Days* fans.

Organization and Coherence

Amy: Give more interesting heading titles. I think you need to show that you're trying to challenge negative ideas about soap fans in each section of your paper, so maybe each heading can mention one of those negative ideas.

Justin: Your questions for each section of the analysis were confusing because you don't really answer them. Like in your section on cultural influences that entice people to watch. You talk about Joe and gender there, but it doesn't seem to fit. Your best organized section is the last one.

Instructor: Restructuring your paper according to your persuasive aim will help you address your reader's needs here. Consider revising your headings to address the cultural assumptions which inform the various stereotypes about soaps which you are attempting to challenge. This should help you avoid repetitious information. E.g., you discuss sensational topics in the "emotionally" attached section, then again in the "skeptics" section. Why not have a separate section that addresses controversial story lines and the way the *Days* group responds to them?

Language Choices

Amy: Good! You seem very enthusiastic and proud to be part of the *Days* group.

Justin: Some of your sentences are long, and you repeat a lot of the same words.

Instructor: See my comments on your draft. It might be easier to make your sentences more concise after your revise your organization.

Conventions

Amy: Good job with MLA cites here. No problems that kept me from understanding what you have to say.

Justin: I fixed a lot of your commas on your paper.

Instructor See my comments on your draft. Very good use of MLA format.

Main Emphasis for Revision

Amy: Reorganize the paper to show what stereotypes there are and then show how the *Days* group meets or doesn't meet those stereotypes. More interesting headings.

Justin: Use your observation notes more so that your readers can understand what you guys do when you get together. Include more information from my interview! (ha)

Instructor: Clarify the persuasive aim of your ethnography by restructuring your paper according to the readers' stereotypes you want to dispel.

To prepare for her writing group's reader response workshop, Terri reread her paper, which she had set aside for several days. That incubation time was important, for it helped her re-see her paper and possibilities for revising it. Moreover, by reading Amy and Justin's ethnographies, Terri got some valuable ideas. For example, she decided to follow Justin's idea to have a separate section of the rationale devoted to describing the culture, its history, and its shared values. In class, Amy, Justin, and the instructor confirmed Terri's ideas for revision, and she was pleased with the advice she received from her group. She had put a lot of work in this paper, and she knew that she had included some good research. But she also knew that reorganizing the essay—as Amy had suggested previously—was her priority for revision.

When Amy and Justin helped Terri devise a new organization plan, they discussed Terri's ongoing dissonance about the soaps. Terri admitted, for example, that she was very disturbed about a study by Beth Olsen showing that soaps promote unsafe sexual practices. This was a very important issue for her readers, but Terri didn't think she had developed her response well enough. She told Amy and Justin that researching and writing about soaps had made her question soap's cultural values and their effects on viewers. But she wasn't sure how to express her doubts without undermining the strength of her argument. The group sought advice from their instructor, who explained that Terri should include her concerns in her ethnography. Such concerns wouldn't undermine her argument; they would make it stronger. As a member of her local culture, Terri could certainly acknowledge her dissonance about it. This would serve to bulwark her credibility and clarify her attitudes toward the *Days* culture. Terri began developing a revising plan based on the advice she had received.

Terri's Revising Plan

Focus: They thought my focus was clear; I just need to follow it more throughout the ethnography. I will keep in mind that my aim is to persuade my readers by describing the *Days* culture and making it more human, rather than stereotyped.

Development for Readers: My research is good, but I don't really relate it to college-age skeptics until later in the paper. I will try to make each section relate to my reader's needs. I will include more observations of my culture.

Organization: This is my big area that needs improvement. I'm going to reorganize the paper around the stereotypical attitudes some people might have about the *Days* culture. My sections will include: Getting to know the *Days* fans; why younger, college-aged viewers like soaps; stereotypes about viewers' gender; controversial topics in soaps; and claims that soap fans are out of touch with reality.

Language Choices: I will hold on to my enthusiastic tone and try to express more why the stereotypes are hurtful to me.

Conventions: I will proofread very carefully.

Priority for revision: Reorganizing the paper for my readers and giving more details about the people in the culture.

After developing her revising plan and explaining it to Amy, Justin, and her instructor, Terri began the process of revising her ethnography. This time, as she wrote, she felt much better about her work, the ideas she was expressing, and her relationship with her readers.

Terri's Revision

Days Culture at the Union

After the heart-wrenching departure of a beloved *Days of Our Lives* character, I looked around to see if anyone else was crying. As I suspected, everyone who huddled around the television appeared to be choked up. Joe and Julie were comforting each other by sitting very close, and Kim was groping for a tissue in her backpack. Angie caught my eye and offered me a consoling smile. Then someone in the crowd mumbled something about "soap-opera heaven," and we all laughed. We had lost ourselves in an hour of outrageous and moving drama, but now we were back in reality, packing our books, and heading in different directions to grab lunch or make it to class on time.

Every weekday afternoon over a dozen avid fans of *Days* meet in the student union to relax and enjoy an hour free from the worries of classes, jobs, and personal problems. We are in good company, because about five million college students watch soap operas at least once a week (Kissinger 100). *Days,* which has been capturing the hearts of Americans for over thirty years, is especially popular among college students, and it is the number-one soap among 18 to 48 year-old women ("Nielsens" 9). But some skeptics say that watching soap operas is for sappy time-wasters who poison their hearts and minds each time they tune in to an afternoon melodrama. It's not unusual for someone passing by to make a rude comment to the soap fans gathered around the TV. I think many people consider soap watchers to be fanatics who have lost all sense of reality and who are addicted to the trashy, mindless dramas of daytime television.

Because I am a member of those accused of being brainwashed everyday that I meet my friends to watch *Days,* I decided to investigate what I will call the "*Days* culture." A close look at the *Days* culture at the Union reveals that college students view soap operas in creative ways which both challenge and uphold cultural stereotypes about daytime dramas and their fans. As I observed this culture, I learned that we see the show as our own, as a part of the days of our lives.

My Experiences as a Participant/Observer

I am a religious *Days of Our Lives* viewer, and I have been since I was ten years old and would watch the show everyday after school with my Grandmother. I now go to the Union so I can watch my favorite show in the company of good friends and fellow soap opera fans. I am one of the many people who got involved with the *Days* culture by chance. They have become my closest friends, and we study, talk, and have fun together. As a member of this culture, I have endured much criticism for my devotion to soap operas. So, an important question that haunted me about this culture was why so many people think that soap operas are socially unacceptable in modern times.

My role in the group and the regularity of the meetings made it fairly simple for me to observe the members of the group. Sometimes it was difficult to concentrate on the group members' behaviors when the show was in progress. It was easy to forget about working and just enjoy myself. But once I shared my research with people that make up the *Days* culture, I found that they were more than willing to participate in my research, especially my interviews. That says something about how the *Days* group is: we are friendly and open to helping each other with school and everyday problems.

Tuning into the *Days* Culture

Let me introduce you to the members of this culture. We are college students between the ages of 17 and 21, and we all enjoy the friendship we have found through our shared interest: *Days of Our Lives*. Depending on the day of the week and people's class schedules, there are anywhere from ten to thirty-five people in our culture, and our numbers keep growing. Since we watch *Days* in the Student Union, many people gravitate to our group when they walk by the large-screen TV and see their favorite soap characters on it. Just about anyone can be a member of our culture. They only have to be friendly and willing to join in the fun that revolves around *Days*.

If you passed the lounge where the *Days* culture meets, you would see a group of people congregating around a TV, laughing, and sometimes even yelling at the actors on the screen. According to Dafna Lemish, who conducted a study of college-aged soap opera fans, the behavior of the *Days* culture at the Union is not that different from other groups who watch soaps in public university places. Lemish found that many loyal viewers talk about their favorite television shows with great eagerness and interest, and his research shows that viewing audiences in college campuses around the nation share certain characteristics. There are, for example, primary viewers, who watch the same show in the same place everyday, and they give their favorite soap all of their attention; then there are secondary viewers who talk, eat, or do homework around the television (281). Among primary viewers, Lemish identified four types: leaders, followers, observers, and challengers (281–3). Leaders are enthusiastic to share knowledge about the history of the show, eager to predict plot development, and they often argue with the television. Followers are active conversationalists who usually ask questions towards the leader. Often, leaders and followers were complete strangers before they settled in to watch their soap together. Observers, on the other hand, rarely initiate conversation, and they tend to focus more on how leaders and followers act during the show. Finally, the challenger is a type of viewer who makes stereotypical, often hostile remarks. Seemingly, this is done to put down the other viewers in order to protect their own image by disassociating themselves from the soap opera (283).

Lemish's categories of viewers fit our group to a T. Though many members of the culture drift in and out, depending on their schedules each semester, there remains a core of leaders, followers, and observers. For example, Kim H. is a leader who plans her class schedule around *Days,* and since she has been watching it for years, she often instigates bets about upcoming story plots, actors' histories, and other important facts about the show. People ask Kim questions, and she'll know or find the answer. Joe L., a long-time member of the *Days* culture, is also a leader in the group. He explained, "The Union is the perfect place for our group, because we can do just about anything and nobody tells us to stop!" For Joe, this means cracking jokes throughout the show. I am a follower to a certain extent. Like many other members of our culture, I like asking questions and talking about anything *Days*! Each member of our culture seems to play a role that they enjoy, and that strengthens their friendship with their fellow die-hard fans.

We try not to let the challengers bother us during our show, but it is not always easy. People feel free to walk by us as we're watching *Days* and to make rude comments or laugh at us. On one day when I observed the group, a student who I didn't recognize was making a sarcastic running commentary on the show, saying things like, "Kiss me, kiss me Sami" about a character who was telling her boyfriend how much she loved him. When Julie, a *Days* fan, politely asked him to be quiet, he just laughed and continued making rude comments until he finally left. Kim says this kind of rude behavior doesn't really bother her, but I disagree. It puts a damper on our group when people feel like they can put us and our soap down. We are loyal fans, but it's not just *Days* we are defending: It is our friends who watch soaps, and it is ourselves. We are not sappy people, out of touch with reality. We are friends who are having fun in front of the TV screen. Maybe if more skeptics understood why members of the *Days* culture act as they do, they would be less likely to judge and stereotype us.

Escaping Reality?

One of the most common reasons people put down the *Days* culture is because they think avid soap fans are out of touch with reality. Justin, a friend who was a soap skeptic, expressed this opinion. "I thought that they watched soaps to escape from reality, and I have to say that I thought most people who are addicted to soaps are not too bright." Certainly escaping reality, along with relieving stress, relaxing, and socially interacting, is a reason people watch soaps (Lemish 276). But is escaping reality the same thing as believing everything you see on a soap?

For example, one day when I observed the *Days* culture, the show featured a woman who got into a car wreck. The character was an evil person who had caused a lot of pain to many other good people in Salem. When the car wrecked, cheers went up among the *Days* fans. Joe yelled, "I hope she dies! She deserves it!" Everyone laughed and agreed.

Now, this scene would probably confirm outsiders' suspicions that we actually believed what was happening on the show. But that is not the case. We were making fun of the show and the character, and we were bonding together in our agreement that she deserved her car wreck. As Joe explained the situation,

> When we yell at the TV, it's not because we actually believe the scene is real. Yeah, sometimes certain characters remind you of people you know, and you react. But the main reason is that we like to entertain each other. Sometimes it's like a contest who can make the most humorous remark.

In other words, we band together when we are watching the soap, and each comment or response from a fan reflects his or her personality. Joe compared it to being at a football game. When you yell about a play, you don't really expect the coach to hear you or take your advice. You are just letting off steam and showing off in front of your friends.

It is true that some soap fans take it too far. For example, when a character on *All My Children* was portrayed with a drinking problem and eventually checked into the Betty Ford clinic, dozens of fans actually sent flowers to the show (Davidson 12)! Now, this is not normal behavior, but considering how many people watch soaps, those who sent flowers were a small percentage of the viewing audience. While those who did are out of touch with reality, most fans do not actually believe the story lines in soaps. As Kim said, *Days* does help her escape the reality of school pressures for one hour a day. But, she explained, "Part of the fun of soaps is the fantasy and the crazy story lines. You're not supposed to take [*Days*] seriously, you're only watching it for entertainment."

The *primary* thing that *Days* viewers get out of the soap is friendship. We build relationships with each other by sharing the *Days* experience, whether it is a sad story or a ridiculous and funny one. Peter Buckman, who wrote *All For Love: A Study in Soap Opera,* found that many soap fans use their favorite shows as relationship-builders. True, they immerse their own problems in someone else's for a short period of time, but they also use soaps as an opportunity to gossip about characters, make sense of their own experiences, and build friendships (210). This challenges the stereotype that soap fans are not living in reality or that they believe everything they see on TV.

Women's Entertainment?

Typically, there are about four times more female than male members in the *Days* culture. And if you passed by the *Days* group, you would probably hear someone remarking how much she likes Carrie's hair or Marlena's outfit. On one day of observation, I heard fourteen comments about the actresses' fashions, home decor, and looks. This might make an outsider think that the old ideas that soaps are only for female audiences is true. Justin expressed this point by saying that men just aren't interested in the lovey-dovey stories on *Days*.

But the *Days* when soaps were only for lonely housewives are over. As communications expert Austin Barbrow argues, young people enjoy soaps because of the social interaction of their peer groups; college-age viewers don't always watch their soaps in isolation, the way that older soap audiences who were mainly stay-at-home housewives did (172). Most people don't think soaps have large male audiences. However, the average daytime drama audience is comprised of a nearly 30 percent male audience (Crispell and Waldrop 30). Despite this fact, the majority of issues soap operas concentrate on are portrayed from a woman's point of view, and most of the advertisements on during afternoon soaps are directed toward a female audience. In an interview, Joe L. explained that it can be uncomfortable being a male viewer. First, the commercials during the soaps are sometimes embarrassing to him. But mostly, people look at him strangely or think there is something wrong with him when he sits with the *Days* group and yells at the screen. Joe, however, has come to enjoy the humorous story lines in the soap, and he tries not to let skeptics bother him. "I think a guy today can watch soaps and not be afraid about his masculinity. A lot of the guys on soaps are strong and good-looking, and it's also a lot of fun to check out the good-looking actresses and their love scenes."

Such a large percentage of male viewers would probably surprise many people who stereotype soap fans as sappy females. Though the content of daytime television is primarily for women, it by no means excludes a male audience!

Do Soap Fans "Buy" It?

Members of the *Days* culture are very aware that soaps do everything they can to keep viewers tuned in. The story lines are alluring to young adults, and soaps have adjusted to the interests of younger audiences, who have specific social needs. CBS recently launched a six-million dollar campaign to have people travel to colleges and deliver the message that it is "cool" to watch CBS soaps (Kissinger 100). When this much money is put into advertising, you know that soaps are trying to cater to young viewers' interests. One way they do this is to show sensational and controversial plots.

Daytime dramas are stereotyped as having a circle of love, marriage, adultery, and murder. *Days* is no exception! For example, one character, Stephano, has "died" several times, but he always returns with stories of amnesia or kidnapping. It is understandable why this kind of unrealistic plot would make non-fans even more skeptical about avid fans' devotion to soaps. But many skeptics think that *Days* fans do not know that the show is out to make a profit. Joe, for example, says, "The more controversial a story line, the more fans get emotionally involved."

With her typical sense of humor, Kim suggested that the main reason for this emotional attachment is that the actors are "really attractive." But when I pushed her to explain more, she said,

> I think we get emotionally involved because we really like the show. We can make fun of the characters who might remind us of people we know, and we can cry when someone dies or has problems similar to our own. It also has to do with the fact that we all

watch it together. We laugh together and wonder what's going to happen next. We feel comfortable with each other.

Kim's comments echo what many soap opera experts, like Lemish, say: college students often watch soap operas because of the social interaction. Perse and Rubin, who studied why audiences get satisfaction from their favorite soaps, say that the way you feel about a certain show is related to your prior expectations and activity before you watch it (368). In other words, Kim enjoyed watching *Days* with her step-mom since she was a kid, and she has come to think of the soap as a never-ending story which she can share with other people. She doesn't really believe the truth of all of the plots and characters' actions. They are just a way of connecting with friends about her "friends" on the screen.

After we *Days* fans get to know a character, we feel like they are just like one of our own friends (or enemies). If a "good" character suddenly commits a crime, for instance, we are shocked and in disbelief. Most soap fans blame the show's writers for this kind of situation (Kennedy 48). That shows that we are not people who, as Justin said, "have no life and want to experience something else." Instead, we just like the experience of getting into a story and relating with some of the problems and joys that the soap characters experience. Lisa Kennedy, writer for the *Village Voice,* says, "Who needs existentialism or Freud's 'Mourning and Melancholia' to make ourselves familiar with loss? Who, when we could simply tune in tomorrow?" This almost sarcastic remark supports my research that there is no harm in having some fun in a different world, the world of daytime drama. We do have lives of our own that we learn from, but we also learn through watching others deal with the conflicts of life.

Fans like Kim say they don't mind that *Days* has sensational conflicts to get better ratings. "All shows want good ratings. *Days* educates people, too, about issues like rape and how to handle it." Research shows that soap fans do receive education about the topics featured on their favorite daytime dramas. A *USA Today* chart called "Fans Say Soaps Educate, Too" was compiled by Scott Boeck and Cliff Vancura. They compiled statistics on the top issues that soap fans have learned about or changed their opinions on, including AIDS, rape, breast cancer, alcohol, spousal abuse, and interracial relationships. This has been true in our group. Joe, for example, said that when he watched a character go through a drug problem a few years ago, he could relate to it. He had a friend in junior high school who got hooked on drugs. Joe said that *Days* portrayed the situation so well, he wished he had seen it while he was in junior high because he probably could have recognized his friend's problem and helped him sooner. It is true, however, that some soaps present controversial topics like drug abuse, homosexuality and abortion just to keep their ratings up.

Valerie Davidson, a writer for *Soap Opera Digest* argues that the bottom line in depicting controversial issues is ratings and revenue (14). She explains that soaps usually play it safe when featuring "hot topics." For instance, characters only have abortions when they have been raped, and all of the AIDS victims on soaps have contracted the disease through heterosexual sex or through IV's, not through homosexual sex (13). Still, as Joe's example shows, soaps do educate their viewers, and that is one reason the *Days* group gets so emotionally involved in the soap.

This is not to say that soaps do not have a negative effect on their audiences. Beth Olsen found out that many soaps portray sexual issues in a very romantic and, therefore, dangerous way. She determined that soap opera viewers may be more likely to ignore the need for contraception and protection against sexually transmitted diseases and are more likely to believe that active sexual behavior is appropriate for unmarried partners (107). Her findings are very troubling because sexually transmitted diseases and unwanted pregnancy are two of the most important problems facing young people, like those in the *Days* culture, and people who watch television shows can't help being influenced by them. But the fact is, no matter what show you watch on TV, you will be somehow affected by it, whether it is a morning news show, an evening sit-com, or an afternoon drama. Soaps are in the business of making money, so they are going to give audience's what they want: sex, romance, and intrigue. I suspect that those are things soap skeptics want too, but they get them from Jean Claude Van Damme movies or rock music videos!

Conclusion

I have shown that soap opera fans have many reasons for tuning in for their daily doses of drama. The negative images of soap fans are everywhere, but with education, skeptics can learn to reevaluate their stereotypes. Justin experienced this. When I first told him that I was interested in *Days* of Our Lives, he was surprised because he didn't think computer programming majors like me would be interested in soaps. But as we talked and he started to understand more of the reasons why *Days* fans are fans, he started changing his perspectives. I think more people should do the same and not be so quick to judge soap fans. As Buckman states, "Soaps are a phenomenon, but that does not make their audiences freaks. The audience becomes not simply viewers and listeners, but story tellers too" (200). Members of the *Days* culture primarily watch to make and interact with friends, so watching the soap is a matter of socializing, not just believing everything they see or losing themselves in the unreality of *Days*' story lines!

The next time you pass by people watching a soap or overhear a conversation about the drama of soap characters' lives, it might help to keep in mind the theme to *Days*:

> Like sands through the hourglass,
> so are the *Days* of our lives.

In other words, life is too short to stereotype people!

Works Cited

Barbrow, Austin S. "An Expectancy-Value Analysis of the Student Soap Opera Audience." *Communication Research* 16 (1989): 155–78.

Boeck, Scott and Cliff Vancura. "Fans Say Soaps Educate, Too." *USA Today* 15 May 1995: 1.

Buckman, Peter. *All For Love: A Study in Soap Opera.* Salem, North Carolina: Salem House, 1994.

Crispell, Diane, and Judith Waldrop. "Daytime Dramas Demographic Dreams." *American Demographic* Oct. 8: 29–31, 58.

Davidson, Valerie. "Abortion, Homosexuality, and Political Correctness." *Soap Opera Weekly* 22 Oct. 1996: 12+.

H., Kim. Personal Interview. 27 Oct. 1996.

Kennedy, Lisa. "Days and Confused." *Village Voice* 8 Feb. 1994: 48–49.

Kissinger, David. "CBS Hopes Soaps Wash at College." *Variety* 3 Sept. 1990: 1, 100.

Lemish, Dafna. "Soap Opera Viewing in College: A Naturalistic Inquiry." *Journal of Broadcasting and Electronic Media* 29.3 (1985): 275–93.

L., Joe. Personal Interview. 30 Oct. 1996.

"The Nielsens." *Soap Opera Weekly* 22 Oct. 1996: 9.

Olsen, Beth. "Soaps, Sex, and Cultivation." *Mass Communication Review* 21.1–2 (1994): 106–113.

P., Justin. Personal Interview. 26 Oct. 1996.

Perse, Elizabeth M. and Alan M. Rubin. "Audience Activity and Satisfaction with Favorite Television Soap Operas." *Journalism Quarterly* 65.2 (1988): 363–75.

After reading Terri's revision, Amy and Justin congratulated her. Both agreed that the ethnography had changed some of their perspectives about soap operas and their fans. In a conference with her instructor, Terri explained that these compliments meant a lot to her, because she knew her group members were, at least initially, soap skeptics, so they were her intended readers. When Terri shared her ethnographic findings with her classmates and instructor, she explained that, while she had learned a lot in the process of her ethnographic research, she felt more dissonance about the *Days* culture—especially concerning the cultural values the soap presented—after writing her ethnography. Now, when she watched *Days,* she was much more critical and conscious of the cultural values it was espousing. Many of her classmates sympathized with her mixed feelings, and Terri's instructor explained that her situation wasn't unusual: if writers engaged in real inquiry about the subjects, the writers' positions were bound to be altered in that process. Terri decided to share her revised ethnography with her fellow *Days* fans, and she promised to tell her instructor and classmates what they thought of it. She left her writing class and rushed across campus to the Union, to her friends, and to today's episode of *Days of Our Lives.*

Questions for Analysis

1. Terri's questions for inquiry changed several times in the process of her ethnographic research. Characterize those changes and their causes. Have you experienced similar shifts in your writing efforts?

2. How did Terri's collaboration with her writing group affect her inquiry and writing process? Do you think her project would have been different had she worked with students other than Justin and Amy? Why or why not?

3. At several points in her writing process, Terri felt overwhelmed and had to make decisions about managing her research data, reformulating her guiding questions, and struggling with her own dissonance about *Days of Our Lives*. She used several strategies to manage that overwhelming feeling. Which strategies seem most valuable or useful to you?

4. When researching a local culture to which you belong, it is always difficult to attain a critical distance, to balance your role as both a participant and an observer in that culture. Where do you see this difficulty surfacing in Terri's research? Do you think she ultimately found a way to reconcile her participant and observer roles?

5. As you review Terri's explorations and observations, can you identify any important issues which don't make it into her final ethnography? Do you agree with her choices?

6. Review Terri's first polished draft and the reader responses she received on the draft. What reader response advice seemed most helpful to you? Would you have offered Terri different responses and suggestions for revision? If so, what?

7. One of the aims of ethnographic research is to balance research collected from a variety of sources. Do you think Terry's revised ethnography reflects a balance between memories, observations, library sources, and interviews? Did Terri ultimately offer you a vivid description of her local culture?

8. The sources which Terri found in the library both supported and challenged her experiences with and observations of her local culture. Assess Terri's skill at incorporating the insights of her library sources. Consider, for example, this *USA Today* chart which Terri briefly mentions in her ethnography. What do the graphics say about the author's

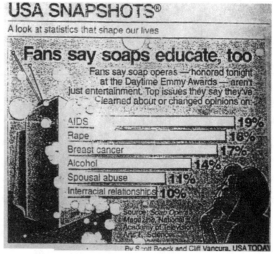

204

attitudes about soap operas? Would you interpret this source differently from Terry? Why or why not?

9. How do you feel about soap operas and avid soap fans? Did Terri's research and ethnography teach you new perspectives about soaps and their fans? Why or why not?

10. When she had completed her ethnography, Terri was surprised to discover that she had more mixed feelings about soap operas than before she started the project! On one hand, she defended the ways soap-viewing can lead to community and new friendships. On the other hand, she could see that soaps promoted negative assumptions about gender, race, class and other important cultural issues. Have you experienced similar mixed feelings about local cultures to which you belong and/or forms of popular culture that you enjoy?

WRITING FOR INQUIRY AND ACTION

YOUR WRITING ASSIGNMENT

In this context you will use ethnographic strategies to research a local culture of which you are a member. If ethnographic research is new to you, it may feel a bit disconcerting for several reasons: you may be unaccustomed to engaging in scholarly research about your everyday experiences and interactions with a group; it might feel strange to assume a participant-observer role, to observe and interview friends and acquaintances who are members of your local culture. The challenges ethnographic research pose are well worth it, for it can be gratifying to engage in inquiry and research strategies that help you understand your local culture—and your role in it—in new ways.

A PROCESS FOR WRITING ABOUT YOUR LOCAL CULTURE

This chapter asks you to begin the process of ethnographic writing by selecting a local culture for inquiry and getting in touch with your dissonance or wonderment about it. In addition to recalling, through memory, feelings and experiences which can guide your inquiry, you will engage in ethnographic strategies that help you understand your culture in action. As a participant/observer, you will observe your local culture on several occasions, taking careful notes and analyzing significant values and behaviors. You will then gather library research, scholarly and popular articles that help you understand your local culture in new ways. After comparing your observations and analyses with others' perspectives, you will interview select members of your local culture to include their voices and opinions in your ethnography.

This process—exploring through memory, observations, scholarly research, and interviews—asks you to continuously test your experiences and perceptions against others' experiences and perceptions, thus making your ethnographic research rich, descriptive, and insightful. Focusing, organizing, drafting, and revising strategies in this chapter help you to negotiate the large amount of research data you'll collect and to write an ethnography that contributes to your and your readers' understanding of your local culture.

Starting
Why raise questions?

Powerful researched writing—writing that teaches you something new about issues important in your and others' lives—begins with powerful questions. When it comes to researching your local culture, developing relevant and insightful questions that guide your inquiry is particularly important. That is, since you are a member of your local culture, you can easily take for granted its daily habits and behaviors. Asking probing (and sometimes difficult) questions, however, can help you understand your membership in your cultures in new ways. This starting strategy is designed to help you do just that.

QUESTIONING STRATEGY
Select a Local Culture / Get in Touch with Dissonance /
Locate Yourself in a Writing Context / Formulate Questions
for Inquiry / Workshop

SELECTING A LOCAL CULTURE FOR INQUIRY

At first, it may be hard to think about *your* groups and organizations as local cultures. Remember, however, that any community of people who share certain values and beliefs can be considered a local culture! Organized, formal groups, such as student clubs, places of work, sport teams, religious assemblies, fan clubs, and academic disciplines or classes are local cultures. But often local cultures are informal communities of people, such as e-mail chat groups, people who work out together, and groups who regularly meet to attend sporting events or to watch favorite television shows. With these possibilities in mind, brainstorm a list of all the local cultures to which you belong, and follow each with a brief comment on your immediate reaction when you think of that culture.

CHOOSE A LOCAL CULTURE FOR INQUIRY

Chances are, you've created quite a list of local cultures! As you choose a local culture for inquiry, you need to keep in mind some practical considerations. Since you'll be engaging in ethnographic research which requires observing your local culture in action and interviewing its members, your local culture must be *accessible*. If the members only meet once a month, it's not terribly practical for investigation. Moreover, if you are an "outsider" to a local culture, it could be difficult or awkward to conduct your research. For example, Mark (whose Questioning Strategy is featured below), considered researching the Asian American Student Alliance because his roommate, an active member, encouraged him to get involved with the group. After careful consideration, however, Mark realized that because he had not hitherto been involved with the group, his presence could be intrusive. To effectively and sensitively research the group's values and interactions, he would have to spend a lot of time getting to know the members, gaining their trust and learning about their goals and concerns. Mark had a realistic sense of the limited time for his assignment. While he began regularly attending the Asian American Student Alliance's meetings, he decided it would be best to conduct his ethnographic research on a local culture with which he was already familiar—his fraternity.

In addition to practical considerations, you should research the local culture that *holds the most consequences for you.* By investigating a local culture, you can learn more about your own values and beliefs, reach new understanding about the cultural influences that inform your role in your culture, and even propose improvements in the way an organization functions. Which culture on your list most influences your current values and activities? Which puzzles, exhilarates, or frustrates you the most? Choosing a culture about which you feel genuine dissonance and curiosity is the first step to conducting valuable research.

GETTING IN TOUCH WITH DISSONANCE

What is it that makes your local culture a *culture*—rather than just a group of people who happen to be in the same place at the same time? The answer lies in the *values* members of your culture share. Shared values influence every local culture's goals, traditions, habits, actions, and ways of seeing the world. College basketball teams, for example, share the values of teamwork, healthy competition, and the desire to win. Sometimes when you are immersed in a local culture, however, shared values tend to become unspoken, even naturalized. They may seem as if they are personal values, a result of individuals' expectations, personalities, and experiences. Yet, shared values also reflect larger cultural values: A basketball player may want his team to win not only for school pride, but also because our society often values winners over losers, no matter how hard losers played or how great their dedication to teamwork! Such a conflict in values is important to investigate, for it might inform your local culture's assumptions and activities.

It is important to make your experiences with and assumptions about your local culture's values explicit if you are to get in touch with the puzzlement, dissonance, or wonderment that may guide your inquiry. As the Questioning Strategy, Part II explains, you might begin by remembering important experiences you've had with your local culture. Next, identify the values those experiences suggest and the cultural sources of those values. Finally, probe for mismatches, gaps, and agreements. What values surface as the most important to investigate? Why?

LOCATING YOURSELF IN A WRITING CONTEXT

Considering which groups of people might benefit most from learning about your local culture is an important part of your planning. Even though you might change your mind about your target readers as your research progresses, it is helpful to narrow your inquiry by locating yourself in a writing context. Identify your possible writing contexts: other members of your local culture? outsiders who have misgivings or misunderstandings about your culture's values? administrators who need to be reminded of the importance of your local culture? Determine the context that best fits your subject.

FORMULATING QUESTIONS FOR INQUIRY

Now that you have explored some of your experiences and feelings about your local culture's values and have considered how your writing context might influence your project, you need to determine what questions will guide your research. When you study a local culture, you could face "information overload." That is, there is a multitude of ways you might investigate a living, changing community of people and its values. You need, therefore, to narrow your inquiry, to research those values or issues which are most meaningful to you.

Your guiding questions might change in the process of your research. But for now, you might begin to narrow your inquiry by posing questions that lead to new understanding, help you recognize the cultural sources of your dissonance, or suggest a course of action or a solution to a problem in your local culture. Select a question or questions for inquiry that help you understand your local culture in new ways, matter most to you and your readers, and are possible to investigate in the time you have available for the project.

Example: Mark Investigates His Fraternity

Possible Local Cultures:

- The fraternity I'm pledging: Will I lose my individuality? My mom thinks all fraternities are "Animal Houses" and that all we do is drink and pick up women. I just saw a news report on hazing in fraternities, and it made it sound like all fraternities abuse their pledges.

- The Pearl Jam Echoes news group: People on the net have intense feelings and opinions about Pearl Jam, but they can be really rude and "flame" each other. Also, it's annoying because a lot of the postings just advertise PJ merchandise.

- The Asian American Student Alliance: My roommate is a member, and he tells me I should get involved. I don't know much about the group or what they want to achieve on campus, but I feel like I should learn because my experiences with that local culture will have a big impact on my life as a college student.

Getting in Touch with Dissonance:

My Experience	*My Values*	*Cultural Sources*	*Dissonance*
At first, I had a negative idea of frats, but I decided to pledge because I thought it would be a good way to meet interesting people. I like the idea of brotherhood—a life-long group of friends who look out for and care about each other. The frat is now my home away from home.	The values of brotherhood fit with the values I was raised with. It is important to have good friends, to be honest with each other, and to have a strong bond with the people you live with.	Pledge histories say that fraternities were established to help create friendship and develop brotherhood and a positive educational experience. College is also a time when you are supposed to make life-long friends.	I don't really have any dissonant feelings. I think the house is what you make of it. Brotherhood is more important to me than ever.
The whole Greek system is always bashed in the media. My mom asks me if I'm drinking and studying enough, and I think she worries about these things because the media gives her a bad impression. You only hear about "Animal Houses" where everybody constantly parties. Yes, we do have parties, but not every day of the week, and if we do drink too much, we take care of each other.	I think a party now and then is fine as long as you don't get too carried away. Drinking with your friends is like a rite of passage: it is a way to become more independent.	The media might bash frats, but they constantly show that drinking is acceptable. Ads that show people having a good time drinking are everywhere. My parents aren't big drinkers, but I know they probably had their share of fun when they were in college!	Sometimes, we do get a little out of hand at parties, and I've seen some people do things under the influence of alcohol that they normally wouldn't do. We all joke about hangovers and "post-party" messes. But partying is not the only thing my frat does! We also sponsor a lot of philanthropic events, we contribute time and money to good causes, and we study a lot.

Possible Writing Contexts:

- Brothers in my fraternity
- Pledges in my fraternity
- The student Greek council that makes decisions about all Greek organizations on campus
- People in my writing class who believe the media's depiction of frats
- A news show or newspaper that only says negative things about frats

I will write to the brothers in my frat house because we are the ones who can challenge the media's "Animal House" depiction of fraternities and fraternity life.

Guiding questions:

1. Why does the media insist on bashing fraternities? Is there any truth to their charges and negative publicity?

2. Why is drinking socially acceptable in college life and in fraternities? How do our attitudes about drinking affect perceptions about fraternities?

3. How can I change the negative views people hold about fraternities?

My central question: How does my fraternity uphold and dispute "Animal House" stereotypes about the use of alcohol, the treatment of women, the individuality of brothers, and the importance of education?

WORKSHOP

1. Discuss the local culture you've selected with your writing group. What makes your subject a *culture,* rather than just a group of people who happen to convene at the same place? Is this a practical local culture to investigate? Why or why not?

2. Discuss your guiding question(s). What dissonance, puzzlement, or wonderment is reflected in your questions? Do the questions seem valuable for inquiry? Why?

Exploring

Why explore?

Your membership in your local culture makes you an expert of sorts: you have first-hand knowledge of your culture's values, concerns, and membership. However, when you are immersed, day-in and day-out, in a local culture, it's easy to start taking many of these issues for granted. Like a person wearing orange-tinted sunglasses, you start assuming that an orange cast to the world is natural. When you explore your local culture, however, you can "de-naturalize" the way you look at and think about it—a very important step in addressing the question(s) which guide your inquiry.

THREE PERSPECTIVES GUIDE
Describe and Distinguish / Trace Moves and Changes /
Map Networks and Relationships/ Workshop

The Three Perspectives Guide can help you think through and become more aware of your role in your local culture, the ways power is shared among members, the values of your local culture, and how those values reflect larger cultural values. You might respond to the following questions in several ways: by brainstorming lists, by freewriting your responses, and/or by writing stories or paragraphs in response.

DESCRIBING AND DISTINGUISHING

- How would you describe your local culture to someone who is unfamiliar with it?
- Describe the shared characteristics of the members of your local culture.
- What physical features characterize your local culture (sights, sounds, locations, etc.)?
- What emotional features characterize your local culture (attitudes, group feelings, etc.)
- What are the day-to-day activities in your local culture?
- What purpose does your local culture serve in your life? In other members' lives?
- How do people become members of the local culture? Are there initiation processes, rituals, or any special requirements for membership?
- How is power distributed in the group? Is there a hierarchy of leadership?
- If you had to choose one adjective to describe your attitude toward your local culture, what would it be? Why?

TRACING MOVES AND CHANGES

- Why and how was your local culture created? Has the purpose for the local culture changed over time?
- Why and how did you first become involved in your local culture? How has your role changed since you first became a member?
- How have your attitudes or feelings toward the local culture changed?
- What larger cultural changes have shaped your local culture (e.g., economic changes, changing roles of women and men at home and in the workplace, changing perceptions of education, new technology, mass media influences, etc.)?
- What are the "traditions" of your local culture? Why and how have those traditions changed? Why and how have they stayed the same?
- Forecast the future of your local culture. How might it change and what will influence those changes? What actions might the members of your local culture take to ensure that it will continue to meet the needs of its members?

211

MAPPING NETWORKS AND RELATIONSHIPS

- In what categories or classifications can you place your local culture? What other local cultures are similar in values and goals? Why?
- What larger cultural values, objects, and/or trends does your local culture reflect? Consider:
  - Assumptions about race, class, occupation, and/or gender roles?
  - Assumptions about relationships (dating, friendships, authority relations, etc.)?
  - TV series or movies? Which?
  - Music? What kind?
  - Advertising? Which ads? Why?
  - Fashions? Which styles? Why?
  - Sports? What kind? Why?
  - Media or community idols? Who?
- What institutional practices (school regulations, business routines, technological procedures, political platforms, city or state laws, church doctrines, etc.) frame the activities and values of your culture? How?
- Create an analogy or metaphor for your local culture. To what object, animal, place, or event would you compare it?

Example: Hanna Explores Her Biker Pack

My guiding questions:

Why are avid motorcyclists stereotyped as immature, sexist, and/or violent? And how does my pack confirm or contradict those stereotypes?

My context:

My fellow classmates who were shocked when I said that I belong to a pack.

Describe and Distinguish:

- A pack is a group of people who ride motorcycles together for fun and safety reasons. Four couples are at the base of the pack, but sometimes other couples join us. My boyfriend, Kevin, and I are the "strange" ones in the pack because we ride a Ninja and the others have Harleys.
- We all love to ride our cycles on the weekend. We all take an interest in bikes. Our ages range from 18 to 45, and we are all Caucasians. We are also all coupled. We wear helmets and an array of biking clothing—leather jackets and some have leather pants or chaps. The leather protects you better than other materials if you are in an accident. All of us work, and most of us have professional jobs.
- Because so many people are prejudiced against bikers in general, we tend to band together in public. The guys in the pack are especially

over-protective of me, since I am the youngest. Another emotional concern is safety. We are careful about where and when we ride.

- We only meet on the weekends when the weather conditions are good. The pack is important in my life because it's like we're all members of a family. I also like moving between two worlds: college student and biker. And it's relaxing to ride after a hectic week.

- To belong to the group, the members must like you, you must have a good bike, you can't be uptight, and you have to know how to ride for safety.

- One guy, Mike, is the oldest and knows the most about bikes, so he's the unspoken leader. Other than that, the guys have most of the power for making decisions. The girls, in all honesty, are for looking good on the back of the bikes.

Trace Moves and Changes:

- Like most packs, we ride together because we're friends and for safety. That purpose hasn't changed.

- Because I was dating Kevin, it was easy for me to become part of the pack.

- At first, their attitude about women bothered me. I had to accept that females are given very little say. If I didn't like it, I wouldn't have to be a part of it. But now, it's really starting to bother me.

- Our traditions stay pretty much the same: we ride for safety, we care about each other like a family, the guys have most of the decision-making power, etc.

Map Networks and Relationships:

- Other packs have similar values and traditions. We might be compared to a family.

- Some tv shows and movies influence us, not because we act like them, but because others perceive us as either Hell's Angels or the Easy Riders! But we are not thugs or "white trash"!

- Most of us wear Harley Davidson clothes. They're fun and they tell other people who we are.

- We follow city/state road rules. Also, we have some pack rules that everyone across the US follows: we respect each other on and off the road.

- A flock of birds. Because they are free and they stick together.

WORKSHOP

1. As you review your exploration with your writing group, highlight the issues that are most important and come closest to answering your guiding question.

    - Which terms or ideas are most prevalent?
    - Of the larger cultural values you've listed, which most govern the values and activities of your local culture?
    - What contradictory values or issues surface in your exploration? What is the significance of these contradictions?
    - As you review your exploration, have any of your original guiding questions changed?

2. Discuss these questions with your writing group to help each other clarify the most important issues for inquiry. Can your writing group offer more details or insights about your local culture?

Exploring through Ethnographic Research
Why explore through ethnographic research?

So far, you have explored your local culture by recalling your experiences and impressions by memory. As you progress with your research, however, you'll need to analyze your local culture's values and actions from a variety of other perspectives. Closely observing your local culture, conducting library research about it, and interviewing its members or associated people allow you to gain a new depth of understanding that can help you answer your guiding questions.

ETHNOGRAPHIC RESEARCH GUIDES
Observe and Take Notes / Compile an Annotated Bibliography / Conduct and Analyze Interviews / Workshop

---

OBSERVING AND NOTETAKING

The opportunity to illustrate the daily behaviors, motives, attitudes, and values of your local culture is one of the greatest benefits of ethnographic research strategies. Indeed, ethnographies are characterized by "thick description," detailed, vivid accounts of peoples' interactions that offer readers powerful insight into your local culture. Observing and analyzing your local culture in action helps you better understand its members—how they negotiate differences, share power, and establish goals.

It's difficult to rely on your memory when you need to record detailed activities. You should observe your local culture on several occasions. When members meet for a business discussion, for example, their concerns and behaviors will be very different than when they meet at an informal party or dinner gathering! By observing your local culture in different situations, you will be able to analyze members' behavior and values from several perspectives.

Since you'll be studying a local culture of which you are a member, it is sometimes difficult to take careful notes because you are a participant *and* an observer.

The more detailed your observation notes, however, the more concrete your discussion of your local culture can be. You might have to distance yourself while taking notes, to become more the observer than the participant. Your notes should include the date, time, and setting of your observation, as well as descriptions of members' daily behaviors, motives and attitudes, methods of communication, interesting quotes or conversations, and approaches to building community by negotiating overt or hidden conflicts. Remember, the things you take for granted or that seem natural about your group are important details to include in your ethnography.

Since you are observing real people in real situations, you might want to inform members of your local culture that you are conducting research. They will certainly notice that you are taking notes, and they might be more forthcoming and comfortable if you share with them the goals of your research. Most people will be happy to be involved and share their insights with you. In rare situations, however, you might wish to keep your ethnographic research private. If that is the case, you must still conduct your research in an ethical manner. For example, you might keep all names and places anonymous, or you might offer a pseudonym for the name of the local culture you're studying.

Analyzing the data you've collected is as important as taking detailed notes on the members' interactions. This is no easy task, for the actions, values and motivations of your local group might seem obvious to you. Begin by searching your notes for resurfacing themes or issues, and analyzing each resurfacing issue according to the questions guiding your research. Here are some questions to consider, but you are not limited to these issues.

- What characteristics do members share (clothing or "style" of dress, language/vocabulary, age, class or socio-economic status, race, occupation, etc.)? What do these suggest about their shared values?

- While observing the members closely, did you notice any contradictions between their actions and the stated values of the local culture?

- Who is in charge of the gathering? Does anyone seem on the "fringes" of the group? Why? How do power relations play themselves out?

- Have any of your observations challenged or contradicted your original assumptions about the group and its values?

Example: Excerpts from Steven's Observations of the First Year Engineering Program

My guiding question: What explicit and implicit values about learning processes and collaboration does the first year Engineering program foster?

Observation situations: A Physics Lecture, a meeting for the Society of Prospective Mechanical Engineers, and the following observation of an Mechanical Engineering examination.

7:00 Thursday, October 15. Lecture Hall 021.

(Note: I wanted to capture the atmosphere of the examination, but I couldn't write down observations during the exam, so I wrote down my impressions immediately before and immediately after taking the test.)

The test tonight, our third written exam, is in three different locations because there are so many different sections of this class. I notice groups of people congregating. They talk with nervous anticipation. Everyone seems to be trudging rather than walking. One pair of guys that passes by is talking about the number of people that have dropped the class so far. One mentions that on Monday, the last day to drop classes, nearly 300 students dropped the course. (Wow!)

When we enter the room about eight minutes before the start time, I am amazed at the space. Maybe the whole rear third of the room is empty. For the last written test, we had trouble finding individual seats about fifteen minutes before the start time. A huge change. One of the TAs (there are six helping with the exam) instructs us to head down front. We find three seats and begin filling out the dreaded scantron forms. The feeling of impersonality washes over me as it does almost every time I fill these things out. This usually happens because I think about the fact that the test is very important to my grade, but it will soon be part of an anonymous stack. Oh well, that's what most of the tests are like in these big freshman courses. The professor has the TAs pass out the exams, and she shouts a few last minute instructions. I am getting a bit nervous, because I never know if I've studied properly for these tests, and they are often tricky and short.

(Later) The test had 20 multiple choice questions, and they were all hard. Many of the questions seemed vague or as if they had a couple possible answers. I had a difficult time with the exam even though I studied intensely. I met back up with my friends. We all walk home, relieved that it's over for now. You'd think we'd want to celebrate, but we all just wanted to go home.

Analysis: The class as a whole was very nervous going into the test. That was definitely the general mood of the group. Most people, myself included, just don't feel ready no matter how much they've prepared. We all feel a lot of pressure to pass, since we can't drop the class. That is a form of the shared value of competitiveness that is pretty obvious in most all Engineering classes. The whole scenario of people first comparing how ready they are, and then asking others how they did is a way to blow off steam, but it's also pretty competition-oriented. Also, the guys that were talking about how many students had dropped the course seemed to think that they were a little better than the rest because they were surviving the class.

The difficulty of the test and the sudden space in the lecture hall seemed to be more connected than I had originally thought. I think the pace has picked up. I think that this course is a prime example of first year Engineering courses that are designed to allow only the strong and proficient to survive.

WORKSHOP

1. Review the observation notes you have written and discuss your most startling, interesting, or amusing observations.

2. Explain how these observations challenge or address your guiding questions. Can the members of your writing group offer alternative analyses or perspectives on your observations? As you discuss these issues, write down your group members' responses and keep them for review.

COMPILING AN ANNOTATED BIBLIOGRAPHY

After you have observed your local culture and have analyzed some of their values and behaviors, you need to test your perceptions against others' research and writing on similar topics. Thus, you'll do scholarly research. The purpose of this research, however, is not only to get hard "facts" on your group; it is also to test your assumptions, to develop new perspectives about your topic, and to develop a well-rounded understanding of the ways your local culture may be related to other cultural groups. In other words, library research is *heuristic*; it helps you reach new understanding.

The annotated bibliography allows you to collect information related to your local culture. Because local cultures are, indeed, *local,* you may not be able to locate material specifically related to your student organization, sports team, club, etc. However, part of doing good research is making connections between your topic (in this case your local culture) and similar topics. For example, if you can't find information on, say, the Single Parent Student Group on your campus, you might find more general research on the challenges single parents face while they are in college, on the kinds of support they find at other universities, or on your school's policies for addressing the needs of single parent students. The goal is to research others' opinions and perspectives about the values and experiences of cultures similar to the one you're researching. Be creative and make connections!

The annotated bibliography is a *working* bibliography; you may not use all of these sources in your final ethnography, but this is your opportunity to learn more about your local culture and other's perceptions of it.

Example: Excerpt's from Mark's Annotated Bibliography on Fraternities

Goettsch, Jane M. and Michael Hayes. "Racism and Sexism in Greek Events: A Call for Sensitivity." *NASPA Journal* 28.1 (1990): 65–70.

Goettsch argues that because Greek organizations often have single-sex and single-race populations, they tend to be sexist and racist. Their levels of sexism and racism often increase through alcohol consumption, initiation procedures, and "little sister" programs. To reduce these problems, fraternities must rely less on stereotypes and start workshops to educate their members.

This author admits that brotherhood is important and that frats do a lot of philanthropic work. Her main assumption is that sexism and racism are wrong, and though frats often deny that they are sexist and racist, they must take actions to reconsider their attitudes toward women and to change sexism. Sometimes her comments are hard to swallow, but there's usually an edge of truth to them.

A section of my paper will be on gender relations fraternities, so this article has a lot of good info. It gives examples of sexist events in fraternities like "flying blue max" (biting women's buttocks at parties) and "sharking" (when pledges have to bite a specific number of women at parties). I've seen these acts at parties, but I didn't know that was what they're called. Potentially useful quote: Page 66: "The culture of many fraternities instills in members a group ethos which objectifies and debases women through language and physical aggression, which lauds heavy drinking and other drug use, and which reinforces group behavior through united behavior."

Lev, Michael A. "Fraternities Fighting 'Animal House' Image—Really." *Chicago Tribune* 10 Oct. 1993: A1+.

Lev looks at the ways fraternities are trying to improve their image and lifestyles. The driving forces behind these changes are the string of expensive law suits against fraternities over issues of rape, injury, illegal drinking, etc. Most of the new restrictions are being strongly enforced by national chapter offices and local governing fraternity bodies. The fraternities are making huge strides in changing their behavior.

The article is very optimistic. Lev seems to assume that fraternity members all have new attitudes, and that new rules will always change people's behavior.

This article will be useful because it lists the regulations that my house should be following. It will be interesting to get my brothers' viewpoints on whether these recent reforms are practiced in the Greek system at this university.

WORKSHOP

1. Review your annotated bibliography. What recurring themes and issues arise? What research did you and your group members find most interesting, troubling, or amusing? Have any of your original assumptions about your local culture changed?

2. With your writing group, discuss the implications of your library research.

CONDUCTING AND ANALYZING INTERVIEWS

After you have completed your observations and have conducted library research, you can develop your understanding of your local culture further by interviewing people who play an important role in it. When you conduct one-on-one interviews, you give individual members of your local culture a voice in your research. You enrich your understanding by comparing interviewees' attitudes and convictions with your own and those you've gathered through library research.

Watch any well-conducted television interview, and you'll see that interviewers establish relationships with their interviewees by being well prepared, putting interviewees at ease, and asking relevant, carefully planned questions. Indeed, while it may seem simple to interview someone—especially a member of your own local culture—this stage of your research poses several challenges: selecting interviewees, scheduling times and places for conducting your interviews, designing effective interview questions, and analyzing the results of your interviews.

Select your interviewees. Decide who can offer the greatest insight into the questions guiding your research. Consider interviewing people who are in various positions of power in your local culture: managers or officers will have very different insights than new members in the group. You might also interview people who don't necessarily belong to your local culture, but who have influence over it (such as school administrators or outsiders who view it differently). The key is to get a variety of perspectives about your local culture. Be sure, also, to take into consideration the practical aspects of interviewing; your interviewees should be easily accessible.

Carefully design your interview questions. Develop questions that build on the research you've already conducted. Review your inquiry strategies, observations, and annotated bibliography to determine which information creates the most dissonance and/or exhilaration for you. As you plan your interview agenda, think about your interviewee's knowledge, and create different interview questions for each interviewee. The questions you'll ask a college administrator or a manager, for example, will be quite different from the questions you'll ask a friend or co-worker who is a member of your local culture. Develop as many questions as you can, using the Three Perspectives Guide, Part II.

Good interview questions are clear and specific, and they should be tailored to your interviewee's position within and knowledge of the local culture. You may want to ask yes/no questions, then ask the interviewee(s) to explain their answers. Don't be afraid to ask difficult or potentially troubling questions, for they can be revealing. It is often valuable to frame challenging questions according to research data you've gathered. For example, if you are researching a fraternity, and you wish to ask about alcohol abuse, you might frame the question thus: "According to Jane Doe, alcohol use is prevalent in fraternities, and it leads to abusive situations. Do you agree with her assessment?"

Conduct your interviews professionally. Make your interview arrangements well in advance. If an interviewee has a difficult schedule, consider a phone interview, but always conduct your interviews at appropriate times and places. Try to set a formal and professional tone so that your interviewees take your research seriously. You may want to use a tape recorder; it can lend a credibility and seriousness to your interviews. If you do not use a recorder, be sure to write your interviewee's responses down as you go along; you want to gather direct quotes, and fresh insight can be too easily lost if you wait too long to transcribe the interviews.

During the interview, give interviewees ample time to respond to your questions. Interviews may not always go as planned, and if an interviewee wanders off the subject, be prepared to bring him/her back around to your most pressing questions. Also, be sure to ask your interviewee(s) for permission to use their responses in your writing. If an interviewee seems hesitant to respond to some questions, you might explain that you can keep his or her identity anonymous in your ethnography.

Transcribe and analyze your interview notes. As you transcribe, include the interviewee's name (or pseudonym), a rationale for choosing to interview him/her, the questions you asked, and a summary of your interviewee's responses (including descriptions of body language, when appropriate). Analyze the responses in relation to your guiding questions and the observations and library sources you've read. Look for commonalties and contradictions in your interviewee's perspectives.

Example: Bernice's Interview with a University Counselor

My ethnography is guided by two interrelated questions: how does racism affect African-American students on this predominately white campus, and how does my local culture—a group of African-American women on my dorm floor—find community and support? I will interview three African-American students and Ms. M., an administrator.

Ms. M. is a counselor in the Dean of Students office. Ms. M. has been a counselor for twenty years, and she is a very sympathetic and dedicated person. I interviewed her in her office on the afternoon of April 21st. I asked her the following questions:

1. Can you give me some facts about the African-American population at this university?

2. Would you say that our university is a friendly environment for non-white students?

3. As a counselor, have you had to deal with many racially-caused incidents? Are there a lot of problems with prejudice on the part of professors or students?

4. Do you feel that many students transfer out of, or never get a degree from, our university because of racial issues?

5. What organizations and activities are in place for African-American students on this campus?

Ms. M. said that 10% of all of the students here are minority students. 4% of those minority students are African-American, and the university has some programs that are trying to recruit and retain a larger African-American student population. Ms. M. would like to say that our college is a friendly environment for non-white students, but she cannot because all non-white students have to face issues and challenges that white students do not face. The administration tries to make the campus a more comfortable place, but there just hasn't been a rise in the number of African-American students over the last year.

As a counselor, Ms. M. works with individual students. She has helped them deal with problems such as depression, family problems, home sickness, death of loved ones, sexual assault—and racism. But no student has filed a formal racial complaint through her, even though she knows that problems which could be formally handled are present. She thinks that most often, students handle racism by going to private counselors, like her, or by talking to their friends. She also admits that, since she is Caucasian, some students might feel like she wouldn't understand their problems.

Ms. M. explains that students themselves must get involved if this campus is going to become friendly to all the multicultural students here. She told me that she is working with some minority students who are putting together a panel on multicultural issues for next fall. Each school does have multicultural groups and organizations to help make life easier. She invited me to take part in those organizations, and I am going to help with the panel next fall.

Ms. M.'s closing remark was this: "Many caring people are concerned about racial issues on our campus. It is hard to have unity when everyone is so different, but if we can come to understand and even appreciate difference, we can learn a lot from each other."

I was surprised that in twenty years as a counselor Ms. M. had never had a student file a complaint about prejudice from a fellow student or professor. But I can see why students wouldn't go to the Dean of Students office. Mostly, racism is subtle, and you always wonder if you were the cause. Many students just feel helpless, and it is easier to keep your head down than stick your neck out.

Ms. M. is a very nice lady, and I look forward to working with her next year. I have made it my personal business to get involved and make our campus more comfortable for all ethnic groups.

WORKSHOP

1. *Before you conduct your interviews,* review questions you've developed with your group. Stage a role-playing scene: each person should try to role-play the identity of an interviewee. As you ask your interview questions in this role-playing situation, consider your interviewee's responses. Are your questions specific enough to engage your interviewees and to get the answers you want? Might any questions be rephrased to avoid offending or confusing your interviewees?

2. *After you have conducted your interviews,* review your transcriptions and analyses. In your group discuss the most striking insights you've gathered, contradictory perceptions by different interviewees who play different roles in your local culture, and facts and opinions that give you a different view of your local culture. Will these issues affect your ethnography? How do they challenge or support the assumptions guiding your research?

Positioning Writers and Readers

Previously, you determined your writing context and who could most benefit from your ethnographic research. Since you have now gathered your research, you can better determine the ways you want to address your readers and to position yourself as a writer. This analysis will help you make important decisions about every aspect of your ethnography—from questions of content to issues of tone and word choice.

Begin by thinking about your position within your writing community and decide which position you'd like to assume and those which you'd like to avoid. Then select the position you want to set for your readers based on their backgrounds and values. See Part II.

Example: Alicia's Writer/Reader Positioning

My Guiding Question: How does the diversity (gender, age, ethnicity, etc.) of the employees in the 24-hour restaurant where I work affect our interactions, and how can we improve our working relations in the midst of such diversity?

My Writing Context: Employees of the Triple B Restaurant. Since I am a member of this local culture, I can share some of my perceptions with my fellow employees. I have not been excluded from any writing positions, but I do need to take care so that I don't offend any of my readers.

I would like to assume the writer position of a caring member of the culture. I am hoping that by sharing information about race relations, gender relations, class relations—in general, relations of power at the restaurant—I can create an awareness of these issues and show both the positive and negative ways they are dealt with in my culture. I think this will be effective because my readers will be able to learn from my information, and they will be praised for their positive behavior, so they won't be as upset by the negative aspects that I will point out.

My reader position will be that of people who are open-minded and want to learn how to improve our working relations by understanding each other's backgrounds and experiences better. The information about race, gender, and class relations should definitely interest my readers because they are a very diverse group of people. Some may find comfort in my findings because they will confirm their own feelings on these issues. Others, however, may not be aware that any power-related problems exist at the restaurant. If this is the case, those members may take offense, but my writer position of a caring member of the group might help the readers be more open-minded.

Selecting a Genre

Your ethnographic research can take any number of genre forms. Sometimes, disciplinary conventions will dictate an ethnographic genre. Suzanne Faber's anthropological research, for example, is in the genre of an empirical case study;

it is structured according to her hypotheses, methods for conducting research, findings, and conclusions. Empirical studies might be the most common genre associated with academic approaches to ethnographic research, but you are by no means limited to that genre. Indeed, the time period over which you've conducted your research, your readers' positions, and the goals of your ethnographic explorations—all affect your genre choice.

If, for example, the questions guiding your research concern understanding the values of your local culture, you may find that a story, narrative of events, or academic essay might be appropriate genres. If your primary goal is to identify ways of improving the communication, efficiency, or working habits of your local culture, a proposal or report might be in order. If you want to dispel stereotypes about or offer "outsider" readers some insight into your local culture, you might choose to create a book, an article for a popular magazine, or even a film documentary that features the results of your ethnographic research. Depending on your goals and your readers' needs, your genre choice might even help you determine which aspects of your research you will emphasize. Interviews with consumers, for example, might be more important than employee observations if your goal is to determine how to meet consumers' needs. On the other hand, if you want to prove that your local culture serves an important function in your community, you might find that readers are more interested in your observations and vivid descriptions of the kinds of services your local culture provides. See Part II.

Focusing

After collecting your research data, you might be suffering from "information overload." Chances are, you have more data than you can possibly include in your final ethnography. Now you have to make decisions about narrowing your focus to include only information that addresses your most pressing and interesting guiding questions.

In the process of conducting your research, some of your original assumptions or opinions about the local culture have probably changed. Your focus should reflect those changes as well as the key issues (of authority relationships, shared values, societal attitudes, etc.) that repeatedly surface in your observations, library research, and interviews. Your focus should include the subject of your ethnography (usually the local culture or its members) and the insight or point of significance you have learned from conducting your research. See Focus Strategy, Part II.

Example: Amy's Focuses

My Guiding Question: Why do my friends and I regularly tan at California Tanning Salon, even though we know that tanning isn't necessarily good for our skin? Should we stop going to the salon?

My Writer/Reader Positions: I am writing as a caring friend who tans, and my readers are in the position of people who should care about their health more than beauty, but too often accept society's definitions of what an attractive woman should look like.

<u>*Possible focuses*</u>

Our regular visits to California Tanning Salon — reflect our culture's pressure on women to feel that our appearance needs to be changed or "improved" constantly.

My friends tan —————————————— because they care more about looking good now than taking care of their health for the future.

I will choose the first focus because it helps resolve my dissonance and the cultural pressures on women to look a certain way.

WORKSHOP

1. Review each focus. Does it reflect a tentative answer to the writer's guiding questions?

2. What reader expectations does the focus generate? That is, what topics for analysis does the focus suggest?

Organizing

An ethnography is often organized according to the process of doing your research and the genre you've selected. Though there are various approaches to organizing the vast amount of data you'll collect, consider including at least three sections in your ethnographic report:

1. A RATIONALE: In this section, you need to offer your reasons for selecting your group, a discussion of the dissonance and questions guiding your research, and any background information you consider important (e.g., the history of the local culture, its original objectives, etc.).

2. A description of your role as a PARTICIPANT/OBSERVER in the group: In this section, you'll need to explain how your role in the group affected your data collection, your guiding questions, etc.

3. An ANALYSIS SECTION: This is the most difficult section to organize, for here you'll include both data you've collected (from observations, library research, surveys, and interviews) and your analysis of that data. It's often useful to organize this section around the questions guiding your research about the group.

As you make organizational decisions, write down the information you might include in the three central sections of your ethnography. Consider what information is most important for your readers, what analysis is most striking, and what observations, library research, or interview excerpts can best support your focus. You might structure your ethnography according to interesting headings, different type fonts, or verbal transitions. See Organization Plans, Part II.

Example: Heather's Plan for an Ethnographic Report
on Incredible Universe

My Focus: Incredible Universe, the appliance store where I work, uses marketing strategies that tap into changes in consumer habits in our image-oriented culture.

"Lights, Camera, Action!"

Rationale:

- Incredible Universe is like Disneyland without the rides. It is a spectacle of fun and entertainment to the point that customers forget that they are spending money!

- Our culture is becoming more consumer-oriented, and some of my sources claim that the line between the image of products and our understanding of ourselves as individuals is blurring. Incredible Universe (IU) seems to be a response to this.

- IU's marketing strategies are becoming popular, and many stores are using them because they are successful.

- Customers need to know about IU's marketing strategies so that they can make informed decisions about what, when, and where to buy items they need.

- Explain my guiding questions:

  What influences does IU's atmosphere and new approach have on customers? Do they buy more, and how do they feel about the store's entertainment marketing strategy? What about people's wants and desires makes IU's approach work?

  What changes in our economic situations and buying patterns influenced IU's new marketing strategies? What do experts think of IU's approach? Why does it work?

  Do IU's values agree with customer and employee's values?

  What effects do IU's wacky language and "culture" have on employees?

- Explain the background (why the Tandy Corporation created IU; how many stores and employees) and description of IU.

  Where and why the language and "culture" of IU was created. Changes in marketing strategies and how people buy more and have a different attitude about what they buy.

Participant/Observer Role:

- I am an employee; being a member of the "cast" allows me to both experience and observe the atmosphere.

- My feelings about IU are constantly changing. First, I was skeptical about the forced friendliness of the store. Then I liked it when I realized most cast members were sincere. Then I became skeptical again when I read more research and found out that customers spend more money and that none of the performances are meant to be serious. I still feel dissonance. On the one hand, the store is fun; on the other hand, there's something about it that seems dishonest.

- Since I am closely connected to some of my interviewees, I've chosen to keep their names anonymous.

Main Issues in Analysis Section:

1. "MIGHTY MORPHIN' MARKETING"

- How IU reflects changes in marketing strategies and cultural changes in attitudes toward buying things. Use customer and employee interviews throughout.
- Store Layout—entertainment
- Thin line between entertainment and consumer goods
- You get what you pay for

2. "HEROES OF THE UNIVERSE: INCREDIBLE UNIVERSE'S CUSTOMERS"

- Effects on consumer buying and satisfaction
- Carnival atmosphere: people don't realize they're spending as much money
- Store set up so people will impulse buy and lose track of time
- Kids have fun in arcades and with shows in the Rotunda

3. "BACKSTAGE: A LOOK BEHIND THE SCENES"

- Effects on employees:
  How they adjust to the "culture"
  How they sell more
  How they feel about mixing entertainment with selling 'props' (like big appliances)

4. "I DON'T THINK WE'RE IN KANSAS ANYMORE, TOTO!" (Conclusion)

- Ethics of IU are both positive and negative. Positive because people do have fun, and they should have control over how much money they spend. Negative because it seems almost dishonest to try to make people spend more by covering up the fact that this is a store, not just a stage.
- Suggestions for customers to handle these new marketing strategies.

WORKSHOP

1. Discuss your organization plan with your group members. Does the organization support the focus? Does the information included in the rationale, participant/observer, and analysis sections make sense?

2. What suggestions do they have for revising your organization plan?

Drafting

After you have developed a satisfying organization plan and have given your ideas "incubation" time, begin writing drafts of your ethnography. Keep your writer/reader position and your guiding questions in mind as you write. As you are drafting your work, new ideas and perspectives may come to you. Do not ignore them if they don't quite fit your organization plan. Instead, write them down, take some time away from your draft, then review these new ideas and where they might be included to support your focus. As you draft your ethnography, keep in mind the importance of correctly summarizing and quoting your library sources and interviews to avoid plagiarism. See Drafting, Part II.

Example: Steven's Polished Draft

A Study of Our First Year Engineering Program

The culture I chose to study is the Freshman Engineering Program at our university. I am heavily involved in this culture because I am a student in this department, and I have completed almost a full year in the program. I believe that this year was an especially good one to study because of the changes the administrators made and the positive and negative results that came from these changes.

The first year Engineering program is an important part of the Schools of Engineering because it is a standard program that all first year students must go through if they want to continue with a specific School of Engineering. We have a very long history with engineering, going back to the fall of 1874. It is definitely one of the most respected engineering schools in the country. The idea with the freshman program is to provide a broad-based initial education that gives students the background for transfer in to any type of engineering school. Some information available from our course catalogue says:

> The Department of Freshman Engineering is the entry point for all new students; initial advising and academic counseling are done there. In 1984 the Freshman Engineering Program was designated a pre-engineering program of study. Qualified students are admitted to the professional engineering programs after satisfactory completion of the pre-engineering program requirements. ("About the Schools of Engineering" 1)

The idea of a separate program for first year students planning on a career in engineering is one that has become increasingly popular over the last decade or so. Many of the top engineering schools in the nation are using this approach to give their engineers some broad-based knowledge. Keeping the first-year students separate from the older engineering students at almost all times allows the freshmen to learn the engineering rules without competing for the time and resources of a non-freshman department. Students aren't pushed to make an immediate decision on what school they want to enter; instead they make the choice over the course of the year as students learn more about each major and what it entails. Many programs are offered by Freshman Engineering as well, such as the popular co-op program, which places students with corporations and gives them valuable work experience.

The overwhelming toll this department takes on the life of a freshman engineering student might be enough to make this program worth studying, but it is the climate the department creates that really seals the deal. The program forces competitiveness because one's future as an engineering student is at stake. The university only admits incoming students to the first year program, not to any other part of the engineering departments. Since one must prove oneself in a variety of large, general classes, many become too bogged down to continue. So, one could make an argument that this freshman program serves as a sieve that only keeps the very best students and sends the rest away in search of another major.

The questions guiding my research boil down to values—the values that the actual freshman department and the individual course departments seem to have about the students and the values I see present within the students themselves. I think that the Freshman Engineering Department is a valuable addition to the engineering curriculum that still has to deal with many of the problems that plague good programs around the country. Students experience a very difficult first year, and there are some problems that need to be addressed.

My role as a participant/observer in this culture is easily defined; I am a student who is currently enrolled in the program, which means I'm a very active participant in the group. I can also easily assume the role of observer by analyzing what is going on in our classes and in the department. This is how I collected my observations and made my analyses—by attending the classes and participating in them, but at the same time taking notes on some of the dynamics happening inside the class. My role as a student made me rather biased, and sometimes the stress of the situation I was observing affected my analysis because I've had an unfavorable view of many of the classes I've taken this year. This, in turn, has led me to think a little less of the overall program. But I did try to focus on both the positives and the negatives.

Values

I have some concerns about what types of values the university seems to telegraph about its students. Since this is such a large university, it can be easy for the beginning students to feel lost in the whole process. The first year Engineering Program (from now on called FYEP) doesn't do a whole lot to help this feeling of anonymity because it uses large, lecture-based courses and multiple choice-style tests. One of the primary things a beginning student can feel is that they don't mater. The university does a fairly good job of combating this because each student takes smaller recitation courses which have typically 20-40 people, depending on the course. But often the TAs in these recitations or labs have not had good training as teachers. I would say that the university is more concerned with making sure that everyone looks equally instructed on paper so that no student can easily prove that they aren't being properly helped. I would say the value that the university is showing here is that they want everyone to be instructed in the same manner but not necessarily equally. This makes sense for the university on a practical level because it is very hard to fill all of the TA positions in a large class. However, the students that must deal with sub-par instruction start to feel resentment and lack of trust for the administrators. The students get a reinforced feeling of not mattering, and their dislike for the program usually grows.

Another value the university appears to have is to only let the strong survive in engineering. They don't do much to nurture along someone who has the skills to be an engineer, but has problems; if that person doesn't work hard to keep his or her grades up during the first year, they will fall by the wayside. This is unfortunate because of the demand for engineering majors, and many fine future engineers fall victim to the "undesigned redundancy" and lack of enthusiasm by instructors in introductory courses (Wineke 6). These students really aren't offered any good reason to plod through. Many instructors and administrators at other colleges have noticed this trend as enrollment in engineering has risen, and they think that many universities are taking on the role of "talent fillers," separating out only the most talented rather than encourage those with ability but without good background in engineering topics. One administrator called for a fundamental change in focus to one that enables students to succeed rather than attempting to "weed them out" (Wineke 6). I think that our school is so worried about letting the quality of their engineers slide that they are content to continue offering only difficult, introductory courses for the freshman year that make it hard for people to succeed. I think students are very aware of this, and they don't like being admitted to a program that drains everything out of them in order to succeed. Everyone gets a chance, but only a few get the chance to succeed.

The values that seem to come from the faculty are more observation and feeling based. My observations of my Physics class showed me that my instructor seems like a nice guy, but his comments reflected a very apathetic attitude to me. He was going to present all the material he wanted to, and it didn't matter if it was registering with the students or not. The professors are all scientists, and they are scientists inside a specific department; therefore, they each seem to have their own agenda with the freshmen, and they don't really care about making sure their class is relevant and appropriately time-consuming. They usually give us brief introductions and then blitz into detailed parts of the subject. I especially feel that the values behind the computer courses and the introductory Physics course are a bit shaky. They are supposed to be designed for the beginner, but they aren't. Physics is a hard level, and interestingly enough, its difficulty doesn't really come from the material in the course. The difficulty comes from the lightening-quick pace of the lectures and the far-removed, incredibly time-consuming labs. Both of these courses were designed by people within these specific departments, and the attitude that I got from both was that we freshmen didn't matter unless we could keep up with them.

The values that emanate from FYEP were summed up quite well by the TA that I interviewed. He said that the program teaches students that it is very demanding and that they must do all the work in order to survive. He said that the program gives students a good work ethic, and he called the whole process "Strengthening by Fire." He said that utilizing groupwork teaches students how to relate with people and to assume leadership. He said he thinks that the FYEP program is doing a good job of stressing environmental values, too, because that is an increasingly large factor in engineering projects. He did a good job of pointing out some of the positive things that FYEP has taught us, namely a good work ethic and to relate to peers in work-based relationships.

Students were the ones who admitted that many of the values they have been exposed to aren't necessarily of the best quality. One of the things that is important in any sort of higher education is a foundation in working ethically, but I had more than one student tell me that they routinely felt the need to violate good, ethical work to keep up with the pace. This is one of the biggest problems I have with FYEP—it is so demanding at times that otherwise intelligent, ethical people feel like they have to break rules to survive. One of the students I interviewed said, "Do what you can in order to get by, not what your parents would want you to do," and "You scrape and claw for every advantage you can get to get the coursework done." These don't sound like the values students should have about their coursework at a top-flight engineering school, and I think they are the direct result of the choices the faculty has made about how to run the program. When students routinely feel forced to accept these values, they become jaded as to their nature and continually accept more of them. Students also often mentioned that they really don't feel important to the program, that they feel like a Social Security number. The problem with having students feel this way is that it is very hard to work continuously for something that doesn't seem to care about you. Many students are motivated when they first start the FYEP, but they become less and less motivated as the feeling of unimportance lingers.

Lastly, one of the people I interviewed had some insight on interpersonal values that I had not thought of before. He said that he really has become prejudiced against people in other majors because of the perception that nobody has to work as hard at the undergraduate level as engineering majors. He noted that he really gets frustrated and angry when he hears people in other majors complain about how hard they have it because he thinks they just don't understand. I think this is a trap that science can really lure people into because I have seen many people put themselves on a higher plane because they work with science; they see others' jobs as less important, even trivial. This attitude is detrimental to the sciences. The book *The Cultures of Science* examines the barriers science puts up, and it explains that science and scientist's attitudes must change in order to include everyone or the field will continue to struggle as people look at fields less insular and elitist (Senechal 2 and 82).

Curriculum

As I mentioned before, FYEP is unique because it is basically a standard, fundamentals-based curriculum that all freshmen must complete to move ahead to the other Schools of Engineering. This is a trend that is very popular at the nation's premier engineering schools. The idea is to stress the fundamentals needed in a variety of other engineering courses and allow the students time to decide on the branch of engineering they want to specialize in ("Freshman Engineering" 1). Another belief that many hold about the program is that it is designed to make the "weed out" process a bit more clear cut. The unspoken consensus among students and faculty is that not everyone admitted to the program has what it takes to complete the requirements for becoming a professional engineer. This is not what prospective students are told, but it is a reality. Since we have such a strong reputation to uphold, many administrators feel they must whittle down the crop to only those who prove through performance that they have what it takes. They make the standard courses just hard enough so that the naturally gifted or people who come from really good high schools survive. Obviously, not everyone is expected to survive, but I think that more can be done to enable those with ability, rather than just make them switch majors. One of the best approaches to getting students to learn anything is to make the material relevant and hands-on. The accepted way of teaching engineering over the last fifty years has been through theory rather than hands-on learning. It was assumed that the latter would come with job experience. But now many universities are trying to give students more hands-on experience (Farrish 6). Since ours is a conservative program, I don't see these changes coming soon, but I do think it is a needed addition to the curriculum. The TA I interviewed called for a change in the freshman seminar to present engineering careers to students, so they understand the available career opportunities. He remarked that it is difficult to see these things when one's class load consists of nothing but fundamentals. He also stated that he doesn't think our freshman base has to be quite so broad.

The reasons that every freshman goes through the same program are well-known. Both the counselor and the TA I interviewed gave me similar answers: it supports students in their first year, it gives them easy access to resources, it offers great background courses, it allows students to decide if engineering is for them, and it teaches the necessary work ethic. I think that most of these are good reasons, and I think the program is beneficial overall, but I also think that there need to be some changes.

For example, our Physics class has given people many problems, and it's a course that many students whom I discussed this project with raised. This class is supposed to be the third-hardest undergraduate class in the nation, and my observations tend to support this notion. The professors

231

move at a lightening-quick pace that almost guarantees that no one can possibly copy all of the notes down in a lecture, let alone grasp them. The notes on the pre-made overhead pages are often written in an illegible green. Our professor made four specific comments in the one lecture that I observed that showed me he was completely apathetic towards the needs of the students. "Did you guys get that? (Pause) Well, I tried." Or, "Now that you're all experts . . ." as he takes something off the overhead that he tried to explain in two minutes. The labs for the course take at least four to seven hours per week, and they are rarely helpful. The lab material we cover is never tested on, and they make us do tons of busywork. It's like having two separate, difficult, four-credit classes rolled into one. This is so stressful. I myself had a strong Physics background, and I should be getting at least a B, but the labs could easily pull me down to a C.

Education Process

Since the classes for the FYEP are very large, the teaching ability of the professors is very important. But how well the TA teaches in the labs or recitation makes or breaks a student because that is where you get the additional help that makes the grades. Many students, however, feel that many of the TAs just haven't been trained well, and they are not good teachers.

Both students and the TA I interviewed saw some spots that needed improvement. The TA explained that because the university is so large, they have to take all the TAs they can get their hands on. He admitted that some have just slipped through the English proficiency exam, and that most have never had a course in how to teach. The students strongly agreed that this was a problem. The obvious solution is more education for the TAs or tightening their admissions. But if they lessen the number of TAs, then they'll also have to cut down the number of first year students allowed in the FYEP.

A big problem with engineering education today is that students aren't taking much of the course information with them. As one expert explains, too often students just don't see that the course information is pertinent (Wineke 1-2) and that many students aren't given a sense of the whole picture and why they're taking the fundamentals courses (Cliff 169). The TA I interviewed agreed that there must be more relevance in the material in the introductory courses. And instructors must show some care for students. One of the students I interviewed claims that he only feels like he has really learned the material from a few courses this year. He admitted that he doesn't have a firm grasp on the material presented in his core engineering courses! I think this points to a real need to change the curriculum and how things are taught.

Overview

The FYEP is a valuable resource for students, and everyone agrees that it does a better job of educating freshmen than a non-standard freshman program would. However, there are many areas of the FYEP that need to be addressed. The students are not learning the material fully because the relevance just isn't there. Studying the program has shown me that it needs some adjustments.

Responding

Why get responses to your drafts?

After you have created a polished draft that reflects your best efforts, you can begin the process of revision by getting response, advice, and encouragement from your instructor, friends, and members of your writing group. The following reader response guidelines can help you and your writing group respond to your ethnographies efficiently. The questions are designed to capture the most common issues for revision that ethnographers face. You might respond to some or all of these questions, or you may develop other questions as each polished draft requires.

READER RESPONSE GUIDELINES

Overall response:
- What did you find most interesting or valuable about the ethnography?
- What did you find most troubling or most in need of revision?

Focus:
- State the focus.
- Is the focus analytical? That is, does it suggest *analysis* about the local culture's values and behaviors?
- One of the most difficult things about ethnographic research is data overload. Has the author narrowed the focus to discuss a particularly important aspect of the local culture?
- Is the focus followed throughout the essay?

Development for readers
- Who are the intended readers for this ethnography? Do you think they will be convinced by the author's focus claim and analysis? Why or why not?
- Has the author offered specific descriptions and examples of the members' behavior, attitudes, etc.? Can you visualize the local culture in action?
- Has the author included data from observation, library research, and interviews to clarify the values of the local culture?
- Has the author clarified his/her role in the local culture, explaining how that role affected data collection, assumptions, etc.?

- Has the author attempted to analyze the group's behavior in terms of our larger society? What are the resurfacing cultural values guiding the group's behavior? Does the author explain what members gain from being part of the local culture?

- Would you have analyzed any of the data differently? Would you advise the author to return to his/her ethnography site to develop more observations and descriptions of the group?

Organization and coherence:

- Has the author included an introductory RATIONALE section which includes guiding questions, assumptions, and dissonance as well as pertinent background information and a rationale for choosing the group? Is that section clear and well-developed? What advice would you offer the writer for improving that section?

- Is the author's discussion of his or her PARTICIPANT/OBSERVER role clear? Does it contribute to the focus? How?

- Has the author offered clear transitions or headings for each section of the ethnography?

- How has the author organized the ANALYSIS section of the ethnography? What questions guide that section?

- How has the author handled "information overload?" Are there any sections of the ethnography that seem repetitive? What are they?

Style and conventions:

- Are the descriptions of the setting and group vivid? Would you recommend stronger word choice to make descriptions clear and vivid?

- How would you characterize the writer's position in the ethnography? Is it appropriate for his/her participant/observer role?

- Has the author correctly incorporated secondary sources? Is it clear which ideas are the writer's and which ideas are from secondary sources?

- Are there any glaring grammatical errors that impede your reading of the paper?

Example: Steven's Writing Group Responds to His Polished Draft

Overall Response:

Isaac: It is a good paper and very informative. But you might work on development. You could explain a lot more about how the FYEP relates to society's ideas of what education should be, how competition should work, etc.

Ellen: You are obviously well-versed in this subject. I don't envy your experiences! I learned a lot from reading your paper, and I think you have a really good reason for writing it. You are not just filling in the blanks.

Focus:

Isaac: Your focus is that the FYEP is valuable, yet has problems that demand attention. You need to connect the values, structures and roles to of the FYEP to larger cultural values. You do a great job showing your dissonance.

Ellen: Your focus is clear. The FYEP has some real problems with the values it is teaching students and with treating students like they are anonymous. This is clear all the way through the paper.

Development for Readers:

Isaac: You could make your first sentence a little more interesting! Besides the rationale being about the problems that have occurred, give specific examples of how students' lives are negatively affected—if possible. Are your readers the Faculty and Administration or are you talking to fellow students? You give your position of a student well. Your claim is strong but could be strengthened by the addition of more specific observations and analysis. You need to describe the situation more vividly so the reader really gets involved. You do a good job of giving your opinion. I think if you cite more library experts, you could support your ideas and claims more. I didn't see a connection between your experiences and larger society.

Ellen: Who are your readers? I know you don't want to write to administrators because you don't want to put yourself in jeopardy, but here you don't seem to talk to anyone in particular. What about writing to people who are thinking about coming to this school and majoring in engineering? I was sad to see that a lot of the good information from your observations (feeling anonymous, like a herd of cattle) gets left out here. No one really seems to have a personality. You don't even explain why you chose to interview the people you did. I think you need to add more of that information to give your ethnography life. Then you won't sound like you are complaining but that you really care about the people who are in the program with you.

Organization:

Isaac: You provide a rationale. You might want to work on making some of your transitions smoother. Your subtitles are too boring. Is there any way to make them more interesting? It might be helpful to place the curriculum section ahead of values to provide a stronger base for your readers to have before you begin with values. Just a suggestion.

Ellen: I think this is your priority for revision. I wrote on your paper all of the places where you repeated yourself. I think that's because of organization problems. You could organize the paper around the different values that you see—being anonymous, learning competition, weeding out students, etc. Your conclusion is really weak. If you write to students who are thinking about the program, you could give them advice on how to survive there.

Language and Word Choice:

Isaac: You may want to describe what a freshman engineering student has to go through by giving more vivid detail.

Ellen: Like I said, give the people more life by including more of what they have to go through. You need to work on your tone; you sound like you are too bitter in some parts here.

Conventions:

Isaac: I marked grammatical errors on your paper.

Ellen: Your sentences are sometimes really long and confusing. I marked typos on your paper.

Priority for Revision:

Isaac: More information from observations and more vivid detail.

Ellen: Organization!

Revising

Study the feedback you received from other writers and create a revising plan to set your priorities for change. See Revising Plans, Part II.

Example: Steven's Revision Plan

Focus: Isaac and Ellen thought my focus was clear. I did too.

Development for Readers: I need to include more of the information from my observations and to make the people in the program seem more human. I agree with this! I also am going to make my readers' positions more clear. I want to teach members of the FYEP how they can improve the system. Maybe I'll just share my findings with some of the TAs that I trust. I also need to use my library research to make more of an impact. I will try to go deeper into what the experts say and compare our FYEP to others around the country.

Organization: I realized that I was organizing the paper around the interviews and observations, rather than around issues. I agree that this is something I really have to work on. I can see all of the places where I was repeating myself.

Language and Word Choice: I was just worried about getting ideas down in this first version. I will smooth things out and write from more of a concerned position.

Conventions: I'll proofread carefully!

Priority for Revision: Including more information from observations and re-organizing the paper.

Chances are your perspectives about your local culture have changed in the process of gathering your research data, writing your ethnography for your intended readers, and revising or "re-seeing" your ethnography. The process of revising is always difficult because it requires that you make decisions about what information to include, exclude, and develop in your project. Remember that there are a variety of approaches to ethnographic research, so as you contemplate the advice and responses from your instructor and writing group, keep your intended focus and readers in mind.

Example: Steven's Revised Ethnography

Students' Experiences In the First Year Engineering Program

The first year of college is typically a difficult one for students. They are expected to deal with major changes—living without parents, a schedule that isn't the same day to day, increased amounts of homework—and to still perform well. A team of researchers recently studied a group of freshmen at a major Midwestern college, and they claim that "adjustment to college is a product of the institutional environment and the person" (Cooper and Robinson 10). These researchers, Cooper and Robinson, chose to study a specific group of freshmen—the engineering majors—to see if there were any differences between these students and those in other majors. One of the first things they noticed was that first year engineering students usually did not enjoy the academic success which they had originally predicted from themselves. In order to explain the phenomenon, Cooper and Robinson claim, "This particularly inflated discrepancy or experience of the 'freshman myth' on academic adjustment is likely a product of the rigorous and demanding technical curriculum" (9). This quote sums up my purpose for researching our university's First Year Engineering Program (FYEP) quite well because it describes two of the most notable effects of the program: that students aren't doing nearly as well as they planned to, and that the program is very rigorous and demanding.

The questions guiding my research boil down to values—the values that the actual freshman department seems to have about students as well as the values that the students themselves have and learn. I want to examine the FYEP's assumptions about how and what students should learn. I also want to examine some of the surprisingly difficult courses the FYEP had for its students this year. Our FYEP is valuable. However, it still has to struggle with general problems that plague good programs around the country. There are specific problems in the FYEP that need to be addressed because students are learning some questionable values.

As a student who is currently enrolled in the FYEP, I am a very active participant in this culture. I collected my observations and analyses by attending my classes and participating in them, but at the same time taking notes on some of the dynamics at work inside the class. My role as a student affected my data collection in that I see things from a student's point of view, and sometimes the stress of the situation I was observing caused my observations to be further biased. I have had many of the same academic troubles that other students have had, and this has caused me to have an unfavorable view of many of the courses I took this year. My bias on this subject is hard to put aside, but I want to stress that I did try to focus on both positives and negatives because overall the FYEP is a good program.

The FYEP is an important part of the Schools of Engineering because it is a standard program that all first year students must go through if they want to continue with a specific school of engineering. The school currently enrolls almost 2,000 students, which is a pretty good chunk of the entire engineering enrollment. Our university has a very long history with engineering going back to the fall of 1874. It is definitely one of the most respected engineering schools in the country. The freshman program is designed to provide a broad-based initial education that gives students the background for transfer into any type of engineering school. Some information available from our course catalogue says:

> The Department of Freshman Engineering is the entry point for all new students; initial advising and academic counseling are done there. In 1984 the Freshman Engineering Program was designated a pre-engineering program of study. Qualified students are admitted to the professional engineering programs after satisfactory completion of the pre-engineering program requirements. ("About the Schools of Engineering" 1)

The idea of a separate program for first year students planning on a career in engineering is one that has become increasingly popular over the last decade or so. Many of the top engineering schools in the nation are using this approach to give their engineers some broad-based knowledge. Keeping the first-year students in separate classes from the older engineering students allows them to learn the engineering rules without competing for the time and resources of a larger department. I interviewed an Academic Counselor for the Schools of Engineering and a TA who were sympathetic to the difficulty of the FYEP. Both agreed that the FYEP has many benefits: Students aren't pushed to make an immediate decision on what school they want to enter, instead the choice is made over the course of the year as the student learns more about each major and what it entails. Many programs are offered by Freshman Engineering as well, such as the popular co-op program, which places students with corporations and gives them valuable work experience. Moreover, the FYEP gives students the one thing they will have to have to pull through: a strong work ethic.

The overwhelming toll this department takes on the life of a freshman engineering student might be enough to make this program worth studying, but it is the climate the department creates that really seals the deal. The program forces competitiveness because one's future as an engineering student is at stake. The university only admits incoming students to the first year program, not to any other part of the engineering departments. Since one must prove oneself in a variety of large, general classes, many become too bogged down to continue. So, one could make an argument that this first year program serves as a sieve that only keeps the very best students and sends the rest away in search of another major. With the forecasted demand for engineers being greater than the supply, it is a commonly held belief among engineering educators that programs such as the FYEP need to transform their role. They must stop being separators and start being enablers, thereby helping students to survive and get enthusiastic about engineering not frustrated with it.

The Courses and The Teachers: How the FYEP Is Organized

A big problem with engineering education today is that students aren't taking much of the course information with them. The experts seem to think that often students just don't see how the course information is pertinent (Wineke 1–2) and that many students aren't given a sense of the whole picture and why they're taking the fundamentals courses (Cliff 169). The TA I interviewed agreed that there must be more relevance in the material in the introductory courses and that instructors must show some care for students. One of the students I interviewed claims that he only feels like he has really learned the material from a few courses this year. He admitted that he doesn't have a firm grasp on the material presented in his core engineering courses! I think this points to a real need to change the curriculum and how things are taught.

One of the best approaches to getting students to learn anything is to make the material relevant and to show them how to do things hands-on. The accepted way of teaching engineering over the last 50 years has been through theory rather than through experience (Wineke 9). It was assumed that the hands-on experience would come with job experience. Many universities are finding it beneficial to make the coursework more hands-on in order to drive the relevance of the material home (Farrish 6). Since ours is a conservative FYEP, however, I do not see these changes coming soon, but I do think they are needed in our curriculum. Many students, including most of those I interviewed, do not know what engineering is about—they just see it as a good way to earn more money because of their science and math aptitude. Something that our FYEP could do as a stopgap measure until further changes come about was suggested by the TA I interviewed; he called for a change in the first year seminar to present engineering careers to students so they can see what opportunities await them. He remarked that it is difficult to see these things when one's class load consists of nothing but engineering and science fundamentals. He also stated that he doesn't think our freshman base has to be quite so broad, that we need to add some relevant classes to capture student interests. I completely agree with his sentiments.

Since the classes in the FYEP are very large (except for the English and Communications courses), students generally agree that the teaching ability of the professor is less important than that one's TA for the course.

People are still dependent on the professor, but the main focus of hands-on activity is in the labs and recitations, which the TAs generally run. The quality of a TA's performance often makes or breaks students' grades for the course in these large (sometimes 500 students) courses. Many students, however, feel that many of the TAs just haven't been trained well, and they are not good teachers. Both students and the TA I interviewed saw some spots that need improvement. The TA explained that because the university is so large, they have to take all the TAs they can get their hands on. He admitted that some had just slipped through the English proficiency exam, and that most had never had a course in how to teach. The students strongly agreed that this was a problem. The obvious solution is more education for the TAs. But if they lessen the number of TAs, then they'll also have to cut down the number of first year students allowed in the FYEP. Perhaps this is the only humane solution, but it does cause a problem: it means less incoming money for the FYEP each year.

As far as the courses themselves go, this year has been difficult because of changes to the plan of study. The first major changes were made with the computer classes. The first semester was comprised of an introduction to UNIX and then studies of the software engineering tools available for use of the Sun stations. The second semester included a computer programming course. Both of these required courses were new, and both gave students a real roller-coaster ride. They were difficult classes, but alone that can't explain why more than half the class ended up dropping the courses before they were over. The big problem was that it consisted of only two lectures per week; there was no lab or a recitation to go over the material in smaller groups. Most people were so busy with other courses that they couldn't handle having to learn something completely new on their own. The weekly homework was difficult, and many students I know were lost from the first week on. And this was a required course, so many students will be forced to do make-up work to keep pace with their plans of study. The counselor I interviewed pointed to this class as a source of many problems for students this year.

Similarly, our Physics class has given people many problems, and it's a course that many students whom I discussed this project with raised. This class is supposed to be the third-hardest undergraduate class in the nation, and my observations tend to support this notion. The lecturing professors have admitted in class that the department instructs them to move at a lightening-quick pace that almost guarantees that no one can possibly copy all of the notes down in a lecture, let alone grasp them. The notes on the pre-made overhead pages are often written in an illegible green. Our professor made four specific comments in the one lecture that I observed that showed me he was completely apathetic towards the needs of the students. "Did you guys get that? (Pause) Well, I tried." Or, "Now that you're all experts . . ." as he takes something off the overhead that he tried to explain in two minutes. The labs for the course take at least four to seven hours per week, and they are rarely helpful. The lab material we cover is never tested on, and they make us do tons of busywork. It's like having two separate, difficult, four-credit classes rolled into one. This is so stressful. I myself had a strong Physics background, and I should be getting at least a B, but the labs could easily pull me down to a C. While our other courses aren't as troublesome, they follow the same rules: move quickly and grade harshly.

Feeling Lost at Sea

I have some concerns about what types of values the university seems to telegraph about its students. Since this is such a large university, it can be easy for the beginning students to feel lost in the whole process. FYEP doesn't do a whole lot to help this feeling of anonymity because it uses large, lecture-based courses and multiple choice-style tests. Beginning students can feel is that they don't matter. Every time a student enters a lecture class, he or she is confronted with at least a hundred other people, usually more. Most professors never connect with students because the lectures are rarely interactive. To combat the impersonality of the lectures, most departments assign each student to a smaller recitation or lab course, which has typically 20-40 people, depending on the course. But since TA's are usually busy as well, few students really feel connected to them. I have never felt like more than a number, and this is not a pleasant feeling. Students also often mention that they don't really feel important to the program, that they feel like a Social Security number.

It is hard to be motivated when you feel unimportant. With so many students in the program, the problem almost seems unreconcilable. However, a study done on predicting the success of freshman engineering students claimed that short, personal interviews conducted by the counseling department during the early parts of the school year helped students to feel like they mattered (Haislett and Hafer 90). I agree that some small, one-on-one style talks could go a long way in bridging the impersonality gap between students and faculty/administrators.

The Drive to Be First

Another value the university appears to have is to only let the strong survive in engineering. They don't do much to nurture along someone who has the skills to be an engineer but has problems; if that person doesn't work hard to keep his or her grades up during the first year, they will fall by the wayside. This is unfortunate because of the demand for engineering majors, and many fine future engineers fall victim to the "undesigned redundancy" and lack of enthusiasm by instructors in introductory courses (Wineke 6). These students really aren't offered any good reason to plod through. Many instructors and administrators at other colleges have noticed this trend as enrollment in engineering has risen, and they think that many universities are taking on the role of "talent fillers," separating out only the most talented, rather than encouraging those with ability but without good background in engineering topics. One administrator called for a change in focus to one that enables students to succeed, rather than attempting to "weed them out" (Wineke 6). I think that our school is so worried about letting the quality of their engineers slide that they are content to continue offering only difficult, introductory courses that make it hard to be successful. I think students are very aware of this, and they don't like being admitted to a program that drains everything out of them in order to succeed. Everyone gets a chance, but only a few get the chance to succeed.

This affects the ethics of the program. Students were the ones who admitted that many of the values they have been exposed to aren't of the best quality. One of the things that is important in any sort of higher education is a foundation in working ethically, but I had more than one student tell me that they routinely felt the need to violate good, ethical work to keep up with the pace. This is one of the biggest problems I have with FYEP—it is so demanding at times that otherwise intelligent, ethical people feel like they have to break rules to survive. One of the students I interviewed said, "Do what you can in order to get by, not what your parents would want you to do," and "You scrape and claw for every advantage you can get to get the coursework done." These don't sound like the values students should have about their coursework at a top-flight engineering school, and I think they are the result of the choices the faculty has made about how to run the program. When students routinely feel forced to accept these values, they become jaded to their nature and continually accept more of them.

The unspoken consensus among both faculty and students is that not everyone admitted to the program has what it takes to become a professional engineer. This is not what is told to prospective freshmen, but it is the reality. Since our program has such a strong reputation to uphold, they feel that they must whittle down the crop to only the strongest. They make the standard courses just hard enough so that many fall by the wayside. Obviously, not everyone in the program can be expected to survive, but I think when you have 300 students drop on the last possible day (as was the case with my Physics class), something is very wrong. When you start seeing yourself as the "weed" that should be "weeded out," it's really hard to keep your motivation up. Students start feeling unnecessary competition with each other; you can sense a feeling of gratification from students who "make the cut," and they seem to think less of others who don't make it.

An Unexpected Consequence

One of the people I interviewed/had some insight on interpersonal values that I had not thought of before. He said that he really has become prejudiced against people in other majors because of the perception that nobody has to work as hard at the undergraduate level as engineering majors. He noted that he really gets frustrated and angry when he hears people in other majors complain about how hard they have it because he thinks they just don't understand. I think this is a trap that science can really lure people into because I have seen many people put themselves on a higher plane because they work with science; they see others' jobs as less important, even trivial. This attitude is detrimental to the sciences. The book *The Cultures of Science* examines the barriers science puts up, and it explains that science and scientist's attitudes must change in order to include everyone or the field will continue to struggle as people look at fields less insular and elitist (Senechal 2 and 82).

Tying It Up

The values that emanate from FYEP were summed up quite well by the TA that I interviewed. He said that the program teaches students that it is very demanding and that they must do all the work in order to survive. The program gives students a good work ethic, and he called the whole process "Strengthening by Fire." He said that utilizing groupwork teaches students how to relate with people and to assume leadership, and he thinks that the FYEP program is doing a good job of stressing environmental values, too, because that is an increasingly large factor in engineering projects. He did a good job of pointing out some of the positive things that FYEP has taught us, namely a good work ethic and to relate to peers in work-based relationships.

The FYEP is valuable. Everyone agrees that it does a much better job of educating first year students in basic engineering courses and about the different types of engineering than would a non-standard freshman program. However, there are many areas of the curriculum that need to be addressed. The students are not learning the material fully because the relevance just isn't there. Studying the program has shown me that it needs some adjustments.

Works Cited

"About the Schools of Engineering." *Course Catalogues—Homepage. Netscape,* 1995.

Cliff, Alan. "A Qualitative Review of Study Behavior Before and During the First Year of Engineering Studies." *Higher Education* March, 1995: 169–181.

Cooper, Stewart E. and Debra Robinson. "Assessing Successful Adaptation to College." A paper presented at the Annual Meeting of the American Psychological Association. August, 1988.

Farrish, Katherine. "Colleges Redesign Engineer Training." *Hartford Courant* 21 February, 1994: 6.

Haislett, Judith and Alex A. Hafer. "Predicting Engineering Students During the Freshman Year." *Career Development Quarterly* September 1990. 86091.

Senechal, Marjorie, ed. *The Cultures of Science.* New York: Nova Science Publishers, 1994.

Wineke, William R. and Phillip Certain. "The Freshman Year in Science and Engineering." National Science Foundation. Washington D.C., 1990.

CONCLUSION

Researching your local culture is no easy task, but it can help you gain new insight about not only the communities you belong to, but the ways those communities intersect with and are influenced by larger cultural values and concerns. The process of ethnographic research is long and can be arduous. If your inquiry has been inspired by real dissonance and wonderment about your local culture, however, few research approaches offer the kind of in-depth understanding and critical engagement that ethnographic research demands.

In this chapter, you have seen work by Marcus, Hanna, Steven, Bernice, Alicia, and Heather. Each of these writers engaged in genuine inquiry about their local cultures, and all learned new ways of seeing and understanding their contexts in action. Some writers, such as Steve and Bernice, used their ethnographic research to propose changes in the actions and values of their local cultures. Steve shared his research on the first year Engineering program with some professors and counselors he trusted, while Bernice made her ethnography available to the Dean of Students Office and other campus organizations interested in changing racist attitudes on campus. Other writers, such as Marcus and Hanna, used their ethnographies to dispel stereotypes about their local culture's attitudes and actions. Marcus's research on fraternities and Hanna's ethnography of a motorcycle pack challenged many of the negative perceptions their reader's had about their local culture. Still other writers, such as Alicia and Heather, found in ethnographic research an avenue for self-understanding and a means of educating the members of their local cultures. Alicia shared her research on tanning salons with her friends who regularly tanned with her, and some changed their tanning behavior based on Alicia's research. Heather used her ethnographic research on Incredible Universe to better understand business ethics, and, since she was a business major, Heather knew that understanding would be invaluable in the future.

As you have engaged in the process of collecting data for and writing your ethnography, you have experimented with a variety of research strategies which are valuable for other writing genres. Interviews, for example, might help you create more solid arguments for readers, while observations might be an integral consideration when developing a proposal for revising business, school, or family interactions. Ethnographic research strategies have a wide range of uses, and they are invaluable for inquiring into your local cultures, your experiences, your life.

6

AREA OF INQUIRY: FIELDS OF STUDY

DEBRA JACOBS

WHY WRITE ABOUT FIELDS OF STUDY?

Fields of study represent an important part of our lives, not only in academic contexts, but in professional, social, and personal contexts as well. Yet despite the significant role fields of study play in our lives, if we took time to reflect on a field of study important to us, we would probably find that there are aspects about the field that puzzle us. Perhaps we feel especially engaged by a certain activity in a field—as if we enter into our own special niche while doing it—but we do not quite understand why. Or maybe something about a field makes us feel especially connected to others, but we are not sure what that something is. There may be ways of learning in a field we hadn't expected or connections to other fields that surprise us. Perhaps we have an interest in a field based on vague notions, but we realize we know little about what the field actually involves. There may be ways that a field challenges certain values we hold or causes us to reconsider certain beliefs, or we might feel alienated or empowered by various social or cultural values and beliefs that a field of study seems to support.

When we write to inquire into a field of study that is important to us, we gain insights that can make what we often consider to be impersonal aspects of a field more intimate to us. Such inquiry is especially relevant to you as students because entering a field of study involves making various kinds of commitments—and certainly making a commitment to something can be considered a highly personal and intimate act. As each of us knows, entering into a commitment without reflection can have painful consequences. Many students, for example, have found themselves in majors that are not at all what the students had anticipated. Unfortunately, the realization that they are in the wrong major often comes well after students have already invested enormous amounts of time and energy—not to mention money—in that major. Or sometimes students drop a course after a term has already begun or decide to stick it out even though they're not happy with it. Investigating options beforehand could help such students make better choices.

Writing as inquiry can help you to understand better what your commitments will involve and to share your understanding with others in a writing context.

EXAMPLES OF WRITING FOR INQUIRY AND ACTION

- James raises questions about the extent to which the field of nursing challenges or reinforces the view of nursing as a female profession. He plans to write to his parents, who have questioned his going into the field of nursing.

- Questioned about her decision to major in accounting, Rhonda writes to inquire into whether accounting is a good choice for her. She chooses to write to students in a chapter of *Future Business Leaders of America*.

- Ronjii is concerned about the extent to which political views of black activists are represented in political science. He chooses to write to members of HOPE, a student organization designed to raise consciousness about race issues.

- Kelly is amazed by how much she gains from discussion groups in history and has decided to examine this experience in the context of her class.

- Lauded for her work in the field of rhetoric and composition, scholar and teacher Janice Lauer writes about composition studies as a "dappled discipline," a discipline that is multi-disciplinary and multi-modal. As a Distinguished Professor of English at Purdue University, Lauer has used writing to investigate ways composition instruction can foster powerful inquiry.

- Writings by William Vickrey, who was awarded the 1996 Nobel Prize in economics, make important connections between theories in economics and public affairs. Vickrey's writing focuses on the importance of using theories from the field of economics for the public good, such as the creation of a practical and socially efficient fare system for public transportation.

- Historian James Axtell, a Distinguished Professor of History at the College of William and Mary, writes about the placement of history in the humanities rather than in the social sciences. Through his writing, Axtell explores similarities between historians and writers, especially with regard to how both must utilize the same invaluable component of their arts, the imagination.

- In an essay that details experiences of African-American students in the composition class, Glenda Gill, Associate Professor at Michigan Technological University, draws from the connections she has made among drama, literature, and the teaching of writing. Also drawing from her experience as an African-American scholar, Gill has found such connections important for bridging what she describes as an oral tradition and the power of the written word.

- Carl Sagan used writing as an opportunity to explore how the study of astronomy can illuminate theological concepts. Renowned for making astronomy accessible to the general public, Sagan championed writing as inquiry, frequently offering personal anecdotes of how writing for the novice led him to new understandings of his field.

READINGS FOR INQUIRY AND ACTION

The classification of an academic discipline can illuminate how that discipline is understood. In the essay that follows, James Axtell uses writing to explore implications of classifying history as part of the humanities.

"HISTORY AS IMAGINATION" *The Historian* (excerpts) by James Axtell

Most historians are professional schizophrenics. Now that the nine-teenth-century chimera of historical "science" has dissipated, their self-identities and allegiances are torn between the humanities and the social sciences. The symptoms of their dilemma are everywhere.

On the one hand, most historians turn to the National Endowment for the Humanities rather than the Social Science Research Council for funding. They regard their writing as a species of literature, and recognize their assumptions about humankind, time and the cosmos as philosophical. . . .

At the same time, in most colleges and universities, history is listed with the social sciences for the purpose of satisfying distributional or "liberal arts" requirements. And many historians are happy with that placement because the dominant mode or fashion in history is social history, which relies heavily on the techniques, methodologies and jargon of the social sciences.

Another obstacle to thinking of history as one of the humanities is the widespread lay opinion that history is a dull, lifeless pile of cold, objective facts about the past, without social significance or human interest. Such a bad press is partly the fault of historians, for their huge audience, throughout its schooling, has been subjected to an unrelenting dose of objective-sounding, fact-ridden textbooks, and bombarded with so-called "objective" tests on an assortment of scarcely related names, dates and events. . . .

Against such odds, can anyone argue persuasively that history in essence is one of the humanities, one of those artful disciplines that explores, explains and celebrates human beings in their full collective and individual humanity? I would like to attempt to make that argument by suggesting that a major component of the historian's equipment, indeed his most important tool, is his imagination, not unlike the poet's or the novelist's.

I realize that some cultural heavyweights would find such a notion strange if not downright ludicrous. Through the mouth of a young divinity student from Salamanca, Cervantes argued that "it is one thing to write like a poet, and another thing to write like an historian. The poet can tell or sing of things, not as they were but as they ought to have been whereas the historian must describe them, not as they ought to have been but as they were, without exaggerating or suppressing the truth in any particular." Dr. Johnson simply snorted that "in historical composition all the greatest powers of the human mind are quiescent. . . . Imagination is not required in any high degree." And from the "scientific" seminars of the nineteenth-century German universities came the Rankean battlecry: Write history *"wie es eigentlich gewesen*—as it had really been," as if total immersion in the archives would skim off any dangerously inventive cells from the historian's brain.

I prefer the notion of history dropped as an aside by George Steiner and supported by a host of practicing historians, past and present. In a review of a book by a French medievalist, Steiner characterized history as "exact imagining," and I know of no better encapsulation. . . .

Most people will have no trouble accepting that historians pursue facts—the "exact" half of Steiner's "exact imagining." That's always the first phase (and, unfortunately, often the last) of what we are taught in academic history courses, certainly as freshmen and as first-year graduate students. Perhaps without ever saluting the tattered flag of positivism, we learn that history is a kind of science, or at least a rigorous methodology, for the collection and verification of facts about the past and their logical and chronological relations. We learn to pray at the altar of Research, as John Livingston Lowes catechized, with "rigorous exactness in both the employment and the presentation of one's facts; scrupulous verification of every statement resting on authority; wise caution in drawing inferences; [and constant] vigilance which overlooks no evidence." We learn to arrange events in strict temporal order so as to be able to distinguish causes from effects. . . .

After shamelessly ransacking virtually the whole university for methodologies and angles of vision, we collect our precious nuggets, those hard-core facts from the past. Contrary to popular opinion, they're not all as desiccated as royal genealogies, Civil War battles or the provisions of the Hawley-Smoot tariff. Perfectly respectable historians have been known to scrounge for "facts" such as lost landscapes in Tahiti, the color of a dead queen's underwear, the death rate of cats in a French working-class parish, the changing price of peasants' bread, gun barrel and pipe stem bores, the salt content of roily river water and the shell content of native pottery, the forgotten meaning of familiar words, and that most elusive of all quests, the motivations behind human behavior, normal and abnormal, individual and collective. These are all "facts," but their mere mention suggests that the search for them is far from simple or dull. . . .

For most historians, the major problem is not research into the past, which despite its myriad enemies always seems to yield an excess of usable facts, but writing about it. "Research is endlessly seductive," as Barbara Tuchman knows, "but writing is hard work." The reason writing is so hard is that it calls upon the historian's imagination at literally every stage.

After our research has been completed and our notecards piled high, the mute data must be summoned to life through active acts of imagination. The first task in writing history is to *reanimate* the known facts, which comes lifeless from the page. We must *revivify, resurrect* and *re-create* the past for ourselves, in our mind's eye, before we can ever hope to transmit that vision to others. We must take the raw materials of our searches, as Paul Horgan has said, "through the crucible fires of our own achieved awareness." Like poets and novelists, we must seize the opportunity, and take the courageous step—to imagine what we know. For "without that intuition which we call 'historical insight,' but which is really a specially controlled exercise of the creative imagination, Garrett Mattingly noted, "most of the past can never be said to exist as history but only as the unorganized material from which history can be evoked." . . .

The main reason we must constantly seek to resurrect and reanimate the past is that, as the novelist L. P. Hartley noticed, "the past is a foreign country; they do things differently there." While people in the past bore familiar human shapes and responded to essentially the same human needs we do, their minds and sensibilities were very different from ours. We simply cannot assume that "human nature" is unchanging and universal, except in the most uninteresting and uninformative generic sense, because cultures and what used to be called *Zeitgeist*—"spirit of the times"—mold and fashion the relatively plastic givens of human psychology and even biology into different species. Without a strenuous act of imagination, how could a modern historian, who has never known hunger for more than a few hours or been wracked by paralyzing fear of the plague or the devils of absolute, pitch-black night, possibly understand the intellectual and emotional climate of a sixteenth-century peasant or a seventeenth-century Huron? . . .

One of the hardest things for historians to remember is that events now long in the past were once in the future. Although history is lived forwards, facing down the stream of time into uncertainty, it is understood and written only in retrospect. We know the end before we consider the beginning, and we can never wholly recapture what it was like to know only the beginning. But there exist two reasons why it is important to "restore to the past its lost uncertainties," in Hugh Trevor-Roper's words, and "reopen the doors which the *fait accompli* has closed."

First, historians no less than other humanists must constantly demonstrate that free will is not a mere philosophical axiom but a fact of life. While it is true that people are bound by the constraints of heredity, society and culture, their choices are almost never limited to one course of action. Only the blessed curse of hindsight prompts us, in moments of intellectual weakness or indolence, to speak of historical "inevitability" and other forms of determinism. . . .

And second, if written history is to capture the raw and complex reality of the past, it must communicate what William Bouwsma calls "the sense of contingency and, therefore, suspense—the sense that the drama might have turned out otherwise—that belongs to all human temporal experience." With imagination applied to deep knowledge, we can establish the real choices that people had in the past, rather than anachronistic, moralistic, or wishful ones. . . .

Thus far we have spoken of imagination's role in ferreting and fleshing out particular historical details. But it has an even more vital part to play in discerning the larger patterns, structures and meanings behind particular events and facts which contemporaries were not able to see. Here hindsight is indispensable for pulling into a single field of vision the beginning and the denouement of the historical plot. But it is largely the synoptic imagination which completes the plot, which sees relations where the eyes see only facts, which sees the lines of form that strike through seeming chaos, which sees underlying unity in apparently diverse phenomena. Imagination has three major functions: (1) to originate, (2) to re-create, and, equally important, (3) to relate diverse elements of life to each other. . . .

With his understanding of the past largely achieved, the historian begins to plan his writing. Again, imagination is indispensable. But even before sketching an outline and certainly well before inserting the first sheet of intimidating, blank paper into the typewriter, he should fix in kind the specific audience he plans to address. This task takes another act of imagination because, as Father Ong has observed, "The Writer's Audience Is Always a Fiction." Not to know for whom you are writing is to invite literary disaster, or at least an unfortunate melange of missed signals and mixed messages. . . .

Since history at its best is shared discovery, the historian's final and most important task is to *translate* his vision, his "achieved awareness" and understanding, of the past for the modern reader. This is far from easy for two reasons. First, the historian's goal must be to tell his story in such a way that the reader will actually *experience* the past rather than simply hear about it. And second, the historian must find a way to translate the foreign idiom of the past into that of his own time, without breaking faith with the past. . . .

Returning from the "foreign country" of the past, the historian confronts an artistic problem similar to that of the anthropologist returning from field work in a foreign culture. Like the denizens of the past, the anthropologist's natives have their own ways of doing things, relating to each other and making sense of the universe. They view the world through unique lenses and classify its movements and parts according to their own consistent schemes. The input of their minds and the output of their tongues are keyed to a complex code of meaning, which can be deciphered only after long study and with great sensitivity. If the participant-observer, the scholar, manages to break the code, to understand finally what makes the natives tick, he must then translate his understanding into the modern idiom of his own culture, which operates according to a very different code. In other words, the historian must respect the contextual integrity of the past while transmuting it through his art. Such a delicate agenda, of course, depends heavily on the writer's imagination. . . .

At every stage the literary genesis of a book of history is a work of the imagination. What matters most in history, Lewis Namier reminds us, is "the great outline and the significant detail; what must be avoided is [a] deadly morass of irrelevant narrative" in between. As for any art, the solution of form for a work of history is the most important of the many aesthetic acts that must be performed. For the past has no shape; as John Updike recognized, "billions of consciousnesses silt history full, and every one of them the center of the universe." Only literature has shape, and historical writing that is not literature is quickly consigned to deserved oblivion.

Questions for Analysis

1. Did Axtell's writing engage him in examining a topic important to him in the context of fields of study? How can you determine if this was an important topic to the writer?

2. Do you think, as Axtell does, that a "widespread lay opinion" about history is that it is "a dull, lifeless pile of cold, objective facts about the past"? To what extent do your academic experiences reinforce or challenge this stereotype?

3. How does Axtell's writing style challenge the stereotype about history as objective, dull, and lifeless?

4. What dissonance concerning the field of history does Axtell discern?

5. What is the focus of Axtell's essay? According to Axtell's understanding of the imagination, how imaginative is Axtell's focus?

6. Why is writing hard for the historian? How does Axtell develop this point?

7. What reader and writer positions are suggested by the essay? How does Axtell suppose his readers will react to his focus?

8. Characterize the kinds of evidence Axtell uses to support his focus. Are Axtell's choices effective?

9. Does anything in the essay surprise you? Trouble you? Anger you? Intrigue you?

10. Relate Axtell's explanation of "exact imagining" to the dilemma he refers to in the opening of the essay. Does the essay resolve the dilemma historians face as "professional schizophrenics"?

A Case RHONDA'S INQUIRY

My younger cousin and I have always been close friends besides being cousins. We live in the same neighborhood, so we've pretty much grown up together. Coming from a family in which she's the only girl, Keandra (my cousin) has also always looked up to me. I have been proud of the way she views me, and I think knowing that she regards me in some ways as a role model has made me more responsible.

I pride myself on my individuality. I'm someone who you might say has pizzazz. I like to be a little bit flashy, but I don't over-do it. I have style. To me, having style isn't just a look or just an attitude. You also have to excel at what you do to have style. In high school, I kept my grades up and worked hard on my studies. Sometimes Keandra and I would do our homework together, and it felt great to be able to help her when she didn't understand something. Both of us had visions of growing up to have exciting, successful lives, and we knew doing well in school would be important for that.

Now I'm a student at the University of South Florida, and Keandra is a junior at our high school. She and I have been growing apart, which I guess is only natural to some extent, but Keandra has also taken on an attitude toward me that I find very hurtful. She looks down on me for the major I have chosen at USF—accounting. She jokes that I'm going to have to get thick glasses and an ugly suit and sit hunched over a calculator all day. She's also made a race and gender issue out of it, thinking that accounting majors are all white males who lack personality—who lack pizzazz.

Keandra isn't the only one who stereotypes people in accounting. I encounter it a lot, even when people just act surprised to learn what it is I'm majoring in. For some, it's just that they dislike math. Others think I should have chosen something more exciting or more glamorous. Basically, they think I've sold out on my dreams and on who I am.

I also have a lot of positive reactions to what I'm doing, and many people support me in the decision I've made. But I'm bothered by the negative responses. I think this writing assignment will give me a chance to think about my major in ways I haven't taken the time to consider yet. I haven't known how to respond to Keandra's jokes or to the stereotypes others have. Mostly, I've just been hurt and defended myself by saying that I like accounting.

Using a questioning strategy helped Rhonda select the topic she most wanted to examine and to think about a context for her writing. Keeping her readers in mind from the beginning helped guide Rhonda's investigation. Rhonda identified experiences and values that she considered to be central to her topic, noticing where her values were out of synch in some way with her experiences. Rhonda also identified some of the important underlying sources for her values. She began to recognize that her values regarding her major in accounting were shaped in various ways by her family and community, by her church and schools, and even by larger cultural forces.

Rhonda's Questions

My Major, Accounting

I keep on feeling like I'm put on the defensive about majoring in accounting. I like accounting and want others to respect my decision.

My Writing Contexts

- Keandra, my cousin
- My composition class

- Friends from high school
- Students at my former high school in Future Business Leaders of America
- My high school math teacher
- Other accounting majors at USF

I will write to students at my former high school in Future Business Leaders of America (FBLA). Keandra could be included in this context, but it enables me to write to others, too.

My Experience	*My Values*	*Cultural Sources*	*Dissonance*
I'm great with numbers and I like working with numbers.	I value enjoying what I do. I think it's important to have a major you like.	Aren't we taught "the pursuit of happiness"? If it makes us happy and it doesn't hurt anyone, why should anyone care?	My value is met. Like I keep telling people, I like accounting. A question I have here, though, is why it's enjoyable.
Some people, like Keandra, seem to disrespect me for making accounting my major. She thinks it's dull.	• being a role model to Keandra • the opinions of others • being someone who is seen as having "star" qualities.	Family—the older looks after the younger. Also church—the Cain and Abel story. My parents—they're always telling me that how you appear to others is important. My peers—I've always been popular for having style.	I'm hurt by Keandra's attitude. I don't like feeling defensive. I want to know what I can say to others to make them see accounting as more exciting.
I encounter surprise or worse (like being made fun of) by majoring in accounting. They seem to think it's not for me because I'm an African-American female.	Having who I am shine through no matter what I do. • not being judged by whether I'm male or female or black or white. • Also, shouldn't stereotype.	Cultural heritage—taking pride in being African-American. Our government—we're all created equal. Also, my church—judge not lest ye be judged.	Again, I feel defensive. I don't like people to get the wrong impression of me, whether because of being African-American, being female, or anything else.
Thanks especially to Mrs. Davis, I got admitted to the College of Bus. Admin. as a freshman. • Felt successful • Am thankful for my high school business prep program.	• She's a role model so I don't want to let her down; I care about her opinion. • I value my accomplishments • I value my high school.	• the idea that you're supposed to give back what you're given. • the idea that you reflect back on those who made you.	My values here are mostly met. The only thing is, I'm not sure Mrs. Davis or my school would *know* that their teaching is paying off.

My Experience	*My Values*	*Cultural Sources*	*Dissonance*
My parents keep questioning me about my major even though I'm doing well.	• My parents' opinions • My parents' judgment • Making my parents proud of me.	We're supposed to respect our elders. • parents are wiser than their children and know what's best for them. "Blood is thicker than water"—means family won't let you down and vice versa	When my parents question me so much, I worry about my decision. I wonder if there's something wrong with my major that won't let me be who I am or who my parents want me to be.
I've always had good things come as a result of doing well. Now it seems like it doesn't matter some people.	• taking pride in what I do especially when I do well; being recognized for doing well; *earning* recognition.	School rewards performance	I'm frustrated my value isn't met outside of school.

My Questions for Inquiry

New Understanding: What is it about accounting that appeals to me? How can I be sure accounting will allow me to be who I am?

Cultural Sources: What does stereotyping accounting as a "male subject" imply about accounting?

Solution to a Problem: What kinds of "rewards" does my major offer that would override my wanting approval from my family and friends?

A Course of Action: What changes can be made in how accounting attracts majors? What can I do to promote accounting as an exciting major?

My Question for Inquiry: Either the first one or the last one. I want to change people's minds, but I also want to make sure accounting is the right choice for me.

In a small group with two other students, Karla and Danielle, Rhonda discussed her problem with articulating a question. She explained that she would like to change people's minds about accounting, but she didn't have much confidence she could do that unless she was sure in her own mind that her major didn't conflict with her sense of identity. For Rhonda, this meant that her major needed to allow for the expression of her dynamic personality and the pride she felt in being an African-American female. Danielle suggested that Rhonda work on making her first question about why accounting appealed to her more specific. Karla thought that Rhonda needed to try to combine the ideas in her first and last questions. Karla also suggested that Rhonda work on her question to reflect cultural sources since, Karla pointed out, cultural sources seemed to play an important part in Rhonda's dissonance.

Rhonda's instructor also collaborated with Rhonda. Having ascertained that Rhonda was still planning to write to high school students in the business prep program, the instructor asked Rhonda if context might be helpful to her in determining a question for inquiry. With her peers' and instructor's comments in mind, Rhonda revised her question to "In what ways can accounting at USF be regarded as an exciting major that allows for individuality?"

With her revised question in mind, Rhonda used the Three Perspectives Guide to continue her inquiry. Rhonda referred to her school's catalog while using this exploring strategy.

Rhonda's Exploration

Three Perspectives Guide

My Question: In what ways can accounting at USF be regarded as an exciting major that allows for individuality?

Describe and Distinguish
The major

- 21 hours of course work in accounting

- course work on taxes and auditing

A person with accounting abilities could be a pretty powerful person, or at least a good person to have as a friend in April. Should make you popular.

- course work in Information Systems

- systems analysis

- database administration

I especially like computer programs in accounting like Quattro Pro. I like making spreadsheets.

- must maintain a "C" average. This doesn't seem very demanding. Maybe some of the upper-level courses are hard, though.

Accounting courses

- learn principles of recording and reporting financial activity

- learn formulas for budgeting and regression analysis

- applications for every kind of business under the sun

- ethics is a part of many of the courses

Learning activities are mostly hands-on. I like this way of learning material—learning by doing. This is one of the things that make accounting fun to me. Who wants to just sit and take notes?

The CPA exam

This takes five years to be eligible. 150 hours instead of 120. I'm not sure what the extra time involves.

Description of accounting

Recording, interpreting, and reporting financial activity. Have to be good with numbers and good at problem-solving.

Recurring images

I see myself in a nice office in a big city. People depending on me to keep their business going.

- These images make me happy, especially because I believe in them. I can make them real.

Trace Moves and Changes

Beginnings

All through school I've liked math and working with numbers, but I'll just go back as far as my junior year in high school. I got involved in Future Business Leaders of America, an extra-curricular organization. My favorite math teacher is one of the teachers who runs the program. I'm sure that's one of the reasons I got involved. I clepped out of a couple math courses and the introductory accounting course here at USF. They admitted me into the College of Business Administration as an accounting major as a freshman, which is really an honor. Not that I'm the only one, but it's still an honor. And more than that, it lets me get started on the courses for my major sooner.

Changes

Keandra's attitudes about me.

- a matter of coincidence that has nothing to do with my major? Maybe. I have gone on to college, and she's still in high school. But she uses my major against me.

My feelings of certainty that accounting is the major for me. Will it lead me down a boring path?

Computer programs are always changing in accounting.

More and more acceptance of technology? Need to be on the cutting edge?

Cultural changes

Minorities in Business majors. It's true there aren't many African-Americans I know who are accounting majors, male or female. There seem to be more A-A females. This is definitely the case in my classes. In fact, there are more females than males in my classes, period!

Why?

A negative way of looking at it is that accountants don't own the store, they help the owners.

Another way of looking at it is that it sure goes against the stereotype that women don't have a head for numbers. There's a classic movie with a line like that in it—"Don't worry your pretty little head about numbers, dear." My experience shows this is ridiculous.

Map Networks and Relationships

Classifications

Accounting is one of the Business majors.

- finance
- marketing

Do these areas seem more "glamorous"?
Accounting is a subject that involves using numbers

- algebra
- calculus

  This is what makes accounting a turn-off to so many people, but I find it to be one of the fun aspects of accounting.

An accountant is a member of a business team

- but not the boss?

Accounting is a subject that involves problem solving

- have to be creative
- have to take initiative
- have to be up on things

All these add up to it being exciting

Similar

Accounting and finance

Opposite

Accounting and Literature

- interpret numbers, not words
- but there is an aspect to accounting that calls for interpreting *situations*. Maybe it's not *opposite* to literature.

Stereotypes

deals with numbers so it's just for men

Accountants are boring

Positive stereotypes?

- have to be a whiz
- ???

Analogy

Going into accounting makes me a traitor. I feel like this a little sometimes.

- sold out on who I am
- maybe it's something about helping someone other than yourself own a successful business
- puts you in the role of being an inferior
- can't express my individuality in a gray suit

Majoring in accounting is like wearing my dressiest clothes.

- shows my self-pride
- well-tailored to fit
- an expression of how I see myself

I feel like this most of the time.

Rhonda's group members noticed that the details and ideas in the two sections, Tracing Moves and Changes, and Mapping Networks and Relationships, best explored her question. They also noted, however, that the details Rhonda included as she described and distinguished were important. Danielle suggested to Rhonda that she think more about the details in terms of her question, though.

Karla pointed out that Rhonda's exploration did not suggest that attitudes about accounting were shaped by the issue of race. Rhonda indicated that she had already thought about this issue. She said that for her being an African-American female was central to her own concerns about expressing herself in accounting. What her exploration made clearer to her, Rhonda reported, was that the experiences she had that contributed to her dissonance stemmed from being a female who cares about leading an exciting life. These insights Rhonda also shared with her instructor, who encouraged Rhonda to examine cultural and social forces relevant to her topic more carefully and to note emerging understandings.

Rhonda's exploration gave her a better sense of what was most important to her about her topic. Still keeping an open mind and jotting down insights as they developed, Rhonda also considered what would be important about her topic and question to her readers. She was assisted in this effort by working through the Writer/Reader Positioning Strategy.

Rhonda's Writer/Reader Positioning

My Question: In what ways can accounting at USF be regarded as an exciting major that allows for individuality?

Positioning Myself

Positions left behind

I've left behind the positions of classmate, high school student, FBLA member, "big-time" senior, "lowly" freshman. Many of the students in FBLA don't even know me, but the teachers still do. Also, I'm no longer the Whiz Kid I used to be thought of now that I'm in college and among a lot of students who are just as good with numbers as I am.

- Can't rest on my "laurels," or at least I couldn't expect anyone to already know my *previous* "reputation."

Positions I have or could have

- Former student
  - Was involved in FBLA and took it seriously. This should make the students in it now know that I can relate to them. Maybe this position would be better if I were writing *about* FBLA, but that's not quite what I was thinking.
- Accounting major at USF.
  - Some of the students will go on to USF since they live here. Again, I can relate to them, and they can relate to me. This position would help me write to them about accounting as someone with qualifications to say what it's like as a college student.
- Peer
  - I could write as someone who is into business just like they are. (If they weren't into it, they wouldn't be in FBLA.) This would help me talk about the kinds of things they're interested in as someone on an equal footing with them. But maybe it would be harder to focus just on accounting or to "sell" them on it. Also, if I wanted to get in the ideas about my identity, maybe peers wouldn't be so good, especially with the males.

    This idea of "selling" accounting is something to think about. Position of salesperson? Well, it's not all there is to it. If they want to actually major in accounting based on what I have to say, great. But mostly I want them to see it in a positive light.
- Professional in an accounting office. Actually, I'm only working part-time as an office assistant in an accounting office.
  - Would help me to talk about stuff on the job end, though I'm only doing a few things accountants do. At this point, I'm not really a *professional* in accounting.
- Female in accounting
  - This gets at part of why I chose this topic. It would help me discuss some of the stereotyping problem I encounter. But if I center on my experiences as a female, would I be able to write to the whole FBLA group? Seems like I would alienate the guys in the group.
- African-American in accounting.
  - As far as the identity issue, it seems like this position would make a lot of sense. But I'm finding that my concerns about identity aren't *specific* to being African-American, even though being able to define my identity includes this. Also, my writing situation. FBLA isn't just for Blacks the way Explorers is.

Position I will adopt

I will adopt the position of accounting major at USF. This position lets me center more on accounting as a subject matter. I don't want to focus so much on me. I mean, I'll be in the text because I'm the writer and it's my way of seeing it that I'll be communicating. But it won't be *about* me exactly. It will be about accounting. This makes the most sense for the writing context, and I'm more comfortable with it.

Positioning My Reader

High school students, FBLA members, peers, teenagers, prospective USF students, learners, prospective business majors at USF.

Choice for my reader

Prospective business majors at USF. It makes the most sense for my topic and writer position. Also, they are interested in business or they wouldn't be in FBLA. By writing to them as prospective majors, I can target accounting and maybe get them to see it in a way they hadn't thought of before. Can be specific about accounting *at USF,* too.

Characteristics of reader position

• Enthusiastic about anything in major, including accounting.

• Some background knowledge (more than the usual high school students not in FBLA).

• Values include getting good grades, being able to use what they already have learned, being able to utilize skills they have (and knowing what skills they need), feeling they are going into the right field.

As prospective business majors at USF, they also would value the reputation of the program.

They have different attitudes, beliefs, backgrounds, and goals, so they will value a major that is flexible and allows them to be who they are (which is the same for me).

The feedback Rhonda received from her group increased her confidence about her ability to write to students in FBLA about accounting. Both peers thought the writer and reader positions helped to construct a realistic writing context. Karla and Danielle questioned Rhonda on the extent to which she thought she would include details specific to being an African-American female, however, given the positions she had set. They also asked Rhonda how she would reach the readers in the position she had chosen for them.

While working through the Writer/Reader Strategy, Rhonda had also been wondering about how she would reach her readers. She had already eliminated some options, such as an academic essay, a letter, and a report because they didn't seem to fit her writing context. Based on her work with the Writer/Reader Strategy, Rhonda had decided that her context for writing suggested that she would be "selling" accounting, as she put it. Therefore, the options she was still considering included writing a speech, a flyer, a pamphlet, or a brochure. Rhonda used the Genre Strategy to help her with her decision.

Rhonda's Selection of Genre

My Possible Genres

- Written speech
- Pamphlet
- Flyer
- Brochure

My Question and Context

I think my question about how to regard accounting as an exciting major and a major that allows for individuality is a question that's looking for aspects about accounting to "sell" it to others. Writing to high school students who might major in it suggests they need to be informed about it also. Any of the genres I'm thinking about could do both of these things.

Key Status

This is a big reason I don't want to do an academic essay. I think mostly professionals in the field of accounting would have the kind of status needed to write that, at least for the students in FBLA. In one way, I could be seen as having little or no status in my field of study. I'm just a student—a beginning one at that. But students often listen to students—about *being* a student. This is even more possible for me writing to students in FBLA because I was a student in FBLA. Now, I'm farther along than they are, so that also gives me a certain kind of status.

Genres in My Context

FBLA is like an "extra" curriculum group even though it's geared toward school. Some genres for the group are newsletters, newspaper articles, and the ones I've thought about—brochures, flyers, and so on. Mostly, genres are used to maintain enthusiasm for the idea of pursuing a major in business and to keep students informed about important topics in business.

My Analysis of Possible Genres

Contexts

Each of the genres I'm thinking about suits the ideas of promoting accounting and informing FBLA students about accounting at USF.

Logistics

The written speech requires that it be delivered. Who would deliver it? I would have to make arrangements to attend a meeting, which I guess would be realistic—except that I really wouldn't want to. I'm not normally shy, but I think I would feel awkward in a speech situation.

A flyer comes across as too casual for this context. And aren't flyers usually used to announce an event of some kind?

A brochure seems a little more formal than a flyer, and it's longer, too. It doesn't take as much time as a pamphlet to produce. Also, it doesn't require me to be there or anyone else to read it out loud.

My Selection and Analysis

My Choice: A Brochure

Writer Position

Will a brochure allow me to write as an accounting major at USF? This could be a little awkward since you might expect a brochure to be written by program administrators or something like that. Why would I be promoting this?

- I want to change stereotypes
- I want to help people who were once like me (FBLA students) to be open to the option of accounting as a major.

Development, Evidence, and Authority

- Brochures are informative, so there should be plenty of information about what the major involves. I'll want to make sure to bring out any ways accounting is exciting. I'll also want to include how it is diverse—which it has to be if it is to allow for individuality. Details about courses, skills, and careers would help here.
- I could help establish authority by referring to the reputation of USF's accounting major.
- Testimonials work in brochures—like the back cover of books or blurbs from movie reviews you see in the paper. These would have to be testimonials of people FBLA students know.
- I'm not sure about the extent to which I could use my own personal experience—as such. Writer of a brochure isn't usually an "I."
- Authority also conveyed by graphs and charts. NUMBERS—and this fits well with my topic of accounting!

Reader Positions

The genre of a brochure puts readers into the position of information seekers *and* persons who might act on that information by somehow supporting whatever is the subject of the brochure. I think this is perfect for my writing context.

Format and Organization

- Most common: a tri-fold. So a brochure usually has 6 panels.
- Front: states topic, captures interest.
- Back: where to go for more info.
- Each inside panel could be on separate ideas.
- Or could fold out like a flyer so each panel is not really a "divider."

Level of Formality

- Well-constructed fragments okay.

- Lists okay.

- Probably will use headings—it won't use transitional sentences the way an essay would.

- Don't want to sound stuffy—will opt for a casual tone, but will also be informational.

- I think talking *to* readers is the way to go—second person. Lots of brochures do this.

Visuals

Brochures often have visuals. Definitely have visual appeal. Could be just font size and style. Ideas that might be conveyed by visuals in my brochure:

- accounting
- education
- excitement
- diversity
- future
- careers
- professionalism
- success
- opportunity
- USF

Variation

My brochure could fold out so inside is basically a flyer. Could be put on a bulletin board in FBLA meeting rooms. Would have to make sure outside panels don't get overlooked.

One panel or more could have fairly lengthy written sections, which would make it essay-like. It still wouldn't *appear* like an essay, though, because of the panels.

Karla and Danielle were enthusiastic about Rhonda's choice of genre. Both could think of brochures they had seen about fields of study, so they were optimistic about the genre being able to assist Rhonda in her writing context. The instructor also thought Rhonda had made an excellent choice. However, she expressed concern about the time involved in creating a brochure. Discussing features of the brochure to help Rhonda assess production considerations, the instructor learned that Rhonda was proficient with computers and experienced with both WordPerfect and Microsoft Word. This proficiency, Rhonda believed, would help to make creating a brochure a practical, realistic option. Rhonda's instructor agreed.

Rhonda understood that issues of design were not the only matters involved in writing an effective brochure. She cared very much about utilizing the brochure to convey the important insights she had been reaching about accounting.

Rhonda's Focuses

My Question: In what ways can accounting at USF be regarded as an exciting major that allows for individuality?

My focuses

Subject	Point of significance
Several aspects of accounting at USF ———	make it exciting and tailored to the individual.
Stereotyping accounting as a male subject —	reinforces the oppressive view of women as not being as logical or as capable as men.
As an accounting student progresses through the core curriculum at USF, ———	his or her individuality shines through.
To be ranked as one of the best accounting programs in the nation, USF's program———	has made sure that it maintains an exciting curriculum that people with diverse talents and goals will enjoy.

Within her writing group, Rhonda indicated her preference for her first focus. She was pleased with it because she believed identifying the aspects would answer her question and be relevant for her readers. Having worked closely with Rhonda throughout her inquiry to this point, Rhonda's peers were a bit surprised that Rhonda was not choosing a focus that reflected her concern about gender stereotyping. Rhonda reminded them that the most troubling experiences that contributed to her initial dissonance involved responses from people such as her cousin Keandra. It was important to Rhonda to focus on accounting as an exciting major.

Rhonda's instructor also wondered if Rhonda was avoiding the important gender issue Rhonda's inquiry had led her to examine. Rhonda considered this possibility. She decided that the focus she selected could include insights about gender because gender stereotypes were opposed by her assertion about individuality.

Rhonda's instructor and her group members encouraged Rhonda to keep this idea in mind as she created different plans for developing her focus. Rhonda based each of her plans on essentially the same focus.

Rhonda's Organizing Plan

My Organizing Plans

Time segments

Focus:

Progressing through the core curriculum in accounting at USF ———	gives students more and more insights about how diverse and exciting accounting can be.

Development

The first courses in financial accounting ——	teach diverse skills in recording, interpreting, and reporting.
Courses in cost accounting —————	show students different ways of assisting management through problem-solving.
Advanced courses —————	place students in diverse and exciting environments.

Parts of whole

Focus:

Several aspects of accounting at USF ——— make it exciting and tailored to the individual.

Development

The core courses ——————————— teach a variety of skills in different environments.

Such electives as Law and Accountancy —— reflect the applicability of accounting to exciting areas.

The faculty ——————————————— come from diverse backgrounds.

The program as a whole ——————— appeals to both males and females and a wide variety of personality types.

Criteria

Focus:

The accounting major at USF——————— meets the criteria of being exciting and diverse.

Development

The variety of skills learned in accounting — makes accounting an exciting field.

The opportunity for expressing individuality whether you are male or female ————— is provided by the diverse careers accounting prepares you for.

Grouping

Focus:

Getting a degree in accounting ————— is like being given a magic wand.

Development

The power to influence lives in important ways ——————————— is exciting.

Options available in accounting ———— ensure diverse career choices.

Karla and Danielle recognized that through her plans Rhonda had furthered her insight about the excitement and diversity accounting offered. However, Karla believed that Rhonda might have closed off opportunities for a different insight by sticking so closely to one basic focus. Karla also commented that Rhonda's plans did not indicate that Rhonda intended to develop any ideas about how cultural, social, or institutional values or practices contributed to her insight. Agreeing with Karla, Danielle suggested that Rhonda could include such ideas with the insight pertaining to diversity. The instructor supported the group's comments and suggestions, but she noted that if Rhonda wished to follow Danielle's advice, Rhonda might need to examine what cultural, social, or institutional forces contributed to her overall focus in order to avoid merely inserting such thoughts.

Rhonda chose to follow her plan on Parts of a Whole to draft her brochure. She also drew upon ideas in her other plans as well as in her work with other strategies. In addition, the drafting process led Rhonda to new ideas. After writing several drafts of her brochure, Rhonda shared a polished draft with her group and instructor.

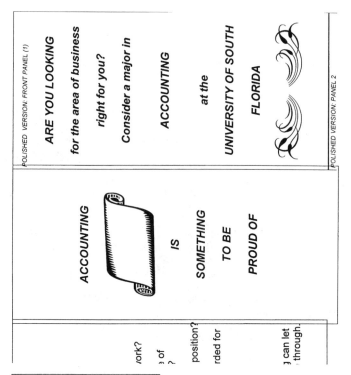

POLISHED VERSION: FRONT PANEL (1)

ARE YOU LOOKING

for the area of business

right for you?

Consider a major in

ACCOUNTING

at the

UNIVERSITY OF SOUTH FLORIDA

POLISHED VERSION: PANEL 2

ACCOUNTING

IS

SOMETHING

TO BE

PROUD OF

POLISHED VERSION: BACK PANEL (6)

Accounting: What's it all about?

Is accounting about some guy with glasses and an ugly suit dwelling in a dark, dank room all day hunched over a calculator? A job with no individuality, no pizzazz?

Of course not!

Accounting is actually one of the most diverse fields in the country, not to mention one of the most highly paid. Accountants analyze and prepare financial records for individuals, companies, branches of government, and non-profit organizations.

Accounting at USF

USF's School of Accountancy was established in 1987 and has become one of the largest programs of accounting education in the United States. It is also one of the most prestigious, which means that you are in a position to benefit greatly from a university with the 4th best placement on the CPA exam.

POLISHED VERSION: PANEL 3

The CPA: Your Gateway

The title of CPA--Certified Public Accountant--is your gateway to pursue a path leading to one of the many diverse fields in accounting, including the following positions:

forensic accountant
IRS auditor
tax accountant
legal auditor
loan officer
purchasing agent

None of these positions fits the stereotype of accounting. The forensic accountant, for example, trains at the FBI academy, has the duty of stopping white collar crime, and travels widely. The IRS auditor is responsible for reviewing and evaluating individuals' and companies' financial records.

Rewards of Accounting

It is estimated that by the year 2000, the mean starting salary of a CPA will be $48,000, one of the highest of all majors.

POLISHED VERSION: PANEL 4

Degree Requirements

Like other programs at USF, a bachelor's degree in accounting requires 120 semester hours. There are 18 hours of required accounting courses and 9 hours of accounting electives. General business courses take up 39 hours, while non-business courses take up 54.

If you are interested in obtaining more information, please contact the following office:

Undergraduate Advising
BSN 1406
College of Business Administration
University of South Florida
4202 E. Fowler Avenue, BSN 3403
Tampa, FL 33620
813-974-4290

Karla and Danielle used the Reader Response Guide to comment on Rhonda's polished version as did the instructor. Because Rhonda used the genre of brochure, her respondents utilized the Reader Response Guide to comment on specific aspects of that genre. The readers addressed issues about form (the panels of a brochure, for example) in the section on organization and coherence. Other comments about genre were discussed in the other sections of the guide as well.

Rhonda compiled the responses she received from her group members and her instructor. She wished to consider them carefully before planning her revision.

Rhonda's Compiled Reader Responses

Overall responses

Karla: The brochure is working well. Looks professional, which goes along well with something you're trying to convey about your topic.

Danielle: Neat idea on the opening question. You cover all the big ideas your readers would want to know about, too.

Instructor: Your concern about your topic is reflected in the polished look of the brochure and the nice coverage you gave the topic.

Focus

Karla: "Accounting is a rewarding major and you can get a good degree in it at USF." The idea about it being exciting isn't central, but you do mention it. Panel four needs to get back to rewards—maybe something again about excitement.

Danielle: "Accounting at USF is exciting and will put you on a road to success." It seems that the main thing you want to say is it's exciting, but it doesn't come across as so exciting. Like when you talk about what accounting is like on panel two. Are these things exciting?

Instructor: "Accounting at USF is a rewarding major that offers something for anyone." The section on accounting at USF in panel two and the section on degree requirements do not convey insights about accounting. Connect details in these sections to your focus. I also wish to note that your focus did not strike me as being as insightful as it could be. You seemed especially concerned about the idea of expressing individuality during your inquiry. I think you mean for your points about diversity to convey such thoughts, but the points you have are connected to careers. Do you think that captures your insights about individuality?

Development for readers

Karla: Readers are those interested in going into accounting. Writer position is spokesperson for accounting at USF. Appropriate details for readers. Maybe readers would want more on courses. Visuals appropriate. Maybe a better visual on the front panel would help get readers' attention.

Danielle: You're writing as college accounting student to people who might be college accounting students. Position's clear and maintained. You have lots of good details. Where did you get all the info.? You probably need a footnote or something. Good visuals.

Instructor: You're writing as an insider in the accounting major at USF who is promoting it to students who are interested in accounting as a major but not yet sure. Your details are informational and appropriate for what your readers need to know. I don't see that you have included details that disprove gender stereotype, which you need to do on at least the second panel, if not throughout. Visuals are effective, but they lack originality. Is there any visual that could better suggest excitement on the first panel?

Organization and coherence

Karla: The parts of the brochure are used and so is your parts/whole plan. The one part that confused me was the CPA section. Is that part of your major? Do you have to get this to have the jobs you list? Also, maybe you need to make all your headings ask a question like your first one.

Danielle: Parts of the whole. You talk about the whole first, then break it up in parts. What happened to the ideas in your plan about courses and faculty?

Instructor: Well-organized brochure that discusses first accounting as a whole, and then parts you consider important. Panel three suggests that the CPA exam is one of the broad parts of accounting. Is this true? Would a different heading make more sense for your organization? Do your headings help you convey your focus?

Language choices

Karla: Casual but knowledgeable. Informal but professional. More specific descriptive words (like "ugly suit") needed.

Danielle: Style jumps around. You "talk" to the reader, but then you get more formal. Degree requirements sound bland compared to the rest.

Instructor: You establish an informal style by using second person, contractions, questions, etc. Sentence variety helps maintain reader interest. Try to use a few more "unusual" words (such as "pizzazz" and "gateway") to convey the kind of individuality the brochure promotes. Reflect on style in section on degree requirements.

Main emphasis for revision

Karla: Organization. Headings and especially ideas for panel three.

Danielle: It's all real good. Just work some on style.

Instructor: Development for readers. Keep focus in mind as you revise for development.

The responses Rhonda received to her polished version led her to review her inquiry. She articulated specific ideas she had for revision and prioritized them according to which would result in the most significant changes.

Rhonda's Revising Plan

My Revising Plan

- I see that I need to keep my focus in mind better as I revise. My main revisions will be in the area of development. I want to add details about excitement such as skills you learn that make accounting exciting.

- My idea about the individuality of accounting needs to come through better. I will include details about course electives and relate them to individuality. I'll also try to make connection about individuality and career choices clearer.

- The CPA section needs to be clearer. I'll focus on the degree instead of the CPA: on the BBA.

- Try to find a better visual for the front panel. But there's a limited number of pictures on my software.

Implementing changes according to her Revising Plan, Rhonda created two revised versions of her brochure before arriving at a revision with which she was satisfied.

REVISION: PANEL 5	REVISION: BACK PANEL (6)	REVISION: FRONT PANEL (1)
Is accounting		**ARE YOU LOOKING**
the right major	**ACCOUNTING**	**for the area of business**
for you?		**right for you?**
		Consider a major in
Do you like exciting work?		
Do you like a sense of accomplishment?	**IS**	**ACCOUNTING**
Do you want a respected position?		**at the**
Do you want to be rewarded for doing well?	**A DEGREE**	**UNIVERSITY OF SOUTH**
	TO BE	**FLORIDA**
Find out how accounting can let your unique talents shine through!	**PROUD OF**	

REVISION: PANEL 2
Accounting: What's it all about?

Is accounting about some guy with glasses and an ugly suit dwelling in a dark, dank room all day hunched over a calculator? A job with no individuality, no pizzazz?

Of course not!

Accounting demands the ability to work as a member of a team gathering data, analyzing problems creatively, and presenting conclusions forcefully and imaginatively. An accountant must be alert, honest, resourceful, and logical (an ability to work with numbers doesn't hurt either).

In addition, accounting is actually one of the most diverse fields in the country, not to mention one of the most highly paid. Accountants analyze and prepare financial records for individuals, companies, branches of government, and non-profit organizations from agribusinesses to zoos.

Accounting at USF

USF's School of Accountancy was established in 1987 and has become one of the largest programs of accounting education in the United States. It is also one of the most prestigious, which means that you are in a position to benefit greatly from a university with the 4th best placement on the CPA exam. Various undergraduate scholarships are available.

REVISION: PANEL 3
The BBA: your Gateway

The degree of Bachelor of Business Administration is your gateway to pursue a path leading to one of the many diverse fields in accounting, including the following positions:
**forensic accountant
IRS auditor
tax accountant
legal auditor
loan officer
purchasing agent**
None of these positions fits the stereotype of accounting. The forensic accountant trains at the FBI academy, has the duty of stopping white collar crime, and travels widely. The IRS auditor is responsible for reviewing and evaluating individuals' and companies' financial records and for upholding federal law.

A BBA does not tie an accountant down to one particular industry, like a degree in engineering means that a person may be working in industry for his/her entire career. An accountant's future is flexible.

Rewards of Accounting

It is estimated that by the year 2000, the mean starting salary of a CPA will be $48,000, one of the highest of all majors. Accountancy can lead to management opportunities, and not just of an accounting department. Some accountants rise to the position of CEO!

REVISION: PANEL 4

Degree Requirements

Like other programs at USF, a Bachelor of Business Administration in accounting requires 120 semester hours. You must complete 18 hours of required accounting courses and 9 hours of accounting electives that enable you to follow your own path. Accounting majors take 39 hours of general business courses and 54 non-business courses.

If you are interested in obtaining more information about a degree in accounting, please contact the following office:

Undergraduate Advising
BSN 1406
College of Business Administration
University of South Florida
4202 E. Fowler Avenue, BSN 3403
Tampa, FL 33620
813-974-4290

Questions for Analysis

1. How did Rhonda's experiences contribute to selecting a topic? Was the topic one about which Rhonda had compelling dissonance? How can you tell?

2. What aspects of Rhonda's writing process contributed most to her inquiry?

3. Was the writing context one that mattered to Rhonda? Did the context help her with her inquiry or hinder her?

4. In what ways did the writer and reader positions Rhonda chose shape her inquiry? Would other positions work better? Why or why not?

5. Reflect on Rhonda's examination of cultural, social, and institutional values and practices. What understandings did she gain with respect to these forces?

6. Evaluate Rhonda's decision to write a brochure. Was this a realistic choice? Were there any insights Rhonda had before selecting a genre that contributed to her choice?

7. To what extent did Rhonda's focus respond to her question? Had she arrived at a significant insight?

8. Did Rhonda's plans for developing her focus further her understanding of her topic? Was the plan she selected the best for her focus? Why or why not?

9. How closely did Rhonda stick to her plan for developing her focus in her draft? To what extent did her decisions in this regard help or hinder her?

10. What advice would you give Rhonda about her polished version? Do you agree with the responses she received from her group and instructor?

WRITING FOR INQUIRY AND ACTION

THE WRITING ASSIGNMENT

You will use writing to inquire about a field of study that is important to you. To conduct your inquiry, consider your context for writing. With whom will you share your insights about the field of study you have selected? Determine your writing context at the outset of your inquiry and keep it in mind throughout the process of inquiry.

YOUR WRITING PROCESS

Using writing to gain insights into the field of study you have selected involves a well-executed inquiry. Your assignments will include your work with a number of writing strategies that will assist you with your inquiry.

Starting
Why pose questions?

Because you are a student, your inquiry in the context of fields of study promises to be especially relevant and valuable to you. Already, you are positioned in this context as, among other things, a learner. Regardless of the extent to which they utilize well-defined strategies to do so, learners have an important activity in common: they all raise questions which will lead them to better understandings. What more appropriate context is there to enact the position of learner than fields of study? Not all learners are equally proficient in articulating good questions, however. Beginning your inquiry in this context well will increase the potential rewards it offers you. Using the Questioning Strategy to help you formulate questions for inquiry is one way to begin well.

QUESTIONING STRATEGY
Select a Subject / Get in Touch with Dissonance / Locate Your Subject in a Writing Context / Formulate Questions for Inquiry / Workshop

---

Because you are a student, your inquiry into a field of study promises to be especially relevant and valuable to you. As you begin to pursue your academic interests, it is worthwhile to probe aspects of a field of study you find intriguing. The

Questioning Strategy assists you in beginning your inquiry into a field of study well. The Strategy will help you determine an important area of puzzlement that will frame your writing experience. Beginning your inquiry well increases the potential rewards writing in the context of fields of study offers you.

SELECTING A SUBJECT IN THE CONTEXT OF FIELDS OF STUDY

It is worthwhile to consider several possible topics in this context to help you to make a well-considered choice. Academic majors, special programs of study, or vocational tracks are obvious possibilities. Are there any others that intrigue you? A particular course within your major or program? A core sequence you will follow? A student seeking certification in electronics wanted to investigate the extent to which courses in a vocational sequence progressed according to skills. Or perhaps you would like to know more about the college, school, division, or program by which your major is classified. Or, like some students, you might be intrigued by how it is you learn a particular subject or how learning is enhanced in a particular course. A biology student, for instance, chose to inquire about the role writing plays in learning biology. A math student wanted to understand how working in groups enhanced learning in a calculus course.

After you have listed possible subjects, jot down your first thoughts and reactions for each about why these are important to you. Include especially aspects about the subjects that evoke strong emotions. This brainstorming work will help you select a topic based on which subject included in the list puzzles you the most, which you would like to understand better, which stimulates the strongest feelings, or which holds the most consequences for you.

GETTING IN TOUCH WITH DISSONANCE

Once you have selected a subject for inquiry within the context of fields of study, reflect on your learning experiences with the subject that particularly stands out for you, as well as any unknowns that strike you as important. Since you might have very little experience at this time in a field, it is especially worthwhile to ask yourself what it is you most want to know about your subject. Why are these unknowns important to you? Identifying values and their sources can help you further in understanding why a subject in this context is compelling to you. In addition, noticing mismatches or gaps between your experiences in a field and your values exposes potential areas of inquiry.

LOCATING YOUR SUBJECT IN A WRITING CONTEXT

Consider readers for whom your writing on the topic you select concerning a field of study is relevant. Readers within academic contexts are likely candidates, such as students in your composition class, students in another course pursuing similar academic or vocational interests, a teacher of a course relevant to your inquiry, students at your former high school who are considering a similar field of study, and so on. Other readers for whom your writing would be relevant include, of course, those who care about you and your ideas, such as family and friends. Also consider persons who can relate to your experiences as a student, such as the readers of a student newspaper or other publication; or perhaps there are readers whose actions you might wish to influence, such as administrators, librarians, or school boards.

FORMULATING QUESTIONS FOR INQUIRY

Alternative questions can be framed in different ways depending on where you might want your investigation to lead. Formulating a question so it will help you to a **new understanding** can be fruitful if you are especially compelled to arrive at an explanation of something you don't know or find confusing about a field of study. You might be uncertain about what kind of major, program, or vocational track best fits with how you see yourself, or maybe you want to know what kind of research skills are required in a field. A **cultural sources** question can lead to inquiry into the cultural, social, or institutional values and practices that affect experiences with or attitudes about your subject, both in and out of a school setting. A question that directs you toward **finding a solution to a problem** can initiate investigation of specific areas you want to find out about with regard to your subject—perhaps the role writing does or should play in learning a given subject or perhaps the degree to which a subject such as math is characterized by objective knowledge. A question that asks what **course of action** to take may help you determine what becoming a professional in a field of study entails.

Deciding which question to choose after you have posed several—at least one of each type—will depend on which you think holds the most chances for leading to new knowledge and which matters most to you and those in your writing context. Of course, you also need to take into consideration the time you have for the project.

Example: Mark's Questions

Fields of Study that Matter to Me

- Fine arts
  Since I'm in college, I'm worried that I don't know as much as I need to about art. I'm no artist myself, but if I'm college educated, how much about am I supposed to know?

- Social science
  I like lots of areas to study in social science. I like anthropology and learning about different cultures. Also, political science. I think governments are fascinating. I might go on to law school, so I'll probably want to take a lot of courses in poli-sci. Of course, history is my favorite. It's going to be my major. I like knowing how things were in the past.

My Choice for this Inquiry: History, My Major

Learning about history is exciting. Of all other subjects, it definitely stimulates the most feeling in me. Putting bits and pieces together from the past to make a picture tell a story is fun. And it's my major. It should matter to me most.

My Writing Contexts

- My cousin: his mother teaches history in the 7th grade, but he thinks it's boring.
- Mrs. Stone's high school history class: these students could benefit from what I have to say.
- Writing class: students are interested in learning about the various academic fields they could go into.
- My current American history teacher.
- History scholars: I wouldn't have much credibility here.

My Choice for Writing Context

Mrs. Stone's high school history class.

My Experience	*My Values*	*Cultural Sources*	*Dissonance*
My history teachers say there are competing theories of history.	Gaining factual knowledge about the past.	In high school history was about names and dates.	I don't know how to decide which theories are right.
My college instructors encourage class discussions of open-ended questions.	Instructors who have a wealth of information, who serve as sources of knowledge. Answers that are right or wrong.	Our society teaches us that adults in leadership positions are authorities.	I wonder how much I learned when teachers expected me to give them back what they gave me.
My American history teacher sometimes disagrees with the textbook.	Texts that provide accounts of how things really happened.	School: in the past, what I have read I have been tested on.	Before this semester I didn't know there was so much disagreement in history.

My Questions for Inquiry

New understanding:
By what criteria can competing historical accounts be evaluated?
What constitutes a reliable source in history?

Cultural sources
Why are students in high school rewarded for knowing just the names, dates, and places of history?
What does the concern with the "facts" of history leave out?

Finding a solution to a problem
What roles do or should teachers and students have in a history classroom?

Course of action
What are the necessary skills a person must possess in order to be called a historian? To succeed as a history student?

My Choice for Question for Inquiry

What are the necessary skills a person must possess in order to succeed as a history student? This question matters most to me because thinking and writing about it will probably help me with my courses.

WORKSHOP

Sharing your work with the Questioning Strategy in a group gives you the opportunity to discuss how you plan to frame your inquiry before you continue. To ensure your group work is helpful, here are some guidelines to follow.

1. Determine if the question will lead to genuine inquiry in the context of fields of study.

2. Determine if the kind of inquiry suggested by the question seems appropriate for the writing context.

Exploring

Why explore?

Sustaining your inquiry by exploring the topic you selected in the context of fields of study encourages you to keep an open mind before reaching your conclusions. Exploring by using the Three Perspectives Guide is one way to help ensure you will conduct a strong exploration. The Guide will help to generate ideas and attitudes you might not have previously examined or even thought to examine, making you more receptive to new insights. If you are examining unknowns in a field of study with which you have had little previous experience, struggling to articulate ideas and details can indicate a need to consult sources.

THREE PERSPECTIVES GUIDE

Investigate from Three Perspectives / Review Ideas and Highlight Those that Answer Your Question / Allow Your Ideas to Incubate / Workshop

---

INVESTIGATING YOUR QUESTION FROM THREE PERSPECTIVES

Before you begin exploring, write down your question and your writing context. You will want to keep them both in mind while you use the Three Perspectives Guide.

DESCRIBE AND DISTINGUISH

To examine your subject from one perspective, you will describe and distinguish it in such a way that it stands out from everything else. What are the significant traits and features that comprise your subject? For a major, these might include required courses, subject matters, and areas of specialization; for a specific course, distinguishing features might be its methods of instruction and assessment, its sources of authority, the skills it fosters or ignores, and the questions it raises. Also consider the values and attitudes that are held for your subject, both by you and by others, as well as the values and attitudes it projects. A reading list in a modern American literature course, for example, might be seen as projecting certain values and attitudes according to the authors it includes and according to those it excludes.

TRACE MOVES AND CHANGES

Another perspective from which to explore your topic asks you to trace moves and changes. How did your interest in your subject begin? How has the field of study changed? How have cultural influences affected the field, or how has a field affected culture? For example, as a result of a heightened sensitivity to and value for diversity, many reading lists in modern American literature courses have been revised to include authors who reflect people's differences in race, class, gender, and sexual orientation.

MAP NETWORKS AND RELATIONSHIPS

Using the third perspective of the guide helps you to map networks and relationships. Three specific ways of doing so are by classifying, comparing and contrasting, and creating analogies. How you perform any of these acts will influence what you will generate in your exploration. Consider different ways you might classify the practice of keeping a log of an experiment for the lab component of a biology course. Perhaps you would classify it as a means for recording data, as a form of busy work, as a way to become disciplined, or as a way to think. Certainly further exploration of these classifications would produce very different results. The classifications would also suggest certain attitudes that might be examined.

REVIEWING IDEAS AND HIGHLIGHTING THOSE THAT ANSWER YOUR QUESTION

As you look over your exploration, be sure you have included details for each perspective about cultural beliefs and values that shape your subject. This involves thinking about stereotypes, habits, assumptions, and so on that derive from various sources in our culture and society, such as family, church, and the media. For example, one of the stereotypes of a science professor—that of the "nutty professor"—is reinforced by various movies, not the least of which is the Jerry Lewis spoof by the same name, which was more recently remade with Eddie Murphy. Although we might acknowledge that the stereotype is ridiculous and, as far as Jerry Lewis or Eddie Murphy is concerned, merely an outlet for their much beloved humor, examining the stereotype and ways it has shaped views of science professors can be illuminating.

ALLOWING IDEAS TO INCUBATE

If you find that sections of your exploration are not very illuminating or that you are unable to highlight emerging insights, it would probably be worthwhile to investigate sources on your subject. Some important sources in the context of fields of study are course catalogs, academic journals, course syllabi, tests, lecture notes, etc. Talking to persons connected to your field, such as students, professors, advisors, or professionals in the work force, is also extremely valuable. Be sure you still take time to reflect on your exploration after you have fleshed out your ideas by consulting sources. Sometimes our best insights are reached when we let our ideas "rest" for a while.

Example: Excerpts from Mark's Exploration

My Question and Writing Context: What are the necessary skills a person must possess in order to succeed as a history student? I plan to write to prospective history majors in Mrs. Stone's history class.

Describe and Distinguish

What is distinctive

The sources of information in history are authentic or what you might call objective:

- diaries
- letters
- first-hand testimony
- objects: uniforms, emblems, furniture, tools, etc.

The instructional methods in history concentrate on the facts:

- lectures
- exam
- lots of reading
- dramatizations: my high school history teacher sometimes did this.

Physical features

In history, all data is taken into account. Anything that you might see, touch, smell, or taste would be important to record. One thing this tells me about my question is that to be good in history, you need to be very observant.

Values

It's always said that those who don't know the past are doomed to repeat it. I don't know how true that is. It seems to me that many people who know the past still repeat it, which is sometimes good, sometimes bad. I think we understand others and ourselves better by studying history.

But maybe as a whole we don't repeat our mistakes. When we're thinking about getting involved in a conflict in another country, Vietnam is always brought up. And then we try not to get involved in an armed combat way, like we're close to doing in Bosnia. But there was Desert Storm. Maybe there it was clear we could get in and out quickly, so it wouldn't be like Vietnam. I bet others can see plenty of similarities, though.

I've always valued the accuracy of history. More and more I'm seeing that for some things, accuracy might be "in the eyes of the beholder."

Activities

Lots of reading and discussion. In history class, it seems like students are talking as much as the teacher. The teacher encourages this, even when there are disagreements. At first this surprised me, and I was kind of bothered that the teacher didn't just set things straight. I mean, it's *his* class, right? Now I've started enjoying some of the arguments. It's not like you can argue that it's sunny when it's raining outside, but sometimes the discussions really make you think. And then if you're not all thinking the same way, it's a matter of deciding what sounds the most convincing. But that's hard.

Images and feelings

It may seem funny, but somehow when I think of history, the first images that pop into my head are American flag, fireworks, and other patriotic things. I feel excited and proud.

Trace Moves and Changes

Beginnings

As a kid, I played GI Joes. I enacted battles I heard about from WWII. I started learning the names of military ranks and different kinds of combat gear, artillery, tanks, etc. I also played board games based on war. I think I absorbed a lot of the history about different wars pretty easily because of my initial interest in war games. Of course, studying history is a lot more than just learning about wars, but that's what got me started, I think.

Changes

- All through school until college, I did well in my history classes. Now I'm still doing okay, but it's harder. Some of the accounts we get about a certain event do not agree with other accounts of the same thing. It seems like it doesn't matter as much, just that I get the material right. Sometimes this bothers me because I think there must be a right answer and a wrong answer. I guess there is, but there's a lot in between.

- How I've changed, how I'm changing, is I'm having to adapt how I learn history. I don't just write things down to memorize and use my imagination just to reconstruct how something "really" was. Now I write more to get down what I'm thinking, and then I ask myself what the teacher might think of my ideas. It's made me feel like I have to be more responsible for what I learn.

- Changes in history can affect society, too. It seems that more and more our society questions the idea of authority. I think history has contributed to this.

Map Networks and Relationships

Similarities and opposites

History and English are similar:

- both involve reading and writing
- both help us understand ourselves
- both involve communicating well
- English: writing essays on your own ideas
- history: presenting convincing arguments for your points of view

History and biology are opposites:

- history is about civilization and society
- biology is about animals and physical life

Classifications according to cultural, social, or institutional assumptions, values, beliefs, and practices

At one time, I thought history was objective. How can truth play favorites? But obviously, there are lots of stories that don't get told. What does get told depends on the values of a society. For example, it seems that a lot of what I've studied in history has the idea of progress in it. This invention led to that positive change in society. We value seeing time in terms of progress. Anyway, maybe if something doesn't seem to go along with a value, it won't "go down in history." Like we're always taught that crime doesn't pay. When criminals make history, you always learn what their punishment was. How many *famous* crimes go without punishment?

WORKSHOP

Sharing explorations in a group can reveal what details or ideas stand out for others as especially significant. Readers other than the writer also can help the writer to see areas he or she overlooked. As you and the members of your group collaborate on each other's exploration, follow the brief list of directives provided below.

1. Identify areas in the exploration that are most connected to the question.

2. Highlight recurring ideas or images and note the writer's emerging understandings.

3. Consider how carefully cultural, social, and institutional values and practices have been examined.

Positioning Writers and Readers

Why position writers and readers?

Setting your writer and reader positions has important consequences for your writing. Inappropriate writer or reader positions could impede your ability to share your understanding about a field of study. On the other hand, thoughtful decisions about writer and reader positions and critical analysis of them can help you to write more effectively. The Writer/Reader Positioning Strategy assists you in this endeavor.

WRITER/READER POSITIONING STRATEGY
Position Yourself as Writer / Position Your Readers / Workshop

---

POSITIONING YOURSELF AS A WRITER

Positioning yourself as a writer in your writing context means determining who you will be in the text you write. Immediately, that decision is constrained by positions you already have or could realistically have in your writing context. In order to think about these positions better, write them down. In addition, list positions you have left behind and those from which you are excluded. What would these positions allow you to write about your topic? What would they prevent you from writing about? Write down your responses to these questions so you can make a thoughtful decision about the writer position you will take in the context you have selected. As an example, consider a first-year student with an undecided major who has been inquiring into the role group work plays in her introductory algebra class. If such a student were to write to students in the class, she could write from the position of, among others, novice math student or group participant. Notice that the first position suggests she will keep to her experiences with math, whereas the other position suggests that she would include other experiences as a student in other classes as well. In the context described, the writer would not be able to take the position of mathematician or expert teacher.

POSITIONING YOUR READERS

Like writer positions, reader positions are constrained by the writing context. But determining a reader position isn't simply a matter of identifying who the readers are given a certain setting. You may be writing to students in your composition class, for example, but you might choose not to position them as students. Instead, you could decide to make the reader position that of peer. Through writing, you enter into a relationship with your readers. As with other kinds of relationships, what position one person occupies has implications for what other positions are available. The student writing as a participant of a group needs to think about what reader positions make sense given the kinds of relationships a participant in a group can have with his or her readers. This writer might choose to position his or her readers as collaborators, as evaluators, or as grade-seekers. Each of these positions enacts a different relationship between the writer-as-participant and the readers. What is important is that the choice of reader position makes sense given the writer's position of participant.

From among the reader positions that are available in your writing context, determine which make sense given your writer position. Write these down to help you make your selection. To decide which position you will choose, consider ways in which the positions might benefit your readers. What might your readers gain by adopting the reader position? How might they be harmed or angered? Reflect on questions such as these in conjunction with the question you are exploring. What reader position best fits your topic and inquiry?

Examining the reader position you have selected can strengthen your writing and enhance your inquiry. With your question and context in mind, jot down values and beliefs that characterize the reader position you have chosen. The position of collaborator can be characterized by the values of cooperation, dependability, responsibility, trust, and so on. What beliefs characterize the position? To examine your reader position, consider also knowledge and background. The position of collaborator suggests someone who knows that collaborating involves working with others and who has experience with sharing responsibility for a collective effort. What knowledge would you expect from the reader position you have set? What background experiences?

Example: Sue's Inquiry into a Nursing Program

My Question and Readers: What image of a nurse does the nursing program at the University of South Florida foster? I am writing to members of the Student Health Care Society.

Positioning Myself

How I have been positioned

I am a student on the basic track in the nursing program. That track means I have to get basic liberal arts courses out of the way before taking the nursing courses.

I took a first aid class and got certified to do CPR.

I gave blood and once bone marrow.

Positions left behind

Someone who knows she wants to be in a caring profession but not sure what.

Someone who knows she wants to go into health care but not sure what.

My Writer Position: An informed applicant.

Positioning My Readers

Positions available

Prospective nursing students

Prospective nurses

Students in health care interested in the nursing program

Students who like competition

My Choice of Reader Position: students in health care interested in nursing—prospective applicants.

Who is excluded?

Only those who know they definitely do not want to go through the program.

I want to make sure I don't somehow make guys think they're excluded.

Who benefits?

The program itself benefits.

Other health related programs might be harmed—lose majors.

Students who are waffling would benefit.

I might benefit by helping to shape others' impressions of the program.

Values and Background of Reader Position

Background

They're familiar with the program. They know there is a program.

They know they're interested in health.

They probably know what a lot of their options are.

Maybe they've heard the things I have about competition.

The nursing program has a good reputation. It's easy to get a job as a nurse once you're through.

Mostly young adults to middle-aged adults. Mostly women?

About half from this area. Others from New York, New Jersey, etc. Some international students.

Probably like people and like to feel needed.

Values

- Health
- Other people
- Life
- Being responsible, being prepared
- Doing well, professionalism
- Learning from experts
- Knowing what to do in a crisis
- If they are undecided, they probably would want there to be some kind of flexibility in the program—transferable credits?

WORKSHOP

Collaborating in a group about your work with the Writer/Reader Strategy can lead to new understandings about your writing context. For discussion, consider the following:

1. Determine how realistic the writer and reader positions are and how effective they will be for the writing context.

2. Describe the relationship suggested by the writer and reader positions. Discuss the implications of the relationship for drafting.

3. Consider how thoroughly the reader position has been described. Note any additional values, knowledge, beliefs, and background experiences that characterize the reader position.

Selecting Genres

Why consider genres?

The form your writing about your topic in the context of fields of study takes—a report, an academic essay, a letter, a pamphlet—contributes to how your insight about your topic is understood. A letter to a friend conveys an intimacy about your insight that a report obscures. On the other hand, a report suggests a kind of professionalism that is not so formally conveyed by a letter to a friend. Because genre contributes to meaning, considering alternative genres can continue your inquiry about your topic; it is not simply an activity to determine how you will present the insight or the content you already have. Also, more than a ready-made form, the genre you choose prompts you to think about specific ways you might utilize, reconfigure, or even ignore its formal or conventional features.

Genre is one of the most concrete ways you contextualize your writing. Taking time to consider carefully the genre you will use affects how the relationship between reader and writer is constructed in your text. The Genre Strategy assists you with the important decisions you make concerning this aspect of contextualizing your writing.

GENRE STRATEGY
Select a Genre / Examine the Implications of the Genre / Workshop

---

SELECTING A GENRE

Texts about a subject in the context of fields of study occur in all types of genres. On a University Expo day at your school, it would not be unusual for there to be speeches, essays, flyers, newsletters, and so on about programs of study, special courses, colloquia, academic student organizations, and numerous other subjects. What are some of the genres you know that you could use in this context? Listing these will help you to realize how different your writing would be for the various genres you could choose.

Think about the genres you have listed in light of your question and writing context. What genre(s) will contribute to your inquiry? What genres are most appropriate for your writer and reader positions? Assessing the compatibility of writer and reader positions with your genre is very important.

If the writer position is that of a novice learner, certain genres help to establish you in that position more readily than others (and some genres could even prevent you from making that writer position clear). The same is true for reader positions. A writer in the position of novice learner could write an academic essay or a research paper for a teacher in the position of evaluator, for example.

To determine how realistic a genre is for your writing context, you will also need to think about some very practical matters, including the constraints of this project and production factors, such as time, cost, and materials. Also, take into account how familiar you are with a given genre as this could help determine how long it will take you to produce your text.

EXAMINING THE IMPLICATIONS OF THE GENRE

Based on this preliminary inquiry, which genre will you choose? Which genre is appropriate for your writing context? Which will best enable you to present your topic in an effective way and help you to establish the writer and reader positions you have set?

A realistic assessment of your familiarity with the genre you have chosen is crucial to estimating well the time it will take you to utilize the genre selected. It is especially important that you think about the implications the features will have for your writing context: such thinking enhances your inquiry. A student who chooses to create a flyer for his or her writing context, for example, will need to make decisions about the use of visuals. Examining how visuals are used in a flyer could lead the writer to discover a feature about the topic that he or she believes captures an important understanding the writer wants to convey. Even if the writer doesn't use a visual to present this central feature, the analysis assisted the writer's inquiry.

Analyzing features of your genre also involves considering the kinds of details, information, evidence, and so forth that are expected. One of the benefits derived from this activity is that it can show you areas you still need to explore or research. For example, if you're writing a brochure on your major, using your own experience as evidence that a degree in that major from your school is well-respected might not be as effective as other kinds of evidence. This is because the brochure usually does not include who you are (aside from your writer position, of course), so you might not be able to make personal details weigh as heavily as other kinds of evidence. Instead, you might need to do some research in order to learn, for instance, a particular national ranking of a program at your school.

Keep in mind when analyzing genre that it can be flexible to your needs. How effectively you have utilized genre for your writing context should be the standard by which you assess ways you might deviate from the usual features of your genre.

Example: Mark's Genre Selection

Selecting a Genre:

- essay
- report
- video
- brochure
- pamphlet
- speech
- dialogue
- flyer

My Question: What are the necessary skills a person must possess in order to succeed as a history student?

Context: Mrs. Stone's history class. I plan to target prospective history majors.

- The oral genres would be okay if I could be like a guest speaker in Mrs. Stone's class. I don't like to have to be up in front of a class, though, so I'd rather do something written.

- I don't have the ability to do much in the way of visual genres. Well, I can do some visual things on my computer like graphs and charts and clip art.

- I was thinking I'd write an essay, though, so I don't think I'd need any visuals.

- Unless maybe I wrote something like a pamphlet.

Revised List:

- essay
- pamphlet
- flyer
- brochure

Preliminary Analysis

- A pamphlet would let me focus on just my topic. But for a pamphlet, I'd have to know about everything there is about history. A pamphlet is dense. It has so much information. I'm not at a place yet in my education to be able to do this.

- An essay reinforces the idea that my readers are students in a classroom. That's good, especially for my subject: skills of a history student. With an essay, I could explain a lot about myself, which I wouldn't do in a pamphlet. I could let them know I used to be a student in Mrs. Stone's class and just come right out and tell them why I'm writing. But I don't know how I'd get around telling them they need to know what I have to say because they won't really learn it in Mrs. Stone's class.

- A flyer or brochure? With those, you're usually promoting something, which is what I guess I'll be doing. One page—a flyer—probably wouldn't cut it. This wouldn't be an *ad*.

- Brochure has the idea of some kind of product or service in it, like it's selling something. But it's not what you usually think of as an advertisement. And it's not like students aren't used to getting brochures once in a while. We got brochures about taking Spanish after school, and I also remember at least one about 4-H.

Choice and Analysis

I had thought I'd write an essay, but maybe it would be interesting to try a brochure. Besides, there can be essay-like parts in a brochure. Also, I can get around the problem of sounding like I'm putting down Mrs. Stone.

Examining the Implications of the Genre

My Choice: A brochure.

Context: Mr. Stones' history class

Details and Authority

A brochure is maybe short compared to an essay, but it's also usually very informational. It's often like a reference source. Readers expect all the basics they'll need. It has to be thorough. If they still have questions about the very basics, then the brochure doesn't establish much authority. The looks of the brochure can also help with authority. Giving very specific information and maybe where to go for more information also helps establish authority.

Reader Position: future history major

Format

Usually tri-fold, but I've seen some that are basically a page folded in half, like a card. There might be headings, bold-faced print, visuals, writing that is in phrases or full sentences. Sometimes each page/fold is a section. The front page/fold catches attention and lets the reader know what the brochure is all about. These features could help me talk about different things without having to connect them the way a reader would have to in an essay. Also, in a brochure I wouldn't have to give background information.

Formality

This depends on the readers to some extent, but a brochure is always a bit formal simply because it presents information in such an organized way. Being organized is really important. It shouldn't look sloppy. But you can be more informal in the language you use. You can use everyday language and talk to the reader, or you can use very formal language, and sometimes technical, depending on what the brochure's for. Mine's not going to be technical, but I don't want to use slang or really informal language either. This *is* about school, so I want it to come across as educational without being boring or intimidating.

Medium

It's written and often has visuals or at least different kinds of fonts and styles. Effect? Could make it interesting. Would help make reading about studying history less boring.

> *Variation*
>
> Brochures can vary a lot by how much writing there is in them. Some have what almost amounts to a fairly long essay, or even short essays. Some have so little they could almost be a flyer that's just one page without any sections. I like how the brochure can overlap with an essay. Some of the ideas I'll want to discuss in some detail.

WORKSHOP

As you collaborate about genre in your writing group, consider the following suggestions.

1. Assess how realistic and practical a genre is for the writing context and for this project in the context of your composition class.

2. Consider ways in which the genre selected will affect the writing context.

3. Address how thoroughly genre has been characterized. Do the details that describe genre suggest the understanding of someone who will be able to utilize the genre effectively?

Focusing

Why focus?

Focusing gives you the opportunity to reflect on your inquiry in order to decide how you will now frame the writing of your text. A student who questioned the kinds of support creative writing students need might find that he or she is primarily concerned about various ways to support the writing of drama. Or suppose a student is motivated to understand better why he or she feels a powerful outlet for the need to be creative in the field of business. This student's inquiry might lead to examining various areas, such as marketing, finance, and accounting. Even if a student was already inquiring about something as specific as, say, the role of the imagination in biology, when focusing, the student might come to the conclusion that the most important insights to emerge from this inquiry concern the role writing plays in fostering creativity in science.

Because an open-ended inquiry into a field of study can lead to many different insights about any number of aspects of your topic, the Focusing Strategy assists you in reaching an understanding you find important for your writing context.

FOCUSING STRATEGY
State Your Focus / Workshop

STATING YOUR FOCUS

To state your focus, it is helpful to restate your question and review your work with the other strategies you have used in the context of fields of study. If you have highlighted insights in your exploration or jotted down emerging understandings elsewhere, gather them together so you can examine them now.

Writing possible focuses in a subject/point of significance format is useful for clarifying your own understanding of what you most want to say in your writing. In the context of fields of study, the subject of your focus should clearly identify an "academic" topic—for example, certain courses, majors, methods of instruction, study skills, thinking strategies—even if your writing context will not involve readers directly connected to academia. Working to ensure that your focus specifies a subject from within the parameters of "fields of study" assures that the insight you articulate helps to illuminate this very important part of any student's life.

Example: Sue's Focuses

Question: What image of a nurse does the nursing program at the University of South Florida foster?

Possible focuses

<u>Subject</u>	<u>Point of significance</u>
The nursing program at USF ——————	upholds the ideals of professionalism.
Being in the nursing program—————	is like being a member of a team.
The nursing program at USF ——————	prepares you to be a member of a team.

Example: Mark's Focuses

Question: What skills does a college student need to do well in history?

Possible focuses

<u>Subject</u>	<u>Point of significance</u>
Studying history in college————————	is not like studying history in high school.
The ability to form good arguments —————	is important for doing well in history.
The skills needed by a college history student————————————	include a mind for details, an ability to interpret, an ability to judge, and an ability to form good arguments.
Studying history in college————————	has a lot in common with English classes.
A successful history student —————————	is like a painter.

My Choice of a Focus

Any of these focuses could be important to the students in Mrs. Stone's class. They all are important to me and show my understanding. What got me started on all this were my mixed feelings about how the teacher encourages us to argue in my history class, so I want to include that, but not just that. My choice will be the third one: "The skills needed by a college history student include a mind for details, an ability to interpret, an ability to judge, and an ability to form good arguments."

Organizing

Considering alternative ways to organize your text about a field of study continues to advance your inquiry. Whether you decide to organize your focus by whole and parts, by time segments, by setting criteria, or by grouping, trying out each of these different ways can bring you to a deeper understanding of your subject. Your inquiry is enhanced in two specific ways. First, you come to understand what stands out for you as the significant components of your subject. To develop a text about nursing by time segments, you will need to determine what aspects of nursing are enhanced by considering them with reference to time. Second, forecasting different ways of organizing your focus can be seen as "pushing" yourself to a deeper understanding of the insight you have reached. As you consider aspects of nursing according to significant moments in time, you are urged to elaborate on the point of significance of your focus for each of those moments. After you have created alternative plans for organizing your text, consider which works best for your focus and genre (see Part II).

Example: Sue's Possible Organization Plans

Whole / Parts

Focus:

The nursing program at USF ————————	upholds the ideals of professionalism.
The faculty ————————————	are experts in their areas.
The core courses ————————	get you ready to be part of a team.
The practicums ————————	make sure you don't just know, but can also do.
Competition in the program ————	can be connected to the importance of having a good team.

Time Focus

The way the nursing program is sequenced —	helps you develop the ideals of professionalism.
The liberal arts requirements taken first ——	make sure you're well-rounded and committed.
Going through the core courses with mostly the same students ————	helps you learn the material and be part of a team.
Advancing to the practicums————	ensures you can perform well in real-life situations.
By the time you're finished, you ———	are able to give the best care to your patients.

Example: Mark's Possible Organization Plans

Whole / Parts

The ability to interpret what you
read or even experience———————— helps you to sort out facts from arguments.

Learning to evaluate arguments———————— helps you compare different versions of the
same historical event.

Learning to write down your own ideas
as well as others'———————— helps you to think better.

Speaking up during class discussions ——— exposes students to different points of view.

Time Segments

Learning facts and dates in history ——— develops a mind for details.

With this background knowledge,
a student ————————— can begin to sort out stories that make the
most sense.

After learning to be critical,
a history student ————————— can think even more independently.

Criteria

Criteria for a skill:

- helps you to do well in school

- strengthens your mind

Having a mind for details ———————— exercises your memory and helps you do
better on objective tests.

The ability to interpret ———————— increases understanding and helps you with
essay tests.

The ability to judge———————— helps you to be critical, to do well on tests,
and to participate in class discussions.

The ability to argue———————— helps you to think on your own, to contribute
to class discussions, and to write papers.

Grouping

Like a painter, a history student——————— notices detail.

Both a painter and a history student ——— try to see different points of view about
something.

Both also ————————— are creative and use the imagination.

WORKSHOP

Share your work with Focusing and Organizing, along with your plans for
developing, in order to determine which of your plans can best help you develop
your understanding of your topic. Use the following directives to guide your
collaboration.

1. Make sure that the focus is written in the format of subject/point of significance. Is the subject a field of study? Does the point of significance
   articulate an important understanding? Refer to the question for inquiry
   and the work with other strategies to offer suggestions.

2. Determine how effectively each organizational plan will assist in developing the focus.

Drafting

Knowing that you will likely write several drafts of your text before writing a polished version is both reassuring and liberating. It is reassuring to know that you have the opportunity to compose your ideas with care but without having to worry that others will see your struggles, false starts, misspellings, and so on. It is liberating to realize you can follow your ideas where they lead you, that your inquiry is still taking place while you draft. Even though you will be drafting to develop your focus and implement your plan for organizing, noticing new insights while you draft is an exciting and rewarding aspect of this part of your inquiry (see Drafting, Part II).

Example: Mark's Polished Version

EXAMPLE: MARK'S POLISHED VERSION

BACK PANEL (4)

Skill 3: Arguing your own point of view

College history majors usually have strong backgrounds in history. Some students have already extensively studied some time period that is especially interesting to them. During class discussions, these students might be best able to present their own points of view. But college professors encourage *all* students to develop and be able to support their own points of view on essay tests and research papers.

Besides reading and listening to pay attention to details, and in addition to understanding different points of view, history majors in college learn to form their own versions of historical events. Keeping weekly journals of your thoughts about what is being studied helps you formulate a viewpoint. In a journal, you might connect what you learn about a historical period or event to your own experiences and interests in order to develop a point of view.

For example, a student in Florida studying the civil rights movement might investigate civil disobedience in Florida during the 1960s, which is often overshadowed by more famous acts in other states. Writing assists you in putting your ideas down in words so you can participate in class discussions and so you have something to start with when it comes time to write a paper. You might be surprised by how much writing you do for your history classes, so be prepared!

Remember, history in college is no longer just memorizing facts. You use writing, reading, listening, and discussing to think for yourself.

FRONT PANEL (1)

THREE ESSENTIAL SKILLS

FOR

HISTORY MAJORS

☑ Paying attention to details

☑ Seeing different points of view

☑ Arguing your own point of view

If you are planning a history major or minor, expect to cultivate three essential skills.

PANEL 2

Skill 1: Paying attention to details

History majors in college are most successful when they learn to do what artists do. Good artists are very observant and notice details others overlook. You are now developing this skill of paying close attention to details in high school. This skill is your anchor. But college level history students have to be more independent and more responsible for their own learning.

Learning to read carefully is one way you develop the skill of paying attention to details. In high school, there are aids to assist you in acquiring this skill. For example, high school textbooks in history contain headings, words in bold-faced print that can be looked up in the glossary, summaries of main points, and review sections. If you only rely on these aids to skim the material instead of learning to read carefully, you will have trouble in college because many college-level history texts do not have so many aids.

In addition to reading carefully, listening well is another key factor in paying attention to details. In high school, the teacher uses handouts and writes important points on the board. Think of these aids as being like training wheels that will have to be taken off in college. College history professors hardly use the board at all, and sometimes what they say in a lecture isn't even in the book. Learn to listen well so you can take good notes. You will find that you study from your notes as much as you do from your textbook.

Last, it is important to begin recognizing the *telling* detail. The telling detail is one in which a person's character can be seen or one that seems to foretell historical events. Hitler, for example, is known to have cherished a monstrous inkwell that he kept on his desk, and he valued highly the overblown architecture of Albert Speer. His bad taste in furniture and the arts is a detail that adds to our historical understanding of him, his actions, and his obsessions.

PANEL 3

Skill 2: Seeing different points of view

Some historians say that the United States was involved in the Vietnam War for a noble reason--to contain communism. Others disagree, viewing the conflict as essentially a civil war in which we had no right to intervene. Suppose both sides have all the same facts and details. Which side is right?

In college, details sometimes become more complicated than they were in high school. Using the very same facts, people can give different accounts of the same historical event. A college history professor might even disagree with what the textbook says. If you have learned the skill of paying attention to details, you will notice these differences, which is important. Seeing different points of view is an important skill for history students because facts and details can't tell a story themselves. It's the historians who put the details together to create a complete picture, which again makes them like artists.

In college, it becomes clear that the pictures created by historians show a certain point of view. It is important to keep this in mind because sometimes there is a version of a historical event that contradicts another. The Vietnam War is an excellent example. There is the point of view of the American military leaders like General Westmoreland, who cannot say that Americans they fought with died in vain. There is the viewpoint of civilian leaders like John McNamara, who regrets his part in what he considers a political failure. There are also the points of view of journalists not involved in the fighting, who could take a more objective look at both sides, the ordinary American "grunt," the South Vietnamese soldier and the South Vietnamese civilian, and the North Vietnamese soldiers and their leaders. To each of these people, details about the war on which people might agree can look drastically different.

291

Responding

Your group members represent excellent critical readers for your text in a field of study. Whether or not you call upon the position of student in your text, your group members' experiences as students will likely help them relate to your work. You will also want to get your instructor's input. The responses that follow were based on the Reader Response Guide (see Part II). This guide can also assist you in constructing your own response to your text.

Example: Compiled Responses (Excerpts) to Mark's Brochure from His Group (Ronjii and Chris) and Instructor

Overall Response

Chris: Going with a bi-fold brochure was a great idea. This lets you present "short essays" on each panel without giving high school students the first impression that they're going to read an essay. Students will learn what you want them to from this and be interested.

Focus

Ronjii: Your focus is straightforward—"Three essential skills for history majors are paying attention to details, seeing different points of view, and arguing your own point of view." Wouldn't these be the same for any student in a history class? You say *major.* I think you should not limit your focus that way. Also, I think the points about writing, reading, listening, and discussing seem like a second focus or a sub-focus. This could be confusing. Can you relate these points to your focus more clearly?

Development

Ronjii: It's clear that your readers are soon to be in a transition from high school to college. Your details that relate to that transition are great. Your readers will feel engaged. But some of your examples might lose them. Who is Albert Speer? Good to include details about civil rights, but why have you mentioned no one who is African-American? Also, no women? One more thing: you give great details about Vietnam, and it might be bad to lose them, but I think the more recent Desert Storm could be better for your readers.

Chris: You are writing to upper level history students in high school. The reader position is that of future major or minor. I question your picture on panel 4. It works great for the idea of arguing, but it kind of goes against what you're saying about class discussions. I think the person standing up would be taken as a teacher figure. That is the person in the picture with the answers. The other two just have questions. Also, a couple things you say might come across as putting down high school, like the "training wheels," the "more complicated" details (panel 3), and the warning at the end.

Organization

Instructor: You have done a superb job organizing your brochure according to parts of the whole. The headings on each panel are effective, and your visuals are incorporated nicely. There is an aspect of your organization that I find confusing, however. Do you mean to suggest that there is a chronological order to reading, writing, and discussing? Notice how you separate these on your panels, indicating perhaps that you see one leading to the next. Is this what you want to suggest? If so, do so more explicitly. If not, you need to reconsider how and when you mention those points.

Revising

Besides giving you the opportunity to communicate your ideas more effectively, revising in a field of study can deepen your awareness of what it means to make a commitment to a field. The Revising Strategy offers ideas that can help you with your revision (see Revising, Part II).

In the example of Mark's brochure, a revision enabled him to incorporate valuable suggestions from his group and instructor. First, he revised to clarify the relationship between the three skills a student of history should cultivate and the activities of writing, reading, listening, and discussing. Mark's revision deepened his own understanding: he revised his panels to show that each activity is relevant to developing each skill, an insight he had not reached when writing the polished version of his brochure.

Mark also tried to be more sensitive to his readers' experiences as he revised, minimizing differences between high school and college and providing more timely examples, such as the United States' involvement in Bosnia. In addition, acting on advice from Ronjii, Mark referred to Martin Luther King, Jr., in the section on civil disobedience and mentioned the need for more female perspectives on the panel "Arguing your own point of view."

CONCLUSION

Mark followed through on his plan to share his brochure with Mrs. Stone's history class. He sent his revised brochure to his former high school teacher along with a letter that thanked her for her guidance. Mark was honored to receive Mrs. Stone's correspondence in return. In her letter, Mrs. Stone told Mark how delighted she was to present his brochure to her class. "You'll be pleased to know," Mrs. Stone wrote, "that my students responded enthusiastically to your ideas. We had a great class discussion as a result of your brochure. How wonderful to know that a former student of mine is continuing to develop as a historian!"

7

AREA OF INQUIRY: TECHNOLOGY

THOMAS CLEMENS

WHY WRITE ABOUT TECHNOLOGY?

*T*echnology is the use of tools or machines to create, maintain, and control actions. Machines make most of our way of life possible. For example, appliances preserve and prepare food and heat and cool our living and working environments. Bicycles and space shuttles are fast, efficient ways of transportation. TVs, videos, telephones, faxes, computers, and satellites transfer and store information. Consequently, many forms of technology help shape the way the world is experienced. In particular, computer and Internet technologies are transforming information production, design, storage, retrieval, and transfer. Internet technologies have created electronic communities with members around the world in business, government, institutions, and private life. The electronic world of "cyberspace" encircles the globe. How different life would be without these technologies? How has computer and Internet technology changed the way human beings sense, feel, and think? How have they helped shape our under-standings of the world and each other? Inquiring into the consequences of computer and Internet technology can help us reach new perspectives of how they help construct what it means to be human.

EXAMPLES OF WRITING FOR INQUIRY AND ACTION

- Mairéad wishes to know if sentencing in the judicial system can be monitored for bias against ethnic minorities. She wishes to research if computer technology could possibly make it possible to record, store, and search data for that purpose. She designs her research as a special handout which her former criminal justice instructor agrees to use in his course.

- Charles is concerned about the destruction of wildlife habitat by urban development. He wants to research the role satellite locating with its enhanced computer technology can play in planning development so both wildlife and human beings can co-exist in the same habitat. He plans to shape his research into a well documented proposal, which he is going to submit to the regional office of the state game and wildlife department in his hometown.

- Ten, a nursing student, collects data on the use of computer diagnosis in pediatrics. Since she works part-time as an aide on a pediatric hospital unit, she received permission from the head nurse to submit her research in the form of an informational report on the state of diagnostic computer technology, so the staff could take new developments into account in their plans for equipment requests.

- Lester Faigley explores how computer aided instruction will reconstitute the voice of students as they are able to engage in written class discussion anonymously without waiting a turn. His research appeared as a chapter in his book, *Fragments of Rationality: Postmodernity and the Subject of Composition*. His inquiry helps him raise questions about the type of writing environment computers establish, and then he tries to answer his questions through observation, learning from other composition teachers, and reflecting on theories of communication.

- Kenneth C. Green wonders why computer technology has not transformed the classroom beyond a minimal level. Thus, he inquires into how science and technology have interacted with economic, political, and social practices, producing a situation in which the anticipated results from integrating technology into education have not been fulfilled. He writes an article in a professionally published newsletter to evoke thinking about his questions among teachers across the country.

READINGS FOR INQUIRY AND ACTION

"TO START A DIALOGUE: THE NEXT GENERATION OF AMERICA'S SCHOOLS" by James A. Mecklenburger

This essay is excerpted from James A. Mecklenburger's "To Start a Dialogue: The Next Generation of America's Schools," which appeared in The Forum: Phi Kappa Phi Journal. *It is included here because Mecklenburger argues for a rethinking of not only how technology is used in schools but for a rethinking of what schools ought to be. In a preamble, Mecklenburger states that the document was written by himself, other consultants in his company, and educators, hence, he uses "we" to represent the voice of authorship. The second reading is a story of Mark's process of writing a research paper. Mark is a student who chose to study how video games have sparked various responses.*

To Start a Dialogue:
The Next Generation of America's Schools

Too much of what is being said and done in the name of education "reform" is not. Words like *reform* and *restructuring* and *transformation*—which are supposed to denote major changes in the life of humankind—are being devalued by their use to describe very modest changes. The powers-that-be are worried about education, but with few exceptions, the changes they foresee mean that when reform is complete schools in the next generation will be much the same as they are today.

We think that pioneering educators, schools, school districts, and institutions in America must begin an earnest and public dialogue that takes the nation and its educators and policymakers far beyond the current politically driven, well-meaning but limited "reform" drumbeat of national goals, outcomes, standards, assessment, and accountability.

Why "Global Village Schools"

Even if current reform agendas succeed at improving the conventional school, which arguably they will, their results will not be good enough. The nation is a decade or more into the information age, a new era for which our schools were not designed and are not suited. Our children—all children—have a birthright to succeed in the information age, and the nation's future economic success requires that they do. Reformed or unreformed, the industrial-age school will not be adequate.

At Global Village Schools conferences and in other forums and activities, educators and others need to discuss what it means to educate in the information age and to think about how to craft and how to implement the next generation of education efforts in America. We should be thinking about schools as if their creation begins on our watch, in our times, and in light of the incredible information and communication technologies that are or soon will be at our disposal.

We suggest that the dialogue be about global village schools (GVS), and we offer the beginnings of a framework of twelve GVS principles as an intellectual point of departure. Initial work on these principles began in 1991 and 1992 under the direction of the Mecklenburger Group [consisting of consultants] and a team of progressive Louisiana educators. The principles have since been elaborated and refined. We have used the name "global village schools" for the phenomenon of information age schooling because the "global village" phrase is rooted in information age history, because it is euphonious, and because it communicates—better than, say, "schools of tomorrow"—something about the outlook, character, and purpose of information age schooling. We are finding that the phrase "global village schools" communicates well with leading-edge educators and the great mass of practicing educators, as well as with policy makers and lay people. We adopted "global village" from the philosopher and scholar Marshall McLuhan, who coined the phrase three decades ago to explain the impact of the information age. But we have discovered that "global village schools" communicates a sense of educating appropriate to today's and tomorrow's world, even to many people who have not heard the phrase "global village" before or who know nothing of its origin.

The GVS Concept

. . . the twelve principles listed below reflect our best thinking so far about the GVS concept. Even as we take some pride in authorship, we acknowledge that these twelve statements are very much a "draft" and a work in progress. Although we assert a copyright to this material to claim credit for authorship where appropriate, we offer these pages as the opening to a dialogue that will surely result in better expressions by us or by others over time.

Education in the Information Age

Like an HMO that is concerned round-the-clock for the health of its clients, a GVS will be concerned round-the-clock for learning. A school building will not define the school; a building may be the "headquarters" of a community of learners but not the sole location. Electronically, through voice mail and various networking schemes, there are many ways even today that home, school, and other institutions near and far can be intimately connected so that the customary distinctions blur.

The hallmark of the information age is that information is no longer scarce because the information that flows through electronic systems, which includes entire books, papers, and magazines, is as commonplace as the air we breathe. Starting with the advent of telegraph and telephone, advanced by film and radio, buttressed by television broadcast and cable TV, by recorded video and audio, by xerography and FAX, and capped by digital information systems, society has changed fundamentally.

Because we now live in an information age and electronic networks are linking the world into a global village, an educated person is becoming one who has the ability to find out what is known, then to think about what is known, to reflect upon changes in what is known, to explore, to share, to debate, to question, to compare and contrast, to solve problems—to engage in what today's educators sometimes call "higher order thinking skills"—and even to contribute to what is known. Creating educated persons for the twenty-first century is unlikely to be the result of schools organized around lecturing, reading and testing, no matter how good the lectures, the readings, and the tests might be.

Strategies of Reform

Global village schools may either be created afresh or be restructured with great effort by leaders of conventional schools or other agencies. Restructuring is . . . merely a strategy for reform and a means of reflecting the educational needs of American citizens in an information age. Starting afresh is another strategy. Privatization is a strategy. Formation of regional and national consortia is a strategy. Home schooling is a strategy. Imitations of elements of other institutions (hospitals, training, franchises, kibbutzim, user groups, for example) is another strategy.

Global village schools will be grounded in visions of successful citizenship, learning, work, and leisure in the twenty-first century—visions that are likely to be quite different from those that informed the design of today's schools in the nineteenth century. And global village schools are likely to be designed around the information tools of the late twentieth and twenty-first century, just as today's schools once were designed around, and continue to reflect, the information tools of the nineteenth century.

A Different Kind of Institution

A global village school will be primarily an enterprise, a community of learners, not merely a place. A global village school will exist in the hearts and minds of the people who work and learn therein.

Global Village Schools Principles

Creating a Community of Learners

To "school" is a congregational act, as with fish that swim and live together. A global village school means a "school" that is a round-the-clock community of learners not necessarily bound by a place or a building—although a building may be a convenience or even an opportunity (just as an office serves a business or a church serves a congregation). The work of a school—the "schooling" of school, the learning that is the mission of school—will occur where it is appropriate: not only at its headquarters but also in the homes of its students, in the activities of its teams and clubs throughout a region and in contests statewide, and in the far-flung sites that a child may reach by ways of field trips, electronic connection, or through the mail.

Succeeding in the Information Age

The test of the success of a global village school or any of its components will be that it assists youngsters to succeed in the information age, which is both their birthright and an economic necessity for the nation. . . . GVS schools will be managed to attend closely to issues of productivity, resource allocation, and educational effectiveness, so that newer practices also will not be sacrosanct, except insofar as they advance the purpose of the school.

Linking Students with the Globe

A global village school respects the information age reality that students not only live in a local village (or neighborhood, town, city, or state) but are linked around the globe. In effect, all people are beginning to live as though the entire planet were but one community. An educated person is becoming one who functions successfully in both the local village and the global one.

Coping with Changing Information

A global village school will respect the information age reality that information and human knowledge grow and change constantly. No human can master it all, and preparation for a lifetime of learning is a major purpose of school. Education will be about exploration, about finding information, and about using information well. When exploration becomes the dominant mode of students' work, an educated person will be one who explores effectively, understands insightfully, and communicates skillfully.

Adults Guiding Students

In global village schools the adults who assist students should themselves be explorers because students will learn by emulating adults. But adults' most important roles are the ones that students only rarely can fulfill: working as "travel agents," tour guides, and expeditionary leaders to arrange for students to learn successfully. Agency, guidance, and leadership—the essential information age "global village" roles for teachers—necessitate major changes in the nature of preparation and in-service and especially in the information and support services that enable adults to be successful agents, guides, and leaders.

Using the Tools of the Information Age

In global village schools, an educated person will be one who uses the tools of the information age well. These tools include the traditional school tools of printed paper and of writing, ciphering, listening, and speaking. But they also include an array of personal information tools including audio and video, music and graphics, computers and cameras, recording devices, and editing equipment. And they include the large-scale broadcasting and computer-based networks that carry information around the globe and from which people learn and to which people contribute. Many of these technologies will be housed in or connected to the school "headquarters," but others are likely to be elsewhere in the community. Exploring for educational purposes the technology in students' homes and communities (or even putting them there when families themselves cannot afford them) will be a vital part of global village schools.

Networking Students

Global village schools will nurture students as network participants. People create and use networks as educational tools, both personally and through electronic means. Students will learn collegial skills; often they will work in teams face-to-face, over time, and over long distances through electronic means. Families will be treated in global village schools as important educational networks for students.

Using the Seven Cs

In the world at large, and in global village schools, an educated person means becoming adept at the Seven Cs: comprehension, creativity, calculation, collaboration, competition, contribution, and communication.

Evaluating Learning

In global village schools learning will be evaluated in many ways, both formal and informal, and by learners themselves as well as by peers, by adults, and by institutions. Traditional modes of evaluation may be acceptable within their limits, but they cannot be allowed to serve as a kind of box score of students' abilities or performance.

Respecting Individuality

Global village schools will respect individuality. . . . students and parents will work with teachers to plan both individual and group-based activities; and they will work together to assess how well students have performed and therefore what students should next engage in. Global village schools will be sensitive not only to students' academic differences and learning styles but also to students' special needs or disabilities. Every child should be expected to reach his or her own fullest potential.

Removing Barriers

Global village schools may function at almost any age. At times, students will likely work with other students of different ages, just as adults (in schools and in life) usually do.

Becoming Colleagues

In global village schools, governance will be structured collegially and with all members of the community participating. The style of a GVS and its electronic networking, its evaluative approach, its emphasis on the Seven Cs, and its close ties to families will reinforce a community-based model of governance. . . . The principal of a GVS will likely be a collaborative leader, nor a hierarchical one. Working with teachers and others, he or she will be a model for the agent, guide, and leader roles that adults will play with students.

Questions for Analysis

1. In what ways does Mecklenburger's essay result from a project of inquiry?

2. What are the persuasive elements in the essay?

3. What can you infer about the readers whom Mecklenburger is addressing?

4. What action do you think Mecklenburger is seeking to accomplish?

5. How effective are the appearance and the organizing strategies of the essay?

6. Which concepts or terms are defined in the essay? Are they effectively defined? Are there others which need definition?

7. What kind of status or authority does the author assign himself in the essay? Evaluate the effectiveness of the strategies that he uses to do this.

8. What claims or assertions does the author make? Which is the one that brings the essay together conceptually and gives it a focus?

9. Evaluate the effectiveness of the reasoning and the evidence that he uses to support his claims. Where do each of his claims receive sufficient support from reasoning and evidence? Where do they not?

10. How would you describe the attitude of the author toward his readers? In what ways does this attitude increase or decrease your trust in his discussion, your willingness to continue reading what he has to say? Do you feel that you are included as one of his intended readers? Why?

A Case   MARK'S INQUIRY

> As a member of the next generation of thinkers and decision makers in an ever changing technological world, I see a lot of negative attitudes toward video games by the older generation, namely my parents' generation. Others feel that video games are useful and sort of a subliminal way of introducing younger kids to this technology. I want to bring these different attitudes out into the open for discussion to see where the problems lie. By researching this subject, I hope to learn more about how people feel toward video games and what people who have studied this widespread technology say about it.

As Mark thought about an inquiry into technology, he recalled several articles in his community's newspaper which reported on the concerns that various people had with video games. Since his experience with video games which began in early childhood did not resemble the negative influences that were attributed to the games by well meaning people in his community, he became curious about the effects of video games on others who grew up with them as he had. At the same time, he wondered how negative attitudes toward video games had developed, especially in parents in his community. Mark decided that the situation formed an effective starting point for an inquiry. He used a questioning strategy to help him clarify the direction that his research should take.

Mark's Questions

Selecting a Subject for Inquiry

Video games present many new and exciting capabilities that could affect my future. As an amateur computer programmer now, I could very well become a video game creator because I have been very creative and good at the few things that I have done in animation and game making. Also, the way that I became interested in majoring in computer science was when I got introduced to my computer through the games I was playing on it. The only problems that surround video games now are that some people see them as destructive to young kids' minds. Other than that, video games are very useful in more ways then most people would think

Getting in Touch with Dissonance

I believe that there is more to video games than what initially meets the eye when you turn them on. Although many believe that they are violent or mindless, on the whole they are very educational and a good social instrument for some people. For example games like Tetris, a very popular game for the Nintendo entertainment system, teaches players shapes and enhances their thinking and reaction times when they are forced to put a weird shape in place in enough time to create a solid line. But does the violence that is displayed in video games bring out aggression in the players of those games? In writing this paper, I hope to enlighten people to the better side of video games, which most people do not consider. I hope to change this stereotypical view of video games, by illustrating the many benefits of video games and their ties to all aspects of the world and life.

Locating Yourself in a Writing Situation

Given this project is an academic research paper, I will write it as a special report to a group of parents. The group that I choose will include my composition instructor and members of college faculty, all of whom are parents. These faculty members are in English, humanities, psychology, history, and sociology.

Formulating Questions for Inquiry

Question: If parents say video games are so bad, then why do they keep buying them for their kids?

Question: Does video game violence suppress or stimulate a child's aggression?

Question: If the violence has an effect, then was there a problem with the player before he/she started playing the game?

Question: Are video games more than just electronic thumb twiddling?

> *Question:* Though perceived to be harmful and destructive by many parents, can video games ever be considered more like a teacher and helpful, changing the way young minds view the world and their place?

Mark's writing group members, Rossi and Stan, thought that Mark had made a good effort to begin his inquiry but wondered aloud if he wasn't committing himself to a definite position too early. They thought that his questioning strategy sounded less like an inquiry and more like he was preparing to martial evidence to argue for his particular point of view. They asked him if he knew what the concerns of the critics are? If he knew what the sources of their concerns were? Moreover, they asked him since he was already an avid player of video games, could he overcome his enjoyment long enough to look at evidence from a range of perspectives before he judged the effects of video games?

In light of his group's suggestions and his instructor's concurrence with the comments of the group, Mark revised his Guiding Question in order to rethink how he needed to come at his research in an inquiry.

Mark's Revised Guiding Question

> What evidence is there that video games can be seen as a normal positive activity for children?

With his guiding question at hand, Mark's next step was to determine what he already knew and what he needed to research. Mark used a Three Perspectives Guide to help him sort out what aspects of his subject he needed to research.

Mark's Exploration

> *My guiding question:*
> Is there any evidence that video games can be seen as a normal positive activity for children?
>
> ## *Three Perspective Guide*
> *Describing and distinguishing*
> Video games have made it possible to have a home video arcade that fits on your television. While requiring very little technical know-how to play, these video games have helped almost everyone who plays them, by helping to educate children using special counting games or shapes and so forth. Video games have also created a kind of social group for people to be associated with. With all the games and game companies out there, they have made a big impact on our economy simply from their design and need for sale. Video games also are a gateway, I believe, to other aspects of technology, like computers for example; I got involved in the other uses for my computer from the increased complexity of the games I was playing and the knowledge of the whole computer that they demanded. Though video games themselves are not dependent upon the Internet for survival, the Internet has supplied a new place for video games to thrive. In return the

lure of online gaming has helped the Internet to thrive also, so they are actually working together. Most of the controversy over video games comes from the violence in them. Most opponents to video games see only the side of video games that they want to, so if they want them to be harmful and destructive, then they concentrate on only the negative aspects of the games. I am intrigued by the fact that so many people can contribute to something they are so against by buying the games. Also, I am curious as to why something that I see as useful can be taken the opposite way by someone else.

Need to research

Any documented evidence of people working with computers now who were influenced heavily and got involved in the field through playing video games. Also get parents' opinion of video games and why they feel that way.

Tracing moves and changes

How this situation started

- In the late '70s and early '80s the first video games were put out in the stores; at first they were nothing more than simple hand-eye coordination, a ball bouncing around the screen was called Pong, put out by one of the early pioneers Atari, Commodore 64, or Coleco Vision, and ripped to shreds by irate mothers and parents who said their kids were spending all of their time in front of the TV playing these games.

- Since the first games, games have become more sophisticated, and some consistently more graphic and violent. This has only fueled the cause of video game opposers.

- Nintendo was the first real big break through in home video game technology.

- New games, like Mortal Kombat and Virtua Cop, are currently under the knife as far as parental and anti-violence censorship goes.

How I have changed my beliefs and attitudes

- I do not think that I really have changed any of my views of video games; ever since they first came out, it was my opinion that they were more beneficial than harmful.

Larger cultural changes that have affected this situation

- The realization that computers are the wave of the future, that technological advancements in the space and other programs spawned the personal computer boom, and games came out for the PCs. Then after the arcade computer games came the home game systems that catered more to the younger audience.

Need to research

Look for game reviews of the most scrutinized games and what the public or press releases said about them. Get information on the development of Internet games and their current popularity and usefulness.

Mapping Networks and Relationships

Video games are used by most as a form of entertainment and are considered valuable by some because of this entertainment quality and at the same time the educational value that they possess. Most opposers of video games say that video games are destructive and used only to rot out kid's minds. Video games can lead to a career in some form of computer field or maybe even to make video games yourself. Though a lot of parents would argue that playing video games will decrease your chances of doing anything with your life, and that they only cause a regression in the mind, I see video games as subliminal alternative teachers, who teach us in ways that we probably never will notice or think twice about.

Need to research

Find articles or such in magazines like PREVENTION, which are geared towards the parents of the world, on the disadvantages of video games. This will help gather evidence on the beliefs about video games that are circulating through the world.

Rossi and Stan commented on how well the Three Perspectives Guide related to Mark's Guiding Question and how well that it sorted out the aspects of the subject that Mark will have to research in order to answer his Guiding Question.

ANNOTATED WORKING BIBLIOGRAPHY

Mark's next step was to explore the range of opinions on video games. He decided to concentrate on two means of obtaining research: **library resources** because he thought that he could find a wide variety of texts describing and predicting the positive and negative effects of video games and the **Internet** because he thought that people interested in computerized games would also be active there.

To keep his exploring organized, so he could keep backtracking to a minimum and use his time as efficiently as possible, Mark decided to construct an Annotated Working Bibliography. A working bibliography provided him with a list of references that represented the best sources he could find that indicated some connection to his subject. He decided to write annotations for each reference in his Working Bibliography by skimming each source and annotating, or recording, an evaluation. His annotations would help Mark decide which of the sources were the most promising for his subject and would guide him to read the most valuable sources first.

Library Research

Mark began constructing his Annotated Working Bibliography by exploring library sources by sitting down at his library's online indexes of periodicals and books. He called up a search screen and typed in the keywords "video games and violence." That called up a number of references including the following, which he recorded in Modern Language Association format.

Munson, Marty. "Kids and Vids: Many Children Like the Nice Stuff Better." *Prevention* December 1995: 36.

Nashawaty, Chris. "Killer Games." *Entertainment Weekly* 11 March 1994: 70–72.

Brody, Herb. "Video Games That Teach." *Technology Review* November 1993: 50+.

Then Mark typed in the keywords "video games and value." With that he received the following reference.

White, William B., Jr. "What Value Are Video Games." *Sports Illustrated for Kids* May 1994: 17.

Mark used a number of keywords in his online searches. Then, he looked up his subject in *The Library of Congress Subject Headings,* a reference work which is like a thesaurus for keywords. It indicates the types of terms that are used to represent a wide variety of subjects. Mark obtained more keywords for his search. Mark continued his search through a number of online indexes, or databases, including *Social Sciences Index, Business Periodicals Index, ERIC, Magazine ASAP, InfoTrac,* and the *New York Times Index* . . .

From such databases, Mark complied a list of references all of which he converted to MLA bibliographic format and placed in alphabetical order. Then, he checked the online index which contained the holdings of the library. For each reference he found in the library's holding, he recorded the call number, or shelf number. For those references which were not in the library's holdings, he set those aside with the idea that if he needed more sources, he would pursue these through the Interlibrary Loan service.

After he organized his list of references in his Working Bibliography by call number, he located them on the shelves and skim-read each of them in order to record his annotations. Mark's annotations included the following information: the extent and manner that his subject was treated in the source, the particular point of view that the source brings to the subject, the degree of credibility that the source establishes, and the limitations of the source (date of publication, degree of discussion about subject, and level of evidence and reasoning for its claims). By using this guide for his annotations, Mark was able to begin indicating if each source was a high, middle, or low priority for careful reading and note taking.

Excerpt from Mark's Annotated Working Bibliography of Library Resources

Munson, Marty. "Kids and Vids: Many Children Like the Nice Stuff Better." *Prevention* Dec. 1005: 36.

Describes the results of a study by Patrick McGuffin, a Ph.D. and the chief psychologist in the Department of Child and Adolescent Psychiatry, Hahnemann University Hospital, Philadelphia. The results are summarized, and the details of the study are not given. The results surprised the author: one-half of the choices were for nonviolent games. A recent study that I can use to support that good games are available and preferred in many instances by children. High priority source.

Internet Sources

After Mark compiled a number of sources and annotations from library sources, he went to the Internet through a private access account. He went to a "Channels" section and clicked on Games Channel. Then he clicked on a number of games that he wanted to research. From there, he clicked through various hotlinks that seemed to relate to his subject. For example, he clicked on Games Channel Newsletter and scrolled through it until he found an article that related to his subject. He downloaded the article. He returned to the Games Channel screen and clicked on Press Releases. Then he searched the choices for ones connected to his subject.

In another session, Mark went to the Internet and clicked on Webcrawler, a software that searches the texts of online documents for the keywords that he typed in the search dialog box. He typed in "video games." He tried each of the sites that were brought up. He accessed several Bulletin Boards and left message postings which requested a response on Game Designers Forum. He requested opinions on the games that the designers release and any arguments against the games. After more searching, using Yahoo!, he entered several Internet sites with annotations into his Annotated Working Bibliography.

An Example of Mark's Annotation of an Internet Site

<http://www.sega.com/segapc/news/releases/orion.html/>

This site explains how companies that make games are developing interactive games that feature letters and numbers instead of weapons and violence. The site is owned by Sega, so the "news release" is actually a marketing device. The games are not described. This source is useful in establishing a new trend in game development, away from violence. Some credibility is indicated by the fact that an advisory panel of ten educators and child psychologists helped create the game for age appropriate use. Launched Fall 1996. High priority source.

NOTE TAKING

After he annotated his working bibliography, Mark placed his references in order of most valuable to least valuable, based on the priority ratings that he included in his annotations. Then, he began reading the sources with the highest priority. As he read each source, he took notes that he felt might contribute to constructing an answer to his guiding question and those aspects of the subject which were indicated in his Three Perspectives Guide as needing research. He focused on summarizing the reasoning and evidence used in making claims about the effects of video games. He kept his notes on note cards because he could easily reorganize his notes before he began to draft his paper.

Example from Mark's Note Taking

Munson "Kids"   vids and violence
Reports that Patrick McGuffin, Ph.D., chief psychologist, Dept. of Child and Adolescent Psychiatry, Hahnemann U Hosp, Philadelphia, conducted a study of the video game preferences of 60 children, ages 6-17, with results that half the time children preferred the nonviolent games. Gender and age produced no differences in choices. Results suggest that many children do not always crave violent action as entertainment. (p. 36)

Example from Mark's Note Taking

"Electronic Games." *Compton's Interactive Encyclopedia,* 1995.
Video games first sold in the early 1970s. Made possible by computer silicon microchips which have large capacity circuitry, storing thousands of bits of memory with visual and sound effects. In the early 1980s there was a shift from arcade parlors to home software games.

After Mark had taken notes on all those sources that he felt might be useful to answer his guiding question, he wrote an analysis of what his position as writer ought to be and how he would position his readers. Mark used the following strategy.

Mark's Positioning of Writer and Reader

My guiding question:
What evidence is there that video games can be seen as a normal positive activity for children?

Positioning Myself:
That of an active video game player and one that has experienced the helpfulness of them.

- I, as the child in this case, want the games that I like to be available to me if I want them, so I feel strongly about people who have not played a particular video game but say how harmful it is and so on.

- I am going to take a tone of some knowledge but not a professional and basically persuasive, from the perspective that I understand the views of the professionals in the computing business.

- I tell them that I am a computer major due to video game influence, and that I personally have tried some of the things said in my paper.

My choice of readers: English instructor and several faculty who are parents and have agreed to read my paper because they are wondering about the value of video games.

Positioning My Readers:

- Most everyone by today has played or at least seen a video game. And with the growing dependence on computers, everyone will be familiar with them at some time.

- Parents, and in this case my instructors, derive their understanding from what has been published about video games and their negative effects on children.

- They have a different value system than we (the younger generation) do. We see that video games have a positive effect on the mindset of the players, as they educate as well as entertain. Whereas parents and instructors see them only as they appear on the surface, as graphics that move and keep us occupied. Parents believe that violence is bad and most of the games involve killing and other violence. Also they (mostly parents) grew up in an age where the only games were board games and reading was the big pastime.

These answers tell me that I have to present the information in this case to an already made-up mind, that of the irate parent, in such a way that while it may not change their mind at first, it will plant a seed that over time will grow. The parents I am writing to are academics from several disciplines. They probably have done some reading on the subject and have access to my sources. I have to be accurate and fair in my representation of the range of opinion. Also, since they are academics, they will value formal research and studies as evidence.

After Mark determined the positions for himself as writer and for his readers, he then generated a list of the possible genres or forms his discussion of his research could take. Mark knew the form of his discussion had to fit his writing situation and the expectations of his readers.

Mark's Selection of Genre

As mentioned before, the aim in my paper is to get the older generation to look at video games in a new light, with me as their guide through these new angles and views towards the subject. Even though my teachers have to read it, it has to be like a real publication since it would be aimed at them anyway and since they are mostly that age which has negative beliefs toward video games. A formal academic paper would fit the expectations of these academic parents. My readers would expect me to demonstrate an ability to present multiple perspectives on the subject and then judge each of them by criteria that I have constructed from my research. Since that is the expectation for a formal academic research paper, I will prepare one for my readers in the form of a research report in the form of a handout.

Once Mark knew the genre of his paper, he organized his notes into categories. These categories helped Mark understand how his research suggested an answer to his guiding question. Mark tried three focuses and found one that his research and his thinking on the subject supported. His focus answered his guiding question and suggested how the rest of his discussion would be developed.

Mark's Focuses

Constructing a Focus Statement:

Subject	*Point of significance*
• Video game economics ——————	means that violence is what sells, but the brilliantly programmed new puzzle and intellectual games are on the rise as well.
• Parents' opposition to these games is ——	well known, but parents keep buying these games for the kids nonetheless.
• Video Games, if properly managed by parents, ——————	offer many educational benefits to children.

My choice: the last one, because it incorporates many different views and angles and still can incorporate all perspectives on the advantages and disadvantages of video games.

Mark's focus, in turn, pointed toward the categories in which he had organized his notes. In order to plan how his paper would be organized, Mark wrote an organizing plan using his categories of notes. Mark reorganized his thoughts and the points at which each of his notes entered into his discussion. By placing his thoughts and his notes on the subject into an organizing plan, Mark achieved a guide from which to draft his paper. An organizing plan shows how both parts of the focus—that is the subject of the paper and its significance—are reflected in each section of the paper through assertions.

Mark's Organization Plan

Focus: Video games, if properly managed by parents, offer many educational benefits to children, despite some worries about their bad effects.

- *Introduction:* Parents' worries about video games.
  - the violent nature of some games.
  - a tendency to cause children to become socially withdrawn.
  - they take away from valuable study time.
  - they inhibit the mind from learning many other things.
- Studies do not support the relationship between video games and violence.
- Video games develop physical skills.
  - hand/eye coordination
  - physical and mental reactions
- Video games help in rehabilitation.
- Video games build social skills among peers.
- Video games encourage family togetherness.

- Video games can lead to computer careers.
- Video games familiarize children with a high tech society.
- Video games involve children in the internet.
- Video games help children with computers in the classroom.
- Video games are intellectually stimulating.
- Video games need parental management.

After Mark wrote his organizing plan, he shared it with Rossi and Stan, members of his writing group. They helped Mark understand where he needed to clarify his assertions in each section of the paper. These assertions act as a link between the focus and each of these sections. Rossi and Stan also helped with his reasoning and representations of the evidence that he located during his research. Once his plan was revised, Mark wrote a draft, which he shared with Rossi and Stan. This gave Mark a chance to review how well his plan organized his thoughts and research. Rossi and Stan pointed out places where there were gaps in the discussion or places where his reasoning and evidence were inadequate. From this feedback, Mark revised his draft with his priorities in the following order: focus, development for readers, organization, style, grammar, research style format, and mechanics. When his paper was "polished" in all these areas, he made copies for Rossi, Stan, and his instructor and invited their written responses.

Mark's Polished Draft

Mark B.
Professor C
English 101-12

Video Games: The Substitute Teacher

Ever since the first video games came from the arcade into our homes, via the early pioneers of this now multi-million dollar industry, like Atari, they have been surrounded by controversy over whether they do more harm then good. Due to the attraction of video games to children, they can become engulfed in them. Many of the people who oppose the contents of video games today are parents of the kids who are playing them. They say that kids spend too much time playing the games when they could be doing something more useful with their time, like reading ("Question" 17). There are people in the world who believe that video games have a tendency to take over a child's life and that the morals displayed in the games themselves are less than humane and, therefore, should not be made and given to a child so they could influence the child with the acts displayed and thinking involved.

They also argue that the violence level in the games is giving children the message that violence is okay ("Question" 17). Parents are worried that their children are getting a warped sense of reality when they see that after a person gets ripped apart by some alien, they come back to life healthier than ever ("Question" 17). The violence shown in the games and the disrespect for human life that is sometimes incorporated into the video games are sometimes blamed for natural human aggression. Opposers of video games attribute the growing rate of violent crimes in America, the rise in illiteracy among adults, and the break down of the communication in the household all to the effect of video games on children.

At the same time, there are those who see that video games are more than just mindless button pushing. Technically, video games have only become better over time in the sense that the graphics used have become increasingly realistic and the computer itself has become more like a real person in the way it uses logic for problem solving. Parents buy their kids video games for several reasons. One of those reasons is the fact that video games are easy entertainment that will require no involvement on the parents' part to organize anything and no rejection for the child. Video games have no preference who plays them, so, therefore, no child can be rejected by one, whereas, if the child put the same amount of energy into getting a group together for a game of baseball, there is still a chance for rejection by the other children. Video games, if properly managed by parents, offer many educational benefits to children despite some worries about their bad effects.

Even the worry over violence is contested by some studies. Studies do not support the belief that serial killers and masked murderers exist because when those kids were young they played games where the object was to kill as many people as they could ("Question" 17). Dr. Silvern, professor of early-childhood education at Auburn University, says: "I have completed two studies on the relationship between game playing and aggression and have not found any direct link. . . . Children are definitely aroused and they may be excited, but I would not say they are violent." People will buy into the theory that a game caused a person to go on a killing spree because it presents an easy scapegoat. This could have been expected though since most people tend to shift the blame of anything as far away from themselves as possible. The blame for these things can not rest solely on the things learned from watching the graphics of a video game. "A lot of people think that kids are going to kill someone or do what the person does in the game, but kids are smarter than that," says Ira Wrestler, a thirteen year-old at Urbana Middle School, in Urbana, Illinois ("Question" 17). There is no real deep down desire for kids to play these violent games anyway, says Patrick McGuffin, chief psychologist in the department of child and adolescent psychiatry at Hahnemann University Hospital, in Philadelphia. A recent study polled 60 kids, who played a violent game and a nonviolent one for one minute apiece, then were asked which one they would want to continue playing (Munson 36). The results came back that half wanted to continue playing the nonviolent game; also, age and gender did not make a difference (Munson 36). Cheryl Handley, an early-childhood education major, agrees that the stupid part about the whole thing is that the parents keep buying the games for their children. So, therefore, how can a person be so against something they apparently support?

When you really step back and look at the whole picture, video games are providing players with more than just entertaining pictures on a screen. One of these benefits is physical coordination. William B. White, Jr., director of public relations and advertising for Nintendo of America, believes that not all the benefits of video game play stem from a challenging bunch of character configurations on the screen or from a good plot of a entertaining game(74). It is true, it has been found that the constant movement of objects on the screen and the hand-eye coordination involved in playing a video game can actually improve your reaction time both physically and mentally (Gutierrez 11). In a study that tested this statement, "60 healthy adults ages 60 to 79 were divided into three groups. One group played video games three hours a week, while another watched movies, and the third had no special activities. After 11 weeks, the video-game players had quicker reaction times, both physically and mentally, than the nonplayers" (Gutierrez 11). There have been many other times video games being used to improve mobility than just this one.

Video games have also been used in hospitals as a part of physical therapy in rehabilitation (White: 74). Paul Echelard, speech pathology supervisor at St. Luke's Hospital in California, which uses video games in the rehabilitation of heart and head injury patients, says that some video games "require memory skills, some require decision-making skills, some visual-perceptual, and some motor control. We are dealing with patients who have problems in [all of] those areas" (White 75). Video games have even been specialized in some cases, becoming a regular part of therapy. One of these cases was the use of video games to treat a condition called amblyopia, or lazy eye, in which one eye does not function as well as the other and needs to be exercised in order to correct the fault (Compton's np). The good eye was rendered useless by a patch so that the other eye had to do all the work while playing the game (Compton's np). The success rate of the use of video games to aid in rehabilitation depends on the severity of the injury and the frequency that a game is used.

In addition to the physical benefits of the actual game, researchers have found a social benefit in video games as well. Anyone who has ever been to a mall knows that kids tend to travel to arcades in groups. Dr. Donald Jackson Jr., director of the psychological services center of Widener University in Chester, Pennsylvania, noted that this simple act of going to the arcade is very helpful, socially, for the children (Golin 122). They interact with one another by bumming quarters from each other and challenging each other for the high scores (122). Also, it is never unusual to see a group of five or six kids huddled around one video game shouting instructions to the one who is playing the game. According to White, video games "foster communication and cooperation between the players, leading to a joint effort to succeed" (74).White reports that as children master a video game, they in turn gain a greater sense of confidence and morale (White 74). This boosted self-confidence then "encourages more socialization" (White 74). Video games "have shown that traditional age and gender gaps in game play of other types are modified or even eliminated during home video games" (White 74).

Not only have video games helped to bridge social gaps between children but in families as well. White contends that it starts with the siblings in the family, if there are any, when they play the games together. I play video games against my brother all the time, at least five times a week, on one of the three video game systems in our house. In a family with siblings, who under normal circumstances beat each other over the head, video games bring them together and promote more interaction rather than the rivalry that often surfaces when they compete (75). I have found even that I can channel some aggression felt toward a member of my family into kicking the stuffing out of them in a video game; it is a great stress reliever as mentioned earlier. The game does not even have to be a violent fighting game. I play my brother in football, baseball, basketball, and racing games in addition to those other games; and I get the same pleasure from a victory in any one of them. There have been many studies done on the effects of video game playing as a family, and the consequent interaction. Some of the most detailed research about structured video games in the family and the consequent effect they have on it has been done by Edna Mitchell, head of the Department of Education, at Mills College (White 75). She observed twenty families over a six month period, interviewing them at the beginning and at the end, to get the prevailing attitudes on the project (White 75). Results of the experiment showed that "families reported playing together, interacting both competitively and cooperatively, communicating and enjoying each other in a new style. They were decidedly enthusiastic about this change in family life" (White 75). Perhaps one of the best things about video games is that they are not biased in the sense that any person can play them if he or she tries.

Gender, age, sexual preference, marital status, grade-point average, none of these things matter when it comes to playing a video game. When it came to family playing, video games helped to "bridge the gap," as one father commented, between fathers and their daughters (White 75). Some fathers found that spending quality time with their daughters by playing video games with them helped to even the one-sided list of activities to do with them, as opposed to the things a father can do with his son. The same thing goes for a mother and her son, and the infinitely more things a mother and daughter do together.

It certainly seems that a person who is playing a video game at this moment cannot possibly benefit any further, but on the contrary they can. With all the new technological advances in the last few years in the way of computers, one might begin to wonder how and why these people, who are making this technology available, ever started thinking about and working with computers. Here again, video games can play a role. White says that "by many accounts, video games are a key element in getting children familiar with and used to an increasingly high-tech society" (74). Video games help introduce children into the world of microcomputers at a time when it is becoming increasingly more important to have those skills (White 74). It is believed that many of the computer programmers and technicians today got their start in computers by playing video games (White 74). Nick Beirnhoff, the person responsible for setting up the Internet provider Dave's World and current networking guru for State Farm's data processing division, gave a presentation to my Introduction to Micro-computer class in which he said that the reason he got into computers was from "playing video games." I am currently working on an associate degree in applied Computer Sciences, and so I looked back on why I ever became involved in computers. My father is a systems analyst at State Farm Insurance, and ever since I can remember, there has been a computer of some kind in my house. When I was little, the only thing that I needed them for was to play those, at the time, cool games. So, therefore, I had to learn to maneuver around the computers operating system by the time I was eight years old in order to make the game I wanted to play run. Consequently, by the time I needed to actually use the other parts of the computer to type my papers, I just seemed to know how to use those applications that I was in. I owe it all to the fact that I wanted to play a video game on my computer and consequently learned how to move around and use the other aspects of the computer.

Another way in which video games are getting children introduced to the computer is through the Internet. In what is called on-line gaming, kids are introduced to a rapidly increasing information center due to a yearning to play a video game with someone half way across the country. At an Electronic Entertainment Expo, Allen Adham, president and founder of Blizzard Entertainment, a leading multimedia studio for educational and entertainment software, said "Internet gaming is the next level in computer entertainment." (Blizzard 1). Starting this past summer, Blizzard offered its customers free access to Internet gaming through the company's battle.net server (Blizzard 1). "Battle.net provides an arena for Blizzard customers to chat, challenge opponents and initiate multiplayer games" (Blizzard 1).

These on-line games are not just games with great graphics that are attracting these kids; in fact most of them are puzzle and strategy type games. Metasquares, a puzzle game much like Tic-tac-toe, was created by Scott Kim, known for his mathematical puzzles, his book of two-way writing called "Inversions," and the computer game "Heaven & Earth", which was Beta tested on the Internet (Starbugsnews 2). That means that it was open for Internet users to play and then report, if they wanted, on the "bugs" or glitches that could then be worked out (Starbugsnews 1). Not only is the game itself educational but the way in which the child is forced to get to the game as well. By learning their way around the Internet to play video games, children are learning valuable skills that will help them in their future school experiences. When it comes time to use the Internet as a source of research for a term paper, they will know how to maneuver around the Internet and find the information needed. Children can recognize that if to get to the video game they played they went through the "Games channel," and then through various other forums and such until they got to the game, then why not go to the economics site to maybe get stock quotes or information on new upcoming companies for an Economics report. Take a look back to where I got the information above; I just got on the Internet and typed in "video games" on the Web Browser and went from there. Though there is still ongoing research into the educational value of video games, I believe that they should be put into practice to find out.

The new technology today should be incorporated into the schools and used to teach kids while they are still young. I have found that since I grew up in a computer centered household, that I am better off when it comes to using a computer in an school environment, whereas, some of the adults, for example, who did not grow up as this technology was coming out are finding it harder to learn to use it. Three young girls, whom I have the pleasure of baby-sitting, are currently six, four, and two years old. They have learned how to count, recognize colors, and shapes and so forth due to computer games where, for example, they have to count the number of star-shaped fish that wash up each time a wave crashes on the shore. When they answer correctly a new wave comes and a different number is there (Handley np). Computer manufacturers and the makers of video games have recognized the concern for the content of video games and have answered it by combining the fascination and excitement of a game with lessons to teach language, mathematics, reading, and science (Brody 50), showing that the makers of the so called violent and harmful games are not some money hungry corporate executives who are out to poison the minds of our youth.

Most of the video games out on me market today are actually intellectually stimulating. "Games such as Lob, where the player has to strategically position cubes to block his enemies but leave himself an open path, resemble nothing so much as an animated IQ test" (Golin 121). Another recent game is the new learning game created by Sega Entertainment in conjunction with Orion Interactive entitled "Sonic's Schoolhouse" (Sega np). "Sonic's Schoolhouse" is Sega's first "edutainment" title and introduces Sega's popular character, Sonic the Hedgehog as the kids' computer friend (Sega np). The game features a 3D schoolhouse and playground with a first person perspective that creates a virtual reality environment for the kids (Sega np). "Sonic's Schoolhouse was designed as a game, but instead of using weapons and enemies, it uses numbers and letters (Sega np). According to Dr. Steven Silvern, professor of early-childhood education at Auburn University, video games allow for problem solving on many levels (Golin 58). "One of the first rules of problem solving is to ask yourself how this situation is like something you already know. In most of these video games, you will find that each successive level of play not only offers the situations that need new techniques but also requires the player to use the knowledge accumulated in overcoming past obstacles" (Golin 123).

True there are still those games that are virtually mindless, and it is the parent's job to steer their children towards those games that are going to be good for them. The question then becomes how to turn your child onto the games that are mentally as well as physically challenging. One way is for the parent to take an active role and actually play the games themselves to see what the effect is on them (Golin 121). This also ties back into the statement earlier about video games bringing parents and their children together like no other entertainment medium can do. Like something that children normally would not go for, if you disguise it so it looks appealing to children they do not know the good it is actually doing them. For example, if you set a five year old down in front of a math book and said do all problems on pages 10 through 100, she would look at you like you had just shot her dog. But on the other hand if you boot up a game where children are supposed to count the number of shells left on the beach each time a wave comes in, they will play it all night, and not think twice about the learning part of it. In an interview with Cheryl Handley, an early-childhood education major at Heartland Community College and experienced baby-sitter for ten years, she agreed with this statement made above. Slowly, people are beginning to see that video games are not just mindless thumb exercises as first believed.

I see video games becoming a bigger part in classroom education in the future, especially in the lower grades, because of their ability to adapt to a different teaching style because they have no other real style to base it against. Other areas like special education I believe will incorporate the use of video games for learning. My mom worked as a teacher's assistant at Bloomington High School, in the Special Education department last year. While there, she was put in charge of the daily supervising and teaching of a child who had cerebral palsy and used a computerized talk-board to communicate. Also programmed into the talk-board were games that were designed to get the child to recognize numbers, letters, and picture icons. These are just some of the many ways that computers and video games help use learn more each and every day. Computers are the wave of the future, and the teachers for the great minds of the future.

Works Cited

"Blizzard Entertainment Introduces Battle.net—A New Concept In Gaming Over The Internet." 16 May 1996. OnlinePosting. Games Channel. America Online.

Brody, Herb. "Video Games That Teach." *Technology Review* Nov 1996: 50 +.

Compton's Interactive Encyclopedia. CD-ROM. Compton's NewMedia, Inc., 1995.

Golin, Mark. "Are Video Games Zapping Your Child's Mind?" *Prevention* Aug 1992: 56+.

Gutierrez, Paul. "Shhh! Don't tell." *Snorts Illustrated for Kids* Sep 1996: 11.

Munson, Marty. "Kids and Vids: Many children like the nice stuff better." *Prevention* Dec 1995: 36.

"Sega Entertainment, Orion Interactive bring fun and games to PC learning software." 10 October 1996.

Online Posting. Games Channel. America Online. Available HTTP://www.Sega.com/segapc/news/releases/onon.html.

"Starbugsnews Review: Metasquares." 22 January 1997. Online Posting. Games Channel Newsletter. Keyword: Metasquares. America Online.

"Question: Are Video Games Good For Kids?" *Sports Illustrated for Kids* May 1994: 17.

White Jr., William B. "What Value Are Video Games?" *USA Today (magazine)* Mar 1992: 74–75.

Mark's instructor had distributed a reader response guide to the class in order to guide the response from the writing group members. Rossi's and the instructor's responses follow.

Example of Two Reader Responses to Mark's Polished Draft

Overall

Rossi: I found your paper interesting, even though I haven't played many video games. I could follow your thinking pretty well. I got off track a couple of times later in the paper.

Instructor: You set up a good argument for the use of video games by bringing in some new information into the debate.

Focus

Rossi: I know that you are writing in support of video games, and I got your focus at the end of the first paragraph.

Instructor: The last sentence in the first paragraph seems to be your focus statement which sets a direction for the reader because it signals all the assertions to follow.

Development for Readers

Rossi: I think that you gave some good reasons why video games can be useful in certain situations, but I am wondering where you are drawing the line between good uses and not so good uses. Explain that more. You have enough discussion and examples about how video game technology can improve education.

Instructor: It is not always clear where the citations of sources begin. This confuses your reasoning with that of the sources. Therefore, clearly reference the beginning of each citation.

- The evidence you provide is useful in supporting your assertions. On the other hand, there are times in the paper when you lead off the discussion of a point by using source materials, and your assertions are only implied. Therefore, clearly state your assertions before using source material.

- Similarly, check your use and placement of sources; the use of sources are only effective when they are used to expand or support an assertion that you have made in your discussion.

- Are there any more studies on video games that you can find? Now that you are familiar with the places where these studies show up, you could search there for more and more links on the Internet. Are there any that show results which conflict with the studies that you have in your paper? Moreover, you could also use more detail in representing the views of those who are opposed to or concerned about video games influences. And once you have represented those views, you might consider countering them more precisely with the evidence that you have found.

Organization

Rossi: Your organization was pretty clear to me. You introduced each section stating the aspect of video games that you would be discussing.

Instructor: Overall, I thought your organization works by parts of the whole. I could follow point by point as you represented the views of those of others and then responded to those negative views with the positive results of playing video games. But I think the discussion of each positive point has to be closer to the corresponding negative point established early in the paper. You lump all negatives together in front of the paper and then discuss all the positives after that. Maybe you need to respond with positives to each negative when it is first mentioned.

- The ending needs a stronger role in the paper.

Language Choices (Words and Sentence Structure)

Rossi: I think that your readers will appreciate the nonjargonistic vocabulary in the paper. I found, however, some sentences difficult to follow. Also, reduce the number of quotations and convert them to summaries in your own words. Most of the quotations you use are not special in terms of their style.

Instructor: You need to reference the beginning of each citation.

- Another stylistic practice you might want to adopt is to consolidate a string of references from the same source into one reference. For example, the first time that you use Golin, you use three notes from him in a row. Since all three notes are consecutive and are contiguous in the source, convert the three citations to one. The reference to the source in the first note can act as an introduction to all three, and the documentation after the third note can serve as documentation for all three.

- Reduce the number of quotations to one or two. Only use a quotation when the style of the author is especially poignant or elegant. The rest of the time refer to your sources through representations in your own words.

- The transitions between your comments and the use of your notes (sources) need to be grammatically and stylistically smooth.
- The informality of "mom" reinforces your personal experience, but what effect does that word have on how serious and thoughtful your paper will be understood as "researched." I'm not suggesting that relating personal experience is inappropriate for your set of readers, but how does your representation of your personal experience fit with the rest of the paper and with your readers' expectations of a "researched" paper?

Conventions

Rossi: I think that your paper is relatively free of errors. Nice job proof-reading!

Instructor: Check your handbook on the use of single and double quotation marks; you have a couple of changes in that area to make. Read through sentence by sentence and check them over.

MLA format

Rossi: The comment by Handley which you represent early in the text is not fully documented. Not all your citations indicate the source at their beginnings.

Instructor: In your Works Cited list, check the completeness of the online references. Also place angle brackets < > around each URL to set them off from any text and punctuation external to the URL. You need to cite the Beirnhoff information and the information from your mother. The former would be cited as a public talk and the latter probably characterized as an interview. Let's talk about that.

Suggestion for Revision Priorities

Rossi: I would like to see you develop your education points more.

Instructor: Get the citations referenced correctly, establish the credibility of your sources, and reorganize so your positives respond directly to each negative point you represent.

Rossi and Stan discussed their responses to Mark's paper with him. Then they gave him their written comments and answered Mark's questions about their responses. After hearing their responses, Mark received his instructor's written and oral response. Mark then made decisions about which advice to incorporate into his revisions. To do that and to help himself identify his revising priorities, Mark drew up a revising plan. Then he followed his plan, rethinking and revising his paper.

Mark's Revising Plan

Focus: I need to make sure every assertion supports my focus.

Development: I need to reference the beginning of my citations and at the same time incorporate my information about each source that will help establish its credibility. I need to begin each section of the paper with my assertions about the subject. I'm going to research for more information on the positive uses of video games and use that to reduce the concerns of parents about the games.

Organization: I think I need to respond specifically to each concern with a discussion. Thus, I have to separate and discuss each concern in terms of the positive information. I need a stronger ending, one that wraps up my discussion as a whole.

Style (Word Choice and Sentence Structure): I need to reduce the number of quotations by transforming them into citations in order to clarify the points of my discussion. I can consolidate sequences of citations from the same source. I have to rethink how I present my personal experience in the paper. Since my readers are faculty who I know, they might accept my experience as a part of my discussion but only as it supports information that I found during my research. I have to connect personal experience to the research.

Conventions: I'll read sentence by sentence for errors and typos.

MLA Format: I need < > around URLs. I need to find out how to cite interviews and public talks.

Mark's Revision

Mark B.
Professor C
English 101-12

Video Games: The Substitute Teacher

Ever since the first video games came from the arcade into our homes via the early pioneers of this now multi-million dollar industry, like Atari, they have been surrounded by controversy over whether they do more harm then good. Due to the attraction of video games to children, they can become engulfed in them. *Sports Illustrated for Kids* reports that many of the people who oppose the contents of video games today are parents of the kids who are playing them. They say that kids spend too much time playing the games when they could be doing something more useful with their time, like reading ("Question" 17). There are people in the world who believe that video games have a tendency to take over a child's life and that the morals displayed in the games themselves are less than humane, and, therefore, should not be made and given to a child so they could influence the child with the acts displayed and thinking involved.

They also argue, according to *Sports Illustrated for Kids,* that the violence level in the games is giving children the message that violence is okay ("Question" 17). Parents are worried that their children are getting a warped sense of reality when they see that after a person gets ripped apart by some alien, they come back to life healthier than ever ("Question" 17). The violence shown in the games and the disrespect for human life that is sometimes incorporated into the video games are sometimes blamed for natural human aggression. *Sports Illustrated* also states that opponents of video games attribute the growing rate of violent crimes in America, the rise in illiteracy among adults, and the break down of the communication in the household all to the effect of video games on children ("Question" 17).

At the same time, there are those who see that video games are more than just mindless button pushing. Technically video games have only become better over time in a sense that the graphics used have become increasingly realistic and the computer itself has become more like a real person in the way it uses logic for problem solving. Parents buy their kids video games for several reasons. One of those reasons is the fact that video games are easy entertainment that will require no involvement on the parents' part to organize anything and no rejection for the child. Video games have no preference who plays them, so, therefore, no child can be rejected by one, whereas, if the child put the same amount of energy into getting a group together for a game of baseball, there is still a chance for rejection by the other children. Video games, if properly managed by parents, offer many educational benefits to children despite some worries about their bad effects.

Even the worry over violence is contested by some studies. Studies do not support the belief that serial killers and masked murderers exist because when those kids were young they played games where the object was to kill as many people as they could ("Question" 17). In an article in *Prevention,* Marty Munson summarizes the results of an experiment done by Dr. Silvern, professor of early-childhood education at Auburn University, who says: "I have completed two studies on the relationship between game playing and aggression and have not found any direct link. . . . Children are definitely aroused and they may be excited, but I would not say they are violent." People will buy into the theory that a game caused a person to go on a killing spree because it presents an easy scapegoat. This could have been expected though since most people tend to shift the blame of anything as far away from themselves as possible. The blame for these things cannot rest solely on the things learned from watching the graphics of a video game. Ira Wrestler, a thirteen year-old at Urbana Middle School, in Urbana, Illinois said when *Sports Illustrated for Kids* interviewed his class about the effects of video games on kids, "a lot of people think that kids are going to kill someone or do what the person does in the game, but kids are smarter than that" ("Question" 17) There is no real deep down desire for kids to play these violent games anyway, says Patrick McGuffin, chief psychologist in the Department of

Child and Adolescent Psychiatry at Hahnemann University Hospital, in Philadelphia. A recent study polled 60 kids who played a violent game and a nonviolent one for one minute apiece, then were asked which one they would want to continue playing (Munson 36). The results came back that half wanted to continue playing the nonviolent game; also, age and gender did not make a difference (Munson 36). Cheryl Handley, an early-childhood education major, agrees that the stupid part about the whole thing is that the parents keep buying the games for their children. So therefore how can a person be so against something they apparently support?

When you really step back and look at the whole picture, video games are providing players with more than just entertaining pictures on a screen. One of these benefits is physical coordination. William B. White, Jr., director of public relations and advertising for Nintendo of America, believes that not all the benefits of video game play stem from a challenging bunch of character configurations on the screen or from a good plot of a entertaining game (74). It is true, it has been found that the constant movement of objects on the screen and the hand-eye coordination involved in playing a video game can actually improve your reaction time both physically and mentally (Gutierrez 11). In a study that tested this statement, "60 healthy adults ages 60 to 79 were divided into three groups. One group played video games three hours a week, while another watched movies, and the third had no special activities. After 11 weeks, the video-game players had quicker reaction times, both physically and mentally, than the nonplayers" (Gutierrez 11). There have been many other times video games being used to improve mobility than just this one.

Video games have also been used in hospitals as a part of physical therapy in rehabilitation (White: 74). Paul Echelard, speech pathology supervisor at St. Luke's Hospital in California, which uses video games in the rehabilitation of heart and head injury patients, says that some video games "require memory skills, some require decision-making skills, some visual-perceptual, and some motor control. We are dealing with patients who have problems in [all of] those areas" (White 75). Video games have even been specialized in some cases, becoming a regular part of therapy. *Compton's Interactive Encyclopedia* describes a case in which video games are used to treat a condition called amblyopia, or lazy eye, in which one eye does not function as well as the other and needs to be exercised in order to correct the fault. The good eye was rendered useless by a patch so that the other eye had to do all the work while playing the game *(Compton's "Video Games")*. The success rate of the use of video games to aid in rehabilitation depends on the severity of the injury and the frequency that a game is used.

In addition to the physical benefits of the actual game, researchers have found a social benefit in video games as well. Anyone who has ever been to a mall knows that kids tend to travel to arcades in groups. Dr. Donald Jackson Jr., director of the psychological services center of

Widener University in Chester, Pennsylvania, noted that this simple act of going to the arcade is very helpful socially for the children. They interact with one another by bumming quarters from each other and challenging each other for the high scores (Golin 122). White also observes that it is never unusual to see a group of five or six kids huddled around one video game shouting instructions to the one who is playing the game. According to White, video games foster communication and cooperation between the players, leading to a joint effort to succeed. White reports that as children master a video game, they in turn gain a greater sense of confidence and morale. This boosted self-confidence then encourages more socialization. Video games "have shown that traditional age and gender gaps in game play of other types are modified or even eliminated during home video games" (White 74).

Not only have video games helped to bridge social gaps between children but in families as well. White contends that it starts with the siblings in the family, if there are any, when they play the games together. I play video games against my brother all the time, at least five times a week, on one of the three video game systems in our house. In a family with siblings, who under normal circumstances beat each other over the head, video games bring them together and promote more interaction rather than the rivalry that often surfaces when they compete (75). I have found even that I can channel some aggression felt toward a member of my family into kicking the stuffing out of them in a video game; it is a great stress reliever as mentioned earlier. The game does not even have to be a violent fighting game. I play my brother in football, baseball, basketball, and racing games in addition to those other games, and I get the same pleasure from a victory in any one of them. There have been many studies done on the effects of video game playing as a family and the consequent interaction. Some of the most detailed research about structured video games in the family and the consequent effect they have on it has been done by Edna Mitchell, head of the Department of Education, at Mills College (White 75). She observed twenty families over a six month period, interviewing them at the beginning and at the end, to get the prevailing attitudes on the project (White 75). Results of the experiment showed that "families reported playing together, interacting both competitively and cooperatively, communicating and enjoying each other in a new style. They were decidedly enthusiastic about this change in family life" (White 75). Perhaps one of the best things about video games is that they are not biased in the sense that any person can play them if he or she tries.

Gender, age, sexual preference, marital status, grade-point average, none of these things matter when it comes to playing a video game. When it came to family playing, video games helped to "bridge the gap," as one father commented, between fathers and their daughters (White 75). Some fathers found that spending quality time with their daughters by playing video games with them helped to even the one-sided list of activities to do with them, as opposed to the thing a father can do with his son. The same thing goes for a mother and her son, and the infinitely more things a mother and daughter do together.

It certainly seems that a person who is playing a video game at this moment cannot possibly benefit any further, but on the contrary, they can. With all the new technological advances in the last few years in the way of computers, one might begin to wonder how and why these people, who are making this technology available, ever started thinking about and working with computers. Here again video games can play a role.

White says that "by many accounts, video games are a key element in getting children familiar with and used to an increasingly high-tech society" (74). Video games help introduce children into the world of micro-computers at a time when it is becoming increasingly more important to have those skills (White 74). It is believed that many of the computer programmers and technicians today got their start in computers by playing video games (White 74). Nick Beirnhoff, the person responsible for setting up the Internet provider Dave's World and current networking guru for State Farm's data processing division, gave a presentation to my Introduction to Micro-computer class in which he said that the reason he got into computers was from "playing video games." I am currently working on an associate degree in applied Computer Sciences, and so I looked back on why I ever became involved in computers. My father is a systems analyst at State Farm Insurance, and ever since I can remember, there has been a computer of some kind in my house. When I was little the only thing that I needed them for was to play those, at the time, cool games. So therefore I had to learn to maneuver around the computers operating system by the time I was eight years old in order to make the game I wanted to play run. Consequently, by the time I needed to actually use the other parts of the computer to type my papers, I just seemed to know how to use those applications that I was in. I owe it all to the fact that I wanted to play a video game on my computer and consequently learned how to move around and use the other aspects of the computer.

Another way in which video games are getting children introduced to the computer is through the Internet. In what is called on-line gaming, kids are introduced to a rapidly increasing information center due to a yearning to play a video game with someone half way across the country. At an Electronic Entertainment Expo, Allen Adham, president and founder of Blizzard Entertainment, a leading multimedia studio for educational and entertainment software, said "Internet gaming is the next level in computer entertainment." (Blizzard 1). Starting this past summer, Blizzard offered its customers free access to Internet gaming through the company's battle.net server (Blizzard 1). "Battle.net provides an arena for Blizzard customers to chat, challenge opponents and initiate multiplayer games" (Blizzard 1).

These on-line games are not just games with great graphics that are attracting these kids; in fact most of them are puzzle and strategy type games. Metasquares, a puzzle game much like Tic-tac-toe, was created by Scott Kim, known for his mathematical puzzles, his book of two-way writing called "Inversions," and the computer game "Heaven & Earth", which was Beta tested on the Internet (Starbugsnews 2). That means that it was open for Internet users to play and then report, if they wanted, on the "bugs" or glitches that could then be worked out (Starbugsnews 1). Not only is the game itself educational but the way in which the child is forced to get to the game as well. By learning their way around the Internet to play video games, children are learning valuable skills that will help them in their future school experiences. When it comes time to use the Internet as a source of research for a term paper, they will know how to maneuver around the Internet and find the information needed. Children can recognize that if to get to the video game they played they went through the "Games channel," and then through various other forums and such until they got to the game, then why not go to the economics site to maybe get stock quotes or information on new upcoming companies for an Economics report. Take a look back to where I got the information above; I just got on the Internet and typed in "video games" on the Web Browser and went from there. Though there is still ongoing research into the educational value of video games, I believe that they should be put into practice to find out.

The new technology today should be incorporated into the schools and used to teach kids while they are still young. I have found that since I grew up in a computer centered household that I am better off when it comes to using a computer in an school environment, whereas, some of the adults, for example, who did not grow up as this technology was coming out are finding it harder to learn to use it. Three young girls, whom I have the pleasure of baby-sitting, are currently six, four, and two years old. They have learned how to count, recognize colors, and shapes and so forth due to computer games where, for example, they have to count the number of star-shaped fish that wash up each time a wave crashes on the shore. When they answer correctly, a new wave comes and a different number is there (Handley np). Computer manufacturers and the makers of video games have recognized the concern for the content of video games and have answered it by combining the fascination and excitement of a game with lessons to teach language, mathematics, reading, and science (Brody 50), showing that the makers of the so called violent and harmful games are not some money hungry corporate executives who are out to poison the minds of our youth.

Most of the video games out on me market today are actually intellectually stimulating. "Games such as Lob, where the player has to strategically position cubes to block his enemies but leave himself an open path, resemble nothing so much as an animated IQ test" (Golin 121). Another recent game is the new learning game created by Sega Entertainment in conjunction with Orion Interactive, entitled "Sonic's Schoolhouse" (Sega np). "Sonic's Schoolhouse" is Sega's first "edutainment" title and introduces Sega's popular character, Sonic the Hedgehog as the kids' computer friend (Sega np). The game features a 3D schoolhouse and playground with a first person perspective that creates a virtual reality environment for the kids (Sega np). "Sonic's Schoolhouse was designed as a game, but instead of using weapons and enemies, it uses numbers and letters (Sega np). According to Dr. Steven Silvern, professor of early-childhood education at Auburn University, video games allow for problem solving on many levels (Golin 58). "One of the first rules of problem solving is to ask yourself how this situation is like something you already know. In most of these video games, you will find that each successive level of play not only offers the situations that need new techniques but also requires the player to use the knowledge accumulated in overcoming past obstacles" (Golin 123).

True there are still those games that are virtually mindless, and it is the parent's job to steer their children towards those games that are going to be good for them. The question then becomes how to turn your child on to the games that are mentally as well as physically challenging. Golin suggest that one way for parents to take an active role and actually play the games themselves to see what the effect is on them (121). This also ties back into the statement earlier about video games bringing parents and their children together like no other entertainment medium can do. Like something that children normally would not go for, if you disguise it so it looks appealing to children, they do not know the good it is actually doing them. For example, if you set a five year old down in front of a math book and said do all problems on pages 10 through 100, she would look at you like you had just shot her dog. But on the other hand if you boot up a game where children are supposed to count the number of shells left on the beach each time a wave comes in, they will play it all night and not think twice about the learning part of it. In an interview with Cheryl Handley, an early-childhood education major at Heartland Community College and experienced baby-sitter for ten years, she agreed with this statement made above. I feel that one's ability to determine whether they are learning something or not rests on a state of mind or opinion of the situation. For example, just about everyone would agree that Chess is a great game for kids to begin to play because it teaches them to think ahead and use strategies to capture the other player's king. What about a game like Tetris, a puzzle game in which different odd-shaped pieces float down from the top of the screen and the object is to use those pieces to make a solid line across the screen and not let them stack up higher than the screen. In Tetris, the player can see what the next piece is so he or she has to place the current one accordingly, much as in Chess when the player knows what can and cannot happen based on the moving restraints of some pieces. Since both games teach almost the same lessons and enforce similar reasoning, then why is Chess not as popular as Tetris is? Because kids do not realize that they are learning while they are playing Tetris. The studies shown above and the observations made by people who work with children demonstrate that video games receive a good deal of support from child care and child development specialists. They, like a growing number of parents, understand that video games are not just mindless thumb exercises, as first believed.

I see video games becoming a bigger part in classroom education in the future, especially in the lower grades because of their ability to adapt to a different teaching style because they have no other real style to base it against. Other areas like special education I believe will incorporate the use of video games for learning. My mom worked as a teacher's assistant at Bloomington High School in the Special Education department last year. While there, she was put in charge of the daily supervising and teaching of a child who had cerebral palsy and used a computerized talk-board to communicate. Also programmed into the talk-board were games that were designed to get the child to recognize numbers, letters, and picture icons. These are just some of the many ways that computers and video games help use learn more each and every day.

Though some people still believe video games to be harmful to those who play them, there are probably an equal amount who believe that video games are beneficial. The fact is though that while there may be some overblown drawbacks which stem from video game play, there are substantially more positive aspects that video games have. While I do not think that the major drawbacks should go unnoticed, I do feel that the positives should be stressed a whole lot more. It seems to me that with anything, no matter how much good it does, the little amount of bad, no matter how small, will always be stressed more. People need to see the good aspects of video games more often because they are going to be around for a long time to come and they have a lot to offer us. We just have to want to see it. Computers are the wave of the future, and the teachers for the great minds of the future.

Works Cited

Beirnhoff, Nick. Lecture. Bloomington, IL, September 23, 1996.

"Blizzard Entertainment Introduces Battle.net—A New Concept In Gaming Over The Internet." 16 May 1996. OnlinePosting. Games Channel. America Online.

Brody, Herb. "Video Games That Teach." *Technology Review* Nov 1996: 50+.

Compton's Interactive Encyclopedia. CD-ROM. Compton's NewMedia, Inc., 1995.

Golin, Mark. "Are Video Games Zapping Your Child's Mind?" *Prevention* Aug 1992: 56+.

Gutierrez, Paul. "Shhh! Don't tell." *Sports Illustrated for Kids* September 1996: 11.

Handley, Cheryl. Personal Interview. 18 November 1996.

Munson, Marty. "Kids and Vids: Many children like the nice stuff better." *Prevention* Dec 1995: 36.

"Sega Entertainment, Orion Interactive bring fun and games to PC learning software." 10 October 1996. Online Posting. Games Channel. America Online. Available HTTP://www.Sega.com/segapc/news/releases/onon.html.

"Starbugsnews Review: Metasquares." 22 January 1997. Online Posting. *Games Channel Newsletter.* Keyword: Metasquares. America Online.

"Question: Are Video Games Good For Kids?" *Sports Illustrated for Kids* May 1994: 17.

White Jr., William B. "What Value Are Video Games?" *USA Today* Mar 1992: 74–75.

Questions for Analysis

1. In what ways would you interpret Mark's paper as an action?

2. Into what writing situations would Mark's paper fit?

3. Which elements in the paper would you interpret as persuasive strategies? How well do they suit the implied readers?

4. How would you describe Mark's attitude toward his readers? Which elements are the basis of your inference? In what ways do these attitudes increase or decrease the readers' trust in his discussion?

5. How effectively is the essay organized? Why?

6. Are there any terms defined by Mark? Are they effectively defined? Why did he define them? Are there any additional terms that need defining?

7. What kind of status or authority does Mark assign himself in the essay? Evaluate the effectiveness of the strategies he uses to do this?

8. What is the main assertion that brings the essay together conceptually and gives it a focus?

9. Where are Mark's reasoning and supporting evidence sufficient for his assertions? Where are they not?

10. How does Mark establish the credibility of the sources he uses? Are his sources effectively used in support of his assertions?

WRITING FOR INQUIRY AND ACTION

THE WRITING ASSIGNMENT

Using a number of strategies in this chapter, inquire into the consequences and implications of a computer or Internet technology. Choose a technology that is meaningful to you and to a disciplinary or occupational field of your choice. Your readers need to be a group of people that share the consequences of the technology. Use methods of inquiry to find out about some cutting edge technology that has changed and is changing the field. Consider how your inquiry can help these readers reach new understandings of how computer or Internet technology changes the ways that tasks are done, attitudes are formed, and values are shaped. All sources have to be up to date and pertinent to a description and evaluation of the cutting edge technology which you are researching.

YOUR WRITING PROCESS

Inquiry begins with your curiosity about the unknowns of a technology. By guiding you through several strategies, this chapter will help you begin and develop your inquiry and then help you turn your inquiry into an effective paper which addresses real readers.

Starting

Why pose questions?

Resources for research, both on the Internet and in libraries, are so numerous that it is easy to become overwhelmed or to overlook resources valuable to your research. With a research plan, you can achieve a systematic approach which still allows you to take advantage of the serendipitous finds that happen along the way. The first step is to choose a subject and then raise questions about it in order to give direction and purpose to your research.

QUESTIONING STRATEGY

Select a Subject for Inquiry / Get in Touch with Dissonance / Locate Yourself in a Writing Context / Raise Questions / Workshop

---

SELECTING A SUBJECT FOR INQUIRY

Within the context of Internet and computer technology, the possible avenues for research go in many directions. For one thing, although technology is a singular word, it actually represents many different technologies. Yet, many technologies are closely related and work together to give rise to new generations of technological developments. Your inquiry begins with a technological development whether you would call it "progress" or a "problem." What new and exciting capabilities do these technologies promise that might affect your future? Or what problems and limitations does the technology present?

For example, developments in data creation, storage, and transfer systems have made possible the Internet and computer systems. These developments have reduced time on task, storage space, and limitations in long distance communication. At the same time, they have reduced the value of human labor, allowed the violation of confidentiality, required constant retraining, and have burdened educational budgets. For more strategies on starting to plan, see Part II.

As you plan your own education, career, and life style, you face a world increasingly organized around Internet and computer technology. List, diagram, or free write about areas of these technologies that because of their possibilities or the problems that they seem to create affect you enough that you are moved to research them. For example, how have the areas of your vocational interests been changed by computer and Internet technology? Or what areas of computer or Internet technology do you face in your college course work? And how has your home life or social life been changed by these technologies?

GETTING IN TOUCH WITH DISSONANCE

For each subject in your list, diagram, or free writing, add some thoughts on the dissonance you feel. Dissonance is a feeling that you lack knowledge and perspective on a particular subject. You feel there is a "gap" between what you know and what you ought to know or would like to know. Use this gap, or dissonance, to help you find an aspect of computer or Internet technology that either interests you because of its exciting possibilities or worries you because of the problems it is or it will be causing. For more information on dissonance, see Part II.

In many ways, Internet and computer technology are making the "rules" of how things will work and be organized. On one hand, these rules will involve greater speed than before, fewer obstacles to communication among people around the world, easy and quick transfers of great amounts of information. Thus, these technologies bring the world "closer together." The technologies have revolutionized games people play, movie effects, publishing, business communications, medical research, weapons, and so forth. These technologies have also pushed their own research and development into the fast lane, creating fascinating new possibilities for more developments. Your dissonance in these cases might grow out of wonder about what is going on now or wonder of what will happen next.

On the other hand, perhaps your dissonance grows out of a concern for the problems that these technologies have created for those trying to maintain confidentiality in communication and personal records, security in governmental and business databases, and jobs in the large-scale downsizing of industry and government. Certainly, in education and in business, the high cost of purchasing, maintaining, and upgrading these technologies has created significant financial hardships.

As you list, diagram, or free write about your dissonance whether it is positive or negative, reflect on the importance of your subject to your values. How intense is your excitement or concern about the aspect of Internet or computer technologies that you are considering for your inquiry? Is either one deep enough to commit yourself to several weeks of research and writing on the subject? Moreover, what kind of action would your writing project seek to accomplish in the world? In other words, what aim would your writing accomplish?

LOCATING YOURSELF IN A WRITING SITUATION

Now that you have chosen a subject which generates significant dissonance for you, consider how to understand your upcoming research and writing as an investment toward an "action" in the real world. To write in the real world means to write to real readers. A writing situation consists of using your writing as an action which you present to real readers in order to have them help you change a situation. Writing as an action suggests that your aim is to make an impact upon the beliefs, attitudes, actions, or values of your readers. A writing situation identifies to whom you are writing, why, and how. Readers do not appear out of thin air, nor can you magically reach them through wishful thinking. Instead, think of your readers as those who pick up and read a campus newspaper, a program newsletter on the job, or a special handout prepared for a course or a club. In other words, as you think of possible writing situations, think of the possible forms in which your writing could actually be packaged and delivered to real readers. List or diagram them.

The academic research paper is not a form of writing readily adaptable to all reader outlets. On the campus, a research paper has its place if the readers are suitable to your subject matter and aim. Your writing, in other words, has to be able to reach the readers who will be able, if receptive to your ideas, to carry out your aim. An academic research paper can have uses beyond earning you a grade. As an action, your research paper could be the vehicle to bring about some change in belief, policy, or practice in your classroom, your major department, your field, your school, your community. Your research paper could serve as a catalyst to begin the ball rolling on developing a new opportunity on your campus or in addressing a problem with respect to Internet and computer technologies. Your aim at this point in your project might be vague, but nonetheless, your aim helps you point your research paper in the direction of a "publication" form of some kind which has real readers on the other end.

You need to consider who is or who ought to be concerned with the subject of your dissonance. Who could effect change? In other words, who are your possible readers? At the same time, consider the means through which these readers would be able to read your paper: handout on a street corner, part of a Website, a packet in a course (with the instructor's permission of course), and so forth. When you begin to see the connections among your subject, your research, and real readers, you will establish motivation for yourself and for your project. Thus, list the writing situations that you understand as possible for you and your project. List the readers and aim that you could accomplish with them. Choose a set of readers that would provide the best chance for you to carry out your aim for your writing project.

RAISING QUESTIONS FOR INQUIRY

By this point, you have chosen a subject for inquiry, the dissonance that motivates your inquiry, and a writing situation (aim, readers). Your subject represents an area which you need to know more about in order to carry out your aim. At this point in an inquiry, you do not know what you will find out from your research, nor do you know exactly know what you feel or think about the aspect of the Internet or computer technology that is your subject. Thus, research is needed. Since the resources of the Internet and libraries are numerous, you need to enter into your research project with a definite plan in mind. By framing your dissonance about the subject in a "guiding question," you are giving your research efforts the direction they need. List or free write questions in which you try to connect your dissonance to knowing more about your subject. Before moving on, choose a guiding question. For more on formulating questions, see Part II.

Example of Joselyn's Questioning Strategy

Aspects of Computer and/or Internet Technology That Matter to Me

- I am interested in future job security in the areas of information systems, local area networks, and networks in general. This includes both manager and staff positions. From previous reading, I know that programming skills are a necessary first step, which leads to system analyst positions, although some starting positions combine the two.

- Another aspect that interests me is how programming languages have changed and simplified the programmer's job. Newer languages allow programmers to reuse chunks of code, rather than having to start over from scratch each time.

- I am interested in the "intranets" that are the rage now. Networking software and hardware have evolved quickly around demand for private information systems on the Internet.

My Choice for This Inquiry

Since I'm interested in a college degree that covers information systems, this cutting edge networking technology of intranets would be a good place to become acquainted.

Getting in Touch with My Dissonance on this Subject

The Internet has evolved into intranets for business data sharing. With that, a move from mainframes to networks to intranets has taken place. So much movement requires a lot of software and hardware movement. Programmers and analysts are needed to keep up with changes from one type of information system to another. Problems with compatibility and regular maintenance keep them hopping. My dissonance comes from my concern with the drawback that all this constant change involves companies in taking risks with new technologies. Because everybody else is going to some new thing, you have to do it, too, just to keep up with the crowd. Businesses of all sizes must be draining their budgets each year to upgrade systems or implement new ones. What I want to know is what is the role of intranets in this rapid turnover of technology and business practices? Networking technology changes so fast that a programmer must remain mobile and committed if he or she expects to climb the ladder. Information system professionals spend short periods of time on one project which then is changed by new technologies and so there is a constant renewing of project focus. Every new technology that comes along has to be mastered immediately and that requires expensive classes or constant self learning. Also information system (IS) professionals could be working on several projects simultaneously. How can one expect to have a life if you're always at work or constantly learning the new stuff?

Locating Myself in a Writing Context

- I can aim to inform other students in their first two years of college who are thinking about programmer/analyst jobs how they can expect to be involved with intranets.

- A researched paper would be effective because then I can document what is happening and not just write from my own personal experience and hearsay.

Possible sets of readers:

- My writing project could be in two steps: One an academic research paper written to my composition instructor and my composition class. From our introductions, I know that there are at least two other students in this room who said they were going into information systems and programming. Other students indicated interests in business, accounting, and public relations. All these areas will probably have something to do with intranets. So this class has people who could benefit from my research.

- The second step could be to write to the readers of the college newsletter that is circulated in the halls. The newsletter often includes information on vocational areas. My research paper could be adapted to the readers of that publication.

- I could write my paper to a computer science class as an informational resource for the instructor. Since the students are learning programming, my paper could be used by the instructor as information on intranets, which is an area that new programmers need to learn about.

<u>*My Choice for a Writing Context*</u>

I choose: Preparing my research paper as a supplement handout in a introductory computer science course.

Formulating Questions for Inquiry

- Why has the Internet generated a need for intranets?
- What kinds of new technologies made this move possible?
- What role has governmental regulation played in the development of intranets?
- What role have security issues played in the development of intranets?
- What implications do these changes have for programmers?
- What kind of issues do people considering programming need to consider?
- What is the impact that Networking and intranet developments have on job security for programmers?

<u>*My Choice for a Guiding Question for My Inquiry and Research*</u>

What is the impact that Networking and intranet developments have on job security for programmers?

WORKSHOP

1. In your group, discuss possible topics about technology for inquiries. What questions and puzzlements do they raise for you?

2. Consider if the inquiry is located within a real writing situation in which your papers will result in some action or new understanding.

For more information on collaboration for this workshop and those that follow, see Part II.

Exploring

Why explore?

Once you have an inquiry question to guide your research, you first need to take stock of what you know about the subject. One way to do that is through the Three Perspectives Guide or other exploratory strategies. This guide will also help you determine what aspects of the subject related to your guiding question require research. After finishing the guide, you are set to begin researching in order to answer your guiding question with the latest, or "cutting edge," information. The two guides following the Three Perspectives Guide help you research the answer to your guiding question through library and Internet resources. In exploring the information on your subject, it is most worthwhile to find and use the latest information and perspectives. That's a purpose of research to provide yourself and your readers with the latest thinking. By including consideration of the most recent critiques of your subject, you are striving make your writing an effective act.

THREE PERSPECTIVES GUIDE
Describe and Distinguish / Trace Moves and Changes / Map Networks and Relationships

---

By coming at your subject from different perspectives, you can discover what you already know and what needs research. The following prompts are meant to trigger responses, whether through free writing, stories, or lists. Feel free to move around randomly and respond to the prompts, returning to earlier responses in order to add or change your responses. Those that you cannot respond to consider as candidates for research.

DESCRIBING AND DISTINGUISHING

Describe the physical aspects of the technology. How does it work? How much is this technology dependent on the Internet?

What new opportunities has the technology generated? What changes has this technology caused or helped bring about in business, education, public affairs, and private lives? What are the negative consequences of this technology with respect to the environment, education, economy, and relations among social groups? For more information on the Three Perspectives Guide, see Part II.

What kind of training does this technology require? What kinds and amounts of resources (material, financial, human) does it require? What role does the technology play in the operations of business, education, public affairs, and private lives? What aspects seem to have the most consequences? Why?

What aspects of the technology interest you the most? Why? Which of the above points and others that you thought of need to be researched in order to help answer and/or change your guiding question?

TRACING MOVES AND CHANGES

What problem or situation led to the development of the technology? Has the technology changed over time? How do these changes relate to the changing needs of business, education, or other public affairs? Which historical events would you compare in significance to the development of this technology? Which preceding technologies made this technology possible? Predict further developments and uses of the technology.

Do any laws, policies, or rules have to be changed to make room for the use of this technology? How has the technology affected economic, social, and political institutions over a period of time? How has the technology affected values in general? values of particular groups? Has the technology allowed any groups to gain or maintain economic, social, or political advantages over other groups? Predict the effects of the technology on the ways people are organized, categorized, governed, or controlled.

When did you first become involved or interested in the technology? Why?

How has your attitude toward the technology changed over time? Why?

What new issues, problems, or controversies has the technology helped create? What issues, problems, or controversies has it helped to solve?

Which of the points above and others that you thought of need to be researched in order to help answer and/or change your guiding question?

MAPPING NETWORKS AND RELATIONSHIPS

In relation to other technologies, how would you categorize or classify the technology? What other technologies have similar aspects or consequences? What is unique about this technology? Why is this technology considered "valuable?"

What are the disagreements over the nature, use, or consequences of the technology? What impact does the technology have on the way people view the development or use of other technologies?

Is the technology associated with any particular fields of study or occupations? How are these associations related to how people value or not value the technology? Are there associations made between the use of the technology and the group identity of the users, for example, the way 1950s boys are associated with hot cars and 1950s girls are associated with dolls and beauty pageants? How is the technology represented in advertising, TV shows, videos, movies, literature, and so forth?

What images or metaphors seem appropriate for your feelings about the technology? For example, do you see it as "a beauty" or "a beast?" Which of the points above and others that you thought of need to be researched in order to help answer and/or change your guiding question?

Example: Joselyn's Exploration

<u>*My Guiding Questions and Writing Situation*</u>

What is the impact that Networking and intranet developments have on job security for programmers? I am writing my research paper as a supplement handout to be used in an introductory computer science course.

Distinguishing and Describing

Physical aspects

Include the software that creates the internal network, the server that manages the software, individual personal computers within a group or organization, various hardware components that allow users to transmit, print, and share data, a separate Web server that provides hyperlinks to various application servers within the organization, the Internet protocols that allow the hyperlinks to exist, and the connections and cables that link these various hardware components together.

How it works

The Web server acts as the mediator between individual PCs and the various application servers; the Internet protocol allows data from the various servers to be shared in hypertext; the intranet software creates the private network; the browser software gives PC users a graphical interface within which to work; a "firewall" prevents anyone outside the organization from infiltrating an organization's servers; the Web server allows users within the intranet network to access the Internet.

New opportunities generated by intranet technology

Corporate information can be shared, interactively manipulated, updated JIT, allowing users to access up-to-the-minute data; intranet software and management of private networks, including implementation, requires new knowledge of networking specific to the intranet software; growing demand for personnel who understand implementing and maintaining these systems; software makers making money hand over foot; adds more jobs to the computing profession pool.

Negative consequences

Software developers are at each other's throats to get the most business; larger companies with a foothold may win this battle and secure their place in governing the computing lives of America and the world; implementing and maintaining networks takes a lot of time, and once these networks are established, they seem to be the backbone of a company, meaning the network must continually work properly or the business may bust; software developers trying to profit the most release new software several times a year which drains corporate funds continually as they try to stay competitive.

Training and resources

Networking requires personnel to solve compatibility problems with software and hardware; networking personnel must work with users to solve their problems or deter the problems that they cause; enormous time demand to implement and maintain keep networkers up all night; knowledge of Internet technology; knowledge of all application server software; this technology costs money and constant issues of new releases keep money flowing out; intranet technology is very popular and will grow immensely and play a vital role in business, etc.

Aspects with the most consequences and why

The fast growth of intranets because high demand for intranet software will keep the software, hardware, implementation and maintenance fields hopping and growing. The ripple effect here is almost endless. The economy benefits as a whole, corporations of all sizes benefit from it, and all the individuals within these industries have opportunity for personal advancement in knowledge, cash, etc.

Aspects that interest me the most and why

The ones that I have little knowledge of: physical connections and compatibility of hardware and software because these areas involve implementation and maintenance. As long as human beings use this technology, there will be a propensity for problems to occur. These realities spell job security for me.

Research needed

How intranets works, software, negative consequences, training requirements. What are the new technologies being developed? What are the problems for the Internet created by the rush to intranets?

Tracing Moves and Changes

Over a period of time

The Internet started booming in 95? maybe 94? Intranets came into existence in late 95 or early 96. In the time since then, the major players and lots of new ones have really cashed in on demand for intranet technology. On the other hand, the PC market, which was all the rage before this technology was introduced, started going south and is still headed that way. PCs are faster and packages are beefed up more than ever—and the prices are lower than ever and still dropping.

The problem that led to development

The situation was a realization that Internet technology could be incorporated into private network software. The hyperlink technology allows users from different platforms (Macintosh, IBM compatible) to access the same data, thus businesses could keep their existing networks and PCs, no matter the platform, and share information without the hassles of separate software and systems that allow cross-platform data sharing.

In addition, many cross-platform problems require separate solutions for hardware and software and for each pair of platforms. Company expense increases exponentially every time a new software is added because it has to be meshed with existing software. Intranet software lets all those applications remain in their separate servers and users can share it all once it's been converted into hypertext. Some folks with intensive needs find the intranet technology too slow and have opted to keep their Lotus applications because they're faster. Software developers are working on solutions for these speed-type problems. Intranet technology has changed in the same ways that all computer technologies have changed in that users and developers discover new needs all the time. Behind all the intranet technology growth is the growth of the Internet.

Comparative historical events

Intranet is just one of the developments that the Internet has brought about. Intranet is a cottage industry that developed within the Internet. Like the Saturn automobile being developed within the General Motors company today. Or the Macintosh being developed within the computer industry. Or the minivan within the automobile industry. Or the Great Society within the Federal government's web of programs.

Future developments and uses

More businesses, educational institutions, and corporations, both large and small, will continue to demand this technology. Professionals predict rapid growth this year and through the year 2000 for intranets. Current developments include data security implementation and integration; software developments that would allow users faster processing time within intranets when intensive tasks are undertaken; intranet and Internet access is being built into more productivity sites and/or operating environments.

It seems as though the Internet technology is slowly spreading down into the PC market. There is development of Network Computers now by several manufacturers that will supposedly give corporate users a less expensive means of accessing the Internet (avoiding expensive PC networks).

The Internet has made object-oriented programming languages, hypertext, and other more universal communication technologies popular. The trend seems to be toward one common and universally compatible technology. If this does in fact occur, it would be the end of PCs as we know them today. A $500 NC would allow access to the Net, where applications could be located, downloaded, used, and then uploaded back to the Net when you're done using them. No more expensive desktop computers and maybe even fewer or no more PC networks as we know them. I better stop there. Networks will probably always be necessary for employees to communicate.

Laws, policies, or rules to be changed

None that I'm aware of. The physical structure and the Internet hypertext technologies were already in place. The idea just used the Net technology and incorporated it into network software. One thing that has become an issue recently is how far Uncle Sam should go to restrict the length of data encryption coding. The longer the code, the more secure the data. Uncle Sam wants to limit coding to about 54 and experts say 75 is more realistic and, in fact, necessary to keep foreign customers from being scared away by hackers. Uncle Sam and law enforcement officers claim that if coding length goes over their 54 limit, they should be provided the key to the code. That way they can keep a close watch on electronic transfers. For example, without the key to longer codes, criminals could wire funds without the IRS ever knowing about it for tax purposes. Other criminal possibilities are probably endless if no one has the code key but the sender and the receiver of the information. Struggle is over how much power the Fed should have. Nothing new there!

Social institutions

Inequality of opportunity certainly holds for some groups.

Political institutions

Have beefed up their tax revenues by opening the Net up to the public. This new technology has generated even more economic activity and tax dollars. What's good for the economy is good for the politicians. Again, certain institutions not adequately funded may suffer inequality of opportunity. In general, this technology would only help institutions.

Values in general

Have risen where efficiency is concerned. Greed has become more evident as everybody wants a bigger piece of the pie. But as the major players continue to integrate each other's products into their own, the compatibility improvements have brought about compromise and unity.

Group advantages

Any group with the money to acquire this technology enjoys an advantage over the groups that can't afford it, especially in the marketplace. The major players in the computer industry enjoy an advantage over small or new companies but not always. One big advantage for the major players is that their products are already widely distributed and their bank rolls are large, which affords them a cushion for error. If a smaller company sticks its neck out for a new technology that flops, they go under. Then again, if a small company's product does well, it tends to increase profits significantly.

Points that need research

Data security, problems that intranets solved, whether new categories of people will/have emerged, social effects, political effects, preceding and enabling technologies, laws that have changed.

Mapping Networks and Relationships

Relation to other technologies

I would class intranets as a network tool for sharing data and as a private Internet.

Uniqueness of intranet technology

It's a private, protected network, as opposed to the general Internet which leaks data.

The value of intranets

It's considered valuable because it allows data from servers running on different platforms to be shared using Internet protocol. This greatly reduces the quantity and complexity of software and hardware compatibility problems. Thus, it has economic value because it opens up access at a cost lower than previous technology.

Disagreements

Include the fight with Uncle Sam over power of access and among major players over which distributed object platforms should be used.

Impact on the way people view the development and the use of other technologies

Greatest impact on PCs. Some impact on other network technologies (LANs). As they become less used, perhaps even less needed, they might become a thing of the past. Positive views on the development of better technologies for intranets: for printers, telephones, fax over the net, long distance calls over the net. These last three will make a big dent in the telephone company revenues.

Associations

With mainly corporate and large businesses, there are massive amounts of data storage. Any big organization, hospital, school, church even. The high value of intranets derives its existence from the nature of such organizations: They all have lots of people and lots of data that need to be accessed from lots of different places, even geographically.

Representation in ads

Same ways the Internet is. Lots of waves with captions "Catch the Intranet Wave," "Here come the Intranets." Always some catchy phrase about productivity or profit increases.

Images for intranets

"Labyrinth" or "web" shielded by an "umbrella" called a "firewall."

Need to be researched

Disagreements over the status of LANs, new technologies spin-offs, and ad images.

WORKSHOP
Help your group members by evaluating the following:

1. Did the writer discover enough aspects of the subject?
2. Is the original guiding question still in line with the interests of the writer or does it need to be changed?

EXPLORING THROUGH LIBRARY RESEARCH
Orient Yourself to the Library / Create a Working Bibliography / Annotate/ Take Notes / Workshop

---

Orienting to the Library

Library searches vary somewhat from library to library. Orient yourself to your library by taking a guided tour, reading over library materials, reading signs and posters, and asking library personnel. By becoming oriented to your library, you will save time and frustration. Most libraries have access to a wealth of information. With an investment of your time in orientation, you will be able to access those resources which will benefit your project.

CREATING A WORKING BIBLIOGRAPHY

A working bibliography is list of references that are related to your subject and to your guiding question. You compile a working bibliography by searching through indexes and bibliographies. After you compile your working bibliography, you want to check the catalog of your library's holdings to see which sources are available in your library and which will have to be obtained through the Interlibrary Loan Service.

Many of the indexes, which list references by field and subject categories, are online (computerized text, often connected to a remote site), on the Internet, or on CD-ROM (compact disk-read only memory). CD-ROM indexes often have their own computer terminals, such as *InfoTrac*. In some libraries, *InfoTrac* has an article print out and save-to-disk capability. The MLA Bibliography can be searched on the world wide web.

Many indexes are called abstracts because they include a summary of each source. Since online indexes are updated continually, they provide the latest in published material. Online and CD-ROM indexes have on screen instructions which tell you what you need to do. Between them and help from the librarian, you will be computer searching in a short time. By making selections and pressing the enter key, in most cases, you will be led to a search window. Here you type in the keywords, which are the words that you feel identify aspects of your subject and inquiry question. Online and CD-ROM indexes use on-screen menus and on-screen directions to guide you. After selecting a particular index, you will be guided to a search screen. For more on constructing a working bibliography, see Part II.

Example of an "Online Resources" Window in a Library

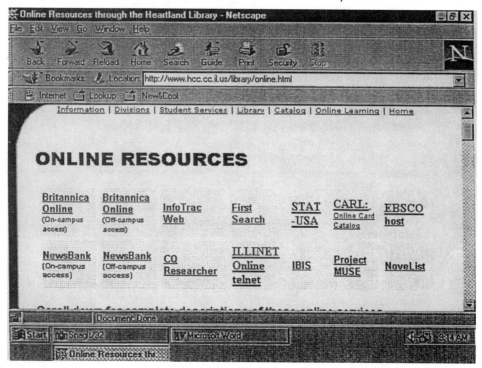

Example of Online Database Windows in Infotrac

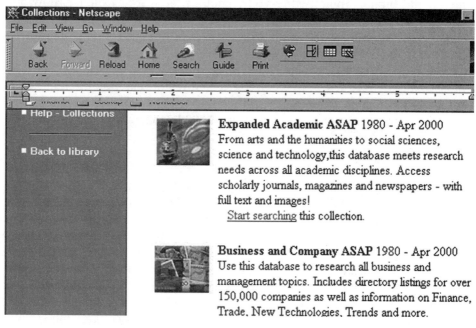

Example of Online Search Screens

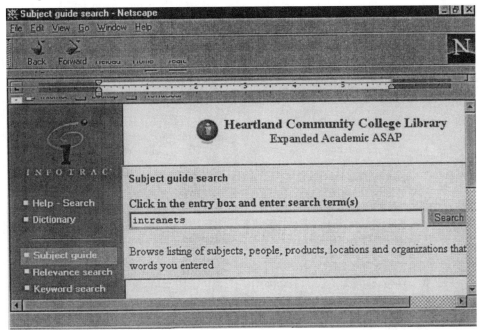

By typing in keywords in the subject search line and pushing enter, you call up all references identified by those keywords. Your choice of keywords is important for conducting a successful search. All the references in the computerized index, or database, are "keyed" to certain descriptive words. Therefore, a variety of keywords will produce more results than one or two keywords. One helpful tool in locating effective keywords is a set of books entitled *The Library of Congress Subject Headings,* which cross references keywords that many databases use.

Excerpt from the Library of Congress Subject Headings

Intramedullary fracture fixation
  (May Subd Geog)
    [RD103.153]
      UF   Fracture fixation, Intramedullary
            Intramedullary nailing
            Intramedullary osteosynthesis
            Medullary nailing
            Nailing, Intramedullary
            Nailing, Medullary
            Osteosynthesis, Intramedullary
      BT   Internal fixation in fractures
Intramedullary nailing
    USE Intramedullary fracture fixation
Intramedullary nails
    USE Intramedullary rods
Intramedullary osteosynthesis
    USE Intramedullary fracture fixation

Intramedullary rods *(May Subd Geog)*
    [RD103.153]
      UF   Intramedullary nails
            Medullary nails
            Medullary rods
            Nails, Intramedullary
            Nails, Medullary
            Rods, Intramedullary
            Rods, Medullary
      BT   Orthopedic implants
Intramercurial planets
    USE Planets, Intramercurial
Intramural sports *(May Subd Geog)*
    [GV710]
      BT   School sports
  —Records *(May Subd Geog)*
      BT   Sports records

Intramuscular injections
    USE Injections, Intramuscular
Intramyometrial coring *(May Subd Geog)*
    UF   Coring, Intramyometrial
    BT   Myometrium—Surgery
Intranasal drugs
    USE Intranasal medication
Intranasal medication *(May Subd Geog)*
    [RM160]
    UF   Drugs, Intranasal
          Intranasal drugs
          Medication, Intranasal
          Nasal medication
          Pernasal medication
          Transnasal medication
    BT   Drugs—Administration
    RT   Respiratory therapy
Intranets (Computer networks)
    (May Subd Geog)
        [HD30.385 (Business)]
        [TK5105.875.16 (Technology)]
        Here are entered works on
        computer networks used by an
        organization to give its members
        access to internal information via
        Internet technology.
    UF   Internal internets (Computer
          networks)
    BT   Business enterprises—Computer
          networks
          Wide area networks (Computer
          networks)
    NT   Intelink (Computer network)
Intraocular fluid
    USE Aqueous humor
Intraocular implant lenses
    USE Intraocular lenses
Intraocular lens industry *(May Subd Geog)*
        [HD9707.5.C65-
HD9707.5.C654]
    BT   Optical trade
Intraocular lenses
    [RE988]
    UF   Crystalline lens prosthesis
          Implant lenses
          Intraocular implant lenses
          Lens implantation

    BT   Aphakia
          Implants, Artificial
          Ophthalmic lenses
  —Complications *(May Subd Geog)*
    UF   Intraocular lenses—Complica-
          tions and sequelae
          [Former heading]
  —Complications and sequelae
    USE Intraocular lenses—Complica-
          tions
Intraocular pressure
    UF   Ocular tension
          Pressure, Intraocular
    BT   Body fluids—Pressure
          Eye
Intraocular pressure, High
    USE Glaucoma
Intraocular pressure, Low
    USE Ocular hypotony
Intraoperative complications
    USE Surgery—Complications
Intraoperative monitoring *(May Subd Geog) [RD50.5]*
    UF   Monitoring, Intraoperative
    BT   Patient monitoring
          Therapeutics, Surgical
    NT   Neurophysiologic monitoring
          Respiratory gas monitoring
Intraoperative neurophysiologic
monitoring
    USE Neurophysiologic monitoring
Intraoperative radiation therapy
    USE Intraoperative radiotherapy
Intraoperative radiotherapy
    (May Subd Geog)
    UF   Intraoperative radiation
          therapy
    BT   Radiotherapy
    SA   *subdivision* Intraoperative
          radiotherapy
          under individual diseases,
          e.g. Cancer—Intraoperative
          radiotherapy

Example of Illinet Search Page

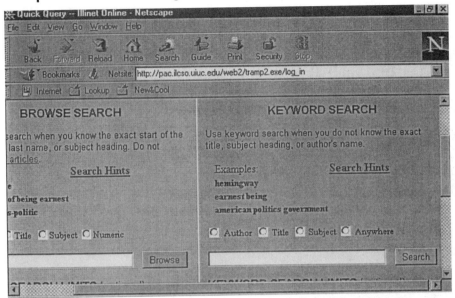

One of the advantages of online indexes is that many of them can be accessed through any computer terminal with internet access.

After the choice of a particular index is made and entered, the computer calls up a search page. Then any number of keyword combinations are typed in. By using the help command, you can call up windows which explain the types of symbols that assist in conducting online searches.

Example of "Limit Search" Screen in the Online Database of Infotrac

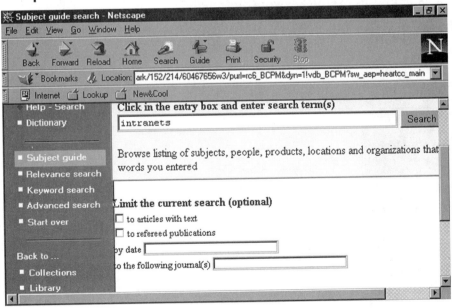

Thus, by following the on-screen directions, you can reach the search window in the index of your choice. By typing in keywords, you will call up the references pertinent to those keywords. By thinking up keywords related to your subject and guiding question, you will be able to locate the references listed under the keywords. Your search might yield references to journal articles, magazine articles, books, video tapes, audio cassettes, CD-ROMs, laser disks, art work, reports, and so forth.

Results by Category in Infotrac Based on the Keyword "Intranets"

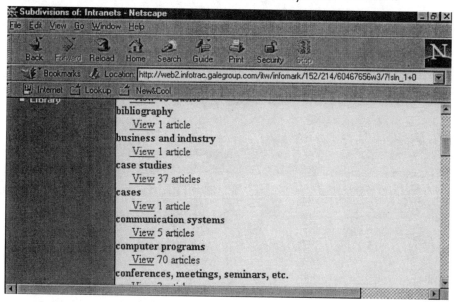

Example of Results for the Keyword "Intranets"

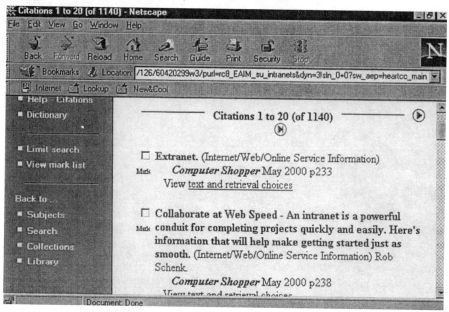

Write your working bibliography in the style format (e.g. MLA or APA) required by your instructor and indicate the call number (or shelf number) of each source, which indicates the location of the source within the library. Periodicals, or serials as librarians might call them, are often found in several locations within the library. The most recent issues are probably in a reading area. The earlier issues are bound by "volume" and located on shelves, perhaps in their own section. Old periodicals are often placed in a special storage unit and accessed through filling out a request form. Sometimes older volumes are converted to "microtext," such as film, card, or fiche. Microtext requires the use of special magnifier reading machines which can be operated with a few instructions from a librarian. Sometimes periodicals are converted to CD-ROMs. In any event, the online or card catalog list of your library's holdings identifies the form of the periodicals.

For those holdings not in computer databases, you need to search through print indexes. These are books in which the sources are listed by subject areas. The search is the same as in online indexes; use your keywords to locate appropriate references. These print indexes can be specialized. Examples are *Architectural Index, Communication Abstracts, Ecology Abstracts, Film Literature Index, Index of Economic Articles,* and *Mathematical Reviews.* This list is just a sampling; there are many more available. Many major newspaper indexes are now available online. Check in your library's reference section for a listing of the library's holdings of indexes and abstracts.

Bibliographies are publications which include lists of references pertaining to a selected subject. You can find the references to bibliographies in the holdings list of the library. A bibliography might appear in one of various forms, such as a book, a periodical, a handout or a website. To find bibliographies, include the word "bibliography" as a keyword in your search.

The reference section of your library has other useful sources. Ones that are particularly helpful to students are *The Congressional Quarterly Researcher* and *The Congressional Quarterly: Weekly Report.* These publications help track the activities of Congress and thus the federal government as a whole. *Facts on File: World News,* a digest with an index, and *Editorials on File,* which published editorials from around the country, records the events and the issues that are finding their way into the news reporting channels. These publications are also a good place to generate ideas for how to approach the subject of your inquiry.

After you have determined which references belong in your working bibliography, arrange your references in a priority order. Your research does not have to be limited to the holdings of the library. For those high priority references which you find in the indexes but which are not in the library's holdings, you can take advantage of the Interlibrary Loan Service, which in some libraries can be accessed from the online index database. This service allows you, often free of charge, to obtain materials from other libraries. Usually you may keep the borrowed material up to two weeks. Since it might take one to two weeks to obtain the material, you need to allow for that in your research plan. Group the references available in your library by call number so you can locate all your sources in the same section at one time.

If any materials are missing or marked "reserved," check with the reserve section of the library. Many libraries allow instructors to take sources off the regular shelves and place them in a Reserve Section so students in their classes may have access. This is to prevent one student from monopolizing a source. Usually Reserve materials are checked out for a restricted time and must stay within the library.

Special collections are materials of singular value that are set off from the regular holdings. They might consist of the working papers of an author or well known person, papers from the archives of an organization or institution, old manuscripts, or other papers or objects of particular value. Hours are usually limited.

Government depository libraries are sites where the US Government Printing Office regularly sends publications. Over 1400 libraries are designated as depository libraries. Not all depository libraries receive all government publications, nonetheless, if your library is designated as such, you have a sizable holding of government publications close at hand. MARGIVE, developed by the Government Publishing Office in 1976, is a CD-ROM index to US Government publications. Another classification system used for federal government publication is a scheme developed by the Superintendent of Documents, known as SuDoc Numbers. Your library probably has a handout to explain how SuDoc works. Publications of the federal government include documents from federal agencies, census, Congress, president, supreme court, regulations, statistics, information on foreign countries, crime, education, health, and patent/trademark information. By using the keywords "government documents and publications" you will reach websites for government documents, including links to local government.

The Congressional Information Service Index, which publishes the working papers of the US Congress, and the American Statistics Index, which includes a guide and index to the statistical publications of the federal government, provides a means of searching among government publications and documents.

Example: References from Carol's Working Bibliography, in MLA Format

1. Journal article

Wells, Susan. "What Do We Want from Public Writing?" *College Composition and Communication* 47.3 (1996): 324–41.

The 47 indicates the volume number and the 3 indicates the issue number. The pages for the entire article are at the end.

2. Magazine article

Max, D.T. "The End of the Book?" *The Atlantic* Monthly September 1994: 61–71.

A reference for a magazine does not include the volume and issue number. Instead the date suffices. Note that if the date included a day (for example, the 26th), it would appear before the month, as in 26 September 1994.

3. Book

Fish, Stanley. *There's No Such Thing As Free Speech: And It's a Good Thing, Too.* New York: Oxford University Press, 1994.

The book reference includes the site of publication, the name of the publishing company, and the year of copyright.

ANNOTATING

After you have located your sources, skim them in order of priority, making annotations, which are brief notes that evaluate the source according to the following criteria: the extent and manner that your subject is treated in the source; the particular point of view that the source brings to the subject; the degree of credibility that the source establishes; the limitations of the source; and a rating of priority.

Credibility is the degree of trust that readers will place in an author and in a text. The readers' trust is encouraged through information about an author's expertise in the subject, perhaps through a job title or a description of the author's research and writing about the subject. Limitations of a source might include the age of its information (date of publication), the brevity by which it discusses the subject, or the lack of trustworthy evidence for its claims.

The purpose of annotating is to efficiently decide which of the references in your working bibliography are worthy of careful reading and note taking. During the skimming of sources for annotation, you can expand your working bibliography if you find promising references in the sources. For more on annotation, see Part II. For more on MLA bibliographic format, see Part II.

Example of Carol's Annotation (Print Source)

Reference to source

Wells, Susan. "What Do We Want from Public Writing?" *College Composition and Communication* 47 (1996): 324–41.

This article provides a framework for locating real audiences for student writers. The article does not directly discuss how computers play a role but offers strategies to find audiences that do not exclude the use of the computer. The article reviews the advantages and disadvantages of four strategies. Wells situates her discussion in relation to discourse ethics, identity politics, feminist principles, and the movement within composition studies to help students write to make a difference in their particular writing situations (all hot topics in the field). Many sources used, most from the mid 1990s. This article would help me set up a conceptual framework to answer my inquiry question. High priority reference.

By writing your annotations on your computer in a file, you could merge your working bibliography file with the annotation file to produce your Annotated Working Bibliography. When you begin drafting, you could cut and paste the bibliographic references into the end of your draft and delete the references that you did not use as sources in the paper. Thus, you will save yourself the type of retyping and formatting.

NOTE TAKING

The point of note taking is to gather information of various kinds that will help you construct an answer to your guiding question. Legally and ethically, you have the right to incorporate the ideas, arguments, and information from sources into your paper as long as you clearly indicate in your text when the borrowing from a source starts and when it ends. This is true no matter if you incorporate a source's question, opinion, statistic, example, or words. Thus, as you read, indicate the source for all your notes, no matter how long. To fail to indicate the beginning and ending of a source's material in your text is plagiarism, the representation of another's text, thinking, or style as your own. Plagiarism can have serious consequences, academically and legally.

The purpose of your notes is to help develop and support your answer to your guiding question. As you read, think through what each source can contribute to that goal. Usually what a researcher/writer needs is the gist of the source's perspective on the subject, that is the argument that the author makes, and notes on the credibility of the source based in part on the information provided about its sources. This might be contained in one note. Certainly helpful statistics or examples should be noted as well, but there is no need to take more than a few notes per source. With few exceptions, you probably do not need the details in a source even if you wish to record the reasoning and summary of the evidence behind the source's argument. For more on note taking, see Part II.

A goal to read and take notes on as many pertinent sources as possible will acquaint you with the range of perspectives on the subject. You will have a better understanding of the subject by reading to understand the differences among experts and their reasoning than by having detailed accounts of a few sources. To cover a wide range of opinion on the subject, it is important to keep moving in your reading and note taking and not to become bogged down with a few sources. You will discover that sources talk about and interpret one another and that their discussions help you come to a better understanding of the subject.

No matter what kind of research you are doing, it is wise to bear in mind the adage, "You can't believe everything you read." The question then is how do you judge, or evaluate, what you hear, view, or read as a researcher? In short, you need to develop a critical position by which to evaluate the source material as you digest it. A critical position is based upon the beliefs that you hold as most reliable based on experience, reflection, and consideration of the conflicting beliefs held by sources. In your consideration of sources, analyze what claims an author makes and the values those claims support, what reasoning and evidence are supplied as the grounds for those claims, and how do sources compare in their claims, reasoning, and evidence.

If nothing can be found at the site on the source of information, you will have to spend some time trying to locate information on the source in the reference section of the library through biographical dictionaries and directories, such as *Biography Index, Biography and Genealogy Master Index, Who's Who in America: A Biographical Dictionary of Notable Men and Women,* and *American Men and Women of Science.* Check your library's holding for such biographical reference works that can provide background information on your sources.

Label your notes with the source, exact page number in the source where the note is found, and a brief descriptive title for the note. The first two are essential in documenting your sources correctly, and the latter is important in helping organize and track your research.

Example Note from Carol's Reading

Wells   Methods of Constructing "Publics" as Audiences

Wells argues that audiences beyond the classroom walls have to be constructed; they are not just sitting there waiting for the student to write to them. She offers four schemes to construct public audiences: the classroom as public, analysis of public discourse, students writing as participants in some public activity and discourse, and students writing in public forums as representatives of their disciplinary fields. (pp. 338–339)

Example Note from Carol's Reading

Wells   On what public writing looks like

She reminds us that as writing goes public, the genre and the style have to fit the writing situation. Thus, the use to which student writing is put determines the genre and the style, or as she puts it, might remind us of magazine or church bulletin instead of an essay. (p. 340)

WORKSHOP

You can help members of your writing group decide if:

1. Each annotation is complete enough to reflect an effective evaluation of the source.

2. The note taking is centering on ideas and arguments from a variety of viewpoints and is geared toward answering the guiding question.

EXPLORING THROUGH INTERNET RESEARCH
Create a Working Bibliography / Annotate / Take Notes / Workshop

Orienting to the Internet

If you have little or no experience on the Internet, it is wise to seek help from your instructor, campus computer center, which might offer Internet short courses, library which might have Internet access, or the designated assistants in campus computing labs. By achieving a general understanding of the Internet, you will be able to adapt to its continuous changes. It is the nature of the Internet to change constantly.

The Internet itself is the electronic web of connections among all the computers connected to it. Travel on the Internet, that is moving from site to site, can happen in various ways, depending on the protocols of a site. A protocol is a set of commands that are required to access a site. A site on the Internet is a stored electronic file in a computer. By following the correct protocols, your computer, in general, can access any file on the Internet.

This section does not have the space to describe all the protocols, software, and means of accessing all sites on the Internet. A general introduction, however, will get you started in researching on the Internet. With the right equipment, you can be researching on the Net in a short time.

CREATING A WORKING BIBLIOGRAPHY

Browser software allows you to access sites on the World Wide Web protocol. The millions of sites on the Web exist as hypertext; that is, they are discrete files, but any one of them can incorporate links to other sites. You can browse on the Web through typing in a site's particular address, called a URL (Uniform Resource Locator) or by clicking your mouse on the highlighted icons and texts in any site, called hyperlinks or hotlinks. If you click on a hotlink, your browser automatically connects to the URL of that site.

For example, if you have access to Netscape Navigator and browser software, you click on its icon on the Program Manager screen in Windows, your computer will call up the Netscape Home Page. A Home Page is an introductory page to many other sites. The hotlinks on the Netscape Home Page are highlighted in blue and underlined (for those black and white viewers).

Partial View of the Netscape Search Window

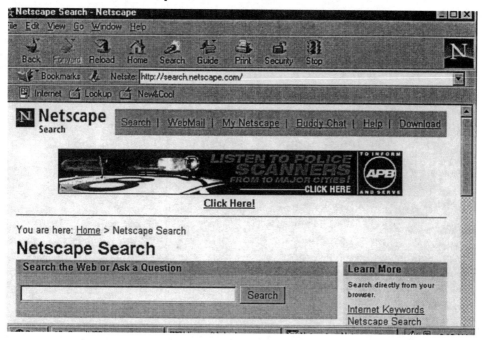

This is how hypertext connections work. You can keep searching through sites until you find information that you feel is useful to answer your guiding question. You may also access Internet sites by typing in a URL in the dialog box or Go To box. As noted above, URL stands for "uniform resource locator," or an Internet address. There are three parts to an URL: protocol, domain, and directory path.

To begin with, the angle brackets at the beginning and ending of the URL are not a part of the address. They are there to set off the URL from surrounding text. Do not type them in when posting an address. The first part of the URL, or protocol, indicates the kind of electronic hookup that is made. For example, World Wide Web sites always begin with <http:>. Other common protocols are <FTP:> (file transfer protocol) and <telnet:>. Each of these protocols has its particular commands to access sites. The second part, or domain name, has two elements separated by a dot. The element before the dot indicates the owner of the Web site or email service, and the element after the dot indicates the type of provider (e.g. com = commercial, edu = educational, net = network management, and gov = government). The third part of indicates the directory path which is the real address part of the URL. This indicates how a particular file is accessed. The slanted lines between the parts of the URL are called "separators." You can learn more about URLs at <http://www.w3.org/pub/WWW/Addressing/Addressing.html>.

Since many URLs are long, they have to be divided when they are represented in text. This is an important point, because for URLs to work they have to be exactly reproduced. Thus, do not break within the protocol abbreviation, the first part of the URL before the //, double separators. Break before a punctuation mark and take the punctuation mark to the next line. Do not hyphenate breaks; the marks between the angle brackets < > should be exact reproductions. Thus, move whole words to the next line or divide words where they normally would be hyphenated, but do not insert a hyphen. [See *Wired Style,* by the editors of *Wired* magazine.]

In researching the Internet, of course, you are looking for text and/or graphics that are related to your guiding question and subject. Fortunately, search tools accessed through your browser help carry out searches for references. Some search tools organize sites by subject, such as Yahoo! <http://www.yahoo.com>, The Library of Congress World Wide Web Home Page <http://lcweb.loc.gov>, and the Internet Public Library <http://www.ipl.org>. Browsers have a "bookmark" function which is located in a pull down menu or pop up window. Bookmarking allows you to electronically mark sites and to record them in a bookmark file. Then you can revisit these sites quickly.

Example of Bookmark Menu

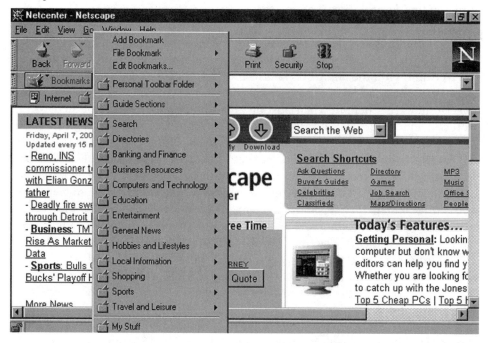

Another type of search tool scans texts of files to come up with matches for any keywords that you specify. Some of the commonly used text searching tools are Magellan <http://magellan.com>, Net Search <http://home.netscape.com>, Savvy Search <http://www.savvysearch.com>, and WebCrawler <http://webcrawler.com>.

Again, the number and sophistication of search tools changes frequently. By accessing the help files of the new tools, you can learn to use them effectively. Whenever you are typing in URLs, make sure that you type them exactly as given.

Within the Internet, there are various methods of travel. Some allow you to read and download (store in your own computer files). Others allow you to exchange electronic messages with networks of groups or with individuals. In any case, sites are added everyday to the Internet. Businesses, organizations, institutions, agencies, and individuals have sites which you can visit, read, download, and some to which you may post.

Thus, the idea of a search on the Internet for references and for sources which you can print out or download is the same as in doing a library search. As in library searching, you need to record the bibliographic information pertinent to any site that you borrow from. A site on the Internet is considered a publication, but it is electronic (virtual or cyber) rather than print. The form that an electronic reference needs to take is still evolving, but the following aspects of the electronic publication you should record and convert to your required style manual form when you list the source in your working bibliography: names of author(s), title of document, URL, date of publication, date that you accessed the publication, part or section heading or number, and any other information that would help someone else find the site. Refer to your style manual for its examples of how to record electronic sources.

In addition to the World Wide Web for getting around the Internet, there are several other protocols for accessing sites. Gopher is a program which allows you access menus which list resources in several levels, By executing the "go for" command, the program accesses the files and displays them on your computer screen. Veronica, available in such programs as Yahoo!, is a search program which can access Gopher sites.

There are several other protocols that probably require some instruction from your campus computer center, your instructor, or students that know the guide ropes. Telnet is a program that allows you to log into another computer. You can download Telnet programs free. FTP (file transfer protocol) allows you to send for files at sites on the Internet. If you have an account with your campus computing center, you will probably have access to email. Email allows you to communicate with other individuals with email accounts around the world. You can also signup for listserv groups through email. There are thousands of listserv groups, each of which supports an ongoing asynchronous (that is the postings do not appear on the screens of other viewers simultaneously but are delayed) discourse on a particular subject. There are listserv groups for every discipline and many for particular interests of their patrons within disciplines.

The Usenet protocol has a similar function to listserv groups, but instead of members posting individual messages which everyone in the listserv group receives as individual mail, the Usenet sites are collections of postings which individuals may access to read. Whereas email and Usenet sites (called newsgroups) are asynchronous, there are two protocols that allow synchronous or real time conversation. IRC (Internet relay chat) allows virtual space on the Internet where people can gather in real time and exchange conversation as a online telephone conversation. The MUD (multi-user domain) and MOO (multi-user domain, object-oriented) protocols provide such sites. A final protocol is HyperNews. HyperNews protocol brings together sites that relate to a particular subject, and it allows ongoing links to be constructed that represent responses to these sites.

There are many help books out on using the Internet for research. Such a book can help you with the finer points of navigating the Net and with helping you find your way to an array of search tools and protocols.

ANNOTATING

After you have downloaded or printed out promising sources, skim them, making annotations, which are brief notes that evaluate the source according to the following criteria: the extent and manner that your subject is treated in the source; the particular point of view that the source brings to the subject; the degree of credibility that the source establishes; and the limitations of the source.

Example from Joselyn's Annotated Working Bibliography

Reference To Source:
Cortesse, Amy, with Bureau Reports. "Here Come the Intranets." Business Week Archives. Monday, November 25, 1996, by bwwebmaster, Copyright 1196, by The McGraw-Hill Companies, Inc. Accessed February 12, 1997. <http://www.businessweek.com/1996/09/b34641.htm>.

Annotation

Presents a comprehensive discussion of why intranets are the wave of the future. Gives examples of businesses that are using intranet technology. Shows how competition among application developers has pushed the development of intranet technology into high gear. Many stats used and examples of companies. Many quotes from players in the competition. Written so managers can gauge how fast intranets are developing and the kinds of applications they can expect. Only limitation is this is a secondary source which has compiled a discussion from short blurbs from primary sources. High priority source for me.

NOTE TAKING

After you have reviewed the note taking guidelines in the Exploring through Library Research section, you might decide to save your notes in a computer file. As you save notes from your reading of all the sources, you could group them in the file according to the aspects of your guiding question to which they relate. Then your notes could be pasted into your draft at the appropriate places. There are applications which help you do this.

Example of Joselyn's Note Taking on Online Source

Cortese "Here . . ." the concept of intranets

These are Web sites that operate within a company. The software permits employees to access the Net from within the company but prevents non-employees from accessing the internal system of the company. Companies are seeing intranets as a way to streamline their internal communications and save money. The result is that many items—manuals, policies, specs, forms, and so forth—that were once paper are being converted to electronic text. Intranets not only speed up communication but also cut space for storage. pp. 1–2 of 7.

EXPLORING THROUGH FIELD RESEARCH
Decide on Appropriate Strategies / Construct an Approach / Take Notes / Workshop

Besides library and Internet resources, there are research strategies that are more person to person. Experts in many fields have developed guidelines for gathering information that can be used to construct knowledge. A short well planned interview with an expert in your subject can save you time in planning your research and/or can contribute as a source to your paper. Observation of activities or people related to your subject can also help develop your understanding. Questionnaires and surveys are means of collecting the opinions or experiences of a certain group or population. To be credible, however, field research has to follow well studied and field tested procedures. For more information on field research, especially interviewing, see Part II.

Positioning Writers and Readers
Why position the writer and readers?

As a writer, you are not alone in the production of your text. There are other voices that need to be heard as the text is "invented" and put on paper. These other voices are your readers. The following strategy prompts you to consider the needs of your readers and to consider how to negotiate with those needs in order to accomplish your aim. Without the readers' consideration of your text, you cannot accomplish your aim. The words you choose, the order you put them in, the appearance of your document, and the overall design of your document reflect your knowledge of and your attitude toward your readers. Simultaneously through the breadth and depth of your discussion, its organization, and the presentation of your point of view, you are constructing a relationship with your readers. Your text will have a "tone" or feeling to it that helps shape your readers' response. In considering what your readers are like, you can best consider which strategies will help bring about a "receptive reading." For more information, see Part II.

WRITER/READER POSITIONING STRATEGY
Position Yourself as Writer / Position Your Readers

POSITIONING YOURSELF AS WRITER

What are the possible positions for you to assume as a writer in relationship to your readers? Can you be a leader or follower; facilitator or critic; expert or beginner; guide or fellow explorer; and so forth? Which of your possible positions best suits the needs of your readers? To which positions do you think your readers would be receptive? Why? Which role do you choose for yourself as writer? Why do you think this is the best position for this writing situation? How can you construct this position in your writing?

POSITIONING YOUR READERS

Who are the possible readers in your writing situation? What possible positions do your readers have in this writing situation? Can they be fellow learners or fellow experts; fellow victims or privileged beneficiaries; and so forth? Which reader positions would best suit your aim and have the best chance to result in a receptive reading? Which reader positions do you choose? Why? How can you construct this reader position into your writing? Which reader values, beliefs, and attitudes do you need to take into account as you construct this reader positions?

Joselyn's Writer and Reader Positions

Post-research guiding question: What are intranets and why did they become such a big deal so quickly?

Positioning Myself

Possible positions

- leader and facilitator or knowledge through examination
- follower, insomuch as a beginner (myself) would follow advice of experts
- a critic only in my capacity as a reporter of expert critique within sources
- guide rather fellow explorer, since I've done the exploring already, a guide position seems more logical

Positions that would best suit needs:

Readers who are novice inquirers would best be suited by my position as an informed reporter, guiding them through the mountains of technical terms, problems, and solutions. Along the way, the focus will be on computer technology that makes intranets possible. Any person with experience in current intranet trends would have prior knowledge of most things I'll cover causing boredom for them and difficulty for me in keeping their attention. It was easy for me to find information on intranets, and I can only assume that currently employed folks have already studied or are studying the trends. Conversely, novice learners or students seem best to an informed writer who explains technology, uses credible and current sources, and who covers all the angles on the way. Basically, I'll stick with introduction to intranets, what caused them, how they're used, some problems, some solutions, and new trends they have caused.

Positioning My Readers

Computer science students with the ability to choose or change their course of study. They must be fellow learners with inquiring minds for my work to have impact. My hope is to spawn interest as well as to inform. Those with their wits about them will be in tune with the importance of these technologies and impact on the future. This is the next wave in computing for all businesses, large and small. I have to gain and maintain interest. I'll need to use experts for support and leave nothing assumed, whether term or concept.

WORKSHOP

Help members of your writing group to:

1. Evaluate the choice of the writer's and readers' positions in terms of the amount of power actually available to the writer in the writing situation.

2. Evaluate the strategies to construct the positions in terms of the readers' values, beliefs, and attitudes.

Selecting Genres

This chapter demonstrates different kinds of research papers. What that means for you is determined by your instructor, your aim, and your writing situation. Commonly, the academic research paper is a longer, formally written report or scholarly argumentative essay. Yet, it can also be a Web site, an essay submitted to an academic journal, an article in a magazine that specializes in cutting edge information, a handout in a course, and so forth. When you select a genre, it has to suit the requirements of your writing situation. For more information on selecting a genre, see Part II.

GENRE STRATEGY
Select a Genre / Examine the Implications of a Genre

What are the possible genres that fit the constraints of your situation? For example, even though your instructor will read your paper in order to evaluate it, you might have permission to choose the students in your composition course as readers. What genre would they find acceptable and readable? If you wish to submit your paper to a journal or a magazine, what kind of genres are acceptable? By reading journal an magazine editorial policies, you can determine the genres acceptable in that forum. In any case, you should choose a genre that is suitable to your readers and writing situation. One factor has been traditionally present in the writing situation of students writing academic research papers: the credibility of the research is linked to its presentation. In other words, the production of a formally written research papers is often seen as a necessary requirement in certifying students as academically able. Even within that genre, however, there exists potential for a creative and appealing presentation of your research. With computer technology, the creation of tables, graphs, illustrations, charts, and diagrams are very possible with a couple of quick lessons in graphics software. These visuals not only are fun to create, but they make research writing much more digestible. At any rate, you need to list the possible genres, or forms, that your paper could take in your writing situation. After considering the advantages and disadvantages of each, you need to select one. For more information on genres applicable to research projects, see Part II.

Joselyn's Selection of Genre

Let's see, I need to stay within the acceptable realms of informative prose. Nearly all sources I have are completely informative; the computing community expects that. Stick with plain reality where problems or controversy are concerned, except where questions of competitiveness and monopolizing are concerned!

Posing questions in the text would be good . . . or it might be too corny. As for opinions—they are out.

Keep coming back to writing the paper as an introductory, informative, current guide to intranets for a student's reference, or that of any novice for that matter, and for the advancement of knowledge. It will be necessary for me to remain neutral in controversy and to avoid any attempt to use emotion as a tool.

It's not feasible for a college newspaper to publish such a paper. Perhaps a magazine or journal might, but then I might not reach my readers or might not get it published. More locally, I could ask my computer science instructor if I could shape this paper into a well-researched report on intranets for use in introductory computer science courses. This technology is so new that it would not be in textbooks yet. Another alternative that I could pursue in the future is to construct my paper as a site on the college's Web site.

For now, I choose the research paper for introductory computer science classes. I could prepare my handout and ask a computer science instructor if this paper would be useful in his or her course.

WORKSHOP

Members of the writing group should help each other to evaluate:

1. The choice of the genre, given the constraints of the instructor and the writing situation.

2. How well the aspects of the genre fit the focus of the writer.

3. How well the writer has analyzed the genre.

Focusing

Why focus?

Now that you have inquired into your subject by exploring as many sources as possible, it is time to develop an answer to your guiding question. This answer represents the understandings at which you have arrived following reflection on your research. This answer provides a base for the discussion that will constitute your paper. Moreover, the focus is the guide rope that will help you determine which aspects of our research paper need to be included in the paper. It is the main assertion that ties together all your other assertions on the subject as an answer to your guiding question. A focus statement is a general statement, one that implies all sections of your paper. It is like the trunk of a tree giving rise to all its main offshoot branches. For more information on focusing, see Part II.

FOCUSING STRATEGY
Restate Your Question / State Your Subject and Point
of Significance

CONSTRUCTING A FOCUS STATEMENT

Your answer to your guiding question has to assert that something is true based on the reasoning and evidence that you present in your paper. Your assertion, in other words, makes a claim by putting the *subject of your research* together with a claim (your opinion on what can be known about it). This second part of the focus, that is your claim, is your insight into some aspect of the subject stated in terms that are *significant to you and your readers*. In addition to including your claim about the subject, a focus statement should be based on the knowledge that your research established in two senses. First, if the answer that you expected to find in the course of your research was not verified by your research, you cannot maintain that expected answer and support it with that particular research. One student who explored the waste disposal problem of nuclear power plants fully expected to find a solution. Instead, her support for nuclear power waned when she discovered the tremendous logistical and scientific problems which prevent a safe disposal of nuclear waste. This led her to write a focus statement that fit her research. Second, your focus statement should not cover more territory than your research permits. In other words, you cannot support claims about your subject unless your research backs you up. A focus statement has two parts:

The subject ———————— and ———————— the point of significance.

Joselyn's Focus Strategy

My guiding question:
What are intranets, and why are they important for new programmers to know about?

Possible answers (focuses) to my guiding question:

Subject	Point of significance
1. Intranets ————————	are unique, private internets.
2. Web technology ————————	makes private networks possible.
3. Intranets ————————	are the current wave in computing for all businesses, large and small.
4. Intranets ————————	are a cottage industry within the computing industry, comparable to Macintosh development within the industry in the 80s.
5. Web technology ————————	allows multiple users of different platforms to access data company-wide.
6. Intranets ————————	empower users through better access to more current information.

My choice:
#3: Intranets are the current wave in computing for businesses, large or small.

> *Rationale:*
> From this statement, I can access every area of my research, from history and development to current solutions and new technologies, in order to answer my guiding question.

WORKSHOP

You can help members of your writing group to evaluate:

1. The presence of a subject and point of significance in the focus.

2. The degree that the focus statement answers the guiding question

Organizing

Why create an organizational plan?

Instead of just beginning to draft your paper, it would be an effective use of your time to organize all that research which you feel must be a part of discussing your focus. Your paper is first of all a presentation of your claims (assertions) that you make about the subject. Thus, although the focus is the main claim, it is not the only claim you make. Think of all the claims in your discussion fitting under the general statement of the focus. The focus statement tells readers what the paper is about generally, but these other claims which are subordinate to the focus create a skeleton for your paper. In short, every section of your paper should be headed up or organized around one of these subordinate claims. The role of research has been, to this point, to help construct those claims through broadening and deepening your understanding and knowledge of the subject. Now as you plan to write your paper, your research has a different role. Its job is to serve as development and support for the claims that you make about the subject. For more information on organizing plans, see Part II.

Thus, the focus statement is linked to all sections of your paper by the particular subordinate claim that each section supports through your reasoning and documented evidence from your sources. Because this is a rather involved process, an organizational plan helps you visualize your paper ahead of time. It is like a pre-print view on a computer. By constructing a plan, you can rearrange the order of your claims, expand your discussion about a particular point, or move evidence to a more effective place. By arranging all your claims, reasoning, and evidence in a plan, you have a guide to follow when drafting, although, like any other plan, it can be changed if you are moved to do so.

Now is the time to consider using visuals, such as tables, graphs, charts, diagrams, illustrations, and so forth, to represent information discussed in the text. Visuals must be fully incorporated into your text through the discussion and reference to them. Each visual should be self-explanatory through its design and caption. Full bibliographic references to visuals (which may be called "figures" and numbered consecutively) are placed in order of appearance on a FIGURES page, which can be placed at the beginning or the ending of the text.

MODAL PLANS

The following are four general organizational schemes that you can consider using. See Part II for more information on each type of modal organization.

1. The subject is divided into parts (of the whole). Each part is discussed in a separate section of the paper.

2. The subject is organized into events that happen in chronological order. Each section of the paper could be a different stage in time.

3. The various facets of the subject are grouped or classified according to similarities and differences. Each section of the paper discusses a different group or classification.

4. The subject is expressed in the form of a judgment (evaluation). The parts of the paper are the reasons or criteria for such a judgment (evaluation).

Joselyn's Organization Plan

My choice of organization: Parts of the whole.

Rationale: I have several different parts of the subject to discuss and to relate to why they are significant to my readers.

Focus: Intranets are the current wave in computing for businesses, large or small.

- Introduction to Intranets: Definition and history
- Intranets are easy to implement. (Strom) (WM)

  The means of building an intranet are readily available.

  There are several physical needs. (See IB; Cortese)

  There are conceptual needs and planning needs.
- They help companies solve problems. (Woodmark; Cortese)
- They are already being used in major companies. (Christensen; Cortese)
- They work better than Lotus. (LPI 8–10) (Cortese 17)
- They are meeting new challenges.

  Data security (Rothfeder; Ubois; Bidzos; McCullagh)

  Domination of Internet market (Lewis; Cortese; Neubrath)

  Standards for intranet software (Snyder; Rothfeder)
- They are setting new trends and changing technology. (Carr; Pulver; Cortese; Lewis; Gross)
- Conclusion

WORKSHOP

Help your group members to:

1. Evaluate if the organizational plan suits the readers and writing situation.
2. Determine if every part of the plan further develops the focus.
3. Decide whether the order works well.

Drafting
Why draft?

Writing is difficult enough without expecting perfection, especially on the first try. An effective research paper manages to foreground a writer's claims on the subject and support those claims through a fair amount of reasoning and evidence, all in the form of a coherent discussion. An effective research paper engages its readers even though they might not agree with all the perspectives of the writer, but they read it nevertheless because they respect the author's efforts to present his or her ideas and supporting research honestly and clearly. Thus, the readers do not feel as if they are being manipulated or being deceived. All of this is a tall order, and it takes time to allow for revisions. For more information on drafting, see Part II.

WRITING SEVERAL DRAFTS

Before you begin drafting, gather together your planning work as guides or plans. Certainly your organizational plan will guide you through the development of your ideas. The following are some guides to help in incorporating research into your paper.

Citations

The use of a source in your text, other than a direct quotation, is a citation. Each citation needs a clear beginning which signals the beginning of the borrowing from a source and needs to be followed by documentation. Thus, citations include references to ideas, questions, assertions, examples, statistics, phrases, and so forth that you took from a source, but they do so without quoting the source.

Effective citations are always in your own words. They do not "shadow" the wording or style of the original source. They begin with an introductory cue, for example, a reference to the author's name, and they end with documentation which is a shorthand reference to the complete bibliographic reference in the list at the end of the paper.

Example Citations from Online Sources

> Peter Lewis says in his *New York Times* article that there is a power struggle between Microsoft and over a hundred companies competing for dominance of the Internet (paragraph 1).
>
> According to Amy Cortese in her article in *Business Week,* intranet technology is simpler than previous technologies and therefore fewer programmers are needed (paragraph 13–17).
>
> Other possible beginning references:
> Fred Smith defined intranets as. . . .
> A study conducted by Jane Marshall

If you plan on using two or more citations consecutively in your text, you might be able to consolidate the citations between one opening reference and one closing documentation. Between this opening reference and closing documentation, continue to refer to the author when necessary to distinguish his or her assertions from your own. In the following example, note the references to the source. These references clarify whose claim or information is being advanced. The point is that you need to clearly establish what information and claims come from you and which come from a source.

Example of Consolidated Citations from Joselyn's Paper

> As Jeffrey Rothfeder points out in his article for *PC World,* entitled "Hacked! Are Your Company Files Safe?" firewalls are often too easy to penetrate because the password system is not complicated enough. What makes matters worse is that software developers are in such a rush to get their products to market that security features are often overlooked (176). Rothfeder is a freelance writer for *PC World* and an author of a book on data security, called *Privacy for Sale.* According to Rothfeder, half the data theft cases are instigated by people with inside access—namely, "dishonest employees" (180). This reality goes along with the fact that most IS staffs are too busy to even track inside theft (Rothfeder 182).

Quotations

A quotation is a word-for-word borrowing from a source, no matter if one word or a paragraph. Shorter quoted passages are set off from the text by quotation marks and longer quoted passages are often set off from the text by indentation (called a "block quotation").

Quotations should be used sparingly and only when they express a point especially well. In any case, immediately before the quotation, you introduce the source of the quotation and the reason for the use of the quotation. The words of the introductory sentence should lead grammatically and stylistically into the quotation.

Example of a Shorter Quotation (Four Lines or Fewer)

> Woodmark Associates in an online seminar describe nine ways how Web technology can help organizations to "increase the ease, frequency, and quality of inter-departmental communication" (Part 2).

Note in the example above that the word-for-word quoting of the source is located within the quotation marks. A block quotation, as illustrated in the next example, is indented ten spaces from the left margin.

Example of a Longer Quotation (More Than Four Lines)

A quotation can be effectively used if the idea it expresses sums up a point under dispute in your sources, especially if the dispute turns on the use of significant words such as in a law, policy, or inflammatory statement. Even then, quotations longer than a few lines should be avoided.

> Lester Faigley speculates that: the Internet will soon be as ubiquitous as cable television as the costs of computers and connections continue to drop. At least ten million people today in the United States are connected either directly to the Internet or to commercial on-line services. Even more phenomenal has been the growth of the World Wide Web, which in months became a major medium of publishing. (37)

DOCUMENTING SOURCES

A style manual is a book written by editors of publications within professional fields. These manuals describe and illustrate the conventions (accepted ways) of writing submitted for publication within their fields. There are variations in conventions from field to field, therefore, your instructor has probably specified a particular style format for your paper. The Modern Language Association (MLA) style manual is commonly used in the humanities; the American Psychological Association (APA) style manual and the CBE (Council of Biology Editors) are commonly used in the sciences.

STYLE IN A RESEARCH PAPER

Depending on your writing situation, you may write in first person ("I") or in third person. In many writing situations, the readers expect a research paper to be written in the third person. If your readers are unfamiliar with any specialized terms relating your subject, you will need to define them. Moreover, If you break your paper into sections with a descriptive header, it might help orient your readers.

Finally, style in the research paper is subject to the expectations of its readers. Your voice as author has to achieve credibility through clearly indicating the beginning and ending of borrowings from sources, the extent and aptness of your reasoning and evidence in support of your assertions about the subject, the degree to which you appeal to your readers' intellectual and emotional receptivity, and the credibility that you establish for your sources.

A STRATEGY FOR DRAFTING

If your planning work culminates in the organizational plan, or outline, organize the research notes that you plan on using in the paper according to their order in your outline. As you begin to write, following your outline, let the construction of your ideas and their development be your main concern. Feel free to move around on your draft, writing wherever your mind keeps generating thoughts. Connections between sections of the paper can be developed later. By plowing ahead and writing a rough draft, you create a text that will probably still need substantial deletions, additions, and changes. The rough draft allows you to "get-it-together," but it is important to see the rough draft as a beginning and not a text that has earned its existence. Revision is the strategy that can make a weak paper excellent, but it requires time, effort, and critical reading on your part.

PRODUCING A POLISHED DRAFT

Revise your rough draft until you have a "polished" draft, that is a draft that reflects your revisions brought to bear on every aspect of the writing process: focus, development, organization, style, and conventions. The polished draft is a draft you can share with others.

Joselyn's Polished Draft

Joselyn H.
Professor C
English 102-04

Intranets: The New Wave

Introduction

The recent popularity and proliferation of the Internet has brought about the discovery of a new technology that generally combines the technologies of the Internet and World Wide Web (WWW) with those of an existing network, including a local-area network (LAN) and a wide-area network (WAN). This new technological configuration can actually be identified by two names, depending on the physical location of the user and the method of access. One of these is called an *extranet,* a label that seems to be entirely secondary to *intranet,* the label most commonly used for this technology. Unless otherwise noted by explicit combination of these two terms, it should be understood that *extranets* and *intranets* are separate things, even though the technology is generally one and the same. Additionally, the term *intranet* will be used in this writing as the primary label for this technology, unless the discussion explicitly pertains to *extranets.*

As its name implies, an *extranet* is primarily for external users. Conversely, an *intranet* is primarily for users who are inside the organization. *Extranet* describes a unique network, usually owned and maintained by a corporation, that allows customers, suppliers, and any others with outside interests to access certain company data through a public Internet gateway. *Intranet* describes a unique network, also typically owned by a corporation, that allows company employees to access certain information about their company, while also providing a gateway to the public Internet. What follows is a comprehensive discussion of this technology that will provide insight into how intranet technology came about, how it works, how it's being used, how to build an intranet, who is using intranets, a comparison of intranets and Lotus Notes, some problems intranets have caused, how they affect the industry, and the future of the technology. The importance of this technology cannot be understated. What will be evident by the end of this paper is that intranets are the new wave in computing for business today.

It is helpful to understand that intranet and extranet technology are based on Internet and WWW technology, which includes many protocols and other dynamic characteristics, all of which are easy to use and allow users to operate from any computer platform. These factors, together with the recent proliferation of corporate LANs, WANs, and web servers, led to the discovery of intranets—a discovery that arose from information access problems. Wordmark, a company in Houston, Texas, began using intranet and extranet technology in August 1994, when they began to publish, train, and consult with businesses regarding this technology (About Wordmark 1). They started several informational web sites, one of which is an online seminar that fills nearly 20 printed pages. In a section, titled, "Traditional Problems with Information Access," they list several problem areas (Building, Traditional 1), indicating that information access problems caused the discovery.

Further clarification of this discovery can be found in an article written by Amy Cortese, Software Department Editor for *Business Week* magazine. According to Cortese's article, "Here Comes the Intranet," the physical requirements were already in place (paragraph 12). Even more interesting is the quote from a manager of marketing for Digital Equipment Corporation, Tom Richardson, who clarifies the fact that even though the primary focus today is on running a business with an intranet, this was not the intention for those who initially implemented the technology (paragraph 6). In other words, uses for the technology were discovered following the discovery of the technology.

Intranet technology, as Robert Christensen states, is almost the same as Internet technology. Christensen developed and marketed software for 16 years before he became an Intranet Consultant in Atlanta, Georgia. In his article, "Intranet: Misspelling . . . or Megatrend?" Christensen identifies the Transmission Control Protocol/Internet Protocol (TCP/IP), E-mail, and WWW standards as requirements for the support of both technologies. The difference between them, he says, is that, "the Intranet is essentially a private Internet" (1). He further clarifies the distinctions between the two by pointing out three advantages that intranets have over the public Internet. In general, intranets transmit data more quickly, a firewall keeps outsiders from entering through the Internet, and the network managers can control the content of information. Christensen goes on to say that workstation platforms supported by intranets are the same universal group supported by Internet standards—Macintosh, UNIX, and Windows (1).

The true power of intranet technology lies in the exacting similarities to Internet standards. The Wordmark online seminar points out that browser software is central to intranet technology. At the heart of browser software is the Hypertext Markup Language (HTML). A detailed discussion of the origin, uses, and components of HTML can be found in the section of the seminar, titled, "Understanding the Technology." Here, it is important to note that anything possible on the Internet is also possible on intranets as long as the network is supported by the TCP/IP protocol (Building, Understanding 1-2). In general, the intranet software runs on any network that's supported by a web server, provided the software is written for the network platform.

Intranets Are Being Used to Solve Problems

As mentioned earlier, information access problems helped bring about the discovery of intranet technology. The section of Wordmark's seminar titled "Traditional Problems with Information Access" lists these common information-sharing problems that exist within corporations today: conflicting format problems; a need to routinely upgrade costly, incompatible viewing devices; printed records that are frequently changed and infrequently used; databases that are hard to access; and information that becomes outdated quickly (1). Recall here that intranet technology is based on Internet and WWW technology. Previous examples from Christensen showed its relationship to Internet technology. What follows is its relationship with WWW technology, courtesy of Wordmark.

Part two of Wordmark's online seminar begins with a section titled "Evaluating Web Technology On Its Own Merits." Here there are 31 beneficial attributes of the WWW that are handed down to intranet technology, all of which help solve the information-sharing problems mentioned above. Conflicting format problems between Windows and Macintosh operating systems, for example, are solved through web protocols that operate efficiently on any platform. The graphical user interface (GUI) incorporated into web browsers negates the need for routine upgrading of costly, incompatible viewing devices. One of the basic advantages of private networks is the replacement of enormously expensive records that were previously in print, records that need to be frequently changed and are used infrequently—a company phone directory, for example. Another empowering use is the replacement of information previously stored in databases that are burdensome and complex to access otherwise. Yet another advantage is the ability to keep information current—updating data on one server instead of meticulously updating several locations (Building, Evaluating 1). It would be cumbersome to list the remaining benefits here. The important thing to see is the vast number of advantages that Internet/WWW technology lend to modern businesses.

One major advantage is cost savings. Cortese points out that paper documents, such as manuals for business processes, training procedures, and the like, are easily converted to electronic data (paragraph 4). For clarification, the section of Wordmark's online seminar titled "The Internal Web," lists the following possibilities: 22 printed documents; six electronic resources, such as templates, utilities, applications, and test data; as well as seven possible two-way communications that could be interactive, instead of being done by phone or fax (1-2). Cortese goes on to say that maintaining applications and hardware is easier with intranets and that programmers won't be necessary in such large quantities (paragraph 16). Yet another advantage, according to Cortese, is the ability to link networks around the world—the global possibilities are endless (paragraph 7).

Process Software Corporation developed Internet software in Framingham, MA. They employ expert developers who use Internet Protocol (IP) and are the creators of the WWW server line called, "Purveyor" (About Process 1). Their web site contains an article titled "*Intranet*—A Guide to 'Intraprise-Wide' Computing," that further stresses the importance of accurate, less costly data that can be accessed easily through intranet technology. They mention advantages over E-mail, which can be quite redundant and burdensome for both reader and sender, and work groups that need private access to sensitive data. Intranets improve these areas as well while providing relief to Information System (IS) management teams, who are generally too busy already (1).

The other important use of this technology, rather than internal use, is for the benefit of external clients, customers, and suppliers. The section in Wordmark's online seminar titled "The External Web," outlines five areas in which corporate data can be supplied to users outside the company. The one key difference between internal and external networks is the type of information that's made available. Extranets can contain product information, including brochures, catalogues, manuals, discounts, frequently asked questions (FAQs), and demonstrations. Customers and suppliers can get support, get questions answered about orders, and file complaints online. Employment advertising can be put on the network and easily updated, which saves advertising costs. Future employees can interview online, cutting costly hiring expenses (Building, External Web 1-3). And one of the great advantages is the built-in log, a standard feature for servers that allows the company to track visitors. For every person who accesses your home page, "there is a time-stamped entry that indicates their domain name (or IP address) and what they looked at" (Building, External Web 3).

Intranets Are Easy to Implement

In a section of Wordmark's seminar titled "Prerequisites for Adopting the New Technology," there are five general requirements described that make implementing intranets easier, all of which are basic features for local-area, wide-area, and web server networks. What's interesting is that most big corporations already have the necessary hardware and software to support an intranet (Building, Prerequisites 1).

Some of the basic features of intranets have been mentioned above as they came up in the opening discussion. It is time to mention the conceptual necessities and some other physical components that are needed to build and maintain a private network, which will put intranets in better focus. Although it is not a simple matter of buying software and installing it on a network server, the general configuration and conceptual necessities are so much common sense to current IS professionals with experience in system design projects. The reason for simplicity in the minds of experienced professionals is that nothing is new for intranets, other than the intranet software itself. Everything else is familiar to the IS staff. Depending on the level of expertise in these areas, however, some companies have opted to hire professional consultants to help them get started. And according to David Strom, an author for *Forbes* magazine, once the company personnel get a few intranet implementation projects under their belts, additions and improvements are relatively easy to handle in-house (paragraph 9).

According to Strom, building an intranet requires both practical technicians and creative thinkers—if the conceptual details of implementation are to move along smoothly. He recommends, however, that the first step should be to decide exactly what the network will be used for since the possibilities are so numerous (paragraphs 1–2). From there, the departments involved in the project will be clear, and the decision as to which department or individuals will manage the project can be made. This conceptual decision must be made early, according to Strom, to avoid confrontation and unnecessary in-fighting in later stages of the project (paragraphs 13–15). In the section of their seminar titled "A Phased Approach to Implementation," Wordmark recommends a 13-step process for getting started (1–2). From these examples it's clear that careful planning is a must!

The five necessary physical components were mentioned earlier and can be found in Wordmark's seminar in the section titled "Prerequisites for Adopting the New Technology." A LAN or WAN based on TCP/IP protocol is the first requirement. Although not every person in the corporation needs a terminal of their own, everyone should have a computer readily accessible that uses a GUI interface, which is requirement number two. Thirdly is a web browser that manages TCP/IP, HTML, and perhaps multimedia files. The fourth requirement is to make fast modems available for persons with legal access, who are geographically distant from the network. The final requirement is a security system—a firewall that uses passwords to verify access to the network (Building, Prerequisites 1).

According to Process, the heart of the intranet is the network server, configured to handle WWW sites. These servers are known as web servers and most corporations already have one—some have two or more. Two advantages of web servers are that they are easy to maintain and use and secondly, since they are part of a LAN on which the bandwidth is wider, applications run faster (*Intranet* 1–2). This speed advantage plays a big part in allowing audio and video to be incorporated into private and public web sites. Process confirms the need for TCP/IP protocol and further explains that network hardware should support, "Windows NT, Windows 95, and/or a UNIX system platform" *(Intranet* 3). In addition to these possible software platforms, web software is needed to manipulate web pages and to create HTML tags that turn word processing documents into web documents. Process lists 14 questions that help to decide which WWW server to buy, based on current and future needs of the company (*Intranet* 4). Choosing a web server is one of the vital areas in planning and implementing that may influence smaller or less experienced businesses to call in a professional consultant.

Process says that intranets are, "an ideal solution for any organization with more than 100 users and/or with remote locations distributed over wide geographical areas" (*Intranet* 2). At the other end of the spectrum, Christensen cites a source, "who designed an Intranet to support over 16,000 users and 450 servers for one Fortune 500 company" (1). In other words, the size of an intranet has a floor, according to some. However, the ceiling seems to be limited only by the needs of the company.

Intranets are Already Being Used in Major Companies

Christensen cites several companies that are currently using and expanding intranets. MCI has an intranet with 12,000 links. VISA links 2,500 employees and 19,000 banks with their intranet. Ford Motor Company implements world-wide intranet access for every employee on a salary (2). Cortese adds to the Ford story when she points out that the 1996 Ford Taurus was designed through interactive intranet sessions involving designers, "in Asia, Europe, and the U.S." (paragraph 8). Anyone with information to share can benefit from intranets.

Cortese outlines the history of intranets at Federal Express Corporation (FedEx) by tracking the development of their network from the beginning. In 1994, FedEx set up their first web server, allowing customers to track their own packages. Cortese reports that FedEx may have saved $2 million each year by replacing human assistants with electronic interaction, provided for the customer's convenience. At the end of 1996, FedEx had 60 home pages on the web and had plans to enable 30,000 world-wide employees to access new internal pages being developed at the headquarters in Memphis, TN (paragraphs 1–2).

The more empowering example comes from Silicon Graphics (SGI), manufacturers of the most powerful and expensive workstations. As Cortese writes, every desk at SGI is equipped with an SGI workstation that costs in excess of $5,000. SGI began experimenting with intranets as soon as the Mosaic browser hit the market. They began using their intranet to publish data that was previously restricted to printed sources. Today, SGI uses intranets to send audio, video, and to link databases. In fact, SGI employees used their world-wide intranet to personally experience President Clinton's tour of the headquarters in 1993 (paragraphs 21–24).

Intranets work better than Lotus Notes

From Cortese we learn that intranet technology has solved the following situation: Over the years, software developers haven't kept their promise to establish viable links to, "computers, software, and databases," enabling employees to access everything from one "single system" (paragraph 5). From the discussion thus far, it is evident that intranets have done exactly that. Cortese outlines three advantages that intranets have over Lotus Notes: the cost is less; fewer programmers are required for intranet software, which is not nearly as complex as Notes coding; and the training required for intranets is far less than the on-going training required for Notes, due to complex coding (paragraph 15).

Process expounds upon each of these advantages and draws further conclusions as to differences between intranets and Notes. There are two key differences, according to Process. The first is the database design of Notes, which duplicates information and provides slow access to geographically separated databases. Intranets, on the other hand, use WWW technology that eliminates the duplication of databases and allows quick access to any database in the world, provided the database is linked to the intranet. The second is that Notes is designed for strictly internal purposes. Conversely, intranets can be used internally and externally (*Intranet 5*).

The cost differences are dramatic—from startup cost and training to maintenance, following implementation. Process conducted a survey among corporations to determine the startup cost for Notes, which is $245,000. Comparatively, an intranet can be set up for $10,000 or less. Web browsers cost around $40 each for intranets, while the Notes equivalent to a browser costs $100 each, or more. Training is labor-intensive and on-going for Notes while intranet training is very similar to that found in classes designed to teach web page creation and basic Internet surfing techniques. The maintenance for Notes also requires extensive technical expertise while intranet maintenance is similar to making changes on a web page. One final contrasting feature is the dial-in charges associated with Notes that can be as high as $80 for each person, per month, compared to legal entry with a password for intranet users from any place in the world (*Intranet 5–6*).

The startup costs mentioned above are verified by LPI Software Funding Group, Inc., a software and hardware leasing company from Wayne, PA, whose largest leasing deal in the last five years was for $10 million (Background 1). LPI posted an article, titled "March Commentary of the Month: The Dominance of the Intranet," which was last updated in December 1996 (March 3). However, they discuss another aspect of the rivalry between intranets and Notes. Notes, because of its complex coding, provides a better medium for collaborating work groups and a higher level of data security than intranets (2). An example of a complex program that requires high security would be a corporate accounting application, for which Notes provides, "impeachable security," to borrow a descriptive phrase from Cortese (paragraph 17).

Intranets are Meeting New Challenges

One of the challenges with intranets is security. What makes intranets secure is a firewall that allows users to enter using passwords. The term "firewall" warrants a clear definition at this point. *Computerworld* magazine maintains a web site at which a glossary of computer terms can be found. That glossary defines "firewall" as, "a gateway between two networks that selectively filters information passing between [them]" (Glossary 2). For the purposes of this discussion, the two networks mentioned in the definition are the public Internet and the private intranet. Cortese adds a bit more to this definition by saying that firewalls allow employees to access the public Internet but they keep Internet surfers from entering the private network (paragraph 3). In contrast, what makes Lotus Notes even more secure is that it is never exposed to an Internet gateway because it is strictly an internal application, eliminating the possibility of unauthorized access through the Internet. But Notes has complicated password coding, which isn't always the case with intranet firewall systems.

As Jeffrey Rothfeder points out in his article for *PC World* magazine titled "Hacked! Are Your Company Files Safe?" firewalls are often too easy to penetrate because the password system is not complicated enough. What makes matters worse is that software developers are in such a rush to get their products to market that security features are often overlooked (176). Rothfeder is a freelance writer for *EQ World* and an author of a book on data security, called, *Privacy for Sale*. According to Rothfeder, half the data theft cases are instigated by people with inside access—namely, "dishonest employees" (180). This reality goes along with the fact that most IS staffs are too busy to even track inside theft (Rothfeder 182).

In addition to theft, Rothfeder deals with one other business problem that's magnified by increased use of the Internet and intranets—virus infection. He states that almost half the virus infections are caused by external access to intranets through the Internet. He goes on to say that most incidents are never reported for fear of losing customers and that the U.S. Department of Defense has a quarter-of-a-million unauthorized accesses each year (172). He provides solutions for large and small companies, the most compelling of which is data encryption. The point is made that stolen data can't be read, especially when the encryption designed, "by RSA Data Security of Redwood City, California," is used (Rothfeder 180). Jeff Ubois is an Internet specialist and freelance writer for *Internet World* magazine, a publication dedicated to following Internet progress. Ubois interviews the CEO of RSA Data Security (RSA), Jim Bidzos, in an article, titled, "Cryptic Minister," in the February issue of IW. Several problems within the data security area are uncovered in the interview. But first, it's interesting to note that RSA encryption is currently built into, "every browser ever made by Microsoft, Netscape, Oracle, IBM, Open Market, Spry, Spyglass, . . . [and] every copy of Lotus Notes" (Ubois 60). So, to backtrack for just a moment, the fact that RSA encryption is part of every copy of Notes explains the superior security features it holds over intranet software and further clarifies the "impeachable security," label given to it by Cortese (paragraph 17).

Ubois' article verifies, like Rothfeder's article does, that new Internet uses have spawned changes, one being the need for security. RSA encryption is already used in software copies that total 90 million. In addition to browsers and Notes, RSA is used to transfer medical records and in pay TV, to name a few. In Ubois' interview, Bidzos outlines problems related to the U.S. government's wish to control RSA because the National Security Agency (NSA) and police departments are unable to break the codes. The NSA is cited as having the world's most proficient ability to monitor electronic data transfers. To allow RSA products to be exported around the world would be to give up their advantage. The police are concerned that criminals using RSA could easily participate in covert activities with no worry of being caught. The other problem is that the computer industry wants what their customers want—privacy with RSA (Ubois 60). Bidzos goes on to say in the interview with Ubois that the government uses three tactics to control RSA. First, and most effective, is their control over exporting RSA products. Second is their power to set standards, which used to be effective back in the 60s when the government was 50% of the computer market, however, it's ineffective today as they're only 2–5% of the market. Industry will listen to the other 95% of the market that wants security. The last area is the government's ability to purchase the technology, which has had no impact on the market so far, according to Bidzos (Ubois 61).

Because the government has adopted their own encryption, called the Clipper Chip, they wish to make it the standard for data security. The computer industry prefers RSA because it is much more effective. The result is that government agencies can't use RSA browsers or Notes because it's against the law for them to do so, even though some offices are bound to have one of the RSA products in use. In addition to government hurting itself in this way, they are hurting the computer industry by controlling the export of RSA products, according to Bidzos who states that government controls slow the development of encryption. Meanwhile, countries around the world are buying strong encryption from businesses outside the U.S., which cuts into the profits of the computer industry, the largest in the U.S. economy (Ubois 62).

Declan McCullagh expands the export control issue in her article, "Encryption Clash," in *IW*. It is stated that the battle over encryption export has been going on for two years so far. In a nutshell, the government wants the keys to the encryption code so that it can continue to monitor the flow of electronic data. Her expansion on the matter details the standard upheld by current law, which allows coding to be 56 bits in length. Security gurus argue that the code length should be at least 75 bits long (McCullagh 18).

Another problem area brought about by new Internet uses is the fight over who will dominate the new Internet market. An article written by Peter Lewis for the *New York Times* mentions that the developers of the UNIX platform were unable to set a standard years ago, which allowed Microsoft to dominate the desktop market. Currently, standards for Internet applications, like Java, are being agreed upon in hopes of keeping Microsoft from dominating the Internet market as well (paragraph 14). While a Microsoft manager says they love and accept Java, they are rewriting portions of the Java code so that it works, "best, or only, with Microsoft's own Windows," a practice referred to by Lewis as, "preferential coding" (paragraphs 5-10). Cortese mentions another angle that Microsoft has taken to gain control of the Internet market. They were giving their web server and browser software away for free, which started a Justice Department investigation (paragraph 36-39). Another tidbit from an article written by Michael Neubarth, Editor-In-Chief for IW magazine, sheds light on how the industry views Microsoft's dominance. The article, "Best Foot Forward," cites Scott McNealy, CEO of Sun Microsystems (developers of Java) as saying, "to kill Microsoft—that's the top priority for all of us" (10). In other words, the industry wishes moral injustices upon Microsoft. This is evident from Lewis' article which states that over 100 computer companies met to discuss setting standards for Java and Microsoft was not invited (paragraph 1).

Another problem is that large software developers, like Microsoft and Netscape, don't always follow the standards that are already in place, according to Joel Snyder. Snyder is an author for *IW* magazine and a senior partner at a law firm in Arizona. Snyder says that Microsoft and Netscape don't take the time to work the bugs out of their products before shipping them to market. He describes some problems that he sees with web page products that allow users, millions of them, to incorporate non-standard features into their web pages (98). David Carr, who specializes in databases and object technology for *IW* magazine, mentions another standards battle between these software giants. Namely, "a universal object standard [that] would enable different computers on the Internet to share all data and programs." A universal standard would allow users to create their own applications, as well as using, "distributed-object communication protocols as an alternative to HTTP" (66). In this discussion, it is mentioned that the web was designed to use FTP, a protocol, "for sharing documents, not objects," and that a distributed-object protocol would solve this problem—if the two big rivals would stop using different standards (67).

Intranets Are Setting New Trends and Changing Technology

In the battle over object standards discussed in Carr's article, he concludes that as long, "as the competing factions," make attempts to merge the different technologies, progress toward, "a universal computing infrastructure," remains a possibility (70). Intranets, as a movement within the Internet market, have caused software developers to bundle their technologies with those of competitors. In fact, Lewis quotes a senior analyst with International Data Corporation (IDC), who says exactly that of Java, a cross-language. The quote makes clear that intranets have caused new, "interest in Java" (paragraph 17). Cortese also says that intranets have caused change for Netscape (paragraph 42). In addition to these two examples, intranets are carrying on the compatibility trends that the Internet started—and it's happening across the board, in every corner of the software market, not just with Java and Netscape.

Jeff Pulver, a former vice president in the information technology industry and a writer for *IW* magazine, maintains his own web site for monitoring, "telephone software products" (104). He makes predictions about the future of products that allow faxing over the Internet using corporate intranets. He also mentions another new technology—voice mail. His prediction for this technology, if it does become popular, is that intranet voice mail may turn, "computer workstations (both at home and in the office) [into] a direct replacement for . . . telephones" (105). Wordmark's seminar agrees with Pulver's telephone replacement theory but takes a different angle of approach. In the section, titled, "Evaluating Web Technology On Its Own Merits," they predict that web browsers may one day, "become the document-based equivalent of the telephone" (1).

Cortese predicts that software companies will concentrate on, "helping corporate customers build intranets," a trend that should boost intranet software sales, "to more than $4 billion in 1997, from $476 million," in 1996 (paragraphs 10–11). More software predictions are made by Neil Gross, Technology Department Editor for *Business Week* magazine. His discussion includes intranets and extranets as the driving forces that will cause Internet software sales to reach $3 billion in 1997 (104).

LPI makes it clear that intranet servers and Internet servers are pretty equal in number right now. However, through the year 2000, intranet servers are expected to outnumber Internet servers by a ratio of 10 to 1 (1). Their figures are based on IDC/Link projections. IDC/Link is one of two research companies owned and operated by International Data Group (IDG), a world-wide corporation that specializes in Information Technology (IT). IDG publishes, "275 magazines and newspapers in 75 countries [including] *Computerworld, Macworld,* and *PC World."* They are the publishers of, "The '. . . For Dummies' series," as well as exposition administrators (IDG 1). As a caution, Rothfeder iterates that growth in intranets should be closely accompanied by a serious interest in data security. As he puts it, "anything less than a full-fledged focus on the issue could be disastrous to the nation's economy" (182).

Conclusion

Intranets are the current wave in computing for business today. Within the Internet age, a new technology has been born. It is expected to grow at phenomenal rates and will probably be a deciding factor in the success of many corporations. What's important to notice in all of this is the propensity of the technology to move toward compatibility in all areas.

The more competitors bundle products, the more the products become the same. Also of importance is the way the Internet WWW technology has simplified computing. As more products become more alike through bundling web technology, we become more efficient. Let's hope that intranets finally bring our computing complications to a manageable and acceptable level.

Works Cited

"About Process Software Corporation." Online. Internet. 27 Feb. 1997. Available. <http://www.process.com/corporate/aboutpsc.htp>.

"About Wordmark.Com." 3 Oct. 1996. Online. Internet. 4 Mar. 1997. Available. <http://www.wordmark.com/about.html>.

"Background: LPI Software Funding Group, Inc." Online. Internet. 27 Feb. 1997. Available. <http://www.lpilease.com/backmsb.htm>.

"Building a Corporate Intranet." Online Seminar. 9 Sept. 1996. Internet. 12 Feb. 1997. Available. <http://www.workmark.com/sem_l.html>.

Carr, David F. "Object Wars." *Internet World* Feb. 1997: 66–70.

Christensen, Robert. "Intranet: Misspelling . . . or Megatrend?" *Atlanta Computer Currents* May 1996.

Online. Internet. 12 Feb. 1997. Available. <http://www.mindspring.com/—rchris/ct00002.htmb>.

Cortese, Amy. "Here Comes the Intranet." *Business Week* 25 Nov. 1996. Online. Internet. 12 Feb. 1997. Available. <http://www.businessweek.com/1996/09/b34641.html>.

"Glossary." Online. Internet. 21 Feb. 1997. Available. <http://www.computerworld.com/intranets/intr&..glossary.html>.

Gross, Neil. "Software." *Business Week* 13 Jan. 1997: 104–05.

"IDG in Brief: Corporate Overview." Online. Internet. 27 Feb. 1997. Available. <http://www.idg.com/profile/overview>.

"*Intranet:* A Guide to 'Intraprise-Wide' Computing." Online. Internet. 20 Feb. 1997. Available. <http://www.process.com/news/intrawp.htp>.

Lewis, Peter H. "Alliance Formed Around Sun's Java Network." *New York Times* 11 Dec. 1996: C2+.

"March Commentary of the Month: The Dominance of the Intranet." 6 Dec. 1996. Online. Internet. 12 Feb. 1997. Available. <http://www.lpilease.com/column.html>.

Neubarth, Michael, ed. "Best Foot Forward." *Internet World* Jan. 1997: 10.

Pulver, Jeff. "Dialing for Dollars." *Internet World* Jan. 1997: 104–05.

Rothfeder, Jeffrey. "Hacked! Are Your Company Files Safe?" *PC World* Nov. 1996: 170+.

Snyder, Joel. "Snubbing Standards." *Internet World* Feb. 1997: 96+.

Strom, David. "Art, Geeks, and Power Ploys: How to Build Your Intranet." *Forbes* Aug. 1996. Online. Internet. 12 Feb. 1997. Available. <http://www.strom.com/pubwork/forbes896.html>.

Ubois, Jeff. "Cryptic Minister." *Internet World* Feb. 1997: 58–65.

Responding
Why seek responses to your draft?

It takes a great deal of work to effectively synthesize your ideas and a mound of research notes into a coherent document. During the process, a writer might lapse into writing for the writer and not for the reader. Thus, reader responses from other students and your instructor can help you evaluate your paper. The following is a set of response guidelines which address the particular needs of a research paper. They, of course, can be adapted to fit various writing situations, aims, and genres. For more information on responding, see Part II.

For the response reader, the writer should identify the writing situation, the readers that are addressed, and the forum in which the readers would see the paper. Thus, the response reader can take them into account.

READER RESPONSE GUIDE

Overall Response
- What are the main strengths of the paper?
- What one or two aspects should be the main concern in its revision?

Focus
- State the focus of the paper.
- To what degree does the focus stand out in the paper?
- Does the focus effectively identify a subject and a claim or point of significance about that subject?
- Which sections of the paper, if any, do not develop the focus?

Development of the Focus
- What shows that the paper is appropriately written for its readers?
- Are there any weaknesses in this respect?
- Where are the subordinate claims not clearly identifiable in each section of the paper?
- Where are the subordinate claims inadequately supported by reasoning and evidence?
- Which reasoning and evidence do you find particularly helpful and effective?
- Which sources lack sufficient background information to make them credible?
- Is there anything inadequate about the beginning of the paper?
- Is there anything inadequate about the ending of the paper?
- How effective are the visuals?

- If visuals are not present, do you think they would increase the effectiveness of the paper? Suggest some examples of where.

Organization and Coherence

- Which organizational pattern do you recognize in the paper?
- Is the order of the sections of the paper effective?
- Where are the parts of the paper that do not seem to relate to the text in front of it or to the text behind it?
- Which paragraphs seem too long or too hard to follow?
- Are the section headings descriptive and effective?

Language Choices

- Which words do not seem appropriate for the readers?
- Which phrases or sentences are particularly effective? Why?
- Which sentences are not effectively worded? Why?

Research Style Format

- Are the beginnings of citations clearly indicated?
- Are citations and quotations correctly documented?
- Is the wording in citations original and consistent with the student writer's style?
- Are quotations effectively introduced and incorporated stylistically and conceptually into the student writer's discussion?
- Are the headers with pagination correct?
- Are the number and length of quotations effective?
- Are block quotations set up correctly?
- Is the title page correctly and effectively set up?
- Is the works cited page or reference page correct?
- Are the headers or footers with page numbers correct?
- Are the margins and spacing throughout the paper adequate?

Conventions

- Are there any patterns of error in grammar, usage, capitalization, punctuation, or spelling?
- How effectively has this polished draft been proofread for typos?

Example: Carol's Reader Response to Joselyn's Polished Draft

Overall:

This is an interesting report on a new technology, one that I never knew existed. I can understand why this subject is important to your readers, beginning students in computer science.

Focus:

I understand that the focus is that intranets are an important new tech-nology, but I was unsure of the particular significance to your readers that your paper should state, it seems to me. I think there should be a state-ment on this significance in the first section.

Development for readers:

- You did an excellent job of explaining intranets—their origins, what they are, their use, and their problems. But I have a couple of observa-tions. At times after a discussion of the technical aspects of intranets, you just stop and do not connect to what you just wrote to any signif-icance for your computer-science readers and/or the focus of the paper.

- In the second paragraph of "Easy to Implement," you refer back to the beginning of the paper but do not summarize what it is that you are talking about. That lost me.

- The end of paragraph 4 in Challenges runs together police concern with RSA and the wants of the computer industry; sort these points out. I don't see how they are related.

- In paragraph 8 of that section, you mention that Snyder sees problems, but you don't tell what they are or how they relate to your discussion.

Organization:

I really like how you divide the report into sections and give each section a heading that indicated what was in the section. This made the paper a lot easier to follow. I like the order of the sections; they kind of build up to the important point of the effect intranets will have on business.

Language choices:

- Generally the words you used seem to fit your readers, beginning com-puter science students, because most would know the terms you used. At the same time, you defined new terms like intranet itself. I could even understand this paper, so I think that they could.

- Some sentences need revision. See my marks in the margins.

MLA format:

You did a great job on this. But in your text you use "Process" as a refer-ence to a source, but I don't see what source that refers to.

Conventions:

Cannot is one word. The only error pattern I note is that you tend to overuse commas. You put them in places where they are not needed.

Suggestions for revision priorities:

Those development problems need work.

Revising
Why revise?

After you have considered the responses from other students and your instructor, you have the opportunity to make changes which will make your paper more credible to the readers in your particular writing situation. Revisions consist of opportunities that you take to make your paper more effective in how it can carry out your aim in writing to your readers. In other words, even though you have a draft, the paper is not finished until you think your readers will give your ideas serious consideration. Your paper is not an end in itself; it is a means to carry out your aim in your writing situation. For more information on revising, see Part II.

REVISING STRATEGY
Study Feedback from Responders / Construct a Plan for Priorities / Revise Your Polished Draft

---

Since revision implies making changes, it is effective to begin with the largest problems and then work down to the level of grammar, usage, and conventions. For instance, it is a waste of time to correct spelling and punctuation in a paragraph that is eliminated during a later revision. An effective order of revision is reflected in the reader response guidelines: focus, development, organization, style, and conventions.

Example of Joselyn's Revising Plan

Focus:

My paper relates to the interests of my target readers, beginning computer science students, but I have to make clearer what intranets mean to them in terms of job preparation.

Development for readers:

I need to go through my paper and make sure every idea / introduce into the paper is explained enough and is connected to the train of thought progressing through the paper.

Organization:

Leave as is.

Language choices:

I have to work through sentence by sentence to clarify how I worded things and to make sure the point of each sentence is clear.

MLA format:

I need to reference Process to its source.

Conventions:

I need to figure out how to use commas.

WORKSHOP

You can help your group members evaluate:

1. How effectively the revising plan responds to the readers' comments.

2. How effectively the revising plan helps the writer achieve a paper which will carry out his or her focus in the writing situation.

Excerpts from Joselyn's Revised Draft

Joselyn H
Professor C. . . .
English 102-04

Intranets: The New Wave

Introduction

The recent popularity and proliferation of the Internet has brought about the discovery of a new technology that generally combines the technologies of the Internet and World Wide Web (WWW) with those of an existing network, including a local-area network (LAN) and a wide-area network (WAN). This new technological configuration can actually be identified by two names, depending on the physical location of the user and the method of access. One of these is called an *extranet,* a label that seems to be entirely secondary to *intranet,* the label most commonly used for this technology. Unless otherwise noted by explicit combination of these two terms, it should be understood that *extranets* and *intranets* are separate things, even though the technology is generally one and the same. Additionally, the term *intranet* will be used in this writing as the primary label for this technology unless the discussion explicitly pertains to *extranets.*

As its name implies, an *extranet* is primarily for external users. Conversely, an *intranet* is primarily for users who are inside the organization. *Extranet* describes a unique network, usually owned and maintained by a corporation, that allows customers, suppliers, and any others with outside interests to access certain company data through a public Internet gateway. *Intranet* describes a unique network, also typically owned by a corporation, that allows company employees to access certain information about their company, while also providing a gateway to the public Internet. What follows is a comprehensive discussion of this technology that will provide insight into how intranet technology came about, how it works, how it's being used, how to build an intranet, who is using intranets, a comparison of intranets and Lotus Notes, some problems intranets have caused, how they affect the industry, and the future of the technology. The importance of this technology cannot be understated. What will be evident by the end of this paper is that intranets are the new wave in computing for business today and that their prominent role in information systems should make future computer programmers and systems analysts should learn as much as they can about them.

It is helpful to understand that intranet and extranet technology is based on Internet and WWW technology, which includes many protocols and other dynamic characteristics, all of which are easy to use and allow users to operate from any computer platform. These factors, together with the recent proliferation of corporate LANs, WANs, and web servers, led to the discovery of intranets—a discovery that arose from information access problems.
* * * *

Intranet technology, as Robert Christensen states, is almost the same as Internet technology. Christensen developed and marketed software for 16 years before he became an Intranet Consultant in Atlanta, Georgia. In his article, "Intranet: Misspelling . . . or Megatrend?" Christensen identifies the Transmission Control Protocol/Internet Protocol (TCP/IP), E-mail, and WWW standards as requirements for the support of both technologies. The difference between them, he says, is that, "the Intranet is essentially a private Internet" (1). He further clarifies the distinctions between the two by pointing out three advantages that intranets have over the public Internet. In general, intranets transmit data more quickly, a firewall keeps outsiders from entering through the Internet, and the network managers can control the content of information. Christensen goes on to say that workstation platforms supported by intranets are the same universal group supported by Internet standards—Macintosh, UNIX, and Windows (1).
* * * * * *

Intranets Are Being Used to Solve Problems

As mentioned earlier, information access problems helped bring about the discovery of intranet technology. The section of Wordmark's seminar titled "Traditional Problems with Information Access," lists these common information-sharing problems that exist within corporations today: conflicting format problems; a need to routinely upgrade costly, incompatible viewing devices; printed records that are frequently changed and infrequently used; databases that are hard to access; and information that becomes outdated quickly (1). These problems drove developers to patch together what became intranet technology, which is based on Internet and WWW technology; intranet development rode piggyback, so to speak. Previous examples from Christensen showed its relationship to Internet technology. What follows is its relationship with WWW technology, courtesy of Wordmark. The following discussion explains how intranet technology is being used to solve problems in information systems.

Part two of Wordmark's online seminar begins with a section titled "Evaluating Web Technology On Its Own Merits." Here, there are 31 beneficial attributes of the WWW that are handed down to intranet technology, all of which help solve the information-sharing problems mentioned above. Conflicting format problems between Windows and Macintosh operating systems, for example, are solved through web protocols that operate efficiently on any platform. The graphical user interface (GUI) incorporated into web browsers negates the need for routine upgrading of costly, incompatible viewing devices. One of the basic advantages of private networks is the replacement of enormously expensive records that were previously in print, records that need to be frequently changed and are used infrequently—a company phone directory, for example. Another empowering use is the replacement of information previously stored in databases that are burdensome and complex to access otherwise. Yet another advantage is the ability to keep information current—updating data on one server instead of meticulously updating several locations (Building, Evaluating 1). It would be cumbersome to list the remaining benefits here. The important thing to see is the vast number of advantages that Internet/WWW technology lend to modern businesses.

One major advantage is cost savings. Cortese points out that paper documents, such as manuals for business processes, training procedures, and the like, are easily converted to electronic data (paragraph 4). For clarification, the section of Wordmark's online seminar titled "The Internal Web" lists the following possibilities: 22 printed documents; six electronic resources, such as templates, utilities, applications, and test data; as well as seven possible two-way communications that could be interactive, instead of being done by phone or fax (1-2). Cortese goes on to say that maintaining applications and hardware is easier with intranets and that programmers won't be necessary in such large quantities (paragraph 16). Thus, computer programmers need to be alert to the premium placed on intranet training and experience. The more global experience the better for still another advantage on intranets, according to Cortese, is the ability to link networks around the world—the global possibilities are endless (paragraph 7).

Process Software Corporation developed Internet software in Framingham, MA. They employ expert developers who use Internet Protocol (IP) and are the creators of the WWW server line called "Purveyor" (About Process 1). Their web site contains an article titled "*Intranet*—A Guide to 'Intraprise-Wide' Computing" that further stresses the importance of accurate, less costly data that can be accessed easily through intranet technology. They mention advantages over E-mail, which can be quite redundant and burdensome for both reader and sender, and workgroups that need private access to sensitive data. Intranets improve these areas as well while providing relief to Information System (IS) management teams, who are generally too busy already (1). Even with all this new technology making problems disappear for information systems, the problem still exists for the computer programmer or systems analyst to keep up with it.
* * * * *

Intranets Are Easy to Implement

Some of the basic features of intranets have been mentioned above in the opening section, but the main features to keep in mind is their use of existing intranet technology with a firewall protection system. Given those physical components, it is time to mention the conceptual necessities and

some other physical components that are needed to build and maintain a private network, which will put intranets in better focus. Although it is not a simple matter of buying software and installing it on a network server, the general configuration and conceptual necessities are so much common sense to current IS professionals with experience in system design projects. The reason for simplicity in the minds of experienced professionals is that nothing is new for intranets other than the intranet software itself. Everything else is familiar to the IS staff. Depending on the level of expertise in these areas, however, some companies have opted to hire professional consultants to help them get started. And according to David Strom, an author for *Forbes* magazine, once the company personnel get a few intranet implementation projects under their belts, additions and improvements are relatively easy to handle in-house (paragraph 9).
* * * * *

Intranets Are Already Being Used in Major Companies

Christensen cites several companies that are currently using and expanding intranets. MCI has an intranet with 12,000 links. VISA links 2,500 employees and 19,000 banks with their intranet. Ford Motor Company implements world-wide intranet access for every employee on a salary (2). Cortese adds to the Ford story when she points out that the 1996 Ford Taurus was designed through interactive intranet sessions involving designers "in Asia, Europe, and the U.S." (paragraph 8). Anyone with information to share can benefit from intranets.
* * * * *

Intranets Work Better than Lotus Notes

From Cortese we learn that intranet technology has solved the following situation: Over the years, software developers haven't kept their promise to establish viable links to "computers, software, and databases" enabling employees to access everything from one "single system" (paragraph 5). From the discussion thus far, it is evident that intranets have done exactly that. Cortese outlines three advantages that intranets have over Notes: the cost is less; fewer programmers are required for intranet software, which is not nearly as complex as Lotus Notes coding; and the training required for intranets is far less than the on-going training required for Notes, due to complex coding (paragraph 15).
* * * * *

Intranets Are Meeting New Challenges

One of the challenges with intranets is security. What makes intranets secure is a firewall that allows users to enter using passwords. The term "firewall" warrants a clear definition at this point. *Computerworld* magazine maintains a web site, at which a glossary of computer terms can be found. That glossary defines "firewall" as "a gateway between two networks that selectively filters information passing between [them]" (Glossary 2). For the purposes of this discussion, the two networks mentioned in the definition are the public Internet and the private intranet. Cortese adds a bit more to this definition by saying that firewalls allow employees to access the public Internet but they keep Internet surfers from entering the private network (paragraph 3). In contrast, what makes Lotus Notes even more secure is that it is never exposed to an Internet gateway because it is strictly an internal application, eliminating the possibility of unauthorized access through the Internet. But Notes has complicated password coding, which isn't always the case with intranet firewall systems.

*****

Cortese mentions another angle that Microsoft has taken to gain control of the Internet market. They were giving their web server and browser software away for free, which started a Justice Department investigation (paragraph 36–39). Another tidbit from an article written by Michael Neubarth, Editor-In-Chief for *Internet World* magazine, sheds light on how the industry views Microsoft's dominance. The article "Best Foot Forward," cites Scott McNealy, CEO of Sun Microsystems (developers of Java) as saying, "to kill Microsoft—that's the top priority for all of us" (10). In other words, the industry wishes moral injustices upon Microsoft. This is evident from Lewis' article which states that over 100 computer companies met to discuss setting standards for Java and Microsoft was not invited (paragraph 1).

Another problem is that large software developers, like Microsoft and Netscape, don't always follow the standards that are already in place, according to Joel Snyder. Snyder is an author for *IW* magazine and a senior partner at a law firm in Arizona. Snyder says that Microsoft and Netscape don't take the time to work the bugs out of their products before shipping them to market. He describes some problems that he sees with web page products that allow users, millions of them, to incorporate non-standard features into their web pages (98). David Carr, who specializes in databases and object technology for *Internet World* magazine, mentions another standards battle between these software giants. Namely, "a universal object standard [that] would enable different computers on the Internet to share all data and programs." A universal standard would allow users to create their own applications, as well as using, "distributed-object communication protocols as an alternative to HTTP" (66). In this discussion, it is mentioned that the web was designed to use FTP, a protocol, "for sharing documents, not objects," and that a distributed-object protocol would solve this problem—if the two big rivals would stop using different standards (67).

****

The problems of intranets, of course, become the problems facing programmers and systems analysts. Whether in applications development or in IS in a company, employers will always be on the lookout for those who can troubleshoot or resolve the many problems or limitations of the technology.

How Intranets Affect the Industry

In the battle over object standards discussed in Carr's article, he concludes that as long, "as the competing factions," make attempts to merge the different technologies, progress toward, "a universal computing infrastructure," remains a possibility (70). Intranets, as a movement within the Internet market, have caused software developers to bundle their technologies with those of competitors. In fact, Lewis quotes a senior analyst with International Data Corporation (IDC), who says exactly that of Java, a cross-platform language. The quote makes clear that intranets have caused new "interest in Java" (paragraph 17). Cortese also says that intranets have caused change for Netscape (paragraph 42). In addition to these two examples, intranets are carrying on the compatibility trends that the Internet started—and it's happening across the board in every corner of the software market, not just with Java and Netscape.

Jeff Pulver, a former vice president in the information technology industry and a writer for *Internet World* magazine, maintains his own web site for monitoring "telephone software products" (104). He makes predictions about the future of products that allow faxing over the Internet using corporate intranets. He also mentions another new technology—voice mail. His prediction for this technology, if it does become popular, is that intranet voice mail may turn, "computer workstations (both at home and in the office) [into] a direct replacement for . . . telephones" (105). Wordmark's seminar agrees with Pulver's telephone replacement theory but takes a different angle of approach. In the section titled "Evaluating Web Technology On Its Own Merits," they predict that web browsers may one day "become the document-based equivalent of the telephone" (1).
* * *

Conclusion

Intranets are the current wave in computing for business today. Within the Internet age, a new technology has been born. It is expected to grow at phenomenal rates and will probably be a deciding factor in the success of many corporations. What's important to notice in all of this is the propensity of the technology to move toward compatibility in all areas. The more competitors bundle products, the more the products become the same. Also of importance is the way the Internet/WWW technology has simplified computing. As more products become more alike through bundling web technology, we become more efficient. Let's hope that intranets finally bring our computing complications to a manageable and acceptable level for IS personnel and the business world alike.

Works Cited

"About Process Software Corporation." Online. Internet. 27 Feb. 1997.
    Available. <http://www.process.com/corporate/aboutpsc.htp>.
"About Wordmark.Com." 3 Oct. 1996. Online. Internet. 4 Mar. 1997.
    Available. <http://www.wordmark.com/about.html>.
* * * *

CONCLUSION

In its usual form, the research paper is a genre in its own right and serves particular teaching goals. In this instance, the paper was read by the instructor and students in the computer science class. Research papers can also be put to good use around campus as supplementary handouts or special reports in courses that have a disciplinary interest in the subject. Thus used, they could bring special focus to important technologies, innovations, or issues within a field. Also, research papers can be components of Websites serving a course or a special area of study. More broadly, though, that does not prevent a research paper, which is the result of genuine and conscientious inquiry and research, from being adapted to other forms of writing which the student could put to use in the world outside the school: letters to the editor, letters to agencies and corporations, reports, and articles submitted to newspapers, magazines, and newsletters. The goal of using the research paper as the basis of some desirable action most likely will result in a more thorough inquiry and a more thoughtful research paper.

8

AREA OF INQUIRY: WORKPLACE PROBLEMS

TIM PEEPLES

WHY WRITE ABOUT WORKPLACE PROBLEMS?

Because the workplace is one context that will almost certainly be important in your life, it offers an ideal site for inquiry and action. Indeed, from the employer's perspective, inquiry and action carried out by employees can develop and maintain the competitiveness of the workplace. But an employee's responsibility to inquire into and act upon workplace problems extends beyond a responsibility to the workplace or an employer. An employee's responsibility to inquire into and act upon workplace problems extends to herself, her co-workers, and her communities. In some cases, and all too many cases, what increases the competitiveness of the workplace does harm to workers and/or the community. For instance, in an attempt to reduce health care costs, a company might choose a health care provider based primarily on its overall cost. This could save a company lots of money, thus making it more competitive. However, the increased competitiveness of the company, in this case, may reduce the health coverage of the employees, which may eventually cause them harm. Your responsibilities to inquire into and act upon this kind of workplace issue may not directly affect the competitiveness of your employer, but it is nevertheless a critical area in which an employee would inquire and act.

EXAMPLES OF WRITING FOR INQUIRY AND ACTION

- Todd, who now lives at home and works on his family's dairy farm, worries about how his parents will keep the farm lucrative after all the children leave. Todd, Valerie, and Eric work together to inquire into the problem of redesigning the family farm in a way that does not require monetary outlay for new employees but will maintain and even increase the profits.

- Audrey, a gymnastics instructor at the YWCA, is fed up with the way she always has to do the work that her supervisor and fellow instructor are supposed to be doing. Audrey and her group members, Sara and Shanna, work together to figure out how Audrey might address this problem at work.

- Loma, who works in the Business School Advising Office, Abby, and Rickie are all students in the business school on a large university campus. Each of them has mentioned to the others how frustrated they are by the lack of advising they get within their major. They decide to inquire into the problem of a lack of advising within their business school.

- Heather has worked at a religious camp for two summers in a row and has become increasingly disturbed by some of the sexist rules at the camp. Pascale and Julie are eager to help Heather inquire into the problem of sexism within this summer camp.

- C. R. Cranston serves as the Director of the Electronic Communications Department of a large, multinational insurance company. Early in 1996, the company developed and made active a main web page for the company. A month later, a division within the company wanted to make their own web page and attach it to the main page. Concerned about protecting the company's image, its employees, and its business, Cranston set up a team from Community Affairs, Commerce, Business Development, Support Services, the Legal Department, and Marketing to work on inquiring into the problems that a web page might cause for the company and to develop any necessary policy statements that would serve to address these problems.

- Erin owned a clothing shop in a small, new shopping complex in a resort town in Florida. The complex was co-owned by the shopkeepers and governed by a committee made up of a sub-group of shopkeepers. The city government had very strict building codes, and new building contracts, even for repairs, could take months to get. The problem was that Erin and several other shopkeepers had noticed that there were leaks in the ceilings of several of their shops. The leaks not only put the inventory at risk, but several of the shopkeepers had noticed that the leaks were close to their circuit breaker boxes. Erin began inquiring into how she might address this problem. One of the complexities was that she needed to address many different readers: the shopkeepers, the complex's governing body, the builders, and the city government.

READINGS FOR INQUIRY AND ACTION

"IT'S JUST A MATTER OF TIME: TWENTYSOMETHINGS VIEW THEIR JOBS DIFFERENTLY THAN BOOMERS"
by Helen Wilkinson

In *The Intimate History of Humanity*, French academic Theodore Zeldin notes that women and young people are leading the movement to win back control of our time from the demands of jobs and bosses. For women time has always been at a premium—more so as growing numbers of women work as well as mother and nurture—and the younger generation has seen the costs of too much work and too little time in the lives of their parents.

His insights reinforce research we are carrying out at Demos, an independent British public policy think tank, on the changing values of today's young people. One central finding of Demos' report, *Generation X and the New Work Ethic,* is that control over one's time is the third most important career goal of British young people today. (The first, traditionally enough, is money; the second is the chance to use their brains.)

The report shows that young people want to work but don't want to overwork; they reject the "time bravado" culture of the past, with its workaholic worship of long hours at the job, in favor of a "life friendly" work culture.

Demos' report also reveals generational tensions between the baby boomer generation, who are now managers, and the young workers they are recruiting or managing. Managers lament the incapacity of today's youth to work hard. One particular issue that seems to vex baby-boom bosses is the realization that the old-style corporation loyalty of the past does not resonate with the younger generation. The assumption among young professionals is that old-style employment relationships simply cannot be trusted today. Young people will constantly ask of an employer, "What have you got to teach me?" They believe that security nowadays comes from the transferability of one's skills to other jobs rather than from advancement in hierarchically managed organizations. Economic uncertainty has bred self-reliance among this younger generation.

Managers also frequently complain that younger employees have erratic timekeeping. They don't understand young people's desire to work from home or late at night rather than according to the fixed corporate hours.

For their part, Generation Xers are critical of the sloppiness of their managers, their laziness for failing to keep up with technology, their reliance on secretaries and personal assistants rather than the Internet, and, crucially, their failure to use time efficiently. Many young people criticize their managers for their "make-work" rather than "real-work" mentality. They have no sympathy with the way their elders spend time in meetings rather than getting down to the job at hand.

What are the reasons for this generational divide in today's offices? Maybe it has something to do with the fact that young professionals in their twenties are the first generation to have been socialized into a work culture where insecurity is the order of the day and where there are no jobs for life.

With a few exceptions, business has been slow to recognize the problems of the "time bravado" culture—the stress that is caused and created by a culture of presenteeism (the workaholic equivalent of absenteeism; you are always at your desk no matter how little you accomplish).

An increasing number of young workers, especially women, have decided to opt out of traditional workplaces. In the United States and increasingly in the United Kingdom, there is no shortage of young women setting up their own businesses: They're no longer prepared to wait for companies who have not been able to change their work culture fast enough. The implications of this attempt to regain control of their time is clear. Women and young people want work to be judged not on input but on output, no longer on the site where work is done, but on how well work is done.

On this point, Theodore Zeldin senses that history might be on our side, since we're now moving away from industrialism and the time culture that was necessary for assembly-line work: "There is a new sensitivity to the texture of time, to what makes it flow smoothly, agreeably, sensuously. People do dream of enjoying their work by doing it at a rhythm which suits them and varying their rhythm for different occupations. This notion of personal rhythm was what the industrial revolution attacked and tried to destroy."

We must ask what needs to be done to speed up the process of breaking free from the tyranny of too little time. For a start, the workplace should allow time out for college courses, community volunteering, and sabbaticals. The sabbatical is close to my heart. After five years working as a researcher and producer of TV documentaries, I needed time for myself, away from my job. I wanted to recharge my batteries, work in a different environment surrounded by different people and learn different skills. I was lucky enough to have a broad-minded manager who could see that this was a necessary stage for me. I was granted a sabbatical last year.

I read Zeldin's history of the sabbatical with delight. He writes: "The weekend is only one half of the Sabbath. God also instructed the Jews to make a sabbatical holiday every seven years, in which they should stop tilling the land, cancel debts, and release their slaves." He goes on to predict that "the sabbatical year may become a human right demanded in the 21st century. . . . Since individuals are increasingly unhappy about wasting talents which they cannot use in their jobs, the sabbatical year might have a future, offering an opportunity to change direction, or simply to do what busy people do not have the time to do, namely, think or take a long promenade." It was precisely in my seventh year of working after college that I felt the need to take a break.

Zeldin goes on to argue for a government role in making sabbaticals compulsory—just as it once decreed the 40-hour week. If sabbaticals are not made compulsory, then taking one might be read as disloyalty and lack of commitment. After all, the paradox of our society is that we have enforced idleness for some (a growing 14.4 percent of British society) and overwork for many.

Somewhere in the middle lies a balance. Women have known the need for it for many years and young people perhaps are now the wisest of us all.

Excerpted with permission from the British magazine The Idler *(Jan. 1995). Subscriptions: £15/yr. (6 issues) from 15 St. Stephens Gardens, London W2 5NA, U.K.*

Questions for Analysis

1. What are some of the workplace problems raised in this article?

2. What is the main workplace problem addressed?

3. Is the main problem addressed a problem where you work or have worked? In what ways is it or is it not?

4. Are you persuaded that there is a problem? Why or why not?

5. What is the article's recommendation for addressing the main problem?

6. Are you persuaded by the recommendation? Why or why not?

7. How would the recommendation be received where you work now or other places where you have worked?

8. In what contexts might this recommendation be most persuasive and lead to the most action?

9. The article has several key terms or concepts, such as control over time, hard work, and real-work. Are these terms problematic? Are they well defined? Do you agree with the ways they are defined and used?

10. The article argues that the younger generation does not conceive of work as something bound by time and place. In other words, an employee can "work" at home in the middle of the night just as well and maybe even better than being in an office from 9–5. What role do you think media technologies, like the World Wide Web, email, and cell-phones, have in changing conceptions of work?

A Case   MYNDEE, NATASHA, AND NICOLE'S INQUIRY

> The other day after being introduced to the new workplace problem context in class, I was on my way to work at The Fifth Street Diner trying to figure out what I could work on for this project. "At least I'm working somewhere right now," I thought. "That gives me a real context." As I thought about Fifth Street—the name most people used to refer to the diner—I could not think of many "problems" there. But I remembered that Tim said we could also focus on a workplace "need," something that could improve the workplace. I decided to consider workplace needs at Fifth Street. That got me to a point where I could start using the Questioning Strategy.

At this point in the project, Myndee was working on her own, as were Natasha and Nicole. Even though they would eventually work together as a co-authoring group for the duration of this project, they started their inquiry process individually. Once Myndee decided to focus on workplace needs at Fifth Street where she worked, she started a list of needs she might address and explored some of her own experiences and values to locate areas of dissonance she felt at work.

Myndee's Questions

Needs at Fifth Street

1. a new menu

2. better advertising on campus

3. better advertising, in general

4. maybe a web page?

In our writing class, we have talked about world wide web pages as things that are "written." I think writing a web page would be really cool. And this might be a time to learn how to write one for a good reason. Fifth Street gets most of its customers from the downtown area, where it's located, but it isn't drawing enough customers outside the realm of just downtown employees. The diner could easily serve and accommodate more customers, but it doesn't. A web page would address the need to advertise for a broader audience by advertising on another level.

Probing for Dissonance

My Experience	My Values	Cultural Sources	Dissonance
Empty seats at Fifth Street	Small, locally owned businesses are important to a town's health	my home town	I want Fifth Street to get more clientele
I have more fun working when it's busy	I like being busy, meeting new people, and talking	My mom	I get depressed when work is slow
Bob and Jaycee, the owners, treat me like family	I want to help friends out as much as possible	Growing up: with only my mom and me, we learned how important helping and being helped by friends is	Bob and Jaycee are more than my employers

Locating in a Context

The context for this project is Fifth Street and its owners. I work for Bob and Jaycee as a waitress, and we're pretty good friends. They have already mentioned the possibility of a web page, so there has been some discussion about this. I think they would definitely put in the money to have a page. Even though I may not be able actually to make the page in this class, I could at least make some recommendations for it and do some preliminary research for them. Since we all get along well and since I'm at school to study food marketing, I have good credibility, too.

Formulating a Question

How will a web page attract more customers for Fifth Street?

As Myndee worked through the first part of the Questioning Strategy, she started to see a pattern. One of the needs at Fifth Street was to draw in more customers, particularly from outside the downtown area. Myndee decided the best kind of question for her to ask right now was one that would lead to a new understanding of how a web page might work for Fifth Street.

Myndee's class was already organized into peer groups. Since this was going to be a co-authored project, she already knew her co-authors, Natasha and Nicole. What they didn't know was whose workplace problem/need they would be inquiring into. After working individually to identify workplace problems and/or needs that mattered to them, their first group activity was choosing whose project idea they wanted to work on as a co-authoring group.

They discovered that choosing a project meant learning a little bit about each others' workplace contexts. Using the Three Perspective Guide as a way to discuss their workplaces, Myndee, Natasha, and Nicole each described their workplace and briefly summarized the problem/need they had identified. They did this in class as an informal discussion. After discussing each person's project idea, they used the three bulleted questions under "Select Workplace Problem/Need for Inquiry" in the Questioning Strategy to evaluate which of their projects they wanted to work on as a team for the next four weeks. Before the end of this class period, they chose Myndee's project idea for their group project. Rather than working individually, they now began to inquire and act as a co-authoring team.

Before going any further, they needed to develop a plan for their project. Having been told that their Project Plans would serve as "contracts" for their group work, Myndee, Natasha, and Nicole decided to start off by writing a brief statement outlining their choices about the ways they would collaborate during the project. They called this their "collaborative contract," and each signed it when they reached agreement on all the points.

Myndee, Natasha, and Nicole's Collaborative Contract

- Even though we know that an integrative team approach to collaboration takes more time, we will try to work as a team on every part of the project. Since we know we work well together from the first project in the class, we think we will do a better job if we work as a team all the time.

- Since we will be working together on every part, we agree that we will each make it to every class and every out-of-class meeting we set up. If we can't make it to a meeting, we will contact the others at least 24 hours in advance.

- Even during the drafting, when it is hardest to work together, we want to try working together instead of "assigning" each other things to do.

- Even though we can all be pig-headed (we saw this in the first project, didn't we!), we still know we can achieve consensus. We can be pig-headed, but we agree not to be judgmental.

Along with their "collaborative contract," they also made a couple of visuals to help them see the overall Project Plan they had developed. The first visual plan they developed is called a Gantt chart. They learned about this kind of chart in class discussion and thought it would help them visualize the overall schedule of their project. At first, but as a group, they simply sketched a chart out by hand in class. Later, Natasha, who had experience with computer drawing software, made the following chart.

Date / Project	Week 1 M T W R F	Week 2 M T W R F	Week 3 M T W R F	Week 4 M T W R F
Research Survey	▬▬▬	▬▬		
Web	▬	▬▬		
Cost	▬	▬		
Interviews	▬▬▬	▬▬		
Positioning, Genre, Focus		▬▬		
Doc. Design		▬▬		
Drafting			▬▬	
Response			+	
Revising			▬▬	▬▬
Final Report				+

When they reviewed their plan, they realized that the Gantt chart helped them list the tasks to be completed, develop a time line, and pretty well identify critical points in the process (the end of each line represented a "due date"). The one thing the Gantt chart didn't do well at all was identify who would do what. Since they had already decided to do everything together, that wasn't a big problem, but they still felt they needed a second kind of visual plan to help them make some more distinctions about deadlines. So they made a simple table with the tasks they needed to complete and wrote out the days when these tasks needed to be done.

Myndee, Natasha, and Nicole's Project Schedule

Finish writing survey	*Friday, Week 1*
Hand out survey	*Monday, Week 2*
Tally survey results	*Friday, Week 2*
Set up initial interview	*Wednesday, Week 1*
Develop follow-up interview	*Wednesday, Week 2*
Set up follow-up interview	*Wednesday, Week 2*

Once they finished their second visual, Myndee, Natasha, and Nicole decided that their Project Plan met the criteria listed in the "Review" section of the Project Plan Strategy.

During the first week and a half of the project, Myndee, Natasha, and Nicole chose the workplace need they wanted to inquire into and made a plan for their project. They also spent a good deal of time doing some preliminary research. They consulted the research strategy section, Part II, to help them out. At the suggestion of their instructor, they wrote out a brief plan of what they wanted to get out of their research.

Myndee, Natasha, and Nicole's Research Plan

Survey:	We think that lots of people who travel, like for family vacations, check out where they're going before they go. And when they check out a place, they look for fun places to go and historical places. Since Fifth Street is one of the oldest restaurants in town, it might be a place vacationers would like to visit. We want to find out if people do check out a place before they travel there, and if they do, do they or might they use the WWW.
Web:	We want to find out how other restaurants in town are advertised on the web. We also want to check out the Chamber of Commerce page, since that is probably the page most travelers would check out.
Cost:	After talking with you, we know it costs money to have a web page. We want to find out how much it will cost Bob and Jaycee to have one.
Interviews:	We want to interview Bob and Jaycee to find out 1) if they have access to a computer, 2) if the computer connects to the WWW, 3) if they want to advertise on the web, 4) if they think advertising on the WWW will increase the number of customers, and 5) if they also think they need to get customers from places outside of downtown.

Even though research was not required of them in this project, Myndee, Natasha, and Nicole found their research to be exceedingly helpful in their inquiry and action. They felt like they had really helpful information for Bob and Jaycee. The whole group was now excited about the project and felt like their project would be able to address Myndee's question. With their research data in hand, they moved on to consider their positioning.

Myndee, Natasha, and Nicole's Writer/Reader Positioning

Writer Position

Myndee hasn't ever actually written anything for Fifth Street, except for some signs to put in the windows. When writing signs, Myndee has been an employee. She has also written to them as friends, like when she wrote a birthday card to Jaycee. The two positions Myndee has written from in this context have been employee and friend. But Natasha and Nicole have never written in this context. Even though we have each been in workplace contexts and written as employees, it doesn't make sense for us to position ourselves as employees.

Myndee has talked with Bob and Jaycee about stuff dealing with the restaurant, so we don't think she is excluded from writing something about our research and recommendations for a web page. Because Myndee is wanting to study the food industry, she wants to leave behind an image of herself as "just a waitress" and wants to position herself as someone who can help. We all want to avoid being "just students" who are "just writing a paper." So even though we are working on this project in our English class, we don't want to write as "just students."

A big problem we're running into is that it's hard to position all of us together as one co-authoring group. If it were just Myndee, she could be an employee, and if it were just Natasha and Nicole, they could be "student consultants" to Bob and Jaycee. Since we can't all take the position of "employee," we will position ourselves as "student consultants."

Reader Position

Our readers will be Bob and Jaycee, not the rest of the staff. Bob and Jaycee could be "owners," or "employers," or "friends." Because we have positioned ourselves as "student consultants," they could be positioned as "clients."

Because we want to help Fifth Street in terms of making a decision about a web page, we need to address the people who will make the decision: Bob and Jaycee. As "owners," they value making money, keeping customers happy, keeping their business, and making their business even better. But "owners" seems like too broad of a position to be helpful. Since we are trying to help Bob and Jaycee, we think that "clients" is the best position for them.

Once Myndee, Natasha, and Nicole had finished considering their positioning, they wrote their focus statement: A web page would be a good way to attract out-of-town customers to Fifth Street. They then moved on to consider their genre choices. Up to this point, they were still considering writing a web page.

Myndee, Natasha, and Nicole's Genre Work

Considering Alternative Genres
- web page
- research paper
- recommendation report
- letter

We are trying to answer the question, "How will a web page attract more customers to Fifth Street?" So far, our response has been, yes; a web page will attract more customers. We have positioned Bob and Jaycee as our "clients." As "student consultants," we are helping them by researching the possibility of writing a web page to attract more customers. We have been wanting to write a web page, but a recommendation report would be better for our focus and our readers. A research paper would put us too much in the position of "students," which we want to avoid. And a letter is too informal. A recommendation report seems to be the kind of thing a "consultant" would write to a "client." The recommendation report makes sense in our context, too.

The web page isn't very practical for us, anyway. None of us knows how to write web pages. We haven't ever written a recommendation report either. But we could write a recommendation report a lot easier than a web page. Since we have already done some research for the project, we also have the kinds of evidence that a recommendation report needs to be believable. The recommendation report has to talk about what kind of research was done to cause the writers to make a certain recommendation. We can talk about our research.

Selecting and Examining the Implications of Our Genre
We have decided to write a recommendation report. To do this well, we are going to get some samples of recommendation reports from our instructor and consult the Genre Strategy in Part II. We know from class discussion that the recommendation report already has a very particular kind of structure, so seeing some models will help us. We will have to look over our research better than we have. When we were thinking about writing a web page, the research was information just for us. Now, it will be a big part of our final report.

Having discovered through the Genre Strategy that a web page wouldn't be the best genre for their project and context, Myndee, Natasha, and Nicole moved on to consider how they might design their recommendation report document. They wanted a document that would "look" good enough to be from "consultants." They also wanted one that Bob and Jaycee could use well.

Myndee, Natasha, and Nicole's Document Design

Positioning: We will write to Bob and Jaycee as clients, and we will position ourselves as "student consultants."

Genre: Recommendation report. The report has to clearly state the need we are addressing, explain the research we have done, discuss what we have found in our research, and make a recommendation.

Focus: A web page would be a good way to attract out-of-town customers to Fifth Street.

Hierarchies of Our Page
We know from the genre that we have chosen that our document can be broken down into an overview, a discussion of the need, our research methods, our findings, our recommendations, and our conclusion. We also know that because of the research we've done, we can break up the research section into survey, web, cost, and interview sub-sections. Under our sub-sections, we can list what we wanted to find out and then in the findings section report what we actually found out. We could use numbers so a reader could quickly cross-check the two sections. We could also list the criteria we used to make our recommendations.

Our Readers

Our readers will be receptive readers at first. When we talked about how Bob and Jaycee would read our report, we first thought they would just be receptive readers, but then Nicole said they may read the report differently the second or third time they read it, like when they are thinking about who they want to hire as their internet service provider. So they might be scanner and search readers, too. At first they will be reading the report to get what it says. Later, they will probably use it to make specific decisions about things. We need to make the whole thing coherent, but we also need to make it so they can find important information quickly and not have to read the whole report each time they use it.

Persuasiveness

Myndee says she has never seen Bob and Jaycee read a recommendation report. Most formal writing comes from the Health Department, which sends regulation stuff now and then to all restaurants, and from food companies who are trying to sell new products to them. It would be weird if we suddenly gave Bob and Jaycee a recommendation report. But since we have already interviewed them and talked with them a lot, they know it's coming. They think it's cool we're doing this for free. So just doing the report already makes it pretty persuasive.

Myndee, Natasha, and Nicole were eager to begin a draft of their report. They had stayed on the schedule they made in their Project Plan and were now in their third week of the four weeks they had for the project. They wanted to get a polished draft to their instructor and another group by the end of the week so they could get some feedback and work on revisions.

Myndee, Natasha, and Nicole's Polished Draft

MEMORANDUM

TO:	Bob and Jaycee
FR:	Myndee, Natasha, and Nicole
DT:	April 13
RE:	Recommendation

Overview

The purpose of this report is to recommend an appropriate solution to The Fifth Street Diner's problem of limited clientele. We will provide you with the results of our research and investigation into developing a web page for the diner. We will first discuss the diner's problem and need and then move on to the research methods we used and what we found. With all of this information in mind, we will then provide an accurate and thorough recommendation that will help satisfy The Fifth Street Diner's current need.

The Need

The current situation at the Fifth Street Diner is that the diner is not drawing in enough customers outside of the local business district. The diner could easily accommodate and serve more customers. However, Fifth Street needs a more effective way of advertising that will attract clientele from out of town. We feel that advertising on the web will solve the Fifth Street Diner's clientele problem.

Research Methods

Our Project Planning Gantt chart shows the research we did for this project. We wrote and handed out a survey for the customers, we looked into how much internet service providers in town charge to rent web space, we found out what kinds of web pages other restaurants in town have, and we did interviews with Bob and Jaycee.

Findings

Survey

Through surveys conducted at the Fifth Street Diner of the business's clientele, we found that 75% of their customers are regulars. We also found that 85% of their customers travel and 75% of those people research their destination before they travel. We feel that due to these high percentages it would be beneficial for the Fifth Street Diner to advertise on the web. Since the majority of the diner's customers do come from the downtown area, a web page could be very beneficial in drawing customers from out of town.

Web

We researched web pages for the area and the Chamber of Commerce when trying to decide between an independent or collaborative web page. The web page in both of these sections for restaurants only allowed for specific information, such as name, address, and phone number. We felt that due to Fifth Street Diner's prominent history it would be more beneficial for the diner to have an independent web page. By advertising this way, they could not only draw customers from the local area, but also those traveling to historical sites throughout the state. Since over twenty million people are connected to the internet, this type of advertising could prove to be very beneficial.

Cost

We called three local businesses that publish web pages to get an idea of what the cost would be to actually publish a web page. The three businesses that we called were Websters, Sitings, and Nothing-but-Net. Websters charged twenty-five dollars for each megabyte of information, plus an additional five dollars for every additional megabyte. Sitings had a six month trial period and then charged three hundred dollars a year (which is the equivalent of twenty-five dollars a month). We found that out of these three businesses, Nothing-but-Net was the least expensive at twenty dollars a month.

Recommendation

After discovering the diner's problem, we established some criteria that needed to be met by a possible solution. The criteria are as follows:

- client accessibility and feasibility
- effective broadening of diner's clientele
- world wide access for travelers and visitors that may be potential customers
- emphasis on diner's historical appeal
- reasonable implementation cost

Then, after our research, we have come to a conclusion about a recommendation for the diner. An independent web page would be extremely beneficial.

With the notes, research, and findings, our recommendation is justifiable. A web page would meet all of the criteria established. Since the manager of the diner has a computer and access to the internet, a web page would be accessible and feasible. Also, since a web page is a form of advertisement, it will definitely broaden clientele for the diner. In addition, the web page will reach potential customers all over the world that may be traveling through the area or may be coming to visit the university. Another benefit of the web is that its content is unlimited. Therefore, the diner's historical appeal can be emphasized, in contrast to the possibility of advertising on the Chamber of Commerce page which only lists addresses and telephone numbers. The cost is also reasonable.

Conclusion

Thus our recommendation is for The Fifth Street Diner to implement a web page. The research is completed. We would be happy to assist you in any other research you need done or even the designing of the web page. The only step that needs to be completed is the actual implementing of the page.

Myndee, Natasha, and Nicole found themselves hurrying through their draft much more than they would have liked and were anxious to receive feedback from their instructor and another co-authoring group within the class. They found that trying to draft all together as an integrative team made the drafting process pretty inefficient. They also found drafting integratively less satisfying than they thought. They couldn't keep a continuous thought, and they had trouble reflecting on the strategic work they had accomplished earlier. As they waited for the feedback, they discussed the revisions they themselves saw they needed to make. Once they received their feedback and analyzed it, they wrote up a revision plan memo to their instructor.

Natasha, and Nicole's Revision Plan

MEMORANDUM
    TO: Tim
    FR: Myndee, Natasha, and Nicole
    DT: April 15
    RE: Revising Plan, Fifth Street Diner Project

Design/Genre Revisions

First, we need to be more specific in our headings. Several readers noticed that our headings are too vague and typical. They aren't specific to our project, so they don't help the readers find and remember information as quickly and as effectively as they might.

Our report heading isn't formal enough. Even though we know Bob and Jaycee personally, we should still use their last names in the report header. Also, we should make the RE: line more specific.

We will break our research methods section into sub-parts, as we mentioned in our document design plan but didn't do in our draft.

Focus

The "Overview" now has us addressing a "problem," but our focus is on a "need." It also says the report will give a solution, but our focus is on a recommendation, not a definitive solution. We will change this to make it consistent with our focus.

Readers

Overall, we need to make the report a little less formal. The tone is kind of stiff. We think this is because we tried to draft it all together.

Our research section also sounds like it is written to our instructor, not Bob and Jaycee. We need to rewrite that section with them in mind.

Organization

We will move our criteria to the overview section since they are pretty important and will help Bob and Jaycee evaluate what the report says as they read through it. In the recommendation section, we can use the criteria to discuss our recommendation.

After finishing their revision plan, they went right to work on their final report. They decided to continue working integratively, even though they thought it didn't work very well during drafting. They thought revision was different enough that it would be good to work integratively.

Myndee, Natasha, and Nicole's Revision

MEMORANDUM
    TO: Bob and Jaycee McNichols, Owners of The Fifth Street Diner
    FR: Myndee, Natasha, and Nicole, Volunteer Researchers

DT: April 18
RE: How would a Web Page Help the Fifth Street Diner Bring in
        Customers?

An Overview of This Project

The purpose of this report is to inform you of the research we have been able to do over the past three weeks on the possibility of The Fifth Street Diner developing a web page to help bring in more customers from outside of the downtown area. We will first discuss the diner's need to bring in customers other than those just within the downtown area and then move on to the research methods we used and what we found. To evaluate our findings and help us make a recommendation, we developed the following five criteria for an effective response to the diner's need to attract more customers from outside of the downtown area:

- client accessibility and feasibility
- effective broadening of the diner's clientele
- greater advertising access for potential customers from outside of the area
- emphasis on the diner's historical appeal
- reasonable implementation cost

Our recommendation will address these five criteria.

The Need the Project Addresses: Drawing in Customers from Outside the Downtown Area

The current situation at the Fifth Street Diner is that the diner is not drawing in enough customers outside of the local business district. The diner could easily accommodate and serve more customers. However, Fifth Street needs a more effective way of advertising that will attract clientele from out of town. We feel that advertising on the web will solve the Fifth Street Diner's clientele problem, so we have researched the possibility of a web page to see if it would be a recommended way to address the diner's need.

What Kind of Research Were We Able to Do?

First, we need to make it clear that we did not have a lot of time to research this need, and we also do not have training in research. We think what we chose to do in our research was good, but someone with training in research might come up with better data to help with the decision.

Our Project Planning Gantt chart shows the research we did for this project. (see Appendix) We wrote and handed out a survey for the customers, we looked into how much internet service providers in town charge to rent web space, we found out what kinds of web pages other restaurants in town have, and we did interviews with Bob and Jaycee.

Interviews—Throughout the project we conducted various personal interviews with you, the owners of the diner. From these interviews we wanted to find out, first, if you thought there was a need to draw in customers from outside the downtown area. We also wanted to find out if you had access to the web and if you were interested in the possibility of developing a web page to help bring in customers from outside the downtown area.

Surveys—We conducted a survey of customers in the diner. We felt that this would help validate the diner's problem with statistical results. Generally, we wanted to find out if most of the customers were from the downtown area and if they ever researched where they would go on vacations. We wanted to find out if people might use a web page to help plan where they might eat and visit, including when they might visit our area.

Internet Research—We conducted some web-page research of various local business pages. We wanted to see what the local options seemed to be.

Internet Service Provider Costs—We made phone calls to local internet service providers (companies that store web pages on their computers). We wanted to find out how much a web page would cost.

What Did We Find in Our Research?

The Findings from Our Interviews

From periodical interviews with you, we not only gained lots of useful information, but we became assured that we were working on a need that they saw was important and a possible solution that they had interest in.

We found that the owners saw a need to draw in more customers from outside of the downtown area. As they pointed out, this would be more and more important to their business as the downtown area continued to get more and more other restaurants. The downtown area had four new restaurants open within two years, and they all competed for a customer base that wasn't growing very fast.

We also found that you have a computer that is hooked to the internet. You see the possibility of a web page as intriguing.

A Survey of Fifth Street Diner's Customers

Through surveys conducted at the Fifth Street Diner of the business's clientele, we found that 75% of their customers are regulars. We also found that 85% of their customers travel and 75% of those people research their destination before they travel. These numbers back up our assumption and your opinion that the diner needs to attract more customers from outside the downtown area.

The Kinds of Web Pages Used by Businesses Within the Area

We researched web pages for the area and those found through the Chamber of Commerce page. We found that there were two kinds of web pages. We call the pages connected to the Chamber of Commerce "collaborative" pages and the others "independent" pages. From what we found, the web pages for restaurants in both the collaborative and individual categories only allowed for specific information, such as name, address, and phone number. However, on an independent web page, the diner could control better what was on the page. We felt that due to Fifth Street Diner's prominent history it would be more beneficial for the diner to have an independent web page. By advertising this way, they could not only draw customers from the local area, but also those traveling to historical sites throughout the state.

The Cost of a Web Page

We called three local businesses that publish web pages to get an idea of what the cost would be to actually publish a web page. The three businesses that we called were Websters, Sitings, and Nothing-but-Net. Websters charged twenty-five dollars for each megabyte of information, plus an additional five dollars for every additional megabyte. Sitings had a six month trial period and then charged three hundred dollars a year (which is the equivalent of twenty-five dollars a month). We found that out of these three businesses, Nothing-but-Net was the least expensive at twenty dollars a month.

Recommendation

To help make a recommendation about the use of a web page to draw in more customers from outside of the downtown area, we used our criteria.

- client accessibility and feasibility
- effective broadening of diner's clientele
- world wide access for travelers and visitors that may be potential customers
- emphasis on diner's historical appeal
- reasonable implementation cost

With the notes, research, and findings, our recommendation is justifiable. A web page would meet all of the criteria established. Since you have a computer and access to the internet, a web page would be accessible and feasible. Also, since a web page is a form of advertisement, it will definitely broaden clientele for the diner. In addition, the web page will reach potential customers all over the world that may be traveling through the area or may be coming to visit the university. Another benefit of the web is that its content is unlimited. Therefore, the diner's historical appeal can be emphasized, in contrast to the possibility of advertising on the Chamber of Commerce page which only lists addresses and telephone numbers. The cost is also reasonable.

Conclusion

As new restaurants open in the downtown area, and as more and more people begin using the world wide web for fun, work, and research, we think a web page for The Fifth Street Diner would be an excellent way to draw in customers from outside of our local downtown area. If you decide that you would like to develop a web page, we have some neat ideas for one that we would like to share with you. If you would like, we might even be able to volunteer to learn some web page writing and help you develop your web page.

Anyway, we would like to thank you for all of your assistance in this project. We know you have said the project has helped you, but it has also helped us. We have learned a lot from this project, and it has been fun doing a writing project that really makes a difference.

Questions for Analysis

1. Do you think Myndee's inquiry is genuine? Is she inquiring within a real context? Is the problem/need genuine for Myndee and The Fifth Street Diner?

2. Myndee jumps pretty quickly to a consideration of a web page. Did she hurt her inquiry by doing so? Would her inquiry have been more helpful if she would have formulated a question that did not include the possible solution of a web page in it?

3. Was the inquiry genuine for Natasha and Nicole? Would it have been better for the group to do the questioning strategy together? How might that have changed their inquiry?

4. Was the inquiry genuine for Bob and Jaycee? How might the project have been different if Bob and Jaycee had been included in the inquiry throughout the project?

5. Do you think Myndee, Natasha, and Nicole were best served by an integrative team approach to the project? Can you identify places in their project where working integratively was beneficial?

6. Can you identify places in Myndee, Natasha, and Nicole's project and their report where a different approach to collaborative management would have served them better?

7. Research was an integral part of Myndee, Natasha, and Nicole's project. This is the case in most workplace writing. How did research help them in their project? What role does their research play in their inquiry process, including the final report?

8. Working through the Writer/Reader Positioning Strategy and Genre Strategy, Myndee, Natasha, and Nicole discover something new. They discover the importance of the diner's history write-up on the back of the menu. This illustrates how inquiry/discovery can happen throughout your writing. What other discoveries do you see them making as they work through the project?

9. How well do you think Myndee, Natasha, and Nicole integrate their discoveries/inquiry work into their report?

10. When drafting their report, Myndee, Natasha, and Nicole ignored several good ideas they had in their document design plan. How could they have taken better advantage of their document design plan? What procedure would you recommend to them?

WRITING FOR INQUIRY AND ACTION

THE WRITING ASSIGNMENT

Conduct a written inquiry into a workplace problem or need. It is best if you inquire into a problem or need at a place where you presently work or an organization to which you presently belong. If you are not presently working anywhere, your inquiry can still be genuine and helpful if you inquire into a problem at an organization to which you belong or a workplace where you have once worked, especially if you plan to return. Choose a problem or need that is most puzzling and/or intriguing to you. If you will be working in co-authoring groups, you will also want to choose a problem or need that will be of interest to the co-authoring group.

YOUR WRITING PROCESS

Writing in the workplace is different in several ways from most academic and personal sorts of writing. First, most workplace writing is done with others, often in co-authoring teams. Also, workplace writing generally requires you to make efficient plans for your longer writing projects as a means of persuading your supervisors that you should have time set aside for your inquiry. Finally, workplace writing generally requires writers to design their documents so they can be effectively used by many kinds of readers. This chapter will introduce you to a number of strategies that will help you approach these workplace writing challenges with more confidence and effectiveness.

Starting

Why pose questions?

Does writing in the workplace really begin with posing questions? Isn't it true that most writing and work done in the workplace is initiated by something your boss has told you to do? Maybe on first impression, but only on first impression. You can look at the way writing starts in the workplace from different perspectives that change this initial impression. First, don't you think your workplace writing and work begin with *someone* asking a question? Isn't there always someone who identifies a problem that needs to be addressed? If so, then workplace writing and work really does begin with questioning. The difference is that you may not always have the authority to initiate the questioning process. Even though you may not have the authority to initiate the questioning process, the best kinds of workers are routinely identified as those who "take initiative." But how? You can take initiative either 1) by identifying a problem or need at a place where you work or an organization to which you belong, or 2) by more critically exploring the tasks your boss has asked you to address. From these alternative perspectives, workplace writing *does* begin with posing questions.

QUESTIONING STRATEGY
Select a Workplace Problem / Need for Inquiry / Probe for
Dissonance / Locate Your Subject in a Writing Context /
Formulate a Question for Inquiry / Workshop

Selecting a Workplace Problem/Need for Inquiry

If you decide to take the initiative by identifying a problem/need where you work
or in an organization to which you belong, you need, first, to select a problem/
need. The best way to start this process is simply to start a list of problems/needs
you have seen. You might make this listing activity an ongoing project. If you
do, you can keep a notebook with your observations and feelings. The notebook functions as an ongoing list of problems/needs into which you would like
to inquire.

If you are just starting such a list, don't jump at the first problem/need you
write down. You want to identify problems or needs that provoke strong reactions. Even though your first problem/need provokes strong reactions, you will
want to create a substantial list before you move on. As you develop your list,
you may discover more critical problems/needs that you would like to address, or
you may begin to notice relationships between the problems/needs in your list
that will help you as you inquire into and act upon the problem/need.

Once you have made a substantial list and maybe even have tried to cluster
your list, you need to choose a problem/need you want to address. Basically, you
need to decide which one is most worth investigating. To help you decide, ask
yourself the following questions:

- Which of these problems/needs most affects you now?
- Which most affects your employer or organization members?
- Which can best be addressed by you? Do you have ample experience?
  Do you have the needed expertise? Do you have relevant authority?

Probing for Dissonance

Workplace problems/needs usually arise as *conflicts* or *gaps*. A conflict arises
when one person's or one group's values *are* met but when, at the same time,
another person's or group's values are *not* met. For example, when your manager
is preparing the work schedule for the next two weeks, her main goal (value) may
be simply to have enough staff for each hour during the next two weeks. However, half of the manager's staff, including you, might be students who have
classes to go to, tests to take, children to get to daycare, etc. What you value most
is a schedule flexible enough to work around your other responsibilities. If your
boss doesn't consider your other responsibilities and values only "covering" the
staff-hours needed at work, her values conflict with yours and cause a workplace
problem. Unlike conflicts, which lead to problems, *gaps* in values can lead to

needs. Contemporary business consultants refer to such gaps as "white spaces." They typically represent areas for improvement. Instead of identifying a problem or conflict, you can identify areas where your workplace or organization can be even better. A need is a kind of positive dissonance. In this case, there is a gap between what *is* now happening in the workplace and what you think *ought* to be happening.

To help you locate your dissonance, make a table in which you write down 1) your experiences with the problem/need you have chosen, 2) your values as they relate to the problem/need you have chosen, and 3) the sources of your values. Once you have written down five or more experiences, along with the corresponding values and sources for the values, reflect on your table by writing out what conflicts and/or gaps you have identified.

Locating Your Subject in a Writing Context

You have already located your problem/need within a general workplace or organizational context. Now, think about the more specific contexts in which your problem/need is situated. Is this a problem/need *within* a single rank of workers? For instance, is your problem/need situated within the context of construction laborers? Maybe the problem/need isn't within the ranks of construction laborers but is a problem/need within a context that *cuts across* the ranks of laborers and foremen. Or perhaps your writing context extends from the workplace across and into the families of the employees? In the workplace and in organizations, writing contexts can be identified by rank, by divisions, by departments, by regions, and many other means.

At this point, you need to identify some more specific contexts in which your problem/need is situated and then determine your writing context. To help you think through this decision, think about the following questions:

- Which context will be most impacted by your inquiry?
- In which context might there already be some discussion about your problem/need?
- In which context is there the greatest possibility that your problem/ need could be addressed?
- In which context do you have the most credibility?

Formulating a Question for Inquiry

By this point, you have chosen a subject (problem/need) for inquiry, identified your dissonance in relation to this subject, and chosen a primary writing context in which your subject is situated. Now, you need to formulate a question to help guide your inquiry. Without a specific question, your inquiry lacks direction, and you won't know when you have reached any sort of satisfying end. Try posing several questions that capture the kinds of responses or answers you seek. You need to ask yourself if you want responses that lead to new understanding, or to the identification of the cultural sources of the problem/need, or to a course of action. In the workplace all too often, people think that the only valuable questions to ask and responses to give are those that lead to direct action. However, sometimes responses that lead to new understanding or the identification of cultural sources of problems are necessary before any sort of "direct action" can be taken. Therefore, do not overlook the value of questions that are not aimed at a course of action.

WORKSHOP

1. The best questions to guide your inquiry are those that a) lead you and your readers toward some new position on the problem/need, b) are narrow enough to lead to a valuable response within your time constraints, and c) appeal most to your co-authoring group (if you are working with one). Evaluate your inquiry question based on the three points above.

2. In your group, write out your responses to these criteria.

Example: Audrey's Starting Guide

Workplace Problems/Needs that Matter

Audrey's Workplace

- YWCA (gymnastics)

Problem

1. instructors lying on time cards
2. instructors not holding up to their responsibilities

Choosing Problem/Need for Inquiry

I think the second problem is the best to address. The first problem affects me a lot, but Beth, the head of gymnastics, has already begun dealing with this. So the second problem will probably affect me the most if it isn't dealt with. The second problem affects the employer most because the employer is sometimes one of the people who doesn't live up to her responsibilities. This could make the second problem a bad choice, because I might get into trouble if I pursue it. Because the first problem isn't one that I can get "evidence" on, it would be hard to address. I also am not in a position to really address this problem. Since I am a senior instructor, though, I am in a position to address the second problem. Both problems would probably be interesting to the group I'll be working on this project with since I assume we all have dealt with both problems and predict we'll deal with the same problems in the future. The second problem seems more challenging, though, and since we are together and have time to work on it, I think if we work on the second problem now, we might be better prepared to deal with it later in our work.

Probing for Conflicts or Gaps

My Experience	*My Values*	*Cultural Sources*	*Dissonance*
• work goes more smoothly when everyone gets along, but even though I got along with Beth at first and even liked her, she has used her position to do less work.	• getting along with people is important to all of our happiness.	• my parents and teachers have taught me to get along with others.	• since summer ended and Beth became Head Instructor, everyone hasn't been getting along.
• when people don't follow regulations it upsets those who do and ends up causing problems, and at work, people are no longer following the regulations of their jobs.	• following regulations is important for the benefit of the entire group.	• I have learned from the laws, school, and parents that I must follow rules. If I don't I am both punished and possibly hurting others around me.	• I have been noticing that everyone at work isn't following what we're supposed to do, and this has made my work harder and less satisfying.
• when the regulations are not followed and people don't get along at work, as it has been for several months now, others have to pick up the slack of what some people aren't doing.	• we should do what we are hired and asked to do.	• not only have family and school taught me this, but my friends have taught me that if we agree to something, we hurt each other if we don't follow through.	• When I was hired, I was told I would have to do certain jobs and took responsibility for those. It doesn't seem others have done likewise, and it is making my job a pain.

Locating My Subject In a Writing Context

- **identify possible contexts**
  - co-workers
  - Beth, head of gymnastics
  - Carol, head of YWCA
  - Jane, head of youth dept.
  - all members of the YWCA
- **determine my context**
  - co-workers would be the most interested in this problem
  - no community has discussed this problem, outside of some under-the-breath grumbling
  - the head of the youth dept. has the most power

> - I have the most influence with co-workers and the head of the youth dept., with whom I have worked for several years and with whom I am a friend
>
> *I will write in the context of co-workers.*
>
> ### Formulating Questions for Inquiry
>
> - **pose questions**
>
>   1. Why does Beth not work when she gets paid for it?
>
>   2. Why does Beth leave her responsibilities to her co-workers?
>
>   3. How much does Beth value her job?
>
>   4. How does Beth feel about her other co-workers?
>
>   5. What about the workplace has caused Beth and some of my co-workers to think they don't have to take responsibility?
>
>   6. Why does Beth think she can get away with not taking responsibility for her work?
>
>   7. Does Beth realize that she is upsetting people by not taking responsibility?
>
> - **choose a question and a context**
>
>   All of the questions lead to other possible positions on the problem, but the sixth question could be especially good in helping me explore if Beth really is the problem or if something else is. It's possible that there are other reasons for the problem, and I am open to new ideas about what they might be. The sixth question helps me get at the understanding I want; the last question is a question I might address in a back-handed way by writing something that Beth sees so she finds out that some people are upset. Once I begin working with my co-authoring group, we will have only about three weeks to work on this, so I can't pick a question that takes lots of research.
>
>   My question for inquiry will be a combination of questions six and seven: How can I persuade Beth, without attacking her, that if she and others pull their own weight at work, work will be a lot better for us all?

COLLABORATION

PROJECT PLANNING STRATEGY

Decide on a Collaboration Management Model / Decide How You Will Deal with Group Conflict / Make a Project Plan / Review Your Project Plan / Workshop

---

WHY PLAN YOUR PROJECT?

Even if you are writing alone, it is helpful to plan your writing projects. However, the model of the individual writer writing in the workplace is rarely the actual case. Most workplace writing is collaborative in some sense. Consequently, it is critical that co-authors develop some sort of plan for their project. Without a plan, their process will most likely be inefficient, which will lose money for the organization or business, and their final document will most likely be less effective than it could have been. Much in this project planning strategy can help you plan your writing projects even if you are not directly collaborating with anyone else and are writing alone. However, the strategy assumes you are working on co-authored projects. If you are working on such projects, you will find the following strategy very helpful in planning your work together.

Deciding on a Collaboration Management Model

There are *three basic models of collaboration management*: the *division-of-labor* model, the *integrative-team* model, and a *combined-management* approach model. A division-of-labor model separates the work that each member of the groups does. In this model, each member of the collaborative writing team works on discrete tasks within the overall writing project. Usually, tasks are assigned according to an individual's areas of expertise. An integrative-team model is the opposite of the division-of-labor model. Instead of separating people and their tasks, the integrative model brings the entire group together. Each member of the group participates in every stage of the writing project. Typically, collaboration works under some sort of combined-management approach model. Under this model, some parts of the project are worked on separately and some are worked on as a collaborative team.

As a group, you need to decide what collaboration model you will use. You might want to start off by talking about any collaborative writing you've done before. What worked well? What didn't work so well? Why do you think things worked as they did? In addition to reflecting on your past collaborative writing experiences, discuss when you think certain kinds of collaboration are most helpful. You need to decide if you will use one model throughout your project or if you will use some sort of combined management approach.

To help you think about when to use what collaborative model, discuss the advantages and disadvantages of each model. For example, what are the advantages of working separately? But also discuss what the disadvantages of working separately are. When you have identified advantages and disadvantages for each of the models, discuss how you might predict and correct for the disadvantages and make the best of the advantages. For instance, if one of the disadvantages of working separately is that your final document sounds like it's written by several different people and doesn't sound like a unified document, how can you plan a way to correct for this disadvantage? And if one of the advantages of working integratively is that you can generate more ideas, how can you plan to take advantage of a high generation of ideas?

Planning for Varied Types of Collaboration

As you can see from the discussion above, collaboration is not always the same thing. There are various kinds of collaboration. Sometimes collaboration means being in the same physical place writing together. But other times it means working in physically separate places but working towards an agreed upon aim. How collaborative writing teams work depends on the group, the project, the resources, the amount of time, and many more factors. This is why it is important that your collaborative writing team work together to plan the ways you will collaborate.

However, there are some general patterns of the kinds of collaboration that go on during the process of writing in a collaborative team. The diagram below shows the kinds of collaboration by levels of collaborative intensity.

Planning Collaboration for Various Stages of Co-Authoring

Stages	Levels of Intensity	Notes/Suggestions
Planning	Heavy	Starting, Exploring, Positioning: this part should be carefully and collaboratively pursued for it lays out the foundation for the entire project
Drafting	Low	The highest collaborative intensity in this stage of the writing process is when you discuss document design. The collaborative team should all share a sense of the genre and the design of the document. You might want to talk about graphics at this point, also.
Critique/Testing	Moderate	This is the stage at which you should plan to ask for responses to your documents. You might even devise a document "test" to see if your document accomplishes what you want it to.
Revising	High	The collaborative team should develop a revising plan that critically reflects the planning and testing the group has done.
Editing	Moderate	You may want to establish different aims of editing for each team member so that each person has a greater critical focus.

Do not follow this chart point for point. It is meant to initiate discussion about how you might plan for the best kind of collaboration at various stages in your project. At this point, you might start to sketch out a general schedule of your project, including in it the levels of collaborative intensity at each stage. Be sure that you include time spent out of class on the project in your overall plan.

Deciding How You Will Deal with Conflict

When collaborating, you can count on conflict. Your collaborative team will need to make decisions about when to get together to work on your project, who will be responsible for what, when to have certain parts of the project completed, what your main goals for the project are, who you will write to, etc. Each of these decisions can lead to disagreements or conflicts. How will you work those out?

The first thing to remember is that all conflict is not "bad." Conflicts over issues of substance, often referred to as "substantive conflict," are good for collaboration. For instance, your collaborative writing team might disagree on the central problem you need to address. If you ignore this disagreement, pushing it under the carpet for the sake of reducing conflict, your project may suffer. It may suffer in various ways: you may actually be addressing a less important problem; members of your team might hold different conceptions of the problem in their minds as they work through the project, which can lead to further conflicts; or your final document might come off as "confused" because the collaborative team never fully discussed different perspectives on the problem/need. In order to avoid these faults, your need to have ways to address conflict in your group.

First, focus on achieving *consensus*. Consensus means that everyone on the collaborative team can *accept* a decision. This does not mean that everyone "gets their way." No, consensus usually means some members of the team, if not all, have to compromise some part of what they want. Consensus also does not mean a majority vote. Most likely you will be working in small teams, maybe with three in a group. A vote by majority could mean that one third of your group is not represented in your decision. Reaching consensus means you will have to discuss your differences.

In this process, avoid judgmental talk, talk that directly attacks another person or their views. Instead of judgmental talk, try making decisions based on previous decisions you may have made in the project, such as your main goal or your context. Use your planning work to help you make decisions. Look over your planning to see what question you have been addressing; review your exploration to review the data/evidence you have on your problem/need; review your positioning to consider how your decisions work within the constraints of your context while also helping you reach the position you want to achieve through the writing. Finally, work at describing the alternative positions that are being raised. It is best to catch alternatives on paper so everyone can refer to them. Each member of your group should be taking notes on the group's discussion, and your group should stop occasionally to summarize what has been discussed and address any issues that have not been resolved.

Making a Project Plan

A project plan is a visual representation of your project. Of course, the plan you make at the early stages of writing may be revised as you work through the project. You may discover that you need more or less time for certain parts of the project, and as you find this out, you can adjust your plan.

The project plan is used in several different ways. For your collaborative team, the project plan functions in two ways. First, it functions as a "contract" for the team's collaborative work. Therefore, it is important that everyone in the group participate in the construction of the project plan. The project plan also functions for your collaborative team as a schedule. Like any schedule, it helps you see what you have already accomplished and what you need to do next. For a boss, manager, or some sort of supervisor, the project plan functions in slightly different ways. At first, the plan informs the supervisor of your work plan, but it also persuades the supervisor that you are ready to begin work on your project. As you work through your project, the project plan works as an evaluative tool. The supervisor can evaluate how well you are reaching your goals.

For individual writers, the project plan functions in a slightly different way. Rather than making a team contract and schedule, the project plan makes a personal contract and schedule. In terms of a supervisor, the project plan works in the same way as described above.

The project plan should accomplish the following:

- list the tasks to be completed
- identify who will be responsible for what
- schedule the tasks chronologically
- identify periodic deadlines (i.e., drafts, peer review, revisions)
- identify the project's final due date

How the Project Plan Can Be Developed

As mentioned earlier, the project plan is a *visual* representation of your project. Therefore, you need to visualize the whole project. To visualize the project you need to 1) decide what *categories* you will use to mark the chronology of your project and 2) determine a way to *illustrate* the overall project.

Typically, the categories used are the *tasks* you have identified as critical to your project. Some of the *tasks* you have been learning as critical to writing in this textbook are differentiated as "writing strategies," such as starting, exploring, positioning, etc. You could use these strategies as your categories. As for ways to illustrate the whole project, a calendar is a simple and familiar tool for visualizing lengthy projects. Two methods used frequently in planning projects are illustrated in the example below. Use these to help you design your own visual representation of your project plan.

WORKSHOP

1. Once you have developed a project plan, review it to make sure it a) lists the tasks to be completed, b) develops a time-line of when tasks will be completed and when the project as a whole will be completed, c) identifies who will be responsible for what, and d) identifies critical points in the process (drafts, research, interviews, evaluations, meetings, etc.).

2. Write a brief evaluation of your project using these five points.

3. Share your plan and your evaluation with a peer group and/or your instructor.

Example: Audrey, Sara, and Shanna's Project Plan

Our Project Plan
- We have decided to work integratively throughout the process, so the project plan below does not distinguish who will do what. As you told us in class, we should try to make our project plans so we have a couple of things going on at the same time so if something goes wrong with one part, the rest of the project doesn't come to a halt. As you can see, we have planned our project so that we're doing exploring and the

beginning of positioning at the same time. The same goes for our polished draft feedback and our revisions. We decided those were the only places we wanted overlap. We also want to point out to you when we want feedback for our planning and our polished draft. On those dates, we will be turning those things into you and another group in the class that we've made a deal with to exchange work for peer review.

Sample Project Plan

Task	Start Date	Due Date
Starting	Wed. Oct 18	Fri. Oct. 20
Exploring	Fri. Oct. 20	Mon. Oct. 23
Positioning	Fri. Oct. 20	Wed. Oct. 25
Focusing	Fri. Oct 27	Fri. Oct. 27
Planning	Mon. Oct 30	Wed. Nov. 01
Polished Draft	Fri. Nov. 03	Fri. Nov. 10
Response and Revisions	Wed. Nov. 8	Fri. Nov. 10
Final Draft	Fri. Nov. 10	Mon. Nov. 13

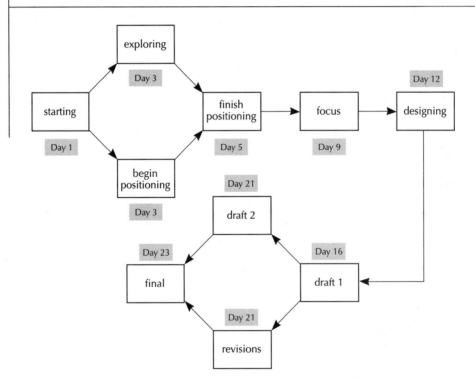

Exploring
Why use the Three Perspectives Guide?

Whether the initial inquiry into your project was done collaboratively or not, if you are working as a co-authoring team, the rest of the team will need to gain some knowledge of the specific workplace context being addressed by the team. To gain that knowledge, you can use the Three Perspective Guide as a means to discuss as a group the characteristics of your team's specific workplace context. This will help everyone become familiar with the team's specific workplace context. The Guide's perspectives can be found in Part II, but you will need to adapt them to your context.

You might return to the Three Perspective Guide to help you look not at the workplace context, as above, but to look at the specific problem/need that has been addressed. In other words, you can use this strategy at different times and in different ways to help you.

Why use library, Internet, and field research methodologies?

This chapter does not focus on any specific research strategies. However, research is often a critical part of workplace writing. Library research and Internet (Part II) helps you bring in expert arguments on various workplace problems/needs. One of the valuable things you can do for your workplace as a way to take initiative is to bring in new ideas from articles and books you would find through library or Internet research. The Field Research strategies (Part II) are very helpful for the kind of field research workplace writing projects might entail. If you have the time, you should consider doing some kind of research to help you develop an effective response to your workplace problem/need.

Positioning Writers and Readers

In any writing context, you are positioned. That means you have a particular role or set of roles in relation to others. Part of what the positioning strategy asks you to look at are the roles you play and the relationships you have within the writing context. These roles and relationships limit or constrain the kinds of things you can do. In workplace contexts, these constraints may be much more obvious and rule bound than in some other contexts. It may seem that because they are more obvious and rule bound that it is less important for you to analyze them. But the opposite is the case. It is even more important that you analyze your position within the workplace writing context. Why? If you overstep your position within the workplace, the consequences could be much greater than in less rule bound contexts where your position is less defined.

But *positioning* does not only mean looking at your roles and relationships. *Positioning* does not only mean finding out how you are constrained so you can "play by the rules." *Positioning* is also an action. In this way, the writer/reader positioning strategy asks you to see how you might act within the constraints of your writing context.

Since positioning in a workplace writing context is so important, you should consider using the Writer/Reader Positioning Strategy, Part II. See also Forum Analysis, Part II.

Selecting Genres

Before you can begin thinking about designing your document, the next strategy to be discussed, you need to consider your genre choices and then choose a genre for your project. One of the constraints of the workplace is the more rule bound positions and roles allowed. You have analyzed this kind of constraint in the Positioning strategy above. Another constraint in workplace writing is the kind of genres typically used and accepted. The Genre Strategy can help you increase the chances of writing a successful document within your specific workplace context. See Part II.

Focusing

By this point in your project, you have spent some time exploring your specific workplace problem/need. If your schedule permitted, you may have even done some research on the problem/need. Before you can begin drafting a response to your initial question of inquiry, you need to clearly identify what you have discovered through your inquiry. To do this, it will be helpful to use the two focusing strategies, Part II.

Designing a Document
Why Design Your Document?

The persuasive effect of whatever you are writing extends beyond the "content" of what you write. Especially in an age of desktop publishing, the "look" of what you write becomes a critical part of the overall effect of your document. This has always been the case. For instance, the teaching of "penmanship" and the choices of what color pen or pencil to write in are each examples of concerns for the "look" of writing. And as you know from experience, these kinds of choices make a difference in the effectiveness of documents.

Document design, though, is much more than making a document "look" pretty. When thinking about the design of documents, you need to think about such questions as: to whom are you writing? how will they be reading what you write? what will they be using your document for? how do you want to position yourself as a writer? and what emotional effect do you want your document to achieve? Document design is a huge field of study and there are organizations that make their entire business the study and production of well designed documents. Obviously you will not be able to address all of the concerns of document design. But in the strategy that follows, you will find ways to think more critically about the ways you shape and design your writing for specific purposes and in specific contexts.

DOCUMENT DESIGN STRATEGY

Write Down Your Planning Decisions / Think about the Page as a Unit of Design / Think about Your Reader / Think about the Persuasiveness of Your Document / Workshop

---

Writing Down Your Planning Decisions

The work of designing documents is not separate from the other work of writing. You need to integrate the planning work you have already accomplished in order to most effectively design your document. To do so, you should start by writing down your inquiry question and the action you want to achieve through the writing of this document. Your document design should also take into consideration your positioning. Instead of simply looking back at the work you did in the

424

positioning strategy, briefly re-describe how you want to position your reader and how you want to position yourself. When describing these choices, be clear about the constraints, too. After re-describing your positioning, write down the genre you have chosen. Genres also constrain what you can and cannot do when writing. When considering your genre, briefly outline the kinds of constraints the genre you have chosen places on you. Finally, write down the focus you have chosen. By this point, you want to have a clear, relatively brief summary of your planning decisions.

As you work through your document design decisions, you must be certain to reflect on the planning and drafting decisions you have been making throughout your project. The shape or design your document takes depends on these former decisions you have made.

Thinking About the Page as a Unit of Design

Writing can be broken down into different size units. For instance, when you first began learning to write, you were very conscious of writing at the level of individual letters. When designing documents, you need to look at writing from the unit of the page. You need to re-see a document as a sort of picture or frame. Have someone take a page of writing and hold it up for you to look at it from across the room, the way you might look at a painting. You are now seeing the page as a unit of design.

No matter if you are writing on a standard sized page, or if you are creating a brochure, or if you are making a flyer for a wall, you need to think about what your readers will see as a unit of design. For a brochure, there are several units of design. For example, the front cover, the inside cover, and the whole brochure opened up are all different page units. When making a document like a brochure, you need to think about the purpose of each of those page units, how they work together, and how they should be designed to achieve your project goals.

The Standard Page

The standard page can be designed in several different ways. In the workplace, you might find the following as the three basic ways of looking at the page as a unit of design.

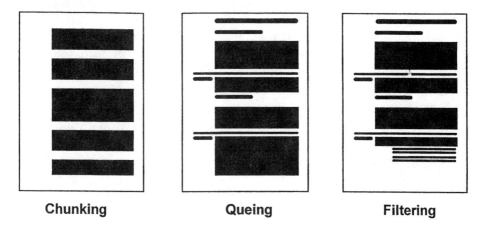

Chunking   **Queing**   **Filtering**

Notice that each general design uses headings, sub-headings, spacing, indentation, and lists or boxes to distinguish parts of the overall document. In addition to these design strategies, what is not so easily identified in the above examples is that headings, sub-headings, and body text are also distinguished by font size and highlighting. These design strategies increase the efficiency of reading and the reader's level of comprehension.

Documents do not "naturally" become "chunked" or "filtered." The -ing on the strategy names emphasizes the *action* writers take to construct documents. You should think about chunking, queing, and filtering not only as adjectives for describing the look of finished documents but also kinds of document design actions you can take.

Determining the Hierarchies of Your Document

To help you *act* as a document designer, you first need to determine the hierarchies of your document. Ask yourself the following questions:

- In what ways can my document be broken down into smaller pieces or categories? In other words, what headings and sub-headings might be appropriate to my document?
- What parts might be broken down into lists?
- What parts of my document might be important enough to be off-set from the rest of the document with boxes or shading?

Thinking About How Your Document Will be Used

The ways you design documents have a lot to do with the ways your readers will use your documents. For example, if you are trying to put together a set of shelves, you do not want the instructions to be in tiny fonts and organized into long paragraphs. In such a case, you as a reader need a document that is designed for easy reading and a document that leads you clearly from step to step. That is why instructions for putting together items like shelves are often written in fairly large print and enumerated.

The typical workplace reader does not have a lot of time. Efficiency is critical. Therefore, you typically want to design workplace documents so readers can find key points and the most important information very quickly.

In general, you can think of the ways your document might be used by considering some of the roles your readers might take when they read your document. Some of these roles, or patterns of use, are described below to help you design your document:

Skimmer: The skimming reader will read your document for the general idea and will spend very little time reading your document. You have to make sure that your document is designed to bring attention to the main points of what you are writing for the skimming reader.

Scanner: The scanning reader will also read quickly, but this reader is looking for specific information. For instance, a manager going through a stack of resumes for the first time is typically a scanning reader, looking for key information to eliminate some of the applicants for the job.

Search Reader: This reader is a scanner, but in addition to scanning, the search reader will give extended attention to some parts of your document.

Receptive Reader: The receptive reader reads for thorough comprehension. This is much the way you read a textbook for a course.

Critical Reader: The critical reader is reading for comprehension, but also reading to evaluate what is written. When you read an editorial in the newspaper, you are probably acting as a critical reader.

As you probably have realized, you will design your document differently for different kinds of readers. In terms of the page designs illustrated above, the skimmer and scanner need documents with much more queing and filtering. These two kinds of readers would generally find documents that lack these design features as unhelpful and even frustrating. Though the receptive reader and critical reader probably need queing and filtering less than the skimmer and scanner, queing and filtering can still increase the comprehension of your readers.

You have already determined a reader position that will help you think about how your document might be used. What the Writer/Reader Positioning Strategy does not help you think about is how your document might be used differently over time or in varying contexts. You should consider whether or not your document will be used differently at different times and in different contexts.

Write down the kind of reader you will be addressing and the context in which they will be reading your document. Write down your reader's goals. Why will they be reading your document? To complete a task? To become aware of a problem? To learn new information? Also, write down what you want your reader to *do*. Finally, make a short list of the kinds of documents your reader might commonly read in your specific workplace context.

Thinking About the Persuasiveness of Your Document

See Persuasive Appeals, Part II

In the process of designing your document, you need to contemplate the credibility, affective, and rational consequences of your design choices. Just by paying attention to design features, you will be positioning yourself in the workplace as more credible. In an academic context, typing a paper gives a student more credibility than handwriting a paper in pencil; in a workplace context, signs that a writer has conscientiously designed a document lend credibility to the writer.

To help you design a more persuasive document, make the following three lists. First, determine the ways credibility is gained in your workplace context. Second, determine the kinds of affective consequences various documents have in your workplace context. Finally, determine the kinds of arguments you are making in your document.

Once you have reflected on the general appeals of documents in your work-place context, you want to analyze your specific design context. Write out brief responses to the following questions to help you make choices about the design of your document.

- How are most documents designed in your workplace context?

- In what ways are documents designed differently by employees of different "rank" in your workplace context?

- What kinds of documents have helped others gain the kind of credibility you want in this context?

- In what ways do different fonts create different emotional responses (e.g., does one look more "technical" than another)? What emotional response do you want to provoke in your readers?

- How can you bring your reader's attention to your more critical arguments? Can you put them all into a list? Can you off-set them in a box or by shading? Have you distinguished separate arguments by headings and sub-headings?

WORKSHOP

1. Review your document design planning by writing out your key decisions. Share these with your group.

2. In addition to writing down your key decisions, make a sketch or several sketches of the "look" your document will take according to your plan.

Example: Audrey, Sara, and Shanna's Document Design

Prior Decisions

Question:	• How can I persuade Beth, without attacking her, that if she and others pull their own weight at work, work will be a lot better for us all?
Writer Position:	• Senior Instructor
Reader Position:	• co-worker
Genre:	• combination of memo and flyer
Focus:	• If everyone does her own work and helps one another, everyone else will be happier and more productive at work.

- **determining hierarchies**
  - A flyer would have some bright colors and big headings to catch people's attention, but a memo would be more subdued. We need to find some balance between these two.
  - A memo would have paragraphs and big chunks of small text to read.
  - Even though a memo might go over a page, we would have to keep our document to a page.

- •A memo would have a heading section identifying to whom the document was addressed. Again, what balance would we need between and memo and a flyer?
- •If we included the Little Red Hen analogy, it would probably go at the bottom.
- •We want to set off the key questions we are asking and some sort of moral or directive.

- **thinking about readers**
  - •At first, our readers would be skimmers, and we would need to catch their attention.
  - •But then we would have receptive and critical readers.
  - •We want our readers to see themselves as somewhat implicated in the problem of some people not doing the work they are responsible for. And we want Audrey's co-workers to change their behavior and attitude.

- **thinking about persuasiveness**

Credibility

- Audrey has first hand experience of the problem, and she has authority because not only has she been there a long time, but she was offered the position of Head Instructor (Beth's position) of gymnastics.
- Audrey has not talked with Jane about the problem and has shown respect for Beth, so no one will see her as being a tattle-tale.

Affective appeals

- We want the co-workers to be sympathetic of Audrey and themselves, not Beth. We want them to relate to the people who have to pick up the slack.
- We want the audience to see us (Audrey) as understanding of the difficulty of the positions everyone holds and the good work they do.

Rational appeals

- Others get mad at Audrey when she has to leave early because it makes them have to put the equipment away.
- Jane could come in and supervise.
- If one person doesn't do the work, someone has to.
- Everyone has other things to do, so they can't keep picking up the slack and interfering in other responsibilities.

Organizing

After planning the design of your document but before you begin drafting, you need to plan the ways you might organize your document. Certainly, your genre and document design decisions help you envision the organization of your document, but you must still make choices about the document's organization if it is to be most effective. Using the organizing strategy in Part II, write out a brief plan of the whole document organization and the section organization as discussed in the strategy.

Example: Audrey, Sara, and Shanna's Organizing Memo

MEMORANDUM
    TO: Tim Peeples
    FR: Audrey, Sara, and Shanna
    DT: Nov. 01
    RE: Organization decisions

We have decided that instead of using the organization strategy as we typically do, we will write a memo to you summarizing our organization decisions. We will be turning in our polished draft on Friday and hope this memo will help you in responding to our draft.

Writing Context

First, we need to summarize some of our reader decisions, considering there have been several changes over the process of writing. We chose to write to Audrey's co-workers hoping that they would become aware of the problem and maybe something would come of it. We also decided to write to Jane, the Head of Youth, because she is in charge and can take control of the situation.

Genre, Design, Organization

We have decided to write a memo that also has some characteristics of a flyer. We want to avoid being positioned as too formal, and we think something that is kind of like a flyer, with some color, would be less formal. But since we are writing from the position of "Senior Instructor," we have the authority to write something formal, like a memo.

Because we're not writing a formal memo, we are not going to have the typical memo heading. Instead, we'll have something like "Attention" at the top. And then at the bottom, we'll have something more like a flyer that sums up the document.

However, we will have a traditionally organized memo in the middle. Our organization will be (1) to make people aware of the problem, (2) to explain the problem in detail, and (3) to express strongly our feelings about the problem.

Drafting

Even the most experienced workplace writers write several drafts when they are writing major reports. Often the process of drafting requires writers to send drafts "up" to one and even many levels of management within an organization. If a document serves as any kind of binding contract between, for instance, the organization and clients, drafts will most likely be reviewed by a legal department or legal advisor. Consequently, many drafts are written for most workplace reports. Making drafting part of your writing process increases the probability that you and your work will be well accepted, clear, and professional in appearance. See Drafting Strategies, Part II.

Example: Audrey, Sara, and Shanna's Polished Draft

ATTENTION
Jane and All Gymnastic Instructors
(From Audrey)

Currently, it has been brought to my attention that some of our fellow co-workers have been slacking off on their responsibilities. It seems to me as if I have been doing certain tasks that are not my responsibility and tasks that are supposed to be shared are left to be done by a *few* co-workers, not *all*. I understand that we all have other responsibilities that we need to tend to. Yet when we were hired, it was made clear to us what our job was and how it was to be done. Lately, this has not been followed through with.

I give credit that everyone met up to the standards of teaching and getting their job done, in the beginning. Lately, though, it seems as though the attitudes and care for how things get done have seriously declined. I understand that with all of us in school it is a challenge to everyone to be as dedicated as we were in the summer, but it is a give-and-take situation. I know that people tend to get upset when I have to leave early to take an exam or go to a study session, but I *make it a point* to make up for this later.

Maybe it is going to take bringing in Jane to supervise us to make us get things done. Is this what we all want, to be treated like little kids? If that is the case, so be it. I feel, though, as if we are mature enough to correct this problem without the intervention of a third party. In conclusion I hope that this can be solved and not turn out like the story of the Little Red Hen.*

*Little Red Hen: It is a story about a hen who asks for all kinds of help from other animals to get materials to make bread. Of course they all say no, and she does it herself. Later the animals need a favor—food— and the little red hen says no. Maybe if they would have helped just a little they would have been rewarded.

Remember:
If everyone does her own work and helps one another,
then everyone else will be happier.

Responding and Revising
Why Respond?

In the workplace, you will receive and give lots of responses to documents. A major difference between typical academic writing and writing in the workplace is that the writing you do in the workplace is "authorized" by the organization/ company for whom you work. In other words, *you* are not the "author." The "author" is the organization/company. Since this is the case, most of the writing you do will be responded to, revised, and worked on by many people. In addition to learning how to receive feedback from others and to incorporate that feedback into your revisions, you need to learn how to offer helpful feedback to others. The Reader Response Strategy (Part II) helps you work through responding to documents in a more organized and helpful way.

Why Revise?

In the workplace, the answer to the question, "Why revise?" can be quite simple: Your job is on the line. Of course, there are other, sometimes equally important reasons. For instance, the documents you produce are a representation of you and the organization for whom you work. If you are not careful to revise, you hurt not only your own professional reputation but also that of your organization. Because organizations are typically in the service of some sort of clientele, it is important that you revise also for the good of your clients. Refer to the Revising Strategy, Part II.

Example: Audrey, Sara, and Shanna's Revision

ATTENTION
Jane and All Gymnastic Instructors
From Audrey

Recently it has been brought to my attention that some of our fellow co-workers have been "slacking off" on their responsibilities. I have to agree that it seems as if I have been spending a lot more time doing certain tasks that are not my sole responsibility. The tasks that I have been spending an increased amount of time working on are those tasks that have been traditionally *shared* tasks done by us all *together*.

I certainly understand all of the other responsibilities that we all need to attend to. At work, we have our own students, their parents, and the gym equipment to attend to. And now that school is back in session, we all have the extra pressures of attending to our school work. During the summer when we all could focus on work and didn't have classes to worry about, there seemed to be no problem. Now that we're all back in school, even though we have more to attend to, it is *because* we *all* have more to attend to that we must be sure to carry our weight at work.

I know we cannot keep on with the way things are; it's not fair, it makes work unpleasant, it affects our ability to do our jobs well, and it might cause us to lose some fine instructors. *I don't think* we want to have to bring Jane in to supervise us to make us get things done: we don't want to be treated like kids, do we? *I believe* we are mature and responsible enough to correct this problem without intervention. I hope that this can be solved by us together and not turn out like the story of the Little Red Hen.*

*Little Red Hen: It is a story about a hen who asks for all kinds of help from other animals to get materials to make bread. Of course they all say no, and she does it herself. Later the animals need a favor—food—and the little red hen says no. Maybe if they would have helped just a little they would have been rewarded.

Remember:
If everyone does her own work and helps one another,
we all will be happier and more productive at work.

CONCLUSION

By this point, you have had the opportunity 1) to read a detailed case of one co-authoring group working through an entire workplace problem/need project, 2) to follow some of the parts of another student co-authoring group working on a workplace problem/need project, and 3) to inquire and act within a workplace context of your own. The strategies you have used throughout this chapter can be adapted to other workplace writing projects, and can help you inquire and act more effectively in those contexts.

One of the surprises that much workplace writing brings is the amount of work that can go into what looks like a simple document. For instance, Audrey, Sara, and Shanna spent a little over three weeks exploring, planning, designing, drafting, and revising a one-page document. This is not always the case in the workplace. Much of the writing done in the workplace becomes routine, just as some of your academic writing does. However, when you are faced with new, or particularly dynamic and volatile workplace problems/needs, you can benefit greatly by more conscientiously inquiring and acting, as you have done in this chapter, and as you have read about others doing.

Part II

Alternative Strategies, Genres, Collaboration, and On-line Resources

9

INVENTION STRATEGIES

JANICE LAUER AND ANDREA LUNSFORD

Starting Strategies

Why Use a Starting Strategy?

Starting to write is daunting for most of us. Because this is often the act that stumps us, there are things you can do instead of staring at the blank page. Some of these are long range strategies like keeping a journal so that you regularly are writing. Other ways to begin are quite informal, like freewriting. Still others give more guidance, like the Questioning strategy below. The technique you use also depends on the type of writing you are doing. While the strategies offered here do not exhaust your possibilities, they offer you a few ways to start.

QUESTIONING STRATEGY
Select a Subject / Get in Touch with Dissonance / Locate Your Subject in a Writing Context/ Raise Questions

---

When you write to inquire, you are using writing to investigate puzzling aspects of your subject. Instead of just communicating what you already know, you can learn something through writing. Inquiry always begins with questions, not answers. But raising good questions is not easy because often your previous education has stressed having good answers, not questions. This strategy is designed to help you shape the direction of your inquiry so that you begin with those aspects of your subject that you find most compelling to further understand. Without a strategy to guide writing as inquiry, you can often waste a lot of time in your investigation. This strategy also helps you to decide what context you will write in: who will be your readers. It is important from the beginning of your writing process to include in your investigation those with whom you will share your new ideas. Since writing as inquiry holds so much potential for you, it is important that you begin well.

The Questioning Strategy helps you undertake these important efforts well. After you list meaningful subjects, the Strategy helps you to identify **dissonances** or clashes—those aspects of your experience that don't quite fit with your values and expectations. You experience dissonances constantly in your life—some important, some insignificant. You are assigned a roommate whose habits and interests are the opposite of yours, yet you think you'll like this person. You expected your boyfriend to be understanding about your college plans, but that has turned out badly. Why? You encounter a theory in your psychology class that challenges your religious beliefs. You meet someone form another country or race that shatters your preconceptions. All of these dissonances are opportunities for not only further understanding these subjects but also yourself and where your expectations and values come from. Dissonances are the driving force behind writing as inquiry because they put you in touch with how you could learn something important to you and therefore make the writing process worth your while.

The strategy activities in bold type give you steps to take as you carry out your inquiry. See the student examples in the shaded boxes for illustrations of how other students have used the strategy in their work.

Selecting a Subject for Inquiry

List subjects that matter

As you begin work in your writing contexts, brainstorm a list of subjects within that context that provoke strong reactions. Try for several subjects. Note down your immediate reaction when you think of the subject. Here are some examples from different areas of inquiry:

Examples:

- soccer coach: I admired him more than anyone else in my life
- my dad: he expects me to study what he thinks is right for his son
- my neighborhood organization: we were frustrated trying to get everyone to clean up the area
- my African-American friends: does rap music still encourage us to hope or does it have a negative effect?
- promotion practice where I work: promotion seems to correspond directly with the amount of formal education rather than the quality of work or commitment to the organization

Choose a subject for inquiry

Which of these subjects puzzles you the most?

Which one would you like to better understand?

Which one holds more consequences for you, if you investigate it?

Which one stimulates more feelings of discomfort or exhilaration?

Getting in Touch with Dissonance

- **Identify experiences in your writing context that puzzle you**
- **Write down your values or expectations that relate to those experiences**
- **Mention some sources of your values**
- **Analyze your dissonance**

> Has your experience challenged your value?
>
> Has your experience fallen short of your value?
>
> Has your experience exceeded your value?

Locating Your Subject in a Writing Context

Writing is done in a context of readers: your family, your class, a group of friends. A writing context includes a group of people who participate in an activity together, such as work or a sport; who share an identity or history; who live in the same location; or who are related. A writing context is a situation in which a group of readers and writers already communicate with one another through writing or who could appropriately do so. You are, for example, already part of a composition course context in which you share papers. You are not yet, however, in a writing context of nuclear physicists. Personal writing contexts are likely to include members of your family or friends. You may be members of political or religious groups to which you belong or readers of publications to which you contribute. In the academic world, your writing contexts are comprised of the professors and students in your disciplinary fields and courses. At work, your writing context may include your superiors and fellow workers. Each of these contexts has its own expectations about writing and its own conventions.

The context, then, has an important influence on how you and your readers will regard your subject: what they will consider important; what they will be willing to read about; what subjects they consider off limits—all of these factors have a bearing on what you can write about. Therefore, choosing possible contexts now will benefit your inquiry by gearing it towards your eventual readers.

Identify the possibilities

Almost all writing has multiple readers and contexts. For example a textbook is written for students and teachers. One is usually primary—the one to which the writer directs the text. The others read knowing that the book is directed to the primary readers. In a writing class, the instructor is always a reader; often the other students are readers. Sometimes department faculty read your text as a part of a portfolio. These are not the only readers, however. This book aims to help you write in situations that involve other contexts as well. In these cases, the instructor and students are secondary readers, coaching you as you interact with your primary readers.

Examples:

- the fast food place where I work: special orders are accepted but prepared inefficiently and usually messed up

- my job at the local plant: even though our building at work is "smoke free," my boss and, consequently, many of my coworkers continue to smoke in the lounge

- the small company I work at: because I've moved out on my own and work full-time, I'm no longer eligible for my parent's health plan, but the small company I work for doesn't provide health care and I can't afford it on my own.

Formulating Questions for Inquiry

Choose a puzzlement you want to investigate

Inquiry can occur when you find yourself in puzzling circumstances such as:

- an encounter that challenges one of your family traditions or values

- a situation in college that doesn't fit your expectations

- new ideas in classes that clash with what you've learned before

- problems in groups to which you belong

- disagreements with friends over the merits of a TV series or a song

These situations, which generate intense feelings that you can't at the moment explain, offer the richest occasions for writing as inquiry. If these disturbing feelings are about matters important to you, they are worth investigating through writing. Posing questions will help you to determine what you don't know yet but want to find out.

Pose questions that capture the kinds of responses or answers you seek

The way you pose your question will lead to different kinds of responses:

- **new understanding**
  What was it about the residents of the nursing home that inspired me even though their circumstances were sad? How could I share this understanding with them in writing

- **the cultural sources (values and practices that affect your subject)**
  What cultural attitudes toward different groups of people prompted my mother to help some but not others? Where do I stand on this? How does this impact my relationship with her? Could I explore this in writing with my family?

- **a course of action**

  In what ways, can I relate to my mother that will help both me and my sister reach our own goals yet still respect my mother's values? Could I write her a letter?

- **solution to a problem**

  What could our volunteer group do to better the conditions in the nursing home?

  How could we communicate our suggestions to the directors of the home?

FOCUSED FREEWRITING

This is another strategy for starting your writing.

- Write for 15 minutes on your topic. Don't control or critique your writing—just write. Keep moving, allowing one idea to lead to another.
- Read your freewriting and star anything that is puzzling or unanswered about your subject.
- Pick an aspect you have starred and freewrite on it again.

PROJECT PLANNING

Project planning helps to guide a group project.

Why Plan Your Project:

As this textbook instructs and illustrates, good writing is more than a grammatically correct final product/document. Rather, good writing is a process of inquiry and action. In any context, it can be helpful to plan one's writing process, but in the workplace and on co-authored projects, it is critical that writers plan their writing projects.

In the workplace, project planning functions in several ways: to guide the writers' work; to propose projects; to make funding decisions; to manage resources; and to evaluate progress. For the writers of a project, the project planning does more than simply map out the steps of production; the project planning is a critical stage where writers discuss and negotiate "How will this group of writers on this project best work together?"

Collaboration

When you co-author, you have to consider carefully the ways you manage your collaboration. As you know from having others comment on your writing, your collaboration with them is negotiated: you negotiate what needs to be changed, not accepting one or the other's opinion without first considering alternatives and discussing your choices. This negotiating process is even more intense when you co-author. Below, you will find some strategies for negotiating your co-authoring process.

Reaching Consensus

One note about the following strategy. Each part raises questions rather than giving you answers. Thus, your co-authoring group will be engaged in responding to questions, and this will lead to discussion and varying opinions. As you work collaboratively, you should try to work toward **consensus**. A position founded upon consensus is defined as a position that everyone in the collaborative group can accept; consequently, consensus usually means that everyone compromises some part of what they want. In your groups, you should work to achieve these kinds of consensual agreements.

Deciding What Kind of Collaboration Management Model You Will Use

There are three basic models of collaboration management:

- division-of-labor
- integrative
- combined

Collaborating under a *division-of-labor* model would have each member of the group working separately on discrete tasks within the overall project. Usually, tasks are assigned according to expertise. Under the *integrative* model, co-authoring work is done together, each member working as an integral part of each stage in the projects process. Under this model, no one is assigned as a specific expert, rather people's roles shift and change throughout the process according to what needs to be done within the group. Typically, collaboration happens in some sort of *combined* management model, some tasks separated and others accomplished in a fully integrated fashion.

What collaboration management model will you use?

Will you use this model throughout the process of your project?

What are the benefits of this model?

What are the disadvantages?

Are there ways to correct for the disadvantages?

Planning Levels/Intensities of Collaboration

Though workplace practices are not necessarily what we *should* imitate, it helps to know how writing is done in the workplace. The diagram below shows the intensity of collaboration as it happens in the typical workplace throughout the writing process. You might use this to initiate ways to talk about managing your project process.

Stages	Levels of Collaboration	Notes/Suggestions
Planning	Heavy	Starting, Exploring, Positioning: this part should be carefully and collaboratively pursued for it lays down the foundation for the entire project.
Drafting	Low	You might want to talk about graphics at this point.
Critique/Testing	Moderate	This is the stage where you should plan to ask for responses to your documents. You might even devise a document "test" to see if your document accomplishes what you want it to.
Revising	High	The collaborative group should develop a revising plan that critically reflects the planning and testing the group has done.
Editing	Moderate	You may want to establish different aims of editing for each team member so that each person has a greater critical focus. In this way, the group works collaboratively to plan who will do what—who will check spelling, who will check comma usage, who will check for parallel structuring, etc.—but then each individual works independently.

Deciding How You Will Deal with Conflict

Conflict is not necessarily "bad." Research in collaborative writing suggests that conflicts that center around personalities and processes of getting work done (process conflict) are negative kinds of conflict. However, the kind of conflict that deals with disagreements about "rhetorical" alternatives—audience choices, persuasive appeals, etc.—can be helpful. With this kind of conflict, you should

- focus on achieving **consensus** (see opening),
- avoid **judgmental talk**, and work at **describing** the alternatives that are being raised.

To help make choices,

- use the planning work you have developed,
- look over your planning to see what question you have been addressing,
- review your exploration to determine what data/evidence you have on your problem/need,
- review your positioning to consider how your decisions work within the constraints of your context while also helping you reach the position you want to achieve through the writing.

Making a Project Plan

A project plan helps you see what needs to be done next, what has been done, and when things need to be done. A project plan should include the following:

- list of tasks to be completed
- who will be responsible for what
- schedule of the process
- periodic deadlines (drafts, comments from teacher, revision, etc.)
- final deadline

The process of developing the project can be traced by the strategy guides you have been using to this point. You can use starting, exploring, positioning, etc. to help you identify discrete stages of your process.

Reviewing Your Plan

Once you have generated a project plan, review it to make sure it achieves the following:

- lists the tasks to be completed
- develops a time-line of when tasks will be completed and the project completed
- identifies who will be responsible for what
- identifies critical points in the process (drafts, research, interviews, evaluations, meetings, etc.)

Exploring Strategies

Why explore?

If you have raised a question that is pressing and genuine, you increase the chances of reaching a satisfying answer if you conduct a thorough investigation. To guide your exploration, you and your group can use sets of directives and questions

- to trigger your memory or stimulate your imagination,
- prompt lines of critique or sharpen your powers of reasoning about your question, and
- direct you to gather further information.

The strategies below can help you conduct a wide-ranging investigation that breaks through your mental ruts and customary viewpoints.

Why explore in writing?

It's a good idea to conduct your investigation on paper because the very act of writing down:

- has heuristic, or discovery, power,

- records your ideas,
- allows you to review and evaluate them.

THREE PERSPECTIVES GUIDE
Describe and Distinguish/ Trace Moves and Changes/ Map
Networks and Relationships

This guide is a powerful one because you can use it in any writing context: Its three perspectives can be adapted to help you recall experiences in detail, to make imaginative connections, and to probe the cultural connections of your beliefs and values. You can use this guide in any order or move back and forth as your ideas come to you. The investigation is for your benefit—to help you reach an understanding that satisfies you and readers in your primary community. Sometimes in the middle of exploring, you will glimpse an insight. Be sure to note it down. But continue because further exploring may challenge this early answer. When using this strategy, write ideas freely without worrying about sentence structure, grammar, spelling, or punctuation.

Investigating Your Question from Three Perspectives
Write down your question and writing context

The questions under each perspective below are an adaptation of a more complex guide, the tagmemic guide, developed in a textbook by Richard Young, Alton Becker, and Kenneth Pike. In each of your writing contexts, it helps if you adapt or tailor the general questions here to fit that context. The examples below are taken from a variety of writing contexts.

Describe and Distinguish

This perspective will guide you to recall aspects of your subject in detail, noting those features that are especially distinctive and vivid in your memory. Some of these specifics might be important in answering your question. Looking closely at your subject also allows you to brainstorm ideas that may be useful later in writing your paper. Putting your memories in words forces you to find your own language for your experience—how do you define your subject? What does your subject look like, smell like, to you, to others.

- What's distinctive to you about your subject? To those in your writing context?
- How would you describe your subject to someone in that context unfamiliar with it?
- What physical features characterize your subject (sights, sounds, etc., emotions, attitudes)? What bearing do they have on your question?
- What sort of day-to-day activities do you associate with this subject?

- What is your attitude toward this value? Acceptance? Challenge? Rejection? Indifference? Why?

- When you think of your subject, what recurring images come to mind? What feelings are aroused? Do others in your context share these emotions?

Trace Moves and Changes

The perspective emphasizes changes that occur either as they are prompted by significant events or as they evolve gradually over time. Here are some questions to pursue.

- How did your experience with the subject begin?

- How has your subject changed? How do these changes relate to the question you are investigating?

- How have you, your attitude, or feelings changed? What about those in your context?

- What larger cultural changes have influenced your subject? (e.g., the changing roles of women, the end of the Cold War, the introduction of VCR's or the Internet)

Map Networks and Relationships

This perspective makes connections between your subject and ideas, subjects, and cultural values and practices.

Group your subject.

Grouping is helpful for understanding your subject. Once you have placed your particular subject in a larger group, you can make connections between your subject and the general characteristics associated with that group. In addition, sometimes describing your subject from within a larger, more generalized framework makes it easier to construct important features. Usually a subject can be placed in many groups.

In what groups can you place your subject? What connections can you make to other subjects in the group?

Compare or contrast your subject.

Comparing your subject to others that are similar or different allows you to generate many new ideas about the features that are alike or different about your subject.

- Identify points of similarity between your subject and others. Then identify points of difference with others subjects.

Create an analogy or metaphor for your subject.

Analogies and metaphors are ways of making connections between your subject and other unusual subjects such as an item of clothing, a location, or a holiday. Feel free to use your imagination to connect your subject to whatever pops into your mind.

- To what object, animal, place, or event would you compare it? Why?
- How would your analogy strike those in your writing context?

Examine cultural narratives.

Cultural narratives are common story lines used throughout a culture, telling how things typically happen. Once you identify some of the cultural narratives that apply to your subject, you can examine them for assumptions and stereotypes. For example, stereotypes, or rigid, generalized ideas about the character or behavior of people with certain identities (boy, girl) are a more particular kind of assumption. As with cultural narratives, you may think you are not affected by these assumptions and stereotypes. However, their pervasive presence in the culture means that everyone is affected by them. Naming these assumptions and stereotypes can aid you when describing the impact of cultural values on your particular subject.

The assumptions operating in cultural narratives found in movie plots and song lyrics also get played out in social practices and social institutions. Social practices are shared, habitual ways of doing things. A variety of guidelines exist for the social practice of dating, for instance: who will initiate the date, who will decide where to go, who will pay. Social institutions are larger, more formalized organizations that direct our shared social structures. Here are some questions to help you explore the cultural connections with your subject:

- How is your subject characterized in your writing context?
- What cultural narratives govern your subject?
- What assumptions, stereotypes, habits, social practices, and institutions frame your subject, questions, and values?
  - Stereotypes about gender roles, "families," "communities"?
  - Habits and assumptions in communicating and learning?
  - Church doctrines or practices? Which? Political parties and platforms? Which ones?
  - World events? Which? TV series? Which? Movies? Which?
  - Books? Magazines? Newspapers? Which ones? Advertising? Which ads? Why?
  - Fashions? Which? Hero figures? Who? Games? Toys? Sports? Entertainment? Which?
  - Family rituals?

Review Your Ideas and Highlight Those That Answer Your Question

You have just generated a lot of material. While you were doing so, you may not have seen connections between the work you were doing, and the question you are raising. Take time now to look over your Three Perspective notes with the idea of searching for pieces of answers to your question. Note those parts that you may be able to use to create an answer.

Allow Your Ideas to Incubate

Inquiry takes place subconsciously as well was consciously. Allow yourself time to set aside your inquiry and let your non-conscious mind explore for answers.

STRATEGIES FOR DEVELOPING AND EVALUATING PERSUASIVE APPEALS
Credibility Appeals, Affective Appeals, Rational Appeals

The following strategies are designed to help you develop persuasive appeals. They are divided into three categories: credibility, affective, and rational. These classifications will help you keep in mind the many assumptions, attitudes, ideas, and feelings people use when they consider the claim you are making in your writing.

Restate your focus and writer/reader positions

Constructing Credibility Appeals

These appeals help to establish your writer position as one who deserves trust and respect. Often you will address readers you have never met, and they will only be willing to meet your challenges to their ideas and values if they can respect the writer position you have set. In your text:

1. Refer to shared values.

2. Refer to shared background and/experience, usually pertaining directly to the issue.

3. Refer to the part of your writer position that will prompt readers to listen to you. What authority, experience, or knowledge will confirm for your readers that you are worth listening to.

Constructing Affective Appeals

We don't really have emotions apart from our ideas and experiences. Consequently, crafting appeals to readers' emotions is more a matter of *how* we present credibility and rational appeals. It also involves avoiding arousing feelings that would alienate or anger readers.

1. Determine what emotional state would prompt your readers to respond to your focus.

2. Identify what emotional state would be most likely to move readers away from your focus.

3. Use connotation, vivid language, and striking examples to invoke those emotions you desire in your readers.

Constructing Rational Appeals

The following list includes many frequently used appeals (arguments). Decide which ones will help you persuade your readers.

1. **USE AN EXAMPLE, STORY, OR NARRATIVE.** When you provide concrete pictures of the ideas you put forth or tell stories that illustrate your point, you are providing examples. Examples are an especially important rational appeal because they can perform so many functions. An example can illustrate shared experiences and values. The way you describe something or tell a story can also raise or quell your readers' emotions. Examples can be as short as a sentence, or your whole text can be one extended story—or narrative—that brings your readers to understand your focus.

2. **PROVIDE A DEFINITION.** Often a problem turns on how the parties involved define an important term.

3. **PROPOSE A MODEL OR A PLAN.** Issues may have been resolved in a different context. The way an issue was dealt with there may serve as a model for your own issue. If you are confronting a specific problem, that plan might serve as the solution to the problem. If you are proposing a solution or plan, the major part of your text may be a description of that plan.

4. **STATE AN IDEAL, PREMISE, OR PRINCIPLE.** These are usually "sayings" or values that both you and your readers share.

5. **DESCRIBE CAUSES/EFFECTS.** Sometimes causes and effects can be explained in one-sentence "If, then" clauses. In other cases historical background may establish a cause/effect relationship.

6. **DESCRIBE CONSEQUENCES.** Like cause/effect, consequences establish a relationship between two things. Consequences differ in that the relationship may not be as direct or immediate. For example, consequences can be something that "may" happen in the future.

7. **ESTABLISH A CONNECTION BETWEEN PERSONS AND ACTIONS OR THE LACK OF CONNECTION.** This appeal may take several forms. You might suggest that a certain type of person or a character trait is associated with a particular action. Similarly, you can suggest that an action is identified with a certain type of character.

8. **RELATE MEANS TO ENDS.** This appeal can be used in a number of ways. It can be simply descriptive or it can express some form of the judgment that an end does or does not justify certain means.

9. **SHOW A DIRECTION IN A STAGE OR PROCESS.** This appeal can be used to analyze a present condition, evaluate what has come before, and suggest what may happen in the future. Sometimes you can suggest that your focus is a step in the direction of a greater change.

10. **USE CLASSIFICATIONS.** This appeal may involve putting your subject or issue in a certain group. Sometimes you may argue that this element or issue has been put in an inappropriate group.

11. **USE COMPARISONS AND CONTRASTS.** Your classifications may provide starting points for comparisons or contrasts that support your focus.

12. **APPEAL TO SHARED AUTHORITY.** This authority can be a person or reference source.

13. **CREATE AN ANALOGY.**

TOULMIN'S SYSTEM OF ANALYSIS

This guide was adapted from the work of Stephen Toulmin, a modern philosopher. His system is particularly helpful in analyzing arguments or in examining your own arguments. We offer here a simplified form of the Toulmin system, which asks that you answer the following questions:

1. What is the *claim* being made?
2. What are the *grounds* or *good reasons* that support the claim?
3. What *underlying assumptions* support the grounds?
4. What *backup evidence* exists to add further support?
5. What *refutations* can be made against the claim?
6. In what way(s) is the claim *qualified?*

As an example, let us assume you have been asked to examine a brief prepared by a striking union on your campus. You could gather information for your analysis by asking and answering Toulmin's questions:

(1) What claim do the strikers make? The claim may well be that the employer should provide increased health benefits, so let's take that as our example.

(2) What are the grounds for this claim? After interviewing union officials, you find that health care is inadequate and that a disproportionate amount of the workers' salaries must go to providing health care; they feel these grounds justify their claim.

(3) This claim and grounds suggest a number of underlying assumptions that you could examine, the most obvious one being that workers at the college have a right to adequate health care. The underlying assumptions are often omitted from an argument because the writer assumes agreement on them, but it is important in an analysis to uncover and evaluate these assumptions.

(4) What backup support could the union offer to support the assumption that they have a right to adequate health care? A clause in their contract, perhaps, or a legal precedent established by other groups in their position? Can you think of any other means of backup support?

(5) If the union's brief is effective, it will no doubt have considered possible refutations to its claim and offered answers to these refutations. Your job is to analyze these answers.

(6) Finally, you should determine whether the claim is qualified in any way. Are there, for instance, any conditions under which the union would *not* press its claim? If so, these are the qualifications.

Answering Toulmin's questions in the way demonstrated here can thus help you gather information necessary to analyze any argument, whether or not it is your own.

A DEDUCTIVE CHAIN

The deductive chain is a widely used informal rational appeal. When you have difficult readers who hold a position opposite from yours, this persuasive strategy helps you establish points of agreement from which to argue. Or when you struggle to reach your own probable judgment, a chain can help you consider your readers' views as you investigate. How does it work?

The chain has three statements:

1. A principle that both you and the reader accept,
2. A linking statement that you must prove, and
3. A conclusion, the focus you want the reader to accept.

If your reader is unlikely at the outset to respond favorably to your focus, you can establish a principle on which you both agree. For example, if you want to persuade your instructor that "final exams are detrimental to students," you will probably not gain immediate acceptance. Such a frontal attack might be fatal. You must search for a principle with which she might agree, such as: "Any educational practice that promotes artificial learning is detrimental to students." If she does not agree with this principle, you must find a different one or try to convince her of it. If she agrees, you can build an argument on this shared belief by creating a link with your subject such as: "Final examinations promote artificial learning." Now you have to prove that final examinations do that. Let's examine the chain you have created:

Principle: Any educational practice that promotes artificial learning is detrimental to students.

Linking Statement: Final examinations promote artificial learning.

Conclusion: Final exams are detrimental to students.

Notice that you have shifted proof from the conclusion to the linking statement. If you can persuade your reader of the truth of this statement, using the three appeals, your conclusion will fall into place. The value of the chain is that you start with a belief shared with your readers. Finding shared beliefs is one of the keys to successful persuasion. You can argue for a conclusion forever, but you may be wasting your breath if you are working within no shared assumptions. Effective persuasion is always collaborative.

You can construct a chain to reach a judgment, to share a conclusion, or both. If you have a focus, you can work backward from it, looking for a link and a principle within which to argue. If you are searching for a focus, you can set shared principles about your subject and work forward to convince yourself of a conclusion.

You can also use a deductive chain to structure whole papers by stating the principle in the introduction, writing the remainder of the paper to prove the linking statement, and then stating the conclusion at the end. These chains can also work within a single paragraph that begins with or implies a principle, elaborates the linking statement, and then advances or implies the conclusion. For example, here are some deductive nuggets from different pieces of writing. Notice that in some of the selections, one statement of the chain is only implied, not stated explicitly.

> "If we accept that a child cannot learn unless taught through the language he speaks and understands . . . then any necessary effective educational program for limited or no English speaking ability must incorporate . . . language arts taught in the child's native language. . . . " (Angelo Gonzales and Luis O. Reyes, "The Keys to Basic Skills," *New York Times*)
>
> "The people who framed the Bill of Rights believed that we had a right to be secure in our homes, our persons and papers and effects, and that the Government had no right to intrude on that area of privacy without probable cause, a determination usually to be made by a judge. We're concerned about the rights of young people in an institutional setting." (Jeffrey Fogel, "An Invasion of Privacy," *New York Times*)
>
> "The bombing of Hiroshima was an act of terrorism; its purpose was political, not military. The goal was to kill enough civilians to shake the Japanese government and force it to surrender. And this is the goal of every terrorist campaign." (Michael Walzer, "Hiroshima: An Act of Terrorism," *The New Republic*)

Deductive Chains and the Evaluative Mode

Deductive chains are especially useful when you evaluate something. To evaluate you need to establish criteria or standards commonly accepted by you and the audience. A deductive chain for a paper evaluating the TV series *Chicago Hope* might contain this:

Principle: Any TV drama that has complex, consistent human characters, a serious theme, a variety of wit and humor, a range of emotion, and a realistic treatment of a subject is a good TV drama.

Linking Statement: *Chicago Hope* has complex, consistent human characters, a serious theme, a variety of wit and humor, a range of emotion, and a realistic treatment of a subject.

Conclusion: *Chicago Hope* is a good TV drama.

When setting up such a chain, you should determine whether the readers will accept your standards for a TV drama. (A writing group can help decide that.) If you cannot anticipate agreement, you have two options. You can revise the principle by changing the standards, or you can argue for the principle itself, showing why these are good standards. The second option requires extra work.

Checking the Deductive Chain

Another advantage of using a chain is that you can check the validity of your reasoning. A valid chain has only three ideas, each repeated twice. Here are the three ideas about *Chicago Hope:*

1. Any TV drama that has complex, consistent human characters, a serious theme, a variety of wit and humor, a range of emotion, and a realistic treatment of a subject
2. Good TV drama
3. *China Beach*

Three types of problems can mar your reasoning.

1. The first occurs when you have more than three ideas in your chain, sometimes caused by an ambiguity in one of the ideas as it is repeated. If so, the reasoning is in trouble. That happens below. Can you find the problem?

Any TV drama that has complex, consistent human characters, a serious theme, a variety of wit and humor, a range of emotion, and a realistic treatment of a subject is a good TV drama.

Chicago Hope has complex, consistent human characters, a variety of wit and humor, emotional scenes, and a realistic treatment of a subject.

Chicago Hope is a good TV drama.

2. Another problem occurs when the conclusion goes beyond the principle and linking statement. Here's an example:

Any TV series that has a serious theme is worth viewing.

Most hospital series have serious themes.

All hospital series are worth viewing.

3. A third problem occurs when a writer tries to make a positive conclusion from a negative principle or linking statement.

All good TV dramas do not have complex, consistent human characters, a serious theme, a variety of wit and humor, a range of emotion, and a realistic treatment of a subject.

Chicago Hope does not have complex, consistent human characters, a serious theme, a variety of wit and humor, a range of emotion, and a realistic treatment of a subject.

Chicago Hope is a good TV drama.

THE JOURNALISTIC FORMULA: WHO, WHAT, WHEN, WHERE, WHY, HOW?

This is probably the simplest and most widely used means of gathering information about a subject, and it has long been used by members of the news media. If you are to write an article for your student newspaper, for example, on a strike that is affecting your campus, the journalistic formula could guide your earliest efforts at gathering information:

1. Who is on strike (what specific groups)?
2. What are the terms of the strike?
3. When did the strike begin and how long is it expected to last?
4. Where are the strikers? Are there picket lines? Where is strike headquarters? Where are negotiations taking place?
5. Why did the strike occur? What issues, demands, or pressures brought it on?
6. How is the strike being conducted? Picket lines? Publicity campaign? Demonstrations?

Answering these questions may well open doors to your subject and help you gather necessary basic information.

THE PENTAD: ACTION, AGENT, MEANS, PURPOSE, SCENE

Kenneth Burke, a modern philosopher, rhetorician, and literary critic, developed the pentad (which is closely related to the questions asked in the journalistic formula) as a tool for analyzing dramatic events, and it can be particularly useful in writing about texts including literary works.

Answer the following questions.

1. What is the action? (What is happening?)
2. Who is the agent? (Who is doing the action?)
3. What is the means? (How is the agent doing the action?)

4. What is the purpose? (Why is the action being done?)

5. What is the scene? (Where and when is the action occurring?)

THE CLASSICAL TOPICS OR "PLACES"

This strategy, which was first developed by Aristotle, involves asking another set of questions about your subject:

1. What is it? (Calls for *definition*.) If you are writing about a campus strike, for instance, definition will probably play an important role in your investigation: What constitutes a strike in this situation? How could the terms and issues of this strike be defined? What are the elements of the strike?

2. What caused it? (Calls for establishing *causal relationships*.) Answering this question will also yield important information for an article on a campus strike and would probably reveal a complex web of causes that may lead to any number of hard-to-identify effects.

3. What is it like? (Calls for *comparison and contrast* and *analogy*.)

4. What do people say about it? (Calls for *testimony*.) Gathering testimony, especially by authorities, experts, or other highly respected people, can often help you investigate a topic. If you choose to use this topic in a paper, however, the testimony you gather must be appropriate to your subject *and* to your audience.

BRAINSTORMING

This technique, often used in business and particularly in advertising, involves listing in writing any ideas that occur to you about your subject in the order in which the ideas occur and as fast as you can. Brainstorming often works particularly well in small groups. You may ask several friends or classmates to spend 30 minutes with you listing ideas about your subject and brainstorming together, with one person acting as secretary and noting down all the ideas you and your friends come up with. Brainstorming can thus be a good means of generating spontaneous ideas that provide raw material for a paper.

SPEED WRITING

This exploratory strategy involves:

1. sitting in a quiet place and writing your guiding question at the top of a sheet of paper,

2. setting an alarm for the length of time you want to speed write (15 minutes is a good length of time) or have someone agree to call you after the time has elapsed,

3. then, concentrating on your question and writing down everything that comes into your mind, and *not stopping* writing until the time is up.

Like brainstorming, this strategy will produce irrelevant material, but it may also lead you to a new and surprising insight.

LOOPING

This technique is a form of directed speed writing. It assumes that you have a topic at hand but that you need help getting good ideas about the topic. Peter Elbow, describing this technique most fully, uses the metaphors of a "voyage out" and a "voyage home" to explain the process of looping. In the "voyage out" you focus on first thoughts or prejudices about your topic, although you are free to stray as far from your topic as you want. The aim of the "voyage out" is to lose direct sight of the topic in order to follow the creative flow of your thoughts. The second part of the loop, the "voyage home," asks you to sort through all the new ideas and examples you have generated, select those that give you a new insight into or are particularly applicable to your topic, and use those to produce a new loop that you can eventually use as part of your essay. As with speed writing, looping will provide you with a mass of raw material, and much will have to be thrown away. More importantly, however, the looping process may lead you to a new insight about your topic or your relationship to that topic.

MEDITATING

This strategy involves thinking in a concentrated yet relaxed way about your subject. You may not think of yourself as using this technique, but most of us do meditate or "think hard" about major problems in our lives, although this activity is seldom visible to other people. When researchers at Harvard's Pre-School Project found that the brightest children spent more time "staring" than they did anything else, the researchers concluded that the children were thinking hard or meditating on some object and that this activity was closely related to how well they learned. If you want to meditate on your guiding question, find an absolutely quiet spot, sit in the position you find most comfortable, and focus your inner attention on your subject until you are lost in thought. This technique may be especially helpful for incubating ideas.

KEEPING A JOURNAL

Write each day in a journal during your writing process. Record any ideas that come to you about your subject: ideas from your remembered experiences, your reading, or your conversations about the subject.

Also record any ideas about your writing context: your readers or the type of writing you will do.

Star any emerging insights or answers to the questions you have raised.

CLUSTERING

Clustering is a visual way of generating ideas. Develop each cluster as the ideas suggest themselves. Expand new clusters from existing ones, going into more details and sub-aspects.

Example:

10

RESEARCH STRATEGIES

JANICE LAUER

Library Research

COMPILING A WORKING BIBLIOGRAPHY

A working bibliography is a list of books, journal articles, newspaper articles, and other references on a subject. There are two major ways of finding these references. The first is printed sources—catalogs, indexes, and bibliographies. The second, is computer data bases—a more efficient way to find references.

Using Printed Sources
References common to all fields

1. **LIBRARY OF CONGRESS SUBJECT HEADINGS**
   A list of the subject headings used in indexes.

2. **FOR BOOKS:** **SOURCES INDEXED**
   Card catalog (subject section)   Books available in this library (See sample cards.)
   Essay and General Literature Index   Chapters or sections of books from 1900 on, especially in the social sciences and humanities

3. **FOR PERIODICALS:**
   Reader's Guide to
   Periodical Literature   About 180 popular magazines.

4. **FOR NEWSPAPERS:**
   The New York Times Index   The contents of the *Times,* in brief abstracts
   Wall Street Journal   Business and financial news, since 1958

5. **FOR GOVERNMENT DOCUMENTS:**
   Monthly Catalog of   Between 1200 and 2200 titles in each issue, on
   U.S. Government Publications   all topics, by the largest publisher in the world

References for specialized fields

For convenience, the following list of frequently consulted, specialized indexes is broken down into the four major modern academic disciplines: the natural sciences, the social sciences, the humanities, and business. Their contents are generally indicated by their titles; where the title may be opaque or misleading, a description has been added.

1. NATURAL SCIENCES

Chemical Abstracts
Biological Abstracts
Applied Science and Technology Index [About 180 periodicals in fields such as computers, energy, fire technology, space science, food industry, plastics, and other industrial and mechanical arts.]
Food Science and Technology Index
Solar Energy Index
Pollution Abstracts
Abstracts on Hygiene
Engineering Index

2. SOCIAL SCIENCES

Psychological Abstracts
Sociological Abstracts
Anthropology Abstracts
Criminal Justice Abstracts
Hispanic American Periodicals Index
Index to Periodicals By and About Blacks
Social Sciences Index [About 260 periodicals in anthropology, economics, environmental studies, geography, law, criminology, political science, public administration, etc.]
Women Studies Abstracts [Books, reports, and about 500 periodicals about women and education, law, mental health, physical health, family, and government affairs.]

3. HUMANITIES

PMLA Supplement [Journals and books on languages and literature.]
Film Literature Index [About 135 periodicals in all aspects of film.]
Art Index
Music Index
Communications Abstracts
Education Index
Physical Education Index
Historical Abstracts [About 2000 international periodicals in all aspects of history.]
Writings on American History [About 400 international American history periodicals in the history of culture, religion, theater, business and industry, etc.]

Humanities Index [About 210 periodicals in classical studies, archaeology, folk-lore, history, languages, literary criticism, performing arts, political criticism, theology, philosophy, etc.]
Abstracts of Folklore Studies
Catholic Periodical and Literature Index
Index to Jewish Periodicals
Philosopher's Index

4. BUSINESS

Business Index [in microfilm only] [Books and about 350 periodicals plus *The New York Times* financial section.]
Business Periodicals Index [Same as above, but indexes 70 fewer periodicals. Its advantage is that it is available in printed form.]
Public Affairs Information Service Bulletin [About 425 periodicals in interna-tional relations, economics, current events, commerce, industry, government affairs, law, etc.]
Sage Public Administration Abstracts [About 275 periodicals in city budgeting and finance, policy making, bureaucracy, etc.]

• DICTIONARIES	ITEMS INDEXED
Oxford English Dictionary 1884–1928; Supplements, 1933, 1972 (A–G), 1976 (H–N)	Variant spellings, etymologies, pronunciations, meanings, quotations from English works
Dictionary of American English on Historical Principles	Words originating in America or relating to American history, etymologies, quotations
Dictionary of Americanisms on Historical Principles	Words or expressions originating in the United States, etymologies, quotations

• BIOGRAPHIES	ITEMS INDEXED
Dictionary of National Biography	Biographies of prominent English people
Dictionary of American Biography	Biographies of prominent Americans
Who's Who	Biographies of prominent living English people
Who's Who in America	Biographies of prominent living Americans
International Who's Who	*Brief biographies of prominent people through-out the world*
Current Biography	Biographies of living international people
Contemporary Authors	Biographies of novelists, poets, playwrights, etc.

• OTHER SOURCES	ITEMS INDEXED
Almanacs and handbooks of facts	Data, facts, names, dates
Atlases and gazetteers	Maps, names of towns, cities, mountains, rivers
Bibliographies	Lists of books on subjects or authors
Concordances and books of quotations	Sources and wordings of quotations
Encyclopedias	Introductory and summary articles on topics
Yearbooks	Articles and bibliographies on major topics of that year

Cards from the Card Catalog

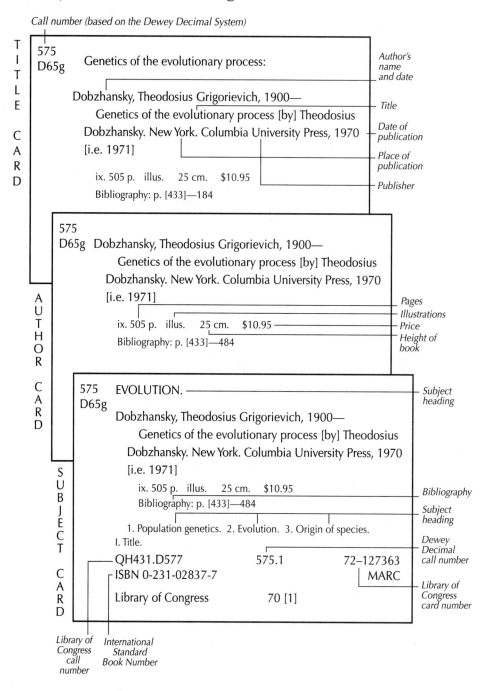

Call number (based on the Dewey Decimal System)

TITLE CARD

575
D65g   Genetics of the evolutionary process:

Dobzhansky, Theodosius Grigorievich, 1900—
    Genetics of the evolutionary process [by] Theodosius
Dobzhansky. New York. Columbia University Press, 1970
[i.e. 1971]

        ix. 505 p.   illus.   25 cm. $10.95
        Bibliography: p. [433]—184

Author's name and date
Title
Date of publication
Place of publication
Publisher

AUTHOR CARD

575
D65g   Dobzhansky, Theodosius Grigorievich, 1900—
        Genetics of the evolutionary process [by] Theodosius
        Dobzhansky. New York. Columbia University Press, 1970
        [i.e. 1971]

        ix. 505 p.   illus.   25 cm. $10.95
        Bibliography: p. [433]—484

Pages
Illustrations
Price
Height of book

SUBJECT CARD

575   EVOLUTION.
D65g

Dobzhansky, Theodosius Grigorievich, 1900—
    Genetics of the evolutionary process [by] Theodosius
    Dobzhansky. New York. Columbia University Press, 1970
    [i.e. 1971]

        ix. 505 p.   illus.   25 cm. $10.95
        Bibliography: p. [433]—484

        1. Population genetics. 2. Evolution. 3. Origin of species.
        I. Title.

    QH431.D577   575.1   72–127363
    ISBN 0-231-02837-7   MARC

    Library of Congress   70 [1]

Subject heading
Bibliography
Subject heading
Dewey Decimal call number
Library of Congress card number

Library of Congress call number   *International Standard Book Number*

Using Data Bases

Most college libraries have access to several data bases, which are primarily indexes and compilations of abstracts in various fields. For example, you may use the *Reader's Guide to Periodical Literature* either in its printed, bound version or on CDROM (that is, a compact disk that stores information in "read-only memory" so that the material can be retrieved but not changed). If your library has the CDROM version, which is updated yearly, searching for material on your subject is easier and faster than using printed versions. But there is a similar data base, the *Magazine Index*, that covers almost twice as many popular periodicals as the *Reader's Guide*. Or you might prefer to use *InfoTrac*, a data base that indexes nearly 400 popular and scholarly periodicals along with the last six months of the *New York Times;* the memory covers the last four years.

Annotating Selected References

In order to determine which sources to read in depth, you can annotate your most promising titles.

1. For each title, note the call number, setting aside those unavailable.

2. Put the available titles into a priority list, arranging those from similar periodicals together to facilitate finding them.

3. Locate and skim these sources in order of priority, making annotations.

   a. Important aspects of the topic the source contained,

   b. Indications of the depth of treatment (length, number of references, statistics, etc.),

   c. The credentials of the author, and

   d. The limitations of the sources.

   The credentials of the author are important to give the paper credibility. If the author is a professor at a well-known university, the chairman of a research institute, the president of a large company, or the leading expert on the subject in question, the writer may want to use that source instead of one by an unidentified author or by a journalist writing on the subject for a lay audience. The limitations of sources may include the date of the article or the fact that it treats the subject in only a minor section or offers a superficial discussion. As much as possible, try to find sources that are recent and reliable (i.e., the evidence is eyewitness, firsthand, or otherwise authenticated).

4. After annotating the sources, select those to be read carefully for note taking.

Sample Annotations

Campbell, Bob. "New warnings given on eating fish from lakes,"
 Detroit (Michigan) Free Press, January 27, 1987 (located in
 NewsBank [microform], Environment, 1987, 11·E3, fiche)

- state warnings on eating fish from lakes St. Clair, Michigan,
 and Superior
   - warnings on various kinds of fish because of chem.
   contamination
   - different warnings on same kinds of fish depending on size
   and age of the fish

Author: Free Press staff writer

Greenpeace, Great Lakes Campaign. Washington, DC:
 Greenpeace, Spring 1988

     - toxic pollution, toxic stress
     - Greenpeace GL campaign
     - toxic politics
     - halting toxic flow
     - toward "zero discharge"

Author: none, pamphlet put out by Greenpeace

Griffin, Melanie, "A double dose of Danger for the Lakes." <u>Sierra</u>,
    November/December 1987, p.47.

"Double Dose" for GL.
  (1) toxic chemicals
  (2) airborne toxic chemicals
     cause for more than 50% of toxic poll. in 3 of 5 GL.
1975 toxic air pollutants became a concern when
  - Lake Superior isolated Isle Royale
    - small island lake had pesticide toxaphene;
      only source - airborne
  - dangers of exposure to toxic chem. to humans

Author: credentials unknown

Behm, Don, "Great Lakes pollution rides wind, study says."
    <u>Milwaukee</u> (Wisconsin) <u>Journal</u>, November 18, 1987 (located in
    NewsBank [microform], Environment, 1987, 79: C10, fiche).

- Canadian & U.S. air quality researchers - airborne pollutants
- air quality advisory board report
    - reports # of lbs. of PBC's and lead dumped on Lakes Superior
      and Michigan by the winds
    - report on how far winds carrying pollutants can travel
      in 1 day & 5 days

Author: credentials unknown

NOTE TAKING

Starting with the most useful titles, read the sources carefully and take notes. The purpose of note taking is to extract the ideas, data, information, and authoritative statements that will contribute to your understanding of your question. Try using the note-taking technique of *key words,* organizing information on each card under an important sub-aspect. For example, below is the key word *toxics* on several note cards to record information from different sources—from Begly, Behn, Greenpeace, Griffin, Meyerson, Ritter, Schmidtke, and so forth. You can then group citations from several sources to back up a point about toxics in the paper.

If you have recorded the bibliographic information (title, author, etc.) on an annotation card or a working bibliography, you only have to connect your notes to that bibliography by the author's name. Or you can use other connecting notations such as numbering references and using the number on the note. When you take notes, be careful to record the page numbers from the source so that you will have them for your citations later. Try to take most of your notes as citations, not quotations.

Taking Notes on Cards

Note taking on cards entails organizing and recording information from sources under key words so that similar information (either from different parts of the same article or from different sources) can be readily combined in the paper. Some notes, showing the use of two key words, *cleanup difficulties* and *toxic winds,* appear on the next few pages. Most of the notes are citations—information from the sources, but not direct quotations.

Notecards offer several advantages:

1. You can think about your sources as you organize the information to help you answer your question.

2. You can interact with your sources, using your own language and organization to see relationships between the information from different sources. You can then work with the sources and not be overwhelmed by them.

3. By recording only the essential information and ideas, you can save time in the long run because you have extracted the material from the sources.

4. Writing down the information and reorganizing your notes can help you see emerging points.

Sample Notecards

Cleanup Difficult   Rebuffoni
24:

    3. Contaminants are entering many other ways
      a. runoff of farm fields / city streets
      b. lakeside hazardous waste dumps and industrial discharge
    4. quantity of fish is much better, however fish are tainted with toxics
    5. many chemicals, ie DDT, PCBs, Dieldrin, although banned over 10 years ago, persist in harbors' and estuaries' sediments, thus contaminating fish - of the 42 listed toxic hot spots around Great Lakes, 38 of them have contaminated sediment showing the enormity of the problem

SEDIMENT

Cleanup Difficult   Rebuffoni
p. 15

   I. Differences in WQ standards (state/federal borders)
    ex. A. Canada   350 ppb trihalomethanes in drinking H_2O
       B. USA   150 "   "   "   "   "
       C. Ontario   0.7 micrograms/L of dieldrin in drinking H_2O
       D. Ohio   0.0007 "   "   "   "   "   "
       E. NewYork .02   "   /L of hexachlorobenzene
       F. Wisconsin .0007 "   /L "   "
  II. Fragmented applications of the regulation laws
    Canadian Environmental Law Association Report
    "One chemical can be strictly controlled as an aquatic discharge but ignored as an air pollutant."

TOXIC WINDS   Behm
2 reasons why airborne pollution is major source of L. Superior's pollution
C/O
   1. Lake's water surface area is so vast 37,700 sq. miles:
       "collection plate" to trap pollutants
   2. Small amt. of land area drains into the lake, therefore
       most of L. Superior's water comes from rain/snow

       Lake Superior largest lake in the world, capable of holding
       all water in Lakes Ontario, Huron, Michigan, Erie plus
       3 additional Lake Eries.

C/O TOXIC WINDS   Behm
Atmospheric pollution of the Great Lakes
IJC (International Joint Commission w/reps from Canada and U.S.)
   International Air Quality Advisory Board
   Report from November 1987:

Lake	substance	amt. dropped from sky	% of total sub. entering from all sources
Superior:	PCBs	1,200 lbs/yr	90% of yearly total
	lead	515 lbs/yr	97%
Mich.	PCBs	875 lbs/yr	58%
	lead	1,135 lbs/yr	99.5%

Taking Notes on the Computer

Computer users who have no access to computers in the library have to photocopy periodical material and work with it at their computers later. Notes taken from Behms article in the *Milwaukee Journal* might be recorded in the computer in the following style:

Toxic winds Behm

A1

There are two reasons why airborne pollution is a major source of Lake Superior pollution: (1) the lake's water surface area is so vast-31,700 square miles-that it acts like a "collection plate" to trap pollutants; (2) only a small amount of land area drains into the lake, and therefore most of Superior's water comes from rain and snow.

A5

Lake Superior is the largest lake in the world, capable of holding all the water in Lakes Ontario, Huron, Michigan, Erie, plus three additional Lake Eries.

    The International Air Quality Advisory Board, an international joint commission of the U.S. and Canada, reported in November 1987 that in Lake Superior, the yearly total of 1200 pounds of PCBs and 515 pounds of lead that dropped from the sky into Lake Superior represented 90% and 97% respectively of the total of those substances that entered the lake. For Lake Michigan, 875 pounds of PCBs and 1135 pounds of lead from the sky for the year represented 58% and 99.5% respectively of the total of those pollutants.

Notice that there is no attempt in these computer notes to separate the information except by topic and pages in the source (A5, for example, means section A, page 5, of the issue of the *Milwaukee Journal* specified in the bib cards). Using the search function, you can return to any topic, word, phrase, or idea. More important, you can try to take notes in complete sentences because the computer will allow you to move the entire sentence or paragraph into a draft without recopying or rewriting. This practice provides an extra protection against plagiarism denied you when working with handwritten notes.

DOCUMENTING SOURCES USING THE CONVENTIONS

You use different types of conventions depending upon which field or writing context you are writing in. The conventions of the Modern Language Association (MLA) are used by many disciplines in the humanities and arts. The conventions of the American Psychological Association (APA) are used by fields in the social sciences and natural sciences. The *Chicago Manual of Style* is used by such fields as linguistics and music. Manuals published by these organizations show you how to cite and quote material (1) in the body of the paper itself and (2) at the end in a page of references or a bibliography.

MLA Bibliographic Form

For more detailed instructions, consult the *MLA Handbook for Writers of Research Papers,* 5th edition (1999).

1. BOOK: _____

Ashworth, William. *The Late, Great Lakes.* New York: Alfred A. Knopf, 1986.

If the publication of the book was more involved, the citation would look like this:

Ashworth, William, and James Todd. *The Late, Great Lakes.* Ed. Sherrill Anderson. 3rd ed. Vol. 2. New York: Alfred A. Knopf, 1986.

Pamphlets are treated as if they are books.

2. PERIODICAL: _____

Cobb, Charles E. Jr. "The Great Lakes: Troubled Waters." *National Geographic* July 1987: 2–31.

Since this is a magazine, not a scholarly journal, no volume number is included.

- For a scholarly journal, the volume number, with no punctuation before or after it, and the year in parentheses follows the name of the journal.
- For journals without continuous pagination through a year's issues, the year is necessary as well.

McDowell, David. "Perspectives on the Great Lakes." *Journal of Applied Philosophy* 12(1988): 24–36.

3. ESSAY IN A BOOK: _____

Dorsey, David. "The Chemical Approach to Conservation." *Essays Presented To Loren Eiseley.* Ed. Paul Craft. Detroit: University of Detroit Press, 1989. 154–96.

4. NEWSPAPER: _____

Rebuffoni, Dean. "Lakes Are Cleaner, But Toxic Woes Remain. "*Minneapolis Star and Tribune* 23 Nov. 1986: A23–24.

5. INTERVIEW: _____

Gorsky, Lt. Todd. Personal interview. 16 April 1988.

If the interview had been conducted by telephone, "Telephone interview" would replace "Personal interview."

APA Bibliographic Form

For more detailed instructions, consult the *Publication Manual of the American Psychological Association*, 4th edition (1994),

1. BOOK: _____

Ashworth, W. (1986). *The late, Great Lakes*. New York: Knopf.

If the publication of the book was more involved, the citation would look like this:

Ashworth, W., and Todd, J. (1986). *The late, Great Lakes* (3d. ed.). New York: Knopf.

2. PERIODICAL: _____

Cobb, C. E. Jr. (1987, July). The Great Lakes: troubled waters. *National Geographic*, vol. 2–31.

An article from a scholarly journal:

McDowell, D. (1988). Perspectives on the Great Lakes. *Journal of Applied Philosophy*, 12(6), 24—36.

3. ESSAY IN A BOOK: _____

Dorsey, D. (1989). The chemical approach to conservation. In P. Craft (Ed.), *Essays presented to Loren Eiseley* (pp. xx–xx). Detroit: University of Detroit Press.

4. NEWSPAPER: _____

Rebuffoni, D. (1986, November 23). Lakes are cleaner, but toxic woes remain. *Milwaukee Star and Tribune*, pp. A23–24.

5. INTERVIEW: _____

Gorsky, Lt. T. (1988, April). [Interview with the author.]

Field Research

Field research strategies are excellent tools for enhancing your understanding of a culture and its values. This kind of research helps you to observe your culture's values and actions *as they occur,* and to test your experiences and impressions against others' who have written about and/or participated in your culture or one similar to it.

Field research requires gathering research data from:

1. *Observations and Descriptions,* often quite detailed, which record your observations of the daily practices, conversations, and values of the local culture.

2. *Interviews* and/or

3. *Surveys*

How Does Field Research Differ from "Traditional" Research?

Field research requires many of the same skills as traditional research: you must make decisions about what aspects of the topic are most important to you, most worthy of inquiry; you must gather, synthesize, and analyze a large amount of data; and you must make decisions about how to organize your ideas for specific readers. However, field research differs from traditional research in that it provides "thick descriptions" of the daily habits and values of a group. While traditional research may require that you assume an objective role or emphasize the validity of published scholarship *above* your own experiences with the local culture, field research begins with you and your experiences. It asks that you use all of your senses—sight sound, feeling, etc.—to gain a new understanding of your subject, why you or someone you care about is involved in it, and how it is related to dominant cultural values.

OBSERVING AND NOTE TAKING

One of the goals of ethnographic research is to capture the daily behaviors, motives, attitudes, and values of your culture. Since you'll be studying a culture of which you are a member, it is sometimes difficult to take careful notes because you are a participant and an observer. Here are some strategies to consider:

Observing Your Culture

Choose your times for observations and note taking carefully

Decide according to the information you wish to gather. Always record the date, time, and setting of your observations.

Consider the ethics of your observations

Since you are observing real people in real situations, you might want to inform members of your culture that you are conducting research. They will certainly notice that you are taking notes, and you might find that they'll be more forth-coming and comfortable if you share with them the goals of your research and the kinds of questions you're asking. Indeed, you might find that they will be happy to be involved and share their insights with you. In rare situations, however, you might wish to keep your ethnographic research private. If that is the case, you must still conduct your research in an ethical manner. For example, you might keep all names and places anonymous, or you might offer a pseudonym for the name of the culture you're studying.

Visit your group and observe on several occasions

Repeated visits are designed for several purposes. For example, depending on the culture you are observing, you might want to collect data during formal and informal business, philanthropic, and/or social events. By attending several events at several settings, you can get a well-rounded view of your culture and have an opportunity to analyze members' behavior and values from several perspectives.

Taking Notes

Record as many details about the local culture as possible

Note taking will help you not only to include specific examples and observations in your ethnography, but also to gain a better understanding of how members of the local culture negotiate their differences, share power, and reflect specific cultural values. Include descriptions of the setting where the members meet, their specific behavior, conversations, and concerns. Take detailed notes. Don't depend on memory when observing. It is easy to forget group interactions, specific behavior, conversations, etc. The more detailed your observation notes, the more concrete your discussion of your local culture can be. Remember, the things you take for granted or that seem natural about your group are important details to include in your ethnography. Keep in mind that your observations should be influenced by your guiding research question(s).

ANALYZING YOUR OBSERVATIONS

Analyzing the data you've collected is as important as taking detailed notes on the members' interactions. This is no easy task, for the actions, values and motivations of your local group might seem obvious to you. But try to question them by considering the ways they reflect larger cultural values. You might structure your notes so that on one side of the page you list the actions and conversations you observe, while on the opposite side of the page, you list your reactions to and analysis of your observations.

Group your observation notes into central themes or issues

Consider what topics or cultural values keep resurfacing in your observations.

Analyze each resurfacing issue

Analyze each issue according to the questions guiding your research. Here are some questions to consider, but you are not limited to these issues.

- What characteristics do members share (clothing or "style" of dress, language/vocabulary, age, class or socio-economic status, race, occupation, etc.)? What does this suggest about their shared values?

- What is the general "mood" of the group? Why?

- Who is in charge of the gathering? Does anyone seem on the "fringes" of the group? Why? How do power relations play themselves out?

- What seem to be the members' attitudes toward the cultural assumptions you're investigating?

- How does the setting of the group (space, intended use of space, etc.) affect the group's interaction?

- Have any of your observations challenged or contradicted your original assumptions about the group and its values?

INTERVIEWING STRATEGY

Why Interview?

Interviewing people who have special knowledge and insight about your subject for inquiry can be a surprisingly efficient and gratifying way of developing your understanding. Contrary to the impression we might get from successful television interviewers, however, conducting an interview is no simple task. It requires a lot of forethought and preparation. A successful interview results from good planning before the interview and fostering active responses during the interview. The following strategies offer suggestions to guide you through planning and conducting your interviews. Select the strategies that best pertain to the context in which you are working.

Setting Goals for Your Interviews

How you prepare for and structure an interview will depend on the questions guiding your inquiry and your goals for writing. For example, a journalistic interview will be different than an employment interview. Similarly, an interview in which you ask for facts and statistics might vary greatly from one in which you ask for advice. In order to conduct a successful interview and to get valuable responses from your interviewees, you need to define the questions guiding your inquiry and to envision the way the interview will contribute to your understanding of your subject.

Review your explorations and the sources of your dissonance, and consider the kind of information you want from your interviewee. Determine how this interview will contribute to your writing project. Is there a specific niche that you want this source to fill? Do you want to gather:

> Statistics and facts? General opinions and perceptions about the subject?
>
> Up-to-the-minute "insider" information that only a face-to-face interview can provide?
>
> Personal experiences and stories that add depth to your inquiry?
>
> Perspectives that conflict with your or other sources' ideas and that offer you a well-rounded view of your subject?

There are many kinds of information you might glean from an interview, and it is vital to have a clear idea of your goals and objectives as you plan for it.

Selecting Interviewees

After you have determined the kinds of information you want to gather from your interviews, you will need to make decisions about *who* can share that information with you. In some contexts, your interviewee choice is clear. If, for example, you are studying a computer programming class to understand why the teacher assigned certain tasks, you will certainly need to interview the teacher to record his or her objectives and impressions. In other contexts, however, your choice is not as clear-cut, and you will have to make careful decisions about selecting your interviewees:

> Who can offer you the most relevant information and insights about your subject?
>
> What credentials will interviewees need if you are going to cite them as authorities? Should they have specialized degrees? Years of acquired knowledge and work in your area of inquiry? Experiences with the group or issue you're investigating? Perspectives that differ from or can embellish other kinds of research you're gathering?
>
> Will your potential interviewees be readily available for and willing to participate in an interview?
>
> What are the ethical implications of your interviewee choices? If you are asking for sensitive information, will you need to keep your source anonymous?

You should consider all of these issues as you select your interviewees. It is also valuable to consider interviewing people who have contradictory perspectives about or hold varying positions of power within the context of your inquiry. For example, in addition to interviewing the computer programming teacher mentioned above, you might also want to interview students in their class to see if their perspectives mesh with their teachers'. The success of your interviews depends, in great part, on your interviewee selection.

Creating Questions for Your Interviews

Developing interview questions that help you reach your writing goals requires foresight and planning. If you omit an important issue or question during your interview, it is rare (though not impossible) that you will have the chance to schedule a second, follow-up interview. Therefore, it is vital to consider your subject from a variety of perspectives to ensure that you develop comprehensive and insightful interview questions.

The Three Perspectives Guide is a powerful tool for helping you prepare your interview questions. When you consider your subject from the three perspectives—describing and distinguishing, tracing moves and changes, and mapping networks and relationships—you increase your chances of covering all important aspects of your subject. Each perspective will help you create different kinds of questions that help you tap into your interviewee's special knowledge.

Describe and distinguish:

This category helps you identify the stable features of your subject and your interviewee's knowledge about those features.

How would your interviewee define the subject or issue? How would his or her perspectives differ from others' definitions?

What are the significant and distinctive features of the subject to your interviewee?

What important statistics or facts might your interviewee know?

Trace moves and changes:

By developing interview questions that examine how your subject has changed over time, you can get your interviewee's perspectives about the history and future possibilities of your subject.

How did your interviewee become involved with the subject? How has your interviewee's interaction with the subject changed over time? Are those changes significant?

What information does your interviewee have about the history of the subject? How does that history affect the subject today?

What are your interviewee's impressions about the future of the subject?

Map networks and relationships:

Developing questions that examine the social influences and relationships that affect your issue can lead to important information from your interviewees. When your interviewee gives you his or her perspectives about the role of your subject within our culture, such as the images and stereotypes associated with it, you gain valuable knowledge important for your writing.

How would your interviewee characterize the role of the subject within their culture?

What social issues (economics, gender, changes in family values, etc.) seem to have the greatest impact on your subject? What would your interviewee say is the greatest effect of that impact?

According to your interviewee, what other subject or issue is comparable to your subject? Why?

Using the Three Perspectives approach will help you develop questions to get in-depth information and responses from your interviewees. You can tailor your questions according to your goals, subject for inquiry, interviewee's knowledge, and writing context.

Reacting and Responding during the Interview

In addition to the pre-planning questions, as the interview progresses, you may want to ask questions that elicit more information or insight into topics you wish to explore. Successful interviewers ask questions intended to evoke a range of responses from short answers to longer examples or stories.

You may encounter a need to ask more questions in areas such as:

- examples or information that supports data you have already gathered.
- an alternative viewpoint to add depth to your investigation.
- narratives or stories to illustrate points you are making, or to introduce other facets of your topic.

Be aware that more than just the "text" of the interview can be useful in your writing project. Often, features of the interview itself (details of the setting, mishaps involved in setting up the interview, information received from colleagues or secretaries etc.) can become valuable parts of your project.

Reading between the Lines

Sometimes you will find that the most interesting material to come out of an interview was not responses to specific questions, but, rather the "chit-chat" that took place before and after the interviewing itself. Often, someone will illustrate his or her point by telling a story, and these stories can be rich sources of information, so rich, in fact, that you may want to solicit a story by asking questions like "What is the strangest route to a career in pharmacy that you have heard of?" or "Have you talked to many students who were in the same shoes I'm in?" By using your pre-developed questions and staying aware of ongoing developments and interesting narratives and points-of-interest, you can ensure a successful interview.

Evaluating Information from the Interview

Try to transcribe the notes from your interview as soon as possible, while the information is fresh in your mind. Then, think about what was said in relationship to the inquiry in which you are engaged. What was the most significant thing you learned? How does what was said affect your project as a whole? Remember that you will be selecting only the most applicable material to include in your draft, so you must evaluate the information you received in light of the goals you have set for your inquiry.

The following questions may be helpful:

- What does this information say about my subject?

- In light of this information, should I reconsider my focus?

- Do I need to look for other sources to confirm or compliment this information?

Incorporating Narratives

If, in addition to gaining answers to your formal questions, you were successful in soliciting a story or narrative about your subject, you must determine how it fits into your inquiry.

Ask questions such as:

- What does this story say about my subject?

- How does this story function within the context in which it is told?

- What appeals to me or bothers me about what the story says or does?

For example, if you are looking at a particular major and the person you interview shares a story that circulates within the discipline, you should look at the way that story helps shape the major, and how it potentially shapes students choosing to enter the field.

USING SURVEYS

Surveys are another good way of collecting information about your culture. They are especially useful for gaining information about large groups who would be impossible to interview. It is important to construct your questionnaire carefully and test it with a pilot group before using it with the people you want to contact for your study.

11

READING AND INTERPRETIVE STRATEGIES

JANICE LAUER

INTERPRETING WRITTEN TEXTS

This strategy was developed by Debra Jacobs.

You will profit from consulting texts that exemplify, discuss, or from which you can infer the character of learning in your discipline. The Interpreting Strategy guides you to consider three broad aspects of a text. The questions posed about each aspect represent some possible lines of inquiry. Your chosen discipline and specific text might suggest other questions.

Analyzing Structures in the Text

Consider what is foregrounded in the text and what is placed in the background

- What is the text's focus and purpose?
- What form does the text take? What are the parts of this form?

The form of a text might be a first-hand narrative, a retelling of events, or an argument about what happened. It might be a report of an experiment.

- What does the focus, purpose, or form suggest about the text?
- What are the recurring terms or concepts? Which of these, if any, are explicitly or implicitly set in an opposition?

When a term or concept is set in an opposition, it is understood in terms of its contrast to something else. Common examples include male/female, life/death, natural/artificial, etc.

- Is one term in an opposition privileged over another? What are the implications of such privileging for understanding the text?

In a history text terms or concepts referring to civilization might recur in opposition to references to primitive life.

In a psychology text, nature/nurture or genetic/environmental.

In a sociology text, conformity/independence. If the history text characterizes civilization as an advancement over primitive life, it might be implying that the historical events most important to the study are those that can be seen as furthering the advancement of civilization.

Analyzing Your Experience of Reading the Text

Consider how you experienced the text.

- What were your expectations for the text and why did you expect what you did?

To what extent were your expectations satisfied?

Sources for your expectations include:

- previous knowledge of the text or its subject;
- impressions based on previous encounters with similar texts;
- the text's opening, layout, or design;
- aspects of the text's publication, such as date, publisher, or editor, etc.
- How are you expected to respond to the text?
  To question or challenge it?
  To be persuaded or moved by it?
  To be informed by it?
- What does your response to the text suggest about questions of authority?

Questions of authority concern who or what decides

- what can or cannot be said,
- who can or cannot speak,
- what is considered important or unimportant.

Analyzing the Cultural/Social Codes and Conditions of the Text

Consider how/why the text reinforces or resists, complements or challenges other texts like it and the tradition in which it can be placed.

- In what tradition/canon can the text be placed? How does it mirror or break the rules/conventions of that tradition?

A psychology text might follow the tradition of behavioral psychology.

A history text might be placed in the canon of political philosophy.

- What is suggested about learning in your discipline when you think of the text as a product?

Who are the text's producers and consumers?

What is its market?

What created a demand for it?

Thinking about a recent popular history text, The Native Americans, as a product would entail noting the following points.

- the book was co-authored by several scholars in history
- it was influenced by dozens of Native Americans who served as consultants and who might also be seen as authors.
- it was produced as a result of revisionary efforts in American history.

Details such as these might indicate that interpretation in history requires multiple perspectives or that writing in history involves collaboration.

- In what ways is the text a potential site of commentary about race, class, gender, etc.

In what ways might the text be considered a site of empowerment or oppression on the basis of cultural, social, or economic conditions?

Regarding a text as a site of empowerment or oppression entails identifying those who profit/benefit from it and/or those who suffer or are marginalized by it.

READING GUIDE

Every strong writer must be a strong reader as well, both of his or her own writing and of writing by others. In fact, much of what you write in college will be related to reading you have done or are doing for a particular class. As a result, you need to make your reading time as effective and efficient as possible, making every reading minute really count. Doing so means, first of all, recognizing that effective reading demands action. The words on a page are just that: black marks on paper. It takes your active mind to fit these black marks together and to embed them in the context of your life and all that you know in order to make them mean something. While we can't provide a course on how to become an effective reader here, we can offer some guidelines to help you exercise your reading muscles and make you a stronger reader. Here they are:

1. Begin by anticipating, by trying to guess from the title or first few paragraphs what the essay, article, or book will be about, what approach it will take, what points it will make. Then see how well the text matches your expectations.

2. Read first of all for the "big picture," the main idea, the gist. Ask yourself, "What is the point of this article or book?" If you can't answer such questions, stop and retrace your steps. Don't forget to ask for the opinions and advice of classmates and teachers.

3. Don't get bogged down by words you don't recognize. If you can get the meaning from the context, keep reading; just make a note in the margin in case you later want to look the word up.

4. As you read, try to relate each point to what has preceded it. If you can't see a relation, pause for reflection. You may have missed a connection—or you may have discovered a weakness in the author's line of thought.

5. As soon as you have read something, take the time to try to summarize it in your own words. If you can do so, you have done an effective job of reading.

6. Develop your own system of note taking, one that will help you remember the most important points in your reading. Some students like to keep a reading log in two major categories: one devoted to summaries, quotations, or memorable words and the other to unanswered questions, reflections on what has been read, and ideas for writing. Once you have a system for keeping notes on your reading, practice it regularly. Chapters 8 and 10 illustrate two different note-taking strategies, one for researched writing and one for essay examinations.

INTERPRETIVE GUIDE FOR A POEM

Reading Closely

1. What are the direct images in the poem? What do they contribute to the meaning of the poem? (A direct image is a reference to things that can be directly encountered by the senses: sights, sounds, etc.)

2. What are the indirect images? What do they contribute to the meaning of the poem? (Indirect images are figures of speech:

   a. personification—turning abstractions or animals into persons

   b. metaphor—an implied comparison between two things of unlike nature that have something in common

   c. simile—an explicit comparison between two things of unlike nature that have something in common

   d. metonymy—substitution of an attribute for what it suggests

   e. symbol—use of a concrete object or action to represent something more abstract

3. Who is the voice or speaker in the poem? The speaker is not necessarily the poet.

4. What kind of language is used in the poem? What do these word choices contribute to the meaning of the poem?

   a. Ordinary words

   b. Unusual words

   c. Technical words like *stanza, rhyme, rhythm, image*

Reading Dynamically

1. What kind of form or structure does the poem have? Stanzas? How long? What does the structure contribute to the meaning of the poem?

2. What kind of rhythm or pattern of movement does the poem have? Regular? Fast? Slow?

3. What kinds of sound patterns are used? What meaning or feeling do these sounds convey?

   a. Repeated consonants?

   b. Repeated vowels?

Reading Holistically

1. What kind of poem is it? Sonnet? Ballad? Lyric? Elegy? Dramatic monologue? What are the features of each of these kinds of poems? How do these features enhance the meaning of the poem?

2. What themes or subject matters can you use to create groups for your poem? Poems about freedom? About death? What other writings can you put in these groups?

3. With what other poems can you compare this one? What are the similarities? How do they help you understand this poem?

4. What analogy fits this poem? Fits your reading of the poem? Fits an image in the poem?

5. What view of politics, culture, economics, class, or gender does this poem embody or critique?

6. What view of what it means to be human does this poem embody?

7. What is the focus, the major theme of the poem, the central statement of meaning that you make of it?

8. How do all the features of the poem contribute to that meaning?

INTERPRETIVE GUIDE FOR A SHORT STORY

Reading Closely

1. a. Who are the main characters? What physical or personality features distinguish them?

   b. What do they contribute to the meaning of the story?

   c. What class, gender, or racial values or attitudes are introduced by these characters?

2. a. What is the setting?

   b. What does this contribute to the story?

   c. What political or economic views are invoked by the setting?

3. What kind of dialogue do the characters use? Why?

Reading Dynamically

1. What is the central conflict of the story? What does it contribute to the meaning?

2. What is the narrative progression? Large segments of time? Flash-backs? What does it convey?

3. What does the ending mean?

Reading Holistically

1. a. What kind of story is it? Historical? Psychological? Mythological? Other?

   b. What are the features of this kind of story?

   c. What do they contribute to the meaning of the story?

2. How can you group your story by subject matter? Stories about adolescence, about overcoming hardship, etc.

3. What are your criteria for a good short story? How does this story meet them?

4. What other stories are similar? How do these similarities help you interpret the story?

5. What analogies for your story or its characters come to mind?

6. What view of what it means to be human do the characters embody?

7. What is the focus, the major theme of the story, the central statement of meaning that you make of it?

8. How do the features of the story contribute to that meaning?

INTERPRETIVE GUIDE FOR A NONFICTION ESSAY

Reading Closely

1. Who is the intended audience? What is the writer's voice or relationship to the audience? How is this expressed in the essay?

2. What kind of language is used? Concrete? Abstract? Jargon? What are particularly good examples of this language? What are examples of connotative language, irony, metaphor, or analogy? What do they mean?

Reading Dynamically

1. How is the essay organized? Is it coherent? If narrative, what are the key moments? If descriptive, what are the significant parts? If classification, what are the features of the class and/or the points of comparison or contrast?

2. What examples, evidence, argument, or appeals are used? Why? What do they contribute to the essay?

3. How did your thinking change as you read the essay?

Reading Holistically

1. What genre or type of essay is this? What are the features of this type of essay?

2. What are the criteria for a good essay? Does this essay meet them?

3. What are the underlying political, economic, gender, or class assumptions of the author? Where are they expressed or implied?

4. In what historical moment was the essay written? How does that affect its meaning? What historical research is necessary to answer these questions?

5. What analogy occurs to you for this essay? For your reading of it? For its subject matter?

6. What view of what it means to be human does the essay convey?

7. What do you conclude is the focus, the major theme of the essay, the central statement of meaning?

8. What feature of the essay contribute to this meaning?

A SEMANTIC CALCULATOR FOR BIAS IN RHETORIC

This strategy was developed by Donald Lazere.

1. What is the author's vantage point, in terms of social class, wealth, occupation, ethnic group, political ideology, educational level, age, gender, etc.? Is that vantage point apt to color her/his attitudes on the issue under discussion? Does she/he have anything personally to gain from the position she/e is arguing for, any conflicts of interest or other reasons for special pleading?

2. What organized financial, political, ethnic, or other interests are backing the advocated position? Who stands to profit financially, politically, or otherwise from it?

3. Once you have determined the author's vantage point and/or the special interests being favored, Look for signs of ethnocentrism, nationalization or wishful thinking, sentimentality, and other blocks to clear thinking, as well as the rhetorical fallacies of one-sidedness, selective vision or a double standard.

4. Look for the following semantic patterns reflecting the biases in No. 3:
   a. Playing up: (1) arguments favorable to his/her side,
      (2) arguments unfavorable to the other side.
   b. Playing down (or suppressing altogether):
      (1) arguments favorable to her/his side,
      (2) arguments favorable to the other side.
   c. Applying "clean" words (ones with positive connotations) to her/his side; applying "dirty" words (ones with negative connotations) to the other side.
   d. Assuming that the representatives of his/her side are trustworthy, truthful, and have no selfish motives, while assuming the opposite of the other side.

5. If you don't find signs of the above strong biases, that's a pretty good indication that the argument is a credible one.

6. If there *is* a large amount of one-sided rhetoric and semantic bias, that's a pretty good sign that the writer is not a very credible source. However, finding signs of the above biases, does not in itself prove that the writer's arguments are fallacious. Don't fall into the *ad hominem* ("to the man") fallacy—evading the issue by attacking the character of the writer or speaker without refuting the substance of the argument itself. What the writer says may or may not be factual, regardless of the semantic biases.

12

SITUATING, DRAFTING, AND REVISING STRATEGIES

JANICE LAUER

Strategies for Considering Readers and Writers

WRITER/READER POSITIONING STRATEGY
Position Yourself as Writer/ Position Your Readers

*P*osition is used here in very specific ways. First, when used as a noun, it refers to a position a person takes on in any given situation. Positions or roles help you know what to do and how to behave in that situation. A few frequently used positions are student, son or daughter, employee, and consumer. Each position is identified by an activity; type of relationship with others; and set of privileges, responsibilities, and restrictions. For example, an activity associated with being a student is taking courses; the student position has a subordinate relationship to her teachers, and a peer relationship with other students; a student has such privileges as using the library, asking the instructor for help; she has responsibilities like attending class and completing assignments; a student is usually restricted from deciding what material will be covered in a course, or from seeing exam questions before a test. In many other areas, positions are also important; for example in baseball each player has a position that entails certain jobs and responsibilities on the team.

In addition to describing activities, privileges, responsibilities, and restrictions, positions carry with them guidelines for behavior, values, and attitudes. Student behavior generally includes being silent during lectures and speaking up during class discussions. The position of student carries with it the valuing of learning and the assumption that schooling will result in more opportunities. Attitudes such as respect for teachers and a desire to do well, perhaps better than anyone else, are associated with the role of student. Positions, then, are important for the smooth operation of the society because they provide stability and continuity. However, positions can also limit unfairly and need to be examined and questioned rigorously.

Second, *position* is used as a verb to name the activity of placing or being placed in a role. You are positioned as a student when you are at school. Others relate to you in certain ways as a result, and the educational institution structures policies that reinforce your positioning. While some of the time you don't have much choice about how you position your self or are positioned, other times you do. You have choices about how you position your classmates, for example. Positioning them as colleagues rather than competitors will have important consequences for your interactions with others.

Positions can also be developed or *invoked* within written texts. In other words, you can place or *position* yourself in a role as you write. In your relationship project, for example, you can compose from the position of friend, or daughter, or employee, depending on the positions you take on in your relationship and some other factors you will read about shortly. The positions you select for yourself and your readers carry with them guidelines for interactions. These guidelines can help you move your readers towards a desired understanding.

Why Writer Positions?

Just as readers are positioned by a writing context, so, too, are writers. These positions constrain you when you write. For example, in your family you probably aren't positioned as a stranger; you can't take that position. You may be positioned as the "youngest" and that constrains you. Through analysis of the context you have selected and its constraints on you as a writer, you can act/write more effectively. That is, analyzing your position as a writer within that context helps you to construct positions from which you can act as a writer.

Why Reader Positions?

When you talk to others, you are sensitive to their differences, e.g., you talk differently to your friends than to your teachers or parents. But being sensitive *in writing* to different readers is more complex. In each of your writing communities, readers are positioned in a certain way. For instance, the writing of the classroom positions you as a student. But when you read a letter from a friend or read an editorial, you are positioned very differently. It is vital that you understand how your context already positions readers so that you can better direct your writing. This strategy will help you to analyze and construct your position as a writer in your writing context. It will also help you to set a position for your readers.

Positioning Yourself

Indicate how you have been positioned in your writing context.

What positions have you written from within this context?

What positions have you been excluded from?

What positions have you left behind you?

Select the position you will take as a writer.

What position will you now adopt within this context?
What will you be to/for others within this context?

What positions will you avoid?

Example:

> In my biology class, will take the position of an innovator, but not a rebel or a naive "up-start."

Positioning Your Readers

Consider the reader positions available in your writing context

- Determine who is excluded (who isn't written to or spoken of)?
- Indicate who would benefit from these positions and who might be harmed or angered.
- Consider what reader position best fits your subject.

Set the position for your readers.

Within your context, then, there are different reader positions. You need to set the one you want for your readers. The question you are exploring should help you here.

Examples:

- In my family, some positions available are: family member, sibling, parent, child, grandparent, friend, rival, role model, disciplinarian, sports enthusiast, workers, neighbors. We never mention my uncle George or hear from him.
- I think my family would be irritated by being put in the position of disciplinarians but they would benefit from the rest of the positions, especially the position of parents, which fits my parents, grandparents, and older sister. Or I might put my parents in the position of sibling rivals because they had this problem in their own family and it might work for my subject.
- In my university , some positions are administrators, faculty, teaching assistants, students, staff , campus police, and service people. Other positions are scholars, learners, educators, facilitators or obstructers.
- Except for "obstructers," readers would benefit from any of these positions, although I don't think faculty and administrators would like to be in the position of campus police.

Characterize the values and backgrounds you would expect from that reader position.

FORUM ANALYSIS

The Forum Analysis was developed by James E. Porter.

Background

- Identify the forum by name and organizational affiliation.
- Is there an expressed belief, editorial policy, philosophy? What purpose does the forum serve? Why does it exist?
- What is the disciplinary orientation?
- How large is the forum? Who are its members? Its leaders? Its readership?
- In what manner does the forum assemble (e.g., newsletter, journal, conference, weekly meeting)? How frequently?
- What is the origin of the forum? Why did it come into existence? What is its history? Its political background? Its traditions?
- What reputation does the forum have among its own members? How is it regarded by others?

Discourse Conventions

Who speaks? Writes?

- Who is granted status as speaker/writer? Who decides who speaks/writes in the forum? By what criteria are speakers/writers selected?
- What kind of people speak/write in this forum? Credentials? Disciplinary orientation? Academic or professional background?
- Who are the important figures in this forum? Whose work or experience is most frequently cited?
- What are the important sources cited in the forum? What key words, events, experiences is it assumed members of the forum know?

To whom do they speak/write?

- Who is addressed in the forum? What are the characteristics of the assumed audience?
- What are the audience's needs assumed to be? To what use(s) is the audience expected to put the information?
- What is the audience's background assumed to be? Level of proficiency, experience, and knowledge of subject matter? Credentials?
- What are the beliefs, attitudes, values, prejudices of the addressed audience?

What do they speak/write about?

- What topics or issues does the forum consider? What are allowable subjects? What topics are valued?
- What methodology or methodologies are accepted? Which theoretical approaches are preferred: deduction (theoretical argumentation) or induction (evidence)?
- What constitutes "validity," "evidence" and "proof" in the forum (e.g., personal experience/observation, testing and measurement, theoretical or statistical analysis?)?

How do they say/write it?

Form

- What types of discourse does the forum admit (e.g., articles, reviews, speeches, poems)? How long are the discourses?
- What are the dominant modes of organization?
- What formatting conventions are present: headings, tables and graphs, illustrations, abstracts?

Style

- What documentation form(s) is used?
- Syntactic characteristics?
- Technical or specialized jargon? Abbreviations?
- Tone? What stance do writers/speakers take relative to audience?
- Manuscript mechanics?

Other considerations?

DESIGNING FOR A READER

The following strategy has been adapted from the strategy developed by Linda Flower.

Analyzing Your Audience

Knowledge

What does your reader need to know?

What are the main ideas you hope to teach?

Does your reader have enough background knowledge to really understand you?

If not, what would he or she have to learn?

Attitudes

What is a reader's image of the subject?

What are a reader's feelings about the subject?

Needs

For what does the reader need your information

What kinds of adaptation will such a need require of me?

Anticipate Your reader's response

Draw inferences and create gists

- Supply a framework for your ideas
- Create and fulfill accurate expectations to help the read anticipate your meaning.
- Make your hierarchical structure clear to the reader

Organize for a creative reader

- State your main idea explicitly in the text
- Focus your paragraph on the topic or main idea
- Use a standard pattern of organization

Focusing Guides

Why focus?

A focus is a response to your question—the result of your exploration, incubation, imagination, and pondering. It represents the gist of writing, your new insight, or solution. Writing as many responses to your question(s) as occur to you will help you to test them. Do they satisfy you? Do they suffice to guide the rest of your composing process? Which one works best?

FOCUSING STRATEGY

Stating Your Focus

A focus sets the stage for the text you will write. A focus is a two-part statement that organizes a text. The first part, a subject, names the situation under investigation; the point of significance expresses an understanding of the situation. The focus serves a couple of vital functions for the text. First, it represents an attempt to answer your guiding question. Second, it announces the content and organization of the text since all material in a text must contribute to explaining the focus and the order must follow the organizing pattern established by the focus.

Restate your question.

Review your exploration and reader/writer positions.

You may have collected a number of partial answers. In order to decide on the main answer, review your exploration again, now that you've had a chance to let your ideas incubate. Do any parts emerge as supplying an answer? Also, keep in mind the writer/reader positions. Of the answers you've reached, which ones would be most appropriate for these positions?

State your subject and the point(s) of significance.

First, determine what **subject** emerges as important. Your original subject as a whole? An aspect of your subject? For example, if you are investigating your ambivalent relationship with your brother, you may conclude at this point that it is your early relationship with him that seems important now.

Second, articulate the **point of significance**, the new insight that you are linking with your subject. For example, you may conclude that your early relationship with your brother gave you a sense of inferiority, a position related to gender attitudes in your family.

Example:

• Many of the editorials, columns, and news stories of the Campus News ———————	have been irresponsible and fostered growing feelings of distrust and disrespect on the campus.
(Subject)	(Point of significance)

Writing out several focuses helps you to clarify your thoughts, to look at alternative meanings. You can ask:

- Do any of these focus statements represent new understandings important to me?
- Do any of these focuses answer questions important in my writing?

If you conclude at this point that you have still not resolved your dissonance, your continuing puzzlement can also be a focus statement such as:

• The affluence of my suburban neighborhood ———————	now embarrasses me even more, but I don't yet fully understand why.
(Subject)	(Point of significance)

Even though this focus statement isn't a final answer, it records your present conclusion. Here you have decided on the aspect of the neighborhood—its affluence—that is important. This focus statement commits you to discuss this affluence and the feeling of being put off, even though you cannot explain why.

FOCUSING STRATEGY FOR PERSUASION

A focus is an answer to a question you find important; it expresses the result of your exploration and summarizes a new insight. When you write to bring about a change in your world, your focus also expresses the response or action you hope to elicit in your readers.

Writing to change your world doesn't mean that your only objective is to prompt your audience to take an action. Sometimes the first step toward action is becoming aware of an issue or a problem; and sometimes a change in attitude is necessary before a more concrete change can take place. Consequently, your focus may be somewhere on a continuum with creating an awareness at one end and eliciting an action on the other end.

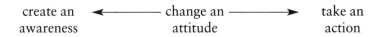

As you prepare to state your focus, consider which type of persuasive response is most appropriate for your subject, the positions of your readers, and your own position as a writer.

Stating Your Focus

- **Restate your question**

- **Review your exploration and writer/reader positions**

- **Formulate responses to your question based on your subject and the point of significance/persuasive response**

Like the focuses in the preceding chapters, a persuasive focus has two parts.

- The first part of your focus defines your subject in a particular way.
- The second part defines your new insight, or the point of significance. In this case, however, your point of significance should also define the persuasive response you hope to elicit from your readers.

NUTSHELLING

Lay out the substance of your paper to yourself in two or three sentences.

Teach a couple of willing friends your nutshell so they get the point.

Organizing Plans

Why organize with a strategy?

While it is possible to draft a paper directly from your focus, you are like a builder constructing a skyscraper without plans; it is possible but costly. Organizing strategies allow you to try different plans for developing your focus before expending the time needed to write several drafts of a text. The following strategies can help you to probe in advance alternative ways of developing your focus. They can be inquiry tools as well, helping you to modify your focus, to sharpen or qualify it., or even reject it.

As the examples below demonstrate, a visual plan of development, helps you to determine if you can develop both your subject and point of significance. But a given focus or writing context may suggest one or another.

This strategy works best if you forecast alternative ways to develop your focus. If you can't find any way to develop your focus, it probably means you don't have a workable focus yet. These alternative ways to develop can be used with larger parts of a text that has an overarching organization such as a persuasive structure or a report format.

MODAL PLANS

Organize by whole and parts

This strategy can be used for any subject. If the subject is physical, parts are usually a spatial sequence : left to right, far to near, up to down, and so forth, from some perspective provided for the reader. If the subject is an idea, a movement, a political issue, or a literary text, parts are aspects of that issue. For example, to explain a management structure to a subordinate you might first use more familiar and then less familiar aspects. To persuade other students to support an event on campus, you might present its features in the order of their attractiveness to students' interests and tastes. To express a mood of joy about a relationship, you might build from the least to most intense parts of the relationship. The strategy involves giving the reader a sense of the whole and delineating the parts and their relationship both to the whole and to each other. Parts are selected in light of your focus, audience position, and writer voice.

Example:

Focus

My family and neighborhood's value
of wealth as a symbol of "the good life" —— is reinforced constantly by cultural
codes on TV.

(Subject)   (Point of significance)

Parts of Whole

Our large homes as status symbols ———— reflect homes on such programs The Rich
and the Famous.

Our latest model cars ———————— are the top line models in the ads.

Our designer clothes ——————— are shown in TV programs & ads.

Our appliances ———————— are like prizes on game shows.

Organize by time segments

This strategy develops by a sequence of time segments. The sequence has many variations in which units of time can be altered, as in flashbacks. The time segments are selected in terms of their relation to your focus. If, for example, you are writing to argue that sexual exploitation in advertising has increased, you can present a history of changing ads, creating a chronology of growing exploitation. To create fictional surprise in a story you might use climactic order of time segments. Cause-and-effect order is a variation of the narrative in which the time segments selected are presented to argue for a causal relation. Process sequence, another variation, emphasizes repeated and repeatable time sequences.

Example:

Focus

Over the years, my family's value
of racial equality ——————— was tested by cultural
practices of racism.

(Subject)   (Point of significance)

Time Segments

In my small grade school, as a member
of the only Asian-American family, I——— was taunted, left out of parties,
and didn't make friends.

Later, in high school,
my sister ———————— wasn't picked for cheerleader,
or nominated for the homecoming court.

Recently my father ——————— didn't get a promotion in his company
where upper management was all white.

Organize by setting criteria

This strategy develops your focus by putting your subject in a category, setting criteria for that category, and then measuring your subject up against these criteria. You can set criteria for any subject—a TV detective show, a political issue like welfare reform, a specific poem, or a biology theory. What you choose as criteria helps you to develop your focus. For example, if you want to evaluate a recent movie, you might first put it in the category of science fiction, then create criteria for good science fiction movies, and finally measure the movie against these criteria.

Example:

Focus

The College Voice ———————————— doesn't measure up as a good campus
newspaper.

(Subject)   (Point of significance)

Criteria

Its national and international news ———— is skimpy.
Its editorials ————————————————— have been irresponsible.
The local news———————————————— is filled with inaccuracies.
Its coverage of entertainment———————— is spotty.
Its sports news ——————————————— only covers men's football and basketball.

Organize by grouping

This strategy develops by putting your subject in a larger group and then relating your subject to other subjects in the group. Yon can group any subject—a friend, an ideology, a poem, a scientific theory. How you choose to define the group helps you to develop your focus. For example, if you want to explain to your classmates a new kind of computer software, you might first put it in the category of learning aids, then create some features of learning aids, and finally explain how your software has these features.

Comparing and contrasting are variations of this strategy because they imply grouping; that is, your basis for comparing or contrasting comes from the similar or dissimilar features two subjects have as members of a group. One way to develop a comparison or contrast is to discuss each similarity or difference, one at a time, in relation to both subjects. For example, if you were creating a new interpretation for a short story, showing that it was a piece of science fiction similar to another story the reader knew, you would first identify several features of science fiction and then show, one feature at a time, how the two stories either had or lacked these features.

Creating analogies is another variation of this strategy. You place your subject in an unusual group, then identify the features of this group, and finally show how your subject shares these features. For example, if you wanted to communicate the apprehension arising from a catastrophic illness when someone doesn't have health insurance, you could liken it to going into bankruptcy. You could organize your essay by first showing the fears connected with bankruptcy, and then illustrating , one at a time, how such an illness would share features of a typical bankruptcy—the feelings of helplessness, the lack of resources to pay the debt, the severity of the situation, and the social stigma attached. Again, this strategy should help you elaborate your focus.

Example:

Focus

Our family's view of career ——————— has been shaped to some extent by success several cultural codes.

(Subject)   (Point of significance)

Categories

My family's view ——————— echoes traditional gender codes about working women: TV working women, wives in political campaigns, etc.

My family's view ——————— buys into the code of the American work ethic.

My family's view ——————— includes the American dream of the self-made millionaire.

ORGANIZING WITH A PERSUASIVE PLAN

Develop an introduction

The introduction of a persuasive paper has at least three functions:

1. it establishes the credibility of the writer;
2. it begins the appeal to the reader's attitudes, values, and feelings; and
3. it announces the writer's focus.

Most of the introduction should be devoted to establishing your credibility. Here you can introduce the appeals that you selected. Normally the introduction concludes with your focus. Remember that your task in the introduction is to bring the readers from their own preoccupations into your subject arena, to begin raising concern about your topic. You must build bridges, indicating why your readers should listen to you and why they should care about your subject.

Think of the reader as needing answers to four questions.

1. Why should I be interested in this *subject?*
2. What are you going to argue about this subject?
3. Why should I listen to *you?*
4. Why should I read this *now?*

Order your appeals

Your proof is the longest section of your paper, usually several paragraphs in length. In this section you concentrate on interweaving your three kinds of appeals. At the core are your rational appeals. But these should be advanced with details, information, examples, and language that work to sustain your credibility and stimulate feelings and attitudes in your reader.

When creating a persuasive plan, you might (1) list all of the appeals you intend to use and then (2) indicate in what order or section of the paper they will be employed. A plan helps you to determine how these appeals fit together, what transitions you will need, and what gaps may exist. A plan also enables you to check that all parts of your argument support your focus.

(Insert a refutation)

Refutation anticipates and answers your reader's objections. It can be made in a separate section or interwoven with the proof. If you have analyzed your reader's views of the subject, you will have some ideas about what can be refuted. Refutation can add to the persuasive force of your paper in several ways. First, you show that you are not ignoring opposing views, thus enhancing the plausibility of your argument. Second, if you state objections fairly and accurately, you add to your own credibility. Third, by acknowledging the reader's emotional involvement in the subject, you can defuse some of the potential hostility.

You can refute by directly attacking an reader's statement of facts or proof. You can *deny* the reader's position and maintain that the opposite is true. You can make a *distinction,* accepting an reader's position in one sense but denying it in another, more important sense. You can *retort,* using your reader's reasoning to draw a different conclusion.

You can also use indirect refutation, attacking the character, credibility, or reasoning of an author with an opposing position, *but only if this person is not your own reader;* otherwise he or she will stop listening to you.

Add a conclusion

The ending of a persuasive paper requires the writer to summarize the proof and restate the major conclusion. In a short paper, these may be included in a single sentence. In a longer paper, the two may require a paragraph. The ending should be as brief as possible because a long summary irritates readers who have paid close attention to your proof.

Example:

Focus:
Discipline at Carver High School should be regarded as one aspect of a student's education that promotes patience, diligence, and responsibility.

Introduction

1. Establish credibility
   - Refer to firsthand experience
   - Acknowledge need for practical policy to show respect

- Identify with reader about need to maintain classroom control
- Refer to reader's knowledge of Professor Cohen's thoughts about discipline

2. Stimulate attitudes and emotions
   - Show sensitivity to values by acknowledging addition of new courses

3. State or suggest focus

Proof

Affective and Credibility Appeals Used with the Following Rational Appeals

Discipline at Carver should promote patience.
- Refer to Spaulding for authority
- Compare/contrast corporal punishment and counseling

Discipline at Carver should promote diligence.
- Classify discipline as training
- Use warden/prisoner analogy

Discipline at Carver should promote responsibility.
- Refer to process of becoming self-reliant
- Provide example of an instructive discipline program

Refutation

Corporal punishment does not enable teacher to maintain classroom control.
- Argue that there could be a waste of investment in educating
- Show effect of aggressive punishment
- Show discipline to be a means, not an end

Conclusion

1. Stimulate emotions and attitudes
   - Use analogy of corporal punishment and Skinner box
   - Imply battle analogy

2. Restate or recall focus
- Refer to Ingram v. Wright to strengthen credibility

3. Call to action
   - Set up model of instructive discipline program
   - Indicate connection between reader's values and actions

SENTENCE OUTLINE

A sentence outline helps you develop both parts of your focus (subject and point of significance) in each section of your writing.

Example:

Focus:
Cleanup of the toxic pollution of the Great Lakes will be a necessary but difficult and complex task.

PURPOSE OF FOCUS: To become culturally aware of the complexity of a subject

Section 1: There are many things at stake if serious and intense cleanup efforts aren't implemented. (Introduction)

1. Size of the Great Lakes makes their cleanup reason enough.

2. Millions of people are dependent on the Great Lakes and are suffering ill effects from the toxic contamination.

3. Great Lakes' animal deaths and severe defects are a direct result of the toxic contamination.

Section 2: The nature of the Great Lakes itself makes cleanup difficult and complex.

1. Volume to surface area ratio makes the GL a toxic "collection plate."

2. Replacement time of water causes complications once substances enter.

3. Ecosystem of the Great Lakes straddles state and national borders, greatly increasing complexity.

Section 3: The nature of toxic pollution causes difficulties.

1. Microcontamination is a much harder problem to clean up than "conventional" pollution was in the sixties.

2. Overwhelming number of toxics creates additional problems.

3. The many sources of entry for toxics cause even more difficulties.

TOPIC OUTLINE

Focus: The college student needs to realize that the credit card industry pours a lot of energy and expense into encouraging the use of credit cards, even though overuse of credit creates a negative impact on the individual consumer, especially college students.

Section 1

    1. The history of credit cards

    2. The use of an advertisement and how it affects the consumer.

Section 2

    1. The impact that credit cards have on college students.

    2. Why credit lenders focus on college students.

    3. What is appealing about credit cards for college students.

Section 3

    1. The average American and how credit cards affect the individual consumer.

    2. Why the credit card industry has had such an impact.

    3. Why Americans are willing to utilize credit cards, even when they know the negative effects.

Section 4

    1. Possible solutions for reducing credit card debts.

    2. Final suggestions for credit card debt prevention.

ETHNOGRAPHIC ORGANIZATION

Creating an Organizational Plan

A ethnography is often organized according to the *process* of doing your research, though there are various approaches to organizing the vast amount of data you'll collect.,

Include at least three sections:

    1. **A RATIONALE:** In this section, you need to offer your reasons for selecting your group, a discussion of the dissonance and questions guiding your research, and any background information you consider important (e.g., when the group started, its original objectives, etc.)

2. A description of your role as a **PARTICIPANT/OBSERVER** in the group: In this section, you'll need to explain how your role in the group affected your data collection, your guiding questions, etc.

3. **An ANALYSIS SECTION:** This is the most difficult section to organize, for here you'll include both data you've collected (from observations, library research, surveys, and interviews) and your analysis of that data. It's often useful to organize this section around the questions guiding your research about the group.

DOCUMENT DESIGN

Why design your document?

The persuasive effect of whatever you are writing extends beyond the content of what you write. Especially in the age of desktop publishing, the "look" of what you write becomes a critical part of the overall effect of your documents. This has always been the case. For instance, the teaching of "penmanship" and the choices of what color pen or pencil to write in are each examples of concerns for the "look" of writing. And as you know, these kinds of choices make a difference in the effectiveness of our documents.

Document design, though, is much more than making a document "look" pretty. When thinking about the design of documents, you need to think about such questions as whom you are writing to, how they will be reading what you write, what they will be using your document for, how do you want to position yourself as a writer, and what emotional effect you want your document to achieve. Document design is a huge field of study and there are organizations that make it their entire business to study and produce well designed documents. So obviously you will not be able to address *all* of the concerns of document design. But in the strategy that follows, you will find ways to think more critically about the ways you shape and design your writing for specific purposes and in specific contexts.

Writing Down Your Planning Decisions

- Write down your question.
- Write down what action you want to achieve through this document.
- Describe how you want to position your reader.
- Describe how you want to position yourself.
- Write down the genre you have chosen.
- Write down the focus you have written.

As you work through your document design decisions, you must be certain to reflect on the planning decisions you have outlined above. The kind of shape or design your document takes depends on these former decisions you have made.

Thinking about the Page as a Unit of Design

The first important step toward designing documents is re-seeing a document as a sort of picture or frame. No matter if you are writing on a standard sized page, or if you are creating a brochure, or if you are making a flier for a wall, you need to think about what your readers will see as a unit of design. For a brochure, there are several units of design: for example, the front cover, the inside of the front cover, and the whole brochure opened up. Depending on the number of folds in a brochure, if you were to design a brochure, you would have to think about several different units of design as well as the whole brochure as one unit of design.

The standard page can be designed in several different ways. In the workplace, you might find the following as the three most basic ways of looking at the page as a unit of design.

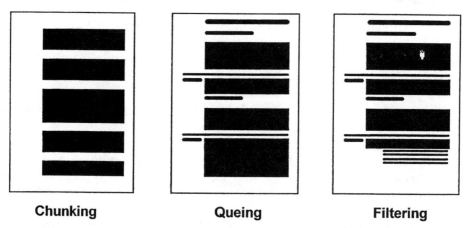

| **Chunking** | **Queing** | **Filtering** |

Notice that each general page design uses headings, sub-headings, spacing, indentation, and lists or boxes to distinguish parts of the overall document. In addition to these design strategies, what is not so easily identified in the above examples is that headings, sub-headings, and body text are distinguished by font size and bolding. These design strategies increase the efficiency of reading and the reader's level of comprehension.

Determine the hierarchies of your document.

At the early stages of your document design, you might ask yourself:

- In what ways can your document be broken into smaller pieces or categories? In other words, what headings and sub-headings might be appropriate to your document?
- What parts might be broken down into lists?
- What parts of your text might be important enough to be off-set from the rest of the document with boxes shading?

Thinking about Your Reader

As it is critical for you to think about what kinds of documents are appropriate for your workplace context, it is critical that you think about the kinds of readers who will be reading or using your document. In the typical workplace, people do not have a lot of time, and efficiency is critical. Therefore, when designing workplace documents, you typically want to design them so your readers can find information and key points very quickly. In general, you might think of your readers falling into one of several categories.

> **skimmer:** the skimming reader will read your document for the general idea and will spend very little time reading your document. Consequently, you have to make sure that your document is designed to bring attention to the main points of what you are writing.
>
> **scanner:** the scanning reader will also read quickly, but this reader is looking for specific information. For instance, a manager going through a stack of resumes for the first time is typically as scanning reader.
>
> **search reader:** this reader is a scanner, but in addition to scanning, this reader will give extended attention to some parts of your document.
>
> **receptive reader:** the receptive reader reads for thorough comprehension. This is much the way you read a textbook for a course.
>
> **critical reader:** the critical reader is reading for comprehension, but also reading to evaluate what is written. When you read an editorial in the newspaper, you are probably acting as a critical reader.

As you probably have realized, you will design your document differently for different kinds of readers. In terms of the page designs illustrated above, the skimmer and scanner need documents with much more queing and filtering and would generally find documents that lack these design features as unhelpful and even frustrating. Though the receptive reader and critical reader probably need queing and filtering less than the skimmer and scanner do, queing and filtering can still increase the comprehension of your readers.

Analyze your readers

- What kind of reader are you writing to?
- What are your reader's goals when reading your document (to complete a task, to become aware of a problem, to learn new information)?
- What do **you** want your reader to *do*?
- What kinds of document designs are commonly read by your reader in your workplace context?

Thinking about the Persuasiveness of Your Document

Just as you need to think about your credibility, affective, and rational appeals in the *language* that you use in your document, you also need to think about these persuasive appeals in the *design* of your document. If this textbook were not type-set but handwritten, what kind of credibility would it lose? How would you *feel* about it? The point is that the design of a document is part of the overall persuasive effect.

In the process of designing your document, you need to contemplate the credibility, affective, and rational consequences of your design choices. Just by paying attention to design features, you will be positioning yourself in the workplace as more credible.

- Determine the Ways Credibility Is Gained in Your Workplace Context
- Determine the Kinds of Affective Consequences of the Documents in Your Context
- Determine the Kind of Arguments Your Are Making in Your Document

You have explored this in detail, already, in the positioning strategy. But at this point in your document design process, you want to think about your persuasive appeals in relation to the "look," or design of the documents in your workplace context.

Analyze the design context

- How are most documents designed in your workplace context?
- In what ways are documents designed differently by employees of different "rank" in your workplace context?
- What kinds of documents have helped others gain the kind of credibility you want in this context?
- In what ways do different fonts create different emotional responses (e.g., does one look more "technical" than another)? What emotional response do you want to provoke in your readers?
- How can you bring attention to your more critical arguments? Can you put them into a list? Can you off-set them in a box or by shading? Have you distinguished separate arguments by headings and sub-headings?

DOCUMENT ORGANIZATION

Why organize?

There are two levels of organization that you should think about when writing workplace documents: whole document organization and section organization.

The broadest level of organization is the organization of the entire document. Often, the genre types in the workplace have already determined this level of organization for you. For instance, if you were writing a progress report—a report that is typically addressed to others within your company/organization with the purposes of informing the others of your progress and persuading them to give you continued support on the project—you would find that the progress report genre usually requires you to organize your report around (1) the work completed, (2) the work remaining, (3) preliminary findings, and (4) preliminary conclusions. One way to think about many of the genres you find in workplace writing is to think of them as *already organized* or *already designed*. Because the workplace depends on efficiency, strict genres, like the progress report, speed up the process of writing and reading reports.

In addition to this first broad level of organization which is often already established, you must think about the ways you will organize the sections and paragraphs within your report. This level of organization is typically **not** already determined.

Document Organization

Following are some of the common workplace genres and their basic organizational principles. Two broad organizational divisions one should be aware of are the direct and indirect organizational approaches. Direct organization is typical in Western cultures and is characterized by "getting right to the point." Indirect organization is less typical in Western cultures and is characterized by a cautious, typically friendly building-up to the point, and the point is often made towards the end of the document.

> *Memo:* A memo is usually an internal document (exchanged *inside* of an organization), and though used primarily to inform, it is used in a variety of contexts. Consequently, the memo has only a few document level organizational principles. It contains a heading that includes from whom the memo is coming, to whom it is addressed, when it was written, and for what reason it has been written. The memo usually follows a direct organizational approach, announcing in what is often called the "overview" the purpose of the memo and a summary of what the memo details. The overview is followed by the details of the memo and often ended with some sort of concluding statement.

> *Proposal:* A proposal works differently in different workplaces. In some workplaces, the proposal functions as a work contract. In other workplaces, the proposal proposes some future work/research that needs to be done. The proposal identifies a problem or need, does a detailed analysis of the problem/need, identifies your qualifications for proposing and maybe addressing the problem, and discusses your rationale for the feasibility of the project you are proposing.

> *Recommendation Reports:* Two common recommendation reports are the feasibility report and the comparison report. The difference between the two is that the feasibility report addresses the feasibility of a single response to a problem/need, but the recommendation report addresses the comparative advantages of several responses to a problem/need. They are similar, however, in that each report is organized around the following six parts: an overview, a problem/need discussion, a discussion of the method of research used in the project, a discussion of the project's findings, a clear recommendation section, and a conclusion.

Section Organization

In addition to the organization strategies discussed in the general strategies section, workplace writing often organizes under the following strategies.

> *Problem/Solution:* Most direct document organization strategies work under the problem/solution strategy, in that they first identify and fully describe the problem before discussing solutions.

> *Elimination of Alternatives:* This organizational strategy works by addressing each of the alternative solutions to a problem, and then

using a clear set of criteria moves from the least viable solution down, eliminating all but the recommended solution.

BUILDING AN IDEA TREE

This strategy is adapted from Linda Flower's work.

Building an idea tree allows you to:

1. visualize the structure of your whole paper
2. see the connection between each part and your focus
3. see the relationship between one part and another.

Put the key ideas of your focus on the top

Arrange the key ideas in a hierarchically organized tree

The following example is a tree of Part II of this book.

Drafting

Why draft?

Coming to a new understanding for yourself is one thing; sharing that insight with your readers is quite different. It's a complex task to explain the subject in sufficient detail; to guide your reader through the organization of your text; to choose language that constructs your attitude in just the right way. When you create a draft and share it with others before sending it to readers in your primary context, you have a chance to step back and consider how well you have constructed a text for your readers.

WRITING SEVERAL DRAFTS

Follow the method of development and organization you have planned.

Follow the method of development and organization you have planned for the genre you selected. Keep in mind the reader and writer positions you set and the focus you are trying to share with your readers. Write freely each section without worrying about conventions. Just get your ideas down. If new ideas or directions suggest themselves, feel free to pursue them. The very act of drafting also brings to mind other ideas and examples. You need to remain open to surprises that occur as you write. You should also be fluid, sensitive to where your writing leads you.

Review your exploration.

Since the process of generating a new understanding of your subject is ongoing, you may want to review your exploration once again, to look for materials that help you answer your question. Remember that your readers need many specifics and reasons for any point you are making. Reread your exploration for ideas, examples, and materials to develop your text, adding new material as it occurs to you. If your genre calls for other kinds of investigation, use the Research Strategies to help you.

USING COHESIVE DEVISES

Use repetition

Repeat something in the preceding sentence or paragraph in the immediate sentence or paragraph. The thing repeated can be a word, a phrase, a clause, or the total statement of an idea. With obvious limits, it can be repeated exactly or approximately. For example, if the repeated element is a single word, you can repeat it exactly, substitute a pronoun for it, or use a synonym for it

Add transition words

Transition words help alert the reader to any of several relationships:

> Contrast: *but, although, yet, however,* etc.;
> Coordination: *similarly, likewise, just as,* etc.;

Consequence: *consequently, therefore, thus, so, as a result,* etc.;

Accumulation: *moreover, furthermore, in addition, for example,* etc.;

Alternation: *or, either,* etc.;

Sequence: *first, second, next, finally,* etc.

Maintain consistency by avoiding abrupt shifts in number, person, or tense

There are only two grammatical numbers in English—singular and plural. Coherence breaks down when, for example, pronouns and their antecedents don't agree in person and number. Person distinguishes the person speaking (first person—*I, we*), the person spoken to (second person—*you*), and the person or thing spoken of (third person—all other pronouns and nouns).

There are six tenses in English: present, present perfect, past, past perfect, future, and future perfect. Fortunately, they are usually easy to keep consistent. Discourse that begins in the past tense, for example, should continue in that tense except when a reference to another time requires a shift.

USING CONCRETE AND CONNOTATIVE LANGUAGE

As you draft, using concrete language will help you to be credible, while general and abstract language will convey vague, unsubstantiated opinion. A persuasive text will also contain an unusual amount of humor, wit, and satire, probably because humor pleases readers and therefore makes them more receptive to the writer. Effective discourse also contains a high proportion of figures of speech, probably because figures of speech are highly connotative. Below are some passages from published persuasive writing, showing concreteness, connotation, and/or humor.

---

1. Quoted from an essay arguing for smokers' rights:

This year, for example, the American Cancer Society is promoting programs that encourage people to attack smokers with canisters of gas, to blast them with horns, to squirt them with oversized water guns and burn them in effigy.

Harmless fun? Not quite. Consider the incidents that are appearing on the police blotters across America: In a New York restaurant, a young man celebrating with friends was zapped across the face by a man with an aerosol spray can. His offense was lighting a cigarette. The aggressor was the head of a militant antismoker organization whose goal is to mobilize an army of two million zealots to spray smokers in the face. (Stanley S. Scott, "Smokers Get a Raw Deal," The New York Times)

2. Quoted in Martin Luther King's "Letter from a Birmingham Jail":

We have waited for more than 340 years for our constitutional and God-given rights. The nations of Asia and Africa are moving with jetlike speed toward gaining political independence, but we creep at horse-and-buggy

---

pace toward gaining a cup of coffee at a lunch counter. Perhaps it is easy for those who have never felt the stinging darts of segregation to say, "Wait." But when you have seen vicious mobs lynch your mothers and fathers at will and drown your sisters and brothers at whim; when you have seen hate-filled policemen curse, kick and even kill your black brothers and sisters; when you have seen the majority of your twenty million Negro brothers smothering in an airtight cage of poverty in the midst of an affluent society; when you suddenly find your tongue twisted and your speech stammering as you seek to explain to your six-year-old daughter why she can't go to the public amusement park that has just been advertised on television, and see tears welling up in her eyes when she is told that Funtown is closed to colored children, and see ominous clouds of inferiority beginning to form in her little mental sky, and see her beginning to distort her personality by developing an unconscious bitterness toward white people . . .—then you will understand why we find it difficult to wait. *(Martin Luther King, "Letter from a Birmingham Jail")*

In these passages are numerous examples of concrete diction and connotation. But connotation can be a two-edged sword, which, if not used skillfully, can alienate a reader by stimulating the wrong emotions.

DRAFTING RESEARCHED PAPERS

Use citations

If you consulted sources for your writing, you will need to document the ideas and information you gleaned. Citing is the method of doing so. Strictly speaking, a *citation* is any reference to a source other than direct quotation. Citations are mentions of or ideas and information from the source that have been recorded in your own words, not word for word from the source. You should use citations in the paper whenever possible. It is wise to let your readers know when material from a source is beginning and ending. Below are sample citations using APA documentation conventions.

Ashworth says the residence time (which is the time for one drop of water to enter and leave through the outlet) for the entire system is close to 500 years (1986, p. 44)

According to Douglas J. Hallett, president of Eco-Logic Inc., the high surface to volume ratio allows the lakes to take in large amounts of toxics from the atmosphere (Schmidtke, 1988, p. 26)

Less than half of 350 U.S. corporations signed an agreement to comply with the Sullivan Principles (Washing, 1988, p. 23).

Pile (1987) gives another explanation of the term saturation or chrome (p. 244).

These citations were effective because they

1. Identified the source at the beginning of the information,
2. Gave the information in the writer's own words,
3. Closed the citation with the author and the page number,
4. Showed where the writer's own text left off and the material from the source began,
5. Did not use the words from the original, only the information, and

- Did not use quotation marks but did identify the source.

Use quotations sparingly

Quotations are exact statements and passages from the source. To distinguish them from citations, put quotation marks around any material quoted directly either as you took notes or as you wrote your paper. Quotations should only be used when the style as well as the substance of the source is needed to make your point. Both style and substance must be documented if used in the paper.

Here is an example:

> As Rev. A. Boesak, a spokesman against apartheid, said, "Apartheid is so intrinsically evil that it cannot be reformed . . . it can only be eradicated" (Kessel, 1986, pp. 28–29).

The best guide for when to use a quotation is to ask whether the material is so eloquently said that both the substance and the style are important to make a point. A quotation can also be used when the quote itself is the object of discussion, as in the example below.

> This conservative engagement policy, as proposed by the Reagan Administration, is as follows:
>
> The prevention of forced removals of black communities; the extension of funds from the Agency of International Development (A.I.D.) to civil rights organizations and drought stricken areas; the press for the release of apartheid detainees; the encouragement of American businessmen to be more socially responsible (Suzman, 1986, p. 16).

A quote of more than four typescript lines is set off from the text by double spacing, indenting, and typing the extract double spaced without quotation marks. If material is to be left out of the middle of a quotation, ellipses (. . .), three periods separated by spaces, indicate where the material is missing.

Avoid plagiarism

Citations help to avoid plagiarism, the undocumented use of a source's style or material. Here are several varieties of plagiarism of an original passage.

The original passage from Randal's article:

> The dilemma of balancing scientific risks and benefits is, of course, a familiar one. In the case of nuclear energy, both the risks and benefits are at least familiar and more or less quantifiable. And when physicists have created new elements, they have done so with the knowledge that their behavior will be highly predictable. By contrast, even the experts can only guess what will happen when germs are provided with exotic genetic material and what trade-off this new technology will require. And whereas radiation generally decays, novel microbes might multiply indefinitely in a hospitable environment.

1. *Paraphrasing,* substituting other words but retaining the ideas and general order without documenting:

> The difficulty of keeping equal scientific hazards and helps is a normal one. In the instance of nuclear energy, both the disadvantages and the benefits are at least known and more or less measurable. When scientists have found new discoveries, they have done so with the understanding that their actions will be very normal. In opposition, even the authorities can only speculate on what will occur when germs are given unusual genetic substance and what exchanges this innovative technology will demand. While radiation usually diminishes and dies, new microbes might increase continuously in a favorable environment.

2. *Stealing key phrases,* without quoting them:

> Genetic engineering is a fascinating new scientific endeavor. Germs are provided with exotic genetic material to discover what the new combinations will produce. Such experiments are different from the work in nuclear energy where the behavior is highly predictable. Radiation generally decays but novel microbes might multiply indefinitely. This potential hazard raises the old dilemma of balancing scientific risks and benefits.

3. *Stealing an entire sentence or section,* without quoting it:

> There are many questions raised about new work in genetic engineering. What will happen when germs are provided with exotic genetic material and what trade-off will this new technology require? And whereas radiation generally decays, novel microbes might multiply indefinitely in a hospitable environment.

Material that is common knowledge to the reader addressed need not be documented. To identify direct quotations, you should put them in quotation marks while note taking.

WRITING ESSAY EXAMINATIONS

Determining the types of examination questions

Examination questions differ in their expectations for focus, development, and organization, depending on the signal words *define, explain, compare and contrast,* and *evaluate.* Answers that are focused and organized indicate that the writer controls the material, shaping it to address the type of question asked.

Define questions

Questions that call for definition or identification demand concise and accurate answers. Long, padded paragraphs not only reveal fuzzy thinking but also waste valuable test time. Definition questions require

1. stating the term to be defined,
2. putting the term into a class, and
3. distinguishing the term from all other members of the class—hence creating a subclass.

Explain questions

Questions that ask for explanation expect an expanded answer, a full account, examples, and important background material. Short answers are not sufficient. Answers can be focused by indicating the direction of the response.

Explanatory answers are generally organized by description or narration, signaled by words in the question itself:

Description:	"Discuss several factors contributing to . . ."
Narration:	"Discuss the history of . . ."
	"Account for the causes of . . ."
	"Explain the ways that news gives shape to reality."

Compare and contrast questions

Questions that call for comparison or contrast are more demanding because they require a good understanding of two or more subjects and also the ability to detect points of likeness or difference quickly. These activities are complementary; they rest on discovering similarities and differences between items or concepts. The focus indicates whether comparison or contrast will be made and on how many bases.

Although two patterns of organizing comparison are possible, the first pattern is infinitely superior:

Pattern 1
Discuss subjects 1 and 2 on the first point of similarity or difference;
Discuss subjects 1 and 2 on the second point of similarity or difference;
Discuss subjects 1 and 2 on the third point of similarity or difference.

Pattern 2
Discuss subject 1;
Discuss subject 2;
Identify the points of similarity and differences between subjects 1 and 2.

Pattern 1 is superior for several reasons:

1. it identifies the points of similarity and difference more clearly for the reader,
2. it relates the two subjects on these points more closely, and
3. it avoids the redundancy of the first pattern.

But Pattern 1 takes more forethought before beginning to write the answer.

Evaluate questions

Questions that ask for evaluation are often the most difficult. Even though they may require knowledge of only one subject, they entail establishing significant criteria by which to measure the subject. Sometimes the criteria have been set in the course; other times the writer must set them during the examination. *A focused answer will specify the criteria early.*

Evaluative questions can be organized by first specifying the criteria and then relating the subject to each criterion in turn.

Agree or disagree questions

The kind of question signaled by "agree or disagree" involves some kind of evaluation of another's ideas, definitions, explanations, comparisons, or solutions to problems. These questions often entail evaluation in combination with one of the types of answers above, depending on the rest of the question.

1. A question can entail *definition* if it says:

    "The author defines jargon as . . . Agree or disagree with
    this definition."
    Here the writer will have to use some kind of criterion for answering and, if disagreeing, will have to offer an alternative definition.

2. A question can require *explanation* by stating:

    "Zhao argues for three effects of smog. Agree or disagree
    with his view."
    In answering this question, a writer must first explain Smith's three effects and then evaluate their adequacy according to some criteria. If disagreeing, the writer must also provide and explain alternative effects.

3. A question can entail *comparison or contrast:*

    "Garcia claims that freedom and democracy are similar.
    Agree or disagree."
    In this case, a writer must use some criteria to evaluate the comparison of Garcia and, if disagreeing, may want to provide a contrast.

Plan during an examination

One of the pitfalls of essay examinations is uneven time distribution. During the examination itself, you would be wise to take time to plan, first determining the kind of questions that are being asked. You need to check to see whether the questions require you to define, explain, compare or contrast, or evaluate. Each of these kinds of questions makes different time demands. Definitions or identifications require a brief time, explanations more, and comparisons or evaluations the most time. Setting a time frame helps the writer to finish all the questions on the examination. At the time of the examination, you have to plan quickly a workable focus and an organizational scheme because no time is available for first versions followed by revisions.

WRITING A PROJECT PROPOSAL

As you engage in field research, it is valuable to articulate for yourself the central issues for inquiry, the position you'll assume as a participant/observer in your culture, and the ways you might approach gathering data, conducting interviews, etc.

Plan a Proposal

1. A rationale for choosing the culture you'll study. Why will it be useful and valuable to research this culture?

2. The questions guiding your research. What you want to find out about the culture and its values?

3. A discussion of your role as a participant/observer in the group.

    a. What is your role in the group?

    b. How did you become part of the group?

    c. How does it serve your interests?

    d. How is power distributed in the group?

    e. How will your position in the group influence your research collection?

4. A discussion of your assumptions about the group.

    a. What values do you hold about the group?

    b. What is the source of those values?

    c. Are your assumptions open to change?

5. A projected plan for research.

    a. What strategies might you use to find source?

    b. Whom to interview, when to observe your local culture, etc.?

Your proposal is exploratory and heuristic. That is, it is an opportunity for you to state your plans for research and clarify for yourself how you might make this ambitious research task manageable and useful.

Responding Guides

READER RESPONSE STRATEGY

Why respond to texts?

You can receive valuable feedback on your writing from several sources: professionals (your writing instructor), your writing group, your reader, and yourself. As the writer, you should have the opportunity to indicate the kind of response you want from your peers and the aspect of your writing on which you need feedback. Your writing group can also offer advice where they think you need help or encouragement. Below is a Reader Response Guide that you can use on your own writing, and give to your instructor and group to organize their response.

Using the Reader Response Strategy

Give an overall response

What is your total reaction to the piece of writing?
Would the intended readers find it powerful? Dull? Confusing? Other?

Comment on the focus

What is the focus?
What sections support the focus?
What sections are unrelated to the point of significance?
How can they relate better to the focus?

Assess the development for readers

What is the genre? Does the writing suit this genre?
What is the reader position being invoked? What sections engage the reader well?
What sections do not fit that position?
What is the writer position? Does the development seem appropriate from this
    writer position?
Is there enough material (details, examples, arguments) to help the reader experi-
    ence the focus?
What sections need more development?

Examine the organization and coherence

What is the genre? Does the organization suit the genre?
What organization is used?
What parts fit well? What sections break the order?
Do the paragraphs help maintain the order?
What can be done to improve the order?
Is the paper consistent in person, number, and tense?
Does the paper have gaps between paragraphs or sentences?
Where are transitions or other cohesive devices needed?

React to the language choices (words and sentences)

What choices of words work well for the genre, focus and reader position? Which need reworking?

Are the sentence patterns effective? Where could improvement be made?

Do any sentences need combining?

Check the conventions
(Feedback on this dimension is best given by your instructor.)

What conventions are required by the genre? Does the writing observe these conventions?

Are there places lacking the conventions of standard written English—grammar, spelling, and punctuation (if SWE is appropriate in this context)?

Indicate a main emphasis for revision

What is the most important thing for the writer to change for the next version?

Tailor the Reader Response Guide
Adapt the guide to your writing context and subject.

As a class or individually, adapt this guide by adding questions or specifying the type of response you need.

Examples:

Focus:
A focus for a report may be a recommendation. For a persuasive essay, it may be a probable judgment.

Development for Readers:
A letter to a family member may require personal examples, while a persuasive editorial may need arguments.

A review of a movie may need specifics from that movie, while a research paper requires citations from sources.

Organization:
The organization of a report has a definite format, while a personal essay may allow for a number of broad types of order such as time segments or whole-parts sequences. A persuasive essay usually requires an introduction, proofs, and a conclusion.

Language choices:
The use of connotative language is important for the affective appeals in persuasion, but is probably not appropriate in a biology report.

Analyze Your Own Text, Indicating Where You are Satisfied and Where You Need Help.

Under each category of the guide, assess your work.

- If you feel confident of your work in a category, indicate what you have accomplished,
- If you need help with specific aspects of your text, direct your readers to give you response on those aspects.
- Share your assessment with your instructor and/or writing group, and indicate the categories in which you would like responses. (They can respond to other categories if they see a problem, but they will know where you want them to concentrate.)

When Responding to Another's Text, Offer Three Kinds of Help.

In each category of the Reader Response Guide, provide three kinds of response.

- **Describe** what you discover in reading their text. For example, state the focus you found in their text , the reader and writer positions their text seems to invoke, the organization the text appears to have. These descriptions can be very revealing to the writer.
- **Categorize** the strengths of the text. Then categorize difficulties you think the intended readers will have with their text and why. Instead of saying, for instance, that there is something wrong with the third paragraph, indicate the type of problem the text posed—that it did not give enough examples or specifics. You can say you can't find a focus. You may tell them that their intended reader position isn't clear. Or you may say you don't see the connection between the third and fourth paragraphs. These types of responses are invaluable because they pinpoint the *kind* of problems that you detect and the places where they occur.
- **Give concrete advice** about ways to remedy these difficulties. You may suggest, for example, that the writer needs to relate clearly and specifically the second paragraph to the focus or that the writer should add specific examples to the first paragraph.

Revising Plans

Why revise?

Revising a text gives a writer a chance to communicate better with her context of readers. Revising may involve making changes to the focus, development, organization, or style, along with correcting any errors in conventions and spelling. Because some revisions change the text more than others, it makes sense to begin with them. A new focus, for instance, can alter every other aspect of a text, so it should be revised first. Different language choices can best be made after all other changes since the writer may decide to eliminate some text. Making revisions is often a complex process because it involves balancing expectations of many people:

- your writing professor
- your peer collaborators
- your writing context
- your writer position, and
- your reader position

The important thing to keep in mind when making revisions is that not all of these people will expect the same things. It's up to you to decide what should be done to make your writing better based on your **reader and writer positions, your focus, and your context.**

REVISING STRATEGY

Constructing a Revising Plan

Study the feedback you received from your responders.

Begin by reviewing the feedback you received. Are there areas of agreement? Conflicting comments? Both situations indicate a possible need for changes. Conflict can indicate that what you have written is not clear. Remember, though, you as the writer are the one making the final decisions. You know best what you are trying to communicate; you most likely know your readers while your group members and instructor do not. Ultimately, the responsibility for your text is yours.

Create a revising plan to set your priorities for change.

A revising plan identifies the changes you plan to make to the text in as specific detail as you can manage. It serves as tool for organizing your revision, helping you to revise the most basic level feature first. It can operate as a check list once you begin.

Start with any needed revisions of focus, organization, or development for audience. Then consider any sentences that need to be combined or changes in word choice. Finally, edit your paper to make sure you have correct grammar, spelling, and punctuation

Carrying Out Your Revisions

To revise problems with focus, consider the following.

If you have a problem with **focus**, that should probably be first on your list. You will waste time adding more development or better organization to an unfocused paper, and you will waste even more time polishing your sentence structure and diction and cleaning up problems of conventions if you don't first address problems of focus. Below are some common types of focus problems and suggested revisions:

a. If your reader cannot find your focus, it may be because you yourself are hazy about it. Your problems may go back to earlier stages when you were unclear about what point of significance had emerged. If so, you will have to return to that point soon. Your writing may have helped you move toward a clearer focus, but you may still have to recast the writing to reflect that understanding.

b. If you write only on a *subject,* with no clear point of significance, your paper will need major repair because it has no center yet. Go back to your investigation and focusing strategy

c. If some of your material does not fit and hence confuses your reader, then you need to remove the irrelevant section or paragraph or sentence.

To revise problems with unity, consider the following:

A If you have a problem with unity, return to your focus which sets the boundaries for the selection of ideas and examples. A focus is also a commitment you make to your readers: it sets up their expectations. When you maintain that commitment, when you satisfy their expectations, the paper has unity. Whenever an idea, example, or fact wanders beyond the boundaries of the first or second half of your focus statement, unity vanishes. As you revise your paper, therefore, ask of any example, detail, or fact if it supports your entire focus.

To revise problems with development and readers, consider the following:

If you have a focused and organized but undeveloped paper, your problem can stem from several resources.

a. If you have not given your readers enough specific material to enable them to understand your focus, you may profit from looking again at your investigation to see if you can find unused ideas, information, analogies, or comparisons that work to communicate your focus. If not, you will need to generate more material.

b. If you have ignored, insulted or bored your readers by giving them information they already have, consider referring to that information instead of telling it. Consult your reader positioning about your reader's background or interview your readers.

c. If you have used examples and details that are inappropriate for the position you constructed for your reader, reexamine your analysis of their position. Then work on your language choices or examples and details.

See strategies for paragraph development below.

To revise problems with organization and coherence, consider the following:

If you have a problem with organization, you often have serious revision ahead. This kind of problem needs to be remedied before addressing problems with word choices or even development. If you'd add more development to an unorganized paper that will only compound your problem. Usually the opening words of each paragraph indicate to the reader the order you are constructing: whole/part segments, time segments, arguments , and so forth.

a. If your readers can discern no organization, you might return to your drafting plans or develop a new organizing strategy to reorder your writing.

b. If your problem stems from a mixture of organizing strategies, you can try shifting your framework to either one or the other. In a long discourse such as a 50-page essay or a dissertation, a writer uses several orders throughout the whole text, but in shorter sections or pieces, such shifts may disorient the reader.

c. If you have an underlying order to your text, but the reader has to wade to the middle of the paragraph to find out the direction of the writing, that problem can be remedied by letting the reader know at the beginning of each paragraph which segment is about to be discussed.

13

USING GENRES

ANDREA LUNSFORD

Why Consider Genre?

You already know quite a bit about genres, those dynamic forms of discourse you use everyday (letters, memos, answering machine messages, to-do lists) to keep communicating. Genres are effective and efficient because they can offer a point of common ground for writers and readers. The genre of report writing, for example, is fairly well established; the writer does not have to invent it anew with every writing and the reader can easily recognize it and therefore read it more easily. Such patterns of recognition underlie much of human communication. But genres are also dynamic, changing over time and under differing influences. (News stories, for example, changed dramatically with the advent of cheap daily papers printed in long narrow columns). Today, contemporary forms of electronic communication show this generic dynamism at work, as accepted forms for e-mail and other kinds of messages slowly emerge. Within the art of fiction, you are also well acquainted with genres: perhaps you prefer the genre of sci fi or mystery over historical romances, for example. Or within contemporary music, several genres may appeal to you—rhythm and blues, rock, rap. And if you rent movies, you know that most video stores depend on genres to classify their products: comedy, drama, thriller, and so on.

Genres often exert silent but powerful influences on us: that's partly why a book and a movie version of it often differ so dramatically, and why some may like one much better than the other. In general, genres exert this power most when they invoke or hail us as audiences, asking that we accept their conventions and forms. As such, genres raise expectations in us, expectations that are either confirmed or broken. When you tune in to your favorite sit-com, you can usually count on its meeting your expectations for that genre: Fraser or Ally McBeal, for example, will not suddenly be delivering your local news live or performing with the New York City Ballet—or even acting out a hospital crime drama. Instead, they will be just what you expect: characters on light-hearted situation comedies.

Not all art confirms our generic expectations, however. In the classic Alfred Hitchcock movie *Psycho,* the genre of "thriller" led audiences to expect that while the heroine introduced early in the movie might be threatened, she would survive through most if not all of the movie. In a bold move, Hitchcock broke this expectation, however, killing off the heroine in one of the first, and surely one of the most harrowing, scenes in the movie. Theater-goers of the time reacted with shock and horror, even outrage; many later said that scene haunted them for years, for according to generic expectations, "it wasn't supposed to be that way."

In choosing a genre to work with you are choosing a powerful set of terms, ones that will raise expectations in your readers and which will serve as both guide and constraint for you as a writer. In the same way that choosing the genre of research report guides a writer about the general elements and order of the report, it also constrains the writer to use, rather than ignore, those guides and to deliver a report rather than a sermon or a poem. Within any genre, however, dynamic latitude and variation exist: mystery novels, for example, come in a dizzying range and variety, from the British village grandmother as sleuth to the hard-boiled big city private eye. And genres blur and overlap as well: look at the blurring of animated and "live" characters in Disney's *The Jungle Boy*, or of historical and fictional accounts in many "docudramas" or in controversial movies like Oliver Stone's *Kennedy* and *Nixon*.

As is the case with the genres noted above, the academic writing you do is characterized by genres that can often blur and overlap, as might happen if you combined a report with a memo. Or you might decide to blend some personal narrative into a research essay in your history class, or to embed a letter to your readers in a report for a business class.

GENRE STRATEGY
Select a Genre/ Examine the Implications of a Genre

Although genres will always be dynamic and permeable, they also provide some key boundaries or guides for writers and readers alike. As such, they are worth your careful consideration in all your writing tasks. The following strategies aim to help you think productively about choosing a genre (or genres) and about the implications of your choice.

Selecting a Genre

Consider several possible genres.

Given your area of inquiry, your purpose and position and your readers, what seem the most likely and appropriate genres for you to use? List three or four possibilities, then analyze them by using the following strategies.

Consider logistics.

Which genre is most practical and realistic for you to use? You can begin answering this question by thinking about whether you have access to the materials and equipment and even the funds necessary to use the genre effectively (will you need a color printer or special software program, for example, or will you need the help of a graphic designer?) Also consider how familiar you are with the genre, how much you already know about how to use it well. Given your time constraints, is it realistic to choose this particular genre?

Consider situation or context.

All genres exist in a context bound by time and space. That is one reason new genres arise—in response to changes that somehow call for them. Is the genre you are seeking characteristic of any particular time and place and *not* characteristic of some other? For instance, what genre might a writer arguing for universal voting rights have had to choose from in 1705, 1905—and today?

Consider readers.

Because genres exert strong appeals to readers, you need to consider how they will react to the genres you are considering. What genre(s) is most appropriate and effective for the group you want to reach?

Examining the Implications of Genres
Consider use of evidence.

Genres have their customary ways of establishing authority, and you should consider these carefully. The biology lab report, for example, establishes it authority through the use of quantitative data and forms of statistical analysis. An ethnographic report, on the other hand, calls for interview data to establish its authority. In developing a genre, then, you need to ask what "counts" as evidence in that genre, which kinds of information are persuasive and which are not. In the chapter on college research essays, you will find student writers choosing their evidence very carefully, always with an eye for what will be most persuasive to a particular field or discipline.

Consider features and format.

Most genres have some common features of format. In business and professional reports, for example, the Executive Summary is a fairly standard feature, as are the use of headings and subheadings. Letters almost always include a salutation or greeting. What formatting features characterize the genre you are using? How will those features help you? In what ways may they constrain or limit you?

Consider level of formality.

Some genres call for a fairly standard level of linguistic formality. The business report, for example, generally demands a formal level of discourse that adheres to the conventions of standard academic English. Other genres exhibit a very wide range of variation in level of formality. Letters, for example, may call for an intimate level of language—or for a highly formal one, entirely depending on the audience and purpose of the letter. In thinking about the appropriate level of formality, then, you need to consider not only the genre itself (letters, for example) but the intended purpose and readers for the genre before coming to a final decision.

Consider medium.

Genres guide communication in all media of communication—oral, written, visual—and in multi-media presentations as well. What medium (or media) does the genre you are using call for? What do you need to know about the demands and constraints of that particular medium?

Consider use of visuals.

Some genres call for visuals; some even demand them. A technical engineering report without graphs and figures is highly unlikely. Other genres may exhibit a very wide range in the use of visuals: a college research essay on the Civil War's impact on the lives of a student's ancestors, for example, might include none at all, or it might include a number of key illustrations. As you study the genre you plan to use, therefore, ask not only whether it demands or invites the use of visuals but also whether it could use visuals to good effect. Such visuals might include charts, graphs, figures, photographs, maps, drawings, and so on. In each case, you need to ask how they are integrated into the text and what purpose they serve.

Consider range of variation.

As many of the examples above suggest, most genres allow for a range of variation—in format, level of formality, use of visuals, and so on. Consider how wide this range of variation is and how well it will allow you to achieve your goals. How far do you feel you can go in "stretching" this genre, or in blurring it with others?

List the features of your genre

The chart below may be helpful to identify the features of the genre you will be using.

GENRE: _____

Contexts	
Logistics	
Writer Position	
Development Use of Evidence Writer Authority	
Reader Position	
Format & Organization	
Level of Formality	
Medium	
Use of Visuals	
Range of Variation	

As this discussion suggests, when you choose a genre or a mixture of genres, you are making a substantial set of commitments. As a result, taking time to explore just what those commitments entail and to analyze the implications of your choice of genre will be time very well spent.

GENRE: Biographies

Contexts	• workplace; family; web pages; community or professional groups
Logistics	• requires extensive knowledge of subject of biography • may require getting access to the person, or materials relating to the person
Writer Position	• admirer and advocate of the subject's importance • reporter giving information on a key subject
Development Use of Evidence Writer Authorit	• use of historical information, concrete descriptive details • long study experience with subject or extensive research creates expertise; one interested in recording an accurate picture of the subject
Reader Position	• those interested in the subject • those in a position to affect the subject • friends, family members, colleagues, enemies
Format & Organization	• depends on medium and purpose of subject, but sometimes organized chronologically or opening with fact-based information and moving then to impressions of the subject
Level of Formality	• depends on purpose, writer and reader positions, or medium
Medium	• primarily written through some biographical sketches exist in song and can appear on radio or TV (as in the A&E series *Biography*)
Use of Visuals	• depends on purpose and accessibility of photographs, etc.
Range of Variation	• very wide, from a biographical sketch included in a news account (such as a human interest story or an obituary) to longer, book-length stories

GENRE: Brochures

Contexts	• settings in which people are gathered due to a common interest that they might pursue in some way: to promote some kind of product or service; to invite attendance at an event; to ask for feedback
Logistics	• requires mailing the document, physically handing it out, or posting it • often created on a computer; often requires color
Writer Position	• an advocate of some kind
Development Use of Evidence Writer Authority	• graphs, charts, statistics • testimonies • "for further information . . ." • visuals can be evidence ("This picture shows how lovely Gatlinburg is in the fall . . .")
Reader Position	• a consumer of some kind • someone who will heed a call to action
Format & Organization	• front panel announces or forecasts subject • back can be used to supply information, or simply contact information: address, phone number, email, company logo • inside panels supply information
Level of Formality	• wide range, but not intimate • lists okay • fragments okay
Medium	• written and visual
Use of Visuals	• there is visual appeal in design, even if actual visual aids are not included
Range of Variation	• overlaps with essays, pamphlets, fliers, and newsletters

GENRE: Essays

Contexts	• a class assignment; a response to a magazine or newsletter; a local or national contest; a diary; a local radio program
Logistics	• need access to information necessary to provide details, examples, etc. • need time to reflect and explore
Writer Position	• depends on focus and readers; possibilities include expert relating personal experience (as in the *Newsweek* column "My Turn"); critic exploring and calling for action or assessing a text; advocate for some issue
Development Use of Evidence Writer Authority	• use of examples and concrete details, including sensory details • use of analysis and arguments • references to personal expertise or research conducted
Reader Position	• may vary widely from self and close friends to readers of a particular magazine, judges of a contest, or teachers
Format & Organization	• depends on purpose and subject. A personal essay might use a format like *Newsweek*'s "My Turn"; columns which are critical essays might be longer and use full documentation; often uses one of the modes of organization.
Level of Formality	• depends on purpose, reader position, and subject matter
Medium	• primarily written, though could be oral like essays featured on NPR, or if delivered to members of some particular group
Use of Visuals	• depends on format constraints and place of publication.
Range of Variation	• very large, from the most personal to the most distant and academic

GENRE: Ethnographic Accounts

Contexts	• local cultures, disciplines, workplaces, groups of any kind, marketing research
Logistics	• requires time to do research for ethnography (observations, library research, interviews, etc.)
Writer Position	• depends on goal of ethnography; some possibilities include caring member of local culture (LC), educator of those unfamiliar with LC, or proponent of change within LC
Development Use of Evidence Writer Authority	• triangulated research and vivid, thick description • participant/observer role requires clarifying: what is the writer's personal investment in or involvement with the LC?
Reader Position	• caring members of LC • skeptics or outsiders who need to know more about the LC • administrators or those with power to impact the LC
Format & Organization	• organized according to research process: rational hypothesis; participant/observer role; data collection; analysis of data
Level of Formality	• depends on reader positions
Medium	• primarily written, but ethnographic techniques also used for visual mediums, including films, documentaries, and news reports
Use of Visuals	• visuals might enhance thick descriptions
Range of Variation	• great variation, depending on reader/writer positions; could be as formal as academic essays, or be blurred into storytelling

GENRE: Essay Exams

Contexts	• school courses; applications for jobs, schools, or scholarships; workplaces
Logistics	• timed writing situations call for maximum efficiency and practice • allow time for editing and proofreading • if not timed, allow plenty of time for peer response
Writer Position	• student being evaluated • applicant being evaluated • prospective employee
Development Use of Evidence Writer Authority	• needs clear thesis, supported with good examples and reasons • authority projected by one who has mastered course material or who can perform well in exam context
Reader Position	• instructor; admission officer; judge; prospective employer
Format & Organization	• easy to read format; organized point by point with reiteration in conclusion
Level of Formality	• fairly formal
Medium	• usually written
Use of Visuals	• limited
Range of Variation	• not great, though somewhat dependent on time constraints, purpose, and writer/reader positions

GENRE: Interviews

Contexts	• online communication; community or interest groups; workplace; family
Logistics	• requires access to and permission of the person or people to be interviewed • requires time to prepare for and arrange interview; some equipment may be needed if the interview will be taped or you plan to type notes • may require some research and arrangements for tape transcription
Writer Position	• depends on purpose; some possibilities include reporter, researcher, supervisor, or newsletter writer
Development Use of Evidence Writer Authority	• usually developed with specific details and examples • questions and answers structure development • extensive use of direct quotation • writer authority depends on position
Reader Position	• interested member of a group in community; co-workers; those in a position to make decisions based on interview data
Format & Organization	• question and answer format; organized in order of importance
Level of Formality	• depends on purpose, medium, and writer/reader positions
Medium	• written (newspapers, newsletters, websites, etc.) or oral (TV or radio programs)
Use of Visuals	• limited, though may include a picture of the person interviewed
Range of Variation	• wide, depending on purpose, format, and writer/reader positions

GENRE: Letters

Contexts	• friends and family; local or student newspapers; business or professional groups; consumer queries or requests
Logistics	• may require time to gather pertinent information • need to know or find out who will receive the letter • if electronic, requires access to a modem and recipient email address
Writer Position	• consumer with a claim, query, or grievance • friend or relative wishing to share information, experiences, or expertise • employee or employer • citizen concerned with public issues
Development Use of Evidence Writer Authority	• uses direct address and closes with signature • evidence depends on context, purpose, and readers • development is often chronological • writer authority comes from position as expert, advocate, or consumer
Reader Position	• interested members of local community • employer, supervisor, or other authority • those in position to respond to queries, complaints, etc. • friend or family member needing advice or desiring communication
Format & Organization	• open with salutation, close with signature • will include addresses of both sender and recipient if letter is formal or business-related • organization is chronological or logical, point-by-point
Level of Formality	• depends on purpose and writer/reader positions
Medium	• primarily written, either in hard copy or online
Use of Visuals	• limited
Range of Variation	• wide, from very informal personal letters or email to friends, to business letters or letters to an editor

GENRE: Newsletters

Contexts	• college courses; student, community, religious, or national groups; workplaces
Logistics	• requires time to gather information necessary for newsletter articles • requires time and knowledge necessary to design the newsletter • requires understanding of possible means of dissemination
Writer Position	• reporter; editor; advocate; concerned reader of the publication; critic
Development Use of Evidence Writer Authority	• depends on purpose, format, and context • development from extensive examples and possibly quotations • writer authority depends on position, such as expert giving information; member of a group reporting on events; advocate submitting an editorial statement; employee assigned to seek out and write up information regarding the place of employment, the products, or human interest stories
Reader Position	• fellow students, colleagues, workers, or group members who receive the newsletter; those who might be interested in receiving it; those who assigned you to work on the newsletter
Format & Organization	• depends on context, purpose, and writer/reader positions • often 8 x 11″ format, designed like a mini-newspaper • often organized on a story-by-story basis, with appropriate headlines
Level of Formality	• usually fairly formal
Medium	• primarily written
Use of Visuals	• can be extensive if equipment and money permits
Range of Variation	• limited; most newsletters are fairly brief and focused clearly on the needs and interests of the readers or subscribers

GENRE: Memoirs

Contexts	• family or group of close friends; larger group of people who share your interests; your own website or other virtual space; radio or television show
Logistics	• requires time for deep reflection and extensive note-taking • may require access to people important to your current or past life
Writer Position	• depends on purpose, reader position, and context; some possibilities include caring family member writing down life memories, apologist for all or part of your life behaviors, or hero of your own narrative
Development Use of Evidence Writer Authority	• often, but not always, developed through narrative • based on memories, interviews, and artifacts you have collected from your life
Reader Position	• family, friends, or colleagues who have an interest in your life; members of the larger public who share your interests
Format & Organization	• may vary; possibilities include letters, lengthy emails, illustrated websites, or full-length books • usually organized chronologically
Level of Formality	• depends on purpose, format, and writer/reader positions
Medium	• usually written, though may be presented orally via radio or TV
Use of Visuals	• will likely include photographs and other personal artifacts
Range of Variation	• very large, depending on purpose, context, and writer/reader positions

GENRE: Multimedia Presentations

Contexts	• college courses; workplaces; community groups or clubs
Logistics	• requires access to hardware and software, as well and knowledge about how to use them effectively • requires familiarity with the place of presentation: will it have all the appropriate wiring and other equipment you may need? • requires time to gather knowledge base or content for the presentation
Writer Position	• expert demonstrating the power or quality of a product • concerned citizen aiming to attract media attention to the subject • employee or student required to present information • advertiser or advocate attempting to influence others' thinking
Development Use of Evidence Writer Authority	• usually guided by order of the presentation; you develop what is presented in graphics, video, overheads, etc. • may call for charts and graphs, taped testimonials, or other graphics • writer authority is that of an expert who has gathered all necessary information; advocate selling a product or idea; student demonstrating mastery of a subject or material; employee assigned to make a presentation to colleagues
Reader Position	• prospective buyers; concerned colleagues and/or citizens; fellow employees or students; those who share—or oppose—your interests
Format & Organization	• depends on purpose, writer/reader positions, and access to appropriate hardware and software • organization often signaled by an overhead slide or visual aid used at the beginning of the presentation, then revisited from time to time to help viewers follow along
Level of Formality	• depends on purpose, format, and reader/writer positions
Medium	• usually combines oral presentation with extensive visual data; may be accompanied by printed handouts
Use of Visuals	• extensive
Range of Variation	• fairly large, from a brief poster-board session you might organize in a class to a hour-long show designed for an entire organization

GENRE: Proposals

Contexts	• workplaces; community, business, or government organizations; college courses
Logistics	• requires time to gather information necessary to make the proposal • may require access to those with technical expertise
Writer Position	• concerned citizen • employee assigned to present a proposal • caring member of a group who wants to improve the group's position or processes • applicant seeking approval or funding for a research project or a major purchase
Development Use of Evidence Writer Authority	• often develops by moving from problem(s) to solution(s) • often includes causal analysis, comparison of alternatives, examples, cost analysis, detailed rationale • authority comes from writer position as an expert whose advice is being sought; a subordinate asked to gather data and make a proposal; a colleague who volunteers to gather pertinent information for a group; consumer or citizen who has studied a problem and wishes to suggest a solution
Reader Position	• supervisor; instructor; or official who has power to act on your proposal; interested colleagues; other concerned citizens or community members
Format & Organization	• may depend on purpose, context, and writer/reader positions • usually follow a fairly standard format in business and government contexts, with sections devoted to background information, the nature of the problem, alternative approaches to the problem, and recommended solutions. Like formal reports, proposals may also include an executive summary and table of contents.
Level of Formality	• depends on purpose, context, format, and writer/reader positions
Medium	• may be written or oral, depending on context and purpose
Use of Visuals	• may be very helpful, depending on purpose, context, and writer/reader positions
Range of Variation	• fairly wide, from a brief oral proposal to a college class to a full written proposal to make a major change in a business procedure

GENRE: Reports (feasibility, business, news)

Contexts	• workplaces; community groups; college courses; home and family
Logistics	• will likely require time to conduct research or gather information • may require access to equipment for taping or recording • may require capability to use graphics and other software
Writer Position	• depends on purpose, reader position, and format; some possibilities include reporter of needed information, provider of needed advice, educator, or employee responding to an employer's request or demand.
Development Use of Evidence Writer Authority	• may require extensive background information • may include interview data, statistics, examples, cost comparisons, or other pertinent data • authority comes from writer position as an assigned researcher, expert reporting information, trusted advisor, or trusted reporter of events
Reader Position	• employer, instructor, or persons in a position to act on your report; interested consumers; interested and/or caring members of a group or of the larger public; family members.
Format & Organization	• depends on medium and purpose • many organizations follow a conventional report format, including predetermined headings and subheadings. Longer reports usually contain an executive summary and a table of contents.
Level of Formality	• fairly formal, depending on format, purpose, and writer/reader positions
Medium	• primarily written, but could be oral if presented to a community, family, or workplace group. • written reports are often accompanied by a briefer and more informal oral presentation of their contents
Use of Visuals	• varies widely, depending on purpose, format, and reader position
Range of Variation	• varies widely in terms of length, format, layout, and purposes

GENRE: Researched Documents

Contexts	• workplaces; community or special interest groups; college courses; websites
Logistics	• requires access to resources, whether in library, on the street, or in person (for interviews, etc.) • requires time to gather and evaluate resources
Writer Position	• depends on purpose and reader position; some possibilities include employee assessing a range of products, parent choosing a school for a child, or a group member sharing information and results with the rest of the group.
Development Use of Evidence Writer Authority	• based on logical chains of evidence • use of multiple relevant sources • writer authority comes from use of full documentation, and position as an informed group member or advocate
Reader Position	• members of a common group; those interested or in need of information in the document; those in a position to act on the document
Format & Organization	• will vary depending on context, purpose of the document, and conclusions reached in the document. Business, professional, and disciplinary groups may have a standard format for such documents. • often uses subheadings to guide the reader's thinking and attention
Level of Formality	• usually formal, though dependent on purpose and reader position
Medium	• primarily written, though could be oral if presented as a report to a group
Use of Visuals	• helpful, but may depend on purpose, context, and format constraints
Range of Variation	• wide, from a brief recommendation report on which of several products is superior, to a lengthy analysis of the rise in local crime rates

GENRE: Reviews

Contexts	• local or student newspapers; appropriate websites; workplaces; newsletters; meetings of clubs or other groups
Logistics	• time to view, read, or study the work to be reviewed very thoroughly • access to multiple viewings/readings of the work
Writer Position	• depends largely on purpose. Some possibilities include that of an expert assessing the quality of a performance or text, a person who makes recommendations about whether others should purchase, read, or watch the product; community member who wishes to praise or blame the work, or to convince others to embrace or reject it.
Development Use of Evidence Writer Authority	• copious examples from the work reviewed • use of comparisons to other works, if appropriate • writers should clarify their relation to and investment in the work. Are you an expert, an informed observer, an advocate, or other?
Reader Position	• potential viewers/audience for the work • those in a position to influence others (those who might buy the work for others or to use in a class or work site)
Format & Organization	• depends on place of publication or delivery. Newspaper reviews are generally brief and simply organized. Magazine reviews tend to be longer and more essay-like.
Level of Formality	• depends on purpose, reader position, and place of publication
Medium	• primarily written, but could be oral if writer is a member of a club or group to which the review is delivered
Use of Visuals	• limited, and dependent on format constraints
Range of Variation	• fairly wide, especially in terms of length

GENRE: Summaries

Contexts	• course exams; reports or proposals; essays; reviews; position papers
Logistics	• requires access to and thorough knowledge of the text to be summarized
Writer Position	• one who wishes to demonstrate understanding and mastery of a text, a subject, or a position • one who needs to give an accurate sketch of something in order to move on to a proposal, review, etc.
Development Use of Evidence Writer Authority	• follows the pattern of the original • taken from the original text only • writer authority comes from the writer's position as an accurate and meticulous reporter on the content of the original text, or as one who seeks to parody, respond to, or criticize the original
Reader Position	• supervisor, instructor, or employer in a position to judge the summary; those interested or invested in the subject summarized
Format & Organization	• depends on the original in terms of length
	• usually follows the same organizational pattern as the original
Level of Formality	• depends on context, purpose, and original
Medium	• may be written or oral
Use of Visuals	• limited, depending on context, purpose, and original
Range of Variation	• wide, especially in terms of length

14

COLLABORATING EFFECTIVELY

ANDREA LUNSFORD

Why Collaborate?

"Collaborate" is a formal term that names what most of us do all the time: work and learn with others. In your college work, you work with others almost constantly. In the texts and course materials you read, for instance, you "collaborate" with the writers of those texts in making sense of them and thinking them over for yourself. In your classes, you "collaborate" with other students and with the instructor in making the class time productive, and in learning the material. Outside of class, of course, you "collaborate" too—with friends and fellow students as you make important decisions that affect your life both in and out of school. In fact, all the talk you do constitutes an important kind of collaboration. In the broadest sense, then, collaboration is necessary to all learning: no one learns much in complete isolation from other people or the natural world.

Why Collaborate On and In Writing?

Certainly the writers featured in this text demonstrate many of the ways college students collaborate, from the reader responses you can see students providing for their peers in every chapter of this text to the co-authored recommendation report. These students' experiences also suggest that collaboration can be extremely helpful in your college writing as well, from the planning you do with others about topics and ideas, to the response others can give to drafts of your work, to the mental conversations you have with writers whose work you are reading or studying or using as sources for your own writing. Part of using collaboration effectively in these ways depends on your ability to listen carefully and to consider varying perspectives seriously. But beyond using collaboration to make your own writing most effective, you can also co-author, producing a document with one or more of your classmates or friends. Research on the writing that professionals do in a number of different fields (from engineering and chemistry to psychology and law) indicates that the great majority of that writing is done collaboratively, in working and writing teams. If you have not had an opportunity to practice collaborative writing, or to work with other people directly on your writing (and theirs), you will want to spend some time thinking about how to approach these tasks in the most responsible and effective way possible. The following strategies provide a means of starting to think about working well with others and a way to monitor how well you are doing as a collaborator, and as a collaborative writer, as well.

COLLABORATIVE STRATEGIES
Establish Your Group / Focus on Effective Group Interactions /
Manage Conflict / Enact Collaboration

The following strategies aim to help you work effectively and efficiently with others.

Establishing Your Group

- Your instructor may assign you to a collaborative writing group. If, however, you are asked to choose your own group, try for a minimum of three members and a maximum of five: finding times to meet together outside of class gets harder as the group gets larger.

- Look for classmates who may be interested in working on subjects or general topic areas you are interested in. Also consider how the strengths of each person can best complement the group. In this text, for example, you can see writers at work on a co-authored project and listen in as they negotiate their duties.

- Consider the kind of collaboration you will be doing in this group. Will you be working on *planning*? On *responding*? On a *co-authored document*? Consider what kind of group will be most effective in achieving your goals.

- Before confirming the group, share class and work schedules to make sure you can find compatible meeting times.

- Set up some system for contacting one another easily and efficiently.

- Set a regular time for your meetings and commit yourselves to those times.

Focusing on Effective Group Interations

- Working together, draw up a set of guidelines or ground rules for your group work. You will probably want to begin with some basics: courtesy and politeness to all members, for example.

- In addition, make a plan to insure that every member of the group gets a chance to contribute.

- Build in plenty of time for talking and listening, and time for each group member to say back or paraphrase to the group what he or she has heard about the assignment under discussion. Doing so will help avoid misunderstandings and also help identify potential points of confusion or conflict. If discussion lags, try summarizing the discussion so far to see if it will lead to new ideas.

- Consider your task carefully. Will you be working on *planning*? On *responding*? On producing a *co-authored document*? With this purpose in mind, negotiate group tasks openly and thoroughly, and plan to share tasks evenly. If materials routinely need to be prepared in advance of group meetings, for example, take turns doing so. If someone needs to take notes during meetings, rotate this duty evenly, and so on.

- Commit yourself to self- and group-evaluation. After every two or three group sessions, respond to each of the following questions: What has this group accomplished thus far? What has each member contributed? What has worked particularly well? What is not working well, or what are you dissatisfied with? What can you propose to make the group more effective?

Managing Conflict

- Whether your purpose is to *plan*, to *respond*, or to produce a *co-authored document*, you will need to prepare for constructive conflict and conflict resolution. Conflicts and disagreements, which arise in almost all group work, can be very constructive: after all, if everyone in the group goes along with a bad idea just to avoid conflict, the result is likely to be less than desirable.

- Find ways to argue out all possibilities—without being antagonistic or mean-spirited. Try having each group member take a turn arguing for a point of view other than his or her own. Doing so can help defuse tensions and sometimes uncover unexpected common ground.

- Get conflicts out in the open and give them a full discussion, remembering that considering varying and diverse perspectives can strengthen your eventual point of view. Take turns putting the conflict or point of contention in the words of each group member. Hearing multiple views of it may help you decide how best to resolve it. In addition, try looking for some common ground between competing ideas or positions and use that common ground as the starting point for a new discussion.

- If seemingly irresolvable conflicts or differences arise, try focusing not on personalities or even on individual responsibilities but on the end result the group is aiming for. What solution will make that end result best? Looking at the conflict from this perspective may help reduce or solve it—if all members remain open to the possibilities of negotiating compromise.

Enacting Collaboration

Planning Groups

- Is the collaboration intended to help with *planning*? If so, organize your sessions for maximum usefulness by using the guides in Part II to focus the work of the group.

- Prepare for the group meeting by asking each group member to bring to the meeting the work with planning he or she wants response to.

- Organize group planning sessions for maximum efficiency by dividing the time you have as evenly as possible so as to focus on each member's issues.

- Try brainstorming together about the questions or issues, with one member taking notes.

- Try asking some key question: What's missing from this plan? What does the writer still need to do to accomplish this task—and in what order?

- End the planning session by giving each group member response to his or her major decisions on how to proceed.

Peer Response Groups

Is the collaboration intended to give responses to help with *revision*? If so, prepare for the revision session carefully and thoughtfully.

- Prepare and distribute xerox copies of drafts to be discussed to all group members in advance.

- Read the drafts carefully before the group meeting using the reader response guide to annotate each one. You can also include a paragraph or two of end commentary in which you give the writer your general response to the entire draft.

- Prepare a series of questions or talking points about each draft, in order of importance to improving the draft.

- For your own draft, prepare a self-assessment, including a series of questions or points you most want response to, in order of importance.

- In the session, concentrate on the most important of your talking points, saving the written comments for the writer to take home after the group discussion.

- During the session, allow time to compare and discuss each member's description of the draft, summary of its major points, and evaluation of its status.

- Compare the concrete advice on how to improve the draft and, if possible, come to some consensus on the highest priorities for improvement.

- Before the end of the session, take stock of where each draft stands and allow each writer to construct a Revising Plan that indicates where he or she intends to go from here.

Co-Authoring Groups

- Make sure to work through the Writer/Reader Positioning Strategy to construct a position for your co-authored text, following the general strategies for effective group work recommended above.

- Don't move too quickly to closure during the planning stages of the collaborative process: the more you talk through your ideas and listen to one another, the better your final product is likely to be.

- Agree on a Project Plan for work to be done and negotiate jobs each group member will be responsible for. During this negotiation, take special care *not* to assign tasks on the basis of stereotypes (men are better at working with statistics, for example, or women are better at keyboarding), for such stereotypes often do not hold up—and may offend some or all group members.

- Set clear and reasonable deadlines for when each stage of the work will be done.

- If you do decide to draft as a group, block out plenty of time and make sure you have a computer at hand. You can take turns keyboarding, with the rest of the group clustered around the computer actually composing the text. If you decide to divide the assignment into sections, draft the sections and make sure each member gets a copy of every section at least a day in advance of your next group meeting.

- Try to share as equally as possible the research and preliminary work necessary to write this assignment. If you need resources, split up the tasks, asking one member to check out library resources while another searches the Internet and still another interviews some key sources. Then reconvene to pool your information. When you feel you have enough information to begin writing, decide whether you will try to write *as a group* from the very beginning, or whether you will divide the assignment into sections and have each member produce a draft of one section. Experienced writers work in both of these ways much of the time. Some tell us, however, that *group drafting* can be very inefficient because it tends to focus attention on debates over individual word choice or other local and stylistic matters rather than getting the "big picture" in focus and the arguments in logical and compelling order. As a result, these writers prefer to do the planning and focusing together, then draft sections individually using the group's organization plan, and finally come back together for group revising and editing.

- Whichever method of composing you choose, schedule at least two or three full group sessions to revise and edit the draft. You may want to have one person read aloud while the rest of you take notes toward revision. You may want to go paragraph by paragraph, reading the paragraph and working together to revise it.

- Consider adding illustrations or art work to your text. If you are fortunate, one or more members of your group may be quite good at producing such work.

- Agree on a final editor and keyboarder to produce the final draft. Then each member should proofread and return final corrections to the editor/keyboarder.

- If your group will be making an oral presentation in class, be sure you know precisely what the assignment calls for. How much time will you have? What are the criteria for evaluation of your presentation? Then decide how each member of the group will contribute to the presentation of your material, making sure that everyone has a role. Then leave time for at least *two* practice sessions.

15

INQUIRY, WRITING, & TECHNOLOGY

WILLIAM HART-DAVIDSON

Overview

Surfing the web can be exciting. Browsing through literally thousands of screens on sites all over the world, on any conceivable topic, it is easy to feel not only exhilarated by all the possibilities but overwhelmed. The terms "surfing" and "browsing" don't always apply when your inquiry project is something more than a casual trip into cyberspace. Whether you are researching techniques for proper stretching before aerobic exercise, perhaps to include in a brochure for the folks who attend your step-aerobics class each week, or whether you are trying to contact the author of an online magazine article about immigration policy in the U.S. to clarify a point, using the available resources of a computer connected to the World Wide Web can present a challenge. Not only must you anticipate what kind of information might be most helpful and narrow your search—to do otherwise, as you may have found out already, is to be inundated with lots of potentially useless information!—but you must also be very careful to check the source of your information and to represent that information carefully depending on the audience you are presenting it to. In this chapter, we will offer you some strategies for taking your inquiry process on line.

The strategies in this chapter have all been adapted from the general strategies presented in Part II. Below, each strategy is listed along with the general strategy it is based upon:

- planning your research on line (questioning guide)
- locating sources (questioning guide)
- sorting and reflecting on your results (focusing guide)
- evaluating and positioning your sources (bias calculator; positioning guide)

Inquiry, Writing, and Technology

A big part of learning how to write effectively in real-world contexts is learning to use the information technologies you have available to you. While you may not always have the latest cutting-edge equipment or the fastest Internet connection, you always need to rely on writing technologies—from pencils, to laser printers, to one of the earliest technological breakthroughs in writing, the alphabet—to carry out your writing process. Increasingly, a networked computer, word processing or desktop publishing software, and high quality printers are the assumed "basics" of writing in academic and workplace contexts. Unfortunately, access to these technologies is far from universal and a lack of access can put writers at a serious disadvantage.

When we speak of access to writing technologies, we don't simply mean the time or money necessary to use the latest machines and software, though these are certainly important. We also include in our definition of access, such things as:

- the ability to recognize when writing technologies may be useful to you (and when they may not be)
- how to use writing technologies to your best advantage
- how to adapt writing technologies for use in a variety of writing contexts

The most powerful aspect of information technology, though, is its ability to connect you to other people and their ideas. As you probably already know, a connection to the World Wide Web can be a tremendous resource for finding information, clarifying or expanding an interest you may have, and even for making direct contact with people whom you want to reach.

The Strategic Use of Writing Technologies

When we think about the ways technology can change the ways we write or the ways technology can help us with any task for that matter, we often think first about the ways certain tasks can be made easier for us. Using technologies to make things easier is sometimes referred to as "automating" a task or series of tasks. One goal of "automating" a task is to eliminate the drudgery of it. While automating can be helpful to writers in this way, it can also be problematic because of a second, often unspoken, goal of automating. Automating doesn't simply seek to eliminate tedious tasks, it often seeks to eliminate the *writer* too, replacing the strategic decision making of the writer with a programmed script or routine built into the technology. Automating, then, is not very sensitive to context.

But not all technologies are designed to automate. Writing technologies such as word processing software, for example, perform only a few automating functions. Counting the words in an essay is one example of an automated task your word processing software can perform. But what makes a word processing program powerful is the way it provides new opportunities for a writer to engage in the strategic decision making of writing. For example, the cut-and-paste feature of word processing software allows a writer to identify sections of text to move, copy, eliminate, or store in a different location for later use.

On the Internet, search tools are great at automating one of the most tedious tasks associated with doing research: searching through an archive to locate information sources. Search engines, one kind of search tool, accomplish this by using complex algorithms that help boost the likelihood that your selection of search terms—keywords, authors, titles—will yield the resources you are looking for. Indexes, whether they are the traditional printed variety found in the back of books or the online variety such as Yahoo!, are another kind of search tool. They work by establishing categories that seem appropriate for the users of the index and then sorting information according to these categories. In most cases, this sorting is done by a group of editors who make the decisions about which categories are needed and which information goes with which categories. When you are working on the web, it is very helpful to know if you are working with a search engine or an index . . . or with some combination of both!

This chapter aims to increase your ability to use search tools and other information technologies strategically. The strategic use of writing technologies takes some time and effort to learn, but it is well worth the effort because, as you will see, the increased ability to connect with up-to-date, real sources in real contexts is extraordinarily valuable in making your writing and inquiry process better.

Simple . . . and Not So Simple Searches

What is the first step in an effective online inquiry? Much like the inquiry process in general, the first step is formulating a good question or questions, sometimes called a "query" if your question is being posed to a database or search engine. Because online searches are becoming easier to do right from our desktops, we don't often take the time to formulate a query very well. And for some tasks, such as finding a specific piece of information, a simple query will work. Let's consider an example of a quick and simple start to a relatively uncomplicated online inquiry process.

Imagine that, for a friend's birthday, you want to make one of her favorite dishes: miso soup. You sit down at the computer terminal, launch your web browser, and head to www.google.com, a search tool that you have used before with some success. When the page loads, you get a simple, easy to use interface that has just one box where you type the words "miso soup recipe . . ."

And after a short time, you get a screenful of links to pages which match the keywords you have chosen. Google's search algorithm incorporates information in addition to the three terms you gave, including information about how frequently other people have used these terms and the most popular, or most commonly accessed, pages that contain these terms. This information is used to rank the results in what is hopefully the order of their significance. The first item, then, should be the best suited to your purpose, etc.

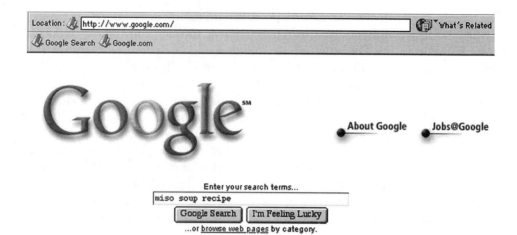

Here's a look at the results you might get from the simple search query above:

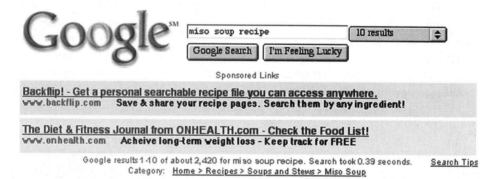

Though it might not be the first piece of information on the page that you notice, near the top Google has returned some data about the number of results your search has generated and where in its catalog you could find information about miso soup. It looks like these three search terms have worked pretty well. There are far more results than you probably want to look at, but the two-thousand four hundred results are, in the world of internet searches, not too bad. Still, even in the first four entries, there are important differences that show up. The fourth one down, for example, is on a site called "vegitarianrecipe.com," and would give you a recipe that uses something other than the traditional fish stock base—known as dashi—for a vegetarian version of the soup. You might have to decide, then, between a more traditional or a modified version. And what if you have trouble finding one of the ingredients? Could you substitute chicken stock for dashi?

Any of these questions, which may or may not have occurred to you as you began your original search, make your search task a little more complicated. But they also make the results you are after more valuable to you. This is why, as you begin any sort of involved inquiry, you should take the time to carefully explore your topic, find the points of dissonance and uncertainty that lurk in that topic, and frame questions that will help you address all the most important issues that arise.

The guide below will help you as you begin to plan your online research. Use it in conjunction with, or prior to, doing one of the "quick searches" such as the one above. Remember, the key is not to get to definitive answers in this first step, but to find out what the most interesting questions might be.

PLANNING YOUR ONLINE RESEARCH
Select Search Terms for Inquiry / Get in Touch with Dissonance

You will recall that the Questioning Strategy helps you to list topics and identify dissonances. In this guide, your topic list will consist of possible search terms. You can express these, as you will see below, in a number of ways depending on the search tools available to you. What is important is to think of terms that are descriptive, including specific names, titles, and keywords associated with your topic. Dissonances in this activity can arise in several ways. One way is not knowing how a particular topic might "fit" under a set of category headings in an index. Another source of dissonance may come from the way the computer automates a search: by searching for examples your search terms in the title or body of a document. This approach could treat a miso soup recipe the same as a document that casually mentions miso soup as part of some other discussion.

The strategy activities are in bold type and give you steps to take as you carry out your inquiry. The examples in the boxes offer illustrations of how others might use the strategy in their work.

Selecting Search Terms for Inquiry

- ## List search terms that relate to your topic

Try to think of terms which name the "basics" of your topic as well as terms that name the more specific features of your topic. It is helpful, too, to list common terms that may be associated with your topic, but which **do not** apply to your search. Here are some examples from different areas of inquiry:

Examples

> - miso soup recipe, traditional, can I use chicken stock instead of fish stock?
> - U.S. immigration policy, agricultural workers, not Canadian
> - neighborhood watch organizations, alternative policing, what is the history of these organizations?, crime rate statistics, participation rates

- ## Choose a search to begin inquiry

Which of your search terms might yield broad results that would point the way to more specific questions?

> Which ones seem like quick searches, which seem more in-depth?
> Which one seems like the most important one for you to locate?
> Which ones represent areas which you are truly curious about?
> Which ones seem most appropriate for keyword-type searches? Which only seem to work as questions?

You should expect your first search to yield more questions than answers. Don't think of it as simply a chance to plug two or three words into a search engine, but rather as a way to begin identifying how you will proceed with your research. You might, indeed, use a search engine to do this because the results will come pretty fast with this method, but you might also choose to begin by sending an e-mail message to someone. In the example above related to "neighborhood watch organizations," the researcher might choose to send an e-mail to his or her local police department through a "contact us" invitation on the department's website and ask for information related to neighborhood watch groups in the area.

Getting In Touch with Dissonance

- ## Try some searches

- ## Take careful notes about the results, especially those that surprise you

- ## Add to your list of search terms

> Where have indexers placed your topic in relation to other categories of information?
> What terms, names, or locations keep popping up that don't seem relevant to your search?

What new descriptors, names, sites, or organizations come up that are helpful?

- **Analyze your dissonance**

    Where did your search surprise you?

    Has your topic shifted on you? Is it larger in scope, or smaller, than you thought?

    Does your expanded list of search terms seem to capture both the certainties and uncertainties you have about your topic?

LOCATING SOURCES
Locate Tools and Sources for More Advanced Searches /
Formulate a Good Query / Organize Your Search Strategy

Locating Tools and Sources for More Advanced Searches

Once you have spent some time working out the most interesting and the as-yet-undefined parts of your search, you can begin a different type of search: a search for tools and sources that will be of use to you. As we have seen, the "simple search" box of a search engine or the main screen of an online directory such as the one shown below from Yahoo!, are good tools for beginning your search.

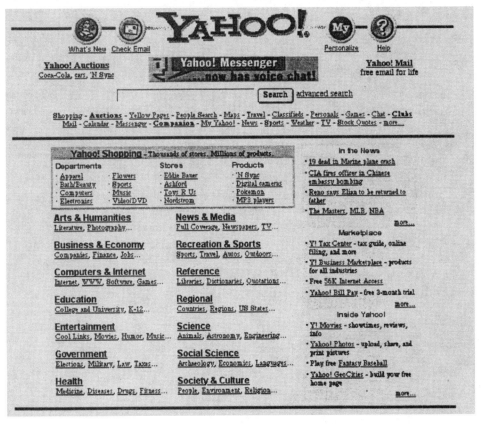

Continuing your search will probably require more sophisticated or more specialized search tools. And it will certainly require sources that can give you more specific and more detailed information. In some cases, this information is just one or two clicks "down" a hierarchy of links provided to you by an online directory. In other cases, the information is more elusive. Answering a question about how patients' rights movements have reacted to a recent report by the National Institute of Health, for example, might require sifting through and summarizing the discussion threads of the three months of postings to an Internet newsgroup.

This strategy will help you to identify the tools and sources that may be of use to you. The goal here, then, is not to answer the questions about your topic directly, but to bring you a step closer to getting those answers by discovering where they might be found.

• Identify tool and resource possibilities

When identifying search tools, think of moving from powerful and broad search tools such as search engines to increasingly specialized tools. You should also think of keyword search tools and direct contact type tools that your Internet connection makes available to you.

Make a list of keyword search tools of the following types:

- **Advanced search features of large search engines.** These are usually available by clicking an "advanced search" or "search tips" link off the main page of a search engine or portal site such as Google or Yahoo!. Performing an advanced search on one of these sites usually involves using Boolean search operators, a set of specialized terms which allow you to customize your search for greater precision. See the step below on "Using Special Operators" for more about Boolean searching.

- **Specialized search tools.** Some search tools, such as deja.com, allow you to focus on a particular type of information. Deja.com provides a way to search Internet discussion groups, also known as newsgroups or usenet groups. Other sites, such as The Macintosh Search Engine at search.applelinks.com, are organized around a particular topic or area of interest. The categories provided on the front page of The Macintosh Search Engine, while similar to those found on other directory sites, are already more specific because each one consists of links related to the Macintosh operating system instead of all computers. A good place to look for specialized search tools is, handily enough, in the "References" category of some of the general search sites.

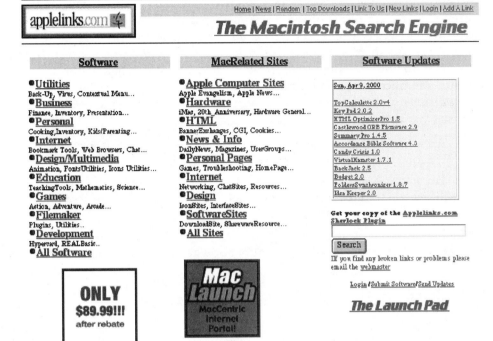

- **Site-specific search tools.** Many sites, particularly those associated with large organizations, have search functions built into them that allow you to search the contents of the site. Most of the time, these search engines are far less sophisticated than the search sites we have discussed previously, but they still can help you to locate important information that you know exists on a particular site. For example, the CNN's site, cnn.com, provides a search feature that allows you to access archived material. This is especially useful since the main function of the site is to provide the latest news. If your project requires you to gather CNN news stories about an event in the past, you will have to search the archives of the CNN site to get that information.

As the example of the CNN web site shows, the more specific and specialized your search tools become, the closer they are to being sources. In fact, it would not be inaccurate to say that CNN's website is one of your sources if your topic involves the researching of archived news articles about a given topic. What makes a search engine on CNN's site necessary, as discussed above, is the way the organization maintains old news items while constantly updating the available news on its site. CNN, like any newspaper, magazine, or journal, is a periodical publication. But their website gives you access to both up-to-date information and archived information. How you go about searching their site depends upon which kind of information you need. This is true for all searches in fact. For this reason, it is useful to construct your list of sources by dividing them into three types: archival, periodical, and direct contact sources.

Following the logic of the Three Perspectives Guide, you can think of your potential sources in terms of what they help you to explore about your topic. Archival sources can help you *describe and distinguish* various aspects of your topic. Periodical sources can help you *to trace moves and changes* in your topic over time. And direct contact sources, while they can also help describe and distinguish and trace moves and changes, offer you the exciting possibility of interacting directly with the communities in which your topic is being shaped.

Consider all three types of sources as you make your list:

- **Archival sources:** single pages or collections of pages that give information about one or more aspects of your topic

- **Periodical sources:** locations, organizations, or publications which allow you to track information about your topic over a period of time or to keep up with the latest updates

- **Direct contact sources:** people, organizations, or sites where you can interact with others who know about or who are also seeking information about your topic

Examples of Tools & Resources for Miso Soup Recipes:

Tools
- from the simple Google search, the category listing for miso soup: HOME>RECIPES>SOUPS and STEWS>MISO SOUP

- Epicurious.com, a recipe and food-related site with "over 10,000" recipes on-line

Resources
- Definitions of ingredients and techniques: The Food Network web site, www.foodtv.com, "Terms, Tips, & Ingredients"

- For my question about substituting chicken stock for fish stock, try posting a question on rec.food.cooking

Formulating a Good Query

• Consider the language constraints of your tool or source

Formulating questions or queries that yield the results you are looking for is not always easy, particularly when you are dealing with a computer rather than a person. You have probably had some experience with search tools that require you to use the special operators AND, OR, NOT, etc. You have probably also experienced frustration when your search yields no results because you misspelled a word. The lesson to take away from both of these experiences is that you should take the time to learn how to best formulate a query that is well suited to your search tool or source.

When your source is a real person, a well formed question is no less important, though a person may be a bit more forgiving if you don't use the word "AND" properly! When sending an e-mail request for information to a busy lawyer's office, you probably won't get far with a question that says "Could you please tell me everything about the Americans With Disabilities Act?" On the other hand, a well-formed question might get you more information than you had expected originally. If you ask "How, in your opinion, has the Americans With Disabilities Act made an impact on the hiring of people with disabilities in our area?" you might get into a conversation which would yield the answer to your question and the opportunity to ask other interesting follow-up questions.

How might you frame the question above for a search engine that uses key words? It might look something like this:

Americans With Disabilities Act AND (Hiring OR Employment) AND Albany, New York

This query uses key terms and Boolean terms to try and locate the answer to the question where Albany, New York is the local community. And what might you expect to get from this query? You might get an answer to the question, though it seems most likely that you will not get the specific answer to your question, but perhaps a source to go to. When this query was plugged into Google, one item that turned up was a national list of ADA consultants that included an expert on the ADA located in the Albany, New York area. This person's office might be a good source for further inquiry.

- ## Create queries that capture the kinds of responses or answers you seek

The way you pose your query will lead to different kinds of results. Consider the various kinds of results that are likely from a given source and consider the kinds of results you'd really like to get. Here are a few types of results that might shape your queries. The sample queries are posed here as questions in natural language. Can you pick out the key terms you might use in a search engine?

- **descriptions or accounts that deal with or mention your topic**

  How has the ADA made a difference in the lives of area residents?

- **discrete facts and figures**

  How many lawsuits were filed under the ADA in the Albany, NY area in the last year?

- **a conversation or initial contact for later follow-up**

  Since the passage of the ADA, how have public-building retrofit contracts been awarded in the Phoenix, AZ area?

- ## Use special operators to ensure the best results

As search tools on the Internet have proven to be generators of revenue because of the large number of visitors they can attract, competition for these visitors has gotten more intense. In order to attract more users, the designers of these search tools have worked to make them easier to use, usually by allowing you, the user, to frame your query in ways that are similar to natural language instead of having to use special search terms. In fact, at least one search tool—www.askjeeves. com—let's you ask questions, just as you would to a person.

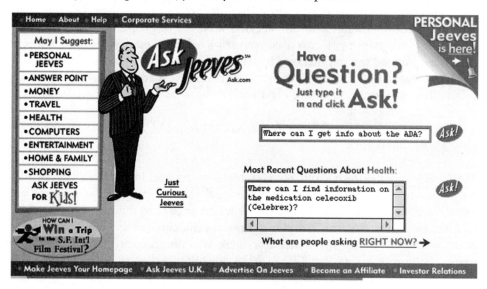

The question "Where can I find info about the ADA?" yields the following result from Ask Jeeves:

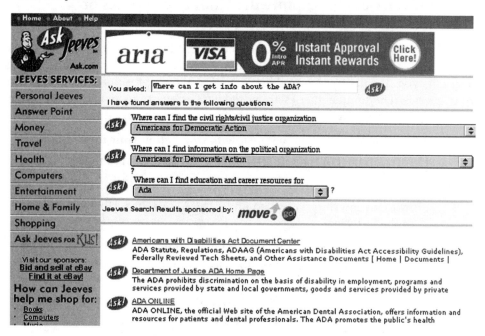

The responses indicate that the abbreviation ADA is a bit ambiguous. It could stand for Americans with Disabilities Act or it could stand for the organization called Americans for Democratic Action. It could also stand for The American Dental Association.

If we wanted to be sure that we got only results that related to the Americans with Disabilities Act, we could, of course, write out the abbreviation. But in most search engines, that would yield results that contained all of those words. The search would probably not be limited to just those words in just that order. In other words, if we enter the phrase

Americans with Disabilities Act

in most search interfaces, this would initiate a search for documents with *any* of those words, including documents that contained only one of the four words. Because most search tools have algorithms which rank the results according to how often, in what order, and how close together the search terms appear in a given document, the first several results returned will probably contain references to the Americans with Disabilities Act. Further down on the results list, though, will be documents that contain only the word "Americans" or, worse, only the word "with!" This is why a phrase like this can yield results in the millions.

The best way to narrow your search for sites that use Boolean operators is to use the special terms AND, BUT, OR, and punctuation such as quotation marks. You can sometimes also use an asterisk to indicate a wildcard, a word or partial word that can vary. Here's a brief description of how to use each of these Boolean terms:

" " **quotation marks:** Placed around a phrase, they indicate that the computer should search for just these words in precisely this order. A search query for "Americans with Disabilities Act" would not return results for documents that contained two or three of these words or contained all of them, but not in their specified order.

AND: used between keywords, AND tells the computer to search for sources that contain both keywords. AND is usually used to narrow a search by requiring both terms to be present. A search for "Americans with Disabilities Act" AND "American Dental Association" would yield documents in which both phrases appeared.

OR: used between two keywords, OR tells a computer to search for documents that contain either of the keywords. OR is usually used to widen a search. In most search tools, when you enter a string of terms, it assumes an OR is between them and will return documents which contain only one of the terms, though these are usually ranked lower on the results list than documents that contain all the terms. OR is especially useful if you want to be sure not to miss a source just because the term you used is not the only relevant one. For example, for a search on soccer, you might want to enter

Soccer OR Football

to get results from both North American and European sources.

NOT: used after a keyword or list of keywords, NOT tells the computer what references to exclude from the search. NOT is usually used to narrow a search, often after a first attempt yields many references to a topic that is not connected to the desired topic. For example, in the search above for information about soccer, we might want to add

Soccer OR Football NOT NFL

to cut down on the amount of sources related to American Football that were returned.

: used anywhere in a keyword, an asterisk or WILDCARD tells the computer to allow anything to substitute for the asterisk. A wildcard is frequently used to search for variations of a word by standing in for several possible suffixes. This is helpful when you are searching for an idea or concept more than a specific term. For example, if you wanted to search for references to the concept of liberty, you might want to also include terms like "liberation," or "liberatory." You could do this with a wildcard. You'd enter liber

Organizing Your Search Strategy

A good search strategy, like a good document draft, is not always easy to produce. It helps to carefully track your research planning process and to write down the important parts of your plan as you develop them. This way, you can revise, prioritize, and seek feedback on your search strategy.

- **Match up questions, terms, sources, data expected, special operators**

Using the chart below, list your questions, writing them out in the form of natural language questions. Next, pick out the important terms in the questions to be used to form queries for online search tools. List likely sources to which you would pose your questions and/or queries next, followed by the kind of results you expect from each. Finally, put down any special operators you might want to try if your search comes back to narrow or too broad.

- **Prioritize your searches**

Each horizontal row on your chart should correspond with a single search. Put the searches in an order that makes sense to you. One thing you may want to consider is how long the search will take. You may want to initiate direct-contact types of questions early since you have may have to wait on a response from a real person. Another thing to consider is the type of result you expect. Are you looking for a lead on additional sources? Then this search should come early on, as it will allow you to add more searches to your chart.

- **Seek feedback on your search strategy**

One of the greatest benefits of writing down the details of your search plan is that you can show it to others who can suggest subquestions, additional search terms, potential sources, and possibly even answers to some of the questions.

Online Research Planning Chart

Questions	Important Terms	Source	Data Expected	Special Operators
How has the Americans with Disabilities Act affected the lives of the disabled in the Lafayette, LA area?	Americans with Disabilities Act Lives of the Disabled Lafayette, LA	Google	More specific sources, either a person I can contact or maybe a news story?	"Americans with Disabilities Act"

SORTING AND REFLECTING ON YOUR INQUIRY RESULTS
Evaluate Your Research Goals / Review Your Search Results / Organize Your Search Results

Evaluating Your Research Goals

Your research goals are benchmarks you set for yourself as you set out to gather the information you need. Because the inquiry process is, by nature, unpredictable and deliberately undertaken with the idea that discovery will change your thinking about a given topic, you research goals may change as you progress. Still, it is a good idea to periodically review your research goals in light of the new results you have obtained. After each research session, use this guide to help you determine where you have been and where you might still need to go in your quest for information.

• Restate your research goals

Look over the chart you made to document your inquiry plan. How many of the searches you planned have yielded the results you had hoped for? How many have led to answers? How many have pointed the way to additional sources? How many remain unanswered?

Make a new chart similar to the last one, this time listing only the questions that remain. Also add any new questions that have arisen. As before, strategize your searches carefully and place them in priority order. This new chart will serve as the plan for your next research session.

• Review Your Search Results

Now it's time to take stock of what the most recent research session you have completed has yielded. During your searches, you may have visited many sites, and you might have engaged in several conversations. Along the way, you might have pursued some tangents and you may have even added to or changed your research questions depending on what information you have found. It is a good idea, therefore, to keep track of where you have been and to evaluate how far along your searches have taken you toward reaching your research goals.

The chart below demonstrates a format you might use to keep track of web sites you have visited. A similar chart might be used to keep track of your contact with other sources, including print documents and field research sources.

WWW RESEARCH CAPTURE FORM

Date: Researcher:

Research Goals:

URL of Site	Site Name/ Organization	Notes

Trends or Tangents Followed:

Research Goals Met/Modified:

Organizing Your Search Results

• Choose an appropriate format

You might have already begun to organize your search results. Perhaps you have downloaded and printed some of the information, storing it in piles according to the research question it responds to. Or perhaps you have taken notes, as suggested in Chapter 7, the Technology Chapter, using notecards. As you surfed the web in search of helpful resources, chances are you "bookmarked" some of the sites, creating a file of links that you can come back to at a later time. These are all good starts.

Another valuable technique, also described in Chapter 7, is to construct a working bibliography, a document that allows you to sort, document, and even add a short descriptive annotation for all of your sources. You can read more about how to do this in Chapter 7.

• Experiment by placing your sources, spatially, in a mock-up of your writing project

The most important thing to remember is that organizing your search results isn't simply a matter of staying organized or neat, though it can help you do these things too. Organizing your results will allow you to begin to see how the information you have collected fits together, how it allows you to describe key ideas about your topic, how it provides you with credibility you might not otherwise have, and how it challenges assumptions you and your readers might hold.

One way to begin seeing these connections is to create a kind of mock-up of your writing project, placing your sources in where they will fit into the text. For example, if you have your sources on notecards, you might just arrange them on sheets of 8 1/2 x 11″ paper, perhaps overlapping sources that respond to one another or constitute "pro" and "con" issues. If you have a working bibliography or bookmark file going, you might copy and paste the references and annotations from the bibliography file into a new file where you can arrange and rearrange them. The added benefit of this approach is that you might use this new file as the basis for the first draft of your document.

EVALUATING AND POSITIONING YOUR SOURCES
Evaluate Your Sources / Position Yourself, Your Readers, and Your Sources

Evaluating Your Sources

Because the information found on the Internet comes from a variety of sources, not all of which are entirely trustworthy, you should be careful to examine your sources (and to the extent that it is possible, your sources' sources!) before you attach your name and reputation to something you find on the Internet. The Internet is a powerfully commercial medium, and even when a site is popular, well-designed, and in other respects trustworthy, you should still be curious about the motives of those who sponsor the publication of information on the Internet. Often, a desire for profit accompanies other, more altruistic desires to educate the public or to provide access to otherwise obscure information.

This guide will help you ask some critical questions about the sources of information you find on the Internet. It has been adapted from the Semantic Calculator for Bias in Rhetoric originally developed by Donald Lazere, Part II.

1. What is the site sponsor/author's vantage point, in terms of social class, wealth, occupation, ethnic group, political ideology, educational level, age, gender, etc.? Is that vantage point apt to color attitudes on the issue under discussion? Does the organization or the author(s) have anything to gain from the position being argued? Are there any conflicts of interest or other reasons that might cause the sponsor or author(s) to include or exclude certain kinds of information?

2. What organized financial, political, ethnic, or other interests are backing the site and the specific information you are accessing? Who stands to profit financially, politically, or otherwise from the site and the information?

3. Once you have determined the sponsors' and authors' vantage point and/or the special interests being favored, look for signs of ethnocentrism, nationalization or wishful thinking, sentimentality, and other blocks to clear thinking, as well as the rhetorical fallacies of one-sidedness, selective vision, or a double standard.

4. Look for the following semantic patterns reflecting the biases in No. 3:
   a. playing up:
      (1) arguments favorable to the sponsors' or author(s') side,
      (2) arguments unfavorable to opposing viewpoints.
   b. Playing down (or suppressing altogether):
      (1) arguments unfavorable to the sponsors' or author(s') side,
      (2) arguments favorable to opposing viewpoints.
   c. Applying "clean" words (ones with positive connotations) or words with favorable commercial value and recognition to the sponsors' or authors' side,

      Applying "dirty" words (ones with negative connotations) or words with negative commercial value and recognition to opposing viewpoints.
   d. Assuming that the representatives and affiliates of the sponsors' or authors' side are trustworthy, truthful, and have no selfish motives, while assuming the opposite of those representing or associated with opposing viewpoints.

5. If you don't find signs of the above strong biases, you can mention this to indicate that the source you are relying upon is a credible one.

6. If there *is* a large amount of one-sided rhetoric and semantic bias, that's a pretty good sign that the site or writer is not a very credible source. However, finding signs of the above biases does not in itself prove that the site or writer's arguments are fallacious. Don't fall into the *ad hominem* ("to the man") fallacy—evading the issue by attacking the character of the writer or sponsor without refuting the substance of the argument itself.

POSITIONING YOURSELF, YOUR READERS, AND YOUR SOURCES

As we have seen, it is important to consider writer and reader positions because they are means of implicitly and explicitly describing activities, privileges, responsibilities, and restrictions, as well as guidelines for behavior, values, and attitudes. And as we have learned in the chapter on communities, doing research such as ethnography brings with it the added responsibility of positioning the participants in your research as well. You have certain responsibilities as a researcher to position your participants and information you gain from them fairly, and you should guard against representations that sacrifice research participants' complexity in the interest of making a compelling argument or telling a fascinating story. When dealing with information sources you have contacted over the Internet through any means of direct contact—e-mail, chat rooms, etc.—you have the same responsibilities for fairly representing your sources.

It can be helpful to consider positioning your sources, that is the people and organizations who sponsor and participate in the sites and forums where you gathered information. Doing this amounts to taking some of the "answers" to the questions 1-6 above and working them into your document in some way.

The Reader/Writer Positioning Strategy (Part II) can help you to see how to do this. Below, the familiar steps of that strategy are presented with only slight changes. A third step is added, though, that will help you make decisions about what information you should disclose in order to position your sources and in order to disclose how you and your readers may be positioned in relation to these sources.

Positioning Yourself

- ### Indicate how you have been positioned in your writing/research context.

   What positions have you written from within this context?
   What positions have you researched from within this context?
   What positions have you been excluded from?
   What positions have you left behind you?

- ### Select the position you will take as a writer.

   What position will you now adopt to represent the information you
      have collected?
   What positions will you avoid?

   Example:

   > As I give the facts about lawsuits related to the Americans With Disabilities Act, I want to seem impartial. The number of lawsuits, in other words, isn't really the problem and I don't want to make it seem like I am giving the number to shock people. I will assume the position of an impartial reporter in that section. This may be tough to do, though, since most of my facts about the cases came from the lawyer's office who tries them.

Positioning Your Readers

- ### Consider the reader positions available in your writing context

  - Determine who is excluded (who isn't written to or spoken of)?
  - Indicate who would benefit from these positions and who might be harmed or angered.
  - Consider what reader position best fits your subject

- ## Set the position for your readers.

Within your context, then, there are different reader positions. You need to set the one you want for your readers.

Example:

> - Since my audience for the ADA brochure consists of the segment of the public who apply for disability, likely reader positions include taxpayer or "the concerned citizen;" friend, family member, or employer of a disabled person; and either a temporarily disabled or permanently disabled person.

- ## Characterize the values and backgrounds you would expect from that reader position

Positioning Your Sources

- ## Consider the mission, funding sources, and activities of the sponsoring organization

  - Determine who is represented, what values are emphasized, what activities undertaken

  - Determine who is excluded (who isn't represented, who doesn't participate)

  - Indicate who benefits from these positions and who might be harmed or angered.

  - Consider what source position is most closely related to your subject

- ## Position your sources in relation to one another

One of the most valuable things you can do for readers is to explain how the various information sources which contribute to your question relate to one another. Try to go beyond simple pro and con relationships, examining, among other things, how the various sources might represent different levels of intensity, different financial or political interests, or even different disciplinary understandings of your topic.

Example:

> - The National Association of ADA Consultants seems to consist mostly of lawyers and other legal professionals whom companies hire to help determine whether or not they are in compliance with the ADA regs. This group does not advocate for the disabled, but they also don't seem to be exclusively on the side of corporations. They are somewhere in the middle, probably equally hated by both groups when a real case goes to trial ☺!

Index

Action, 1, 13, 62, 115, 163, 246, 295, 393
Affective appeals, 125, **147–9**, 343
Analogies, 22, 43, 127, 139, **151**, 213, 258, 342
Annotations, 178–9, **351, 358, 464–5**
APA bibliographic form, 471
Areas of Inquiry, xvii
Argument, *see* persuasive appeals
Ask Jeeves, 560
Audience, *see* Writer/Reader
Authority, shared 127, **149**, 150,

Bibliography
annotated, **217–8**, 306–8, 358
working, **343, 349–50, 354, 459–61**
Biographies, **528**
Bookmark, 356
Brainstorming, 455
Brochures, 262, 266–9, 292–3, **529**

Card catalog, 462
Causes, Effects, 122, 125–6, 139, **147**, 150
Citations, **366–7, 511–2**
Classical Topics, 455
Classifications, 122, 126, 138, **148**, 150, 279
Clustering, 456–7

Coherence and cohesion, 29, **153–5**, 509–10
Collaboration, 1, 8–10, **543–8**
collaborative contract, 399
collaboration management model, **418**
types of, **418–9**
conflict, 419–20
Comparison and contrast, similarities and differences, grouping, 42, 121–2, 138, **150**, 151, 174, 213, 258, 279, 290
Composition theory, xvi
Conclusion, **152**
Concrete language, 156–7, 512–3
Connotation, 146, 510–1
Consequences, 126, **150**
Contexts, writing situations, 1, 5–7, 18, 34, 81, 103, 120, 133, 171, 207–8, 209, 252–4, 272–3, 333, 335, 414
Contrasting Strategy, 77–8, **97–101**
Contrasting terms, 97, 99
Conventions, 29
Credibility appeals, 124, **144–5**, **448**
Criteria organization, 51, 289
Critical essay, 82–6, 87–90, 108–9, 111–4

Cultural assumptions, 3–4, 22, 43, 138
  cultural changes, 22
  narratives, 22, 43, 138
  cultural sources, influences, 21–2, 35, 171, 174–5, 208, 253–4, 274, 415
  cultural values, 16, 174

Databases, **344**, **350–1**, **463**
Deductive chain, 451–4
Definition, 125, **147**, 150
Designing for a Reader, 491–2
Development for readers, 27
Direction in a process, 126, **150**
Dissonance, 21–2, 33, 35, 133, 171, 207, 253–4, 274, 303, 332, 334, 398, 413, 416, 554
Document design, 403, **424–9**, **503–6**
Document Organization, 506–7
Drafting, **52–3**, **107**, **153–5**, **366–9**, 431, **509**
  polished draft, 26–7, 84–6, 108–9, 128, 154–5, 185–92, 227–33, 267–8, 291, 312–9, 369–80, 404–6, 431

Essay, **530**
Essay exams, , **514–6**, **532**
Ethnography, 196–203, 227–33, 237–43, 360, **472–8**, **531**
  ethnographic research, **214–5**
  ethnographic organization, 502–3
Examples, 7, 125, **147**
Exploration, 20–2, 35, 172–5 212–3, 255–8, 277–9, 304–6, 338–42, 422

Fields of Study, **245**, 252, 273
Field Research, *see* Ethnography
Flyer, 432–3
Focus, focusing, 25, 49–50, 83, 105–6, 124, 182, 223–4, 267, 287–9, 311, 363–4, 424
  focusing strategy, 25, 49–50, **142–4**, 287–9, **492**

Focused freewriting, 441
Forum analysis, 490
Four Worlds, 4–5
Free Time, 61–3

Genre Selection, 24–5, **46–8**, 48, 82, 104–5, 124, 141–2, 222–3, 261–3, **310**, 361–2, 402–3, 423–4
Genre Strategy, **523–6**
Genres, xvii, 2, **523–4**
  level of formality, 47
  range of variation, 47
  format, 47
Google, 552–3
Grouping organization, 51, 83, 264–5
Groups
  interactions, **544–5**
  conflict, **545**
  planning groups, **546**
  peer response groups, 546-7
  co-authoring groups, 547–8

Idea Tree, 508
Ideal, 125, **147**, 150
Incubation, 39
Indexes,
  on-line, **343**
  CD-ROM library, **344**, 349–50
Inquiry, 1–4, 13, 17, 61, 75, 115–6, 119, 161–2, 169–70, 245, 251–2, 296, 302, 393–4, 397
Interaction, xv
Internet, 353–7
  sources, 308
Interpreting written texts, **479–81**
Interpretive Guide
  Poem, 482–3
  Short Story, 483–4
  Nonfiction Essay, 484–5
Interviews, 181–2, **218–20**, **474–8**, **533**
Introduction, **151**, 311
Invention strategies, 437–57
Issues in groups, 115, 120

Journals, 456
Journalistic formula, 454

Key terms, 96, 99

Language choices, 29
Letters, **534**
  personal, 26, 30, 53, 58
Library Research, 306–7, **343–4,**
  459–61
Local Culture, 161
Looping, 456

Macintosh Search Engine, 556
Means/End, 126, **150**
Meditating, 456
Memoirs, **536**
Memorandum, 407, 408–11, 430,
  433
MLA Bibliographic form, 470
Modal Plans, 50–2, 83, 264–5, 289,
  365, **495–8**
Model, 125, **147**, 149
Multimedia Presentations, 537

Networks, 22
Newsletters, **535**
Newsletter or newspaper article,
  124, 128
Note taking, 214–6, 308–9, **351–2,**
  358–9, **466–9**, 473–4
Nutshelling, 495

On-line resources, 2
Observations, 175–7, 215–6,
  473–4
Organization, organizing, 26, 28,
  50, 51–2, 106, 289
  ethnographic organization, **224**
  organizing strategy, organizing
    plan, 26, 83, 127, 184–5,
    264–5, 311–2, 364
  organizing memo, **430**

Packages, 75, 93
Participant/observer, 162
Pentad, 454–5

Persons/Actions, 126, 150
Persuasive plans, **151–3,**
  498–500
Persuasive appeals, **448**
Plagiarism, 512–3
Point of Significance, 25–6, 50,
  143–4, 288, 311, 364
Positioning, *see* Writer/Reader
  Positioning
Project planning, 399–400, **417–22,**
  441–3
Project proposal, 516
Proposals, **538**
Puzzlements, 78, 94, 100–1

Questioning Strategy, 17–9, **33–5,**
  35–6, 132–5, **206–8, 273–5,**
  331–2, **413–5, 437–41**
Questions, 3–4, 17–9, 35–6, 80,
  102, 120, 171, 208, 252–4,
  273–5, 303, 334–5, 398
Quotations, 367–8, **512**

Rational appeals, 125–7, **147–51,**
  449–50
Readers, *see* Writer/Reader
  Positioning
Reading Guide, 481–2
Reading and Interpretive strategies,
  479–86
Refutation, **152**
Relationships, 13
Repetition, **154**
Reports, **539**
Researched paper, 312–9, 322–30,
  369–80, 385–90
  documents, **540**
Research plan, 401
Research strategies, 459–78
Responding, 86–7, 110, 129,
  157, 193–4, 234–6, 267–8,
  292–3, 319–21, 382–3,
  432–3
  Reader Response Strategy, 28–9,
    54–5, 56–7, **156–8, 233–4,**
    382–3, 517–9
Reviews, **541**

Revising, revisions, 29–30, 57–8, 88–90, 111–4, 130–1, 158–9, 196–203, 237–43, 269, 293, 322–30, 385–90, 407–11, 432–3, **520–2**
   revising plan, 29, **57**, 111, 158, 194, 236, 269, 322, 384, 407, **520**
Rhetorical appeals, 124–7, **144–5**

Searches, online, **551–63**
   search screens, **344**, 347–8, 354
   search terms, 554
   tools and sources, 555–8
   queries, 558–9
   special operators, 559–62
   research planning chart, 563
   research goals, 563–4
   evaluating sources, 565–6
   positioning sources, 567–8
Self-assessment, 27–8, 56, 88
Semantic Calculator for Bias for Rhetoric, 485–6
Sentence Outline, 501
Shifts, person, number, gender, **154**
Situating, Drafting, and Revising Strategies, 487–522
Social practices, 43
Speedwriting, 455–6
Starting, 33, 92, 132, 206, 271, 331, 412
   Starting Strategy, 75–6, 331
Stereotypes, 22, 43, 122, 257
Story telling, 75–8, **94–5**, 100–1
Story-telling Strategy, 94–5
Strategies, xvi–xvii, 1, 6–7

Subject selection, 25, 33, 95, 132–3, 206, 272, 275, 331, 414
Summaries, **542**
Surveys, 478

Target Group Analysis, 79–80, 100–1
Technology, **295, 549–68**
Terms and Contrasts, 77
Three Perspectives Strategy, **37–9**, 40–3, 121–2, 136–9, **210–2**, 255–8, 275–7, 336–42, 445–8
Time Segments Organization, 51
   narrative plan, 83, 290
Topic Outline, 502
Toulmin's Analysis, 450–1
Transitions, **154**

Values, 16, 36, 106, 120, 134, 141, 171, 209, 253, 274, 398, 416

Whole/Part Organization, 51, 290, 365
Workplace Problems, **393**
Works Cited, 203, 243, 318, 380
   format, **350**
Writer/Reader positioning, 23–4, 43–4, 81–2, 103–4, 123, 140–1, 182–3, 222, 258–60, **280–1**, 309–10, 360, 401–2, 423, **487–9**, 567–8
Writing Processes, xvi, 1, 33, 92, 132, 205, 271, 331, 412
Writing to inquire, 3–4, 413
Yahoo!, 555